THE ROUTLEDGE COMPANION TO DIGITAL ETHNOGRAPHY

With the increase of digital and networked media in everyday life, researchers have increasingly turned their gaze to the symbolic and cultural elements of technologies. From studying online game communities, locative and social media to YouTube and mobile media, ethnographic approaches to digital and networked media have helped to elucidate the dynamic cultural and social dimensions of media practice. *The Routledge Companion to Digital Ethnography* provides an authoritative, up-to-date, intellectually broad, and conceptually cutting-edge guide to this emergent and diverse area.

Features include:

- a comprehensive history of computers and digitization in anthropology;
- exploration of various ethnographic methods in the context of digital tools and network relations;
- consideration of social networking and communication technologies on a local and global scale;
- in-depth analyses of different interfaces in ethnography, from mobile technologies to digital archives.

Larissa Hjorth is Distinguished Professor and Director of HDR in the College of Design and Social Context at RMIT University and (with Professor Heather Horst) was co-founding Director of RMIT's Digital Ethnography Research Centre (DERC).

Heather Horst is Professor in the School of Media and Communication at RMIT University and Director, Research Partnerships in the College of Design and Social Context at RMIT University. She was the director of DERC from 2012–2015.

Anne Galloway is Senior Lecturer in Culture+Context Design at Victoria University of Wellington, New Zealand.

Genevieve Bell is currently a Senior Fellow and Vice President at Intel Corporation where she works in their Corporate Strategy Office, driving long-term strategic visioning and insights.

THE ROUTLEDGE COMPANION TO DIGITAL ETHNOGRAPHY

*Edited by Larissa Hjorth, Heather Horst,
Anne Galloway, and Genevieve Bell*

Routledge
Taylor & Francis Group
LONDON AND NEW YORK

First published 2017
by Routledge

2 Park Square, Milton Park, Abingdon, Oxfordshire OX14 4RN
52 Vanderbilt Avenue, New York, NY 10017

Routledge is an imprint of the Taylor & Francis Group, an informa business

First issued in paperback 2019

Library of Congress Cataloging in Publication Data
A catalog record for this book has been requested

ISBN: 978-1-138-94091-8 (hbk)
ISBN: 978-0-367-87358-5 (pbk)

Typeset in Bembo Std
by Swales & Willis Ltd, Exeter, Devon, UK

CONTENTS

CONTENTS

CONTENTS

CONTENTS

FIGURES

CONTRIBUTORS

Crystal Abidin is an anthropologist and ethnographer who researches Internet culture and young people's relationships with social media, technology, and devices. Her current work focuses on the history of a vernacular form of commerce known as 'blogshops' around South East Asia, the culture of Influencers and Internet celebrity, and grief and vulnerability in digital spaces. Crystal is Postdoctoral Fellow in Sociology at the National University of Singapore, and Affiliate Researcher with the Media Management and Transformation Centre at Jönköping University. Reach her at www.wishcrys.com.

Yoko Akama is Associate Professor in the School of Media and Communication at RMIT University, Australia and Co-Leader of Design and Social Innovation in Asia-Pacific network. Her design research practice is entangled in social "wicked problems," for example, to strengthen adaptive capacity for disaster resilience, and to contribute towards the efforts of Indigenous Nations to enact self-determination and nation building. She is a recipient of the British Council Design Research Award (2008); was a Finalist in the Victorian Premier's Design Award (2012); and won two Good Design Australia Awards (2014).

ken anderson is an anthropologist and Principal Engineer at Intel Corporation. Over the last 20 years, his research has explored the relationship between identity, culture, and technology. His current work highlights key changes in cultural values with the emergence of a digital society and the importance of these changes for the product and business innovation and corporate strategy. Ken's career has included positions in the labs of AT&T, MediaOne, US West, and Apple Computer. He is co-founder and on the board of EPIC (Ethnographic Praxis in Industry Conference). His work has appeared in a wide range of academic and business publications, as well as the popular press.

Tom Apperley is an ethnographer, researcher, and consultant on digital media technologies. His previous writing has covered digital games, mobile phones, digital literacies and pedagogies, and social exclusion. He is Senior Lecturer at UNSW Australia. His book *Gaming Rhythms: Play and Counterplay from the Situated to the Global* was published in 2010 by the Institute of Network Cultures. Tom's more recent work has appeared in *Digital Creativity* and *Games and Culture*.

Elisenda Ardèvol is Associate Professor in Social Anthropology at the Department of Arts and Humanities, at the Universitat Oberta de Catalunya and Director of *Mediaccions* Digital Culture Research Group at the Internet Interdisciplinary Institute in Barcelona. She has been Visiting Scholar at the Visual Anthropology Center of the University of Southern California and EU Centre Visiting Fellow at the Digital Ethnography Centre at the RMIT, Melbourne. Her main research lines are related with digital culture, visuality, and media in everyday life. Currently, she is exploring design, creativity, and collaborative practices in digital technologies. Her publications include "Digital ethnography and media practices" in Darling Wolf, *Research Methods in Media Studies* (2014); editor of *Researching Media through Practices* (2009) and the books (in Spanish) *Key Debates* (2014); *A Gaze's Quest* (2006); and *Representation and Audiovisual Culture in Contemporary Societies* (2004).

Michael Arnold is Associate Professor in the History and Philosophy of Science Program at the University of Melbourne. His ongoing teaching and research activities lie at the intersection of contemporary technologies and our society and culture. In recent years, Michael's research projects include studies of social networking in six locations across the Asia-Pacific; high-speed broadband in the domestic context; ethical and governance issues associated with the electronic health record; digital storytelling by young aboriginals; and digital commemoration.

William Balmford is a PhD candidate at RMIT University. Will's thesis is focused on how the digital distribution Steam platform is shaping household gaming practices around Melbourne. Also, he is the Melbourne-based research assistant for Games of Being Mobile, an Australia-wide investigation into the modalities and contexts of mobile game practices.

Veronica Barassi is the convenor of the BA Anthropology and Media Program in the Department of Media and Communications, Goldsmiths, University of London. She is one of the founders of the Goldsmiths Media Ethnography Group and principal investigator on the "Social Movements and Media Technologies: Present Challenges and Future Developments" ESRC Seminar series. Her work has appeared in top-ranked international journals and she is the author of *Activism on the Web: Everyday Struggles against Digital Capitalism* (Routledge, 2015). Her current research explores the relationship between family life, data cultures, and digital citizenship.

Anne Beaulieu is Program Manager of Energysense, a comprehensive knowledge infrastructure with information on energy consumption, attitude, and behavior in households. She joined the University of Groningen in 2011 as project manager of the Groningen Energy and Sustainability Program, following several years as Senior Research Fellow at the Royal Netherlands Academy of Arts and Sciences (KNAW), notably at the Virtual Knowledge Studio for the Humanities and Social Sciences. Her research follows two main lines: the study of the use of databases and networks in knowledge creation, and the development of new ethnographic approaches to cultural and social phenomena in mediated settings. She is co-editor of *Virtual Knowledge* (MIT Press) and has been guest editor of special issues for the following journals: *Theory and Psychology*, *Social Epistemology*, *Journal of Computer Mediated Interaction*, and *Forum Qualitative Research*.

Richard Beckwith is Research Psychologist in Intel Labs. Beckwith has been with Intel since 1996. He publishes primarily on language, education, sensors, and privacy. Recent work has focused on the human impact of community-based sensing schemes. Before coming to Intel, Richard has worked at Princeton University's Cognitive Science Lab and Northwestern University's Institute for the Learning Sciences. He received his PhD in Developmental Psychology from Teachers College, Columbia University in 1986.

Genevieve Bell is a cultural anthropologist who works at the intersection of technology development and cultural practice. She is currently Senior Fellow and Vice President at Intel Corporation where she works in their Corporate Strategy Office, driving long-term strategic visioning and insights. She started Intel's User Experience practice and helped mainstream social-science research in Silicon Valley. She holds a PhD in Anthropology from Stanford University.

Marsha Berry is Program Manager for the creative writing degree in the School of Media and Communication at RMIT University, Melbourne. She is co-editor of the book, *Mobile Media Making in an Age of Smartphones* (2014). Since 2004, she has been researching the connections between mobile media, place, memory, collaboration, and creative practices and has published her work extensively in international journals as well as in edited books. She is also a writer and artist whose practice includes filmmaking, participatory art projects, poetry, and new media.

Georgina Born is Professor of Music and Anthropology at Oxford University and Professorial Fellow of Mansfield College, Oxford. In the 1980s and 1990s she pioneered the ethnographic study of computer cultures. She directs the European Research Council-funded research program "Music, Digitization, Mediation: Towards Interdisciplinary Music Studies" which involves studies of digital music practices in six countries in the developing and developed worlds and two online ethnographies. Her recent books are *Music, Sound and Space* (ed., 2013), and *Interdisciplinarity* (ed. with Andrew Barry, 2013). *Improvisation and Social Aesthetics* (ed. with Eric Lewis and Will Straw) will be published by Duke in 2016, and *Digital Musics: A Global Anthropology* in 2017. In 2014 she gave the Bloch Lectures in Music at the University of California, Berkeley; the same year she was elected a Fellow of the British Academy in anthropology, and in 2016 she was awarded an OBE.

Alexandrine Boudreault-Fournier is Assistant Professor in the Department of Anthropology at the University of Victoria. She has been conducting fieldwork in Cuba, mainly on the eastern end of the island, since the year 2000. Her research interests are digital media, infrastructure, visual culture, and arts-based research. In 2010, with partial funding from the National Film Board of Canada, she directed the film *Golden Scars*, which tells the story of two rappers from Santiago de Cuba. More recently, she co-directed the film *Fabrik Funk* (2015), an ethno-fiction about funk music on the periphery of São Paulo.

Jenna Burrell is Associate Professor in the School of Information at UC Berkeley and the author of *Invisible Users: Youth in the Internet Cafés of Urban Ghana* (MIT Press). She has a PhD in Sociology from the London School of Economics. Before pursuing her PhD she was an Application Concept Developer in the People and Practices Research Group at Intel Corporation. For over ten years she has been studying the appropriation of Information and Communication Technologies (ICTs) by individuals and groups on the African continent. Recently, she has begun to investigate questions of digital inequality in the USA.

Elizabeth Chin is an anthropologist whose practice includes performative ethnography, writing experiments, and, increasingly, technology hacks. She has conducted fieldwork in the urban United States, Ecuador, Peru, and Haiti. Her work is always concerned with race and social inequality, and she specializes in children and childhood, consumption, and popular and material culture. She is editor of *Katherine Dunham: Recovering and Anthropological Legacy, Choreographing Ethnographic Futures* (SAR Press, 2014). Her book *Purchasing Power: Black Kids and American Consumer Culture* (Minnesota, 2001) was a finalist for the C. Wright Mills Prize. *The Consumer Diaries: My Life with Things* is forthcoming from Duke University Press.

Xi Cui is currently Assistant Professor in the Department of Communication, College of Charleston. He studies media rituals from a sociological perspective exploring issues such as social identity, social solidarity, and emotions. His research topics range from ceremonial events to mundane but ritualistic media uses in various media especially in the contemporary Chinese context.

Ursula Dalinghaus is a postdoctoral scholar at the Institute for Money, Technology and Financial Inclusion, housed within the Department of Anthropology at the University of California, Irvine. She completed her PhD in Anthropology at the University of Minnesota, Twin Cities, specializing in economic anthropology and ethnographic approaches to money, currency unions, and central banks. Since 2005, and based on five years of fieldwork in Germany, her research has examined expert–public communications work around the single European currency (the euro) at the German Central Bank to understand how monetary policy is connected to and made intelligible in everyday social worlds. Her research interests include histories of monetary change and crisis, post-socialist transformation and European integration, and cross-cultural theories of money, accounting, and exchange. She is currently working on a second project that examines German–Greek relations in the European sovereign debt crisis, and preparing a book manuscript based on her PhD thesis, *Accounting for Money: Keeping the Ledger of Monetary Memory in Germany.*

Mirjam de Bruijn is Professor in Contemporary History and Anthropology of Africa at Leiden University and senior researcher at the African Studies Center Leiden (ASC). In her work she focuses on the interrelationship between agency, marginality, mobility, and communication in the context of political and social change. Her specific fields of interest are: mobility, youth, social (in)security, marginality/exclusion, human rights, and Information and Communication Technologies (ICTs). She has been head of several research programs, including "Mobile Africa revisited" (2008–2013), and is now heading the research program "Connecting in Times of Duress" (2012–2017). Both programs look at the interface between communication technologies, mobility, social and political change in Africa and were funded by NWO (Dutch Research Foundation). She has been part of other collaborative programs funded by Volkswagenstiftung, the Dutch Ministry of foreign affairs, and CODESRIA (Council for Development of Social Sciences in Africa). Recently she started a new research program, www.Voice4Thought.org, that envisages the translation of research results from her programs into a public presentation and archive.

Jennifer Deger is an anthropologist, filmmaker, and co-founder of Miyarrka Media, a digital arts collective based in the remote Aboriginal community of Gapuwiyak in northern Australia. A research leader at the Cairns Institute, James Cook University, she publishes in the areas of visual culture, experimental ethnography, and indigenous aesthetics, and has been awarded a number of major research grants including an Australian Research Council Future Fellowship (2012–2016). Her creative work with Miyarrka Media includes the films *Manapanmirr, in Christmas Spirit* (2012) and *Ringtone* (2014), and the installation works *Christmas Birrimbirr (Christmas Spirit)* and *Gapuwiyak Calling: Phone-Made Media from Aboriginal Australia Land.*

Guillaume Dumont is a social and cultural anthropologist. His research focuses, broadly speaking, on the transformation of work and labor in the creative economy with a special interest in creative work, reputation, and self-branding. He is Research Associate at L-VIS–Claude Bernard University Lyon, France, and *Mediaccions* Digital Culture Research Group at the Internet Interdisciplinary Institute in Barcelona.

Paolo Favero is Associate Professor in Film Studies and Visual Culture at the University of Antwerp. A visual anthropologist with a PhD from Stockholm University, Paolo has devoted the core of his career to the study of visual culture in India. Presently he conducts research on image-making, politics, and technology in contemporary India as well as on questions of ontology and methodology in the context of emerging digital visual practices and technologies at global level.

Heather Ford is Fellow in Digital Methods at the School of Media and Communications, University of Leeds and a founding editor of www.ethnographymatters.net. An ethnographer and former Internet rights activist, she studies the construction of knowledge and realignments of power in online systems.

Kim and Mike Fortun Kim Fortun is a cultural anthropologist and Professor of Science & Technology Studies at Rensselaer Polytechnic Institute. Her research and teaching focus on environmental risk and disaster, and on experimental ethnographic methods and research design. Mike Fortun is a historian and anthropologist of the life sciences, and Associate Professor of Science & Technology Studies at Rensselaer Polytechnic Institute. From 2005 to 2010, Kim and Mike Fortun co-edited the *Journal of Cultural Anthropology*, and became vocal advocates of open access publishing in the field. Currently Mike Fortun and Kim Fortun lead development of *The Asthma Files*, a collaborative ethnographic project to understand how air pollution and environmental public health are dealt with in different contexts, and on design of the Platform for Experimental and Collaborative Ethnography (PECE), an open source/access digital platform for anthropological and historical research. Mike and Kim Fortun also co-chair the Research Data Alliance's Digital Practices in History and Ethnography Interest Group.

Isabel Fróes is Lecturer and a PhD candidate at IT University of Copenhagen and Visiting Lecturer at the Information Experience Design Program at RCA, London. She holds a BA in psychology from PUC-Rio and a Master's in interactive telecommunications from ITP, NYU. She has taught many courses related to play and interaction design in various universities in Denmark and abroad. Her research looks into how technologies and playful interactions encountered in our everyday lives touch the ways relationships and activities are socially and culturally developed.

Anne Galloway is Senior Lecturer in Culture+Context Design at Victoria University of Wellington, New Zealand. Leading the More-Than-Human Lab (morethanhumanlab. org), her research examines assemblages of people, nonhuman animals, and technologies, and explores creative methods for ethnographic storytelling and public engagement around related matters of concern. When not teaching courses in design ethnography and speculative design, Anne spends as much time as possible at her rural home, where she shepherds small flocks of rare-breed sheep and ducks.

luke gaspard received his doctorate from the School of Media and Communication at RMIT University, Australia and is now a tutor and researcher in the same school. His work focuses on how how children and youth incorporate and exploit digital technologies, particularly centered around the televisual, in their everyday lives and contexts.

Haidy Geismar is Reader in Digital Anthropology and Material Culture in the Department of Anthropology at University College London where she co-directs the Centre for Digital

Anthropology. She is founding editor of www.materialworldblog.com, associate editor of the *International Journal of Cultural Property*, and co-editor of the *Journal of Material Culture*. Her research interests span critical museologies, material culture studies, comparative object politics, and the digital analog interface that extends to the anthropology of intellectual and cultural property. She has undertaken extensive fieldwork in museum collections and in the South Pacific.

Martin Gibbs is Associate Professor in the Department of Computing and Information Systems at the University of Melbourne. His research covers a range of topics associated with the social use of digital technologies. He has written and continues to write about computer games and has a specific interest in the ways game designers and game players use games to commemorate and memorialize the dead. He was the co-editor of the book, *From Social Butterfly to Engaged Citizen*, and he also co-edited the May 2013 special issue of *The Information Society*, on the *Death, Afterlife and Immortality of Bodies and Data*.

Edgar Gómez Cruz is Research Fellow at RMIT, Melbourne. He has published widely on a number of topics relating to digital culture, ethnography, and photography. His recent publications include *From Kodak Culture to Networked Image: An Ethnography of Digital Photography Practices* (2012) and *Digital Photography and Everyday Life: Empirical Studies in Material Visual Practices* (2016, with Asko Lehmuskallio). Current research investigates screen cultures and creative practice, which is funded through Research Councils UK (RCUK) and Vice Chancellor research grants.

Sharon Greenfield is a PhD researcher in the Digital Ethnography Research Centre at RMIT University where her dissertation focuses on young people as they engage with digital media during bereavement. Her research interests include place making, technology and material cultures, and digital bereavement. Prior to pursuing her PhD she was a researcher in the People and Practices Research Group at Intel Corporation.

Christopher Haworth is Lecturer in Music at the University of Birmingham. His current research is focused on the changing uses of the Internet in underground music, and the application and development of online ethnography methods to analyze these changes. Christopher's work has been published in many journals and edited collections including *Computer Music Journal*, *Organised Sound*, *Leonardo Music Journal*, and the *Oxford Handbook of Algorithmic Music*. He is the editor of *Array*, the journal of the International Computer Music Association, and is also active as an electronic musician and sound artist.

Christine Hine is Reader in Sociology in the Department of Sociology at the University of Surrey. Her main research centers on the sociology of science and technology with a particular interest in the role played by new technologies in the knowledge production process. She also has a major interest in the development of ethnography in technical settings, and in "virtual methods" (the use of the Internet for social research). In particular, she has developed mobile and connective approaches to ethnography which combine online and offline social contexts. She is author of *Virtual Ethnography* (Sage, 2000), *Systematics as Cyberscience* (MIT, 2008), *Understanding Qualitative Research: the Internet* (Oxford, 2012), and *Ethnography for the Internet* (Bloomsbury, 2015) and editor of *Virtual Methods* (Berg, 2005), *New Infrastructures for Knowledge Production* (Information Science Publishing, 2006), and *Virtual Research Methods* (Sage, 2012).

Larissa Hjorth is an artist, professor, and digital ethnographer. Since 2000, Hjorth has been researching the gendered and socio-cultural dimensions of mobile media and gaming cultures in the Asia-Pacific—these studies are outlined in her books, *Mobile Media in the Asia-Pacific* (Routledge, 2009), *Games & Gaming* (Berg, 2010), *Online@AsiaPacific* (with Arnold, Routledge, 2013), *Understanding Social Media* (with Hinton, Sage, 2013), *Gaming in Social, Locative and Mobile Media* (with Richardson, Palgrave, 2014), *Digital Ethnography* (with Pink, Horst, Postill, Lewis, and Tacchi, Sage, 2016), and *Screen Ecologies* (with Pink, Sharp, and Williams, MIT Press, 2016). Hjorth is currently first CI on two Australian Research Council (ARC) grants: one Linkage with Intel, Locating the Mobile, on locative media in Japan, China, and Australia (with S. Pink and H. Horst) (LP130100848): http://locatingthemobile.net/; one Discovery (with I. Richardson) Games of Being Mobile: mobile gaming in Australian everyday life (DP140104295): http://gamesofbeingmobile.com/.

Heather Horst is Professor in the School of Media and Communication at RMIT University and Director, Research Partnerships in the College of Design and Social Context at RMIT University, Australia. She was also Founding Director (2012–2015) of the Digital Ethnography Research Centre. Heather's research focuses upon understanding how digital technologies, mobile phones, and other forms of material culture mediate relationships, learning, and mobility. These themes are reflected in her publications which include *The Cell Phone: An Anthropology of Communication* (Horst and Miller, 2006, Berg), *Living and Learning with Digital Media: Findings from the Digital Youth Project* (Ito, Horst, et al., 2009, MIT Press), *Hanging Out, Messing Around and Geeking Out: Kids Living and Learning with Digital Media* (Ito, et al., 2010, MIT Press), *Digital Ethnography: Principles and Practices* (Pink, Horst, et al., 2016, Sage), and an edited book *Digital Anthropology* (Horst and Miller, 2013, Berg), which was recently translated into Chinese and Arabic. Her current research, funded by the Australian Research Council, the European Union Horizon 20/20 Program, and industry partners, explores transformations in the mobile telecommunications industry and the emergence of mobile, social, and locative media practices across the Asia-Pacific region.

Wendy F. Hsu is a researcher, strategist, and educator who engages with hybrid research and organizing agendas for equality in arts, technology, and civic participation. Hsu researches the relationship between street sound, low-resource technology, and informal economy in Los Angeles and Taipei. A former ACLS Public Fellow, Hsu currently works as the digital strategist of the City of Los Angeles Department of Cultural Affairs, providing research and strategy to redesign the department's data and knowledge architecture.

Kat Jungnickel is Senior Lecturer in the Sociology Department, Goldsmiths, University of London. Her research explores mobilities, DiY/DiT (Doing-it-Together) technology cultures and inventive methods. She is the author of *DiY WiFi: Re-imagining Connectivity* (Palgrave Macmillan, 2014). Her current ESRC-funded research explores the history of women's cycling through radical forms of cycle wear and interweaves STS and archival research with the sewing of Victorian convertible costumes from the 1890s. www.katjungnickel.com.

Brendan Keogh is Adjunct Research Fellow in the School of Media and Communication at RMIT University, and Lecturer of Game Design at SAE Creative Media Institute. His research focuses on the intersection of phenomenological, textual, and cultural aspects of videogame play and production. He is also a videogame critic who has written for a variety of publications including *Polygon, Overland, Ars Technica, Kotaku, Reverse Shot,* and *The New Statesman*. He is the author of *Killing is Harmless: A Critical Reading of Spec Ops: The Line*.

Hannah Knox is Lecturer in Digital Anthropology and Material Culture at University College London. She has published widely on the anthropology of infrastructure, technology, environment, and expertise. Her books include *Objects and Materials: A Routledge Companion* (2013) and *Roads: An Anthropology of Infrastructure and Expertise* (2015).

Tamara Kohn is Associate Professor of Anthropology in the School of Social and Political Sciences, University of Melbourne. Her research interests are in identity, trans-cultural communities of practice, mobility, death studies, institutional ethics and research methods, and the anthropology of the body and senses. She is a Chief Investigator on two Australian Research Council projects: "Digital Commemoration" and "Sonic Practice in Japan."

Jordan Kraemer is Visiting Scholar in Anthropology at New York University and an anthropologist of media and technology. Her current work addresses social and mobile media, transnationalism, and place making among urban European middle classes. She earned her PhD in cultural anthropology from the University of California, Irvine in 2012, and writes about the production of space, place, and scale, technology design, media infrastructures, and contested understandings of sociality, mobility, and personhood.

Patricia G. Lange is an Anthropologist and Assistant Professor of Critical Studies (undergraduate program) and Visual & Critical Studies (graduate program) at California College of the Arts (CCA) in San Francisco, California. Her areas of expertise include studying technical identities, mediated interaction, and YouTube. She is the author of the book *Kids on YouTube: Technical Identities and Digital Literacies* (Routledge/Left Coast Press, 2014). The book draws on a two-year ethnographic project on YouTubers and video bloggers to explore how video creation and sharing are used in informal learning environments. She also produced and directed the film *Hey Watch This! Sharing the Self Through Media* (2013), which was screened in Paris at Ethnografilm, a festival showcasing ethnographic films that visually depict social worlds. The film provides a diachronic look at the rise and fall of YouTube as a social media site. Currently, she is researching video rants and how they facilitate civic engagement. At CCA, she teaches courses on digital cultures, anthropology of technology, new media and civic action, and ethnography for design. Her website is www.patricialange.org.

Débora Lanzeni is Researcher at the IN3 (Internet Interdisciplinary Institute) at the Universitat Oberta de Catalunya and member of *Mediaccions* Digital Culture Research Group. As an anthropologist also trained in filmmaking, she has been doing fieldwork among technological corporations in Buenos Aires and Barcelona, incorporating visual and digital anthropology. Her current research focuses upon understanding how digital technology and its processes of creation, imagination, and production are being made in the context of Urban Labs. She is currently focusing on developments at the interface of Smart City and Internet-of-things, the study of digital materiality, labor, and moral order. Her publications include "Digital visualities and materialities: paths for an anthropological walk" (2014); "Technology and visions of the future: imagination in the process of digital creation from an ethnographic approach" (2014) and "Materiality and experience in the Smart Future-Present of urban design" in Pink, Ardèvol and Lanzeni, *Digital Materiality: Anthropology and Design* (forthcoming).

Christian Licoppe, X (76), ENST (81), a sociologist trained in history and sociology of science and technology, is currently Professor of Sociology at the Social Science department at Telecom Paristech, after managing social science research at France Telecom R&D, and acting as head of the department for several years. Among other things he has worked in the field of mobility and communication studies for several years. He has used mobile geolocation and communication data to analyze mobility and sociability patterns of mobile phone users. He has studied extensively one of the first location-aware communities (the Mogi players in Japan 2003–2008) and the rich configurations of augmented encounters its evolving culture supports. He has also developed ethnographic approaches of complex activity systems relying on innovative use of communication technologies, at the intersection of sociology of work, organization studies, and anthropology of activity. He has extensively studied call centers (in the telecommunications and banking sectors) and legal activities (such as courtroom hearings relying on the use of videoconference), and is currently developing a general analysis of interactions in telepresence settings.

Mirca Madianou is Reader in the Department of Media and Communications at Goldsmiths, University of London where she co-founded the Media Ethnography Group. She has published extensively on the social consequences of social and mobile media especially in relation to processes of transnationalism and migration. She currently directs the ESRC program "Humanitarian Technologies" which investigates the social uses of communication technologies in disasters and humanitarian emergencies. She is the author of *Mediating the Nation: News, Audiences and the Politics of Identity* (2005) and *Migration and New Media: Transnational Families and Polymedia* (2012, with D. Miller) as well as editor of *Ethics of Media* (2013, with N. Couldry and A. Pinchevski).

George E. Marcus is currently Chancellor's Professor and Chair of the Department of Anthropology at the University of California, Irvine. In the 1980s and 1990s he led a small anthropology department at Rice University known for its development of research as critique, and the emergence of new strategies in the writing of ethnography. He has continued this work through a Center for Ethnography at UCI with new and longtime associates. The emphasis is on producing "intermediate" forms of ethnographic expression stimulated by collaborations with designers, artists, and informatics scholars and technicians.

Crystle Martin is Postdoctoral Research Fellow for the Digital Media and Learning Hub at University of California, Irvine. She finished her PhD in Curriculum & Instruction specializing in Digital Media from the University of Wisconsin–Madison. Her dissertation focused on learning and information literacy practices in the community of the massively multiplayer game *World of Warcraft*. It is published as a book entitled *Voyage Across a Constellation of Information: Information Literacy in Interest-Driven Learning Communities*. Her research focuses on youth learning in informal spaces, specializing in information literacy and connected learning, and how those skills, if valued in academic settings, can create a more equitable education system. She is currently exploring computational thinking and future paths in the online Scratch community, as well as methods for equitably implementing coding programs in public libraries.

Bill Maurer is Professor of Anthropology, Law, and Criminology, Law, and Society at the University of California, Irvine. Since 2013, he has served as Dean of the School of Social Sciences at UC–Irvine. He is considered one of the leading cultural anthropologists of money, economic processes, and financial practices, and is the founder of the subfield of anthropology of finance. He is founding director of the Institute for Money, Technology and Financial Inclusion, funded by the Bill and Melinda Gates Foundation. He is the author or editor of nine books, including the soon to be released *How Would You Like To Pay? How Technology Is Changing the Future of Money* (Duke University Press), and regularly provides expert consultation for industry, government, and non-profit bodies seeking to use technology to enhance financial inclusion. He holds a PhD and MA in Anthropology, both from Stanford University.

Tom McDonald is Assistant Professor at the University of Hong Kong. He obtained his PhD from University College London in 2013, where he also worked on the Why We Post project. He has conducted extensive ethnographic research in rural China, and has published papers in *Ethnos* and *Information, Communication and Society*. His first solely authored monograph, *Social Media in Rural China: Social Networks and Moral Frameworks* (UCL Press), was published in 2016.

Sheba Mohammid is a PhD candidate in the Digital Ethnography Research Centre at RMIT University. Her research focuses on notions of the "knowledge society" and on the ground practices and tensions in digital media and knowledge creation, sharing, and use. She has worked for over ten years in digital media and development policy and interventions. She has been named an Emerging Leader for the Digital World (EU/ACP Program/ DiploFoundation), and has served as ICT policy specialist, digital inclusion coordinator, e-learning practitioner, and e-participation expert in organizations ranging from government to NGOs and academia. She coordinated the creation of the National Knowledge Gateway of Trinidad and Tobago. She has designed and implemented e-learning initiatives for audiences in over 50 countries across the world.

Katherine Moline is Senior Lecturer in research practices at the University of New South Wales, School of Art & Design, Sydney. Katherine explores the crossovers between avant-gardism in visual art and contemporary experimental design. Her focus is how experimental practice reformulates the social pacts of art and design. Since co-convening the symposium "sds2k4: Experimental and Cross-Cultural Design" (2004), she curated the exhibition "Connections: Experimental Design" (2007) and introduced international leaders in experimental and critical design to Australian audiences. More recent exhibitions she has curated or for which she has led curatorial teams after completing her doctorate include "Feral Experimental" at UNSW (2014), "Experimental Practice: Provocations" at RMIT (2015), "Experimental Thinking" at Griffith University (2015), and "Climactic: Post Normal Design" at Carnegie Mellon University, Pittsburgh (2016).

Julien Morel is Associate Professor SES, TelecomParisTech, France. He studies the natural organization of face-to-face and mediated interactions (mobile conversations, video communication, location-aware communities, and augmented reality games). He also develops new video methodologies to study the uses of ICT in situations of mobility.

Bjorn Nansen is Lecturer in Media and Communications at the University of Melbourne, a Melbourne Network Society Institute Digital Media Fellow, and a member of the Research Unit in Public Cultures and Microsoft Social NUI Research Centre. His research interests include technology adoption, home media environments, young children and mobile media, digitally mediated death, and post-digital interfaces. He currently holds an Australian Research Council-funded Discovery Early Career Researcher Award.

Amani Naseem is a designer and researcher from the Maldives currently based in Melbourne. She works with creative people from different disciplines in the intersection of art and technology. Her work has been shown internationally at festivals and exhibitions such as the 55th Venice Biennale. A member of the Copenhagen Game Collective, she maintains collaborations with various actors within the Copenhagen arts, games, and interactive scenes. Amani is pursuing a PhD at the Royal Melbourne Institute of Technology where she works with art, games, activism, and context creation within the emerging worldwide movements working between interactive art, performance, and games.

Taylor C. Nelms is Postdoctoral Researcher at the University of California, Irvine, where he also earned his PhD in Anthropology. His research concerns money, law, technology, and the state, especially in the context of efforts to reimagine economy and society in Latin America and beyond. He has written about dollarization, the solidarity economy, and post-neoliberal governance in Ecuador, as well as "zombie banks" and Bitcoin. He has also worked at the Institute for Money, Technology and Financial Inclusion supporting research on mobile financial services and everyday money practices.

Razvan Nicolescu is Research Associate at University College London. Trained both in telecommunication and anthropology, he has conducted ethnographic research in Romania and Italy. His research interests focus on visibility and digital anthropology; political economy, governance, and informality; feelings, subjectivity, and normativity. He is currently part of the Why We Post project and has completed the volume *Social Media in Southeast Italy: Crafting Ideals* at UCL Press.

Didem Özkul is Lecturer in Media and Communications at the London College of Communication, University of the Arts London, and a visiting fellow at the Department of Media and Communications, London School of Economics and Political Science. Her research focuses on mobile media and communications, different aspects of place and meaning-making through the use of mobile communication technologies and their location-aware features, and mobile app ecosystems and the economic and societal dynamics behind the production, ownership, and control of location data.

Tom Penney is a lecturer and Industry Fellow in Digital Media and Games at RMIT University, where he is also a PhD candidate. His art practice involves 3D imaging, games technology, and digital design. Tom's current research project Critical Affection investigates an expanded notion of "critical play" and affect through digital contemporary art practice through a subversive representation of online dating apps. His academic work has been published through journals and conferences including *Media International Australia*, *The Feminist Journal of Art and Digital Culture*, *The International Journal of Contemporary Humanities*, and the International Symposium of Electronic Art.

Sarah Pink is RMIT Distinguished Professor and Director of the Digital Ethnography Research Centre, in the School of Media and Communication at RMIT University, Australia. She is also Visiting Professor at the Swedish Centre for Applied Cultural Analysis at Halmstad University, Sweden and in the Schools of Design and Civil and Building

Engineering at Loughborough University, UK. Her research is interdisciplinary and brings together academic scholarship and applied practice. Her recent co-authored and co-edited books include *Digital Ethnography: Principles and Practice* (2016), *Digital Materialities* (2016), the *Un/Certainty* iBook (2015), and *Media, Anthropology and Public Engagement* (2015).

John Postill is Vice-Chancellor's Senior Research Fellow at RMIT University, Melbourne, and Digital Anthropology Fellow at University College London (UCL). His publications include *Localizing the Internet* (2011), *Media and Nation Building* (2006), and the co-edited volume *Theorising Media and Practice* (2010, with Birgit Bräuchler). Currently he is writing a book about digital activism and political change in Indonesia, Spain, and globally, as well as the co-edited volume *Theorising Media and Change* (with Elisenda Ardèvol and Sirpa Tenhunen).

Stephen C. Rea has been Visiting Assistant Professor of Anthropology at Bucknell University since 2015. He received his PhD in Anthropology from the University of California, Irvine in 2015. From 2010 to 2015 Stephen worked as a research assistant with the Institute for Money, Technology and Financial Inclusion, where he developed an interest in the social, cultural, political, and infrastructural factors incumbent upon mobile financial services (MFS) deployments. He has also conducted extensive fieldwork in South Korea on that country's information infrastructure and online gaming culture.

Ingrid Richardson is Associate Professor in the School of Arts at Murdoch University, Western Australia. She has a broad interest in the human–technology relation and has published on topics such as scientific technovision, virtual and augmented reality, urban screens, wearable technologies, the phenomenology of games and mobile media, digital ethnography, remix culture, and web-based content creation and distribution. She is co-author with Larissa Hjorth of *Gaming in Social, Locative and Mobile Media* (2014).

Juan Francisco Salazar is an anthropologist and media producer. He currently holds an associate professor position in both the School of Humanities and Communication Arts and the Institute for Culture and Society at Western Sydney University. He is co-author of *Screen Media Arts: Introduction to Concepts and Practices* (2008, Oxford University Press, with H. Cohen and I. Barkat), and co-editor of *Anthropology and Futures: Researching Emerging and Uncertain Worlds* (Bloomsbury, forthcoming, with S. Pink, A. Irving, and J. Sjoberg). His research interests and expertise center on media anthropology; visual/digital ethnographies; citizens' media; Indigenous media and communication rights in Chile and Latin America; documentary cinemas; environmental communication; climate change; future studies; and cultural studies of Antarctica.

Christo Sims is Assistant Professor in the Department of Communication at the University of California, San Diego. He is also a founding member of the UCSD Studio for Ethnographic Design and the University of California Collaboratory for Ethnographic Design. His research focuses on the interweaving of morality, politics, and technology, and, in particular, techno-centric attempts to "do good." He is the author of *Disruptive Fixation: School Reform and the Pitfalls of Techno-Idealism* (Princeton, 2017), an ethnography about the design and launch of the first school in the United States to organize its entire curriculum to be "game-like." Between 2005 and 2008, he was a researcher for the Digital Youth Project, the largest qualitative study of young American people and new media to date, and a co-author of the project's final book, *Hanging Out, Messing Around, and Geeking Out* (MIT Press, 2010). He received his PhD from the University of California, Berkeley's School of Information in the summer of 2012.

Jolynna Sinanan is Vice-Chancellor's Research Fellow in the Digital Ethnography Research Centre at RMIT. Prior to this appointment, she was Research Associate in Anthropology at University College London, where she was part of the Why We Post project. She is currently completing the volumes *Visualising Facebook: A Comparative Perspective* (with Daniel Miller) and *Social Media in Trinidad* for UCL Press. Her most recent book is *Webcam* (Polity), also co-authored with Daniel Miller.

Sirpa Tenhunen is an anthropologist who teaches in the University of Jyväskylä as Professor (interim) and university lecturer. She has also taught anthropology in the University of Helsinki and worked as a researcher in the Academy of Finland. In addition to new media, her research interests cover gender, work, and politics in India.

Susana Tosca is Associate Professor at the IT University of Copenhagen, Denmark, where she is a member of the Culture and Communication research group. She is currently teaching the Digital Experiences and Aesthetics Course (BA) and its specialization on Creative Digital Practice (MA), at ITU. Her research interests include digital storytelling, transmediality, computer games, digital aesthetics, hypertext, popular culture, and IT in the primary school.

Luke van Ryn is a PhD candidate in the School of Culture and Communications at the University of Melbourne. His current research focuses on the intersection between media technologies and everyday life, and he is completing a thesis on issues of environmental sustainability in media production.

Cara Wallis is Associate Professor in the Department of Communication at Texas A&M University. She studies the social and cultural implications of emerging media technologies, with a particular focus on how uses and understandings of technology both reproduce inequitable power relations and open up spaces for individual and collective agency and thus, social change. She is the author of *Technomobility in China: Young Migrant Women and Mobile Phones* (NYU Press, 2013), which is an ethnographic exploration of the use of mobile phones by young rural-to-urban migrant women working in the low-level service sector in Beijing.

Emma Witkowski is Lecturer at RMIT University, Melbourne with the Games Design Program. She earned her PhD in Game Studies from the IT University of Copenhagen in 2012, taking a phenomenologically inspired sociological approach to the study of high performance team play in networked computer games. She contributes to the Digital Ethnography Research Centre by running the Media Methods node and her most recent research explores the production of masculinities in e-sports, women and live-streaming, and running with mobile gaming/fitness technologies.

ACKNOWLEDGMENTS

The editors would like to acknowledge the Australian Research Council linkage with Intel, Locating the Mobile (LP130100848), as well as the Digital Ethnography Research Centre (DERC) and the School of Media and Communication at RMIT University. We would like to thank the tireless Esther Pierini for keeping everything in check and to Klare Lanson for a final double check of the manuscript.

ABBREVIATIONS

ANT	Actor Network Theory
BBS	Bulletin Board Services
DIY	Do It Yourself
ICTs	Information Communication Technologies
IRC	Internet Relay Chat
ISP	Independent Service Provider
Keitai	Japanese word for mobile phone
Locative media	Media of communication bound to a location
LOS	Line of Sight
MMOB	Multi-Media on Board (Hong Kong public transport)
MMORPG	Massively Multiple Player Online Role Playing Games
MMS	Multimedia Messaging Service
MUDs	Multi-User Dungeons
SMS	Short Message Service (text messaging)
STS	Science and Technology Studies
UCC	User Created Content
UGC	User Generated Content
VPN	Virtual Private Network
WiFi	Wireless Fidelity
WWW	World Wide Web

INTRODUCTION

Larissa Hjorth, Heather Horst, Anne Galloway, and Genevieve Bell

As the digital becomes increasingly entwined within everyday life, ethnography's value as a key methodological and analytical approach to understand the ways in which digital media technologies are changing how we live, work, and play has increased (Pink et al. 2016; Hine 2015). Bringing together scholars from a variety of disciplines including anthropology, sociology, media, communication, and cultural studies, the *Companion* reflects upon and seeks to assess the past, present, and future of digital ethnography. Through a series of key rubrics—Debating Digital Ethnography; Relationships; Visibility and Voice; Place and Co-presence; Play; Arts; Infrastructures; Politics; and Design—*The Routledge Companion to Digital Ethnography* considers the interdisciplinary role of digital ethnography as we move into progressively more complex digital entanglements within the everyday.

In this Editor's Introduction we outline the nine rubrics and the attendant 44 chapters that constitute the current state of digital ethnography research. We conclude by introducing three provocations for the future of digital ethnography. The *Companion* begins with a section dedicated to Debating Digital Ethnography that contextualizes contemporary debates about the consequences of digital media technologies for ethnographic practice from different disciplinary vantage points. The first chapter by anthropologists Mike Fortun, Kim Fortun, and George E. Marcus provides a short history of computers in anthropology that stems back to Clifford and Marcus' *Writing Culture* (a seminal text in defining the politics and practices of ethnography and fieldwork) to contextualize new modes of ethnographic research, collaboration, and expression. Similarly, sociologist Christine Hine draws from a decade and a half of ethnographies focused on the Internet to consider how digital media cultures have shaped ethnography as a practice, reflecting upon the changes and continuity within the academy. Science and Technology Studies scholar Anne Beaulieu follows Hine with a discussion of how computationalization shapes some of the adaptations of ethnographic methods, a framework that ethnomusicologist Wendy F. Hsu also explores through her discussion of performance. Hsu further questions "the purpose of writing as the predominant expression of ethnographic knowledge" within the context of digital media.

Debating Digital Ethnography continues with reflections by two contributors, Jenna Burrell and John Postill, who consider how the digital media technologies in our fieldsites and fieldwork represent continuity rather than rupture with previous ethnographic practice.

Burrell, for example, highlights how online practices make visible the notion of "the fieldsite as a network" that is meaningfully constructed through the ethnographer's experience. Postill also argues for continuity, noting that ethnography has long involved studying at a distance, but digital media technologies make researching from a distance—doing remote ethnography—easier. The section concludes with a chapter by Georgina Born and Christopher Haworth who reflect upon the meaning of digital ethnography itself. As they highlight, digital ethnography has a double meaning—it refers to deploying the ethnographic to understand digital culture as it does apply to the use of digital methodologies increasingly within ethnographic research.

The next section, Relationships, focuses upon the different forms of sociality that are being mediated through digital media cultures—especially social media. It begins with a contribution by Tom McDonald, Razvan Nicolescu, and Jolynna Sinanan who draw upon their participation on a large, collaborative project of social media use in nine fieldsites to reflect upon how social media is shaping, and being shaped by, small communities around the world. Moving from communities to families, Mirca Madianou examines how Filipino transnational family practices are being transformed in light of the ubiquitous presence of communication—what she calls "polymedia" environments. Luke van Ryn, Tamara Kohn, Bjorn Nansen, Michael Arnold, and Martin Gibbs consider how the practices around memorialization and death rituals are being altered and amplified by social media, with particular attention to how people continue to form relationships with the dead through social media profiles and pages that often persist after their death. The final chapter by Guillaume Dumont turns our attention to the possibilities of social media to move beyond kinship or place-based social ties to develop new relationships. Dumont illustrates how professional rock climbers use a variety of social media strategies, especially self-branding, to cultivate their relations with fans, their sponsors, and other professional climbers.

The third section, Visibility and Voice, attends to the potential and the limits of digital media technologies to transform who, when, and how people are seen and heard, and how digital media cultures may replicate or transform existing offline forms of inequality and participation. The chapter by Cara Wallis and Xi Cui turns our attention to the social media site Weibo in China. Building upon Couldry's definition of voice, Wallis and Cui highlight the ways in which Weibo both amplifies and silences voices in China and the implications of this for developing an online public sphere in China. Patricia G. Lange reconsiders the agency of YouTube video creators, in a context where videos posted online are perceived as collective property that can be remixed or even deleted. These conditions complicate and, in some cases, counteract the agency and self-expression enabled through sites such as YouTube. Crystal Abidin's chapter, by contrast, chronicles how a small community of commercial "lifestyle" microcelebrities engaged in self-branding in Singapore used a range of social media to transform themselves from mere "bloggers" to "influencers" using their visibility and voice for economic gain. The final chapter by Sheba Mohammid and Heather Horst on amateur musicians in Trinidad and Tobago suggests that while YouTube and other sites may assist with skills development and exposure to new audiences, many musicians still feel their voice and visibility is limited unless they migrate internationally.

Part IV investigates the overlay between Place and Co-presence. Co-presence has been a useful concept in the rise of online and mobile media to consider the various forms of presence whereby face-to-face (f2f) is not taken as superior or unmediated. Rather, all forms of communication are mediated—if not by technology, then by gestures, memories, and emotions. Jordan Kraemer's chapter considers the role of ethnography to reflect upon culture, selfhood, and place through the emergent European transnationalism on social media in

Berlin during the #JeSuisCharlie hashtag campaign of 2015. Kat Jungnickel's chapter critically examines the cultures and practices of a grassroots hand-made version of the Internet in suburban Australia, highlighting the value of these practices for helping to imagine new ways of deploying the online and attendant forms of agency within everyday life. The following chapter by Christian Licoppe and Julien Morel turns our attention to the role of locative mobile media in "the development of unplanned, fleeting encounters with pseudonymous strangers, and virtual acquaintances in urban public places," a finding that builds upon yet also challenges Goffman's theory of frame analysis. The last two chapters of this section consider the role of mobile media in challenging notions of place. Ingrid Richardson and Brendan Keogh, for example, approach mobile media as an itinerant interface—between ethnography and phenomenology—that traverses and interweaves material, corporeal, networked, online, and offline contexts. The final chapter by Didem Özkul attends to the critical role of mobile communication as a practice of place making.

Part V, Play, focuses upon the intersection between the contexts and practices of play. Tom Apperley's chapter begins with his examination of gaming as a localized cultural practice through the case study of a Venezuelan cybercafé in which he reflects upon how play can afford spaces for social inclusion in technologically constrained environments. Crystle Martin's chapter on World Wrestling Entertainment (WWE) and its fandom shifts this section to forms of play that often do not receive the attention of gaming scholars yet represent some of the most popular forms of play globally. The next contribution by Emma Witkowski attends to the location-based running mobile app, *Zombies, Run!*, and the ways in which the app draws upon women's feelings of vulnerability in public space. Building upon her phenomenological study of running, gender, and play, Witkowski argues that understanding these playful movements in public spaces can help to rethink the relationship between the body and locality. The final chapter by Isabel Fróes and Susana Tosca examines children's practices in and around emergent mobile technologies (especially tablets) through a focus upon the role of children's hands. Together, the work by Witkowski, Fróes, and Tosca combines phenomenological and digital ethnographic approaches to advance our understandings of play and the body.

The *Companion* then turns its attention to the interplay between digital ethnography and the Arts. The chapter by Paolo Favero reflects upon the ethnographer's role as increasingly like that of a curator whereby they are exhibiting "the ethnographic" in new open-ended modes that reflect the "multimodal, non-linear, relational, and materic engagements with the visual world that characterize the habitats of contemporary art." Larissa Hjorth, William Balmford, Sharon Greenfield, luke gaspard, Amani Naseem, and Tom Penney's contribution explores the role of digital and non-digital play through a series of workshops with young people. The chapter considers how participatory design and art practice can inform ethnographic methods (and vice versa). Drawing upon long-term ethnographic research on digital photography, Edgar Gómez Cruz explores what he terms the "(be)coming of selfies"—that is, the conditions and processes that configured the development of imagery as a central element in online practices. Marsha Berry looks at the emergence of mobile filmmaking, with particular attention to the ways in which smartphones are affording new types of curation and transmedia filmmaking. The final chapter of this section, by Jennifer Deger, returns to the theme of curation through a discussion of her collaborative work on mobile phones with remote Aboriginal communities across north Australia. Deger posits an integration of visual and digital ethnographies that provoke and enable new forms of ethnographic poetics.

The next section, Infrastructures, considers the multiple dimensions and roles of infrastructure (social, material, immaterial to name a few) in thinking through the politics and practice of digital ethnography. Building upon the previous section's focus upon curation and the arts, Haidy Geismar interrogates the emergence and use of Instagram as a platform, software, and archive. Taking an anthropological perspective on smartphone photography and social media, Geismar argues that a study of Instagram as archive should

> embed this technological practice and digital infrastructure in broader issues about the representation of culture and the culture of representation, the epistemologies of social media archives, and the form of collecting and exhibiting popular and personal photographs both online and on mobile platforms.

Alexandrine Boudreault-Fournier's work on digital music circulation in Cuba shifts our attention from platforms and software to use, through an analysis of digital music technologies. Boudreault-Fournier argues that digital music technologies have enabled alternative networks to emerge to counteract the limits and restrictions on media circulation in contemporary Havana, and concludes the chapter with a reflection on the changes these music technologies have made to the practice of (digital) ethnography.

Hannah Knox's chapter takes an "infrastructural approach to digital ethnography" in order to understand social change. Drawing on her fieldwork on domestic energy use, Knox argues that an infrastructural approach enables insights into the interplay between the technical, the material, and the social. The next chapter by Stephen C. Rea, Ursula Dalinghaus, Taylor C. Nelms, and Bill Maurer analyzes both technical and social infrastructures for "financial inclusion" through mobile payments. Comparing three financial inclusion efforts—Kenya's M-Shwari, Reserve Bank of India's "payments banks," and the Central Bank Ecuador's mobile payment system—Rea et al. demonstrate how mobile payment systems "ride the rails" of other infrastructures. This section concludes with a chapter by Juan Francisco Salazar on "polar infrastructures." As Salazar observes, "infrastructures are built networks that facilitate circulation of goods, people, and data and allow for their exchange over space." In Antarctica, there are multiple national infrastructures that underpin Antarctica's mobile telecommunications networks whose operations require an understanding of the other infrastructures that shape life on Antarctica.

The next section in the *Companion* is focused upon Politics. Sirpa Tenhunen begins by reflecting upon the interplay between mobile phones in India and the long history of engagement in local politics in rural West Bengal, India where she has been working for over a decade. The implications of new mobile telecommunications infrastructure for political engagement continue in Mirjam de Bruijn's chapter on mediated political agency in contested regions of Africa. Focusing on mobile social media, de Bruijn highlights how it is opening up spaces for sharing opinions and dissent in ways not possible in public spaces in conflict areas of central and southern Africa. Veronica Barassi then turns our focus to a series of three political groups in Europe to understand the complexities of activism through social media. In particular Barassi draws attention to the tension between collective social movements through social media and the corporate entities that own the platforms and infrastructures for social media activism.

The chapter by Heather Ford continues this thread through a focus on Wikipedia participants in Nairobi, Kenya. Specifically, Ford reflects upon the "authoritative" and seemingly inclusive force of Wikipedia and what gets rejected and silenced by today's knowledge production machine. The final chapter of this section by Richard Beckwith and ken anderson explores the role of environmental sensing and control in the context of Portland, USA. Focused upon the ways in which different stakeholders emerge around access, use, sharing, and ownership of sensor data, Beckwith and anderson consider the productive tensions between civic engagement, participation, and the emergence of "data citizens."

The *Companion* concludes with a section on Design, especially the intersection between design and the future of ethnographic practice. Christo Sims begins this with his chapter "The Politics of Design, Design as Politics." Through fieldwork on a recent design project—a new public school in New York City—the chapter proposes ethnography has much to learn from design practice and failure. The next chapter, by Elisenda Ardèvol and Débora Lanzeni, reflects upon their fieldwork with digital designers in Barcelona, Spain, arguing that ethnography is a process of knowledge not about the world as it is, but the universe that we learn with others. The following three chapters explore the possibilities between design and ethnography through an exploration of three interventions that take a speculative approach to design. The first of these, by Yoko Akama, Katherine Moline, and Sarah Pink, considers "disruptive interventions with mobile media" through *Design+Ethnography+Futures*, a research initiative to explore how a future orientation to research could invite new forms of change-making. The next chapter by Anne Galloway focuses upon the creation and aspirations of the More-Than-Human Lab which seeks to explore sustainable possibilities for people to live with animals, plants, and the land. The final chapter, by Elizabeth Chin, poetically brings together the politics of design—especially the erasure of race—with the speculative turn by using wearables to examine inequality through design, enabling participants to re-imagine what is and what can be. Collectively the projects reflect upon the limits and possibilities of design for engaging social change.

Provocations: The Future of Digital Ethnography

As in any field-defining endeavor, this *Companion* does not and cannot include every domain or dimension of digital ethnography. Rather, it seeks to provide readers with positioned perspectives on key debates in and around digital ethnography as a field, frame, and set of methods. Over the 44 chapters that constitute this volume, we have identified nine key rubrics that represent important conversations in this interdisciplinary field, ones that we view as moving the field forward in productive ways. In this concluding section we briefly outline three areas that have emerged from this *Companion* that we believe are fruitful directions for digital ethnography.

Interdisciplinary Iterations

Throughout the chapters in this *Companion* many of the authors articulated the need to consider the ways in which ethnography—and digital ethnography—is shaping our methodological practices as well as the epistemological frameworks that we operate within. The first section of the *Companion*, Debating Digital Ethnography, includes provocative chapters by Hine, Postill, and Hsu as well as Born and Haworth that all directly address how the practice of ethnography is changing due to an engagement with digital environments. However, many of the chapters in the Art and Design sections also draw our attention to the ways in which the interdisciplinary spaces through which we operate spur further thinking about the utility and usefulness of ethnography. We see this process in Deger's collaboration and curation of an exhibit that is now travelling globally, or in Favero's discussion of open modes of curation. We also gain insight into new possibilities through Ardèvol and Lanzeni's discussion of openness and ongoingness in their engagement with designers. The chapters by Hsu on performance and Chin on wearables and performance provoke ethnographers (and designers) to use these technologies to explore possible futures, opening up new forms of engagement with arenas such as "data" (see below). In effect, design and art can provide spaces for speculation and for creative, even playful explorations of ethnography as a series of changing approaches, theories, and probes. Continued commitment to these interdisciplinary conversations is critical for the vibrancy of digital ethnography as a field and practice.

Data Ethnographies

While not designed into the original call for contributor papers to this *Companion*, throughout the volume there is evidence of an increasing engagement with "data," including different forms of so-called "big data." With a few notable exceptions (e.g. Boellstorff and Maurer 2015a, 2015b; Nafus and Sherman 2014), ethnographers have been somewhat reluctant to engage with the spate of research on big data. In part this is due to an ongoing commitment to stay attuned to the everydayness of our engagement with digital media technologies. Data—big, better, small, rotten, or uncooked (Boellstorff and Maurer 2015a, 2015b)—is becoming part of day-to-day life for many people around the world (see Beckwith and anderson, this volume). Many researchers are exploring the limits of Big Data (boyd and Crawford 2012; Lupton 2016) as well as deploying ethnography to understand Big Data as a type of storytelling that consists of the gaps, biases, and power relations (Watts and Nafus 2013).

Indeed, at the Digital Ethnography Research Centre (DERC) where two of the editors (Hjorth and Horst) work, a series of workshops was convened to focus upon "data ethnography." Workshop participants have to date explored the emergence of data in everyday life through studies of self-tracking technologies, the shift to mobile data in small island developing states, the role of data in games and playful media, the relationship between data and selfies and a range of other topics (see Pink, Horst, and Hjorth 2016 in preparation). We have also been interested in what it is like to live, feel, and imagine with data. While engaging with big data analytics may be part of this discussion, an ethnographic approach to understanding data (of whatever size or scale) promises to yield new insights for our understanding of data, and the practice of digital ethnography.

Making and Theorizing Change

Finally, it is clear that ethnography is not merely a useful tool to describe everyday practice; it is also playing a critical role in intervening in the world. Drawing from the empirical, ethnography can provide insight into motivations and practices that in turn shape future directions for digital media. This is made most explicit in the chapters in the three sections on Politics, Infrastructures, and Design. For example, Akama et al.'s *Design+Ethnography+Futures* initiative and Galloway's More-Than-Human Lab all seek forms of intervention in the world to enable and enhance change-making. Hjorth et al.'s exploration of the intersection between play, art, and design through workshops with young people considers how ethnography can enable reflection and change with formal and informal contexts. Barassi's account of political groups in Europe also looks to the possibilities of social media for making change. Yet, these moves to shift ethnography and ethnographers toward the practice of intervention carefully hinges upon a sustained commitment to understanding the realities of digital media's shaping of the world, and theorizing of social change more broadly.

The focus upon the hidden infrastructures in Rea et al.'s account of mobile money and financial inclusion efforts reinforces the need to understand the structural and regulatory environments that create conditions of use. Many of the chapters also interrogate the design and ownership structures of the corporations such as Instagram and, in Ford's study of Wikipedians, the structures of participation that shape use. In the studies of self-branding by Dumont and Abidin and the studies of visual cultures and user agency by the likes of Berry and Cruz, we see how consumption and production practices are changing. Wallis, Xi Cui, and de Bruijn's chapters highlight the seminal role of the state—and state restrictions and prohibitions—in making different platforms meaningful. Others account for changes and resistances to digital media across different cultural contexts reinforcing the importance of attending to history and context. Digital ethnography will only be effective inasmuch as it makes a commitment to understanding, making, and theorizing change alongside the commitment to deep, thick readings of nuanced practices. Meaningful interventions—even methodological interventions—must be situated within the broader social and historical contexts. Research focused upon understanding how, when, and why change occurs also requires an openness to working with this knowledge—and the collaborators with whom we engage in the field, online, in the academy, and in the world—to engage in change-making. This productive tension is key to digital ethnography's own future as a field.

References

Boellstorff, Tom and Bill Maurer. 2015a. "Introduction." In *Data, Now Bigger and Better!*, edited by Tom Boellstorff and Bill Maurer, 1–6. Chicago, IL: Prickly Paradigm Press.

——. (eds.) 2015b. *Data, Now Bigger and Better!* Chicago, IL: Prickly Paradigm Press.

boyd, danah and Kate Crawford. 2012. "Critical Questions for Big Data." *Information, Communication & Society*, 15(5): 662–79.

Hine, Christine. 2015. *Ethnography of the Internet*. London: Bloomsbury.

Lupton, Deborah. 2016. *The Quantified Self*. London: Polity.

Nafus, Dawn and Jamie Sherman. 2014. "Big Data, Big Questions| This One Does Not Go Up To 11: The Quantified Self Movement as an Alternative Big Data Practice." *International Journal of Communication*, 8: 11.

Pink, Sarah, Heather Horst, John Postill, Larissa Hjorth, Tania Lewis, and Jo Tacchi. 2016. *Digital Ethnography: Principles and Practice*. London: Sage.

Watts, Laura and Dawn Nafus. 2013. *Data Stories*. Orkney: Sand14/Brae Editions. http://sand14.com/data-stories/

Part I

DEBATING DIGITAL ETHNOGRAPHY

1

COMPUTERS IN/AND ANTHROPOLOGY

The Poetics and Politics of Digitization

Mike Fortun, Kim Fortun, and George E. Marcus

Introduction

The Use of Computers in Anthropology (Hymes 1965) is a massive volume stemming from a 1962 Wenner-Gren symposium held in their Austrian castle. The book is rich with diverse and provocative articles detailing early experiences—experiments, even—with computers among anthropologists.[1] The collection is headed by an un-sourced quote from Claude Levi-Strauss: ". . . the fundamental requirement of anthropology," this epigraph reads, "is that it begin with a personal relation and end with a personal experience, but . . . in between there is room for plenty of computers" (Hymes 1965, 5).

Both volume and epigraph seem worth quoting at the opening of a chapter for a companion to digital ethnography—for substantive reasons as well as more theoretical or methodological reasons. Substantively, the quote and the volume itself point to the capacious, plentiful "room" in which anthropology finds itself in the company of computers—in 1965, 2015, and any time in between and beyond. There is lots of room in anthropology—digital and otherwise—for lots of computational devices, and each of these multitudes can be put into lots of configurations. It is once again, as we will argue here, a time (1965, 2015, 2065 . . .) ripe for experimentation, when anthropologists have ample tools and ample spaces in which to work and play with them, toward multiple theoretical and practical ends. And they have ample opportunity and need to do so, we will also argue, within new forms of collaboration.

The quote and volume also reference a formal, structural, or infrastructural concern, which in turn points to an important difference between 1962 as a time of "the computer," and the digital anthropologies of 2015 and beyond. The Levi-Strauss quote—and it is clearly a quote, with quotation marks and ellipses—is un-sourced. Was it spoken or written? When, where, to whom, in what context? That data—or more accurately, that metadata—is not provided in the 1965 volume on anthropology, computers, and the emergent field of new data, methods, and theories. A quick and easy search of the Internet in 2015, however, turns up . . . only a reference to this very 1965 volume, in an informative series on the history of computers in anthropology by Nick Seaver, written for the important, long-running blog-experiment in digital anthropology *Savage Minds* (2014). We learn a great deal about the long history of computers in/and anthropology there (well worth reading but which we cannot recap here), but nothing further about the Levi-Strauss utterance.

This Levi-Strauss quote points to important differences marking the contemporary period in this history of computers in/and anthropology, as well as some enduring features. What we would today call the *provenance* of the Levi-Strauss quote is lost in the 1965 publication. The individual articles in that volume present fascinating accounts of early anthropological experiments with computers, in some cases complete with elaborate fold-outs of machine diagrams and programming matrices, along with finely crafted summaries of the wide-ranging and at times probably heated discussions that took place in 1962—but not actual transcripts that would allow us now, in their future, to attribute and re-consider exact phrasings, or to re-interpret the interactions, exchanges, and movements that occurred between the presentations. The socio-technical infrastructure that could make that kind of data archiving and sharing possible, and thus desirable, both for anthropological work and for anthropology itself, is only now becoming available.

So at this very different infrastructural moment in the human sciences, we can nevertheless reiterate Dell Hymes' earlier conviction that "the computer" offers an opportunity for "heightening the quality of work" in anthropology. As it was then, it is now an opportunity that demands "increased attention" to two things. The first is "the logic and practice of quantitative and qualitative analysis," the second "the forms of cooperation and integration needed to make our stores of data systematic, comparable, accessible to each other and to theory . . . The story of the computer in anthropology will be the story of how these two demands are met" (Hymes 1965, 31).

It is a remarkable and enduring insight. We continue the story here, heeding the same call to attention but now shifting the demand away from how "the computer" of 1962 (when "the" IBM 790 or 7090 was indeed becoming increasingly common, but nevertheless remained "the" singular machine on a small number of major campuses) asked anthropologists to rethink their forms of analysis and cooperation, and turning to the more multiple, omnipresent, and interlaced digital technologies of the contemporary moment—no doubt an even more plentiful situation than Levi-Strauss might have imagined, but a situation calling, still, for attention to how anthropology might be rewritten in this roomy space filled with new digital technologies, new logics and practices of analysis, and, perhaps most importantly, new forms of data. Paying attention now means remaining open to new forms of theory and new ways to collaborate. It also means re-scripting, rewriting, or redesigning the digital platforms, or cyberinfrastructure, to support those new collaborations and theories.

Digital anthropology has taken and continues to take many forms: writing experiments in the form of blogs (e.g. *Savage Minds*[2]), video mashups (e.g. the work of Michael Wesch[3]), online ethnographies as well as ethnographies of the online (e.g. Chris Kelty,[4] Gabriella Coleman,[5] and Tom Boellstorff[6]), multimedia-enhanced journal portals (e.g. culanth.org[7]), new publishing collectives (e.g. limn[8]), and various forms of hypertexts and "enhanced media" projects (e.g. Povinelli and Cho 2012). All of these writing experiments are enabled in part by new forms of technical writing, new codes and languages from XML to WordPress, tools that are written *in* or *into* rather than simply on digital media. Such experiments in digital anthropology are amply and ably covered elsewhere, including in this volume, so we do not review them in further detail here.

Most of these, and similar digital anthropology projects, important and innovative as they might be, do not call for redesign of digital platforms—the rewriting of what we call the digital form. They can thrive quite well within the current, complex digital ecology. They also remain, by and large, in the mode of the individual anthropologist that has been the dominant methodological form for much of the history of the discipline.

Our focus here is on the need to experiment with digital form in ways that promise to rewrite ethnography and the ethnographic archive, entailing the redesign of the digital infrastructure on which they will exist. We look forward to digital anthropology projects that, by re-animating the ethnographic archive in a variety of ways, will also demand and enable new forms of collaboration among anthropologists. They will also enable and leverage new, more collaborative relations between anthropologists and other researchers not only in the human sciences, but also in computer, information, and data sciences as well.

Writing Cultural Critique, **Digitally**

To put that somewhat differently: the distributed digital technologies of the early twenty-first century *reiterate* the structural—and therefore also the experimental—conditions enabled by the mainframe computer of the 1960s, rather than simply repeat them. Those conditions are: a renewed attention to and questioning of what anthropological theory is and how it gets made, a renewed attention to and questioning of the forms (technical and textual infrastructures) that shape and carry anthropological theory, and a renewed possibility of and need for new forms of collaboration. Similarly, important experiments in digital anthropology also reiterate the arguments and proposals put forward in the mid-1980s signified by the publication of *Writing Culture* (Clifford and Marcus 1986) and *Anthropology as Cultural Critique* (Marcus and Fischer 1986), which we combine here under the heading of *Writing Cultural Critique*. The *Writing Cultural Critique* tradition in cultural anthropology attends to the implications and limits of form—a poetics and politics of ethnography powered, in large part, by poststructuralist understandings of language developed through new exchanges with literary theorists, semioticians, philosophers, and others in the humanities from the 1980s onward.

One thread of the critique focused on the singularity and authority of the ethnographic voice in writing about other peoples, often with considerably less privilege or power. Another thread of the critique focused on time—the way both rhetorical conventions and the material form of the published book or article froze the people being represented in history, restricting recognition of both the ongoing development and the limits of ethnographic analysis of that development. The ethnographic monograph or article literally became the end of analysis. A third thread focused on problems of scale, calling for new forms to write the ways individual cultural actors embody, reproduce, and iterate the nested, often contradictory, cultural and political economic systems they inhabit and which, in turn, inhabit them.

Digital anthropology provides opportunities to reiterate and transform all of these threads of the *Writing Cultural Critique* of ethnographic form, and thus extend the tradition of experimentation they have engendered. The critical and experimental promise of digital anthropology, in our view, lies largely in the potential to enable more collaborative and open-ended ethnographic work/writing—across time, space, generations, and "cultures."

This next generation of digital platforms in anthropology can re-purpose work over the last few decades in *Writing Cultural Critique*, work that foregrounded how cultural critique, innovation, and change emerge, in the world and in the discipline alike, while foregrounding the poetic and political force of the genre forms through which culture is expressed and understood. This now-extensive literature in cultural anthropology has drawn on literary and language theory to address the significance of genre forms both in everyday enactment of culture in different settings, and in scholarly representations of culture.

As the "computer form" opened new possibilities for anthropology in the 1960s, visible in the projects of the Hymes volume, the new digital forms of contemporary anthropology plat-forms can re-purpose anthropological writing into new experimental veins in the twenty-first century. In order to do so, however, anthropologists will have to instantiate—in digital form—elements of the language ideology on which the 1980s legacy systems of anthropology drew. In other words, we have to read digital forms and infrastructures "against the grain," and thus work to rewrite and redesign them. The "computer form" of the 1960s opened up new possibilities for data collection, its analysis, and for collaboration; it also harbored a language ideology that assumed the unmediated representation of pre-existing stable forms, through terms that were transparent and fully present to the ethnographer and ethnographic subject. The computer form meshed beautifully with the pre-Geertzian 1960s cultural anthropology of the Hymes volume, in which "interpretation" has only two brief index entries. Decades of developments in com-puter, data, and web sciences have mostly solidified such a code-centric language ideology, in large part through increasingly elaborate yet precise ontologies (sets of terms with definitive uses) used in projects of "knowledge representation."

Poststructural, anthropological understandings of language, meaning, and culture are still at odds, then, with the language ideologies or assumptions that persist in most digital ("informa-tion" or "data") infrastructure. Digital "tools for humanities work have evolved considerably in the last decade," notes Johanna Drucker, but their "epistemological foundations and fun-damental values are at odds with, or even hostile to, the humanities . . . because of the very assumptions on which they are designed: that objects of knowledge can be understood as self-identical, self-evident, ahistorical, and autonomous" (Drucker 2012, 85–6).

In other words, there is a politics to the "digital form," but the form can always be read "against the grain" and thus—partially, iteratively—rewritten. Through such efforts, today's "digital forms" can open up new possibilities for re-coding an information infrastructure that can harbor a language ideology more attuned to current understandings of both language and anthropology, in which sense disseminates and coalesces from the differences populating the system, from the changing relations by which those "differences make a difference," and from the absences, limits, and aporias that configured the parameters of the system and its operation in ways that may not be fully assayable, but can be experimented with—worked and played with—productively and collaboratively.

This is where digital anthropology theory and practice could orient the development of new digital infrastructure that is "deviously designed," as Lindsay Poirier phrases it, "lever-aged . . . in ways that create tensions against its logics," which it must simultaneously retain (Poirier 2015). We continue this chapter by describing our efforts to develop such "devious" digital infrastructure, the Platform for Experimental Collaborative Ethnography (PECE[9]), and the lessons learned as a result about both anthropology and digital infrastructure, and how it might support new forms of collaborative inquiry, data production and sharing, and similar innovations within and across diverse research fields.

From Open Access to Open Data

Digital forms in contemporary anthropology are generally more "open" than their predecessor "computer form" of the 1960s. The proliferation of various kinds of open access projects—blogs, websites, and journals—is an exciting development and has certainly contributed to a sense of new possibilities in digital anthropology. The legal copyright form and similar forms of digital rights management have been the most significant impediment, and Creative Commons or other "copyleft" licensing forms have been the most important solutions. Combined with readily available open source programs such as Wordpress or Open Journal Systems, that need no fundamental technical reconfiguration, multiple new anthropologies are open and available through this "front end" of digital anthropology platforms.

Opening up the "back end" of digital anthropology—where our data are first collected, produced, and analyzed in the form of fieldnotes, interviews, collected documents, photographs, and so on—is a different challenge and continues to face numerous obstacles, including technical ones. Working through those challenges and around those obstacles has been a primary motivation for developing the open source (Drupal-based) digital platform, the PECE, which supports multi-sited, cross-scale ethnographic and historical research. For PECE to realize its main goals—providing a place to digitally archive and share primary data generated by anthropologists and other empirical humanities scholars, facilitating analytic collaboration that values difference and open-endedness, and encouraging experimentation with diverse modes of publication—it both takes advantage of the capacities of the digital form, and takes on their "devious" reforming and redesign. We describe several aspects of this double strategy below.

The PECE project has been informed in part by our own fieldwork among biomedical, public health, and environmental scientists, for whom the ability to generate new quantities and kinds of data, and to openly exchange and recombine that data, has been transformative for their own work, and for their disciplines. Yet even these researchers, who work primarily with quantitative data that more readily conform to the epistemological foundations and assumptions of the digital form as discussed above, are still engaged in constant redesign of their own digital infrastructure to facilitate their analyses and collaboration. Through developing PECE we have learned how much more difficult this is for qualitative data, which require new technical and cultural protocols to encourage data sharing.

Every day, the world's ethnographic archive increases, as everyone from anthropology graduate students to field elders orchestrate interviews, write up notes from a conversation or experience, photograph or video an encounter with a new person, place, or thing, in any of thousands of places around the planet, concerning anything from a virus to "neoliberalism." Yet even when digitized (which still remains relatively rare), this archive is fragmented, individualized, and inaccessible, and is often closely guarded ("my data") until parts of it might finally be released, in thoroughly cooked and digested form only, in formal publication. The logics here are as evident as they are understandable, and we recognize that large-scale, widespread change in anthropology's own research culture is unlikely to occur easily and even, in some cases, is undesirable. However, the opportunities for experimentation here seem vital to us, and PECE tries to affect a partial shift of anthropology's research culture by easing some of the technical challenges of data sharing and analysis.

The basic unit or "data object" in PECE is an *artifact*: a text, image, audio or video file representing anything from an interview or fieldnote, to "gray" or found documents and objects, to published journal articles. Any and all such data objects must be "modeled," meaning that they need to have written into them the kinds of metadata that would allow a researcher to characterize the provenance—source, history, context—of any ethnographic object (like the Levi-Strauss utterance regarding computers mentioned above), and that would allow for other researchers to discover those objects. Consent, permissions, and other ethico-legal data must also be delineated and made part of the data object, and this often requires rewriting digital tools developed for the natural sciences, where such issues have been less formative. Some digital infrastructure (Omeka,[10] Mukurtu,[11] or the Reciprocal Research Network,[12] for example) now has some capacities such as these, but these kinds of experiments need to be further multiplied and extended if the world's ever-increasing wealth of ethnographic data is to exist as more of a collective rather than an individualized entity.

Interpretation and Annotation as Data in a Feverish Archive

Data in the natural sciences tend to retain stable identities, even if they are complexified and enriched by new forms of metadata. They conform to archival logics in their strictest sense, compiling into an authorized, authoritative, and unchanging foundation of reference. Digital anthropology needs this capacity but it also needs something else: the ability to supplement or augment data through interpretation, in a way that preserves the "original" data while, simultaneously and paradoxically, creating new data. The archives for digital anthropologies need to be the vital, always-emergent and transforming archives (Derrida 1998)—originary and authorizing while always open to new "impressions" and destabilizations.

Here too, designing PECE has taught us both how easy the "digital form" makes it to annotate a data object, but also how that digital form limits interpretive possibilities in particular ways, calling for "devious" rewriting. The need and desire to explain texts and other media are enabled by a growing number of digital modules and applications, many of which were developed specifically for digital humanities platforms, but almost all of these still retain the archival logics of the digital platforms of the natural sciences. "Data" remain data and are privileged as foundational, while comments, annotations, and other forms of interpretation remain a distinct object within the digital domain, linked to data but not handled or treated as data themselves. PECE is rewriting the digital protocols to allow for and encourage a different kind of interpretive annotation, one that acknowledges the interlacing of interpretation and data, reading and writing—that data are only "data" when they are read, that they can always be re-read and thus, re-data-ed.

A PECE "collaborative analytic" credits this creative act of reading in several ways and toward several effects. Unlike almost all comment or annotation functions, which essentially give users a blank slate, PECE uses what it calls "light structures" to create, in this case, "collaborative analytics" that prompt users with a series of questions developed for different types of data objects. These open-yet-closed structures—readers can still respond at any length, in any way, may skip questions entirely, and may also create questions of their own to be added to the light structure—function as tagged data fields for each response within a collaborative analytic. They store metadata about the creator and their interpretive habits, allowing the annotation as a whole or in parts to be treated as both interpretation of existing data, to which it remains attached, and as new data in its own right, and thus available in a structured way for recombination with other collaborative analytics attached to other materials, always open to further re-interpretation in the future.

This allows researchers to see how other researchers have responded to particular questions in the collaborative analytic as they complete their own, and to pull together aggregations of question responses so that they can see the interpretations of many different researchers, and of many different artifacts, in one view. The intent is double: to expose interpretive analysis as an ongoing collaborative process that is constantly re-generating data, and to create, in the process, new reflexive ethnographic insights about the interpretive patterns and genealogies of ethnographers themselves.

PECE thus leverages the affinities for data archiving and sharing, collaboration, and openness-to-the-future (or differential reproduction) that the digital form promises even as it also, in part, resists. This is a matter of engaging the language ideologies in play, working them to different effect.

Collaboration and Explanatory Pluralism

An admirable aspiration toward collaborative anthropology is (again) growing (see e.g. Lassiter 2005), and the capaciousness of the digital form as well as its wide accessibility is conducive to the growth of collaborative digital anthropology. The Digital Himalaya project, for example, began as an effort to digitize a few extant ethnographic collections and relatively quickly turned into a noteworthy and ongoing collaboration among anthropologists and their interlocutors alike, generating a wealth of newly digitized material, including journal articles long out of print or otherwise inaccessible, as well as other more recent "born digital" data (Turin 2011).

The digital form itself, however, does not always ensure collaborative effects, which require some redesign of digital tools and infrastructure to facilitate experimental collaborations. The high costs of entry (in terms of both overall production and operation, but also in terms of aesthetically alluring but difficult and daunting interfaces) that are imposed by some digital platforms can, especially in combination with the enduring figure of the solo virtuoso ethnographer, can render group efforts collaborative in name only. PECE works to keep collaborative practices from either being too difficult or over-determined and to do this it has played with the digital form to produce and steward "explanatory pluralism."

PECE's design structure seeks to leverage difference—different artifacts and data, different annotations from different researchers, different explanatory paradigms—into insight, through a variety of display mechanisms. These mechanisms include artifacts-with-annotations, timelines, and "collages" of mixed materials at different stages of analysis, from different researchers, focused on different issues, levels, or aspects. New understandings of an event such as the Fukushima disaster, for example, are generated not through their conformity with items that might be found in a Chernobyl data set, but by foregrounding through juxtaposition their differences on multiple registers, across scales, or within different interpretive frameworks. The platform is designed not to solely develop a concise and consistent view of an object, phenomenon, or problematic situation, but rather to produce and explore multiple views of such phenomena. PECE seeks to leverage for anthropology the kinds of "explanatory pluralism" that feminist philosopher and historian of biology Evelyn Fox Keller argues "represent[s] our best chance of coming to terms" with "inherently complex" processes and phenomena such as biological development (Keller 2002, 300).

PECE helps address the global challenge of creating research infrastructure to support deeply interdisciplinary and international research that addresses complex problems such as global environmental health[13] and disaster prevention, response, and recovery.[14] The multisite, multi-scale, multi-interpretive dimensions of such problems require not so much the integration, but the simultaneous presentation and juxtaposition of diverse forms of data and analyses from the humanities, social and natural sciences, and engineering. This requires robust digital infrastructure for humanities researchers, designed to be interoperable with research infrastructure developed for other fields.

Digital anthropology needs infrastructure that reflects, enacts, or embodies poststructural theories of language, and postcolonial and feminist understanding of the politics of language. This approach acknowledges the ways power is woven into language, common sense, and communicative practice, and demands real, ongoing collaboration. When languages—and the digital systems deploying language—are understood as an open system of disseminating meanings that are labile, ambivalent, dynamic, and transformative, allowing researchers to encounter the continual layering of different interpretations from multiple collaborators, this system enables the way to robust, ever-"thicker" ethnographic knowledge.

It is not only ethnographers who, immersed in dense information flows laced with conflicts of interpretation and interests, can benefit from improved digital means for deploying and developing their hermeneutic sensibilities, and for growing collaborations within our own discipline. Digital anthropology platforms such as PECE can assist the collaborator-interlocutors in their "home" domains, not only in carrying out concrete tasks, but also for thinking through what tasks should be carried out, how they should be prioritized, and how problem identification both directs practical work, and quickly makes alternative pathways invisible. PECE provides a space to experiment with and examine different forms of collaboration and thus can result in research findings with clear relevance to capacity-building efforts in various practitioner communities.

Valuing Noise and Kaleidoscopic Logics

The contemporary—globalized, high-tech, anthropocenic—world generates complex risks and problems at an unprecedented pace. This phenomenon calls for new levels of operational coordination within and across disciplines, and between researchers and practical decision-makers working at many scales (local to transnational). Given the scientific, technical, and cultural complexity of contemporary problems, there is a special need for anthropology's ability to cultivate and sustain "explanatory pluralism," different ways of thinking about problems. Researchers thus need to develop modes of work—and supporting infrastructure—that enable deep and complex collaborations of different kinds, and the "explanatory pluralism" of which they are capable. However, this is where another contradiction of the digital form becomes evident, the last one we will consider here, involving the deep play between, or imbrication of, signal and noise.

The scope of most digital anthropology infrastructure, even that for cultural heritage projects, is almost always limited in advance: data on the global textile trade, for example, is likely to have no place in a digital platform documenting and analyzing indigenous Indian or Andean weaving. Ethnographers, however—especially those in the tradition of *Writing Cultural Critique*—have a long history of fieldwork methodologies that insist they attend to more of the world than they think they are supposed to, that insist they collect more data on more people and things and their relationships than they think they need. Digital tools can assist this "deliberate attempt to generate more data than the investigator is aware of at the time of collection," as Marilyn Strathern describes the discipline's signature "open-ended, non-linear methods of data collection" (Strathern 2004, 5–6). PECE facilitates projects with ever-expanding and evolving groups of collaborators, who contribute different data sets and different interpretive habits and goals. PECE allows for and encourages the continual addition of new types of data, representing new topics and domains, not previously defined as significant or pertinent. In its capaciousness, the digital form can easily handle these multiple forms of data, multiple interpretive annotations, and multiple explanatory frames—even if some "devious" design is necessary to more fully realize these capacities or affinities of the digital form.

Even thus pluralized, however, what we have called the dominant language ideology of the digital form—its poetics and politics—still privileges integration, synthesis, and similar forms of sense-making that are notoriously inept at acknowledging what it thereby marginalizes or excludes. The digital form tends to cancel or filter out the "noise" from which all information systems want to extract the "signal" of truth and established meaning. Existing digital infra-structure developed for the natural sciences privileges identification, equation, integration, selection, simplification, condensation, and synthesis as primary modes of analysis; becoming part of the "language ideology" that carries over into digital anthropology projects as well.

PECE has been designed to work against this logic, although here we must admit to being at the experimental limit of what it is possible to do. We are attempting to make PECE present a researcher, at various moments of the research process, with unexpected data or analysis from other researchers working in a different area. Someone researching the development of immunological theories of asthma, for example, might have their attention drawn to an interview with an atmospheric chemist who studies ozone levels in Houston. PECE tries to leverage or augment the differences that already populate the data, differences that already exist in greater quantities than any researcher knows what to do with, asking researchers to invent new analytics for something they had not expected.

As one strategy, PECE meshes the design principle of explanatory pluralism with the potentials of collage that have long animated ethnographies in the tradition of *Writing Cultural Critique*, aiming for what we call "kaleidoscopic logics" in which configurations of disparate elements are open to sudden change and shifts. Through a variety of display mechanisms, PECE's design structure seeks to leverage difference—different artifacts and data, different annotations from different researchers, different explanatory paradigms—into unexpected insight. The goal is to use the affinities of digital media to "leave manifest the constructivist procedures of ethnographic knowledge," as James Clifford has put it, "to avoid the por-trayal of cultures as . . . worlds subject to a continuous explanatory discourse," in part by always including "data not fully integrated within the work's governing interpretation" (1981, 563–4).

For digital anthropology to do something like this, it will require computational advances that support open-ended, underdetermined engagement with digital content that enables (even encourages) drift and transmutation in the way content is identified and taken up in analysis. The reiteration of digital anthropology will thus also require new collaborations with data scientists and software designers. Not simply as experts, or "tool-builders," or developers-for-hire, but as active co-inquirers who bring their "paraethnographic" curiosity and sensibilities to shared questions concerning the limits and possibilities of digital forms of writing (Holmes and Marcus 2006, 2008).

Notes

1 KF and MF thank Luis Felipe Murillo for his gift of this hardcover volume to them.
2 http://savageminds.org/
3 http://mediatedcultures.net/michael-wesch/
4 http://kelty.org/
5 http://gabriellacoleman.org/
6 http://faculty.sites.uci.edu/boellstorff/
7 http://culanth.org
8 http://limn.it/
9 http://worldpece.org/
10 http://omeka.org/
11 http://mukurtu.org/
12 www.rrncommunity.org/
13 theasthmafiles.org
14 disaster-sts.org

References

Clifford, James. 1981. "On Ethnographic Surrealism." *Comparative Studies in Society and History* 23(4): 539–64.

Clifford, James and George Marcus. 1986. *Writing Culture: The Poetics and Politics of Ethnography*. California: University of California Press.

Derrida, Jacques. 1998. *Archive Fever: A Freudian Impression*. Chicago, IL: University of Chicago Press.

Drucker, Johanna. 2012. "Humanistic Theory and Digital Scholarship." In *Debates in the Digital Humanities*, edited by M.K. Gold, 85–95. Minneapolis, MN: University of Minnesota Press.

Holmes, Douglas R. and George E. Marcus. 2006. "Fast Capitalism: Para-Ethnography and the Rise of the Symbolic Analyst." In *Frontiers of Capital: Ethnographic Reflections on the New Economy*, edited by M. Fisher and G. Downey, 33–57. Durham, NC: Duke University Press.

Holmes, Douglas R. and George E. Marcus. 2008. "Para-Ethnography." In *The Sage Encyclopedia of Qualitative Research Methods*, edited by L. Given, 596–8. Thousand Oaks, CA: Sage.

Hymes, Dell H., ed. 1965. *The Use of Computers in Anthropology*. London: Mouton.

Keller, Evelyn Fox. 2002. *Making Sense of Life: Explaining Biological Development with Models, Metaphors, and Machines*. Cambridge, MA: Harvard University Press.

Lassiter, Luke E. 2005. *The Chicago Guide to Collaborative Ethnography*. Chicago, IL: University of Chicago Press.

Marcus, George and Michael M.J. Fischer. 1986. *Anthropology as Cultural Critique: An Experimental Moment in the Human Sciences*. Chicago, IL: University of Chicago Press.

Poirier, Lindsay. 2015. "Devious Design: Digital Infrastructure Challenges for Feminist Hermeneutics." Paper presented at Annual Meeting of the American Anthropological Association, November 18–22, Denver, CO.

Povinelli, Elizabeth and Peter Cho. 2012. "Digital Futures." *Vectors* 3(2). Accessed October 12, 2015. http://vectors.usc.edu/projects/index.php?project=90&thread=AuthorsStatement.

Seaver, Nick. 2014. "Computers and Sociocultural Anthropology." *Savage Minds*. Accessed September 26, 2015. http://savageminds.org/2014/05/19/computers-and-sociocultural-anthropology/.

Strathern, Marilyn. 2004. *Commons and Borderlands: Working Papers on Interdisciplinarity, Accountability, and the Flow of Knowledge*. Oxford: Sean Kingston Publishing.

Turin, Mark. 2011. "Born Archival: The Ebb and Flow of Digital Documents from the Field." *History and Anthropology* 22(4): 445–60. doi: 10.1080/02757206.2011.626776.

2

FROM VIRTUAL ETHNOGRAPHY TO THE EMBEDDED, EMBODIED, EVERYDAY INTERNET

Christine Hine

Introduction

My first online ethnographic experience happened over twenty years ago in a real-time text-based virtual reality setting called a MUD (Multi-User Dungeon). At the time I was working on a conventional ethnographic study of two fieldsites that were involved in the production and use of software systems for biologists. One of my key informants at the software production site invited me to try out this new (to me at least) form of interaction that he thought I might find interesting, arranging to meet in the MUD on one of the days when I was not physically present in the fieldsite. The technology was clunky and the experience bewildering, and my informant delighted in confusing me by playing tricks with multiple logins. I could not even work out how many people I had met, never mind fathom how I might make enough sense out of what had gone on to produce anything coherent in the way of fieldnotes. As I continued to reflect on what had gone on, however, I came to see that this initial puzzling experience offered a glimpse of the possibility of ethnographic immersion in a space of interaction that did not have a physical grounding.

The key starting point for developing an ethnographic perspective on this kind of space was to dispense with any notion that we might need to judge *a priori* whether or not this form of interaction was sufficiently rich or meaningful to form a basis for ethnographic enquiry. It would be important to take the setting on its own terms, just as any ethnographer within an unfamiliar culture would do. If this were the form that presence took in this kind of setting then the ethnographer could aim to be present in that way too, and the ethnography could focus on how people got on with things in the conditions that were created there. Being immersed in the setting meant being able to experience those conditions and to learn how to live among those who did so alongside them, and thus provided a fairly recognizable mirroring of a standard ethnographic stance.

In the intervening years I have engaged in many different kinds of online interaction and have stuck with this basic ethnographic intuition that our task is to understand ways of life as they are lived, and not to worry too much about whether any specific kind of interaction is "good enough" for ethnographic immersion. If people do it, then that is enough to make it a legitimate focus for ethnography. The task, as I understand it, is to explore the way that life is lived and relationships enacted, through whatever medium is used by the people concerned. Along the way, however, some additional complexities have come to the fore. While glibly I might have set out to study life as lived within the setting, quite patently people do not live out their lives in an online setting alone. In many cases then, to understand that "life as lived" it becomes necessary to extend studies to other spaces, and other media. A multi-modal, multi-sited study brings fresh practical and analytic challenges, as we must decide how and when to follow informants between settings and which of the many possible connections between those settings to pursue.

My more recent ethnographic studies have encompassed online and offline, following practices of meaning-making as people draw on their online experiences within offline contexts (and vice versa). I have found myself looking in depth at online experiences themselves and also within the institutional, domestic, and policy contexts where these experiences have to make sense in order to be sustained. The Internet has changed, as new platforms and new devices have been developed and as the cultural significance of the Internet has evolved. Without necessarily buying into a clear epochal rift between web 1.0 and web 2.0 it is apparent that a cultural shift has happened in the extent to which online activities are expected to be embedded within other aspects of users' lives. Ethnographers engaged with the Internet are increasingly moved to respond to the considerable spatial and temporal complexity occasioned through embedding of online activities within other contexts, with research designs not confined *a priori* to online settings. It has also been necessary for ethnographers to adapt their notions of presence to suit the conditions offered up by various forms of mediated interaction and the contingent connections forged between them.

My personal ethnographic journey has therefore taken me from conventional place-based studies into online-only fieldwork, and from there into a more complex interconnected web of online and offline fieldwork, always focused around making sense of what people think they are up to when they use the Internet. The organizing principles of these studies have, along the way, relied upon enduring principles of ethnography as an immersive form of research focused on knowing through close and sustained proximity and interaction. The form of the studies has, however, been diverse, as different research questions and the very different ways of living and working with Internet technologies that different groups have adopted have prompted different kinds of fieldwork in these uniquely constituted settings.

In the remainder of this chapter I will outline three key sets of ideas that have underpinned my ethnographic practice as it has developed across twenty years of engagement with online ethnography. First, I outline the work in Science and Technology Studies (STS) that shapes expectations of the Internet *as a technology* and suggests some fruitful directions for ethnographic engagement. Second, I discuss the notion of the fieldsite, and explore some different ways of conceptualizing the field that have emerged as we have moved away from wholly online single-sited notions of the online field. In this section I highlight some of the scholars whose ethnographic work in online spaces has inspired and informed my own. Third, I discuss the contribution made by reflexivity to ethnographic studies of wholly and partially online spaces. Finally, the concluding section reflects on the prospects for continued evolution in ethnographic approaches to the Internet.

Science and Technology Studies (STS)

Beyond an adherence to broad principles of ethnography as a means to develop a rich understanding of activities on their own terms, the specific theoretical and methodological resources offered by STS have defined my approach to online ethnography. A key conceptual idea underpinning my approach to the technologies of the Internet is "social shaping" (MacKenzie and Wajcman 1985): the idea that technologies are not the inevitable product of social trajectories of innovation, but are instead thoroughly social in both their development and their use. Applied to the Internet, this perspective suggests that we can usefully attend to the conditions within which the Internet and the many platforms that depend upon it and devices which populate it come to be, because these conditions will be constitutive in some way of the technologies that result. Thus, the ethnographer's role need not be confined to studying impact, but can also be usefully focused upstream, upon the conditions under which technologies come to be as they are.

The interest in how technologies come to be is not only confined to the study of backroom research and development environments. STS also has provocative things to say about the role of users in the innovation process (Oudshoorn and Pinch 2005) and the extent to which users have agency in technological outcomes via the meanings they attribute to technologies, through processes of interpretive flexibility and stabilization (Bijker et al. 1987). This perspective on technologies as products of social construction underpins an ethnographic approach to the Internet that understands things could have been otherwise: this particular set of technologies need not have developed, and they need not have been used in these precise ways.

Rather than studying how the affordances of a particular technology shape what people can do, we are also, to a large extent, studying how people, through their social practices, shape what the technology can do. An STS-influenced approach encourages the treatment of media technologies as socio-material complexes (Gillespie et al. 2014). It also highlights the extent to which a singular, closed notion of the meaning and purpose of a particular technology is always to some extent in doubt. Recent work in STS has explored the notion of ontological multiplicity, suggesting that a given object may be intrinsically multiple, existing in different incarnations in different places (Mol 2002). Viewed from this perspective, we may expect the Internet and its various constituent platforms to take on quite different identities in different contexts, constituted in each place through the specific sets of practices through which they acquire meaning. This focus on the agency of users and the significance of practices in constituting—in a thorough-going way—what a technology is, offers a rationale for conducting ethnographic studies as a means to find out exactly what that technology becomes in each specific context of use. Rather than reading off the likely social consequences in advance from the technology in itself, a detailed study of actual circumstances of use is required.

A further set of inspirations for an ethnographic study of the Internet comes from work in STS on the sociology of infrastructure (Star and Ruhleder 1996). Infrastructural technologies are, by their nature, often overlooked. These technologies provide a basis or framework for other, more immediately noticeable technologies to work upon. An infrastructure (for example a utility, such as electricity, water supply, or Wi-Fi) relies upon agreed standards or conventions that must be shared in order to make use of it. Infrastructures often require considerable "invisible work," both to keep them running and in order to make the messy everyday world fit in with the assumptions built into the infrastructure. Because infrastructures are so taken-for-granted they can risk being overlooked both by participants in the setting and by ethnographers. Bowker and Star (2000) proposed that we should aim to operate an "infrastructural inversion" whereby the background infrastructure would be brought into the foreground of our study with the goal of bringing into view the otherwise overlooked consequences of the infrastructure and the work that sustains it. This provides a provocation for ethnography of the Internet, to focus not only on those aspects that are in some way "spectacular" and commented upon by participants but also those features that go unremarked and become an unspoken part of routine usage (Star 1999; Star and Bowker 2006).

A final concept from STS useful for ethnographies of the Internet is the sociological study of claims-making about the future. The development and uptake of technologies in the present is often informed by and shaped by claims being made about what the future will be like (Brown and Michael 2003). This "anticipatory knowledge" (Nelson et al. 2008; Selin 2008) is a situated phenomenon and it is therefore important to study closely what claims are being made by whom and to what effect. The Internet, the various devices that enable it, and platforms that are supported by it have been rich sites for claims-making about the future. As an ethnographer focused on understanding the meanings surrounding any use of these technologies in the present, it is important to be alert to the claims that are being made regarding the future and to explore how they shape the present. These sets of expectations might be highly significant in shaping the Internet as a cultural artifact (Hine 2000) for those adopting—or indeed rejecting—it in the present.

None of these concepts tell us how to do an ethnography, or what we should expect to find, but I have found them useful as sensitizing concepts, providing foreshadowed problems that give clues about what may be interesting places to look or useful assumptions to subject to a critical gaze. My set of organizing principles for ethnography of the Internet derived from STS sensibilities would include:

1   Take all experiences seriously on their own terms and do not aim to judge whether what people say and do is correct by any external criteria.
2   Explore technologies as cultural artifacts, expecting them to acquire meanings in use, specific to particular contexts.
3   Aim to examine taken-for-granted assumptions and to highlight invisible work that might be unremarked by participants but is essential to keep technologies running smoothly.
4   Critically examine claims-making as an intrinsic part of technological development and uptake.

Fieldsites in Various Forms

The core principles of ethnographic study have remained recognizably the same throughout my twenty years of involvement in ethnography of the Internet. Nonetheless, there have been changes in the way that these studies have been organized and among the most striking developments have been the changes in constitution of the fieldsite. Some of the early studies that were inspirational for me in establishing that an online space could be deemed an appropriate place to do ethnography focused on a defined online group, such as Baym's (1995, 2000) ethnography of a soap opera discussion group and Kendall's (2002) exploration of gender within a MUD. Subsequent notable online ethnographies include Boellstorff's (2008) anthropological exploration of Second Life. The ethnographic focus in these examples was on understanding in detail and in depth how these sites developed their own distinctive cultures.

In subsequent years the notions of online spaces, and online fieldsites in particular, have remained important organizing principles for ethnographers interested in finding out exactly how people make sense of life lived in this medium. Boellstorff (2010) has argued convincingly for the acceptance of online space as a legitimate focus for ethnography, if the goal is to understand that space. However, some key cultural and technological developments have meant that the Internet increasingly seems embedded into diverse aspects of everyday life. Mobile devices mean that the Internet can be used in more locations and on-the-move, and social networking sites have been adopted as technologies that allow us to keep in touch with our existing networks of social contacts, blending our online and offline lives into an inseparable mesh of connections. For an ethnographer interested in exploring how online activities make sense it is, therefore, often hard to treat the fieldsite as confined to a single online space. Increasingly fieldsites are not easily located either online or offline (Garcia et al. 2009) but involve tracing networks of connection through online and offline space (Leander and McKim 2003).

As ethnographers have looked outside the confines of online space for practices that make sense of online activities, a variety of organizing concepts for defining the fieldsite have emerged. Marcus' (1995) multi-sited ethnography provides a model for studies that pursue a topic or theme across more than one connected site, such as Larsen's (2008) study of digital photographic practices. Burrell (2009) construes the field as a network of interconnected sites. Postill and Pink (2012) outline a form of ethnography that explores messy webs of interconnection across online and offline space. The connections explored by the ethnographer might take very different forms in different settings: Geiger and Ribes (2011) outline a trace ethnography that takes seriously the role of computer logs of activity in coordinating action between sites. Within these fields participant observation still plays a role but participation in human activity is supplemented with attention to the traces of activity maintained by machines. Similarly, Beaulieu (2005) highlights that following hyperlinks and interrogating the circumstances of their production may also count as ethnographic fieldwork. Even apparently "machine generated" aspects of the setting are significant for an ethnographer.

The field, then, can take many forms, and it is not always helpful to bound a study in advance through a focus on either online or offline. As Atkinson (2015) highlights, fieldwork is an active process, and rather than the field pre-existing before the work, that work brings the field into being. It is our preoccupations, our theoretical curiosity, and the trails we choose to follow in the field that bring the fieldsite for a particular study into being. Sometimes we may pre-define the field according to a bounded location, whether online or offline, or through our desire to follow a particular group of people, wherever their activities take place. These are, however, choices that the ethnographer has made.

In my own recent work I have explored some quite different forms of fieldsite since my original foray into an online-only field. *Virtual Ethnography* (Hine 2000) made a point of exploring the mass media representations that constituted the Internet as a cultural artifact and informed the development of online discussions and websites. My study of the practices of contemporary systematists (biologists concerned with the classification and naming of organisms) occasioned fieldwork that spanned historical work on the forging of the discipline and its expectations of new technologies, face-to-face ethnographic observation in institutions, close attention to policy documents and the claims about present and future that they portrayed, and online ethnography in diverse contingently connected settings (Hine 2008). My study of the online gift-giving network Freecycle began with ethnographic observations in a single online space, but moved into observation of other online spaces in which participants discussed their activities, and into interviews online and face-to-face and into auto-ethnographic reflection on participation (Hine 2015). In each case, the initial sets of online activities that formed the spark for the study were embedded in multiple other contexts and developing a sufficient understanding for my purposes involved pursuing multiple frames of meaning-making.

Immersion and Reflexivity

Immersion for sustained periods of time has been an important benchmark for the ethnographic methodology. Through being in the setting, however it may be constituted, the ethnographer is able to learn about life from the perspective of participants, and through being there over a period of time is able to conduct research that goes beyond isolated impressions, fleeting encounters, and retrospective reporting. Ethnographic insights are developed over time and tested out in ongoing encounters within the field. Immersion within the setting offers the prospect of developing an embodied knowledge of the setting that goes beyond formal knowledge and verbal accounts of the setting to provide insights into how it feels to live this way of life.

Venkatesh explains that there are many different ways in which a first-person perspective contributes to ethnography, including "to draw on direct experiences in the field in order to access knowledge of the subject's world that might otherwise be unavailable or extremely difficult to access" (2013, 5). Immersion in the field, therefore, offers one way of dealing with the "'silence' of the social" (Hirschauer 2006, 414), a term capturing the concern that many aspects of the field of most interest to us are beyond the ability of participants to describe. This should not be taken to imply that the ethnographer's insight is to be taken as a uniquely privileged or objective insight, but rather that through focused reflection on experience the ethnographer is able to put into words some aspect of the field otherwise left unspoken. The ethnographic self becomes a resource in the research (Collins and Gallinat 2013) through insights derived from being in the field, through recognition of moments of experience shared with participants, and even through acknowledgment of struggles to understand.

Across each of the studies I have conducted within and around online fieldsites it has been important to incorporate a strong reflexive dimension to the fieldwork and the subsequent ethnographic writing. Markham (1998) made an important early intervention by highlighting that reflexivity was a powerful part of the online ethnographer's toolkit, as a corrective to the tendency to assume that we could know in advance what being online was like. This kind of reflection on how a particular form of mediated interaction feels and how it feels to navigate between various forms and sites of interaction has been an important component of developing a deeper understanding of the Internet, predicated on the idea that ethnographic insight is about studying a form of life in its own terms.

Where the field is constituted through some combination of online and offline spaces, the reflexive element allows for the ethnographer to consider what the experience of navigating this contingently connected space is like. Where the ethnographer experiences uncertainty about where to go, or who people really are, it is important to reflect on whether this experience is shared by the participants whose way of life we are hoping to understand. The field, in this kind of study, is constituted through the ethnographer's agency in making choices about which connections to follow rather than through tracing out a pre-existing location or bounded set of connections. Reflexivity involves examining choices and assumptions and reflecting on modes of experience and movements within the field.

Conclusion

Across twenty years of ethnographic study of the Internet, there has been considerable continuity in my reference to theories from STS, my consciousness of the field as a construct, and my reliance on reflexivity as an intrinsic part of the ethnographic endeavor. There have, however, been shifts of emphasis, as scholarship in each of these areas has advanced, and as the Internet itself has changed. Three aspects of the contemporary Internet have proved particularly significant in shaping the ethnographic strategies that I have adopted in recent years:

the embedded Internet makes sense as it participates in multiple frames of meaning-making, few of which are confined to particular bounded online spaces; the embodied Internet has become a part of our way of living our lives, experienced not just as a tool for communicating but as a way of being ourselves and becoming present to one another; and the everyday Internet has become part of the infrastructure of our social existence, often taken-for-granted and only occasionally noticed as an topic of discussion or an influence to be questioned (Hine 2015).

These aspects of the Internet have occasioned studies that move between online and offline as necessary to make sense of the particular ethnographic questions being asked, and which focus on the ethnographer's embodied insights as one experiencing the setting and navigating contingent connections between different forms of activity. The everyday Internet occasions research strategies that seek both to uncover the assumptions inherent in the taken-for-granted infrastructure and to explore the situated nature of claims-making about the past, present, and future of the Internet. This is an ethnography that is rarely now confined within the Internet, but remains oriented towards understanding the Internet as a significant element in the constitution of what contemporary society is and can be.

It would be inappropriate to make too certain a prediction about where the Internet and its ethnography are headed next, given the inherently social nature of claims-making about the future. Nonetheless, it is probably wise to attend to developments that are on the horizon and to make some tentative preparations. One development that provokes and challenges ethnographic attention is the Internet of Things. This promise of an ever-more embedded Internet requires a close examination, inspired by the sociology of infrastructure, of the assumptions becoming embedded in new infrastructures and the power relations that emerge when the objects around us become ever smarter on our behalf. Another set of developments for ethnographers to be attentive to is the increasing retreat of online activities into closed worlds (Lievrouw 2012) of commercially owned, password-protected spaces and the proliferating domain of ephemeral app-based interactions that elude archives and search engines. It will be a challenge to develop ways to be ethnographic about increasingly embedded, ephemeral, and personalized forms of online communication. Fieldsites promise to fragment more than ever before and reflexivity will remain a key resource in articulating how it feels to navigate this complex world.

References

Atkinson, Paul. 2015. *For Ethnography*. London: Sage.

Baym, Nancy. 1995. "The emergence of community in computer-mediated communication". In *Cybersociety*, edited by Steve Jones, 138–63. Thousand Oaks, CA: Sage.

———. 2000. *Tune In, Log On: Soaps, Fandom and Online Community*. Thousand Oaks, CA: Sage.

Beaulieu, Anne. 2005. "Sociable hyperlinks: an ethnographic approach to connectivity". In *Virtual Methods: Issues in Social Research on the Internet*, edited by Christine Hine, 183–98. Oxford: Berg.

Bijker, Wieber E., Thomas P. Hughes, and Trevor J. Pinch. 1987. *The Social Construction of Technological Systems: New Directions in the Sociology and History of Technology*. Cambridge, MA: MIT Press.

Boellstorff, Tom. 2008. *Coming of Age in Second Life: An Anthropologist Explores the Virtually Human*. Princeton, NJ: Princeton University Press.

———. 2010. "A typology of ethnographic scales for virtual worlds". In *Online Worlds: Convergence of the Real and the Virtual*, edited by William Sims Bainbridge, 123–33. London: Springer.

Bowker, Geoffrey C. and Susan Leigh Star. 2000. *Sorting Things Out: Classification and Its Consequences*. Cambridge, MA: MIT Press.

Brown, Nik and Mike Michael. 2003. "A sociology of expectations: retrospecting prospects and prospecting retrospects". *Technology Analysis & Strategic Management* 15(1): 3–18.

Burrell, Jenna. 2009. "The field site as a network: a strategy for locating ethnographic research". *Field Methods* 21(2): 181–99.

Collins, Peter and Anselma Gallinat. Eds. 2013. *The Ethnographic Self as Resource: Writing Memory and Experience into Ethnography*. New York: Berghahn Books.

Garcia, Angela Cora, Alecea I. Standlee, Jennifer Bechkoff, and Yan Cui. 2009. "Ethnographic approaches to the Internet and computer-mediated communication". *Journal of Contemporary Ethnography* 38(1): 52–84.

Geiger, R. Stuart and David Ribes. 2011. "Trace ethnography: following coordination through documentary practices". *Proceedings of the 2011 44th Hawaii International Conference on System Sciences*, IEEE Computer Society: 1–10.

Gillespie, Tarleton, Pablo J. Boczkowski, and Kirsten A. Foot. Eds. 2014. *Media Technologies: Essays on Communication, Materiality, and Society*. Cambridge, MA: MIT Press.

Hine, Christine. 2000. *Virtual Ethnography*. London: Sage.

——. 2008. *Systematics as Cyberscience: Computers, Change and Continuity in Science*. Cambridge, MA: MIT Press.

——. 2015. *Ethnography for the Internet: Embedded, Embodied and Everyday*. London: Bloomsbury Publishing.

Hirschauer, Stefan. 2006. "Putting things into words. Ethnographic description and the silence of the social". *Human Studies* 29(4): 413–41.

Kendall, Lori. 2002. *Hanging Out in the Virtual Pub: Masculinities and Relationships Online*. Berkeley, CA: University of California Press.

Larsen, Jonas. 2008. "Practices and flows of digital photography: an ethnographic framework". *Mobilities* 3(1): 141–60.

Leander, Kevin M. and Kelly K. McKim. 2003. "Tracing the everyday 'sitings' of adolescents on the Internet: a strategic adaptation of ethnography across online and offline spaces". *Education, Communication & Information* 3(2): 211–40.

Lievrouw, Leah A. 2012. "The next decade in Internet time: ways ahead for new media studies". *Information, Communication & Society* 15(5): 616–38.

MacKenzie, Donald A. and Judy Wajcman. 1985. *The Social Shaping of Technology: How the Refrigerator Got Its Hum*. Milton Keynes: Open University Press.

Marcus, George. 1995. "Ethnography in/of the world system: the emergence of multi-sited ethnography". *Annual Review of Anthropology* 24: 95–117.

Markham, Annette. N. 1998. *Life Online: Researching Real Experience in Virtual Space*. Walnut Creek, CA: Altamira Press.

Mol, Annemarie. 2002. *The Body Multiple: Ontology in Medical Practice*. Durham, NC: Duke University Press.

Nelson, Nicole, Anna Geltzer, and Stephen Hilgartner. 2008. "Introduction: the anticipatory state: making policy-relevant knowledge about the future". *Science and Public Policy* 35(8): 546–50.

Oudshoorn, Nelly and Trevor J. Pinch. 2005. *How Users Matter: The Co-construction of Users and Technology*. Cambridge, MA: MIT Press.

Postill, John and Sarah Pink. 2012. "Social media ethnography: the digital researcher in a messy web". *Media International Australia Incorporating Culture and Policy: Quarterly Journal of Media Research and Resources* 145: 123–34.

Selin, Cynthia. 2008. "The sociology of the future: tracing stories of technology and time". *Sociology Compass* 2(6): 1878–95.

Star, Susan Leigh. 1999. "The ethnography of infrastructure". *American Behavioral Scientist* 43(3): 377–91.

Star, Susan Leigh and Geoffrey C. Bowker. 2006. "How to infrastructure". In *Handbook of New Media*, edited by Leah A. Lievrouw and Sonia L. Livingstone, 230–45. London: Sage.

Star, Susan Leigh and Karen Ruhleder. 1996. "Steps toward an ecology of infrastructure: design and access for large information spaces". *Information Systems Research* 7(1): 111–34.

Venkatesh, Sudhir Alladi. 2013. "The reflexive turn: the rise of first-person ethnography". *The Sociological Quarterly* 54(1): 3–8.

3

VECTORS FOR FIELDWORK

Computational Thinking and New Modes of Ethnography[1]

Anne Beaulieu

Researchers using ethnographic methods have traditionally claimed that the way methods are closely entwined with the field and objects of concern is a distinctive trait. The extent of this entwinement can vary; from co-construction, where methods, objects, field and even ethnographer emerge as part of ethnographic practice (Tsing 2005), to more instrumental versions of this entwinement, where a researcher will expect certain topics or issues of interest to become visible in the course of fieldwork (Shaffir and Stebbins 1990). In this chapter, I will propose an approach to understand accounts of methodological adaptations in ethnographic research, in order to contrast different adaptations to digital tools and networked relations within a framing of computationalization (Hayles 2002).

Readers of this *Companion* will most likely already have particular attachments to ethnographic methods. Or perhaps some might feel some reluctance to embrace these methods in their own work—or that of their students—and have picked up this *Companion*, seeking orientation to ethnographic approaches. In any case, ethnographic methods will be associated with research practices, experiences of fieldwork and immersive ways of being a researcher. Ethnographic research is predominantly discussed as a process, a way of learning through doing, rather than simply a set of methodological prescriptions and a means to an end. This is the reason why the key intellectual and cultural movements in Western academia of the past decades— feminism, post-colonialism, post-structuralism, queer theory, etc.—have meant not only a focus on new objects or a revisiting of canons, but also deep questioning of the very process of doing ethnography. As such, adaptations and reflections on ethnographic methods pursued in relation to digital tools and networked relations could be seen as one more foil, against which ethnography rethinks its value, analyzes its processes and reconsiders its contributions.

This chapter focuses on ethnographic accounts in relation to the regime of computation, defined as the import of patterns of information as a basic unit and of computers as universal machines, a dominant cultural condition of our times (Hayles 2002). As Pink et al. (2015) highlight, ethnography has different meanings in different disciplines and these differences are represented in this volume. In Science and Technology Studies (STS), ethnographic methods— particularly participant observation—have been used to understand knowledge production. Being in the lab has been used as a strategy to document how social and cultural processes are entwined with epistemic claims, and to situate scientific activity as continuous with other cultural spheres and social institutions. Fieldwork has been invaluable to show the diversity of meanings attached to technologies and artifacts (Beaulieu et al. 2007), and to understand the transformations in knowledge production as a result of informationalization (VKS 2008). My own ethnographic practice has been shaped by STS, where co-presence in the lab (Beaulieu 2002, 2010; de Rijcke and Beaulieu 2014) has been a core strategy to understand the visual culture of laboratories and the epistemic power of informational and computational objects.

As noted, there have been crises and challenges enough in ethnography, and the approach has been reinvented and reshaped to address literary/feminist/queer turns and twists. There is, however, a particular way in which the computational challenges ethnographic work. In terms of a method where the "ethnographer is the instrument," some of the central claims of computational regimes pose a radical challenge. Presence and engagement, two key elements of ethnographic approaches, have been formulated according to the liberal humanist tradition that links the ethnographer as investigating, learning and knowing subject to embodiment. In a computational regime, where informational patterns are privileged over material instantiations, bodies matter less and less (Hayles 1999), therefore posing a challenge to ethnographic traditions. We will return to this issue, to consider how different starting points for presence (Beaulieu 2010) and engagement (Hayles 1999; de Rijcke and Beaulieu 2014) can actually enrich rather than threaten ethnographic approaches, and how that interfaces where bodies and information meet could actually be of particular interest (Hayles 1999). For now, the point is that one important challenge of computational ethnography is that not only the methods but also the ethnographer as instrument is problematized, and that this problematization takes the form of an opposition between physical embodiment and informational modes.

Rethinking Ethnography and Digital Technology

There is no dearth of reflections, explorations and experiments in ethnography, in relation to digital technologies and networked contexts. Prominent works that have explored the feasibility and consequences of embracing these new forms abound, among which the seminal "proof of concept" *Virtual Ethnography* (Hine 2000) that put forth a number of adaptations of ethnographic methods to the Internet. Several collections on methods to study digital practices and virtual settings have included ethnographic methods as an important part of the researcher's "toolbox" (Markham and Baym 2009; Hine 2005). Digital and networked settings and practices have been the focus or part of ethnographic research for well over a decade, even in the most traditional bastions of anthropological work. A diversity of ethnographic approaches has also widely been recognized as providing valuable insights into the study of Internet and digital culture, broadly defined. Among all this literature, richly documented across this volume, some authors insist on the continuities in cultural practices that endure into the digital (Miller and Slater 2000), while others stress the novel possibilities for human culture (Boellstorff et al. 2012).

But across this divide between those who would signal discontinuities and breaks, and those who insist on the robustness of cultural forms, all authors share a commitment to ethnographic approaches and faith in the resilience of the approach to successfully meet any challenges an informational world might throw at it. More interesting than the potential of ethnographic methods to fail or succeed are the accounts of the value of ethnography for doing work in digital settings or with digital objects.

As widely noted, there are many different contexts and many different disciplines in which ethnography is used. But besides this diversity of theoretical frameworks and epistemic goals for ethnography, there is also a certain hesitation, maybe even a taboo, to pin down ethnographic methods too tightly. This is attributed to the openness of ethnographic approaches to its object, its potential to be adaptive, and to the iterative nature of doing fieldwork well. While there is no shortage of discussions of ethnographic methods, there is generally a reluctance to articulate ethnographic approaches in too explicit terms, a resistance to giving in to post-hoc, "just so" accounts of data gathering (see Hammersley and Atkinson (1983) and the revised introductions to the editions of 1995 and 2007). There are good reasons to fear the instrumentalization of an approach whose strength is learning by doing, of insight through experience.

Yet, while there will rarely be a methods section in ethnographic writing (with possible exceptions in some fields of communication studies and sociology), there are ways in which we transmit, communicate and debate methods. And understanding these accounts is a powerful way of following what is happening to ethnographic methods in their encounters with digital tools and networked settings. Indeed, even if method is implicit, emergent, never prior to engagement with the field, evolving across the research process and into the "-graphy" moments, there are recognizable ways of talking about method. I want to suggest that a focus on the *tropes* used in ethnographic accounts is a useful handle on the dynamics of methods. Tropes are elements of expressive language that have to do with an agreed-upon shorthand. They are different from, say, definitions, which articulate particular features of objects that situate these objects in specific spheres (Beaulieu 2016). Tropes similarly focus attention, but do so not in a lexical manner, in relation to a word, but in terms of narratives. Tropes are shorthand for common story-telling patterns that an audience will recognize and immediately understand. For the purposes of the discussion in this chapter, I consider a trope as an element used to describe an adequate ethnographic approach, open to contestation, but generally taken to be reasonable, valuable starting points.

Tropes are therefore a way to empirically anchor this analysis of changing ethnographic methods. Tropes have been used to analyze aspects of ethnographic work. For example, Rumsey looks at macro-tropes, at a level that shapes entire books. This enables him to address how ethnographies can differ in their forms and relate to differences of theoretical orientations and different forms (Rumsey 2004). Pratt (1987) has also looked at tropes in ethnographic writing to explore the relationship between ethnographic authority and personal experience and to link ethnographic writing to other kinds of writing (in her chapter, travel/explorer writing). Like these authors, I'm interested in exploring the epistemic authority of ethnographic approaches, but do so here by focusing on methodological discussions as part of ethnographic accounts. The focus on tropes enables me to embrace the narrative, contextual mode of accounting for methodological choices in ethnographic work, while being able to focus on methodological investments and changing commitments of various forms of ethnography.

Field of Tropes

A different review of recent work would reveal fields of tropes, for example, as illustrated in Figure 3.1.

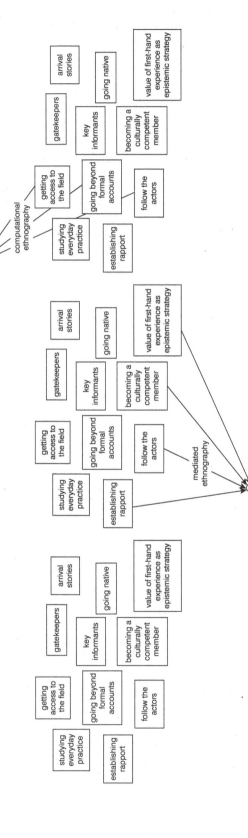

Figure 3.1 A field of tropes (left), and their relative prominence in mediated ethnography (center), and in computational ethnography (right)

Indeed, such an inventory would be a useful pedagogical exercise to underpin a discussion of methods, or as a reflexive move to consider one's own accounts. These tropes serve as ways to anchor one's commitments to ethnographic approaches and the kinds of insights they yield. Across my own work, "going beyond formal accounts" has been a recurring trope (see, for example, Beaulieu 2002), one deeply embedded in the STS tradition in which I was trained in the 1990s, where going into the lab was meant as a way to access practice.

My suggestion is that an analysis of tropes can be a useful way to understand how ethnographic work is changing. In particular, tropes can help characterize computational ethnography as an emerging approach. The aim here is to contribute to the description of computational ethnography, but also to illustrate how tropes might be a useful way to contrast ethnographic approaches. Other fields could be generated, and other vectors could be identified. For example, digital ethnography is a term that has been used to label very different approaches that place different emphasis on aspects of digital technologies and electronic networks—whether ethnographies of screens, networks, interfaces, databases, code, algorithms. The point of a field of tropes is to show how different approaches have contrasting (and partly overlapping) emphasis on different processes as both means and object of ethnography. In the rest of this chapter, I will contrast mediation and computation. The goal is not to classify for the sake of classification, but to understand how different equipment in the epistemological sense (Rabinow 2003) is part of different modes of problematization in regards to ethnographic methods.

Mediated Ethnography

From the earliest work, in computer-supported cooperative work (CSCW) or virtual ethnography, fieldwork that approaches the virtual was articulated with mediation as a major concern. Some of the worries: Can field relations be such that they provide sufficiently authentic rapport? How can the ethnographer whose participation in a setting is mediated speak with authority? What proportion of face-to-face interaction is "still" needed to count as proper ethnography? In this line of thought, ethnographers are eager to set out what happens when mediation is a prominent part of their fieldwork and field relations. Accounts stress the value of engaging with digital technologies as a way of *establishing rapport*, of *following the actors*. Accounts will also tell of the months of learning needed to *become a culturally competent* blogger or gamer. Or they will provide vignettes of "teaching moments," where fieldwork meant confrontation with their own incompetence or moments of recognition of their newly acquired digital savvy. *Being there*, in spite of mediation, or through mediation, or thanks to mediation are all shown as valuable ways of making use of firsthand experience to learn about a particular cultural setting or set of practices (see also chapter by Postill, this volume). Mediated ethnography is also concerned with the tension between analog and digital. The explorations in digital ethnography can have far-reaching consequences, for example, leading to new modes of ethnographic research, where sharing of materials and distributed analysis decenters the personae of the fieldworker (Horst 2016) or where new kinds of accounts become possible (Underberg and Zorn 2014). This tension is further discussed by Chin (this volume), and reviewed in Beaulieu (2010).

Computational Ethnography

In contrast, computational ethnography focuses not on the mediation via the digital, but on the informational dimension of Internet settings, big data and digital tools. As such, computational ethnography stands in tension not so much with the analog, but rather with the narrative, the unfolding of events, which is central to ethnographic practice and accounts. In computational ethnography, code as an instrumental form of language, and computation (rather than representation or interaction) becomes much more prominent. Algorithmic interactions, calculation and generative potential are prominent, with consequences for being in the field and for the objects of ethnographic inquiry.

For example, for a time, hyperlinks were considered to be "authored" or intentional components that structured the web (Beaulieu 2005; Foot et al. 2003). Early approaches to issue mapping (Rogers and Marres 2000) and social network analysis also followed this approach (Wellman 2001). But as the Internet and our interfaces to it developed, new ways of structuring the web have appeared, where authored hyperlinks have largely given way to algorithms, profiling and scripts. As such, the computational aspects of code and of networks have become worthwhile objects of concern for ethnographers. Another aspect of computational ethnography is the way suites of technologies, rather than a specific application, become part of the fieldwork means and context (Hand 2008). Objects and settings of concern have a networked character, which poses particular challenges for the fieldwork. It is in meeting these challenges that computational approaches are put forth as valuable tools for ethnographers. A number of tropes can help guide us in thinking through the adaptations of computational ethnography.

Getting Access to the Field

Getting access has been a long-standing concern in ethnography. With regards to computational ethnography, what is particularly interesting is the way "capture" functions as a strong orienting concept. Computationally apprehending the field, producing one's own archives (Marres and Weltevrede 2013) and delving into the generative potential of digital contexts (Waterton 2010) become core strategies for getting access to the field. Computational tools become a way to study the development of communities, whether in terms of their social (Arnold et al. 2010) or spatial relations (Hsu 2014; see also Burrell, this volume).

Getting access is thus formulated in terms of being able to capture interactions or behaviors of interest. For some researchers, computational ethnography offers the possibility of doing this unnoticed. The idea of unobtrusiveness, of accessing the field without disturbing it has been a recurring fantasy of some ethnographers (Paccagnella 1997). This idea was prominent in some of the early virtual ethnography writing, where being a fly on the wall seemed realizable with participant observation in mediated settings. In computational ethnography, this promise is fueled by tracking devices that map out interactions and the wealth of traces generated by informational contexts—possibly even prior to any elicitation by ethnographers (Neuhaus and Webmoor 2012). Data are collected in situ, more or less surreptitiously and without explicit elicitation (see also Going Beyond Formal Accounts, below).

Follow the Actors

In ethnographic projects that focus on socio-technical systems, such as virtual working environments, large-scale data infrastructures or collaborative platforms (e.g. Wikipedia, open source software), ethnographers have been exploring the power of the computational as a way to better follow the actors. There has been a range of uses of these computational tools; whether to zoom in and out (Ducheneaut et al. 2010) and deal with massively distributed actors, or to focus on how individuals find their ways into these large projects. Logging data, for example, enables ethnographers to zoom in on specific individuals within these larger settings (Geiger and Ribes 2011). Another interesting development with regards to computational ethnography is that non-human actors might be leaving as many interesting and relevant traces as human actors in the field. Deciding which actors to follow might not be a novel dilemma in fieldwork, but computational ethnography tends to broaden the candidates in the direction of technological suites (Hand 2008).

Going Beyond Formal Accounts

The possibility of *going beyond formal accounts*, getting access to what people actually do, rather than what they say they do, is also seen as a powerful way to understand behaviors, institutions and culture ethnographically. Current discourse (for example, EU funding policy) that puts users, consumers or citizens center-stage are fueling these adaptations of ethnographic methods. Computational ethnography, therefore, seeks to identify what people might want or do or prefer, through tracing human behaviors. In addition, computational ethnography can unearth the dynamics of search engines and other algorithmic technologies and interfaces that might otherwise remain unarticulated. Ethnographers have developed software tools as ways of exploring the field, in the process also finding that these tools can act as very valuable probes to go beyond the scripts open to an embodied user, to "reach beyond the end-user experiences of technology" and to see aspects of the field revealed, such as software-imposed boundaries or structuring devices (Hsu 2014). That it would take lots of time to discover these through interrogating interfaces, or that such structuring elements would remain invisible (or at least, not explicit) to an embodied user, are put forth as arguments by ethnographers for enriching modes of fieldwork using bots, scraping scripts and other forms of automating of interaction with the field.

This adaptation of ethnography does meet with criticism from those who develop their ethnography as giving voice to human actors who may be silenced by dominant structures. Researchers who invoke this trope often do not reject elicitation (for example, photo elicitation, a well-known strategy in visual ethnography and sociology) but draw the line at using means that are outside those of the embodied actors in their fields (see Fuller (2011) for a discussion of "giving voice" in relation to ethnographic knowledge claims in an STS tradition).

Studying Everyday Practice

Another growing approach in computational ethnography falls under the label of "sensing." The widespread presence of sensors (for example, in smartphones) seems to provide an easily available informational infrastructure for fieldwork; actors in the field will often already be in possession of sensing technologies. While this type of data may be relatively new to ethnographic data gathering, it can be related to other ways of getting close to the *everyday practices* and experiences of individuals, such as diary writing, and is often put forward as a way of enhancing, intensifying or augmenting participant observation. The possibility of 24/7 data acquisition is presented as a radical complement to (embodied) fieldwork strategies (Entwistle et al. 2013). Whereas the ethnographer's time, attention and presence are limited, sensing approaches can capture traces across the entirety of the "everyday."

Furthermore, given the density and granularity of the data collected, computational approaches are rather obvious ones to turn to when it comes to analyzing field notes and data from the field—data mining, data visualization and pattern recognition. These tools bring in analytic frames that may be novel to social research (Marres and Weltevrede 2013) and to ethnography in particular, and might stretch the expertise required of ethnographers beyond what can easily be found in a single researcher. Unsurprisingly, projects that invest heavily in this approach tend to be pursued by multi-disciplinary teams.

Conclusion

This brief overview of a set of recent trends in ethnographic methods has taken tropes of fieldwork as its anchor, to address innovations that fall under the label "computational ethnography." To end, it is worthwhile to reflect on the epistemic and political issues that can be associated with this approach to fieldwork.

First, let us contrast once again the issues that ethnographers themselves may raise. With regards to mediated ethnography, issues such as the validity of interacting with informants by email, the quality of rapport established in a virtual world or the authority of the ethnographer's web presence tend to be prominent. For ethnographers reflecting on how they can come to know by embracing computational methods, concerns about what is being filtered in/out by algorithms, or regarding the different ways in which platforms shape participants' experiences and promote particular kinds of social and cultural expression are more prominent. The promise of enhancing access to the everyday, and of capturing experience and behavior at a very fine level of granularity in order to enhance participant observation, fuels efforts at deploying sensing to extend observation of the everyday. The ethnographer might remain central as epistemic instrument, but it is a version of the ethnographer as distributed, interfaced—one suited to doing fieldwork in a post-human setting.

A focus on traces and infrastructures, rather than on mediation, tends to bring in different kinds of formalizations to ethnographic work (Beaulieu et al. 2007; van Zundert et al. 2011). The importance of traces might not only shift the forms in which ethnographies are circulated and shared, but they could also change the relative importance of humans and non-human actors in the field. Such trends have been noted by Tironi and Sánchez Criado (2015) in the context of "intelligent urbanisms" (a label used to denote "smart city" activities), where it is assumed that human and non-human actors all have the potential to generate traces that can be perceived as patterns or metrics. As noted above, such assumptions might meet with critique or even backlash from ethnographers who fear the overvaluing of traces, especially when it is felt that these are not accessible to the actors in the field, and that they might detract from a commitment to *giving voice* to human actors.

Another implication of the importance of traces in computational ethnography is that it brings ethnographic work closer to other spheres. Again, to take the example of smart cities as a trend where grassroots, governmental and corporate activities all come together (Tironi and Sánchez Criado 2015). The same could be said of other areas where sensing and big data practices dominate: computational ethnography comes to share major elements with marketing (Center for Media Justice et al. 2014), political campaign strategy (Nickerson and Rogers 2014), and share in the promise of a better public life (boyd and Crawford 2012). As such, ethnography comes to be highly familiar, leaving behind the trope of travel to faraway places and access to spheres unattainable for the reader (Pratt 1987).

Besides changes in the landscape of ethnography given an increased contiguity of "the field," the timescape of ethnography may also be changing. Whereas ethnography was typically research with a fairly long cycle, where period of travel, immersion in fieldwork, writing up of notes, analysis and the production of a monograph typically spanned years, the use of computational tools could provide the basis for a different time cycle in ethnographic work. Marres and Weltevreden (2013) term this "liveness," the ability to do more real-time data analysis and sharing. Whether this will lead to more superficial research, or to more responsive and accountable research, or both, remains to be seen. On the one hand, being able to provide social scientific insights into rapidly developing phenomena (weather emergencies, epidemics) could be a powerful tool to respond to crises. On the other hand, issues regarding accountability of researchers due to the nature of the data (from commercial services/for research), its scope across platforms and over time in a context of "massified data" (Neuhaus and Webmoor 2012) may be further exacerbated by liveness.

As ethnographers may be increasingly investing in speeding up the responsiveness of their work, and in sensing, harvesting and capturing of field traces, the mutual constitution of fieldwork and of the field remains a valuable concern. Sensors, like any other ethnographic device, must rely on infrastructural layers and histories of constitutive entanglements. Patterns of interaction with specific information infrastructures matter for using them effectively (Almklov et al. 2014). Since the situatedness of computational ethnography might be one that links informational practices to interfaced, post-human fieldworkers (on their own or more often than not in a networked team), it remains important to understand these practices of knowledge-making in relation to the traditions of ethnography.

Note

1 Discussions on this topic with participants of a seminar at the Swedish School of Library and Information Science on December 16, 2016, Boras University, Sweden were helpful in clarifying the points discussed here.

References

Almklov, Petter, Thomas Østerlie, and Torgeir Haavik. 2014. "Situated with Infrastructures: Interactivity and Entanglement in Sensor Data Interpretation." *Journal of the Association for Information Systems* 15(5). http://aisel.aisnet.org/jais/vol15/iss5/2.

Arnold, Michael, Damodar Shenviwagle, and Levent Yilmaz. 2010. "SciBrowser: A Computational Ethnography Tool to Explore Open Source Science Communities." In *Proceedings of the 48th Annual Southeast Regional Conference*, 26:1–26:6. ACM SE '10. New York: ACM. doi:10.1145/1900008.1900045.

Beaulieu, Anne. 2002. "Images Are Not the (Only) Truth: Brain Mapping, Visual Knowledge, and Iconoclasm." *Science Technology & Human Values* 27(1): 53–86.

———. 2005. "Sociable Hyperlinks: An Ethnographic Approach to Connectivity." In *Virtual Methods: Issues in Social Research on the Internet*, edited by C. Hine. Oxford and New York: Berg.

———. 2010. "Research Note: From Co-location to Co-presence: Shifts in the Use of Ethnography for the Study of Knowledge." *Social Studies of Science* 40(3): 453–70. doi:10.1177/0306312709359219.

———. 2016. "What Are Smart Grids? Epistemology, Interdisciplinarity and Getting Things Done." In *Smart Grids from a Global Perspective: Bridging Old and New Energy Systems*, edited by Anne Beaulieu, Jaap de Wilde, and Jacquelien Scherpen. New York: Springer.

Beaulieu, Anne, Andrea Scharnhorst, and Paul Wouters. 2007. "Not Another Case Study: Ethnography, Formalisation and the Scope of Science." *Science, Technology and Human Values* 32(6): 672–92.

Boellstorff, Tom, Bonnie Nardi, Celia Pearce, T. L. Taylor, and George E. Marcus. 2012. *Ethnography and Virtual Worlds: A Handbook of Method*. Princeton, NJ: Princeton University Press.

boyd, danah, and Kate Crawford. 2012. "Critical Questions for Big Data." *Information, Communication & Society* 15(5): 662–79. doi:10.1080/1369118X.2012.678878.

Center for Media Justice, ColorofChange, and SumofUs. 2014. "13 Consumers, Big Data and Online Tracking in the Retail Industry—A Case Study of Walmart." www.academia.edu/19526538/13_Consumers_Big_Data_and_Online_Tracking_in_The_Retail_Industry-A_Case_Study_of_Walmart.

Ducheneaut, Nicolas, Nicholas Yee, and Victoria Bellotti. 2010. "The Best of Both (Virtual) Worlds: Using Ethnography and Computational Tools to Study Online Behavior." *Ethnographic Praxis in Industry Conference Proceedings* 1: 136–48. doi:10.1111/j.1559-8918.2010.00013.x.

Entwistle, Johanne Mose, Henrik Blunck, Niels Olof Bouvin, Kaj Gronbaek, Mikkel B. Kjærgaard, Matthias Nielsen et al. 2013. "Computational Environmental Ethnography: Combining Collective Sensing and Ethnographic Inquiries to Advance Means for Reducing Environmental Footprints." In *Proceedings of the Fourth International Conference on Future Energy Systems*: 87–98. Berkeley, CA: ACM Press.

Foot, Kirsten, Steven M. Schneider, Meghan Dougherty, Michael Xenos, and Elena Larsen. 2003. "Analyzing Linking Practices: Candidate Sites in the 2002 US Electoral Web Sphere." *Journal of Computer-Mediated Communication* 8(3). http://onlinelibrary.wiley.com/doi/10.1111/j.1083-6101.2003.tb00220.x/full.

Fuller, Steve. 2011. "Science and Technology Studies and Social Epistemology: The Struggle for Normativity in Social Theories of Knowledge." In *The Sage Handbook of the Philosophy of Social Sciences*, edited by Ian C. Jarvie and Jesus Zamora-Bonilla, 665–82. London: Sage.

Geiger, R. Stuart, and David Ribes. 2011. "Trace Ethnography: Following Coordination through Documentary Practices." In *Proceedings*. Hawaii: IEEE Computer Society Press. www.stuartgeiger.com/trace-ethnography-hicss-geiger-ribes.pdf.

Hammersley, Martyn, and Paul Atkinson. 1983. *Ethnography: Principles in Practice*. London: Routledge.

Hand, Martin. 2008. *Making Digital Cultures: Access, Interactivity and Authenticity*. Aldershot, UK: Ashgate.

Hayles, N. Katherine. 1999. *How We Became Posthuman: Virtual Bodies in Cybernetics, Literature, and Informatics*, 1st edition. Chicago, IL: University of Chicago Press.

——. 2002. *Writing Machines*. Cambridge, MA: MIT Press.

Hine, Christine. 2000. *Virtual Ethnography*. London: Sage.

——. 2005. *Virtual Methods*. Oxford and New York: Berg.

Horst, Heather. 2016. "Being in Fieldwork: Collaboration, Digital Media and Ethnographic Practice." In *eFieldnotes: The Makings of Anthropology in a Digital World*, edited by Roger Sanjek and Susan Tratner, 153–68. Philadelphia: University of Pennsylvania Press.

Hsu, Wendy. 2014. "Digital Ethnography towards Augmented Empiricism: A New Methodological Framework." *Journal of Digital Humanities* 3(1). http://journalofdigitalhumanities.org/3–1/digital-ethnography-toward-augmented-empiricism-by-wendy-hsu/.

Markham, Annette, and Nancy Baym, eds. 2009. *Internet Inquiry: Conversations about Method*. London: Sage.

Marres, Noortje, and Esther Weltevrede. 2013. "Scraping the Social?" *Journal of Cultural Economy* 6(3): 313–35. doi:10.1080/17530350.2013.772070.

Miller, Daniel, and Don Slater. 2000. *The Internet: An Ethnographic Approach*. Oxford and New York: Berg.

Neuhaus, Fabian, and Timothy Webmoor. 2012. "Agile Ethics for Massified Research and Visualization." *Information, Communication & Society* 15(1): 43–65. doi:10.1080/1369118X.2011.616519.

Nickerson, David W., and Todd Rogers. 2014. "Political Campaigns and Big Data." *The Journal of Economic Perspectives* 28(2): 51–73.

Paccagnella, Luciano. 1997. "Getting the Seat of Your Pants Dirty: Strategies for Ethnographic Research on Virtual Communities." *Journal of Computer-Mediated Communication* 3(1).

Pink, Sarah, Heather Horst, John Postill, Larissa Hjorth, Tania Lewis, and Jo Tacchi, eds. 2015. *Digital Ethnography: Principles and Practice*. Thousand Oaks, CA: Sage.

Pratt, Mary Louise. 1987. "Fieldwork in Common Places." In *Writing Culture: The Poetics and Politics of Ethnography*, edited by James Clifford and George E. Marcus. Berkeley, CA: University of California Press.

Rabinow, Paul. 2003. *Anthropos Today: Reflections on Modern Equipment*. Princeton, NJ: Princeton University Press.

Rijcke, Sarah de, and Anne Beaulieu. 2014. "Networked Neuroscience: Brain Scans and Visual Knowing at the Intersection of Atlases and Databases." In *Representation in Scientific Practice Revisited*, edited by

Catelijne Coopmans, Michael Lynch, Janet Vertesi, and Steve Woolgar, 131–52. Cambridge, MA: MIT Press.

Rogers, Richard, and Noortje Marres. 2000. "Landscaping Climate Change: A Mapping Technique for Understanding Science and Technology Debates on the World Wide Web." *Public Understanding of Science* 9: 141–63.

Rumsey, Alan. 2004. "Ethnographic Macro-Tropes and Anthropological Theory." *Anthropological Theory* 4(3): 267–98. doi:10.1177/1463499604045565.

Shaffir, William, and Robert A. Stebbins. 1990. *Experiencing Fieldwork: An Inside View of Qualitative Research*. Newbury Park, CA: Sage.

Tironi, Martin, and Tomás Sánchez Criado. 2015. "Of Sensors and Sensitivities: Towards a Cosmopolitics of 'Smart Cities'?" *TECNOSCIENZA: Italian Journal of Science & Technology Studies* 6(1): 89–108.

Tsing, Anna L. 2005. *Friction: An Ethnography of Global Connection*. Princeton, NJ: Princeton University Press.

Underberg, Natalie M., and Elayne Zorn. 2014. *Digital Ethnography: Anthropology, Narrative, and New Media*. Reprint edition. Austin: University of Texas Press.

Van Zundert, Joris, Smiljana Antonijevic, Anne Beaulieu, Karina van Dalen-Oskam, Douwe Zeldenrust, and Tara Andrews. 2011. "Cultures of Formalisation: Towards an Encounter between Humanities and Computing." In *Understanding Digital Humanities: The Computational Turn and New Technology*, edited by David M. Berry, 279–94. London: Palgrave Macmillan.

VKS (Virtual Knowledge Studio). 2008. "Messy Shapes of Knowledge—STS Explores Informatization, New Media, and Academic Work." In *The Handbook of Science and Technology Studies*, 3rd edition, edited by Edward J Hackett, Olga Amsterdamska, Michael Lynch, and Judy Wajcman, 319–51. Cambridge, MA: MIT Press.

Waterton, Claire. 2010. "Experimenting with the Archive: STS-Ers as Analysts and Co-Constructors of Databases and Other Archival Forms." *Science, Technology & Human Values* 35(5): 645–76. doi:10.1177/0162243909340265.

Wellman, Barry. 2001. "Computer Networks As Social Networks." *Science* 293(5537): 2031–34.

4

A PERFORMATIVE DIGITAL ETHNOGRAPHY
Data, Design, and Speculation

Wendy F. Hsu

In a riverside park in Taipei, I heard a small ensemble of musicians playing and singing through a PA system. This was Friday night. I stood there listening in the parking lot for a while until I spotted the site of the performance. Through the amplified speakers, I began hearing the brilliant footsteps of dancing couples, shuffling and swiveling deftly in a crowd of over 50 individuals. The dimness of streetlights seemed to obscure the identity of the dancing bodies. Amplified music and dancers' steps permeated a pastoral soundscape, a space of collective leisure insulated by the river embankment, away from the urban hustle and bustle of the city. I turned on my audio recorder to capture this sonic oasis. A man who saw my recording gear asked, "Is that video? Are you with the news?" I reassured him that I was documenting the sound for the purpose of research. This uneasiness, I found out later, stemmed from a fear of the city policing their unsanctioned use of public land. Recording while retaining the anonymity of the individual participants protected the privacy of participants and their interpersonal dynamics with one another. I gathered the sense that the participants of this community did not want to see themselves in public media representation, digital or analog.

A partial truth. As ethnographers, we are trained to work through the tension between part and whole. Moreover, we have reached a level of comfort intellectualizing partial truths and epistemic relativism. The humanist approach to presenting research as an interpretation of partial truths has driven the critical turn in anthropology and related disciplines such as ethnomusicology since the publication of the now-classic *Writing Culture* (Clifford and Marcus 1986) and *The Interpretation of Cultures* (Geertz 1977). Issues related to the representational politics of fieldwork (Kisliuk 1998) and the ethics of media documentation (Pink 2015; Stoller 2011) in ethnography have taken up much of the methodological discussions. We know the ethics of when to turn on and off our recording devices. Editorial decisions regarding what to leave out in media representation of the field experiences (Feld 1987) in our published work have been informed by scholarship and to an extent, more practically, by the human subject protocol regulated by organizations such as the Institutional Review Board (IRB).[1]

Anthropologists of digital culture have elucidated the ethical implications of interacting with online communities, while offering practical (e.g. Boellstorff et al. 2012; see also Burrell, this volume) and technical tips (Hsu 2014a) about conducting fieldwork in digital spaces. For the most part, this conversation explores the changing dynamics of participant observation in digital contexts but hardly remarks upon the digital as a platform for delivering and communicating our research. Tricia Wang (2012), along with proponents of open access publishing (Miller 2012; Hsu 2014b), has argued for an open ethnography that is based on the distributed openness of digital media while invoking its democratizing potentials for reaching of a wider audience. Sarah Pink (2015) has explored the multimedia affordances of digital media, advocating for the digital and its ability to capture more than one dimension of sensory experiences of the field. The preference of sensory multiplicity over singularity is further reinforced by scholars who emphasize the relational qualities of digital media including integration, hypermedia, and immersion as a means to create a "real-world" simulation in the ethnographic narrative (Underberg and Zorn 2013, 28).

In the museum world, Geismar has noted a stream of practices that have leaned on the deployment of augmented reality and immersive media to display objects and "activate the objects' true meaning and purpose" (2012, 268). This imperative to simulate or virtualize sites of field research is based on a realist ideology, in my opinion, that runs the risk of substituting the part for the whole of the experience of a cultural system. Efforts to carry out a realist sensory immersion can reify a constantly shifting and dynamic culture. With the postmodernist understanding of ethnography, virtual representations of field materials should be situated knowledge with a contextual explanation of the content and form including aesthetic approach and chosen medium.

Delving deep into partial truths, or in the case of my project, an epistemological impasse, could be the start of a fruitful inquiry. In the ethnographic moment that I invoked earlier, the sonic part of the story is a partial truth. My limited access to the informants' identity has helped me explore an epistemology particular to the experience of the urban working and underclass in Taipei; those whose livelihood and leisure depend on reclaimed public spaces. This epistemological perspective—both public (in terms of its use of physical space and sound) and private (at the individual level) at once—is a critical necessity in the social life of members of the urban working community in order to continue to thrive in the city, in the face of the changing policy and commercial development. This emplaced and embodied epistemology nuances the story about Taiwan's sound culture and the critical mobility of the urban underclass. What is recorded or represented is always a partial story. Illuminating partialness of this knowledge and its role within the cultural system is critical to ethnographic understanding.

Performative Materiality and Design

Digital technology affords us the ability to radically transport, manipulate, and reconstitute research materials with ease. This digital transformation is not necessarily different from analog ethnography, especially in terms of content, but the scope and scale may exceed its analog counterparts. The speed of production with the digital is also faster and less resource-intensive. Because digital production falls outside of the scope of traditional scholarly expertise, it often opens up opportunities for content-and-form collaboration between scholars and makers of digital projects including designers, developers, librarians, and archivists.

What is lost in the shuffle—between the many moving parts of these individual and collective acts of recontextualization—is a continual, close attention to the dynamic relationship between part and whole, object and context, content and form. In a digital production, decision-making often is focused on the objects with less attention on how meanings shift from one context to another. What do we do with the objects? How should we organize, group, and present them? Which tags do we use? Where do we place them? How do we organize the objects into a hierarchy? An overemphasis over objects and things could deprioritize contexts. The preoccupation over objects is not new and has taken a prominent role within the work of physical artifact collection for quite some time. This object-centric thinking, however, persists even in the practices and discussion about digital collections. Within the latter, the object at stake could be the digitized version of the physical artifacts or the digital devices and media (Issac 2008, cited in Geismar 2012, 267–8).

I call for an explicit foregrounding of interpretive perspective in digital expressions of ethnography. Widening the aperture to focus on the performativity of knowledge, seeing what the knowledge *does* instead of its ontology alone, can be productive. It can inform how we reconsider the digital and the interpretive role as we approach the making of digital ethnographic knowledge. In her well-cited article, Johanna Drucker (2013) highlights a theoretical distinction between ontology and performativity, a framework for rethinking materiality in the digital realm. Extending Matt Kirschenbaum's conceptualizing of digital materiality (2008), Drucker emphasizes "the performative dimension of materiality . . . suggest[ing] what something *is* has to be understood in terms of what it *does*, how it works within machinic, systemic, and cultural domains" (2013, 4). Instead of thinking of digital entities as a set of physical properties and capacities, Drucker wants us to reconceptualize the digital as events in which digital processes occur. An event-based approach to digital ethnography suggests a time-based, in-flux engagement with field materials, one that embraces liveness, spontaneity, and openness to uncertainties in execution (p. 12).

Drucker's take on digital performativity is rooted in an analytical commitment to examine digital forms of knowledge; what it is doing interpretively, how it expresses an interpretive rhetoric, exposing its process rather than showing it as a finished product. For ethnographers, digital knowledge is complicated and nuanced by the social structures in and of their field research. The digital materializes in the form of technological infrastructure, content (cultural artifacts and social relations), and social context (Miller and Horst 2012). So an ethnographic engagement with materiality encompasses not only the performance of the authorship, i.e. the writing of the ethnographic text, but also the performative, in-situ interactions with individuals, communities, and artifacts, i.e. how ethnographers "perform" fieldwork (Burrell 2013). Drucker's performative materiality can help us think of the continuum from fieldwork to ethnographic writing as an iterative process of continuous research and knowledge making and sharing. Time-bound, event-based expressions of cultural knowledge can account for the dynamic nature of culture. This interpretive explicitness translates into design decisions that end up producing digital artifacts, social relations, ethnographic writing or representations; all are aspects of ethnographic knowledge that invoke social particulars including time, place, and sharing protocols within the material parameters of digital expressions.

I take an interface example as a brief illustration of the interpretative explicitness in design. Designing an interface constitutes a series of choices regarding what is seen and unseen. Layering and grouping content in ways that architect the experience of site navigation creates epistemological tension and resolution, setting the stage for coming to terms with knowledge and information. This dramaturgy that shapes the temporality and path of knowing, I argue, helps us think about the interaction with the interface as a performance. Kim Christen and Chris Cooney's piece entitled "Digital Dynamics Across Cultures" (2006) is an exploration of techniques for interface and information design that evokes Christen's previous field experiences and grounds a particular visuality principle—in making a cultural object either visible or invisible—within the social and epistemological protocols of Warumungu people. "Barring access to specific images or performances, in a manner consistent with the logics or protocols of the Warumungu people," this design resists the seduction of digital media to virtualize the experience of the Warumungu people, "the impulse to simulate an experience for the viewer to 'become Aboriginal' or to assume another's identity, that avatar-based standard of so many products of digital culture" (Vector's Editorial Staff 2006). This digital interface not only highlights the partial and embedded truths of Christen's ethnography but also invokes the potentially exploitative consequences of universal access to indigenous knowledge. Drucker encouraged us to create interpretive interface that "exposes, calls to attention, its made-ness—and by extension, the constructed-ness of knowledge, its interpretative dimensions" (2013, 41). Displaying knowledge as partial and constructed truths produces material friction. Setting itself against the colonialist appetite for indigenous knowledge, this interpretive interface grounds the partial truths of ethnography within what can be seen as a universalizing digital sphere.

In the remaining part of the chapter, I highlight examples of content platform, licensing protocols, and data practices that articulate digital ethnographic knowledge with performativity. Through the relationship between digital design and performance, I will also elicit the political potentials of speculative, in-process cultural knowledge production in the digital realm.

In-Process Engagement with Digital Fragments

Performance, according to Richard Schechner, is always a twice-behaved behavior (2003). What makes a performance is not its reference to an authentic original, but its iterative nature of being re-performed, re-experienced, and re-lived. This iterative quality is commonly seen and practiced in rituals and in everyday life. Similarly, digital information is always a copy without an original. Each instance of its download, upload, rename, move, and undo is a replication of something that was at once there (with a time stamp or a specific reference to a locale within the digital machine) and not-there (its locale is relational and dependent upon the location of other digital components such as files and applications).

Digital things are not inherent objects, just as performances are not inherent objects. Constituents of digital systems are parts that are not only interrelated within a machinic environment but they also exist in a particular time-space (Drucker 2013). The temporal understanding of the digital as events means that digital information happens in time. Even after the digital event is over, there are traces that point to a time-based actuality. Each execution of a task, i.e. user searching for information in the database or clicking on page links, is an event with a history. Not only that, the ending of each event generates potentials for change within the larger system in the future. Within the performative framework, each object (a file) and its relationship to the whole are constantly shifting in time and over space.

The interrelation and temporality of digital bits of information has implications for the epistemology of a postmodern ethnography. In the "crisis of representation" debate in anthropology, scholars challenged authorial privileges and critiqued the objectifying effects of previous ethnographic discourse. Reflexive rhetoric became a stream within this discussion as scholars argued for critical self-positionality in ethnographic narratives (Hahn 2007; Kisliuk 1998; Marcus 1994). Michelle Kisliuk evokes a performance paradigm in order to foreground the author's social position in ethnographic narratives. She wrote, "A performance approach suggests that the ethnographer should be as explicit as possible about the conditions that delimit her inquiry—in this case, the conditions of field research" (1998, 13). This emphasis on authorial contingency and the limitations of interpretive claims undermines the previous understanding of ethnography as objective truth. It also calls into question the academic impulse to generalize on the basis of one interpretive situation. The authorial voice, according to Kisliuk, should be contextualized within the explicit conditions of a researcher's inquiry and process.

The issue of authorial contingency is related to the spatial and temporal order in which a research event occurs. Prior to this work, Kisliuk points out the permeability of the separation between "the 'field' and the space of writing; we write when we are doing research, and research while we write" (2008). The dynamic tension between field research and ethnographic composition, however, is in tension with the process of producing print-based scholarship. The temporal arc of producing a long-form ethnographic monograph, a process that can last over a decade from fieldwork to the publication of a book, is at odds with the ideal synchronicity between field research and ethnographic knowledge production. By the time the book is out, the narrative has lost its relevance for the cultural community at stake (see Hsu 2014b).

The flexibility of linking digital objects within a database environment has made possible a (near) synchrony among a multiplicity of research activities including organizing, sharing, annotating, analyzing, and interpreting field content (the Tibetan and Himalayan Library, for example). This digital system affords scholars a time-space in which to engage with the iterative cycle of observing, documenting, organizing, field note taking, annotating, reflecting, analyzing, writing, etc. A significant advancement in ethnographic database design is the ability to present field recordings and interpretive content—of both primary and secondary sources—in one space. This multi-tier database structure invites the users to engage with content in exploratory and argumentative pathways. Made possible by the digital affordance of relationality, a multi-tier database has social ramifications. According to Geismar, "the relational knowledge fields converted into binary and remediated by digital technologies are not fixed, but rather are continually emergent out of preexisting fields, power relations, modes of social engagement" (2012, 268).

The Ethnographic Video for Instruction and Analysis (EVIA) Digital Archive is a great example of a multi-tier ethnographic database that serves the three-prong interpretive function of preservation, annotation, and publication. The site's content is clustered as video collections; each created and organized by an ethnographer with particular subject specialty. A collection consists of a series of event-based videos with detailed annotations, along with a long-form narrative that encapsulates the scope of the collection and contextualizes it in social, historical, and geographical terms. Within a single collection, readers could freely skip across events or scenes; or alternatively, readers might browse content at the pre-curated, collection level, starting with the collection-level background narrative, then working their way down to each of the video events that are further subdivided into scenes. In an exploratory mode, users can experience the site using a query-based search function to explore video based on metadata selection organized by geography and style of performance. This feature makes possible the comparison of field recordings across geographical and stylistic categories.

In this environment, each instance of navigation can be considered as an interpretive event within a specific time-space. The path through which a reader engages with site content creates a unique interpretive event. Knowledge produced through engaging with the site content is iterative. Re-engaging with the same content in a different order between items within a collection or between the primary and secondary source levels can generate performative results, making the experience of re-reading content active and participatory. The performative nature of reading and browsing through different phases of research and with other scholars' research would be amplified, I think, if the site gave the readers the capability to save and comment on their paths of reading.

I should mention that I elicit the EVIA Digital Archive to illustrate a particular approach to ethnographic database design as fodder for future thinking on database projects. Database design itself is an interpretive intention. As Deb Verhoeven says, "databases are not (just) a system for ideas. They are also an idea for a system" (2014, 208). EVIA's multi-tier feature is one among many ways to provide a generative environment for performative reinterpretations of ethnographic materials. And other design considerations, for example reader-defined tagging system, crowd-sourced documents, and user annotations at the level of navigation path, would add to the vision of performative ethnographic epistemology.

Research events designed as digital events can be transformative for the individual browsing the site or for the collective knowledge of ethnographic literature. This transformation implies a process-based thinking to create cultural knowledge,[2] rendering the unfinished idea of research as "in beta mode" (Verhoeven 2014, 216). At the meta level of scholarly discourse, the highlighting of the acts of knowledge production over finished products has implications for at once building up and breaking down the history of Western accumulation of non-Western cultural knowledge. Ethnographic databases allow the users, both researchers and readers, to continually engage with field materials. This dynamicism stands in contrast with conventional collections—in analog form such as a book or a journal article in print or ephemera in a museum collection—that are fixed and museumized. The reanimation of field objects can mitigate rarefication of culture, a risk that we take while creating any ethnographic representations.

The continual engagement with the changing content and form of ethnographic materials destabilizes the notion of a single human history; a concept based on linearity driven by and reinforcing the positivist ideology of modernist knowledge systems (Barkan 1995). The potentials for deriving new interpretive insights on a multiplicity of histories from the field documents, especially when given access to communities without previous access to producing scholarly discourse, can foster the emergence of new and nuanced human narratives with disparate time(s)-space(s) as origin and trajectory. With this, we can also begin to challenge the un-varied notion of the user and potentially design for the postcolonial user.

Speculative and Participatory Ethnography

Digital media have blurred temporal orientations, changing users' relationship to the here and now of cultural materials. Diana Taylor (2010) proposes a theory about the digital while drawing on her previous work on the distinction between archive and repertoire. The digital, according to Taylor, troubles the dichotomy between archive—a fixed entity with a past orientation that is authorized by institutions—and repertoire—a live, embodied, and collectivist practice that is focused on the here and now. The reason is that the rapid transmission of digital information creates a "temporal dislocation [that] perfectly captures the moment in which we currently find ourselves in relation to digital technologies—the feeling of not being coterminous with our time—the belatedness and not-there-yet quality of the now" (Taylor 2010, 2). This belatedness, I argue, can be the foundation for thinking performatively about the emergent qualities of digital media. It is precisely the digital's emergent characteristics that empower new forms of archives and repertoires, with an orientation toward the future. These new knowledge practices yield potentials to challenge the dichotomy between fixity and embodiment.

With the future orientation and the immediacy of digital production of cultural information, we can begin to reconsider the relationship between cultural knowledge and social action.

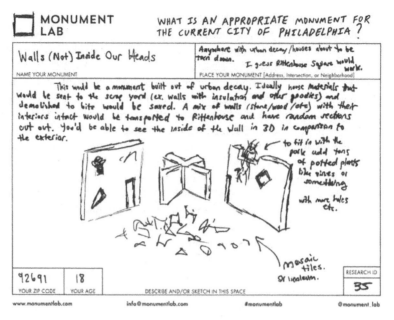

Figure 4.1 Monument Lab survey example (photo by author)

As an example, Monument Lab is a civic art project in which residents and visitors of the city of Philadelphia gathered in a classroom-like space in the City Hall courtyard to speculate and co-design the future monument for the city. Curators of Monument Lab shift the definition of art from a physical object to a site of civic dialogs, with programming of lectures and conversations on the fraught history and politics of the city with community thought leaders and artists. As a core experience of the project, residents, passersby, and civic and community leaders of Philadelphia shared their vision for the city on pieces of survey paper including a box for participants to visually depict their ideal civic monument (Figure 4.1). A team of students led by a digital humanities librarian from Haverford College transcribed, digitized, and aggregated the participants' notes and published them as a public dataset on the OpenDataPhilly website (Allen 2015), a repository of public data about the city.

The project's contribution to a public data catalog demonstrates an unusual approach to rethinking sites of knowledge production. On the one hand, the physical site in which live conversations and data capturing took place is meaningful and to a large extent informs the project's place-based, civic framing and demonstrates public participation and shared spaces. The project also asked the participants to imagine the site of their ideal monument—thus shifting the notion of physical sites into community sites that may be physical (i.e. a particular street corner) or imagined (with answers like "anywhere") or between physical and imagined ("anywhere with urban decay/houses about to be torn down"). Finally, once all the participants' notes became aggregated for the public data catalog online, this digital site of information now carries with it the previous sitedness from municipal architecture to imagined spaces for civic art, stewarding these layers of sitedness within the digital sphere. The project's contribution to the open data repository re-embeds this public knowledge into the digital sphere for further imagining and collective cognition or potentially social action such as contestation. OpenDataPhilly is a community site with a public mission to spur further community actions either digital or physical. Within this social and technological space, the collective data from the Monument Lab is poised to interrogate civic and aesthetic possibilities related to the city, a unique critical role within the digital infrastructures that serve mostly technical and non-humanist data for the tech, startup, and civic technology communities.

The speculative nature is designed to be an intrinsic part of this body of cultural information. As a form of emergent knowledge (Ingold 2011, 158), this dataset illustrates an epistemological shift toward a postmodern "non-retrospective ethnography" (Schneider 2011, 188), a fruitful departure from the backward-gazing and past orientation of cultural critique (Felski 2012). Evocation, a postmodernist rhetorical position "that makes available through absence what can be conceived but not presented" (Tyler 1986, 130, cited in Mjaaland 2013, 54), can create speculative, emergent knowledge within anthropological discourse. A future orientation that is based in the here and now of multiple sites—physical, imagined, and digital—of knowledge production, is at once an archive and a repertoire. It straddles the official domain of civic municipality by its proximity to the City Hall building and embeddedness within OpenDataPhilly, an institutionally legitimated data repository; at once the unofficial, grassroots collective inquiries and contestation against the city government's policies that led to inequitable land use. The data's potentials for prodding community actions make it an ethnography of the possible (Halse 2013). The potential actionability of this cultural knowledge challenges the archival model of fixity and past orientation by unlocking the relationship between ideologies, practices, and institutional status. This act of knowledge retooling builds the form and the platform of social actions, thus recomposing the scripts of social performance.

Retooling ethnographic preservations as a design practice is another type of digital intervention of ethnography. Design is an expression of intention (Wahl 2006), a performed utterance that leads to potential alternative social possibilities and consequences in the future. "Using design to open up all sorts of possibilities that can be discussed, debated, and used to collectively define a preferable future for a given group of people: from companies, to cities, to societies" (Dunn and Raby 2013, 6). Christen Kim's software design project Mukurtu[3] (Mook-oo-too) is a free and open-source "community archive platform" built for indigenous communities to preserve, manage, and share their own heritage content. An outcome of decades of collaboration between an ethnographer and a particular community (Christen 2012), Mukurtu comes with a set of fine-grained levels of access allowing the users to manage the flow of their information based on protocols that reflect the social relations and values such as intellectual property rights of the Warumunga community. The bespoke design of licensing protocols is critical intervention of the history of indigenous knowledge production. Multi-authorship and information access protocols are products of a postcolonial critique of the representational practices about a subaltern community engaged by a dominant culture. Members of the Mukurtu project have re-instrumented the ways for indigenous and previously disenfranchised communities to seize control over the ownership and transmission of cultural knowledge in their present and near future.

Considering design as an ethnographic practice, I add to Kisliuk's list of four dialogic levels within the performance framework for ethnography (1998, 14) to include one that concerns the conversations between the community and their audiences in the post-research near future. The retooling of communications engages with the material and cultural politics around authorship, access, and other informational practices, epistemological remnants of the history of colonization. This, I hope, is a part of the continued efforts that shift the course of power *vis à vis* a past impacted by Western/northern-hemispheric/First-World representations of non-Western/southern-hemispheric/Third World.

Conclusion: From Ethnography to Social Actions

The digital has opened up possibilities for rethinking the methods of expressing ethnographic research and, in doing so, offered some alternatives for repurposing ethnographic information for social and collective actions. The repositioning of data as the basis for community actions (as explored by Beckwith and anderson in this volume) and for civil imagination (examined by Geismar through her analysis of Instagram in this volume) makes up a new frontier for digital ethnography. These emerging modalities of digital ethnography have widened our understanding of ethnography as a set of dynamically and socially engaged knowledge production practices; and prompted the rethinking of the role of ethnographic data and design in the postmodernist epistemology. My hope is that within these discussions, we as ethnographers may consider the digital not just as an information infrastructure or content objects. Beyond the technical considerations are important ramifications for how the digital can performatively remediate the meaning of knowledge production within the machinic, cultural, and social domain of our time and space. Thinking about what the digital does as an interpretive intervention materialized as an interface, event, database, and site of social action can help clarify our decisions regarding the form, content, tool, expressions, and potential consequences of ethnographic knowledge.

To conclude, I will divulge a little of a dream for an ethnographically inspired social performance that I have. After I came back from Taipei, I became frustrated by my inability to contact the members of the ad hoc street music community that I befriended. It was in the Mengjia (or Mongka) district in Taipei where I hung out with a group of elders, musicians, and other members of the homeless, impoverished, and disabled underclass. I collected field recordings of some of the ad hoc street performances by the nakashi musicians. In particular, my main informant, a grandma-aged woman who took me in as her "god-daughter," refused to give me her address and told me that she is sick. I am not sure what that meant, but I could tell that she, along with others in the group, prefers face-to-face interactions to other mediated forms of contact.

If I had the means, I would like to go back to Mengjia to set up a mobile karaoke cafe with Internet for this transient but socially intact community. I will make available a few computers and facilitate those in the community with an interest in digital communications to get set up on a platform to document and share their day-to-day special events and memories. I will stage a speculative design event series inviting the participants to co-imagine a space of belonging for this transient community. Maybe the aggregation and sharing of these digital documents will engender collective reflection as they face the silencing effects of gentrification and urban renewal. Maybe these digital creations will give them a sense of control over their changing environment and provide documents and evidence as they rally for rights and combat evictions.

Notes

1 The IRB (Institutional Review Board) is the name of human subject review committees at US-based research institutions. The purpose of the IRB is to evaluate ethical considerations and approve research agendas that involve human subjects. This type of committee exists in other countries with names that vary.
2 Jenna Burrell evoked the idea of "performing the fieldwork experience for audiences—raw data, transparency, and visuals" by talking about the affordances of a blog for sharing the process and artifacts of field research. For more, read Burrell (2013).
3 See www.mukurtu.org/

References

Allen, Laurie (maintainer). 2015. "Speculative Monuments for Philadelphia," Datasets, *OpenDataPhilly*. www. opendataphilly.org/dataset/speculative-monuments-for-philadelphia (accessed November 14, 2015).

Barkan, Elazar. 1995. "Introduction." In *Prehistories of the Future: The Primitivist Project and the Culture of Modernism*, edited by Elazar Barkan and Ronald Bush, 1–22. Palo Alto, CA: Stanford University Press.

Boellstorff, Tom, Bonnie Nardi, Celia Pearce, and T. L. Taylor. 2012. *Ethnography and Virtual Worlds: A Handbook of Method*. Princeton, NJ: Princeton University Press.

Burrell, Jenna. 2013. "May 2013: Persuasive Formats," *Ethnography Matters*, May 10. http://ethnographymatters. net/blog/2013/05/10/persuasive-formats/ (accessed November 14, 2014).

Christen, Kim. 2012. "Does Information Really Want to be Free? Indigenous Knowledge Systems and the Question of Openness," *International Journal of Communication* 6: 2870–93.

Christen, Kim and Chris Cooney. 2006. "Digital Dynamics Across Cultures," *Vectors*, Fall, 2(1) *Ephemera*. http://vectors.usc.edu/projects/index.php?project=67 (accessed January 22, 2011).

Clifford, James and George Marcus. 1986. *Writing Culture: The Poetics and Politics of Ethnography*. California: University of California Press.

Drucker, Johanna. 2013. "Performative Materiality and Theoretical Approaches to Interface," *Digital Humanities Quarterly* 7(1). www.digitalhumanities.org/dhq/vol/7/1/000143/000143.html (accessed November 11, 2015).

Dunn, Andrew and Fiona Raby. 2013. *Speculative Everything: Design, Fiction, and Social Dreaming*. Cambridge, MA: MIT Press.

Ethnographic Video for Instruction and Analysis (EVIA) Digital Archive, 2015. www.eviada.org/ (accessed October 15, 2015).

Feld, Steven. 1987. "Dialogic Editing: Interpreting How Kaluli Read Sound and Sentiment," *Cultural Anthropology* 2: 190–210.

Felski, Rita. 2012. "Critique and the Hermeneutics of Suspicion," *M/C Journal* 15(1). http://journal.media-culture.org.au/index.php/mcjournal/article/viewArticle/431 (accessed November 11, 2015).

Geertz, James. 1977. *The Interpretation of Cultures*. New York: Basic Books.

Geismar, Haidy. 2012. "Museum + Digital = ?" In *Digital Anthropology*, edited by Heather Horst and Daniel Miller, 266–87. New York: Bloomsbury.

Hahn, Tomie. 2007. *Sensational Knowledge: Embodying Culture through Japanese Dance*. Middletown, CT: Wesleyan University Press.

Halse, Joachim. 2013. "Ethnographies of the Possible." In *Design Anthropology: Theory and Practice*, edited by Wendy Gunn, Ton Otto, and Rachel Charlotte Smith, 180–98. New York: Bloomsbury.

Hemispheric Institute's Digital Video Library. http://hemisphericinstitute.org/hemi/en/hidvl (accessed November 14, 2014).

Hsu, Wendy F. 2014a. "Digital Ethnography Toward Augmented Empiricism: A New Methodological Framework," *Journal of Digital Humanities* 3(1). http://journalofdigitalhumanities.org/3-1/digital-ethnography-toward-augmented-empiricism-by-wendy-hsu/ (accessed November 14, 2015).

——. 2014b. "A Wider and More Transparent Ethnographic Feedback Circle," *Ethnomusicology Review*, 19. http://ethnomusicologyreview.ucla.edu/content/wider-and-more-transparent-ethnographic-feedback-circle (accessed November 14, 2015).

Ingold, Tim. 2011. "Introduction." In *Redrawing Anthropology: Materials, Movements, Lines*, edited by Tim Ingold, 1–20. Farnham: Ashgate.

Issac, Gwyneira. 2008. "Technology Becomes the Object: The Use of Electronic Media at the National Museum of American Indian," *Journal of Material Culture* 13: 287–301.

Kirschenbaum, Matthew. 2008. *Mechanisms: New Media and the Forensic Imagination*. Cambridge, MA: MIT University Press.

Kisliuk, Michelle. 1998. *Seize the Dance: BaAka Musical Life and the Ethnography of Performance*. New York: Oxford University Press.

———. 2008. "Un(doing) Fieldwork: Sharing Songs, Sharing Lives." In *Shadows in the Field: New Perspectives for Fieldwork in Ethnomusicology*, edited by Gregory F. Barz and Timothy J. Colley, 183–205. New York: Oxford University Press.

Marcus, George E. 1994. "On Ideologies of Reflexivity in Contemporary Efforts to Remake the Human Sciences," *Poetics Today* 15(3): 383–404.

Marcus George E. and Michael M. J. Fischer. 1991. *Anthropology as Cultural Critique: An Experimental Moment in the Human Sciences*. Chicago, IL: University of Chicago Press.

Miller, Daniel. 2012. "Open Access, Scholarship, and Digital Anthropology," *HAU: Journal of Ethnographic Theory* 2: 385–411.

Miller, Daniel and Heather Horst. 2012. "The Digital and the Human: A Prospectus for Digital Anthropology." In *Digital Anthropology*, edited by Heather Horst and Daniel Miller, 3–35. New York: Bloomsbury.

Mjaaland, Thera. 2013. "Traversing Art Practice and Anthropology: Notes on Ambiguity and Epistemological Uncertainty." In *Anthropology and Art and Practice*, edited by Arnd Schneider and Christopher Wright, 53–62. New York: Bloomsbury.

Monument Lab, 2015. http://monumentlab.com (accessed November 11, 2015).

Murkutu, 2015. www.mukurtu.org/ (accessed November 11, 2015).

Pink, Sarah. 2015. *Doing Sensory Ethnography*. Thousand Oaks, CA: Sage.

Schechner, Richard. 2003. *Performance Theory*. New York: Routledge.

Schneider, Arnd. 2011. "Expanded Visions: Rethinking Anthropological Research and Representation through Experimental Film." In *Redrawing Anthropology: Materials, Movements, Lines*, edited by T. Ingold, 177–194. Farnham: Ashgate.

Stoller, Paul. 2011. *The Taste of Ethnographic Things*. Philadelphia: University of Pennsylvania Press.

Taylor, Diana. 2010. "Save As . . .: Knowledge and Transmission in the Age of Digital Technologies," *Imagining America*. Paper 17. http://surface.syr.edu/ia/7 (accessed August 22, 2016).

The Tibetan and Himalayan Library, 2015. www.thlib.org/ (accessed November 14, 2015).

Tyler, Stephen. 1986. "Post-modern Ethnography: From Document of an Occult to Occult Document." In *Writing Culture: The Poetics and Politics of Ethnography*, edited by James Clifford and G. E. Marcus, 122–40. Berkeley: University of California Press.

Underberg, Natalie M. and Elayne Zorn. 2013. *Digital Ethnography: Anthropology, Narrative, and New Media*. Austin: University of Texas Press.

Wahl, Daniel Christian. 2006. "Design for Human and Planetary Health: A Holistic/Integral Approach to Complexity and Sustainability." PhD Diss., University of Dundee.

Verhoeven, Deb. 2014. "Doing the Sheep Good: Facilitating Engagement in Digital Humanities and Creative Arts Research." In *Advancing Digital Humanities: Research, Methods, and Theories*, edited by Paul Longley Arthur and Katherine Bode, 206–20. New York: Palgrave Macmillan.

Wang, Tricia. 2012. "Writing Live Fieldnotes: Toward a More Open Ethnography," *Ethnography Matters*, August 2. http://ethnographymatters.net/blog/2012/08/02/writing-live-fieldnotes-towards-a-more-open-ethnography/ (accessed November 14, 2014).

5

THE FIELDSITE AS A NETWORK
A Strategy for Locating Ethnographic Research

Jenna Burrell

This chapter draws on theories about networks and ethnographies of the Internet to address issues of fieldsite selection in ethnographic research. Interest in ethnography—a complex of epistemological framings, methodological techniques, and writing practices—has spread into many domains and disciplines beyond its roots in cultural anthropology. It has been directed increasingly toward pragmatic outcomes beyond academic knowledge production ranging from political action and the development of social programs (Brydon-Miller et al. 2003; Madison 2005) to product design (Lewis et al. 1996; Salvador et al. 1999). It is now firmly entrenched within a range of disciplines, including sociology, media studies, education, science and technology studies, and more. It has long since branched out of academia and become incorporated (with varying degrees of acceptance) into the corporate world (Orr 1996; Suchman et al. 1999; Jordan and Dahl 2006) and international development institutions (Tacchi et al. 2003). Ethnographic practice has been reconsidered and reconfigured at different times and in different domains to meet the diverse sets of interests represented by these various spheres. Some of the convenient fictions that facilitated ethnographic approaches in the past have been less applicable to the new issues, theoretical and pragmatic, undertaken by researchers.

The term *fieldsite* refers to the spatial characteristics of a field-based research project, the stage on which the social processes under study take place. For ethnographers, defining this space is an important activity that traditionally takes place before and in the early stages of fieldwork. It involves identifying where the researcher should ideally be located as a participant observer. Once fieldwork concludes, an ethnography cannot be written without at some point defining this spatial terrain where the social phenomenon under study took place. This is both an act of exclusion and inclusion, indicating what the research does and does not cover. An awareness that the fieldsite is in certain ways constructed rather than discovered is crucial to contemporary practice. Yet the practical work of constructing a fieldsite has not often been discussed. This article will review some of the fieldsite configurations researchers have developed in recent years and will explore a promising one: the fieldsite as a heterogeneous network. The advantages of this particular configuration and the on-the-ground practical and logistical concerns involved in constructing such a fieldsite will be explored in detail.

Over the course of several decades of methodological reflection, ethnographers have called into question the traditional conception of the fieldsite as a bounded space containing a whole culture (Gupta and Ferguson 1997). In the anthropological tradition, fieldwork frequently took place in a village in a remote region. There were advantages to the construction of such a bounded and disconnected fieldsite. It put anthropologists in a position to make strong arguments about cultural difference that unseated presumptions of the universal or biological basis of social practices. Reliance on a bounded fieldsite did not extend as far as claiming complete disconnection from external forces, but the influence of what was "external" to the fieldsite was treated as secondary.

As anthropologists moved to take on new social issues, they began to propose new configurations of the fieldsite. In 1986, Marcus and Fischer, reflecting on neo-Marxist movements, most notably world-systems theory, pointed to an awakening interest among anthropologists in "how to represent the *embedding* of richly described local cultural worlds in larger impersonal systems of political economy" (Marcus and Fischer 1986, 77; emphasis added). Changes in the structures and interconnections of late capitalism, they argued, had increased the scale and complexity of social processes. The containment of a culture within a small bounded space such as a village, was, therefore, increasingly less accurate. In later years, ethnographers joined the debate to suggest that such a containment of culture did not necessarily even occur in traditional studies of an out-of-the-way place (Clifford 1992; Tsing 1993; Piot 1999). Such a challenge to ethnographic practice arose not simply from rapid, global social change but also from theoretical developments, the draw of new objects of anthropological inquiry, and (one can speculate) the incursion of disciplinary outsiders.

However, this view of ethnographic work as the study of global processes as they are experienced locally did not suggest that the global might somehow be studied directly. Marcus, in a later book, revised his earlier writing on "knowable communities in larger systems" (Marcus and Fischer 1986, 77) that relied on notions of "embedding," in favor of studying the "larger system" itself through an "ethnography in/of the world system" (Marcus 1998, 79). In this newer conception, the movement of objects, of individuals, of ideas, of media, and of the fieldworker is attended to, uncovering insights and objects of inquiry that were not visible in studies that assumed culture was spatially fixed. Marcus (1998, 79) directly addresses the matter of fieldsite configuration, suggesting several possible modes that lend coherence to research projects without being spatially bounded. They include "follow the person," "follow the object," and "follow the metaphor," among other configurations, all lending an overarching cohesion to "multisited" ethnographies. These arguments highlight how movement is central to social practice but also that coherent cultural processes can take place across great distances, linking up disparate entities. They can also take place on the move.

Challenges to locating fieldsites are not limited to the understanding that social processes could take place over vast physical terrain. Hannerz, in a compatible argument, draws attention to the heterogeneity of culture. He notes that within contemporary societies cultural processes register in the lives of individuals to varying degrees. Exposure to a diversity of meanings in such societies produces members who determine and define cultural membership for themselves (Hannerz 1992a). Therefore, an attempt to describe the culture within a bounded space, whether a village or a nation state, elides the inconstancies that exist within any heterogeneous population. The practical problem for researchers becomes the challenge of foregrounding—how to pull something coherent forward from such overlapping and intertwined social terrain.

These studies provide the foundation of a contemporary understanding of how culture is (and is not) located. However, with the exception of Marcus's proposal for multisited ethnography, they do not explain how *fieldwork* may consequently be located. Given the arguments for the vast terrain and complex intermingling of cultural spaces, it is clear that fieldsite selection must become something that is done continually throughout the process of data gathering. It cannot be decided once and for all in the early stages. In deciding what to include and what to exclude, some difficult, strategic choices must be made. A further elaboration on Marcus's proposal to "follow" the objects of ethnographic research will be undertaken here in an effort to make these conceptual developments available to practitioners of ethnographic work.

Locating the Field in Cyberspace

The argument for an alternate configuration of the fieldsite presented in this chapter is built on the new ground established by Marcus, Gupta and Ferguson, Hannerz, and others discussed above, but it also draws from new methodological approaches devised to study the Internet. As the Internet emerged in the early 1990s, a distinct set of debates arose around its status as an object of research. Concerns about how to define the fieldsite and fieldwork—issues about the relationship between social phenomena and space—were again central.

Emerging online spaces of the Internet appeared to belong to an entirely new category of space. Online discussion groups and text-based virtual worlds presented compelling new settings of social activity. The Net exhibited non-Cartesian properties, and the activities there did not conform to standard laws of physics. Mitchell (1996) described the Net as, "profoundly antispatial. . . . You cannot say where it is or describe its memorable shape and proportions. . . . But you can find things in it without knowing where they are" (p. 8). The Net frequently produced (especially among new users) a profound sense of spatial disorientation. Researchers experimented with research practices in online realms, formulating the concept of virtual ethnography (Hine 2000; Ruhleder 2000) or cyber ethnography (Ward 1999). Technical properties and social practices in online spaces allowed for research explorations that straddled the physical and the imaginary.

Methodological debates around the Internet were complementary to the ongoing effort to treat global processes as the proper subject of ethnographic fieldwork. Yet the case made for virtual ethnography had certain strengths that were lacking in this other set of critiques. First and foremost, it was well grounded in empirical work. Through participation, close observation, and interviews, researchers showed how inhabitants experienced certain virtual sites and certain forms of engagement on the Internet as both profoundly spatial and social (Rheingold 1993; Baym 1995; Turkle 1995; Watson 1997). This was justification for ethnographic, site-based approaches to the study of what took place online.

Virtual ethnographies were able to show how individuals made sense of ambiguous, non-Cartesian social terrain in the course of lived experience. As Hine (2000) notes, this form of fieldwork did not require the corporeal displacement of the researcher but was, rather, a mental immersion and an engagement with the imagination. T. L. Taylor (1999) describes the "plural existence" of the researcher as simultaneously an online "avatar" and an offline body. Virtual ethnographies demonstrated the possibility of awareness and analysis of spaces beyond what can be physically inhabited. This insight makes it possible to conduct fieldwork on social phenomena that take place across vast distances and in unconventional spaces.

A chorus of voices has also challenged an assumed division between online and offline (Henriksen 2002; McLelland 2002; Leander and McKim 2003; Carter 2005; Wilson 2006; Jurgenson 2012). Miller and Slater (2000) suggest that alternately, "we need to treat Internet media as continuous with and embedded in other social spaces" (p. 5). In their study of the Internet in Trinidad, Miller and Slater conducted household surveys and spent time observing sociability in Internet cafés and other spaces to understand norms of Trinidadian social life that extended into online spaces. Similarly, in a study of knowledge production about genetic disorders, researchers sought "nodes" that served as points of intersection between online and offline worlds and worked back and forth between the online (i.e., websites) and offline (i.e., laboratories and support groups) to develop a more comprehensive picture of knowledge practices (Heath et al. 1999). The network form advocated in this chapter is another structural concept that, like landscapes and nodes, can guide thinking and shape methodological practice in ways that escape strong offline–online divisions.

Constructing a Fieldsite: Lessons Learned

The issue of logistics is a major concern in this movement toward mobile, multisited, and virtual ethnography. If sociocultural processes are taking place across vast terrain, how do we, as researchers, cope with the inevitable limits in time and funding? How do we gain deep knowledge through fleeting social encounters or interactions with the ambiguous inhabitants of ephemeral, virtual spaces and where these "sites" might disappear altogether? The acknowledgment that researchers now often study "parts" rather than whole cultural processes is one logistical accommodation. To address this concern, I will include some suggestions about how spatially vast fieldsites can be understood where the researcher physically inhabits only certain parts of the space.

The case in question is a study of the social appropriation of the Internet in Accra, Ghana, that involved an eight-month period of fieldwork from October 2004 to June 2005. I was interested, in particular, in understanding how the Internet was described and spoken about among users. I hoped to better understand the process users went through to learn how to manipulate this complex technology. I selected Internet cafés in part because they were publicly accessible. Furthermore, these cafés represented a model of shared access that some argue is particularly well suited for the developing world where the Western norm of personal computer ownership was out of reach for most. By looking at Internet cafés, I was positioned to respond to debates in development and technology studies.

Initially, the Internet café itself seemed promising as a stand-alone fieldsite. I could select several of these small businesses and simply spend my days inside these air-conditioned oases observing activities, perhaps providing technical assistance, and gaining an understanding of social processes shaped by the café environment. Yet it became clear early on that I had overestimated the role of these spaces as a socialized place with any cohesive, communal sensibility. Customers came irregularly and often for only short periods of time. I could not count on encountering anyone on a regular basis aside from the operators who worked there. Internet café users similarly noted that they had made no friends or contacts (in face-to-face interactions) at these cafés.

Yet from observing people in these cafés sitting, attentively observing the computer screen, often deaf to any surrounding noise and activity, it appeared that many were engaged in deeply immersive, social experiences in a virtual space. Their physical presence in the café became muted and hollow. These social experiences were frustratingly difficult for me to observe as a researcher, materialized primarily as scrolling text in a small window. I could intervene in such a social engagement from only one side and thereby risk obliterating the interaction in a quest to understand it.

I found that observing the customer circulations through the Internet café alone was insufficient for my purpose: to better understand the role of Internet use in the everyday lives of the urban inhabitants of Accra. The Internet cafés were encompassed within neighborhoods, the neighborhoods within the city. I began to follow people from the café, starting out by arranging an in-depth interview often staged at a nearby eating spot. Ultimately following these Internet café users led me to homes, churches, schools, foreign countries, into the future (if only imagined), and back to the Internet café where I was ultimately able, in a few cases, to observe more closely the immersive social encounters of these Internet users.

In one sense, my fieldsite broadened out to become the city of Accra, as all the Internet cafés I studied, homes I visited, and roads I traveled doing my fieldwork were within the city or its suburbs. However, the city was paradoxically both too complexly heterogeneous (too inclusive) and simultaneously too geographically limited (too exclusive) as a unit of analysis.

It was too inclusive in the sense that it was composed of layer upon layer of intersecting and overlapping activity. Most of this activity, however, had little relevance to my main research interests. It was necessary to more selectively define the fieldsite, outlining its social and material shape within the city, making the social phenomenon visible within a complex social space.

The boundaries of the city were also too exclusive because a variety of locales, institutions, and people near and far have a direct bearing on the appropriation and use of the Internet in Accra. For example, the foreign chat partners of Internet café users, their family members living abroad, and the immigration regulations of countries such as the United States and the United Kingdom are among the many relevant constitutive forces that define Internet use in Accra. Therefore, the fieldsite must be defined without relying on broad territorial boundaries that are too imprecise.

To reconcile these spatial complexities, I conceived of my fieldsite as a network composed of fixed and moving points including spaces, people, and objects. In a "fieldsite as network," the point of origin, the destination(s), the space between, and what moves or is carried along these paths is of interest. It is an approach

> designed around chains, paths, threads, conjunctions, or juxtapositions of locations in which the ethnographer establishes some form of literal, physical presence, with an explicit, posited logic of association or connection among sites that in fact defines the argument of the ethnography.
>
> (Marcus 1998, 90)

Defining the fieldsite as a network is a strategy for drawing the social phenomenon into view by foregrounding it against the social complexity of its urban setting. To foreground is to draw the contours of the phenomenon, distinguishing it from the competing and intersecting activities also taking place within the spatial field that is defined by the territorial boundaries of the city. The term *contour* best describes the outcome of this act of foregrounding by indicating that greater precision is achieved than would be obtained relying on the boundaries of the city, the country, and so forth. At the same time, this term preserves the quality of irregularity and the notion that the social phenomenon is outlined rather than detached from its context.

In translating the many theoretical arguments for mobile and multisited ethnography into a practical reality, I arrived at several strategies that I will detail here. These strategies draw, in part, on some practices that are well established in ethnographic research but are here reframed, related to the demands of contemporary practice, and connected to some novel techniques. This is an attempt to extend and render concrete some of Marcus's suggestions for multisited ethnography. The following are some proposed steps (roughly sequential) for fieldsite construction in contemporary ethnographic practice:

1   *Seek entry points rather than sites.* To study the fieldsite as a network, the researcher must also make a strategic decision about what position(s) to take within the network. I found that this was a matter of searching for entry points rather than bounded locations (Green 1999; Couldry 2003). Hine similarly suggests that ethnographers "might still start from a particular place, but would be encouraged to follow connections made meaningful from that setting" (2000, 60). In this study, I sought to trace out a fieldsite using Internet cafés as a starting point. One way I did this was by tracing paths through the city defined by Internet users to get a sense of their everyday lives. For example, I followed a young woman from the Internet café where she chats with her foreign husband, to the market where she is apprenticing with a hairdresser in preparation for her move abroad, to the Western Union office where she receives money from her husband earmarked for the purchase of a flashy, new cellphone. This approach provided a rich sense of the interconnections between Internet use and other aspects of Internet users' lives. The Internet café, with its frequent circulation of users and digital objects, had great potential for spinning out these broad webs across urban and virtual terrain.

2   *Consider multiple types of networks.* Marcus encourages fieldworkers to follow people, objects, and stories but does not describe the pathways that are traversed. Existing infrastructures for transporting people, goods, and digital objects come in a number of overlapping forms, some of which are already understood as networks. These include phone networks, other telecommunications networks (such as the Internet), transportation networks (such as airlines), road networks, and social networks. By identifying these various networks, they, too, become foregrounded in the fieldsite and can be understood as constraining and facilitating particular movements. By considering this multitude of networks up front, the many possible directions that could be followed are laid out for the researcher to consider. In traversing these networks, the fieldsite becomes a *heterogeneous network*. This incorporates a mapping of the social relations of research participants and their connections to material and digital objects and physical sites. Hannerz (1992b) notes that such a network analysis will engage with the way meaning flows through other relationships, such as the state, market, and media. Accepting heterogeneity preserves the possibility that the social phenomenon under study may be defined not only by social networks but also by material flows and other modes of connection.

3   *Follow, but also intercept.* Another issue is that of more distant locales and of spaces more geographically ambiguous than the city, where activities of following and inhabiting are less feasible. I took the approach advocated by Marcus (1998) to study a single site with an *awareness* of its multisite context. I interpreted this to mean that the Internet café could be treated as a point of intersection where an understanding of the Internet was produced in part by the conversations and circulation of data through these computers. Doing this from a stationary position was a way to avoid the unwieldiness of expanding the fieldsite into multiple countries.

Internet cafés experience constant circulation. Studying the café as a point of intersection meant attending to the connections from this site to other distant sites as well as tracking the movement of material and digital objects and people circulating through the café. The origins or circulation record of these objects, if available, is also of interest, although as I have previously acknowledged, this is often ambiguous. Using this perspective, I found that Ghanaian Internet café users exchanged messages with an extraordinarily wide range of chat partners online, including people not only from the United States and Europe but also from Pakistan, India, Israel, Hong Kong, and many other locations. They sought out mass media imagery of major news events (like the 2005 tsunami and the war in Iraq). They also acquired American hip-hop and rap music and videos. The result was a vision of a chaotic, destructive, and glamorous world outside of the African continent.

4   *Attend to what is indexed in interviews.* Language can be instrumental in providing clues about things to follow and sites to visit. Through language, speakers often construct associations to and between spaces. Paying close attention to references to space and place in speech (or texts) earlier on can also be a guide to the further movement of the researcher. These references map out how the social phenomenon is perceived spatially. For example, in the course of interviews on Internet café use with young people, I heard stories about the schoolyard and the classroom as spaces where students discussed their forays on the Net. Without necessarily visiting these schools, I came to understand how the school, a space where similarly aged young people met and socialized, played an important role in how the Internet was collectively understood. References to places also served as suggestions for new locales to physically visit. For example, interviews with Internet users in one neighborhood yielded references to "bases," informally organized groups of youth who created hangouts on roadsides and in unfinished buildings in the surrounding neighborhood. These informal organizations turned out to be significant sites where technical knowledge about the Internet and cellphones was passed along. Through speech, these spaces were brought forward out of the complexity of the urban neighborhood as sites of technology appropriation. They would otherwise likely have gone unnoticed.

5   *Incorporate uninhabitable spaces.* Use of the Internet frequently involves an engagement with the imagination and the production of imagined spaces because there is much that this medium conceals. Imagined spaces are "social imaginaries" (Anderson 1983; C. Taylor 2002) conceived of in spatial terms. For example, Ghanaians constructed a notion of cyberspace and who was in it from their experiences and other sources of information. From conversations, it became clear that many Internet users conceived of chat rooms, dating websites, and other online spaces designed for mixing and mingling as providing access to philanthropists, potential business partners, and wealthy older people. Yet these expectations did not mesh with their experiences. Internet users tended to encounter teenagers and twenty-somethings in these spaces. The particular technical configuration of chat rooms where the bodies of participants were concealed, where ambiguous screen names were used, and where an unknown number of individuals could be "lurking" without speaking facilitated such speculative imagination.

Besides cyberspace, geographic territories such as foreign countries were also imagined by Internet café users. Their fantasies were constructed partly from what they encountered in mediated form through Internet chat partners, websites, the news media, music videos, TV shows, movies, stories told by Ghanaians returned from abroad, encounters with foreigners in Accra, and rumors. Appadurai (1996) argues for greater consideration of the fantasies people construct through engagements with mass media because they shape aspirations and real-world activities. In Ghana, there was a consequential impact of these imagined spaces, as they were frequently treated as real and correspondingly acted on.

6 *Know when and where to stop.* The potentially infinite size of the network and the lack of a natural stopping point present problems for researchers (Strathern 1996). Practically speaking, one simple way of determining when to stop is when time runs out. As Hine (2000) points out, if one embraces the notion that ethnographic work is no longer about studying cultural wholes, then the question of completeness becomes unproblematic; one stops when one must. The dilemma becomes how to strategically construct the selected part in a way that produces something coherent, and some approaches to this have been detailed above. Meaning saturation is one well-established approach that does not rely on spatial boundaries to define the ending point of research. When interviews with new people and observations in new locales yield a repetition of themes, this may indicate that the research process has come to a natural conclusion. Additionally, research that follows connections may move into a site where there are less and less frequent encounters with the topics of interest. This might not mean stopping the research entirely but rather that the researcher ought to return to the fieldsite's starting point to pursue another set of connections and move in another direction.

Conclusion

By defining the fieldsite as a network in accordance with the guidelines described above, the fieldsite transitions from a bounded space that the researcher dwells within to something that more closely tracks the social phenomenon under study. This site is constructed in terms of how such a phenomenon is perceived and acted on by participants. Ultimately, this approach is in keeping with the *emic* ideal of ethnographic practice. The fieldsite comes to be defined by the physical movements, places indexed in speech and text, and social imaginings produced by research participants. The researcher still, of course, plays a role in the siting of research interests, and the resulting fieldsite is a collaboration between researcher and researched groups. Through an openness to following participants through space as well as in language, there is potential for empirical surprises and novel insights.

In my own fieldwork experience, Internet cafés served as an especially productive entry point for research into the appropriation and use of the Internet in Accra. Strategically, they served as an accessible public space where people could be recruited for interviews. The cafés were focal points of circulation and intersection from which I was able to expand outward, tracing the contours of the social phenomenon of Internet use. This was accomplished by both following the movement of Internet users through the city and by intercepting the flow of media through the Internet as it arrived in the Internet café. This made it possible to narrow the scope of the fieldsite considerably, while still acknowledging how forces from various locales near and far were incorporated into the setting.

Logistics are an often inadequately acknowledged dimension of field-based research. I referred to a number of accommodations in my own fieldwork experience. I advocated staying in place to "intercept" circulations of data, people, and goods rather than following them. I suggested that a spatial mapping could be drawn out, in part, through references to place in language (in interviews and conversations) without visiting each and every one of these locales. The strategic selection of a site (the Internet café) where several networks converged, where people and objects came to me (rather than the other way around), also aided this effort. The work of "efficiently" defining a fieldsite as a network involved conserving movement while switching between directions and objects of interest. Although not applicable to all field-based research, this approach is likely to be particularly useful to certain topics of social research, including migration, new communication technologies, broadcast media, transnationalism, and global institutions, among many others.

Acknowledgment

An earlier iteration of this piece appeared in *Field Methods* (May 2009) 21: 181–99.

References

Anderson, Benedict. 1983. *Imagined Communities: Reflections on the origin and spread of nationalism*. London: Verso.

Appadurai, Arjun. 1996. *Modernity at Large: Cultural dimensions of globalization*. Minneapolis: University of Minnesota Press.

Baym, Nancy. 1995. "From Practice to Culture on Usenet." In *The Cultures of Computing*, edited by Susan Leigh Star, 29–52. Oxford: Blackwell.

Brydon-Miller, Mary, Davydd Greenwood, and Patricia Maguire. 2003. "Why Action Research?" *Action Research* 1(1): 9–28.

Carter, Denise. 2005. "Living in Virtual Communities: An ethnography of human relationships in cyberspace." *Information, Communication and Society* 8(2): 148–67.

Clifford, James. 1992. "Travelling Cultures." In *Cultural Studies*, edited by Lawrence Grossberg, Cary Nelson, and Paula Treichler, 96–116. New York: Routledge.

Couldry, Nick. 2003. "Passing Ethnographies: Rethinking the sites of agency and reflexivity in a mediated world." In *Global Media Studies: Ethnographic perspectives*, edited by Patrick Murphy and Marwan Kraidy, 40–56. New York: Routledge.

Green, Nicola. 1999. "Disrupting the Field: Virtual reality technologies and 'multisited' ethnographic methods." *American Behavioral Scientist* 43(3): 409–21.

Gupta, Akhil and James Ferguson. 1997. "Beyond 'Culture': Space, identity, and the politics of difference." In *Culture, Power, Place: Explorations in critical anthropology*, edited by Akhil Gupta and James Ferguson, 33–51. Durham, NC: Duke University Press.

Hannerz, Ulf. 1992a. *Cultural Complexity: Studies in the social organization of meaning*. New York: Columbia University Press.

——. 1992b. "The Global Ecumene as a Network of Networks." In *Conceptualizing Society*, edited by Adam Kuper, 34–56. London: Routledge.

Heath, Deborah, Erin Koch, Barbara Ley, and Michael Montoya. 1999. "Nodes and Queries: Linking locations in networked fields of inquiry." *American Behavioral Scientist* 43(3): 450–63.

Henriksen, Dixi L. 2002. "Locating Virtual Field Sites and a Dispersed Object of Research." *Scandinavian Journal of Information Systems* 14(2): 31–45.

Hine, Christine. 2000. *Virtual Ethnography*. London: Sage.

Jordan, Brigitte and Brinda Dahl. 2006. "Persuasive Encounters: Ethnography in the corporation." *Field Methods* 18(4): 359–81.

Jurgenson, Nathan. 2012. "When Atoms Meet Bits: Social media, the mobile web and augmented revolution." *Future Internet* 4: 83–91.

Leander, Kevin M. and Kelly K. McKim. 2003. "Tracing the Everyday 'Sitings' of Adolescents on the Internet: A strategic adaptation of ethnography across online and offline spaces." *Education, Communication, and Information* 3(2): 211–40.

Lewis, Scott, Michael Mateas, Susan Palmiter, and Gene Lynch. 1996. "Ethnographic Data for Product Development: A collaborative process." *Interactions* 3(6): 52–69.

Madison, D. Soyini. 2005. *Critical Ethnography: Methods, ethics, and performance*. Thousand Oaks, CA: Sage.

Marcus, George. 1998. "Ethnography in/of the World System: The emergence of multi-sited ethnography." In *Ethnography through Thick and Thin*, edited by George Marcus, 79–104. Princeton, NJ: Princeton University Press.

Marcus, George and Michael M. J. Fischer. 1986. *Anthropology as Cultural Critique: An experimental moment in the human sciences*. Chicago, IL: University of Chicago Press.

McLelland, Mark. 2002. "Virtual Ethnography: Using the Internet to study gay culture in Japan." *Sexualities* 5(4): 387–406.

Miller, Daniel and Don Slater. 2000. *The Internet: An ethnographic approach.* London: Berg.

Mitchell, William. 1996. *City of Bits: Space, place, and the infobahn.* Cambridge, MA: The MIT Press.

Orr, Julian. 1996. *Talking About Machines: An ethnography of a modern job.* Ithaca, NY: Cornell University Press.

Piot, Charles. 1999. *Remotely Global: Village modernity in West Africa.* Chicago, IL: University of Chicago Press.

Rheingold, Howard. 1993. *The Virtual Community: Homesteading on the electronic frontier.* Reading, MA: Addison-Wesley.

Ruhleder, Karen. 2000. "The Virtual Ethnographer: Fieldwork in distributed electronic environments." *Field Methods* 12(1): 3–17.

Salvador, Tony, Genevieve Bell, and ken anderson. 1999. "Design Ethnography." *Design Management Journal* 10(4): 35–41.

Strathern, Marilyn. 1996. "Cutting the Network." *The Journal of the Royal Anthropological Institute* 2(3): 517–35.

Suchman, Lucy, Jeanette Blomberg, Julian Orr, and Randall Trigg. 1999. "Reconstructing Technologies as Social Practice." *American Behavioral Scientist* 43(3): 392–408.

Tacchi, Jo, Don Slater, and Gregory Hearn. 2003. *Ethnographic Action Research.* New Delhi: UNESCO.

Taylor, Charles. 2002. "Modern Social Imaginaries." *Public Culture* 14(1): 91–124.

Taylor, T. L. 1999. "Life in Virtual Worlds: Plural existence, multimodalities, and other online research challenges." *American Behavioral Scientist* 43(3): 436–49.

Tsing, Anna L. 1993. *In the Realm of the Diamond Queen: Marginality in an out-of-the-way place.* Princeton, NJ: Princeton University Press.

Turkle, S. 1995. *Life on Screen: Identity in the age of the Internet.* New York: Simon and Schuster.

Ward, Katie. 1999. "Cyber-Ethnography and the Emergence of the Virtually New Community." *Journal of Information Technology* 14(1): 95–105.

Watson, Nessim. 1997. "Why We Argue about Virtual Community: A case study of the Phish.Net fan community." In *Virtual Culture: Identity and communication in cybersociety,* edited by Steve Jones, 102–32. London: Sage.

Wilson, Brian. 2006. "Ethnography, the Internet, and Youth Culture: Strategies for examining social resistance and 'online–offline' relationships." *Canadian Journal of Education* 29(1): 307–46.

6

REMOTE ETHNOGRAPHY
Studying Culture from Afar

John Postill

It was a tense event. I was sitting in a classroom at Goldsmiths College, University of London, near the front. The speaker was the ex-Muslim and feminist author Maryam Namazie. She was here as a guest of the university's Atheist, Secularist and Humanist Society (AHS) to speak about blasphemy and apostasy. The audience consisted at this point of some 25 souls, including a contingent of young Muslim women seated toward the back of the room. Normally at a university lecture one assumes the audience will be reasonably quiet and respectful—you would certainly not expect to have to contend with hecklers bent on disrupting the session. But on this occasion that was exactly what was in store for Namazie. After a brief introduction by a young, bespectacled AHS member, Namazie wondered out loud whether she should sit or stand, eventually choosing the latter. About ten minutes into her talk, half a dozen young bearded men—presumably from the university's Islamic Society—entered the room and sat along the front row, a mere few feet away from the speaker. One of them began to laugh as Namazie related the recent murder of Bangladeshi bloggers critical of political Islamists. The speaker asked him whether he found it amusing that people were being "hacked to death."

Shortly afterwards, another bearded student started to interrupt Namazie, to which she responded by shouting numerous times "Be quiet or get out!"—alas to no avail. Tongue in cheek, the student replied that he felt intimidated by Namazie who immediately retorted: "Oh, you're intimidated? Go to your safe space." Refusing to be silenced by the constant interruptions and irritations (e.g. loud ringing tones), Namazie pressed on with her presentation and even managed to hold a Q&A session at the end, by which time the troublemakers had already left the room.[1]

★★★

I folded my laptop, got up from the sofa, went downstairs to the kitchen and made myself a cup of tea. I had been glued to the screen for almost two hours without a break. I was not in

London. I was at home in Melbourne; 17,000 kilometers away. What's more, I was not even following the lecture in real-time, for it had been recorded and uploaded onto YouTube the day before (I learned about this video via Twitter). And yet it *felt* as if I was present there and then, in the thick of it, as much a member of the audience as anyone else. I felt the palpable tension, the anger, the fear, the dogged determination, and the final triumph of argument over intimidation. Perhaps it did not feel exactly as if I had been there at the time, but no leap of the imagination was needed to feel a great sense of immediacy—even intimacy—with a recorded event that took place a world away.

A Problem of Legitimacy

This tale of entry was inspired by a draft article by Patty A. Gray (2016) titled "Memory, body, and the online researcher: following Russian street demonstrations via social media," published in *American Ethnologist*. I had the good fortune of being one of the paper's six reviewers. I say good fortune because this reviewing assignment coincided with the early preparations for the present chapter. This gave me an ideal entry point into the question of how we might go about doing ethnographic research remotely in the current age of nearly ubiquitous digital media. Gray opens her article with the following passage:

> It is a crisp winter day in Moscow: brilliant blue sky, bright sunlight, dazzling white snow shovelled into piles along the streets. We are driving along the Garden Ring, the circular road that belts the city of Moscow. Normally on a Sunday this road would be relatively empty and quiet—certainly not the traffic gridlock that paralyzes the city on any given weekday. But on this sunny Sunday in January, the road is full of muscovite cars of all imaginable makes circling the city, making one full turn of the Garden Ring, then another, round and round as they are joined by more and more cars. It is easy to spot who you are looking for, because their white emblems are displayed as visibly as possible on their vehicles: flowing white ribbons; white balloons; a white umbrella sticking through a sun roof; someone's white blouse fluttering out a window; a white stuffed rabbit strapped to a side view mirror. One car is tiled with pieces of white paper, and another has simply piled high its roof with snow. This last example is the most literal emblem, because this has been dubbed the "Snow Revolution," Russia's contribution to the so-called "colored revolutions."
>
> (Gray 2016, n.p.)

Just like me, Gray is referring to an event that she only took part in remotely—in her case in real-time. While I was "transported" from Melbourne to London, she was "driven" around snowy Moscow from her Dublin home: "I am not in Moscow, I am in Dublin; but it *felt* like I was in Moscow, and I want to go back."

Although a long-time specialist in Russia, Gray did not set out to conduct research into the Russian protests remotely—or indeed at all. Yet once she had followed the first protest, she became "hooked" for months on end, joining the action as it played out "from start to finish, spending hours at each sitting." She describes the experience as being "exhilarating and often great fun," albeit as exhausting as traditional anthropological fieldwork. At the same time, this protracted activity raised the thorny issue of whether it could be considered "real" fieldwork given the absence of a "being there" (Geertz 1988) dimension.

The aim of Gray's article is to explore the meaning of "being there" and "being then," and especially the use of social media "to remotely study offline social phenomena." She suggests that ethnographers experience and remember online social media encounters just as they do offline encounters, that is, "in the body." If this is the case, says Gray, the epistemological implications are significant for all ethnographers, including those like her with no particular interest in studying digital media. In this chapter I wish to continue the conversation, so to speak, with Patty Gray on this problem of how to go about studying local phenomena from afar. To this end I will take up a number of the points advanced by Gray and discuss them one by one, starting with the idea of remote fieldwork as a safer way of conducting research in conflict-ridden or otherwise hazardous locations.

From a Safe Distance

One unexpected bonus of doing remote research for Gray was that, as a US citizen, doing fieldwork on the ground in Russia entails a degree of potential risk and harassment:

> [E]ven if I had been free to jump on a plane at the first sign of activity and spend the next several weeks in Moscow researching this phenomenon first-hand, it would have been risky for me to do so [. . .]. As an American citizen, I am a lightning rod for negative attention from Russian authorities.

There is a venerable precedent here. It is commonly thought that "being there" has been the sine qua non of anthropological research ever since Malinowski's "fieldwork revolution" in the early twentieth century (Geertz 1988). Yet during World War II, leading US-based anthropologists such as Mead, Bateson, and Benedict had no alternative but to study the cultures of Japan, Germany, and other nations "at a distance," through media formats such as films, novels, and poetry (Mead and Metraux 2000). After the war, most anthropologists once again lost interest in studying media as relatively peaceful conditions returned to their chosen fieldsites. It was only from the late 1980s that a growing number of them would take up the study of media; often after their research participants had literally turned their backs on them to watch TV or listen to the radio (Peterson 2003).

Of course, there is no guarantee that a presently peaceful locale will remain so forever. Thus in the mid-1990s, as I was preparing for doctoral fieldwork in West Kalimantan, Indonesian Borneo, the country entered a phase of turmoil that culminated in a mass protest movement against the military regime of Suharto, who was forced to step down in 1998. In view of these circumstances, I decided to conduct fieldwork into media and nation building north of the border in Sarawak, Malaysian Borneo (Postill 2000, 2006). Meanwhile, a fellow PhD candidate at University College London, Andrew Skuse, faced a similar challenge as large parts of Afghanistan came under the control of the Taliban. But rather than turn his attention entirely to neighboring Pakistan, where he found himself stranded, Skuse persevered with his plan of studying radio reception in Afghanistan remotely, through local research assistants whose presence was inconspicuous (Skuse 1999). Unlike Gray, who in the early 2010s had access to a wealth of telematic media with which to study unfolding events in Russia from afar, in 1990s' Afghanistan—a media-poor time and place—Skuse had to resort to hiring research proxies.[2]

Ontologically, there are ambiguous situations in which anthropologists who were hoping to conduct fieldwork in a given physical locale (or set of locales) become stranded not offline but online, with less real-time access to physical spaces than that enjoyed by Gray. This was particularly the case in the late 1990s and early 2000s, before the current global boom in web-enabled mobile devices. For example, Birgit Bräuchler (2005, 2013) was hoping to conduct field research in Maluku, Indonesia, but instead had to make virtue (or virtual) out of necessity by focusing on the "cyberspace" created around the bloody religious conflict that pitted Maluku Christians against Muslims from 1999 to 2002. Although most of her research took place online, Bräuchler also managed to conduct some fieldwork on the ground.

In yet other cases, anthropologists have found that their target fieldsites are beyond direct reach owing not to war but to a natural disaster. This was the challenge faced by Jonathan Skinner during fieldwork on the Caribbean island of Montserrat following a volcanic eruption in 1995, when most residents, including Skinner, had to be evacuated at short notice. The instant diaspora was scattered across Canada, the United States, Britain, and other countries. Some of them decided to keep in contact online via an Internet newsgroup they named the Electronic Evergreen. This pre-Facebook social media network allowed displaced Montserratians to recreate the style and rhythm of the erstwhile co-present sociality of their distant homeland. Skinner (2007) was compelled to follow suit, interacting with his research participants at once remotely and online.

Here we can begin to see the varied ways in which anthropologists and other ethnographers have conducted fieldwork safely from afar. For Mead and Bateson, this meant studying media content originating in Japan, Germany, and other nations at a distance as well as after the fact, owing to the wartime impossibility of traveling to those countries. Over half a century later, Gray, Bräuchler, and Skinner were able to follow events "on the ground" in real-time—or close to real-time in some cases, through asynchronous forms of mediated interaction such as online newsgroups. The case of Montserrat is curious, albeit increasingly common among diasporic groups, in that the anthropologist—like his informants—socialized through a remedial technology that recreated the experience of being there prior to the volcanic eruption. By contrast, Skuse conducted his research vicariously, not via telematic media but rather through local research assistants able to work in his target fieldsites.

Planned and Unplanned

Remote ethnography can be planned and unplanned. With the recent proliferation of digital media and the growing political turbulence around the world (Postill 2015a), more and more ethnographers are increasingly unable—or unwilling—to declare an end to their primary research on leaving "the field." Thus in her discussion of how she came to study Russian protests from afar, Patty Gray explains that she was

> not consciously doing *research*—it was not planned, and in the beginning it could not have *been* planned, because even the protesters themselves did not know they would come out onto the street for that first mass demonstration on the fifth and sixth of December 2011.
>
> (Gray 2016, n.p.; emphasis in original)

This Russian specialist unexpectedly resumed her previous on-the-ground work through Internet-mediated research from Ireland thanks to the ready availability of digital technologies at both ends. Similarly, after concluding my Spanish fieldwork into Internet activism in the summer of 2011, I could not help but monitor events from abroad as the *indignados*/15M movement continued to evolve month after month. I did this first from the UK and later from Australia, where I currently live, as well as from Indonesia during fieldwork there.

Gray describes Twitter as a manner of "wormhole" leading to a multitude of social media platforms through which she could keep abreast of the Russian protests. Likewise, elsewhere

I have described Twitter as my very own "human-mediated RSS feed," that is, as an efficient way of channeling the deluge of information related to my research by following a manageable set of informants (Postill and Pink 2012).

There are also times when ethnographers can prepare in advance for periods of long-distance research. For instance, during my 2003–2004 fieldwork into local activism in the township of Subang Jaya, Malaysia, I built into the research design a number of breaks from the field to attend to parental responsibilities in the UK. Interestingly, during these "absences" from Malaysia I was able to devote more time to the wider network of local residents who were active on the local web forum than when I was physically there, occupied with "following" key informants from one offline setting to another (Pink et al. 2016, 134).

Being Then

Gray argues that there is nothing new about remote anthropology itself. The novelty lies in the fact that anthropologists can now access remote sites *in real-time* through social media. She supports this point with the example of an Instagram image tweeted from inside a police van in December 2011 by the Russian activist and blogger Aleksei Navalny, just after Gray and others had witnessed live his arrest along with that of other demonstrators. Navalny's tweet read: "I'm sitting with the guys in the riot police bus. They say hi to everyone." The Instagram photo showed the smiling faces of a group of protesters, some of them flashing the victory sign.

> The tweet and the image are now in my digital archive of that event, so I can refer to them at any time. However, there is no replicating the realtime adrenaline kick of the (being-then) moment when that tweet appeared in my Twitter feed and I read the words, not at all expecting that when I pulled up the image on Instagram I would see what resembled a moment of giddy communitas rather than an experience of repressive police detainment.
>
> (Gray 2016, n.p.)

Gray goes on to argue that "being then" in real-time framed her subsequent interpretations of the evolving riot police practice of detaining protesters in Moscow. Had she merely retrieved the image and tweet from an online archive, the "adrenaline kick" of having lived that intense moment would be missing. Gray concludes that social media are "experienced—and remembered—*in the body* in ways that challenge the distinctions we might otherwise make between virtual and physical encounters."

There is no denying that real-time experiences can indeed be powerful and shape the researcher's understanding of subsequent field events. I for one went through the transformative experience of sharing a common strip of time-space with Plaça de Catalunya occupiers in Barcelona in mid-May 2011, which I described as an awakening for me and countless others across Spain after decades of political slumber (Postill 2014)—an experience that Gray includes in her article. At the same time, we must be careful not to replace one dubious panacea of anthropological research ("being there") with a seemingly more current, yet equally problematic, alternative ("being then").

There are two main reasons to be cautious. First, not all "being then" experiences have to be "adrenaline kicks." One can share experiences with others in real-time at very different tempos, and with widely varying emotional qualities. In my own remote research over the years, I have experienced all manner of emotions ranging from excitement, joy, and even bliss at one end of the spectrum to boredom, frustration, and apathy at the other, with fast-moving phases of intense engagement invariably followed by quiet periods (Postill and Pink 2012). Moreover, different (sub)cultural universes of practice will privilege certain forms of time-bound emotions over others. Compare, for instance, the high risk-taking "edgework" of base parachute jumpers (Ferrell et al. 2001) with the more sedate activities of lawn bowls players or weekend anglers.

Second, whatever the temporal and affective quality of the remote event in question, it is still possible to extract valuable insights from archived moments, even from moments that we never experienced live. For example, in a series of posts titled "Freedom technologists" that I am currently publishing on my research blog,[3] I draw from digitally archived interviews by and with Spanish *indignados* to, among other things, recreate some of the defining moments of their protest movement. Thus many interviewees refer to a collective act of civil disobedience carried out by tens of thousands of occupiers of Madrid's Puerta del Sol Square in May 2011. I might not have been there or then, but through their vivid recollections of this collective rite of passage, and my own comparable experiences in Barcelona, I was still able to imaginatively relive this turning point *almost as if I had been there and then*. Arguably this is not quite "the real thing," as defined by Gray, but it more than suffices for my writing purposes, namely to sketch the early stages of the *indignados* movement through (para-)ethnographic means.

Twin Anxieties

All this suggests that there may be two related anxieties at play in the increasingly common practice of long-distance fieldwork. We could call them (a) the ethnographic fear of missing out, and (b) the anthropological aversion to thin descriptions. As regards missing out, take the angst I felt in March 2011 as I attended an event in Barcelona from afar, via a networked computer from my home in England. The meeting was the third in an itinerant series known by the Twitter hashtag *#redada*. These were sessions organized by free culture activists battling the Spanish government and culture lobbies over the future of the Internet. Participants coordinated these sessions via social media. Those unable to attend in person could do so free of charge by means of a live streaming platform. They could also put questions to the panelists over Twitter.

When I realized that my short trip to the UK clashed with the first ever *#redada* to be held in Barcelona, I was bitterly disappointed. For a moment, I had forgotten that much of what goes on within the world of free culture activism in Spain actually takes place remotely, especially via Twitter. Like me, not everyone can attend all events in person. At times, they may have to, or even choose to, attend telematically. How much did I miss by not "being there" in the flesh? I probably missed a few chances to network with participants, perhaps over a cold beer and tapas or dinner after the event. On the other hand, from the comfort of my English study, undisturbed by the rich contextual cues of a physically co-present interaction (Kiesler and Sproull 1992), I could pay close attention to other features of the event—not least to the social media uses of Internet activists that formed an integral part of my research. Besides, if necessary I could always revisit the archived tweets and video footage at a later point in time.

As for the fear of not being able to live up to the hallowed anthropological ideal of writing "thick descriptions" (Geertz 1973; Ponterotto 2006) based on first hand research, in this respect remote fieldwork is no different from on-the-ground fieldwork: not all texts—or sections in a text—will warrant ethnographic thickness. In some pieces of writing, and for a host of reasons (space constraints, uneven materials, editorial requirements, etc.) anthropologists will alternate between thick and thin descriptions. In other writings, they will spread the ethnographic butter more evenly—and thinly. Thus in a chapter of my monograph *Localizing the Internet* (Postill 2011) titled "Internet Dramas" I weave into the narrative two protests involving residents of the Malaysian suburb of Subang Jaya. While I witnessed the first protest there and then, the second was based on materials I gathered remotely from the UK, mostly online and after the fact, but nonetheless sufficiently detailed to serve my textual ends (Postill 2009). In other words, there is no substantial difference between the remote and on-site sections of the chapter in terms of their descriptive thickness.

That said, there are certain situations in which remote fieldwork is better suited to the task of producing thin descriptions than on-site fieldwork. Although epistemologically, as we have seen, there are no grounds for favoring one modality of data-gathering over the other, logistically it is often not possible for the researcher to return physically to the field in order to answer a fresh question raised by the analysis or writing of the materials, which leaves remote fieldwork as an equally valid alternative. This can result in either thick or thin descriptions, depending on the nature and quality of the materials and the demands of the piece of writing in question.

The crucial point here is triangulation, that is, the ethnographic imperative to gather primary and secondary materials on a given question through as rich a variety of sources as possible (Ortner 1998), including the ever-expanding ways of being there. Relying solely on physically co-present, non-digital fieldwork, or solely on telematics is still theoretically possible, but in most research settings it no longer makes sense to do so.

Conclusion

With the continued diffusion of networked technologies, the remote study of social practices is once again on the agenda—only now with far greater media resources at our disposal than those available to Mead, Bateson et al. in the 1940s. This state of affairs creates both opportunities and challenges for social scientists who wish to adopt ethnographic methods. I argued that there is nothing inherently inferior or illegitimate about researching local issues remotely, or indeed retrospectively, especially for ethnographers with previous local experience. The main challenge is precisely how to overcome this misconception and make adequate provision for remote ethnography in our research designs and practices.

As we saw earlier, Patty Gray (2016) asks herself whether her long-distance monitoring of Russian protests is a legitimate mode of anthropological inquiry, or whether it is "cheating" because there is no "being there" component. She is not alone in her epistemological angst, for it is now gradually becoming rare for ethnographers *not* to use telematic media as part of their research repertoire.

In this chapter I have answered to Gray's concerns with an unequivocal "Yes": it is indeed legitimate to conduct anthropological fieldwork from afar. For one thing, anthropological research is a technologically plural, open endeavor—we use whatever technical means will help us gain insights into the lives and deeds of our research participants (provided they are ethical). Remote fieldwork is more than a remedial measure, a "second best" choice for anthropologists unable to reach their fieldsites for reasons of safety, illness, or disability. It often helps us to observe familiar people and things from a different perspective, thereby creating a richer engagement with the worlds of our research participants. Moreover, as growing numbers of people around the globe take up telematic media such as webcams, live streaming, or live tweeting, "being there" from afar is becoming an ever more integral part of daily life.

It follows that we must make room in our research proposals for both scheduled and unscheduled phases of remote ethnography, something ever more doctoral students and their supervisors are now coming to realize. As more researchers with familial and work-related obligations engage in ethnographic research, and as conditions on the ground in many parts of the world become more uncertain, the overlooked practice of remote ethnography is likely to gain more visibility and methodological sophistication in the coming years.

Notes

1 I have written this para-ethnographic tale of entry by drawing from a YouTube video of the event (see www.youtube.com/watch?v=-1ZiZdz5nao&feature=youtu.be) as well as from a December 4, 2015 report in *The Independent* (UK): www.independent.co.uk/student/news/muslim-students-from-goldsmiths-university-s-islamic-society-heckle-and-aggressively-interrupt-a6760306.html.
2 This raises the complex question of collaborative research that I cannot pursue here. At any rate, it is important that we do not overlook the crucial role played by research assistants in many anthropological and interdisciplinary projects, particularly in cases where the principal researcher is unable to be physically present in "the field." There are also numerous projects in which translocal collaboration was an integral part of the research design and development from the outset: see, for instance, Horst (2016) for a discussion of collaboration where being "in fieldwork" is but one element of the research process, and Nafus and anderson (2009) on the mediated materiality of partly ethnographic research in the corporate sector.
3 See "'Freedom technologists series'," *media/anthropology* blog: http://johnpostill.com/category/freedom-technologists-series/.

References

Bräuchler, Birgit. 2005. *Cyberidentities at War: Der Molukkenkonflikt im Internet*. Bielefeld: transcript.
———. 2013. *Cyberidentities at War: The Moluccan Conflict on the Internet*. Oxford: Berghahn.
Geertz, Clifford. 1973. "Thick description: Toward an interpretative theory of culture." In *The Interpretation of Cultures*, 3–30. New York: Basic Books.
———. 1988. *Works and Lives: The anthropologist as author*. Stanford, CA: Stanford University Press.
Gray, Patty A. 2016. "Memory, body, and the online researcher: Following Russian street demonstrations via social media." *American Ethnologist* 43(3): 500–10.
Ferrell, Jeff, Dragan Milovanovic, and Stephen Lyng. 2001. "Edgework, media practices, and the elongation of meaning: A theoretical ethnography of the Bridge Day Event." *Theoretical Criminology* 5(2): 177–202.
Horst, Heather. 2016. "Being in fieldwork: Collaboration, digital media, and ethnographic practice." *EFieldnotes: The Makings of Anthropology in the Digital World*, 153–68.
Kiesler, Sara and Lee Sproull. 1992. "Group decision making and communication technology." *Organizational Behavior and Human Decision Processes* 52(1): 96–123.
Mead, Margaret and Rhoda Metraux. 2000. *The Study of Culture at a Distance*. New York: Berghahn Books.
Nafus, Dawn and ken anderson. 2009. "Writing on walls: The materiality of social memory in corporate research." In *Ethnography and the Corporate Encounter: Reflections on research in and of corporations*, edited by Melissa Cefkin, 137–57. New York: Berghahn.
Ortner, Sherry B. 1998. "Generation X: Anthropology in a media-saturated world." *Cultural Anthropology* 13(3): 414–40.
Peterson, Mark A. 2003. *Anthropology and Mass Communication: Media and myth in the new millennium*. Oxford: Berghahn.
Pink, Sarah, Heather Horst, John Postill, Larissa Hjorth, Tania Lewis, and Jo Tacchi. 2016. *Digital Ethnography: Principles and practice*. London: Sage.
Ponterotto, Joseph G. 2006. "Brief note on the origins, evolution, and meaning of the qualitative research concept thick description." *The Qualitative Report* 11(3): 538–49.
Postill, John. 2000. "Borneo again: Media, social life and nation-building among the Iban of East Malaysia." Unpublished PhD thesis, University College London.

——. 2006. *Media and Nation Building: How the Iban became Malaysian*. Oxford: Berghahn.

——. 2009. "What is the point of media anthropology?" *Social Anthropology* 17(3): 334–7.

——. 2011. *Localizing the Internet: An anthropological account*. Oxford: Berghahn.

——. 2014. "Democracy in an age of viral reality: A media epidemiography of Spain's indignados movement." *Ethnography* 15(1): 50–68.

——. 2015a. "Public anthropology in times of media hybridity and global upheaval." In *Media, Anthropology and Public Engagement*, edited by S. Abram and S. Pink, 164–81. Oxford: Berghahn.

Postill, John and Sarah Pink. 2012. "Social media ethnography: The digital researcher in a messy web." *Media International Australia* 145: 123–34.

Skinner, Jonathan. 2007. "From the pre-colonial to the virtual: The scope and scape of land, landuse and landloss on Montserrat." In *Caribbean Land and Development Revisited*, edited by J. Besson and J. Momsen, 219–32. Palgrave Macmillan.

Skuse, Andrew. 1999. "Negotiated outcomes: An ethnography of the production and consumption of a BBC World Service soap opera for Afghanistan." Unpublished PhD thesis, University College London.

7

MIXING IT

Digital Ethnography and Online Research Methods—A Tale of Two Global Digital Music Genres

Georgina Born and Christopher Haworth

Introduction

Digital ethnography has, in principle, a double meaning. It refers to the ethnographic study of digital cultures, but can also refer to the development and application of digital methodologies to enhance ethnographic research. If the first meaning has received significant attention in anthropology (Pink et al. 2015), then the second has been less widely embraced. One of the reasons concerns the largely quantitative orientation of existing uses of digital methods for social and cultural research. Anthropology has privileged the qualitative study of social and cultural processes, an approach replicated in the burgeoning subdiscipline of digital anthropology. So while the impact of digital technologies and infrastructures on ethnographic practices of observation, data collection and writing has been well documented (Murthy 2008; Pink et al. 2015), the application and refinement of computational methods to serve or complement ethnographic research have been less explored.

A second reason concerns divergences in the way anthropologists and sociologists have responded to the term "network," a key organizing concept in much digital sociology (Marres 2006; Rogers 2013; Severo and Venturini 2015), particularly in the study of online cultures. However, as Postill (2008), Miller (2012) and Pink et al. (2015, 101–7) contend, the privileging of the network metaphor is problematic, and digital anthropologists have rightly favored approaches that examine the great varieties of relationships, socialities and "social worlds" (Pink et al. 2015, chapters 5 and 6) in which our ethnographic subjects are engaged (Miller 2012, 147), whether mediated by digital technologies or not. Indeed, for Miller (ibid.), the ethnographic study of social networking sites should be aligned with long-standing anthropological research traditions such as kinship.

One manifestation of these tendencies is arguably a divergence between digital anthropology and digital sociology in the past decade—as evident in the contrast between the different research directions fostered by two leading international centers: the Digital Ethnography Research Centre at RMIT University in Melbourne, and the Centre for Interdisciplinary Methodologies at Warwick University, UK.[1] We propose in this chapter that this divergence might be unproductive. Through a case study, we indicate how digital anthropology might now fruitfully adapt some of the digital research methods stemming from digital sociology, while nuancing how those methods are employed. We advocate, then, a mixed methods approach in which digital ethnography is augmented through the use of quantitative online methods, in turn expanding and rendering a more subtle interpretation of those methods. Such a methodological move is particularly necessary, we suggest, when analyzing cultural practices that are deeply enmeshed in, and mediated by, the Internet.

The theme of this chapter is therefore how computational methods can enhance digital ethnography. Specifically, we adapt the Issue Crawler software, a "medium specific" tool for analyzing and visualizing multilateral patterns of hyperlinking between actors using the World Wide Web. Richard Rogers developed Issue Crawler for mapping issue-based controversies online.[2] In his account, Issue Crawler embeds itself within the ecology of the Internet so as to "follow the evolving methods of the medium" (Rogers 2013, 15). We offer a critical and reflexive introduction to the uses of Issue Crawler for the study of online cultures, showing how it can complement online and offline ethnographic research. Our ethnographic focus is on how the Internet is mediating contemporary musical practices through a comparison of two "global" digital music genres, both of which are deeply enmeshed in the Internet: microsound, a long-standing and influential genre with pre-Internet roots, and vaporwave, a spectacular contemporary genre that emerged on the Internet in the early 2010s.[3]

As we will show, by tracing online the nature of hyperlinking practices, Issue Crawler makes it possible to visualize and make available for analysis the relations between some of the key entities associated with the two genres—among them musicians, critics, bloggers, fans, labels, platforms, venues, festivals, distributors, funding bodies and other cultural institutions. When coupled with other sources of ethnographic insight into the two genres, such visualizations of their distinctive hyperlink ecologies significantly deepen the material available for analysis. Given the methodological caveats we set out below, our larger message is that the use of quantitative digital tools like Issue Crawler can be generatively transposed into other spheres of ethnographic enquiry involving online and offline, and hybrid online-offline, manifestations.

Enhancing Issue Crawler: Digital Anthropology Meets Digital Sociology

The Issue Crawler software (henceforth IC) has become a staple of digital sociology (Rogers and Marres 2000; Bruns 2007; Rogers 2010; Marres 2015). When using it, one starts with a list of URLs representing 10 to 20 key webpages, known as "nodes" or "actors," associated with whichever culture, field or social group—in this case, Internet-mediated music genres— is the focus of the study. For our purposes these starting URLs were drawn from multiple sources: a genre website, a leading critic's overview article and other sources of authoritative knowledge about the two genres. IC then crawls through the webpages associated with these starting URLs and stores in a database any hyperlinks that direct the user to another destination on the web. For higher "crawl depth" settings IC does this again, analyzing the outlinks from the first set of results for crawl depth 1, the second set for crawl depth 2, and so on (see Figure 7.1). In this process of "co-link analysis," any webpage that receives two or more

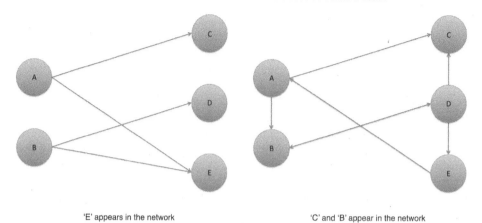

'E' appears in the network   'C' and 'B' appear in the network

Figure 7.1 (a) Visualization of co-link analysis with a crawl depth of one; (b) Crawl depth of two: A and B are starting links; C, D and E are the sites they link to

"inlinks" from within the same group or social network is deemed "significant." The results are then plotted in a 2D visualization that displays the inlink and outlink relations in the form of a pattern among key webpages. The relative x-y positions of the nodes on the map indicate their "relatedness," i.e. how frequently links are exchanged between them (Figure 7.2); while the size of each node corresponds either to the number of inlinks the site receives, the number of outlinks it makes, or a combination of both, depending on the user's choice. Effectively, the resulting visualization portrays patterns of hyperlink relations between nodes that in some cases are purely online entities (mailing lists, blogs) and in other cases are hybrids—online entities that may be both extensions and representations of offline entities (musicians, labels, festivals, galleries, funding bodies and so on).

 H receives four inlinks from the crawled population, so it appears in the network. However, C, E, P, and B do not link to it, nor does it link to them.

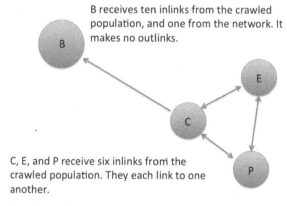

B receives ten inlinks from the crawled population, and one from the network. It makes no outlinks.

C, E, and P receive six inlinks from the crawled population. They each link to one another.

Figure 7.2 Visualization of Issue Crawler results

What, then, is productive about using IC? We want to point to three ways in which the software can assist the ethnographer's work. First, the IC visualizations expand our awareness of the nature of key actors associated with the particular culture, field or group being studied. The crawl for microsound, an established music genre, points to the pervasive online presence of mainstream actors—festivals, galleries, promoters, ticketing agencies and so on. In comparison, the vaporwave crawl highlights vividly, through the very different actors that appear in the visualization, its radically different nature as a "DIY" genre in which the production of user-generated content by a fan subculture is to the fore. The "actors" that appear in the crawl are a multitude of sites hosted by the amateur net-based platform Tumblr, sites that operate as pseudonymous avatars for the members of this subculture (cf. Baym 1999). We will show that vaporwave evidences little separation between producers and fans, approaching those "self-sufficient" publics characteristic of avant-gardes that Bourdieu identifies as "producers who produce for other producers" (Bourdieu and Johnson 1993, 50–1).

Second, IC visualizes the specific hyperlink ecology generated by the hyperlinking practices of key actors associated with the culture or group at issue. Two dimensions are worth noting. On the one hand, the IC results for our case study highlight the diversity and singularity of the hyperlink ecologies of the two music genres; indeed, each hyperlink ecology has a distinctive gestalt, an overall "look," which is itself interpretable (see Figures 7.4 and 7.5). On the other hand, IC allows us to examine the nature of the relations revealed by co-link analysis, and by drawing on other ethnographic and historical sources, we are able to pursue this more acutely than in previous uses of the software. In particular, we probe the social relations apparently manifest in these hyperlinking practices. Where previous researchers using IC depict hyperlink relations as relatively uniform components that together form what appears to be a stable network, our material shows that it is imperative to analyze the differences in hyperlinking practices.

In diverse ways, the hyperlinking that we trace indicates how the actors in each genre are commonly engaged in the reciprocal or bilateral exchange of resources, through a mutual valorization that may be symbolic and/or material—via the exchange of symbolic, cultural and/or economic capital. Indeed, the ease with which actors can participate in hyperlinking suggests that the web assists in accelerating this ecology of mutuality in which two or more parties co-consecrate one another (cf. Bourdieu and Johnson 1993, 76–7). In this sense, the web's propensity to speed up and intensify the exchange of hyperlinks engenders an online version of what Born (1995, 91–4) identifies in an earlier study as an inflationary cycle of prestige, charisma and legitimation characteristic of musical and artistic fields, but more widely applicable, in which actors—musicians and artists, intermediaries (critics, managers, agents, etc.) and institutions (labels, galleries, concert organizations, publishers and so on)—engage in a spiral of mutual endorsement and valorization.

However, a striking finding from our microsound case study is that hyperlinking also engenders uses that are *not* bilateral. Holding the IC results up against additional ethnographic and historical data on the genre points to what might be called aspirational hyperlinking:[4] the anticipatory, protentive (Born 2005, 21) creation by one party of wished-for relations with and valorization by another—relations that are not (yet) reciprocated or actualized, but in which the potential to inflame an inflationary cycle is sought.[5] This is particularly characteristic of musicians and labels from genres such as microsound that, as we will show, aspire to "crossover" from pop to art, seeking to accrue legitimation, new kinds and degrees of cultural and symbolic capital by creating associations with established artists and cultural institutions. In both senses, then, reciprocal and non-reciprocal hyperlinking, the web becomes the medium for the performance of a complex and dynamic prestige economy.

In marked contrast, the visualization of vaporwave's hyperlink ecology is shaped by a particular facet of the way that IC interacts with Tumblr—a platform that IC reveals as central to the genre's participatory subculture. In regard to Tumblr, IC has no way of distinguishing between hyperlinks that are purposefully made by a page owner in order to create a relation, and hyperlinks that are automatically created when a fan or other interested party "likes" or "reblogs" the page owner's page. These "likes" and "reblogs" appear on the visualization as hyperlinks *back* to the Tumblr page of the individual "liker" or "reblogger," in effect reversing the phenomena that IC is designed to portray: thus, frequent "likers" appear on the map as though they were prominent actors, while the actor that is "liked" might not appear at all. As a result, a blizzard of enthusiastic "likers" appears in the visualization in proximity with established artists, illuminating the frenetic nature of the subcultural practices characteristic of the genre.

A third way in which IC can support the digital ethnographer's work, illustrated in our case study by the comparison between microsound and vaporwave, is through its contributions to illuminating a critical dimension often overlooked by previous uses of IC and similar online methods, as well as by digital anthropology and digital sociology; the dynamic, evolving nature both of Internet technologies and of the cultures of Internet use. By employing IC in conjunction with other ethnographic and historical data, our case study captures aspects of their complex and synergistic co-evolution. Indeed, the comparison of microsound and vaporwave highlights how, given the two genres' origins in different phases of the net, both Internet technologies and the cultures of Internet use have evolved between them: from early-adopters' experiments in orchestrating online discussion and debate, in microsound, to a contemporary phase characterized by a reflexive and politicized material and aesthetic play with the very historicity of the Internet, in vaporwave.

In all these ways, as our case study shows, IC proves to be a powerful means of illuminating core dimensions of the cultures, fields or social groups in which the Internet plays a decisive mediating role. Yet limitations become apparent when using the software, prompting us to suggest methodological revisions. First, IC visualizations provide far from exhaustive representations—in our case study offering only a partial image of the life of the two genres. Moreover, the results of IC are very much an artifice of the algorithm employed: IC does not capture important aspects of the genres, and some of the hyperlinks that appear in the visualization are contingent by-products of running the algorithm. Together, this foregrounds the need to draw on additional ethnographic and historical material to discriminate between more and less significant IC findings—a mode of triangulation that can productively be generalized to other quantitative online methods.

A second limitation is that IC operates in a strictly synchronic mode: it performs co-link analysis on all the web data that has been accumulated at the point when the algorithm is run, bracketing questions of temporality and history (Marres and Weltevrede 2013; Rogers 2013). While one can schedule co-link analysis at specific intervals and thereby compare IC visualizations over time, and while other recent quantitative online tools (such as Twitter Capture) allow crawls to cover particular date ranges and thus time distributions, it is not possible to do historical crawls on the public Internet. This signals a wider limitation on all Internet and web-based research, for the net and the web are extremely unstable as environments, subject to relentless churn and renewal; webpages and net platforms appear and disappear regularly without being traceable (Rogers 2013, 24). This is despite the development of Internet archiving projects that attempt to counteract the synchronic orientation and historical "blindness" of the Internet by archiving single pages and sites,[6] for what is lost by such archiving is the intrinsic embeddedness of websites in larger hyperlink ecologies. Thus, with regard to microsound, actors (whether musicians, labels or software) whose contributions to the genre preceded the advent of the Internet, or those no longer active who nevertheless continue to influence the genre, do not appear in the IC results. Since many music genres (and online cultures) enact strong genealogical ties to the past, this blindness to temporal depth is a serious restriction on analysis. It demands, again, recourse to other sources of online and offline ethnographic and historical data to contextualize the synchronic "snapshot" provided by IC.

We therefore advance a series of methodological principles for global digital ethnography going forward: that it should employ quantitative online methods such as IC while being fully cognisant of their limitations—limitations that can in part be counteracted by recourse to complementary research findings from (online and offline) ethnography and history. Indeed, we contend that drawing on such qualitative resources is not only helpful but necessary in order to hone the interpretation of the data generated by IC and similar quantitative tools. In this sense, digital anthropology and digital sociology can enhance one another methodologically. But in addition, we highlight the need to address the Internet as an evolving medium, one that—importantly—has fostered an increasingly reflexive sense of its historicity among recent generations of users. In vaporwave, we will show, such reflexivity is particularly marked, taking the form of aesthetic and political engagements with the earlier materialities and cultures of Internet use.

Proceeding in this way, in what follows we outline for the two music genres, first, their nature and genesis; second, their distinctive uses of the Internet; and third, we give an analysis of the IC visualizations as they illuminate the core actors, relations and creative practices characterizing each genre. We bring out three significant findings: (1) how microsound and vaporwave manifest distinctive eras in the evolution of the Internet as a digital-cultural medium; (2) how they exemplify (at the same time) changing cultures of Internet use; and (3) how they illuminate, through music, the expanding, increasingly reflexive aesthetic and political uses being made of the Internet.

Microsound: Modernism Migrates and Expands Online

The origins of microsound lie in post-War academic computer art music, where the term was identified with a style, technique or compositional philosophy. From the late 1950s through to the 1980s, computer music was modernist in its aesthetic orientation and nurtured within academic and research institutions (Born 1995). For the composer Iannis Xenakis, whose 1963 book *Musique Formelles* coined the term (1963, 68; 1992), microsound named the microtemporal realm of sound related to timbre, and his book proposed a number of strategies for composing at this temporal and perceptual scale. One of these strategies was taken up and extensively developed by computer musicians Barry Truax and Curtis Roads, becoming known, partly through the influence of Roads' 2001 book *Microsound*, as "granular synthesis." From the 1990s, however, a series of computer music scenes developed in parallel outside academia, also adopting the term microsound for their music. They included prominent musicians who drew aesthetically on both modernist elements and popular electronic dance musics of the period, releasing recordings on underground record labels like 12K, Line and Mille Plateaux. In 1999 key figures from these non-academic scenes created the hugely popular email list *.microsound*, a participatory multimedia platform and a forum for the discussion and exploration of a shared "digital aesthetic," accelerating the genre's emergence (Cascone et al. 1999).

The *.microsound* email list began as one of seven genre mailing lists hosted by hyperreal,[7] an online organization for experimental cultural practices with roots in the 1990s San Francisco rave scene. A pronounced facet of the list was discussion of the new aesthetic forms and practices afforded "by the proliferation and widespread adoption of digital signal processing (DSP) tools" (Cascone et al. 1999). Such DSP tools were originally developed in research institutions, but the rise of affordable consumer music technologies over the 1990s led to their commercial development and growing availability outside academia. It was in these conditions that microsound came to be associated with the previously mentioned granular synthesis techniques: newly circulating online in the guise of research articles, software patches and code, these techniques were the driving force in the cultivation of a common microsound aesthetic.[8]

Microsound's Internet-based resources also encompassed two other Internet architectures, each of which contributed to the genre's development. The first was an FTP server. Ordinarily a mundane protocol used to transfer files on a computer network, in microsound it was inventively repurposed as a platform for collaborative, geographically distributed processes of music composition—a relayed creativity (Born 2005). Using a shared sound file as source material, hosted on the FTP server, members responded to creative "challenges" akin to Fluxus event scores issued by other members, uploading the resulting compositions to the microsound server from where they could be downloaded or streamed as online compilation albums. The second Internet architecture exploited was the World Wide Web, which in 1999 was used to curate a webpage listing URLs for what were held to be representative musicians and labels. Mixing present-day musicians with historical forebears, the list performatively constructs a genealogy of labels, academic and non-academic composers that define the genre (Figure 7.3).

Striking in this genealogy is how lesser-known contemporary musicians are set in close association with elected "ancestors"—now-canonic electronic composers including Xenakis, Brün, Francois Bayle and Bernard Parmegiani—in this way aspiring to share in their cultural and symbolic capital. Already evident is a feature of microsound's development that is magnified by the IC results; how, through the *.microsound* list and uses of the web, non-academic musicians have engaged in sustained efforts to access the software, knowledge and aesthetic resources of academic computer art music, while projecting genealogical links to established ancestors and emulating the creative practices of earlier avant-gardes. In these ways they attempt to reduce

---

.microsound related links

---

this is the list of related artist and labels as it was on the old website. in the next few days we'll have a new updated list with the appropiate links.

artists	artist, cont'd	labels
aube	phoenecia	12k
ramon bauer/general	peter rehberg/pita	ina-grm
magic/rehberg & bauer	/rehberg & bauer	mego
francois bayle	jean-claude risset	microwave
frank bretschneider/komet	curtis roads	mille
herbert brun	snd/shirt trax	plateaux/ritornelle
kim cascone	tom steinle	rastermusic
richard chartier	nobukazu takemura	touch
farmers manual	terre thaemlitz	
fennesz	barry truax	
bernhard gunter	voice crack	
hecker/cd_slopper	trevor wishart	
christoph heeman	iannis xenakis	
ryoji ikeda		
infotron		
tetsu inoue		
zbigniew karkowsi		
monolake/robert henke		
carsten nicolai/noto/produkt		
/signal		
oval		
bernard parmegiani		

Figure 7.3 The original *.microsound*.org links page (1999) (image courtesy of Eloy Anzola, John Saylor, Paulo Moaut, Kim Cascone and the *.micorsound* community)

the erstwhile technological, aesthetic, discursive and social distance between the popular and art poles of computer music. These efforts are visible in the IC visualization for microsound (Figure 7.4).[9] The 1999 .*microsound* links page of key artists and labels (Figure 7.3) provided indicative starting URLs for running IC; but since some of the pages are now inactive, and newer artists are missing, we updated it with working links and, where necessary, contemporary replacements. Of the 39 original actors (URLs), just nine appear in the IC results: five are labels or institutions (12k, Raster Noton, Mego, Touch, INA-GRM), and four are artists (Ryoji Ikeda, Christian Fennesz, Richard Chartier, Mark Fell/SND). The wholesale change of core microsound actors since the 1999 webpage suggests a genre that is evolving expansively, an impression confirmed by the prominence of the established actors mentioned earlier: major festivals, promoters, ticketing agencies, etc. But the most remarkable IC finding is the apparent evidence of the success of the aspirations of popular microsound artists and labels to achieve a crossover for their work: from popular electronic music to computer art music and sound art. This is suggested by the appearance on the map of influential cultural institutions including the world-leading Parisian academic computer music centers IRCAM (ircam.fr) and INA-GRM (inagrm.com), the CDMC (cdmc.asso.fr), a French state-funded archive of contemporary art music, the prestigious Austrian Ars Electronica festival for digital arts (aec.at), the Tokyo Museum of Contemporary Art (mot-art-museum.jp) and the Thyssen-Bournemisza Foundation (tba21.org), a leading private patron and collection of experimental art.

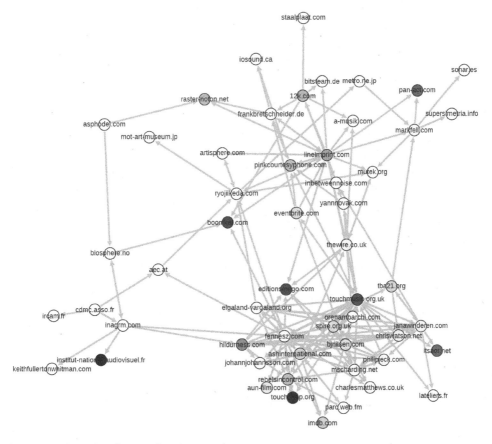

Figure 7.4   Issue Crawler map for microsound

Despite their appearance on the IC map, the question arises: how far are the putative links to these institutions, and to the contemporary art music world, actually achieved, and how much are they aspirational? The IC method provides ways to answer this question. By analyzing the direction of hyperlinking among relevant actors and their frequency—IC's measure of "relatedness"—as well as the types of inlinks actors receive from the crawled population, we can infer which links are expressions of a desired-for connection (non-reciprocal linking) and which represent "real," reciprocal relations. Through this analytical lens, it is clear that IRCAM and CDMC stay firmly within their own contemporary music milieu; they appear as actors only because of the inclusion in the starting URLs of composers Xenakis and Trevor Wishart (who, however, do not appear in the map). In general, the map reveals few hyperlink exchanges between the dense subsets of nodes in the bottom and top right, and the sparser subset in the bottom left, the location of IRCAM, CDMC and INA-GRM.

Yet two cultural institutions do make connections to the denser parts of the map, providing insight into the extent and success of microsound's crossover attempts. The first is the Ars Electronica festival. The international prize hosted by the festival, the Prix Ars Electronica, has overseen major shifts in the aesthetic economy of computer music, specifically the changing articulation between its art and popular poles. In 1999, for the first time, academic computer musicians were ousted from the top prizes by non-academic exponents—"music from the bedroom studios" (Eshun 1999). Microsound was centrally implicated, with several of the genre's core crossover artists and labels gaining prizes (Bernhard Gunter, Terre Thaemlitz, Mego). Initially, these events caused rifts between academic and non-academic microsound scenes; 15 years on, the shift has been metabolized. In accord with this history, the IC map shows Ars Electronica spanning the art–pop divide, receiving inlinks from both CDMC and crossover musician Christian Fennesz, while itself linking to sound artist Ryoji Ikeda.

The second institution, the world-leading Parisian electroacoustic music research studio INA-GRM, exhibits more active hyperlinking. As well as receiving inlinks, it makes outlinks to a number of non-academic microsound artists (Keith Fullerton Whitman, Biosphere, Fennesz and Hildur Guðnadóttir). This is a highly significant finding, showing that some level of robust reciprocal exchange occurs between these musicians and INA-GRM. It is borne out by wider ethnographic observations: two of these artists have held residencies at the studio, while others have performed in recent years at its Présences Électronique festival. Together, these findings suggest that the drive since the late 1990s among non-academic microsound musicians to establish relations with international academic and art music institutions, forging a pop-art crossover and garnering greater prestige and legitimacy for their work, has in part been achieved. If the existence of aspirational hyperlinking is strongly evident in the 1999 .microsound links page, this strategy was emblematic of the genre's early life. It is a sign of the present-day confidence and "arrival" of non-academic microsound artists, in terms of their entry into art music circuits, that their current webpages no longer link to "classic" composers, having no further need to accrue prestige and legitimacy by association. Analyzing the IC results through the lens of ethnography and history therefore reveals a major finding: microsound as a key genre in which the boundaries between art and pop, academic and non-academic computer music are being strenuously reshaped.

Vaporwave: Tumblr as a Parodic and Politicized Creative Platform

Vaporwave presents stark contrasts with microsound. If microsound migrated online in an early phase of the Internet, by the time of vaporwave's emergence in 2011 the net was firmly established as a cultural medium. Commentators expressed growing dissatisfaction with any idea of a rigid separation between online and offline life (Coleman 2010, 492; Lehdonvirta 2010; Rogers 2013), and concepts like ubiquitous computing (Bell and Dourish 2006) and post-Internet (McHugh 2011; Archey and Peckham 2014) arose to reflect an age in which we no longer "log on" but are always connected. Vaporwave is a product of this age: cultivated almost entirely within the medium of the Internet, and remarkable for the extent to which the net is embraced not only as a cultural and social but as an aesthetic medium, visual as much as musical. In vaporwave, novel subcultural practices are developed around "natively" digital objects such as hashtags, hyperlinks, tag clouds and so on, accreting layers of value and meaning.

While in microsound, these net-native technologies were exploited practically to proffer new modes of collaboration, vaporwave exhibits an extraordinarily acute awareness of the historicity of the Internet as an unfolding medium, manifest in the way that old and obsolete Internet platforms, architectures, graphics and cultural practices make ironic returns in new guises. Surreal stylizations of net-native practices—making and following hyperlinks, or surfing from one point in cyberspace to another—are focal for the "vernacular creativity" at the heart of the genre (Burgess 2007).

In place of the standard division of labor in microsound—musicians, intermediaries (critics, managers, agents) and institutions (labels, venues, festivals)—vaporwave is defined almost entirely by its online subculture. Although the genre has produced "stars"—artists such as Vektroid and James Ferraro—and an emblematic label—the Bandcamp-based "Beer on the Rug"—these actors are dwarfed online by the pervasive presence of its hyperactive subculture. The subculture, as mentioned before, manifests a weak separation between producers and audiences, its practices riffing implicitly on notions of DIY, the amateur or "dark matter" (Sholette 2010). Peopled by obscure, pseudonymous avatars that pass for "subjects," with long and unpronounceable strings of symbols and characters for names, the subculture exemplifies but also parodies the participatory, user-generated content ethos of web 2.0.

The emergence of the genre highlights its web 2.0 ethos. "Vaporwave" is a pun on "vaporware," the name for commercial software that is publicly announced but never goes into production; its first reported use was in an anonymous 2011 blogpost, a review of the album "Surf's Pure Hearts" by the little-known artist Girlhood (Harper 2012). When the term came to more widespread attention, it was as an unexplained hashtag accompanying anonymously uploaded soundfiles, images, GIFs and other media. The media posted under this tag were distinctive in audiovisual style. Musically, they included samples of derided music sourced from the Internet and then re-uploaded with little in the way of modification: 1980s "muzak," soul and funk, advertising soundtracks for consumer electronics, luxury hotels and other icons of consumer capitalism, computer game soundtracks and sonic idents. Visually, they featured anachronistic juxtapositions of images of Greek and Roman antiquity with 1990s computer graphics, isolated Japanese cityscapes, leisure advertisements, images of luxury apartments and other signifiers of global capitalism. Vaporwave's coalescence as a genre was therefore "bottom up" fuelled by the decentered and ostensibly democratic practice of social tagging (or folksonomy).

Vaporwave's cultural practices knowingly replicate and parody the addictive, almost compulsory participation that feeds social networks, where the voluntary labor of the user community drives the system and generates value (Mejias 2013). Anyone with a computer and Internet connection can produce vaporwave—there is even an ironic YouTube "how to" video explaining it[10]—and it is shared free through distribution platforms such as Bandcamp and Soundcloud. Indeed, vaporwave circulates more like a "meme" than a music genre, its

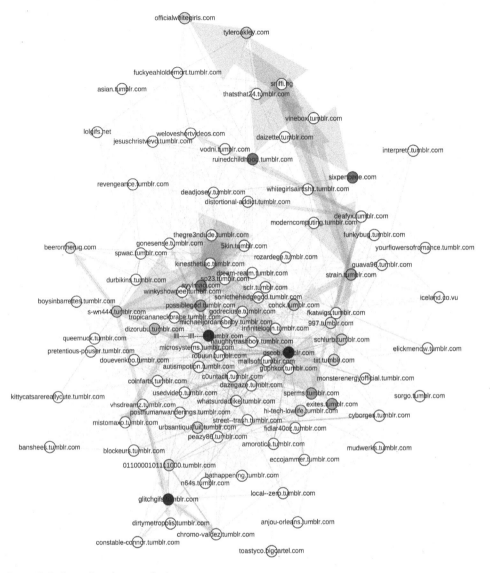

Figure 7.5 Issue Crawler map for vaporwave

profuse user-generated content marked by rigid sonic and visual conventions. The uniformity of these memes is encouraged by their rapid imitation among the genre's hyperactive online subculture, fueled by affective contagion (Tarde 1903, 1969; Shifman 2014; cf. Wiggins and Bowers 2014). This account of the genre is compounded by the IC results (Figure 7.5). Without exception, all of the 100+ actors that appear in the visualization subscribe to the same platform, Tumblr. This is astonishing given that just one of the 19 starting URLs was a Tumblr page, and it is largely an artifact of the way that IC interacts with the Tumblr architecture. The effect, as mentioned before, is that a Tumblr user who "likes" and "reblogs" frequently effectively outranks the actor that s/he likes or references. In a sense this is a methodological anomaly resulting from use of a tool developed in the "age of the hyperlink" (Weinberg 2010) to study a platform that exemplifies "the age of the like button" (Gerodimos and Justinussen 2015). Yet this anomaly is a happy accident for our purposes, since what results is rich evidence of vaporwave's pseudonymous online subculture, its members appearing in the guise of congeries of "likes" for particular artists, tracks and webpages.

Clicking through the nodes that appear in the IC results takes one deep into the genre's amateur net art culture. Participants enthusiastically mimic the vaporwave aesthetic, crudely cloning the genre's kitsch, multimedia, collage-based net art in their Tumblr pages. Signs of the purportedly open, decentralized and egalitarian nature of the Internet celebrated by vaporwave are apparent in the way that, just as fans frenetically "like" musicians and labels associated with the genre, so well-known vaporwave artists and labels link to fans' Tumblr pages, affirming that fan art has considerable "in-genre" prestige. All of this testifies, again, to the horizontal nature of the subculture and the permeable border between artists and amateurs. The effect is that the perfect storm of Tumblr "liking" at the heart of the visualization pushes other actors—stars, labels, key critics, Soundcloud and Bandcamp—to the edges of the map.

Vaporwave's "memetic" subculture, dramatically visualized in the IC map, also portrays a profound shift in the material mediation of music online. Where in microsound hyperlinking practices take place in public web space, in vaporwave they manifest fidelity to a single commercial network. O'Reilly's (2005) account of the transition from "web 1.0" to "web 2.0" characterizes it as a shift from individual public webpages to social network-based blogging; what we see in the map is the successive stage—from blogging to micro-blogging. Known for its cryptic, minimal design, Tumblr is especially conducive to uploading multimedia content such as images, GIFs and short videos. It affords rapid content update and personalization of webpages, a practice abandoned by corporate-monopoly SNSs such as Facebook in their enforcement of a uniform site and page design. Vaporwave participants have created a very singular culture of Tumblr use. As Figure 7.6 shows, a garish collage aesthetic abounds, comprised of found and recycled digital images and clips—the visual detritus of the commercial online world. Users typically appropriate "bad art" such as dated computer graphics, GIFs or icons from historical operating systems. Characteristic motifs are the Windows 95 desktop interface, visual signifiers from the dial-up era of the net, the amateur web design of the Geocities network, and the recovery of obscure injunctions to "interact" with the web manager via a text box.

In this sense vaporwave participates in a broader "Tumblr aesthetic" that has become fashionable in recent years in underground digital music and art scenes (cf. Valiquet 2014, 197). Vaporwave's adherents manifest a shared absorption in the particular ways that Tumblr's materiality mediates what is uploaded there, along with a reflexive intensification of this very material mediation. The dense interconnections in the IC visualization attest to how much the genre is constituted by an energetic, almost purposeless play with the material and aesthetic affordances of Tumblr.

Vaporwave is therefore characterized by an intense material and citational reflexivity in relation to the Internet. Indeed, the genre is a product of the net, which acts at once as content source, creative medium, means of delivery and communication, and as a concept informing all these practices. Central to the genre's aesthetic elevation of the net, as indicated, is a reflexive awareness of the historicity of the net, apparent in the citation of audiovisual signifiers from prior phases of web history (Windows 95 graphics and startup sounds, outdated visual signifiers of "cyberspace" and so on) and in the ironic re-adoption of "obsolete" Internet practices such as hyperlinking itself. If microsound manifests "aspirational" hyperlinking, the explosion of hyperlinking in the vaporwave map shows this earlier culture of Internet use returning in parodic form.

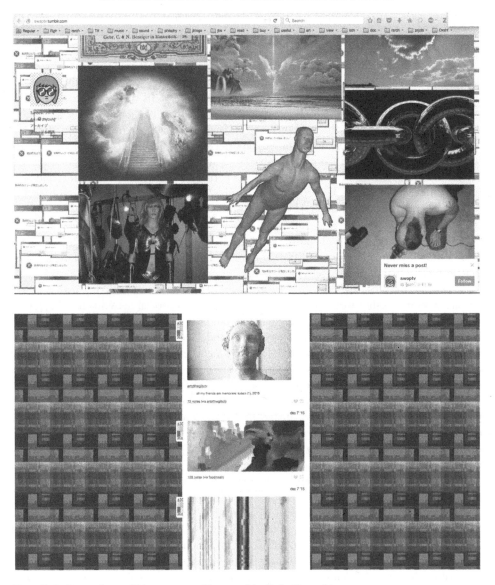

Figure 7.6 Screenshots of (a) swaptv.tumblr.com; (b) glitchgifs.tumblr.com

The frenetic nature of the subculture's imitative mining of parody, irony and surreality points finally to the genre's politics: for vaporwave luxuriates in an unruly and ambivalent celebration-cum-critique of late consumer capitalism. Tracks such as "Utilize your impact" and "Global connections" from Internet Club's *Redefining the Workplace* parody the business-speak of the neoliberal workplace, while James Ferraro's *Far Side Virtual* features automated voices addressing the listener as consumer ("Sir, would you like to read the New Yorker directly on your i-tablet?"). When critic Adam Harper (2012) wrote the definitive article on the genre, he equated it with Accelerationism (Mackay and Avanessian 2014): a radical political theory positing that capitalism should not be resisted but accelerated until it is pulled apart by its own contradictions. In this way he articulated an incipient cultural politics among the genre's adherents, unleashing in turn a wave of content ambiguously celebrating a dystopian capitalism. Vaporwave, therefore, shows both the extent to which music genres are migrating online, and the effects in transforming the nature of music genres today.

Conclusions

Through the use of IC in conjunction with (online and offline) ethnography and history, we have shown how microsound and vaporwave manifest distinctive eras in the evolution of the Internet as a digital-cultural medium; how the two genres exemplify at the same time changing cultures of Internet use; and how they illuminate—through music—the increasingly reflexive aesthetic and political uses being made of the Internet. We have also highlighted core dimensions of the Internet as yet little recognized by digital anthropology: the Internet as not only a social, cultural and political but an aesthetic medium; and the need to engage with the historicity of the Internet—a historicity with which our ethnographic subjects are themselves increasingly reflexively and creatively engaged.

In neglecting to attend to the historicity of the Internet, previous uses of IC and similar online methods have ignored the ongoing transformation both of Internet technologies and of the cultures of Internet use. By comparing microsound and vaporwave we can decipher these transformations as they mediate the two genres. It is because the genesis of the two genres is separated by over 15 years that we are able to illuminate extraordinary differences in their engagements with the Internet: microsound the product of an early experimental phase of Internet use, vaporwave exemplifying a subversive and ironic "post-Internet" net culture. Across the two genres we have demonstrated how computational methods such as IC can enhance the study of digital cultures, supplementing ethnographic and historical method.

The hyperlinking practices that IC was developed to analyze thrive in public web space. With the rise of proprietary social networks and mobile computing, the web is increasingly compartmentalized as platforms aspire to operate as self-contained ecosystems. The hyperlink is a casualty of this increasingly privatized Internet: while the clickable link remains the medium of Internet flow ("surfing" the web), movement is often now contained within the bounds of a commercial platform. As vaporwave shows, commercial platforms like Tumblr can assume such dominance among participants that there remains almost no "outside": the platform is equated with the entire web. In this new ecology, digital methods must increasingly probe music's mediation by social media, and many such tools are already in use—Netvizz, Twitter Capture, Instagram Scraper and so on.

Yet vaporwave enjoins us to remember that technologies and corporations are never the sole drivers of change. One of many captivating things about the genre is participants' subtle and discerning awareness of the historicity of the Internet. The Tumblr-based pseudonymous actors of vaporwave therefore share with Internet researchers a keen interest in periodizations such as "the age of the hyperlink," but they express this reflexive knowledge through inventive creative practices—ironic hyperlinking, for instance—rather than scholarly publications. Quantitative computational methods will always be inadequate for capturing this kind of vernacular creativity, with its effervescent and labile aesthetic and political qualities. If this realization has been absent from digital sociology, it may be because hyperlinks, hashtags, "likes" and so forth are rarely considered vehicles for inventive creativity. We therefore end by stressing again the need for mixed methods. If computational methods extend the reach of the ethnographer, in an important sense such methods will always lag behind the creativity of our ethnographic subjects.

Notes

1 www.digital-ethnography.net and www2.warwick.ac.uk/fac/cross_fac/cim, accessed April 4, 2016.

2 www.govcom.org/Issuecrawler_instructions.htm, accessed April 4, 2016.

3 The case study derives from a larger project employing IC to research Internet-mediated music genres (Born and Haworth, forthcoming). This project, in turn, forms part of a transnational ethnographic research program, funded by the European Research Council Advanced Grants scheme under the European Union's 7th Framework Programme (2007–2013), ERC grant agreement no. 249598. The research program, "Music, Digitization, Mediation: Towards Interdisciplinary Music Studies," was directed by Georgina Born between 2010 and 2015 and based at the University of Oxford. See http://musdig.music.ox.ac.uk, accessed April 4, 2016.

4 The analysis of different hyperlinking practices remains undeveloped in the work of key writers on IC. Rogers and Marres (2000, 9–12) identify two "styles" of hyperlinking among organizations engaged in climate change debates: cross-linkers or reciprocal linking, and non-cross-linkers or non-reciprocal linking. They relate non-cross-linking to a "neo-pluralist gap" (note 46) but take this no further. Rogers (2010) does identify non-reciprocal "aspirational linking," in which smaller organizations make links to established ones to try to secure affiliation, but does not pursue the interpretation. Our analysis of non-reciprocal linking developed independently, and we take this analysis further than these earlier studies.

5 The distinction we are opening up here between reciprocal hyperlinks that in some way actualize a mutuality in social relations and aspirational hyperlinks that, by protending relations with another entity, attempt to bring them into being, but in which there is no certainty that this will be achieved, is a critical rejoinder to notions of performativity which assume that by performing or "enacting" social relations they actually come into being (cf. Law 2004, 56; Latour 2005, 34–5).

6 See, for example, the Wayback Machine, a digital library project that periodically archives webpages, allowing one to search the history of the Internet: https://archive.org/about/, accessed April 4, 2016.

7 www.hyperreal.org, accessed April 4, 2016.

8 Cascone's album *Pulsar Studies* exemplifies the microsound aesthetic and its basis in the material mediation of musical sound afforded by DSP tools (Cascone 2000; Haworth 2015).

9 The shading of a node indicates how many inlinks it receives – darker nodes receive the most. Arrowheads on the edges (or lines) between nodes show the direction of a hyperlink, with double arrowheads indicating reciprocal hyperlinking. The breadth of the edge is a measure of how frequently a site links to another (visible in Figure 7.5). In Figure 7.5, semi-transparent edges were used to improve legibility.

10 www.youtube.com/watch?v=wyt_87yCyNw, accessed April 4, 2016.

References

Archey, Karen, and Robin Peckham. 2014. "Art Post Internet," http://ucca.org.cn/en/exhibition/art-post-Internet/, accessed April 4, 2016.

Baym, Nancy K. 1999. *Tune In, Log On: Soaps, Fandom, and Online Community*. London: Sage.

Bell, Genevieve, and Paul Dourish. 2006. "Yesterday's Tomorrows: Notes on Ubiquitous Computing's Dominant Vision." *Personal and Ubiquitous Computing* 11(2): 133–43.

Born, Georgina. 1995. *Rationalizing Culture: IRCAM, Boulez, and the Institutionalization of the Musical Avant-Garde*. Berkeley, CA: University of California Press.

———. 2005. "On Musical Mediation: Ontology, Technology and Creativity." *Twentieth Century Music* 2(1): 7–36.

Born, Georgina, and Christopher Haworth. Forthcoming. "From Microsound to Vaporwave: Internet-Mediated Musics, Online Methods, and Genre."

Bourdieu, Pierre, and Randal Johnson. 1993. *The Field of Cultural Production: Essays on Art and Literature*. New York: Columbia University Press.

Bruns, Axel. 2007. "Methodologies for Mapping the Political Blogosphere: An Exploration Using the IssueCrawler Research Tool." *First Monday* 12(5). http://firstmonday.org/ojs/index.php/fm/article/view/1834, accessed April 4, 2016.

Burgess, Jean Elizabeth. 2007. "Vernacular Creativity and New Media." PhD Thesis, Queensland University of Technology. http://eprints.qut.edu.au/16378/, accessed April 4, 2016.

Casacone, Kim. 2000. "The Aesthetics of Failure: 'Post-digital' Tendencies in Contemporary Computer Music." *Computer Music Journal* 24(4): 12–18.

Cascone, Kim, Paulo Mouat and John Saylor. 1999. "microsound Mailing List." http://microsound.org/, accessed April 4, 2016.

Coleman, Gabriella. 2010. "The Hacker Conference: A Ritual Condensation and Celebration of a Lifeworld." *Anthropological Quarterly* 83(1): 47–72.

Eshun, Kodwo. 1999. "Music from the Bedroom Studios." Ars Electronica Archive. http://90.146.8.18/en/archives/prix_archive/prixjuryStatement.asp?iProjectID=2598, accessed 4 May, 2016.

Gerodimos, Roman, and Jákup Justinussen. 2015. "Obama's 2012 Facebook Campaign: Political Communication in the Age of the Like Button." *Journal of Information Technology & Politics* 12(2): 113–32.

Harper, Adam. 2012. "Comment: Vaporwave and the Pop-Art of the Virtual Plaza." *Dummy.* www.dummymag.com/features/adam-harper-vaporwave, accessed April 4, 2016.

Haworth, Christopher. 2015. "Sound Synthesis Procedures as Texts: An Ontological Politics in Electroacoustic and Computer Music." *Computer Music Journal.* Cambridge: MIT Press.

Latour, Bruno. 2005. *Reassembling the Social.* Oxford: University of Oxford Press.

Law, John. 2004. *After Method: Mess in Social Science Research.* London: Psychology Press.

Lehdonvirta, Vili. 2010. "Virtual Worlds Don't Exist: Questioning the Dichotomous Approach in MMO Studies." *Game Studies* 10(1). http://gamestudies.org/1001/articles/lehdonvirta, accessed April 4, 2016.

Mackay, Robin and Armen Avanessian (eds). 2014. *#Accelerate: The Accelerationist Reader.* Falmouth, UK: Urbanomic Media.

Marres, Noortje. 2006. "Net-work is Format Work: Issue Networks and the Sites of Civil Society Politics." In *Reformatting Politics: Information Technology and Global Civil Society*, edited by Jodi Dean, Jon W. Anderson, and Geert Lovink, 3–17. London: Routledge.

——. 2015. "Why Map Issues? On Controversy Analysis as a Digital Method." *Science, Technology & Human Values* 40(5): 655–86.

Marres, Noortje, and Esther Weltevrede. 2013. "Scraping the Social?" *Journal of Cultural Economy* 6(3): 313–35.

McHugh, Gene. 2011. *Post Internet.* Brescia: Link Editions.

Mejias, Ulises Ali. 2013. *Off the Network: Disrupting the Digital World.* Minneapolis, MN: University of Minnesota Press.

Miller, Daniel. 2012. "Social Networking Sites." In *Digital Anthropology*, edited by Heather A. Horst and Daniel Miller, 146–62. London: A&C Black.

Murthy, Dhiraj. 2008. "Digital Ethnography: An Examination of the Use of New Technologies for Social Research." *Sociology* 42(5): 837–55. doi: 10.1177/0038038508094565.

O'Reilly, Tim. 2005. *What Is Web 2.0?* O'Reilly Media, Inc.

Pink, Sarah, Heather Horst, John Postill, Larissa Hjorth, Tania Lewis, and Jo Tacchi. 2015. *Digital Ethnography: Principles and Practice.* London: Sage.

Postill, John. 2008. "Localizing the Internet beyond Communities and Networks." *New Media & Society*, 10(3): 413–31.

Roads, Curtis. 2001. *Microsound.* Cambridge, MA: MIT Press.

Rogers, Richard. 2010. "Mapping Public Web Space with the Issuecrawler." In *Digital Cognitive Technologies*, edited by Bernard Reber and Claire Brossaud, 89–99. London: John Wiley & Sons, Inc.

——. 2013. *Digital Methods.* Cambridge, MA: MIT Press.

Rogers, Richard, and Noortje Marres. 2000. "Landscaping Climate Change: A Mapping Technique for Understanding Science and Technology Debates on the World Wide Web." *Public Understanding of Science* 9(2): 141–63. doi: 10.1088/0963–6625/9/2/304.

Severo, Marta, and Tommaso Venturini. 2015. "Intangible Cultural Heritage Webs: Comparing National Networks with Digital Methods." *New Media & Society* (January 14), 1–20.

Shifman, Limor. 2014. *Memes in Digital Culture*. Cambridge, MA: MIT Press.

Sholette, Gregory. 2010. *Dark Matter: Art and Politics in the Age of Enterprise Culture*. London: Pluto Press.

Tarde, Gabriel. 1903. *The Laws of Imitation*. New York: Holt.

——. 1969. *On Communication and Social Influence: Selected Papers*. Chicago, IL: University of Chicago Press.

Valiquet, Patrick Joseph. 2014. "'The Digital Is Everywhere': Negotiating the Aesthetics of Digital Mediation in Montreal's Electroacoustic and Sound Art Scenes." PhD Thesis, University of Oxford. http://ora.ox.ac.uk/objects/uuid:356cdab4-c690-4eb8-9558-3ae80e51d2df, accessed April 4, 2016.

Weinberg, David. 2010. "Knowledge at the End of the Information Age." Bertha Bassum Lecture, Faculty of Information, University of Toronto. https://archive.org/details/KnowledgeAtTheEndOfTheInformationAge, accessed April 4, 2016.

Wiggins, Bradley, and G. Bret Bowers. 2014. "Memes as Genre: A Structurational Analysis of the Memescape." *New Media & Society* 17(11): 1886–906.

Xenakis, Iannis. 1963. *Musiques Formelles: Nouveaux Principes Formels de Composition Musicale*. Special issue of La Revue Musicale, nos. 253–4. Paris: Editions Richard-Masse.

——. 1992. *Formalized Music: Thought and Mathematics in Composition*. New York: Pendragon Press.

Part II

RELATIONSHIPS

8

SMALL PLACES TURNED INSIDE-OUT

Social Networking in Small Communities

Tom McDonald, Razvan Nicolescu, and Jolynna Sinanan

Introduction

In smaller communities with small populations—as opposed to large cities and metropolitan areas—social life is characterized by a strong sense of mutual familiarity: people knowing (or at least knowing of) one another through extended families, work or vocational networks. This chapter argues that for such "small communities," social relations are relatively more intense and confined, and these dynamics play out in particular ways over uses of social media, where people both conform to norms, expectations and values which they share with others and express their individual opinions and aspirations at the same time, often through careful navigation of private and more public-facing platforms.

The findings and illustrations for this chapter are based on 15 months of ethnographic fieldwork, carried out by the authors as part of the *Why We Post* project, a cross-cultural, comparative study of social media in small towns worldwide conducted by nine anthropologists based at University College London.[1] Between 2012 and 2014, McDonald, Nicolescu and Sinanan conducted their fieldwork in rural China, southeast Italy and Trinidad, respectively. All three places were towns that could be classed as "small communities," however the populations of these settlements varied: 20,000 inhabitants in the Italian site, 18,000 in the Trinidadian site and 6,000 in the Chinese site.

Cross-cultural studies have generally posed a challenge for social scientists, due to the difficulties of conducting comparative fieldwork in, and comparing qualitative data from, drastically different cultural contexts. George Marcus' (1995) key essay on the emergence of multi-sited ethnography and Appadurai's (1996) work on the global flows of culture paved the way for new forms of ethnographic enquiry.[2] Despite these advances, anthropologists face significant challenges in balancing the need to follow the movements of people and goods across different cultural contexts with the requirements for deep ethnographic description that are often best met through prolonged engagement in a single locale.

In anthropology, this resulted in a recent series of cross-cultural comparative projects and also in calls for further comparison and public responsibility within the discipline (see Gingrich and Fox 2002). Reflecting these concerns, this chapter is based on the first truly global comparative long-term ethnographic research in digital anthropology, the results of which are summarized in *How the World Changed Social Media* (Miller et al. 2016) as well as online.[3] This project builds on several pioneering monographs, which have made significant contributions to this field (e.g. Boellstorff 2008; Miller 2011; Coleman 2012; Postill 2011), as well as more general works exploring the relationship between ethnography, theory and methodology (Horst and Miller 2012; Boellstorff et al. 2012; Miller et al. 2016; Pink et al. 2016).

Conducting ethnography is key to understanding both how and why people use social media and digital technologies. In addition to analyzing posts on more public-facing social media platforms such as Facebook and collecting data through surveys and questionnaires, living in the town for an extended period of time also allowed us to actively engage in the everyday lives of the communities we worked with, including understanding participants' extended relationships, everyday interactions, as well as less overt online activity which could only be viewed by "friending" informants on the social media platforms they used. This was particularly the case in McDonald's fieldwork, as his participants were especially averse to posting updates on public platforms such as microblogs, instead preferring to use more "closed" platforms such as QQ and WeChat where updates are typically only shared with authenticated contacts, most of whom were known personally to the participants.

One of the main ways in which ethnographic fieldwork allowed us to understand the specific effect of social media in small towns was to show how within the context of navigating social relations that most of the community is (or tries to be) aware of, participants use social media in order to construct a permeable intermediate layer between the personal and more public social relations. More than in metropolitan places, uses of social media in small communities reflect how residents are more attentive in how they respond to distinct sets of relationships that are oppositional as well as complementary: the personal and public. On the one hand, there are intimate and private relationships which are usually more informal, but also uncommitted and disputed. On the other hand, some relations are more public such as those with work colleagues; the permanent contacts parents maintain with their children's school teachers; or periodic connections adults preserve with their former classmates, who now live in other parts of the country. This last set of relations may be formal and expresses either individuality or conformity, or a balanced combination between the two. For users in small places, social media brings together personal and public relations, individuality and conformity in a unique constellation, and allows users to navigate these relations in a way that is rarely found elsewhere in their lives.

Comparative Ethnography

Adopting a comparative approach added a valuable dimension to our ethnographic study of social media. This built on other multi-sited studies where ethnography became a method for understanding movement. For example, migration can be better understood by widening research beyond the home region to the host destination (see Gallo 2014; Gomes 2015; Madianou 2015). In addition to Marcus (1995), Gupta and Ferguson (1997), Hannerz (2003) and Falzon (2009) have emphasized the importance of multi-sited ethnography for understanding how relationships are formed and transform across space. Similarly, in studying uses of social media, the relationships that people have with their contacts range from those they know very well (especially in small towns), to strangers whom they might not know at all. Further, communication on social media is not limited to text alone; visual communication through sharing photos, images and video created by either oneself or others is common, with the varieties of content shared also reflecting contemporary events and popular culture. Thus, the discussions around globalization that were relevant to the emergence of multi-sited ethnography also resonate with researching uses of social media.

In addition to conducting participant observation in each of our fieldsites, we drew on existing ethnographic literature so as to also compare with what other scholars had learnt conducting research in similar cultural contexts. Prior research in Trinidad conducted by Birth (1999) on village life, Miller (1994) on consumption, Olwig (2007) on Caribbean migration and Munasinghe (2001) on Indo-Trinidadian and Afro-Trinidadian relations highly influenced how Sinanan analyzed what she observed in Trinidad. Trinidadian scholars such as Mohammed (2002), Singh (1994), Khan (2004) and Hosein (2010) were also valuable for understanding the historical, economic, political and social relations that shape some of the dynamics of social media use in Trinidad and, especially, what is displayed on Facebook. In China, while few comprehensive ethnographic studies have been conducted on the impact of social media on rural populations to date (as noted by Oreglia 2015), studies on rural migrants in China's cities (Qiu 2009; Wallis 2013) highlighted important themes around mobility and gender that contribute to McDonald's study. Similarly, the few ethnographic studies on social media in Italy focused more on young people and were conducted in the north of Italy (e.g. Giaccardi 2010; Gui 2013; Bonini 2011; Micheli 2013). Nicolescu considered these studies in conjunction with works on media (Vereni 2008), appearance (Sassatelli 2010; Pipyros 2014) and classical anthropology of the greater Mediterranean. Becoming familiar with scholarship on each country allowed each researcher to better observe the more parochial setting of each town, and to be more confident with regards to which phenomena were distinctive to that context when it came to cross-cultural comparison between the fieldsites.

In relatively small communities, people build social relations based on traditions and institutions which include the shared consumption of time and socialization in a way that is largely unavailable in big urban or metropolitan centers, an idea that originated from Simmel (e.g. Lynch 2005; Jacka 2005; Zhang 2001; Birth 1999; Hannerz 1980; Fox 1977; Lewis 1968; Redfield 1947). What emerged from the "small community" fieldsites of the *Why We Post* project is that uses of social media platforms in these places generally reflect and strengthen the values of these communities, rather than gravitating toward global forms and tastes. This is particularly important as it contrasts one of the main assumptions that sees social media as bringing more homogenization and globalization (see Rantanen 2005).

This was especially clear in the case of when young people adopt such global forms and expressions, as they frequently do as an aspiration to share with peers, again reflecting more local practices and values. For example, McDonald's (2016a) research in rural China shows how aspects of "traditional" family life are seen as an aspiration in itself, expressed through images of their babies and posts on the importance of family values on QZone (a popular Chinese social media platform). By contrast, in the project's other China fieldsite, an industrial Chinese factory town, Wang (2016) shows how it is more common for young migrant workers in factory towns to share postings expressing material aspirations for a perceived modern and comfortable life, such as images of cars or clothes. They associate material comforts with earning through labor, as demonstrated in the country's more affluent urban centers. By comparison, in the Italian fieldsite, most people want their online presence to be viewed as consistent with how they are seen on an everyday basis by the rest of their community. Finally, in Trinidad young people have aspirations for a specific kind of social visibility which maintains both respectability and reputation; for example, one day a young person might post images of himself being active in his Hindu temple and the next day, an image of himself and his friends at a party. All of the above examples co-opt global forms for distinctly local purposes.

In the sections that follow, we present comparative illustrations of how residents in small towns use social media to navigate personal relationships, manage their public appearance, strengthen their sense of community and balance demands of both individuality and conformity in a way that generally avoids confrontation, while also allowing exploration of new forms of sociality.

Cases from Small Places: Communities, Non-Confrontation and Experimentation

Strengthening the Community—Southeast Italy

Nicolescu conducted his research in an Italian town situated in the southernmost region of Apulia. This region is characterized by strong relations within the nuclear family and a very specific lifestyle which combines austerity and self-restriction within the household with particular concern around one's public appearance and behavior.[4] Nicolescu (2016) shows how most people (with the notable exception of teenagers) in this fieldsite use social media to support their specific sense of sociality: they seek to associate with their immediate networks and relationships, rather than trying to enhance or expand them.

Facebook is perceived as a *very public* platform, where appropriate conduct means demonstrating conformity and agreement within the already existing social groups. Most residents shy away from posting images of themselves or status updates whose content may be interpreted as self-aggrandizement. They were extremely cautious when sharing a photo of themselves or personal accomplishments online, for fear of being accused of "showing off." Such posts would contradict the average persona that is aspired to and enacted day-to-day, so they would be viewed as out of character and may attract mocking or ridiculing comments online.

In this context, more intimate, personal and complex issues were discussed either offline or over dyadic media such as phone conversations and instant messaging platforms such as WhatsApp. WhatsApp in particular does not simply mark the boundary between public and private, but it also allows one domain to penetrate the other. For example, young women set up large WhatsApp groups with their female friends to support their individual romantic relationships through permanent exchange of information about their respective partners, but also recommendations regarding clothing and hairstyle. At the same time, on Facebook, people might post personal photos and write status updates that only some of their online connections could decipher because they have privileged access to particular offline information.

This became clear in the case of Salvatore. Similarly to others in the town, Salvatore viewed social media as a means to express different aspects of himself, but was also frustrated by not being able to communicate with his contacts in a way that he would have liked. For example, he never posted photos from parties after drinking too much or behaving "stupidly" on Facebook, even though he was having a good time. His close friends who often accompany him on these outings respect his concerns and never tag him in photos which they think Salvatore would not wish to be published online. These behaviors reveal two contradictory concerns: how Salvatore is perceived by his wider community, but also the close friendships he has within the community of people who know him very well. Comments, banter and mocking on Facebook show the levels of friendship between individuals: the closer they are, the more they ridicule each other in public. Ridicule is thus a form of inclusion among closest groups, but it can also have an impact on how the person is perceived by their wider circles and could result in forms of exclusion by others.

Salvatore also works as an IT consultant for a medium-sized company in the nearby city of Lecce. In his hometown, he is known for being a quiet and refined person. Salvatore does not have any inclination to challenge the image that people in his hometown have constructed of him and held for almost four decades of his life. He commutes to work every day and on some weekends he stays in the city with friends. He feels that in Lecce he can have another persona and can even be an entirely different person (un'altra persona). However, he does not want any aspect of his Lecce persona to appear on social media and contradict the image of him in his hometown. As a consequence, Salvatore's posts on Facebook are generally normative and mundane, intentionally crafted to avoid attracting attention and invoking the gossip, moral judgment or ridicule of others.

Salvatore's story might be consistent with common social mechanisms in different social groups in many societies, but the way it was employed on public-facing social media in southeast Italy might have different consequences. First, as the dominant social media platform in the town, Facebook can also be understood as the largest space where different groups congregate at different times and each person has a different degree of visibility. Residents therefore tailor their public Facebook postings to resonate with each individual in their network while adhering to the wider sense of group norms that are reflective of the town itself. The relationship that the person has to the wider community is just as important to uphold and maintain as the relationship between individuals.

Second, because of Facebook, communication and visibility is able to reach multiple social groups concurrently. This meant that for the first time, people had to constantly differentiate between the levels of commitment to each of their social groups. Many felt constant efforts needed to avoid such "context collapse" (boyd 2014) to be extremely annoying and tiring, and so chose to use Facebook as little as possible, or adopt one neutral attitude throughout all their online interventions. For example, local political leaders generally posted in an "official" tone, and young people in a humorous one. People also have to show different levels of support and approval to the multiple concurrent social groups that are present online, most commonly through "liking"—the highest level of approval is through commenting—while disapproval is shown by not acknowledging the post at all. People then use these sorts of feedback as a mechanism to consider and filter their further online interventions.

The third consequence is the increased popularity of more private social media such as WhatsApp. What this platform actually did in the Italian site was to absorb most of the burdens, anxieties, but also needs for individual differentiation from Facebook. In this respect, other public-facing platforms such as Instagram and sometimes Twitter[5] were used by young people to complement, explain or detail some of their posts on Facebook. It is the avalanche of small conversations through text and photos on all of these platforms that allows for the normative and relatively calm aspect of Facebook.

There is also a sector of the town's society who privilege their contacts from larger metropolitan centers over their local ones, such as people who underwent their graduate studies in places such as Rome, Bologna and Milan. After having spent years living and working away, some decide to return and live in their hometowns in south Italy, but they find local social life extremely constricting, so many prefer the prestige, company and opportunities that can result from associating with their urban connections rather than local ones. For example, these alumni might personally know prestigious members of urban arts and humanities circles and invite them over to give public presentations, or those with higher computational skills can collaborate with online entrepreneurial activities started in the north of Italy. These connections represent not only a permanent and most visible relationship with metropolitan areas, but also with the main political, economic and environmental activities generated in these places.

Although there are arguments that it is *because of* social media that people are made more aware of global issues, in this case it is this relatively thin layer of highly educated persons in the town who are the gatekeepers of the trends and discussions from metropolitan areas. For them, Facebook is crucial because it facilitates maintaining their relationships with friends who live in urban areas. But they often feel conflicted in their personal use of Facebook as they have to both address the local norms of posting, which they might find restricting and limiting, while also displaying their cosmopolitan interests and perspectives that characterize the social life of these university cities. Several people therefore accepted a much higher proportion of Facebook contacts from their urban-based friends than from their rural ones. One woman commented: "I prefer to meet them and talk in person. I find it strange to friend [on Facebook] people who pass in front of my door."

In summary, in southeast Italy, social media reflects the constant struggle to keep the balance between personal relationships and the social commitments to the rest of the community. In Trinidad, Facebook is a less conformist platform but nonetheless remains non-confrontational and appeals to a shared sense of identity.

Non-confrontational Public Social Media: Trinidad

Adhering to a shared sense of values was as important in the Trinidadian fieldsite as in the Italian case; yet, being able to express one's opinions and sense of individuality was equally necessary. The balance was achieved by expressing oneself in a non-confrontational manner.

The Trinidadian fieldsite is in one of the least developed parts of the country, over an hour's drive from the next urban center. The population of the town is 18,000 inhabitants; 20,000, including those living in the surrounding villages. The most dominant social media platform throughout the duration of the fieldwork was Facebook and, by mid-2013, WhatsApp had increased in popularity to replace BBM (BlackBerry Messenger). Sinanan (2016) describes how strikingly clear expectations of conduct dictated use of different communication forms, whether everyday face-to-face conversations, private communication over WhatsApp, or posting and sharing on Facebook. Face-to-face communication was seen to be the most acceptable for dealing with any kind of topic. WhatsApp was for private conversation that could, to an extent, substitute for face-to-face conversation. Facebook was seen as the most public form of communication and, consequently, where individuals self-censored to a high degree. Yet, self-censoring was a deliberate form of negotiating privacy, where the permanence and accessibility of social media postings was also associated with having the least control of how content would be received by others.

The clearest example of this spectrum is on the topic of politics. When asked about discussing politics "online," most participants responded, "I don't talk about politics," or "I'm not interested in politics." Yet, in private homes, small businesses such as shops or salons (where owners and customers know each other well) and in more public social areas such as bars, residents of the town would openly discuss the latest political scandal or news story. This was especially the case if surrounded by peers who shared the same political views. Furthermore, although politics is openly discussed among peers, it is usually the politicians as individuals who are discussed, their activities or what they had said or done, rather than policies and their effects.

In the town, politics is mostly spoken about in terms of the individual personalities involved as gossip and scandal, rather than as political activity or activism. Political activism itself is a form of identity that is not aspired to in the town and is associated with university students, those in artistic circles and urban elites. As the town is far from these urban centers and is considered as in the hinterlands (or "real bush" in local dialect) by many Trinidadians who live outside of the town, residents pride themselves on having retained simple country living, family orientation and community values.

Facebook Messenger or WhatsApp were preferred for conversations between close friends or relatives on more sensitive topics such as politics, as it was felt more divergent opinions could be expressed on these platforms. WhatsApp, as a more private form of communication, but also a platform where people can communicate in groups can also substitute for face-to-face and dyadic communication. Chat groups between family members and friends were popular, especially during slower hours of the workday. WhatsApp chat groups were used to organize activities and other logistics among peers, but also to exchange gossip, share photos taken by individuals, humorous memes, songs and links to videos. Among these groups, for more serious or complex discussions, a face-to-face get together was preferred.

In this context, Facebook in Trinidad was similar to that in southeast Italy: it was the most public-facing social media platform, where people maintained contacts from different social networks, hence becoming a conservative space. For example, there was very little political commentary, and on the rare occasions where political viewpoints were expressed, it was mostly in the form of humor, such as through sharing amusing memes. Unlike the serious political conversation that occurred in private offline spaces among peers, in the more open and visible space of Facebook, witty exchange about politics is preferred over coming across as being political through serious commentary. Scandal and gossip can be shared and enjoyed as spectacles, as opposed to posting controversial and divisive opinions. However, displays of values and moral views as a form of everyday concerns and politics were far more common.

From observing the timelines of different research participants in the Trinidadian fieldsite, memes appeared as frequently as images taken by individuals. Unlike the Italian fieldsite, showing photos of oneself drinking, dancing and at parties, or in attractive (and sometimes provocative) outfits before an evening out is generally acceptable and not viewed as controversial, offensive or shameful. Yet, reinforcing social norms and codes of acceptable behavior through humor and moralizing memes was a popular activity. These memes usually emphasized the values of good relationships, such as marriage, family and friendships.

Rose, for example, works in her daughter's salon in a busy mall in the center of the town. Usually there are very few customers in the morning and Rose and her daughter spend the time talking to each other or looking at Facebook on their phones. Most days, Rose will share a greeting on her timeline, such as a meme with a picturesque background and text that says "Good morning," which attracts at least a handful of "likes." She also shares motivational or religious memes, with text such as "A Strong Person is not the one who doesn't cry. A Strong Person is the one who cries & sheds tears for a moment, then gets up and fights again" [sic] or "God is stronger than your circumstances."

Rose and her daughter know their customers fairly well as they have lived in the same area for years, and are friends with many of them on Facebook and WhatsApp. Most of their conversation with customers is catching up on news and gossiping about people they mutually know. Rose reflects that even though she knows a lot of people, she keeps her circle of close friends to a select few as she has fallen out with too many others in the past. Sometimes when she feels unfairly treated by others, she posts another type of meme, an "indirect" (a message posted publicly but which leaves the intended recipient unclear). For example, "Any friend that turned into an enemy has been hating since day one." These sorts of indirect posts serve as a moral commentary on the state of friendships. Only a close group of friends would know the situation referred to, but other social media contacts would share the general sentiment. Therefore, such memes are a visual way to express values and opinions without being too explicit, direct or confrontational, thus reducing potentially undesirable social consequences, such as being avoided or causing a quarrel, for those who post them.

Exploring New Sociality: Rural China

The cases of both Italy and Trinidad explored above have emphasized how social media use in small places is often characterized by the transferral of existing offline social norms and constraints that are strongly experienced in small communities onto these new online domains. In contrast, the evidence from rural China showed how social media also enabled people in small communities to explore new types of sociality in conjunction with separate online activities that still stressed the normative expectations of these communities. This was especially seen through the way different social media platforms mediated rural residents' links and migrations between their rural hometown and nearby urban places such as larger towns and cities which lead participants to use social media as a way to think through their own experience of rurality, and to experiment with other possible alternatives, even from within the town itself.

It should be noted that the social media ecology in China differs entirely from that described in the other two fieldsites. China has developed its own social media platforms while also creating a technical system that effectively prevents its citizens from accessing most non-Chinese social networks (including, at the time of writing, Facebook, Twitter and Instagram).[6] There are two main platforms that dominate the social media market—QQ and WeChat—both of which are owned by the Tencent company. QQ is the comparatively older platform, with its roots tracing back to 1999 when it launched as an instant messaging platform. It has since mushroomed to offer a variety of features including QZone, a web-based social networking platform. WeChat, by contrast, was released in 2011 and is largely a mobile messaging platform (users require a smartphone/mobile phone number to log in), albeit with several social features.

The contrast between these two platforms became particularly clearly expressed through examination of how the town's young people gradually increased their interactions with individuals from outside the town as they became older. McDonald's fieldsite contained only a junior and middle school, so after graduating from middle school (at around 14 years of age) most young people migrate to nearby urban areas in order to attend high school or vocational colleges, before ultimately entering university or employment in the cities. Initially students typically returned to their hometown regularly at weekends, however the frequency of return visits often decreased as time went on.

Gradual migration away from the town was also accompanied by a transitioning in the types of social media platforms that young people used. Several members of this group were already versed in social media, as within the town, Internet access could be obtained either through borrowing smartphones owned by friends or relatives, Internet cafés, school computer labs or, increasingly, broadband connections at home. In this case, migration did not entail a transition from offline to online[7] but rather the transition from rural to urban was accompanied by a second general migration between two different Chinese social media platforms: from QQ to WeChat.

Prior to migration, many students attending primary and middle school in the town itself made significant use of QQ, chiefly to engage in communication with their own classmates. This communication between classmates was facilitated by the popular practice of forming class-based "QQ groups" using QQ's Instant Messaging software. Although QQ groups could, in theory, be formed of any persons, it remained especially popular to base membership of these groups on one's school class. However, as these young people migrated to urban centers, in addition to maintaining their QQ use and forming new groups based on their new classes and institutions, they started to experiment with WeChat, provoked by the realization of its prevalence among urban users and their classmates. Partially this was also related to the fact that these young people started to view QQ as slightly "childish" (*youzhi*) or "unrefined" (*tu*). Thus their adoption of this new platform went hand-in-hand with their urban migration, and the need to appropriately communicate with the new individuals they met in these places. This transition also provoked a re-evaluation of their previous communication methods in the world they left behind.

A further enabling factor was a change in the *way* they accessed the Internet following their migration to the town. Prior to their migration, it was common for young people in Anshan Town to have to share resources in order to gain access to the Internet, for example sharing a computer at home, borrowing others' mobile phones, or visiting friends' homes or Internet cafés. Parents generally felt that mobile phones distracted from schoolwork and from other forms of learning and so sought to prevent their children from owning them (McDonald 2016b).

However, once young people arrived at vocational college and university, there was an enormous rise in the number of students who had access to mobile phones in comparison to middle school students.[8] Parental attitudes toward mobile ownership by their children shifted from one of concern over control to a desire that their children possess such devices in order to ameliorate the disconnection between themselves and their children that accompanied migration (McDonald 2016b). Eventually, many parents purchased such devices for their offspring. This was a further significant factor with regards to the migration from QQ to WeChat, as WeChat required a smartphone in order to log in to the account, so device ownership further paved the way for this migration between platforms.

By examining young people's social media use in the rural China fieldsite, and comparing it with nearby urban areas, we have been able to observe not only the importance of acknowledging the specificity of social media use in small places, but also how people from such places make use of social media to navigate interactions with people from within and outside the town. These new modes of connection also opened up new possibilities with regards to relationships. For example, many students spoke of the role of social media in establishing relationships through interacting with strangers, some of which were romantic in nature. This reveals a further capacity of social media: to allow types of sociality and relationships to occur that might otherwise be difficult to experience within the (sometimes constraining) environment of a small place.

Even while attending middle school in the town itself, many students spoke of indiscriminately adding contacts in their QQ account. When young people started vocational college or university, their parents—who had previously worried that dating would distract their children from studying—generally became more relaxed about their offspring engaging in such relationships. Social media was also seen by students as, among other things, helping to overcome anxiety with regards to talking to potential partners. For example, Wang Gaoshan, a final year university student from the town who returned home one summer explained the ease with which students in urban areas took to online dating through social media platforms.

Dating online is very fashionable in China, you know? Falling in love online, it's just chatting with strangers online. Chat, chat, chat. Then just say, "Let's meet up," you meet, and . . . success! Or, let's say the two of us don't know each other, we are both of the opposite sex. I'll tell you a few things, get a few things off my chest.

Chatting to strangers at universities was also facilitated by a fortuitous combination between technology and urban geography, further reflecting how certain social media might produce very different experiences when used in small places than in large cities. Many social media platforms featured location-based services, which enabled users to find and converse with talk to nearby strangers. Because the majority of universities had relocated their campuses from city centers to large, self-contained campuses outside the cities, the concentration of students in a single locale meant that using these functions was almost guaranteed to return search results almost entirely comprised of university students. Wu Haoran, a male university student from Anshan Town who attended university there explained to me that whenever he switched on the "People Nearby" function on his phone while on campus, he was able to ascertain simply by looking at the distance of the individual, even whether prospective partners were members of his own school or the neighboring colleges. Li Yan, a 21-year-old female from the town who attended university in Shanghai also spoke of "indiscriminately adding" (*luan jia*) new contacts when she was at university.

These examples show how social media is used to both navigate transitions between rural and urban environments, and also to experiment with conversing with strangers. This final feature of social media, the ability to see and explore new forms of sociality and human experience that come to challenge the existing traditions and norms, is also an especially striking effect that it has on small places.

Conclusion

In this chapter, we have drawn on ethnographic fieldwork to explore the dimensions of social life and social media in small towns. Whereas the examples from southeast Italy and Trinidad illustrate how different ways of conforming to a group's values remain as important as maintaining relationships between individuals; by contrast, in rural China, the transition from residing in the town and migrating to an urban area transforms one's relationships as well as the relationship to sociality itself, particularly when becoming more familiar with those who occupy the category of stranger. What all these examples point to, is that for those living in smaller places, uses of social media reveal it to be both an extension of the dynamics of small town life, while also representing a strong intensification of the existing sociality. It is the diversity of uses of new media that allows for navigating between these two simultaneous constraints.

The second argument that should be made is that these two commitments have always been the two landmark poles of social relations: they could mark the permanent tension between private and public, delineate household boundaries, assign gender roles, or facilitate constructing ideas about the nation state. However, social media has created the conditions in which these two poles became attracted *within the same environment*, to an extent that people had to find ways to employ the available platforms and technologies in order to recreate the boundaries they thought were blurring.

In "small communities" this was reflected in a relatively more cautious engagement with public-facing social media and a much more individualized use of the private aspects of social media (i.e. one-to-one messaging, stranger finding services) than in metropolitan spaces. Our ethnographic material suggests that neither of these ways of engaging online resembled the offline relationships. Rather, it was the particular combination of use of the more public and the more private media that responded to the specific requirements for socialization in these communities.

Notes

1 This research was funded by the European Research Council (Grant number: 2011-AdG-295486 SocNet).
2 Such as multi-sited ethnographies (Marcus 1995; Gupta and Ferguson 1997; Hannerz 2003) and transnational migration (see Gallo 2014; Gomes 2015).
3 See the project website at www.ucl.ac.uk/why-we-post.
4 See for example Silverman (1975), Pipyros (2014) and Nicolescu (2016).
5 Even though Instagram and Twitter were used less among adults, they experienced increased popularity among teenagers: 31 percent of students in the last two years of the secondary schools in the Italian fieldsite were using Instagram and 18 percent used Twitter.
6 Government censorship over these platforms is known as the "Great Firewall of China."
7 Although in our industrial China fieldsite Wang (2016) argues that for rural migrant factory workers a "parallel migration" from offline to online also accompanied the physical migration from rural to urban.
8 Nearby urban high schools, too, had slightly higher phone penetration rates among pupils than the middle school in the fieldsite did.

References

Appadurai, Arjun. 1996. *Modernity at Large: Cultural Dimensions of Globalization*. Minneapolis, MN: University of Minnesota Press.

Birth, Kevin. 1999. *Any Time is Trinidad Time: Social Meanings and Temporal Consciousness*. Gainesville, FL: University Press of Florida.

Boellstorff, Tom. 2008. *Coming of Age in Second Life: An Anthropologist Explores the Virtually Human*. Princeton, NJ; Oxford: Princeton University Press.

Boellstorff, Tom, Bonnie Nardi, Celia Pearce and T. L. Taylor. 2012. *Ethnography and Virtual Worlds: A Theory on Method*. Princeton, NJ: Princeton University Press.

Bonini, Tiziano. 2011. "The media as 'home-making' tools: Life story of a Filipino migrant in Milan." *Media, Culture & Society* 33(6): 869–83.

boyd, danah. 2014. *It's Complicated: The Social Lives of Networked Teens*. New Haven, CT; London: Yale University Press.

Coleman, Gabriella. 2012. *Coding Freedom: The Ethics and Aesthetics of Hacking*. Princeton, NJ: Princeton University Press.

Falzon, Mark-Anthony, ed. 2009. *Multi-Sited Ethnography: Theory, Praxis and Contemporary Research*. Surrey: Ashgate.

Fox, Richard. 1977. *Urban Anthropology: Cities in their Cultural Settings*. Englewood Cliffs, NJ; London: Prentice-Hall.

Gallo, Ester, ed. 2014. *Migration and Religion in Europe: Comparative Perspectives on South Asian Experiences*. Farnham: Ashgate.

Giaccardi, Chiara, ed. 2010. *Abitanti della rete. Giovani, relazioni e affetti nell'epoca digitale*. Milan: Vita e Pensiero.

Gingrich, Andre and Richard G. Fox, eds. 2002. *Anthropology, by Comparison*. New York and London: Routledge.

Gomes, Catherine. 2015. "Where to next after graduation: International students in Australia and their aspirations for transnational mobility." *Crossings: Journal of Migration and Culture* 6(1): 41–58.

Gui, Marco, ed. 2013. *Indagine sull'uso dei nuovi media tra gli studenti delle scuole superiori lombarde*. Regione Lombardia.

Gupta, Akhil and James Ferguson, eds. 1997. *Anthropological Locations: Boundaries and Grounds of a Field Science*. Oakland, CA: University of California Press.

——. 1980. *Exploring the City: Inquiries towards an Urban Anthropology*. New York: Columbia University Press.

Hannerz, Ulf. 2003. "Being there . . . and there . . . and there! Reflections of multi-site ethnography." *Ethnography* 4(2): 201–16.

Hasebrink, Uwe, Sonia Livingstone, Leslie Haddon and Kjartan Ólafsson. 2008. *Comparing children's online opportunities and risks across Europe: Cross-national comparisons for EU Kids Online*. 2nd edition. http://eprints.lse.ac.uk/24368, accessed September 18, 2015.

Horst, Heather and Daniel Miller, eds. 2012. *Digital Anthropology*. London: Berg.

Hosein, Gabrielle. 2010. "'Insider' Experiences and Ethnographic Knowledge: Reflections from Trinidad and Tobago." In *Fieldwork Identities in the Caribbean*, edited by Erin B. Taylor, 27–54. Coconut Creek: Caribbean Studies Press.

Jacka, Tamara. 2005. *Rural Women in Urban China: Gender, Migration, and Social Change*. Armonk, NY; London: M.E. Sharpe.

Khan, Aisha. 2004. *Callaloo Nation: Metaphors of Race and Religious Identity among South Asians in Trinidad*. Durham, NC and London: Duke University Press.

Lewis, Oscar. 1968. *La Vida: A Puerto Rican Family in the Culture of Poverty—San Juan and New York*. New York: Vintage Books.

Lynch, Kenneth. 2005. *Rural-Urban Interaction in the Developing World*. London: Routledge.

Madianou, Mirca. 2015. "Polymedia and ethnography: Understanding the social in social media." *Social Media + Society*, April–June: 1–3. doi: 10.1177/2056305115578675

Marcus, George E. 1995. "Ethnography in/of the world system: The emergence of multi-sited ethnography." *Annual Review of Anthropology*: 95–117.

McDonald, Tom. 2016a. "Desiring mobiles, desiring education: Mobile phones and families in a rural Chinese town." In *Mobile Communication and the Family: Asian Experiences in Technology Domestication*, edited by S.S. Lim, 13–32. Springer: Dordrecht.

——. 2016b. *Social Media in North China: Social Networks and Moral Frameworks*. London: UCL Press.

Micheli, Marina. 2013. "Facebook, adolescenti e differenze di classe." In *Mediascapes Journal* 2: 91–105.

Miller, Daniel. 1994. *Modernity: An Ethnographic Approach*. Oxford: Berg.

——. 2011. *Tales from Facebook*. Cambridge: Polity.

Miller, Daniel, Elisabetta Costa, Nell Haynes, Tom McDonald, Razvan Nicolescu, Jolynna Sinanan, et al. 2016. *How the World Changed Social Media*. London: UCL Press.

Mohammed, Patricia. 2002. *Gender Negotiations among Indians in Trinidad 1917–1947*. London: Palgrave Macmillan.

Munasinghe, Viranjini. 2001. *East Indians and the Cultural Politics of Identity in Trinidad*. Ithaca, NY: Cornell University Press.

Nicolescu, Razvan. 2016. *Social Media in Southeast Italy: Crafting Ideals*. London: UCL Press.

Olwig, Karen Fog. 2007. *Caribbean Journeys: An Ethnography of Migration and Home in Three Family Networks*. Durham, NC and London: Duke University Press.

Oreglia, E. 2015. "The 'Sent-Down' Internet: Using information and communication technologies in rural China." *Chinese Journal of Communication* 8(1): 1–6.

Pink, Sarah, Heather Horst, John Postill, Larissa Hjorth, Tania Lewis and Jo Tacchi. 2016. *Digital Ethnography: Principles and Practice*. London: Sage.

Pipyros, Stavroula. 2014. "Cutting *bella figura*: Irony, crisis, and secondhand clothes in south Italy." *American Ethnologist* 41(3): 532–46.

Postill, John. 2011. *Localizing the Internet: An Anthropological Account*. New York: Berghahn Books.

Qiu, Jack L. 2009. *Working-Class Network Society: Communication Technology and the Information Have-Less in Urban China*. Cambridge, MA: The MIT Press.

Rantanen, Terhi. 2005. *The Media and Globalization*. New York: Sage.

Redfield, Robert. 1947. "The Folk Society." *American Journal of Sociology* 52: 293–308.

Sassatelli, Roberta. 2010. *Fitness Culture: Gyms and the Commercialisation of Discipline and Fun*. Basingstoke: Palgrave Macmillan.

Silverman, Sydel. 1975. *Three Bells of Civilization: The Life of an Italian Hill Town*. New York: Columbia University Press.

Sinanan, Jolynna. 2016. *Social Media in Trinidad*. London: UCL Press.

Singh, Kelvin. 1994. *Race and Class Struggles in a Colonial State: Trinidad 1917–1945*. St Augustines: University of the West Indies Press.

Vereni, Piero. 2008. *Identità catodiche. Rappresentazioni mediatiche di appartenenze collettive*. Roma: Meltemi Editore.

Wallis, Cara. 2013. *Technomobility in China: Young Migrant Women and Mobile Phones*. New York: New York University Press.

Wang, Xinyuan. 2016. *Social Media in Industrial China*. London: UCL Press.

Zhang, Li. 2001. *Strangers in the City: Reconfigurations of Space, Power, and Social Networks within China's Floating Population*. Stanford, CA: Stanford University Press.

9

"DOING FAMILY" AT A DISTANCE

Transnational Family Practices in Polymedia Environments

Mirca Madianou

This chapter explores a specific type of relationship—that between parents and children who live apart from each other. The proliferation of communication platforms has contributed to the transformation of the experience of parenting and intimacy at a distance. Communication technologies allow transnational families to come together through sets of mediated practices. This chapter will report on long-term ethnography with UK-based Filipino migrants and their children who remain in the Philippines. Participant observation including online environments (Hine 2015; Pink et al. 2016) has been critical for understanding the intimacy and complex emotions involved in family relationships, especially in the context of separation. Multi-sited ethnography (Marcus 1995) has also been vital for understanding the transnational nature of family dynamics. The chapter will relate some of the key findings of this research (which are reported extensively elsewhere: Madianou 2012, 2014, 2016; Madianou and Miller 2012) to the particular approach followed. The ethnography on which this chapter is based has also provided the foundation for developing a new theory of polymedia and the chapter will conclude by reflecting on the role of ethnography for theory building.

Transnational Families, Polymedia and Ethnography

It is important to explain the particular type of relationship that this chapter investigates. Transnational families are not new (Thomas and Znaniecki 1984), but the increase in, and feminization of, global migration have made family separation quite common (Parreñas 2001). The Philippines has pioneered the phenomenon with over nine million overseas workers and nine million children growing up without one or both their parents (Parreñas 2008, 68). Transnational mothering—and the children they leave behind—are usually referred to as the social cost of migration that developing countries have to pay in exchange for the remittances that keep their economies afloat (Hochschild 2000). While most research on transnational mothering has foregrounded the political economy of global care and the power asymmetries of care provision in conditions of globalization, the experience of those most affected has received less attention. Putting the experience of transnational families at the heart of the analysis, as this chapter does, matters for a number of reasons. Ethnography is suitable for understanding migrant subjectivities within conditions of power. Ethnography can also reveal the complex and ambivalent emotions relating to separation, reunion, and family life more generally.

Recent work in family sociology has shifted our understanding of the family from a static entity to a "set of practices" which is performed by family members (Morgan 1996). Family members "do" family through their daily activities that extend beyond the confines of the family home (Morgan 1996; Wajcman et al. 2008). Transnational families crystallize this trend. In the absence of physical co-presence transnational family members can only "do family" through daily practices that are typically mediated by communication technologies. Making a phone call, sending a text message, or uploading a photograph on a social network site can bring transnational families into being. The research on which the chapter is based has investigated how families are constituted through their communication practices over a range of devices, platforms, and applications.

In order to understand the uses and consequences of communication technologies I draw on a sociotechnical approach that places equal weight on both the social relationships and the design features of social and mobile media. The discussion that follows pays special attention to affordances—essentially understood as the opportunities for action enabled by digital media platforms and applications (boyd 2014; Hutchby 2001). For example, a platform with asynchronous temporal structure (e.g. email) can afford its users more control over their self-presentation (Baym 2015). Synchronous platforms such as video calling afford users less control, but potentially increased emotional immediacy. Of course, the actual emotional consequences of digital media depend on their uses by people, which is why a sociotechnical perspective looks at the intersection of a range of factors that include design features, socio-economic infrastructure, cultural norms, and relationship expectations. In the final part of the chapter I will reflect on how ethnography has contributed to the study of affordances by developing a new theory of polymedia (Madianou and Miller 2013).

The Empirical and Research Contexts

The Philippines is one of the most intensive migrant countries, with over 10 percent of its population working abroad sending over 24 billion USD in remittances during 2012 (Pew Research Center 2013). The dependency of the Philippine economy on remittances explains why migration is an official economic policy and why the state actively promotes and regulates migration (Asis 2008). The demand for care and domestic work in the so-called "global north" has contributed to the feminization of migration, the fact that women are as likely to migrate as men (Parreñas 2001). Given that many of these female migrants are mothers, the Philippines has come to exemplify the phenomenon of "transnational mothering" (Hondagneu-Sotelo and Avila 1997; Hochschild 2000; Parreñas 2005).

Conservative estimates report a UK Filipino population of 200,000. The UK is a popular destination for Filipino nurses and caregivers (POEA 2010)—most of whom arrived between 1999 and the mid-2000s during a systematic recruitment by the UK's National Health Service. There is an additional population of domestic workers, nannies, and caregivers some of whom are undocumented and for whom travelling to the Philippines is almost impossible (at least until they acquire legal status). For undocumented migrants the dependence on mediated forms of communication is higher given the lack of face-to-face contact. The high presence of

Filipino migrants in the UK's care and domestic sector confirms earlier statistics that indicated a high female population (POEA 2005).

The research that informs this chapter consists of participant observation, interviews, and online ethnography which took place between 2007 and 2010 and has continued intermittently to the time of writing (2016). The first period of research (2007–2008) was UK-based and consisted of 53 interviews with Filipino migrants, mainly women with children left behind. During this time we spent time with our participants on their days off. We also frequented Filipino associations and centers in London and Cambridge. This first research phase was followed by fieldwork in the Philippines during 2008/9 consisting of 53 in-depth interviews and participant observation with the (young adult) children of some of these mothers as well as other left-behind children. We also met several other participants (family members, carers, and younger left-behind children) as part of the ethnographic encounter, while I also interviewed representatives from government agencies and regulatory bodies dealing with migration as well as officials from migration agencies, advocacy groups, and telecommunications companies. I also attended the mandatory "Pre-Departure Orientation Seminars" organized by the Philippine Overseas Employment Agency (POEA) for migrants prior to their deployment to the UK.

On returning from the Philippines, several of our key participants were re-interviewed. Online ethnography, especially through Facebook, has taken place throughout all research phases and continues until today as I maintain contact with a dozen of the initial participants (online and face-to-face) as well as their families in the Philippines. This chapter is informed by my long-term immersion in the lives of these transnational families, some of whom I have known for over nine years. The next two sections summarize the perspective of the migrant mothers and the children who remain in the Philippines, respectively.

The Migrant Mothers

What emerged clearly from the fieldwork with migrant mothers is an enthusiasm for new communication technologies as opportunities to perform "intensive mothering at a distance" (Madianou 2012). Mothers with young children found webcam invaluable as it enabled communication that is synchronous and visually rich. Mothers appreciated the fact that they were able to see their children in a period of rapid development. Equally important was the feeling of being recognized as mothers. This observation becomes evident if we compare the simultaneous and visual communication through platforms such as Skype to the earlier period of letter writing when mothers returned to the Philippines after several years overseas to find that their children no longer recognized them. Sandra, a domestic worker in her 40s and mother of two still recalls that moment as a painful rejection.

As the children grow older, practices of intensive mothering involve a range of platforms and applications. Several mothers used Instant Messaging (IM) platforms in order to help with homework, while email worked well for sending detailed instructions or explaining bills. Mothers spend a significant proportion of their time on social media and much of it is dedicated to parenting or even micromanaging their household. I'm still surprised with the level of detail that mothers know about their families' daily activities: participants can often recount the weekly menu, their children's latest school assignment, and the neighborhood gossip. It is common for migrant mothers to put together shopping lists, send detailed instructions for repairs or recipes and generally micromanage the household remotely.

Increasingly, much knowledge about family or neighborhood news is the result of the peripheral awareness afforded by social media rather than direct interpersonal communication.

The popularization of smartphones and tablets as well as wireless services have made possible an "always on" culture of ubiquitous connectivity where being online increasingly becomes taken-for-granted. Functionalities of social network sites such as the "news feed" combined with the portability of internet-enabled devices means that users can be peripherally aware of the actions and daily rhythms of their distant relatives and friends, contributing to a new form of mediated co-presence which I have theorized as "ambient co-presence" (Madianou 2016; see also Hjorth and Richardson (2014) who have developed the concept of "ambient play" to understand parallel developments in gaming). Online ethnography, which includes hanging out and interacting with key participants in social media, is key for understanding the practices that sustain ambient co-presence. Yet despite the different kinds of mediated co-presence that are supported by digital communication media it is important to recognize their limitations. Many mothers of young children told me that frequent communication was a reminder of the geographical distance and the fact that it's still not possible to hug or smell your children on Skype.

Apart from their role in intimacy and care, mobile and social media are tools for social surveillance and monitoring. The increased social cues afforded by a combination of platforms provide migrant women with evidence of life back home. Monitoring is a form of control that explains some social media practices, such as scouring children's Facebook profiles or waiting for their Skype status symbol to become green (a sign that a son or daughter has returned home at the agreed time). Participants were in favor of the opportunity to know what happens in their households, which they contrasted to the past situation when migrants often returned home to a markedly different situation from the one that had been described in letters. Micromanaging a household at a distance can be fraught and participants often describe how the increased cues on social media have triggered family conflicts.

Some participants reported that frequent communication often amplified conflict—if not with their children, then with other family members. While in the past problems were hardly ever reported in letters, in situations of frequent communication it is harder to keep family secrets. But there are further burdens associated with this "always on" culture of connectivity. The expectation of availability and the associated expectation of financial help often put a strain on migrant women who cannot refuse requests from wider family contacts. These requests for help were so frequent that they represented a significant proportion of some of our participants' monthly outgoings. Even with close family members we often observe an ambivalence resulting from the double burden of caregiving (performed via digital media) and breadwinning (the daily job that produces remittances) (see Parreñas 2005; Rakow and Navarro 1992). Ethnography—including online—was ideal for capturing the nuances of this maternal ambivalence as it is performed through and in digital media (Madianou 2012).

The "Left-Behind" Families

If mothers were enthusiastic about new communication technologies, their left-behind children were more ambivalent about effects of long-distance communication in the context of their relationships. For about half of our participants, social and mobile media offered meaningful ways for communicating with their migrant parents and even improving their relationships. For the remaining half, social and mobile media did not actually represent an improvement in their relationship with their parents.

Four parameters were found to play a role in determining the success of transnational communication. First, most of those for whom new media did not work were very young (typically under 10 years old) at the time of their mothers' migration. That time was typically before the popularization of mobile phones and the arrival of web 2.0 so for years these families relied on infrequent and expensive communication. It seems that during this time a gap was formed that was hard to fill even with the advent of new media. So the second parameter is the availability of communication technologies. The remaining factors are the quality of the pre-existing relationship and the quality of transnational care arrangements.

A clear pattern emerged among the now adult left-behind children whose mothers migrated when they were young and who for years relied on expensive and infrequent communication such as the weekly call or the monthly letter. Most of these participants were teenagers when social and mobile media became popular. These platforms introduced changes in the relationship with their parent as they catalyzed a power shift from a situation of limited and pre-planned communication (such as the 10-minute-long Sunday afternoon phone call), to the unpredictability of frequent mobile phone calls, SMS, or social media requests which were often experienced as intrusive and as a form of monitoring. Such was the experience of Ricardo, whose parents migrated when he was three years old and who for years communicated with him via monthly letters and infrequent calls. These highly regulated communication practices changed with the arrival of mobile phones, which his parents embraced enthusiastically. Ricardo experienced his mother's frequent and unplanned calls as a form of unwanted surveillance and disciplining.

For many families technological changes mapped onto already asymmetrical—and often strained—relationships thus catalyzing a need for the renegotiation of power within each relationship. Through online ethnography we were able to observe the mediated practices through which participants tried to take control over the relationship and claim some space for privacy or autonomy. I will return to this point at the end of the chapter, as these practices constitute a key feature of the theory of polymedia.

By contrast, those for whom digital media provided some kind of solution to their relationships were typically older at the time of their mothers' migration (usually in their teenage years). The mother's migration usually followed the arrival of social and mobile media so communication among these pairs of mothers and children was more frequent and affordable. What seems to have happened among many teenagers or young adults in this group is that they developed an "ideal distance" with their parents especially when the pair already enjoyed a strong pre-existing relationship.

Digital media allowed many of these participants to focus on each other freed from some of the burdens of everyday life. Teenagers or young adults were able to derive emotional security at a time of rapid changes and challenges, made possible through frequent mediated communication. Cecilia's story exemplifies the experiences of participants within this group. Cecilia, who describes her mum as her "best friend," became closer to her mother following the latter's migration. Cecilia hardly saw her mum when they both lived under the same roof because of her mother's long shifts and commuting. Following her mother's migration, the two women made an effort to carve out time in their busy schedules to talk to each other and even do fun things together, such as go shopping for clothes while visiting the same websites. Cecilia was able to support her mother during a serious health issue, while her mother offers relationship advice and support to Cecilia.

Polymedia and Ethnography

The comparison of the perspectives of migrant mothers and their left-behind children suggests that new media cannot solve the problems of family separation. While for some families new media constitute solutions, for others they reveal problems that had hitherto been concealed.

New media can even heighten conflicts. Yet, one of the most important consequences of communication technologies is that they become constitutive of how relationships are enacted and experienced (Madianou and Miller 2013). In other words, even though technologies do not solve problems, which are fundamentally social, they do become a constitutive component of these relationships. In the absence of face-to-face contact our participants exploit the affordances of communication technologies in order to manage their relationships. In the era before mobile phones and web 2.0, when users typically relied on a single medium in order to keep in touch (e.g. letters), the particular properties of that medium shaped interactions in specific ways. For instance, the fact that letters took up to four weeks to arrive meant that any "news" reported by letter was always a few weeks old. Although letters are fondly remembered, their asynchronous temporal structure caused frustration among letter-writers (Madianou and Miller 2011).

However in the present situation when users typically have access to myriad applications, platforms and devices, we observed that they begin to exploit the qualities or affordances of each platform in order to compensate for the limitations of other platforms. Choosing one medium or platform over another acquires emotional intent: the ways in which participants navigate the media environments they have access to become as meaningful for their relationships as the actual content that is exchanged through these platforms.

Ricardo's earlier example illustrates this point. The way he decided to deal with his parents' monitoring phone calls was to respond via email, which gave him more control over how he presented himself. Ricardo could take his time to reflect on how to best answer his parents' questions. The asynchronous temporality of email afforded Ricardo more control, which helped him renegotiate the power balance with his parents. A similar renegotiation of power is evident in Aira's communication with her mother. Unlike Ricardo, who for years relied on old media to keep in touch with his parents, Aira has always used Skype with her mother who works in the UK. But as she became a teenager she found that webcam could be too intrusive, especially when the visual cues prompt her mother to ask "annoying" questions such as "why the living room is untidy." So Aira has renegotiated a new balance with her mother to reflect this new phase in her young adult life. Because of her mother's prolonged absence and infrequent visits this renegotiation is conducted through digital media platforms. Aira prefers messaging services, such as Facebook's Messenger or WhatsApp to keep in touch with her mother—a change that is not lost on the mum who prefers the immediacy of video calling.

The theory of polymedia was developed to explain the ways in which users navigate an environment of digital media in order to manage their relationships (Madianou and Miller 2012, 2013). Polymedia shifts our attention from social media as discrete platforms, to understanding social media as part of a composite structure of converging communicative opportunities. In this context, social media are defined relationally within this integrated structure from a user's viewpoint. For Aira, webcam is not simply a means to keep in touch: it is also not an IM or a post on a social network site, which in turn is not a phone call. Understanding the micro-workings of mediated communication casts light not only on our understanding of technological change, but also on the question of power in personal relationships and the ways in which social relationships and digital technologies are mutually constituted.

Ethnography is crucial for capturing the nuances of media uses and their relational implications. In particular, it was the combination of participant observation with online ethnography that revealed the micro-workings of mediated communication or else, the practices theorized as polymedia. It is important to recognize here that ethnography was not exclusively digital nor was it exclusively about the digital. A polymedia approach entails an understanding of communication environments that encompass older technologies and media, such as the earlier mentioned phone calls, letters and the ways these are remediated through new technologies (Bolter and Grusin 2000).

The story of Janice and her daughter Lisa illustrates how ethnography was integral to understanding polymedia. Janice has lived in London for over 10 years, working in various domestic and caregiving jobs following a stint as a domestic worker in Hong Kong. Janice left the family home in a province near Manila without telling anyone about her plan to migrate. For her this was an escape from an abusive relationship with her ex-husband and Lisa's father. Janice told her children that she was off shopping but she never came back. Lisa was five years old at the time and for a long time was unable to forgive her mother for not keeping her promise to return that day.

"I hated her for not keeping her promises. . . . I waited for such a long time and she never came back." For years Lisa refused to speak to her mother on the phone. This changed when Lisa was in her late teens and discovered the circumstances behind her mother's migration. It was only then that Lisa understood why her mother had to leave, but she was not able to communicate this to her mother. When I first met Lisa at the age of 21 her anger towards her mother was still palpable, although by that point they were at least on speaking terms, exchanging emails and messages. Through my friendship with the two women I have been able to observe the gradual melting of the ice through a number of mediated practices.

Shortly after I first met Lisa she started scanning old family photographs and letters into collages. Lisa had found a way to retell the family history that was cathartic. I first saw these collages in her mother's bedsit in London where they were proudly displayed and explained to me in great detail. Every time an email delivered her daughter's digital artwork, Janice felt the ice melting bit by bit. When Lisa's messages became more frequent Janice was delighted. Was her daughter saying, "I understand"? The other shift took place when both mother and daughter bought smartphones and immersed themselves in an "always on" culture of connectivity. Of course, both Lisa and Janice interact with several friends and relatives, but they also use social network sites to keep in touch with each other.

Their Facebook interactions over the years reveal an increasingly warm, witty, and playful relationship. Janice has discovered a friend in Lisa, and Lisa knows her mum is her greatest supporter. When Janice posts pictures of her dressing-up parties in London, Lisa makes playful comments about her mother's looks. Lisa gives relationship advice to her mother, while Janice reposts and promotes Lisa's posts about her new business. Janice walked Lisa down the aisle at her wedding and when Lisa's difficult pregnancy meant she had to stay in bed for months, she spent hours talking with her on Skype every day for moral support and to relieve her boredom. Janice works as a cook and keeps her tablet or smartphone on the kitchen counter all day long. Some days mother and daughter will exchange dozens of messages while Janice is at work.

I have known Janice and Lisa for over nine years and their relationship has transformed during this time. Although digital media did not cause this transformation they have been constitutive in this process. From the reluctant phone calls and the scanned photos and collages sent as email attachments, to the daily Skype calls and playful banter over a series of messages, we can see how communication practices have both revealed the relationship dynamics, but also helped to shift them. The scanned photos were not just digital photos but also signs of rapprochement, while the playful banter and generous Skype calls mark the consolidation of new-found mother–daughter solidarity. I would not have become aware of these transformations without a long-term immersion in the life of this particular family.

The long-term nature of the research is not only relevant in terms of capturing change. It also matters in terms of developing a rapport with participants. I recall that Janice recounted the full story of her migration after we had met several times and after I had visited her family in the Philippines. Similarly, I would not have understood the relationship dynamics if I did not know and keep in touch with both mother and daughter. Multi-sited ethnography and long-term immersion has been key in this research. Also key has been the combination of participant observation, interviewing, and online ethnography. Interviews were invaluable for capturing the life history of migrants and their children as well as their account of their relationships, including the role of technology. Participant observation contributed an understanding of the context of migration, the family dynamics in place, and the actual uses of technologies, both old (such as letters and photographs) and digital media. It has been important that the research was conducted online and face-to-face as the two approaches complement each other, just as people move seamlessly between online to offline environments.

Online ethnography was invaluable for capturing the micro-workings of mediated interactions. Through online ethnography we can be part of the playful banter, we can try to make sense of the frequency of "likes," the announcement of location through locative media (Licoppe 2013), or the reaction to an embarrassing post. Understanding how users navigate the environment of polymedia requires attention to detail: the switching between platforms, the use of emojis, or even silence. Online ethnography, like all ethnographies, is participatory in the sense that the researcher draws on her immersion in and experience of the social media world to understand and write about it. Polymedia is an example of how long-term and multi-sited ethnography in different settings, whether mediated or face-to-face, can generate theory.

Apart from being a theory that explains the micro-workings of mediated communication, polymedia is also attentive to wider questions of social change. The wide lens perspective of ethnography is essential for tracing the consequences of mediated communication not just at a micro but also at a macro level. Apart from the constitutive role of social and mobile media in the experience of family relationships, ethnography revealed a further consequence for transnational families, namely the ways in which the availability of communication technologies function as a justification for decisions around migration. Participant observation and interviews with migrant women revealed a plethora of personal reasons behind their motivations for migration and settlement in the UK, not least the degree of recognition and respect that came with the sending of remittances.

Despite the difficult and exploitative conditions of domestic or care work, for many migrant women migration is experienced as a new sense of autonomous personhood which is hard to give up, even when the economic reasons that propelled them to migrate have been met. Yet, this is not readily acknowledged as a motivation for prolonging one's stay. Instead, a more common justification for decisions to prolong migration is the ability to practice intensive mothering at a distance. This discourse echoes a popular view within the Philippines (found in advertising but also government policies) regarding the optimism about new communication technologies for transnational mothering (Madianou 2014).

The ethnography revealed that social and mobile media do not solve the problems of family separation. Yet the discourse about the power of technologies to do so remains powerful and prominent. Practicing intensive mothering at a distance through new media provides women with a socially acceptable justification for decisions around migration that are deeper and more personal. Popular assumptions about new communication technologies become implicated with decisions about return, thus creating new migration patterns. But perhaps ethnography's most important contribution is not its account of social change or how it links the micro processes of family interactions with wider accounts of social transformation. Ethnography gives voice to the migrants themselves—and their children—and shows how they navigate the contradictory positions and stereotypes about "heroes of the economy" and "exploited workers"; "bad mothers" and "light of the home"; "breadwinners" and "caregivers."

Acknowledgments

Fieldwork in the early stages of the research was conducted jointly with Daniel Miller. I would like to acknowledge the support of the ESRC in funding the study "Migration, ICTs and the Transformation of Transnational Family Life" (RES-000-22-2266).

References

Asis, Maruja M. B. 2008. "The Philippines," *Asian and Pacific Migration Journal*, 17(3–4): 349–78.

Baym, Nancy. 2015. *Personal Connections in the Digital Age*, second edition. Cambridge: Polity.

Bolter, Jay David and Richard Grusin. 2000. *Remediation*. Cambridge, MA: MIT Press.

boyd, danah. 2014. *It's Complicated: The Social Life of Networked Teens*. New Haven, CT: Yale University Press.

Hine, Christine. 2015. *Ethnography for the Internet: Embedded, Embodied and Everyday*. London: Bloomsbury.

Hjorth, Larissa and Ingrid Richardson. 2014. *Gaming in Social, Locative and Mobile Media*. London and New York: Palgrave.

Hochschild, Arlie. 2000. "Global care chains and emotional surplus value." In *On The Edge: Living with Global Capitalism*, edited by Will Hutton and Anthony Giddens, 130–46. London: Jonathan Cape.

Hondagneu-Sotelo, Pierrette and Ernestine Avila. 1997. "'I'm here, but I'm there': The meanings of Latina transnational motherhood," *Gender and Society*, 11(5): 538–71.

Hutchby, I. 2001. "Technologies, texts and affordances," *Sociology*, 35(2): 441–56.

Licoppe, Christian. 2013. "Merging mobile communication studies and urban research: Mobile locative media, 'onscreen encounters' and the reshaping of the interaction order in public spaces," *Mobile Media and Communication*, 1(1): 122–8.

Madianou, Mirca. 2012. "Migration and the accentuated ambivalence of motherhood: The role of ICTs in Filipino transnational families," *Global Networks*, 12(3): 277–95.

——. 2014. "Smartphones as polymedia," *Journal of Computer-Mediated Communication*, 19(3): 667–80.

——. 2016. "Ambient co-presence: Transnational family practices in polymedia environments," *Global Networks*, 16(2): 183–201.

Madianou, Mirca and Daniel Miller. 2011. "Crafting love: Letters and cassettes in transnational Filipino family communication," *South East Asian Research*, 19(2): 249–72.

——. 2012. *Migration and New Media: Transnational Families and Polymedia*. London: Routledge.

——. 2013. "Polymedia: Towards a new theory of digital media in interpersonal communication," *International Journal of Cultural Studies*, 16(2): 169–87.

Marcus, George E. 1995. "Ethnography in/of the world system: The emergence of multi-sited ethnography," *Annual Review of Anthropology*, 24: 95–117.

Morgan, David H. J. 1996. *Family Connections*. Cambridge: Polity.

Parreñas, Rhacel. 2001. *Servants of Globalization, Women, Migration and Domestic Work*. Stanford, CA: Stanford University Press.

——. 2005. "Long distance intimacy: Class, gender and intergenerational relations between mothers and children in Filipino transnational families," *Global Networks*, 5(4): 317–36.

——. 2008. *The Force of Domesticity*. New York: New York University Press.

Pew Research Center. 2013. *Changing Patterns of Global Migration and Remittances*. Washington, DC: Pew Research Center.

Pink, Sarah, Heather Horst, John Postill, Larissa Hjorth, Tania Lewis and Jo Tacchi. 2016. *Digital Ethnography: Principles and Practice*. London: Sage.

POEA. 2005. 2005 Overseas Employment Statistics. www.poea.gov.ph/ofwstat/ofwstat.html (accessed 28 July 2016).

——. 2010. 2010 Overseas Employment Statistics. www.poea.gov.ph/ofwstat/ofwstat.html (accessed 28 July 2016).

Rakow, Lana and Vija Navarro. 1992. "Remote mothering and the parallel shift: Women meet the cellular phone," *Critical Studies in Media Communication*, 10(2): 144–57.

Thomas, William I. and Florian Znaniecki. 1984. *The Polish Peasant in Europe and America: A Classic Work in Immigration History*, edited and abridged by E. Zaretsky. Urbana, IL: University of Illinois Press.

Wajcman, Judy, Michael Bittman and Jude Brown. 2008. "Families without borders: Mobile phones, connectedness and work-home divisions," *Sociology*, 42: 635–52.

10

RESEARCHING DEATH ONLINE

Luke van Ryn, Tamara Kohn, Bjorn Nansen,
Michael Arnold, and Martin Gibbs

Death now knocks in a digital age. When the time is nigh, whether from natural causes at a ripe age, or from accidents or illness when young, the word goes out through a range of technologies and then various communities gather offline and online. Digital ethnography in this "death" sphere has been growing in form and possibility over the past two decades as various platforms are designed and become occupied with the desires of the living and dying. Online funerals and commemorative activities are now often arranged alongside the perhaps more somber rites of burial or cremation (Boellstorff 2008, 128). Services such as LivesOn promise that we shall be able to "tweet" beyond the grave; members of online communities encounter each other on commemorative online sites where they grieve for a shared friend but never meet each other "in person"; and it is predicted that soon there will be more Facebook profiles of the dead than of the living.

This phenomenon creates myriad new converging ideas, behaviors, and capacities that raise many evocative questions in and around digital ethnography: What does it mean to die when we continue to be present and enlivened through such media? What responsibilities and rights do those left behind have to their loved ones' posts, tweets, profiles, and avatars? How can we trace the relationships that gather around the sphere of death when family ties, media platforms, and online communications are so thoroughly entangled?

Just as the Internet is thoroughly implicated in changing customs and rituals of socializing in the developed and developing world, it is now clearly entwined with changing customs and rituals of death, memory, and commemoration. Following the emergence of online memorials or so-called "virtual cemeteries" in the 1990s, practices of online memorialization have diversified in form, spread across multiple platforms, and become popularized, particularly through the re-purposing of social media profiles. Alongside these developments, scholars from a range of disciplines have become increasingly interested in the digital mediation of death, dying, and memorialization. Research has examined issues such as digital legacy management, how grief and social support take shape in online networks, and how the dead persist and continue to participate as social actors through the platforms and protocols of social networking sites.

This chapter provides an overview of digital ethnographic approaches to online commemoration, and possible future directions for research in this field. It draws on the case of Zyzz, an amateur body builder and online celebrity whose death in 2011 provoked a great deal of contested memorialization across Facebook, YouTube, and more targeted websites. It shows how memorialization online can be a fragmented, controversial, and complicated practice, and points to challenges that this practice poses for digital ethnographic research.

Within digital ethnography, scholars interested in death have researched topics including the memorialization of celebrities online (Garde-Hansen 2011), the use of mobile media applications such as Instagram to share photos from funerals (Gibbs et al. 2015), and commemorative participation and memorialization in virtual worlds such as *World of Warcraft* (Boellstorff 2008, 128; Gibbs et al. 2012). As increasing numbers of people with social media profiles die, the profiles that they leave behind and the way that their loved ones engage with them challenge researchers to account for changes in practices of commemoration, caring, and communication.

Early research into online commemoration investigated the "digital cemeteries" of the World Wide Web. In the same way as cemeteries are spaces delineated from everyday life, early online memorials were standalone pages that were dedicated to an individual, and unconnected to other pages around the Web. Knowledge of coding, a source of data hosting as well as uncertainty around etiquette were substantial barriers to online memorials in this period, making them uncommon and often unwieldy sites. Research describing and analyzing Web 1.0 digital cemeteries generally focused on these digital environments as entirely separate from, rather than embedded within, the physical world (Roberts and Vidal 2000).

As social media platforms such as MySpace and Facebook ("Web 2.0") have evolved in increasingly interconnected and interoperable ways, so too has digital commemoration and memorialization become threaded across multiple platforms and increasingly connected to ongoing social experiences in the physical world. Death Studies researchers with an interest in the ways digital technologies are effecting and affecting grieving, memorialization, and commemoration have explored the layering of online commemoration within and alongside physical spaces (Hutchings 2012).

Commercial developers and design researchers have also experimented with the digital augmentation of physical artifacts of commemoration (such as gravestones, coffins, and urns). These continue a lineage that has inserted photo frames and television screens in headstones, but they also change the nature of the relationship of mourners to the object of commemoration. QeepR, for example, marks gravestones with a QR code to allow visitors to a physical grave to access an online social network centered on the deceased person. In this way, traditionally isolated and demarcated spaces and objects are enabled to communicate, to connect, and to converge with other forms of technology.

Persistence and Personhood through Social Media

One of the main threads of this research has been concerned with how the dead continue to persist and participate within the platforms and protocols of social media (Brubaker and Hayes 2011; Karppi 2013; Marwick and Ellison 2012; Stokes 2012). Researchers have considered the social implications of the now all-too-familiar automated prompts on Facebook to get back in touch with deceased friends, questions around inheritance of media libraries through iTunes, Kindle, or Steam, and orphaned profiles that are difficult for executors to identify, access, and shut down (Carroll and Romano 2011; Gibbs et al. 2013).

Pragmatic issues of management are also connected to more abstract ideas about identity and personhood: the ways in which our selves are constituted through a variety of technological prostheses, through our relationships with other people, and through our posts to social media platforms. After death, the digital selves that survive us are assembled by many different authors, and distributed across many different servers and services. In particular, the polyvocal possibilities of online memorials have been seen in controversies around trolling and vandalism (Kohn et al. 2012; Phillips 2011), demonstrating the way in which etiquette around online memorials remains fluid. More generally, the persistent and scalable properties of social media memorials raise questions about post-mortem identity curation, authorship, and authenticity (Marwick and Ellison 2012). An additional concern is the durability or desirability of memorials tied to particular social media platforms; hosting memorials on a particular platform may unwittingly "lock out" friends and family who are not members, or who quit the network (Fordyce and van Ryn 2014, 47–50). New technologies also affect experiences of mourning, and the ways in which social support can take shape in online networks (Moss 2004; Veale 2004; Williams and Merten 2009).

Ethnographers who examine these many issues see, on the one hand, how the designs of new memorializing technologies, in and of themselves, readily reveal some of the ways people imagine, and then open up a path to, open-ended futures for themselves (Ingold 2012, 27). On the other hand, they also understand that the digital ethnography of death and commemoration is not isolatable from the non-digital. Digital ethnography is not a bounded method or technique but is a process that is inseparable from the materialities of life (Pink et al. 2015) and, we would add, death. A person may visit and interact with an online memorial site for a loved one over many years, but this does not mean she will not also physically tend to the body of the deceased and its final resting place, and the material belongings and meaningful memorabilia left behind.

Another may express feelings of loss on a Facebook site that might not match the way they express that loss face-to-face. When Tom Boellstorff (2008) describes attending a funeral in SecondLife, he notes its resemblance to an "offline" funeral in the way the service is arranged, in the way attendees dress, and in the way they address each other. Though many of the mourners did not know each other in a more traditional face-to-face way, nevertheless they came together to celebrate their friend. Gatherings like the one Boellstorff describes are only really possible because of digital media, and need to be understood in terms of the way they interweave communities, technologies, and rituals. Where the digital and material either seamlessly converge or rub up against one another is a fascinating and important site for research. Working with people who are planning for their own death or with the grieving families or publics left behind, as well as with people in death and technology industries who are working to meet people's needs and desires, brings many methodological challenges. In the next section we consider some of these.

How to Study the Dead Online

Studying online memorialization raises challenges for researchers (Bollmer 2013; Brubaker and Hayes 2011; Graham et al. 2015). These include (among many others) defining the field of enquiry, accessing informants or social media content, and conceptually grasping the large bodies of data regularly posted in public online. There are a number of entry points into any chosen field: through those who participate in digital commemoration practices via Facebook or purpose-built websites; through industry professionals; and through exploration of the platforms themselves.

For our current research project in this field, we began with a series of informal conversations (for example, during participant observation at large industry events such as International Expos in the US, UK, and Australia for people working in or providing for the funeral industry). These were then followed by semi-structured interviews with those working with new technologies in the funeral industry: funeral directors, funeral home owners, funeral celebrants, cemetery and crematorium workers, technology entrepreneurs and innovators, and activists wishing to subvert "death denial" in groups such as "Death Salon." The interviews, mostly conducted "face-to-face" on Skype, sought to understand the changes in the professional and industrial field, the values that professionals brought to bear in their dealings with technologies and memorialization, and the visions of the future that these entail.

A difficulty in conducting ethnographic enquiry in this space is that many of the actors involved are interested primarily in their own enterprise, and commercial interests can prevent conversation evolving beyond the sales pitch. Research informed by those with a self-interest, in this case in the virtues of a product or service, is perhaps more overt and sharply defined where one's informants are drawn from industry sources, but in a broader sense the phenomenon is generic to all ethnographic work and all research work. All participants in research occupy a position from which they speak—a position in time, in space, and in relation to all others in the field at that time and in that space—and that position is of necessity partial. As Haraway observed (1988), there is no "God-trick," no "God's eye view" which sees a world complete as it is in itself, or sees a world that is not shaped by perspective or interest. All knowledge is situated, and in the sense that our industry informants were clear and plain in their interests in respect of memorial technologies and services, and thus overt in their partiality and perspective, our fieldwork was made easier.

Users of digital commemoration services provide another avenue to understanding what is at stake in online forms of memorialization and post-mortem sociality. A common methodological approach in this area has been data collection and analysis of public statements (such as posts on social media, and comments on websites), which we have similarly undertaken, though we have also begun interviewing people to explore in a different way how individuals reflect upon their experiences with digital commemoration, their motivations in using online memorials, and the ways that they maintain relationships with the deceased and the broader community. Identifying and contacting the bereaved poses ethical questions about the risks of research participation, as well as disciplinary debates about how purposive such contact should be.

A more materially oriented approach to ethnography, what Star (1999) refers to as an ethnography of infrastructure, approaches this space by attending to the intermediary role and affordances of the technological platforms for commemoration, whether these are purpose-built (in the case of HeavenAddress) or adapted from more mainstream uses (Facebook, Instagram). Spending time analyzing the ways people engage with the *#funeral* hashtag on Instagram offered a way of understanding the "platform vernacular"—how users work to make themselves present in discussions around death online (Gibbs et al. 2015). There is an abundance of material constantly being added to online commemorative spaces, which can be accessed and studied fairly unobtrusively. Such a method minimizes the disturbance to the bereaved, but can miss a sense of the way in which the bereaved make judgments about how and why to participate online. New media platforms such as Twitter and Instagram and their application programming interfaces also enable "big data" approaches. Gathering large volumes of posts on a particular topic can aid researchers in isolating themes and assessing the expressed mood of various communities, even if such researchers risk limiting their immersion in the material to a brief dip.

In the rest of the chapter, we illustrate the points made above by presenting an analysis of the social media commemoration of Zyzz, an amateur bodybuilder and minor celebrity whose sudden death was felt (and whose achievements in life were celebrated, questioned, and contested) in different ways across a variety of online platforms, forums, and communities (explored in greater detail in Nansen et al. 2015).

Social Media Commemoration: The Case of Zyzz

Aziz Sergeyevich Shavershian, known as Zyzz, was an amateur bodybuilder who built a degree of celebrity on Facebook, YouTube, and other social media. He had more than 50,000 followers on Facebook, and a branded protein supplement. He died suddenly in 2011, aged 22. Immediately following his death, online communities were filled with comments of grief, support, remembrance, and anger. Zyzz's death was made the subject of an Australian national radio program discussing drug abuse and male body culture. The tone, focus, and sentiment of these comments varied greatly from platform to platform.

Through an iterative qualitative analysis of posts across six sites, we built an understanding of the themes around which discussion gravitated; the ways in which norms and policies were flouted or asserted; and the forms of address particular to each site. The analysis showed that digital memorialization is fragmented across different platforms, contested by speakers with different relationships to the deceased and with different relationships to drugs and bodybuilding, and difficult to unify into a coherent "grand" narrative. Indeed, the case showed that digital memorialization exists as a host of contested, polyvalent conversations.

Comparative Analysis of Different Platforms

We undertook a comparative analysis of commemorative posts across a number of different platforms, from hobbyist or "passion-centric" (Ploderer et al. 2010) websites such as body-building.com and simplyshredding.com to tributes created on Facebook and YouTube. The large volume of posts to these different sites made a comprehensive analysis difficult; instead we engaged in digital observation and qualitative sampling across multiple sites and conversations to explore in detail the contested discourses that constituted and reconstituted the collective memory of Zyzz.

On niche bodybuilding websites—such as bodybuilding.com and simplyshredding.com—fans and friends of Zyzz left messages of admiration, and commitments to pursue their own fitness goals. These messages frequently featured subcultural jargon, and were policed heavily by moderators in order to maintain respect and support for Zyzz and bodybuilding in general. Drug use was generally implicit in or absent from these discussions; references to "bicycles" (cycles of anabolic steroid use) offered an example of such knowing circumlocution. We see here how the theoretical openness of communication on the Internet is limited to certain permissible forms.

The affordances of Facebook for commemoration have changed over time, and vary from country to country. After Zyzz's death, eight different tribute pages were launched. Such pages can be created and posted to by anyone, resulting in a more fragmented memorialization (Karppi 2013). These vary in their popularity, their focus, and their claims to authority (one was titled "official Zyzz RIP Facebook" despite all such pages on Facebook being *unof-ficial* in Facebook's terms). As a result, the conversation was much more contested than on dedicated bodybuilding sites. These pages attracted posts from Facebook users with wildly different relationships to Zyzz, from family and friends to tourists and trolls. While these

Facebook pages lacked the explicit insider focus of the niche websites, we still found revision and consensus-building through appeals to "respectful" behavior.

When we looked at the YouTube video *Zyzz – The Legacy*, that Zyzz's brother Said uploaded, the case was very different. The cacophonous comments repeat several themes found across the Facebook and bodybuilding site tributes. However, rather than cohering around these themes they explode into an unmanageable, irrecuperable storm of differing opinion, tone, hostility, and seriousness. Many of the comments undermine the dominant narrative of Zyzz as an athlete who passed away too soon, through accusations of steroid use, insults based on his congenital heart condition, and criticisms of his masculinity: "thank you zyzz for dieing. now we have one less steroid junkie on this earth and one less person to pass abysmal genes (mental and physical genes) to future offspring. RIP where you belong" (*Zyzz – The Legacy*, YouTube).

The affordances, pleasures and values of YouTube vary greatly from other media platforms, and it is perhaps not surprising to see the most vitriolic comments appear on this site as opposed to Facebook, for example. Yet another forum for remembrance is worth mentioning here, which has its own unique place in the social media ecology: Squidoo. Before its purchase and closure by HubPages in 2014, this site allowed users, termed "lensmasters," to aggregate content from around the Web in a single page, or "lens." Lensmasters earned revenue from embedded advertisements, of which Squidoo took a 50 percent commission. A user created a lens called *Zyzz RIP – The "YOU MIRIN" Memorial Gallery *UPDATED WITH ALL PICTURES EVER**, filled with images of Zyzz to attract traffic, motivate fans, and monetize the memory of Zyzz through selling protein supplements.[1] The explicit commercialization of Zyzz's image post-death was met with some resistance by visitors: "bahahaha . . . after all those photos 'buy whey protein'. If this website was accurate it would say 'buy anabolic steroids'" (Squidoo).

In this moment we see the tension between the contemporary Web's demand for traffic, the desire to pay tribute to friends, and the selling of miracle substances in pursuit of idealized bodies. Across these online platforms we see a contested, fragmented, and polyvocal memorialization happening. Individuals seek to build group cohesion, express their sympathies, or debunk the figure of Zyzz. The legacy is subject to debate without resolving to a coherent picture; instead the conversation differs from platform to platform. The presentation of this legacy also changes over time, as social media algorithms seek to vary and refresh the content served, and as advertisements adapt to visitors' own browsing history.

Media, Death, Memory

For hundreds of years there has been a tension between media technologies and memory; Aristotle famously worried that the new media technology of writing would weaken our skills of remembrance. The birth of photography also witnessed the rise in hauntings, especially in the form of ghostly auras (Linkman 2012). One of the first imagined-use cases for the phonograph was the recording and playback of the voices of the deceased. Likewise, radio technology was often deployed in search of a means of communicating with the dead (Sconce 2000). While digital platforms such as Facebook, Instagram, and YouTube extend the possibilities for memorialization through multimedia compositions, graphing social relationships and cloud storage, they simultaneously challenge that commemoration: through dispersing authorship among myriad users, through ranking contributions according to opaque algorithms, and through their mapping of social connections in a much more explicit way than has historically been possible.

Dead individuals may be remembered in different ways on different platforms, for different ends, by different publics. Digital ethnographer Penelope Papailias (2016) delicately unpacks this complexity in her study of vernacular and online commemorative practices in the wake of a fatal bus crash in Greece. Papailias' analysis shows how "mediated witnessing" in the digital age connects to public mourning, producing a two-fold representation of the deceased. In the case of Zyzz, people witness his biography and character-portrait while, at the same time, contributing to the shaping of normative responses to that biography. In this way, both the witnessing and the testimony of the witnesses are critical to the commemorative practices we observe.

As we have seen in the case of Zyzz, witnessing is attenuated across several platforms and through degrees of separation from Zyzz—some "first order" witnesses expressing a direct phenomenological connection to Zyzz and existential response to his death, and other "second order" witnesses connecting to Zyzz and his posthumous representation through testimony that reflects dialogically and dialectically on first order testimony. And so the mediatization of the materialization of Zyzz and the meaning that might be extracted from his life is informed by the logic of the database that attests to Zyzz. The network of his memory extends to intimates who knew him, to strangers who knew of him, to ethnographers who, through Zyzz's database and the online testimony of attenuated witnesses, know of him and others who know of him.

On Facebook tributes Zyzz is remembered as an elite athlete and inspirational figure who sadly died at a young age. On YouTube his memory is constructed in terms of drug-fueled excess and narcissism. Users of Squidoo sought to aggregate images they had collected and drive traffic through their now-lost pages. These conflicting images of Zyzz are interwoven through users posting and commenting across platforms, through the interoperability of the social Web and Application Programming Interfaces (API), and through the open questions about how we ought best to remember people in a time where so many of our thoughts seem destined to be shared online.

Take-Homes for Digital Ethnography

Digital ethnography as a holistic practice (see Horst and Miller 2012, 15–18) is well placed to attend to a range of issues, in ways that interviews of individuals, surveys of populations, or analyses of datasets are unable to get at separately. Each of these techniques has something to add, but it is in attention to the interplay of various scales of commemoration elicited through different methodological means that we are best able to understand what is emerging in this space.

Indeed, digital ethnography reaches beyond its attention to research techniques (ethnographic methods) and beyond the production of rich descriptive and analytic texts (ethnographies). The field of digital ethnography is made up of multiple ontological layers, which mesh with each other in many ways. Social media does not just sit "on top" of existing means of mourning and remembering the dead—rather, it appropriates, extends, and transforms those practices. It makes little sense to speak of Zyzz's online memorials as being "in addition to" various offline memorials for those who knew him best; the many different sites, pages, and posts were made by people with wildly varying acquaintance with him, fighting over what his legacy ought to be, creating a controversy that continues to generate revenue for advertisers in a gesture analogous to Zyzz's own self-promotion.

The "online commemoration" we research, then, is not simply exploring the ways in which the act of (offline) commemoration is translated into online forums. Rather, it explores how new technologies are radically remaking processes of memorialization. This remaking is ongoing as we go about our lives, releasing a digital trail in our movement across the

Web (Stiegler 2009). This occurs in the immediate aftermath of our death, as those around us negotiate and authorize our biographical narratives and what they mean, now, and into an imagined distant future, where our digital personas sit on a server farm, waiting, hoping, to be refreshed by the next passing visitor.

Conclusion

The emerging practices of online commemoration have a great deal to say about contemporary relationships with death. New technological advances have made it possible to maintain technologically mediated relationships with and through the dead, to mourn and memorialize people in virtual environments, and pass on rich digital legacies. These developments challenge traditional notions of personhood, sociality, and inheritance, transforming rituals around death as they facilitate, extend, and adapt them. Digital ethnography's attention to the overlapping logics of communities, platforms, and algorithms is well suited to understanding what is at stake in these critical moments.

In the case of Zyzz, we find cacophonous voices leaving their note of support, claiming to see through Zyzz's self-presentation, and making money for themselves through association, advertising, and aggregation. These differing voices are filtered through each platform's technological affordances, form of sociality, and presentation of content; what a particular user might see on any given day could differ greatly from what they see on another day, or from what another user sees. The rich field of online memorialization gives us clues about what it means to live and die at this point in time.

Note

1 We note here that this archive has not been accessible since HubPages acquired Squidoo. This highlights that, while online platforms promise the ability to store, share, and scale our memories, they too are susceptible to loss when businesses change hands, data becomes corrupted, or new legislation is adopted.

References

Boellstorff, Tom. 2008. *Coming of Age in Second Life: An Anthropologist Explores the Virtually Human.* Princeton, NJ: Princeton University Press.

Bollmer, Grant. 2013. "Millions Now Living Will Never Die: Cultural Anxieties About the Afterlife of Information." *The Information Society* 29(3): 142–51. Accessed January 18, 2016, http://dx.doi.org/10.1080/01972243.2013.777297

Brubaker, Jed R. and Gillian R. Hayes. 2011. "'We Will Never Forget You [online]': An Empirical Investigation of Post-Mortem MySpace Comments." In *Proceedings of Computer Supported Cooperative Work CSCW 2011,* 123–32.

Carroll, Evan and John Romano. 2011. *Your Digital Afterlife: When Facebook, Flickr and Twitter Are Your Estate, What's Your Legacy?* Berkeley, CA: New Riders.

Fordyce, Robbie and Luke van Ryn. 2014. "Ethical Commodities as Exodus and Refusal." *Ephemera* 14(1): 35–55. Accessed January 18, 2016, www.ephemerajournal.org/contribution/ethical-commodities-exodus-and-refusal

Garde-Hansen, Joanne. 2011. *Media and Memory.* Edinburgh: Edinburgh University Press.

Gibbs, Martin, Joji Mori, Michael Arnold, and Tamara Kohn. 2012. "Tombstones, Uncanny Monuments and Epic Quests: Memorials in World of Warcraft." *Game Studies* 12(1). Accessed January 18, 2016, http://gamestudies.org/1201/articles/gibbs_martin

Gibbs, Martin, Craig Bellamy, Michael Arnold, Bjorn Nansen, and Tamara Kohn. 2013. "Digital Registers and Estate Planning." *Retirement and Estate Planning Bulletin* 16(3): 63–6.

Gibbs, Martin, James Meese, Michael Arnold, Bjorn Nansen, and Marcus Carter. 2015. "#Funeral and Instagram: Death, Social Media, and Platform Vernacular." *Information, Communication & Society* 18(3): 255–68.

Graham, Connor, Mike Arnold, Tamara Kohn, and Martin Gibbs. 2015. "Gravesites and Websites: A Comparison of Memorialisation." *Visual Studies* 30(1): 37–53. Accessed January 18, 2016, http://dx.doi.org/10.1080/1472586X.2015.996395

Haraway, Donna. 1988. "Situated Knowledges: The Science Question in Feminism and the Privilege of Partial Perspectives." *Feminist Studies* 14(3): 575–99.

Horst, Heather, and Daniel Miller (eds). 2012. *Digital Anthropology*. London and New York: Berg.

Hutchings, Tim. 2012. "Wiring Death: Dying, Grieving and Remembering on the Internet." In *Emotion, Identity and Death: Mortality across Disciplines*, edited by Douglas J. Davies and Chang-Won Park, 43–58. Farnham: Ashgate.

Ingold, Tim. 2012. "Introduction: The Perception of the User-Producer." In *Design and Anthropology*, edited by Wendy Gunn and Jared Donovan, 19–33. Farnham: Ashgate.

Karppi, Tero. 2013. "Death Proof: On the Biopolitics and Noopolitics of Memorializing Dead Facebook Users." *Culture Machine* 14. Accessed January 18, 2016, www.culturemachine.net/index.php/cm/article/view/513/528

Kohn, Tamara, Martin Gibbs, Michael Arnold, and Bjorn Nansen. 2012. "Facebook and the Other: Administering to and Caring for the Dead Online." In *Responsibility*, edited by Ghassan Hage, 128–41. Parkville: University of Melbourne Press.

Linkman, Audrey. 2012. *Photography and Death*. London: Reaktion Books.

Marwick, Alice E. and Nicole B. Ellison. 2012. "'There Isn't Wifi in Heaven!' Negotiating Visibility on Facebook Memorial Pages." *Journal of Broadcasting and Electronic Media*, 56(3): 378–400.

Moss, Miriam. 2004. "Grief on the Web." *Omega: Journal of Death & Dying*, 49(1): 77–81.

Nansen, Bjorn, Michael Arnold, Martin Gibbs, and Tamara Kohn. 2015. "Remembering Zyzz: Distributed Memories On Distributed Networks." In *Memory in a Mediated World: Remembrance and Reconstruction*, edited by Christine Lohmeier, Andrea Hajek, and Christian Pentzold, 261–80. Basingstoke: Palgrave Macmillan.

Papailias, Penelope. 2016. "Witnessing in the Age of the Database: Viral Memorials, Affective Publics and the Assemblage of Mourning." *Memory Studies*. Accessed February 15, 2016, http://dx.doi.org/10.1177/1750698015622058

Phillips, Whitney. 2011. "LOLing at Tragedy: Facebook Trolls, Memorial Pages and Resistance to Grief Online." *First Monday* 16(12). Accessed January 18, 2016, http://firstmonday.org/article/view/3168/3115

Pink, Sarah, Heather Horst, John Postill, Larissa Hjorth, Tania Lewis, and Jo Tacchi. 2015. *Digital Ethnography: Principles and Practices*. London: Sage.

Ploderer, Bernd, Steve Howard, and Peter Thomas. 2010. "Collaboration on Social Network Sites: Amateurs, Professionals and Celebrities." *Computer Supported Cooperative Work*, 19(5): 419–55.

Roberts, Pamela and Lourdes A. Vidal. 2000. "Perpetual Care in Cyberspace: A Portrait of Memorials on the Web." *Omega: Journal of Death and Dying*, 40(4): 521–45.

Sconce, Jeffrey. 2000. *Haunted Media: Electronic Presence from Telegraphy to Television*. Durham, NC: Duke University Press.

Star, Susan Leigh. 1999. "The Ethnography of Infrastructure." *American Behavioral Scientist*, 43(3): 377–91.

Stiegler, Bernard. 2009. "Teleologics of the Snail: The Errant Self Wired to a WiMax Network." *Theory, Culture & Society* 26(2–3): 33–45.

Stokes, Patrick. 2012. "Ghosts in the Machine: Do the Dead Live On in Facebook?" *Philosophy & Technology*, 25(3): 363–79.

Veale, Kylie. 2004. "Online Memorialisation: The Web as a Collective Memorial Landscape for Remembering the Dead." *Fibreculture* 3. Accessed January 18, 2016, http://three.fibreculturejournal.org/fcj-014-online-memorialisation-the-web-as-a-collective-memorial-landscape-for-remembering-the-dead/

Williams, Amanda L. and Michael M.J. Merten. 2009. "Adolescents' Online Social Networking Following the Death of a Peer." *Journal of Adolescent Research*, 24(1): 67–90.

11

RELATIONAL LABOR, FANS, AND COLLABORATIONS IN PROFESSIONAL ROCK CLIMBING

Guillaume Dumont

Introduction

> Dawg, this dude keeps texting me on Facebook! Now, he asks where we gonna climb tomorrow and if he could join us . . . what the hell should I say? We aren't even friends . . .

Sitting on the couch of a cozy apartment in Fontainebleau, France, 25-year-old Michael[1] looks a little upset. iPhone in hand, he deals with the dozens of messages he received today via Facebook. This well-known professional climber from the US is on a three-month trip and met "the dude" this morning while warming up before climbing. As with the many climbers he meets, they briefly exchanged a few words. But the intimacy afforded by social media can render brief encounters into "friends." For Michael—with his 75k Facebook and 44k Instagram followers—these disconnected encounters often happen.

Four years ago, Michael started gaining a strong visibility in media through appearances in several major climbing movies and videos. Since then, he has built his reputation as a well-rounded climber respected for his international travels and hard ascents. Indeed, in every area we visited, climbers came along to say "hi." A few asked for autographs while many took pictures with him (later posted on Facebook and Instagram), but it did not seem to bother him too much. As he says, "It's not that I like all this fame but you get used to it because you gotta deal with it anyway."

However, now he feels pressed to give Marc ["the dude"] an answer, especially since Marc knows that he read the message. Indeed, the latter is marked as "seen" on Facebook. "Just tell him we gonna have a 'rest day' tomorrow" says Luc, the photographer providing Michael with media coverage during the trip. "And what would I say if we meet in the forest?" replies Michael. We laugh in concert and Luc adds: "Cmon, the forest is so vast, he won't even know that we are climbing!" Michael answers: "Hell yes, but what happens if I post something on Facebook then . . ." Indeed, he posts on his athlete Facebook page every day. "Will do it later," he concludes.

For Michael the situation becomes somehow critical. On the one hand, he does not want to meet with Marc and share information about his upcoming plans, but he doesn't want to lie either. On the other hand, he feels the pressure to reciprocate the fan's message posted on social media. While being pleased by his fan's attention, extending those relationships to other grounds remains troubling. Nonetheless, as a professional climber sponsored by climbing companies (to enhance their brand's image and to promote their products), he swings between what he calls "acting professionally" (e.g. in this case writing back and meeting) or following his own desire (e.g. avoiding any kind of conversation).

This chapter explores the labor dimension involved in the creation and management of these "ongoing relationships," mostly via social media. It draws on ethnographic fieldwork with professional rock climbers whose job relies on the management of manifold working activities in which climbing has gained, at some point, a more peripheral place (Dumont 2014, 2015b). Indeed, building visibility and reputation are of major importance to catch sponsors' and followers' attention in order to secure sponsorship contracts with climbing companies. They provide climbers with monetary and non-monetary rewards in exchange for labor of various kinds, primarily oriented toward media production, in addition to performing as a climber. Central to the production and diffusion of stories to followers are climbing media and social networking sites. Indeed, these climbers build on their Facebook, Instagram, Twitter, blog, and website (along with other specialized platforms) to sustain and develop interactions and relationships by publishing what Marwick (2015) calls "aspirational content."

In addition, the companies providing sponsoring opportunities envision, create, and diffuse a glamorous image of these climbers for advertising purposes. They are pictured as talented and gifted individuals living an idealized lifestyle revolving around constant global travel to pursue their passion for the sport. This image of professional climbers developing their communication with fans around a "mobile" lifestyle can be evidenced in Figure 11.1, a screenshot from American climber Paul Robinson's Instagram account. Both cases involve different strategies of presentation, self-presentation, and relationship building. Marketing (e.g. Weber 2007) and social media scholars (e.g. Baym 2012) have underlined the significance of developing and sustaining these relationships to foster reputation building and loyalty with fans. Yet, deploying such strategies is not totally pleasurable or satisfying and, as Michael's example stresses, raises interpersonal challenges.

A part of the job is, thus, to communicate and develop ongoing interactions with fans-as-followers, practices that Baym coined "relational labor" (2015). Contributing to the growing conversation on the establishment of online relationships between "practitioners" and "followers," this chapter aims to examine the collaborative dimension of this labor. The concept of relational labor emerges from a growing body of research primarily focusing on the "fan" and the "celebrities" or "microcelebrities" in relationship building. Notwithstanding, it has been shown that producing the "celebrity"—whether it is an artist, a model, a musician, or a climber—entails the collaboration of different actors who frequently remain hidden behind the scenes (e.g. Becker 1982; Mears 2011).

In the following sections, I explore how online relational labor involves a number of key actors whose participation is notably made visible by the operation of referring (@username).

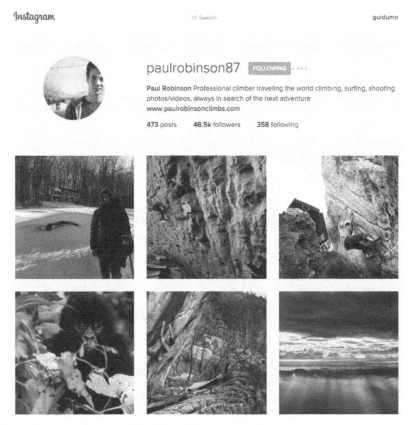

Figure 11.1   American climber Paul Robinson's Instagram main page

I begin with an outline of recent research discussing online relationships between "fans" and "practitioners." I then discuss the context of production of this labor to consider the different relationships at play. This chapter suggests that an investigation of the creation of online relationships needs to acknowledge and to examine the context of labor production to provide a better understanding of its forms, features, and implications.

Building and Managing Relationships with Fans

With visibility and reputation building becoming pivotal indicators of social and sometimes economic success, the digital increasingly plays a key role in the shaping and fostering of one's public image. However, social media also blurs the boundary between the public and private spaces, a practice that impacts upon the divisions between celebrities and their fans. Indeed, research focusing on the interactions between fans and famous people demonstrates that, in traditional settings, the scope of the creation and development of interactions and relationships is limited and controlled, for instance, during autograph signing or ceremonies, competitions, and other events (Marwick and boyd 2011). While arguably still presenting some form of control, especially when intermediaries such as social media agents manage these interactions (e.g. Lizé et al. 2014; Marwick and boyd 2011), digital settings provide easy-to-use tools and a vivid environment to create relationships as well as to support discourse circulation.

More recently, this focus has shifted to the features and meanings of these relationships in the context of celebrities and microcelebrities (e.g. Baym 2012, 2015; Beuscart 2008; Senft 2008; Marwick 2013). This celebrity-based literature highlights the increasing presence of "normal" or ordinary people deploying such strategies (Marwick 2013), practices closely intertwined with the digital context that provide many opportunities to do so (Thumim 2012). The rise of this phenomenon relates to different transformations in labor markets frequently anchored in the increasing popularity of self-branding practices (e.g. Shepherd 2005; Hearn 2008; Marwick 2013) of the so-called "reputation economy" (Gill 2014), "name economy" (Moeran 2003) or "like economy" (Gerlitz and Helmond 2013).

An example of this literature is Baym who explores how musicians interact with fans on Twitter to analyze the "ongoing communication over time to build social relationships that foster paid work" (2015, 17). She draws on Hochschild's (1986) research on "emotional labor," a popular concept among scholars investigating the transformation of work and labor in the contemporary economy (e.g. Gill and Pratt 2008; Entwistle and Wissinger 2006). It describes the induction or suppression of feelings "to sustain the outward countenance that produces the proper state of mind of others, in this case the sense of being cared for in a convivial and safe place" (Hochschild 1986, 7). By referring to emotional labor, Baym aims to acknowledge the labor involved in building relationships with fans as continuous. In this context, "the shift to media that enable continuous interaction, higher expectations of engagement, and greater importance of such connections in shaping economic fortunes calls for new skills and expertise in fostering connections and managing boundaries," writes Baym (2015, 18).

In an earlier paper (2012), Baym notes that these relationships tend to move into the realm of friendships to describe that, before a show, musicians connect and meet with their audience in specific locations of the city. In fact, they try to develop "real social connections" by meeting with their fans. Here, the pleasurable dimension of these interactions seems to overcome the amount of labor involved. While these musicians struggle to build "real social connections" (to use the Baym term), in their research focusing on celebrity and Twitter Marwick and boyd (2011) show that the intimacy built between celebrities and fans remains relative and, often, illusory. Nonetheless, the illusive nature of intimacy strengthens the potential of emotional ties. Marwick and boyd thus argue for a change in the expectations of intimacy via social media leading to an evolution of the landscape of online relationships. To describe the popularization of self-presentation strategies, Marwick refers to the work of Senft (2008) and the concept of microcelebrity (see Marwick 2013). Marwick and boyd coin the latter as a "mindset and set of practices in which audience is viewed as a fan base; popularity is maintained through ongoing fan management; and self-presentation is carefully constructed to be consumed by others" (2011, 140). Instead of creating and sustaining an untouchable position, celebrity practitioners must maintain ongoing affiliations and connections with fans (2011, 157).

More importantly, they have to fill fans' expectations. Contrary to Baym's description of musicians and their fans navigating on the same ground or, at least, that "the positioning of audience is continuously negotiated" (2012, 289), Marwick and boyd emphasize the asymmetrical status that characterized celebrities. In fact, they advocate that celebrity is notably maintained "through mutual recognition of power differentials by fan and practitioner" (2011, 140). Furthermore, exploring the rise of Instagram, Marwick (2015) suggests that microcelebrities are slightly changing due to the visual nature of the content published online and the opportunity to attract mass audiences via the application. Convergences between Baym, Marwick, and boyd can be found in their discussion of social media use by public figures as a dual process whereby "they do not just affect audiences. Audiences affect them" (Baym 2012, 312).

These scholars provide us with a detailed analysis of the practices occurring through these platforms and the self-presentation strategies at stake. Yet, they almost systematically examine the use of social media individually (Twitter, or MySpace, or blogs, or Facebook, and so on), as they do with the interactions between "fans" and "practitioner." Nevertheless, when the creation and development of online relationships are closely (but not exclusively) related to certain forms of economic vitality, these platforms are more likely to be used simultaneously, similarly to the multimedia environment both climbers and followers are using daily.

In addition to the fans and the practitioners, multiple actors are involved in the process. On the one hand, users navigate in a complex ecology of social media, using the sites to publish and re-publish content presenting minor or no variations. On the other hand, whether they address multiple audiences, their "relational labor" relies on various collaborations with other professionals. Marwick and boyd (2010) remind us that while studying self-presentation strategies, Goffman (1959) shows that identity building is a collaborative process during which individuals work together. This process can be extended to the production of relational labor, I suggest. Not only do they work closely with professional media producers, climbing companies or other professional climbers, but also these relationships are incorporated in online publishing via referring strategies.

A Glimpse into Relational Labor

I first met Michael in southern California in January 2013 when conducting ethnographic fieldwork in Western Europe and the USA to explore the work and lives of professional rock climbers. I was interested in understanding what being a professional climber meant and undertook almost two years of participant observation, conducted semi-directed interviews, and compiled and analyzed a large body of written and visual information (Dumont 2014, 2015a, 2015b). Professional climbers, as well as climbing company members and media producers embark on a journey across the globe and develop an intense activity on Facebook, websites, Instagram, Twitter, and other social network sites. Indeed, before our first encounter I was a perfect stranger to Michael. However, due to his visibility, I was aware of his climbing achievements and several facets of his everyday life he distilled in articles and videos, also via his blog as well as his Facebook and Instagram accounts.

While conducting digital ethnography, I quickly acknowledged the constant flow of information delivered by social media and websites on climbers' activities. Getting to spend time with Michael illuminated the labor involved in planning and publishing media content of different kinds. Indeed, sustaining a high publishing level is taking up an important part of his job (including training, traveling, climbing, shooting, editing, managing interactions, business relationships, etc.), as are the building and development of these relationships. Given the inextricable mobile nature of everyday life and work, my fieldwork was therefore highly multi-sited and digital. Mobility and the digital world converge in fostering intimacy among individuals geographically widespread (DeNicola 2012). Nevertheless, it would be wrong to associate the increasingly mobile and digital nature of the field with a denial of the materiality of the digital world (Horst and Miller 2012). Rather, what emerges from the combination of these two dimensions is the materiality of contexts (DeNicola 2012) as well as the highly material nature and practical implications of everyday practices. And this is precisely what is at stake in the labor of building online relationships to sustain and foster economic vitality.

GUILLAUME DUMONT

Social Media, Relationships Building, and Economic Vitality

Research on relationships building focuses on cases where establishing online relationships with followers and building reputation rarely involve an economic dimension (with notable exceptions, see for example Beuscart 2008; Abidin 2014). Conversely, a large number of the professional climbers have their sponsoring contracts evaluated on their aptitudes to produce such labor successfully. For instance, the number of "likes" or visits on their personal page levers economic rewards. In some cases, online posting is included in the terms of the contract as points out Jason, a friend of Michael: "I have a spread sheet with different columns, I need a certain amount of posts on my blog, 8a.nu[2] updates, like videos, photos and their Facebook page."

In addition to climbing magazines, professional climbers publish content on multiple platforms. As a result, climbing companies' expectations toward athletes are high when it comes to generating visibility and reputation as well as gaining fans' attention. Indeed, discussing the issue at an outdoor industry trade show, a team manager from a major European climbing company stated that: "We expect them to be ambitious, and charismatic, and to reach out, be really an ambassador or a speaker." Companies' expectations vary according to the different categories of sponsorships, contracts, and amount of money involved. In the complex process of estimating and fixing the value of climbers, not only do the latter have to perform at the top level; building visibility, reputation, and demonstrating the aptitudes to create a wide and loyal fan base are essential skills to demonstrate (Dumont 2015b). Indeed, companies approach fans and followers as consumers in their own right.

Similarly to Michael, Julie recalls that exposure needs to be combined with what she calls "accessibility." On the one hand, as a professional climber she is prompted by her sponsors to show that the activity is accessible to anyone. On the other hand, she has to act and present herself as though she is easily reachable and "equal" to her followers. Notwithstanding, her climbing abilities and lifestyle are presented and promoted as "unique." Paralleling Marwick and boyd's (2010) observations, online presence combined with a series of tools, the production of aspirational content, and the possession of key information (often recognized through "likes," comments, etc.) help to create the sensation that "the" professional climber is not as unattainable as they are supposed to be. Similarly, this feeling is eventually enforced by displaying personal contact information (including personal phone numbers, email, and street address) on their website and blogs, in addition to the opportunity to contact these climbers via private messaging as on Facebook.

Encouraged by a team manager telling me that "his" athletes were easily reachable via email, social networking sites, or phone, I tried to contact them. My attempts (as well as those of a few friends I asked to try[3]) had zero results. A few months later, I was introduced to one of these climbers by a friend. We spent time together climbing, conducted an interview, but we never mentioned his non-responsiveness to my earlier attempts. One day I asked and was told: "Yep, you know, I've got so many emails and stupid messages via Facebook that I've got to the point that I scan almost everything and rarely write back to anyone."

Providing opportunities for direct contact and making these relationships visible leaves the door open to critics and comments on the information published online. As Michael explains below, the management strategies deployed toward these relationships involve a strong emotional dimension. This is where the concept of relational labor suggested by Baym stands out: "There has definitely been times that I have been like oh man, that sucks, people just gonna be super annoying," says Michael. He adds: "You get all this hate on the Internet by lots of people saying random crap about you and you never meet them." As much as Michael was

RELATIONAL LABOR

SIERRA
BLAIR-COYLE

PROFESSIONAL ROCK CLIMBER FROM SCOTTSDALE, AZ

ASK   ARCHIVE   RANDOM   RSS   SEARCH   TWITTER

ASK ME QUESTIONS :)

I'm not a robot

reCAPTCHA
Privacy - Terms

Ask anonymously or login

Ask

Figure 11.2   Front page of pro climber Sierra Blair-Coyle's "Ask me questions" on Tumblr

hesitating between acting professionally and not contesting, he knew that, for his reputation and the companies sponsoring him, "It would be really bad if [I] just say shut up, you know, or I just tell someone to shut up."

First, the use of social media and websites is incorporated into the labor relationships between professional climbers and their sponsors. Second, it is oriented toward the production of visibility and reputation and, finally, sponsors have strong expectations that climbers break the glass and "make themselves available" (in Julie's terms). These expectations are closely related to the role assigned to climbers as brand ambassadors. They are not only implicitly or legally obliged to communicate via social networking sites and media but also have to manage their reactions toward their audience involving the emotional dimension of this relational labor.

Notwithstanding, beyond these professional duties and the economic viability of such practices, most of the climbers interviewed identify a certain pleasurable dimension in sharing information on their new climbs, travels, and other matters as well as to receive attention. Indeed, Julie adds: "But at the same time it's kinda like, it's not like it's enjoyable but it's kind of like self-rewarding you know." Not that they wish to establish "real social relationships" as Baym's (2012) musicians do, nor do they wish to delve much into online relationships as Michael's example shows. Nonetheless, these "demonstrations of attention" acknowledged by the number of "likes," visits, comments, or re-tweets provide climbers with non-direct economic rewards (and a proportional amount of useful information) encouraging the production of new content, thriving publishing strategies, and the acquisition and improvement of communication skills.

The Collaborative Labor of Online Refereeing

Life and work revolve around collaborations with other professionals who, by working together, create, craft, and diffuse these glamorous representations. Whether "relational labor" is, at the very least, a two-party process, it systematically involves either photographers, professional climbers, or, in relatively rare cases, social media agents caring for online relationships. This is to say that, in order to produce relational labor successfully a number of key actors have to be identified and involved. Beyond the self-centered nature of climbers' publications (to the point that a few climbers called themselves "egocentric"), relationships with fans are related to the labor of other parties. Until recently the focus of attention was primarily on "fans" or "followers" but producing relational labor addresses a wide scope of participants. In the present case, four main types of relationships can be identified: companies (sponsors), media producers, other professional climbers, and fans.

Direct participation emerges primarily from fans. As Sierra Blair-Coyle's "Ask me questions" page showed in Figure 11.2, climbers are encouraged and stimulated to express and share their opinion online by writing comments, asking questions, re-tweeting content, or "liking." From her "Tumblr Tuesday" when she patiently answers the hundreds of questions posted on her wall, to the Instagram contests organized by professional climbers Paul Robinson or Sasha DiGiulian, fostering fan participation not only contributes to enlarging the scope of professional climbers' visibility but also helps in reputation building. When they go on climbing trips, travel to competitions, and attend events, professional climbers spend most of their time with other climbers and media producers (see Dumont 2015b) and systematically refer to them in their online publications.

Whether they share close relationships or not, they make these associations visible via pictures, video-clips, movies, or articles posted on their websites and social networking sites. Not that these media show the photographers or company members at work, but they systematically refer to them via the @username on Instagram, by mentioning friends' and contributors' accounts on Facebook or via a hyperlink on the website. Nonetheless, in this process "hash tagging" is not as important as "referring" because most of the professional climbers have little chance to reach out away from the climbing community (see Figure 11.3).

By referring to their sponsors, they make visible and communicate on their connections but also provide these companies with up-to-date information about their activities, demonstrating that they are fulfilling part of their duties as sponsored athletes. By referring to other media producers, they extend the scope of diffusion of their work and enjoy the connections brought by their own networks of diffusion. By referring to other professional climbers, they reveal their affinities and communicate with each other publicly. In any case, the operation of "refereeing" allows extending and substantively multiplying the diffusion of content and the opportunities of future participation.

In sum, the relational labor of establishing and sustaining ongoing conversations to build intimacy via social networking sites is somehow expected by fans (Marwick and boyd 2011),

Figure 11.3   Screenshot of pro climber Nina Caprez's Instagram account

fulfills personal needs (Baym 2015), or is intertwined with formal or non-formal labor obligations (Dumont 2015b). In doing so, climbers demonstrate their skills and aptitudes in undertaking relational labor—increasing their value to the sponsors and media producers they work closely with. Indeed, as Menger (2002) describes, reputation building is anchored in a process of selective matching leading to the "transfer of reputation." Finally, whether responsiveness remains highly variable, it is also highly selective: professional climbers almost exclusively engage discussion on their social network sites with other professional climbers, companies, or media producers, and rarely address the comments of their fans.

Conclusion

By drawing on the case of professional rock climbers engaging with relational labor, this chapter provides a brief discussion of the collaborative dimension of the latter, yet restricted here to the operation of media production and the process of online referring. It has shown that building, sustaining, and fostering online relationships is at the heart of their labor and anchored in their positioning as brand ambassadors. Climbers have to present themselves as "accessible," regardless of their wishes to actively participate in these relationships. Here, I underline how, through this process, referring online to the companies, media producers, and other professional climbers collaborating in the production of labor is the norm.

While, until now, the focus has been confined to "fans" and "practitioners," the venue offered by online relationship building gives to these "others" a significant role to play and needs to be acknowledged. However, while the concept of relational labor opens the door to further explorations, it needs to be framed and positioned in regards to other analytical tools. In particular, it needs to be anchored in the contemporary transformation of work and labor described as creative, cultural, relational, emotional, or aesthetic labor. Although these are not directly discussed here due to the focus of the chapter, these transformations of work and labor constitute the starting point of this concern for relational labor. Indeed, as the literature shows, these practices are increasingly extending to "normal" or "random" people in many fields.

This discussion is closely linked to self-presentation strategies and, to a certain extent, the question of self-branding which is presented and promoted as an essential asset to secure work opportunities, both by marketers, public speakers, and a few academics (e.g. Kaputa 2006). Authors note that the techniques used to generate attention and popularity are similar to the ones used by companies to market their brands (e.g. Marwick 2015; Grindstaff and Murray 2015; Hearn 2008). Nonetheless, the labor involved in creating and sustaining relationships (whether the latter are essentials or not in gaining fans or in creating a group of loyal consumers) is not systematically planned as a self-branding strategy, nor does it lead to the production of a self or personal brand.

Where self-branding has become a leitmotiv for many, the border between the practices described here and the creation of a self-brand remains unclear rather than blurred. In fact, while creating and fostering these kinds of interactions are definitely central in self-branding strategies, we still do not know much about the forms and features of the latter. For instance, while relational labor is sometimes understood as self-branding, why use—almost systematically—the terms fans, audiences, or followers, and not consumers?[4] These questions rise from both relational labor and the labor of self-branding and prompt us to consider in detail the connective nature but also the differences between these forms of labor. In doing so, it aims to analyze more precisely their scope and implications, a task to which digital ethnography constitutes a key approach.

Notes

1 All names are pseudonyms to maintain participants' anonymity.
2 A climbing media website where climbers have a public profile and can upload their climbs.
3 I asked a few friends to contact these climbers by using a different presentation from mine (I was presenting myself as a researcher).
4 For a similar perspective in the field of celebrities, see Heinich (2011).

References

Abidin, Crystal. 2014. "#In$tagLam: Instagram as a Repository of Taste, a Brimming Marketplace, a War of Eyeballs." In *Mobile Media Making in the Age of Smartphones*, edited by Marsha Berry and Max Schleser, 119–28. New York: Palgrave Pivot.

Baym, Nancy. 2012. "Fans or Friends? Seeing Social Media Audiences as Musicians Do. Participations." *Journal of Audience & Reception Studies* 9(2): 286–316.

———. 2015. "Connect with Your Audience! The Relational Labor of Connection." *The Communication Review* 18(1): 14–22.

Becker, Howard. 1982. *Art Worlds*. Los Angeles: University of California Press.

Beuscart, Jean-Samuel. 2008. "Sociabilité En Ligne, Notoriété Virtuelle et Carrière Artistique. Les Usages de MySpace Par Les Musiciens Autoproduits." *Réseaux* 6(152): 139–68.

DeNicola, Lane. 2012. "Geomedia: The Reassertion of Space within Digital Culture." In *Digital Anthropology*, edited by Heather Horst and Daniel Miller, 80–100. London: Berg.

Dumont, Guillaume. 2014. "Entre Mobilité, Virtualité et Professionnalisation: éléments Méthodologiques et Conditions de Réalisation D'une Ethnographie Des Grimpeurs Professionnels." *Recherches Qualitatives* 33(1): 188–210.

———. 2015a. "Co-creation and New Media: The Entrepreneurial Work of Climbing Photographers in Digital Times." *Anthropology of Work Review* 36(1): 26–36.

——. 2015b. "Professional Climber: Creative Work in the Field of Sport." Doctoral dissertation, Lyon/ Madrid: Université Claude Bernard Lyon 1 and Universidad Autónoma de Madrid.

Entwistle, Joanne, and Elizabeth Wissinger. 2006. "Keeping Up Appearances: Aesthetic Labour in the Fashion Modeling Industries of London and New York." *The Sociological Review* 54(4): 774–94.

Gerlitz, Carolin, and Anne Helmond. 2013. "The like Economy: Social Buttons and the Data-Intensive Web." *New Media & Society* 15(8): 1348–65.

Gill, Rosalind. 2014. "Academics, Cultural Workers and Critical Labour Studies." *Journal of Cultural Economy* 7(1): 12–30.

Gill, Rosalind, and Andy Pratt. 2008. "In the Social Factory? Immaterial Labour, Precariousness and Cultural Work." *Theory, Culture & Society* 25(7–8): 1–30.

Goffman, Erving. 1959. *The Presentation of Self in Everyday Life.* Garden City, NY: Doubleday.

Grindstaff, Laura, and Susan Murray. 2015. "Reality Celebrity: Branded Affect and the Emotion Economy." *Public Culture* 27(1): 109–35.

Hearn, Alison. 2008. "'Meat, Mask, Burden': Probing the Contours of the Branded 'Self.'" *Journal of Consumer Culture* 8(2): 197–217.

Heinich, Nathalie. 2011. "La Consommation de La Célébrité." *L'année Sociologique* 61(1): 103–23.

Hochschild, Arlie. 1986. *The Managed Heart: Commercialization of Human Feeling.* Los Angeles: University of California Press.

Horst, Heather, and Daniel Miller. 2012. *Digital Anthropology.* London: Berg.

Kaputa, Catherine. 2006. *U R a Brand! How Smart People Brand Themselves for Business Success.* Mountain View, CA: Davies-Black Publishing.

Lizé, Wenceslas, Delphine Naudier, and Séverine Sofio. 2014. "Introduction: Les Intermédiaires Culturels: Des Experts de L'économie Des Biens Symboliques." In *Les Stratèges de La Notoriété. Intermédiaires et Consécration Dans Les Univers Artistiques*, edited by Wenceslas Lizé, Delphine Naudier, and Séverine Sofio. Paris: Editions des Archives Contemporaines.

Marwick, Alice E. 2013. *Status Update: Celebrity, Publicity, and Branding in the Social Media Age.* New Haven, CT and London: Yale University Press.

——. 2015. "Instafame: Luxury Selfies in the Attention Economy." *Public Culture* 27(1 75): 137–60.

Marwick, Alice, and danah boyd. 2010. "I Tweet Honestly, I Tweet Passionately: Twitter Users, Context Collapse, and the Imagined Audience." *New Media & Society* 13(1): 114–33.

——. 2011. "To See and Be Seen: Celebrity Practice on Twitter." *Convergence: The International Journal of Research into New Media Technologies* 17(2): 139–58.

Mears, Ashley. 2011. *Pricing Beauty: The Making of a Fashion Model.* Los Angeles: University of California Press.

Menger, Pierre-Michel. 2002. *Portrait de L'artiste En Travailleur. Métamorphoses Du Capitalisme.* Paris: Seuil.

Moeran, Brian. 2003. "Celebrity, Culture and the Name Economy." *Research in Economic Anthropology: A Research Annual* 22: 299–321.

Senft, Teresa. 2008. *Camgirls: Celebrity & Community in the Age of Social Networks.* New York: Peter Lang.

Shepherd, Ifan D. H. 2005. "From Cattle and Coke to Charlie: Meeting the Challenge of Self Marketing and Personal Branding." *Journal of Marketing Management* 21(5–6): 589–606.

Thumim, Nancy. 2012. "Introduction: Self-Representation and Digital Culture." In *Self-Representation and Digital Culture*, by Nancy Thumim, 1–18. New York: Palgrave Macmillan.

Weber, Larry. 2007. *Marketing to the Social Web: How Digital Customer Communities Build Your Business.* Hoboken, NJ: John Wiley & Sons, Inc.

Part III

VISIBILITY AND VOICE

12

"OUR MEDIA"?

Microblogging and the Elusiveness of Voice in China

Cara Wallis and Xi Cui

Much attention paid to the Chinese Internet has focused on two areas: the formation of online communities and modes of sociality (Damm 2007; Giese 2004; Hjorth and Gu 2012), and the role of the Internet in the transforming relationship between state and society in a tightly regulated media environment (Yang 2009; Zheng 2008).[1] With the appearance of microblogging (*Weibo* in Chinese), especially Sina Weibo ("China's Twitter"), which launched in 2009, much scholarship has tended to focus on this latter area.[2] Academics in and outside China have analyzed the use of Weibo (used interchangeably with microblog hereafter) during societal crises to spread information, expose government corruption, and/or force greater transparency and accountability from the party-state (Bondes and Schucher 2014; Qu et al. 2011; Yang 2013). During such extraordinary events, microblogging has indeed served as a platform for citizens to have a voice that is heard even in the midst of official media censorship.

The Internet in general, and microblogging in particular, has definitely reconfigured the traditional form and manner of mediated communication in China. However, scholarship on microblogs has analyzed Weibo-enabled activism through relying methodologically on data mining, yet qualitative—and distinctly ethnographic—research on everyday uses of Weibo is rare. Similarly, with few exceptions (Svensson 2014), users who are less politically motivated and/or socially and economically marginalized are missing from the literature. Thus, a lingering question is how do such people understand Weibo as a force for social change? Furthermore, how do they use Weibo and perceive its ability to give them a voice in the larger society? This chapter uses the theoretical concept of voice (Couldry 2010) to provide some answers to these questions. Based on ethnographic research among three groups of ordinary Chinese—young white-collar workers, university students, and migrant workers—we argue that although Weibo has provided an important platform to amplify the voices of China's netizens, this voice is often diffuse, silent, or constrained for myriad reasons. Assumptions about why people lack a voice online in China usually center on the government's extensive censorship regime, which has intensified in recent years. Although we address this issue, our focus is not on state control. Rather, we situate people's use of Weibo within their own perceptions and discursive construction of voice and efficacy in China's online sphere.

In what follows, we first review prior research on the Chinese Internet and microblogging before laying out the theoretical framework and methodology of the study. We then discuss three themes: Weibo as "our media"; Weibo as providing voice without a voice; and Weibo, social differentiation, and the denial of voice. Ethnographic research cannot make grand claims regarding the majority of Weibo users. Rather, our goal is to provide one lens into an understudied aspect of Weibo in order to contribute to the ongoing conversation on the connection between social media and social transformation in China.

The Chinese Internet: From Bulletin Board Systems to Microblogs

Large-scale surveys undertaken by both official government bodies such as the China Internet Network Information Center (CNNIC) and Chinese researchers (Guo 2007) as well as initial scholarship on Bulletin Board Systems (BBS) (Damm 2007; Giese 2004) showed that the majority of Internet users in China go online primarily for entertainment and sociality. Despite this fact, much research on the Chinese Internet prior to microblogging focused heavily on the connection between online activity and the growth of a virtual public sphere (Lagerkvist 2006; Tai 2006; Yang 2009). Through analyses of heated social issues and "mass Internet incidents," different views emerged as to whether the Internet offered a "safety valve" when contentious issues were raised online and whether it could promote, if not greater democratization, then at least greater political liberalization and a form of civil society (Esarey and Xiao 2011; Hassid 2012; MacKinnon 2008; Yang 2009; Zheng 2008). Simultaneously, a rich body of research looked at social, as opposed to political, uses by groups such as students (Hjorth and Gu 2012; Liu 2011; Wang 2013), elite gamers (Lindtner and Szablewicz 2011), and migrant workers (Gao and Yang 2013; Peng 2012).

When microblogging arrived in China in 2007, and particularly with the rise of Sina Weibo, the use of microblogs to expose corruption and high-profile scandals brought renewed interest in how digital media could be a positive force for transforming Chinese society. Thus, research on microblogging has for the most part followed the strain of political communication research outlined above, with reliance on big data, for example, to analyze people's use of Sina Weibo in the wake of the Wenzhou train crash (Bondes and Schucher 2014); distinguish various types of public sphere formation (Rauchfleisch and Schäfer 2015); or trace how those with a collective identity, such as homeowners, use microblogs, as well as other forms of digital media, to form online networks that could lead to collective action (Huang and Sun 2014). Scholarship has focused in particular on microblogging by public opinion leaders to determine whether and how their use of microblogs enables counter-hegemonic struggles during moments of contestation, including forced evictions, perceived corruption, or food safety incidents (Tong and Lei 2013; Wang and Yang 2012; Yang 2013).

As might be evident by the discussion above, Sina Weibo was initially taken up by predominantly educated, urban, and young users. From the outset, Sina Weibo (and other microblog platforms) courted athletes, movie stars, and other celebrities—who quickly became so-called Big Vs (verified users with over a million followers)—and public opinion leaders (there can be overlap between these two categories).[3] Moreover, China's digital inequality—especially manifest in a sharp divide between developed urban and underdeveloped rural areas—also played a key factor in Sina Weibo's aforementioned initial user base. However, this did not prevent a popular discourse forming around its potential as "grassroots" media and a "voice" for "ordinary" Chinese. Yet, a 2013 study by Fu and Chau revealed that only about 13 percent of Sina Weibo's registered users were active in making original posts and roughly five percent contributed about 80 percent of original content. Furthermore, the scant studies on the potential for Weibo as a means of empowering the marginalized in Chinese society, in particular migrant workers, have found that very few of their voices appear on Weibo (Liu and Tian 2007; Zhang 2013). For the most part, the voices of China's marginalized are amplified only when public opinion leaders or non-government organizations take up their cause (Gleiss 2015; Svensson 2014).

Such research offers an important corrective to some of the hyperbole surrounding the effects of microblogging in Chinese society. Yet, as Fu and Chau (2013) note, their findings do not shed light on why so many accounts remain dormant (apart from the so-called zombie accounts) or why so many users do not post their own thoughts. Moreover, apart from Svensson (2014), who interviewed ten migrant workers, and Li and Lin (2015), who interviewed 15 educated youth regarding posting anxiety on Sina Weibo, scholars have not engaged in qualitative research that includes participants' understanding of their Weibo usage (or non-usage) and virtual ethnography of their Weibo posts.[4] Although government crackdowns on online expression and the rise of WeChat (a mobile social networking platform by rival company Tencent) have led to predictions about Sina Weibo's demise, by the end of 2015 the platform had 100 million daily active users, 222 million monthly active users, and over 600 million registered users, with only 3 percent being outside China (eMarketer 2016). Although usage has gone down since its peak in July 2013, Sina Weibo's user base has expanded from large metropolises to smaller and less-developed urban areas (CNNIC 2014, 2016), providing further reason to determine why so few voices dominate Sina Weibo.

Theorizing Voice

Voice has been theorized in numerous ways in sociological, philosophical, and postcolonial studies. In this chapter, we draw upon Nick Couldry's (2010) work on voice, where he distinguishes between "voice as process" and "voice as value." The former, which is relatively straightforward, refers to the way that humans narrate their lives, or give "an account of themselves and their place in the world" (Couldry 2010, 1). It is probably safe to say that most people desire to have a voice and to know that it is heard and that it matters. More complex is the notion of voice as value, which Couldry defines thusly:

> Treating voice as a value means discriminating *in favor* of ways of organizing human life and resources that, through their choices, put the value of voice into practice, by respecting the multiple interlinked processes of voice and sustaining them, not undermining or denying them.
>
> (2010, 2)

To value voice, then, means to focus attention on which conditions enable voice as a process to flourish as well as to determine and try to minimize the forces, organizational forms, and circumstances (subtle or not) that weaken "or devalue voice as a process" (Couldry 2010, 2). Couldry elaborates on his two-order analytic of voice in the context of US and UK neoliberalism, where an emphasis on market rationalities as the explanatory factor for nearly all social, cultural, and political processes has created what he calls a "crisis of voice" (Couldry 2010, 2). Although the Chinese context is quite different, certain neoliberal tenets, including greater privatization, marketization, and linkages with global capitalism have become predominant along with the elevation of consumption as a marker of individual identity, status, and value. Furthermore, the increased commercialization of the Chinese Internet, including Sina Weibo, has shifted the online terrain as Internet companies of all stripes focus increasingly on generating revenue. Finally, processes initially assumed to accompany market liberalization—greater political freedoms and democratization—have been denied by the party-state and thus the government's censorship regime affects both voice as a process and voice as a value in China, online and off. In this context—what we call neo/non-liberal China—Couldry's two-part notion of voice can be a useful tool for untangling the myriad conceptions and utilizations of voice on Weibo.

Methodology

Methodologically, this research draws inspiration from the work of Miller (2011), Horst and Miller (2006), Hine (2015), Wallis (2013), and others who engage in digital ethnography, or the study of how new media technologies are embedded in everyday life in a particular context. We used multiple methods including participant observation offline, analysis of virtual texts (Weibo posts), and semi-structured face-to-face interviews with 42 participants in Beijing during fieldwork by one of the authors in 2013, 2014, and 2015. Interviews focused on a wide range of topics and social media use, not only Sina Weibo. Interviewees included ten graduate students, ten undergraduate students, ten white-collar workers, seven rural-to-urban migrant workers from villages and small towns (three construction workers, two employees at a beauty salon, and two domestic workers), and five urban-to-urban migrant workers with some vocational education or a few years of university who were employed in small shops. The participants ranged in age from 19 to 29 and were roughly divided equally by gender. One urban-to-urban migrant worker and all of the rural-to-urban migrant workers did not use any microblogging platforms. The other participants had been using Sina Weibo since at least 2011 along with other types of social media (RenRen, QQ, WeChat, etc.).

The ethnographic portion draws upon participant observation of social media use in dorm rooms and work places and virtual ethnography of Sina Weibo in the form of analysis of (and conversations about) postings by a subset of the participants (four graduate students, six undergraduates, five white-collar workers, and two urban-to-urban migrant workers) during an 18-month period from April 2013 through September 2015.[5] Among participants who posted occasionally (once a week or less) all posts and comments were viewed. With participants who were more active (daily posts), we used the navigation bar on Sina Weibo's homepage to view the first page of each month (a maximum of 45 posts and comments were shown). We then organized our findings into various themes that included lifestyle (fashion, beauty, food); travel; social relationships; social issues; positive thoughts/energy; and political issues (there were very few in this latter category). The discussion below focuses on students, white-collar workers, and urban-to-urban migrants, yet although labor migrants did not use Sina Weibo, this lack of representation did not lessen how microblogging was constructed by our informants as being for "everyone," nor did it mean that migrant workers were left out of the conversation altogether, as we discuss in the last section.

Weibo as "Our Media"

As mentioned earlier, a dominant discourse that quickly arose around microblogging as it grew in China was that it was a form of "grassroots" media and a space for ordinary people to voice their views and opinions. In conversations, our informants described Weibo variously as "our media," "grassroots media," and a "melting pot" of ideas, and they initially expressed generally positive comments about the role of Weibo in their own lives and in society at large. Exemplifying this, Lily, a graduate student in international finance, said,

> Weibo totally changed Chinese society . . . We don't have very efficient ways to know what is happening in society. We get limited information from the TV and newspapers, so we need these new media channels because everybody can take pictures and upload them, even though sometimes five minutes after they are uploaded they get deleted. But I think at least the minute they're uploaded, a lot of people can share them. It's a way that . . . every person can have a say.

In noting the positive uses of microblogging, informants often mentioned different Weibo campaigns, such as "Take a Photo, Save a Child," an account registered by the scholar Yu Jianrong in early 2012 to help parents try to find their missing children. They also noted other types of campaigns for social good, such as charitable donations to earthquake victims, although none had participated in such campaigns. Many also mentioned instances where Weibo had helped expose the misconduct of privileged members of society or where it had been utilized to force greater transparency on the part of government officials, such as in the case of the Wenzhou train crash.

Although nearly all of the informants were interested in the importance of microblogs as offering a collective voice to hold government officials accountable, they framed this interest as a concern for social issues or "social justice" rather than an interest in politics. Their Weibo posts for the most part confirmed this distinction. For example, participants posted on high-profile cases of corruption or injustice, such as a watermelon vendor from a rural area who was beaten to death by "urban management" agents in a city in Hunan province in July 2013. In calling Weibo "our media," participants appreciated its power for mobilizing around grievances, yet nearly all of the participants, especially the undergraduates, expressed disdain for more benign types of dissent if they felt it was done without just cause. For example, commenting on Photoshopped images that portrayed government officials in a bad manner, Paul said, "I don't think this is good for our country." On the other hand, our informants appreciated favorable images of police or leaders (e.g., a real photo of two policemen on motorcycles protecting a small child on a tricycle that circulated on Sina Weibo).

Early in our research, the most "political" issue that came up during interviews, and was shared online by participants, was Xi Jinping's spring 2013 visit to Africa. According to Allie, who worked in an advertising agency in Beijing, this was not because of an interest in foreign diplomacy but "because of the fashion of his wife," Peng Liyuan. This focus on fashion, as opposed to geopolitics, as a hot topic on Sina Weibo could be written off as users only being interested in entertainment and celebrity. However, an alternative interpretation is that Peng Liyuan, as the first Chinese first lady to have such a prominent public persona, signifies subtle changes in China's mode of foreign diplomacy and soft power. In contrast, China showed off its hard power through the Military Parade on September 3, 2015, and images of the parade accompanied by expressions of pride also appeared on several of our informants' Weibo (and WeChat) even though earlier they had expressed a lack of interest in politics. Explaining this seeming contradiction, Wang, an undergraduate, said, "This is different. It's difficult not to feel some pride. And anyway, that's all the news is about."

In thinking about voice as process and value, clearly microblogging has allowed more space for diverse voices and opinions. Some of our informants followed certain critical journalists and online public opinion leaders known for writing social critiques, yet when asked the top three Weibo accounts they followed, these were almost always celebrities (movie stars, TV hosts, athletes, singers), friends, brands, and only in some cases online public opinion leaders. Furthermore, many said that even if they read negative news, they consciously tried to post positive stories and messages. For example, Edward, a senior graphic design major, wrote posts such as "Positive energy!" and "Give life a thumbs-up no matter whether you are in a good or bad mood."

Although young people in China are said to love digital media and embrace it uncritically, early in the research nearly every participant remarked that much on Sina Weibo was "shallow" and "disorderly," and all but one participant mentioned the problem of fake news and rumors, which were viewed as bad for society and for the country. Given this concern and their interests in lifestyle and consumption, several informants were unfazed, and some thought it was a good thing when the government cracked down on "rumors" on microblogs in August 2013 (in contrast to Western journalists' focus on censorship). When asked how they could determine the veracity of a Weibo post, no one had a firm method. Some said they went to major news sites. Others said they trusted celebrities, not necessarily a reliable method given the minor uproar caused when Peter Ho (He Rundong), a Tawianese-American film star, appeared to post something fed to him by CCTV that was critical of Apple on Consumer Day (March 15).[6] Thus, while the market was earlier seen as a positive force for freeing the Internet from state control, greater commercialization has also led to the manipulation and the diminishment of voice as a value, a theme to which we now turn.

Weibo as Voice without a Voice

If Sina Weibo is truly "our media," it would seem that one of its main functions would be to enable users not only to have a voice and narrate their lives in various ways, but also to feel their voice is valued. Like social networking sites, Sina Weibo allows users to post thoughts and feelings; however, its very public nature also means that it is different. In general, much of what is posted and forwarded on microblogs concerns news about current events, fashion, entertainment, videos of cats doing funny things, etc. Sina Weibo's "Big Vs" are quite prolific in posting their thoughts on an array of issues, from the profound to the banal. In contrast, although some informants posted their personal feelings, updates on their daily life, or photos of themselves, several said they only forwarded other posts, posted links with no commentary, or made no posts whatsoever. In other words, paradoxically, on the biggest platform where they claim to have a personal voice, they lack a complete one.

Numerous factors might contribute to why people feel they do not have a voice on Weibo, and we will first discuss the reasons that might seem intuitive yet did not emerge as significant. First, several informants mentioned feeling overworked or overly busy, yet none felt they were too busy to compose their own posts or comments. Second, all participants stated that they were avid Sina Weibo users and checked it anywhere from twice a day to constantly. Even when over time some of our informants spent less time on Sina Weibo than in the past (because their interest had shifted to WeChat), they still checked it a couple of times a day, so disinterest was not a factor. Furthermore, a shift toward another application does not necessarily explain how they used Sina Weibo when they were logged in. Finally, only two informants mentioned a concern with privacy, and they were the only informants who used their real name; the rest used pseudonyms.

The reason for our informants' lack of personal expression on Sina Weibo speaks to Couldry's notion of voice as a value. For example, Li, an undergraduate who had no posts and no fans said, "I don't really talk on Weibo. I just see what others talk about." When asked why, he replied, "I'm not an interesting person . . . I have no experience." Another undergraduate, Xiao Gao, was quite passionate in her insistence that Weibo is "media for normal people to express opinions and talk about what they see and do every day. It's their voice." However, she later stated, "I forward (posts) but I don't comment because no one will notice." Another undergraduate said she did not write much because "it has no effects." Comparing Sina Weibo to Renren (popular with students in 2013 but less so in 2015), she said, "Weibo is less efficient than Renren. You might post several messages on Weibo and maybe one person notices." Such feelings of inexperience or that their voice has no effect could be attributed to their status as undergraduates. However, many white-collar workers and urban-to-urban migrant workers expressed the same sentiment. Even Xiao Ding, a white-collar worker who had nearly 600 fans and more than 2,500 posts by September 2015 said three-quarters were forwarded. When asked why she said, "I follow people who have sharp ideas and some important celebrities. . . . I'm not a person who is original . . . I'm boring." Yet, some of her original posts and comments on forwarded news about social inequality, for example, were often quite insightful.

Paradoxically, as much as our informants believed microblogs were "our media," their deeper reflections revealed that this grassroots media did not necessarily enable the complex processes of not only narrating one's life but also feeling valued and validated as a "common person." Most of our informants looked to the Big Vs for thoughts, knowledge, and ideas while devaluing their own voice. On the one hand, this is understandable given that the celebrities and public opinion leaders on Sina Weibo have cultural capital and thus the ability to say things that others might not be able to (within limits). However, this has not necessarily resulted "naturally." Instead, it is connected to the emphasis on status and social stratification more generally found in China, where "VIP" has been attached to everything from rooms in restaurants, to China Mobile lounges in airports, to club memberships. Sina Weibo's early recruitment of celebrities built on this trend, rendering the "value" in voice as equivalent to that which is monetized, which perhaps provides one explanatory factor for the "speaker's corner" phenomenon that Fu and Chau (2013) discovered.

Still, a few informants did post personal things on Sina Weibo. Tina, who had 700 fans and nearly 9,000 posts by September 2015, explained, "When I first started using Weibo, I wanted to write the perfect Weibo, with words and sometimes pictures, but then I changed my mind because it was a waste of energy." For some, the marketing logic of Weibo had an inverse effect; that is, they found it freeing. For example, Zhou, who worked in a small shop, stated, "Famous people don't care about our grassroots common people, so I post more private things on Weibo" (a perusal of his posts showed that they were peppered with profanity in English and Chinese). For others, the anonymity provided by microblogs was similarly liberating. As Xiao Sui, a first-year master's student, said:

> I have a separate Weibo where I post negative thoughts and my true feelings. I don't want to share this with my friends, and if anyone follows me I delete them. It's like a diary, but it is safer because someone could find a paper diary if you left it out by accident. On Weibo I can say whatever I want, and it's just for myself.

Weibo clearly promotes voice as a process, but despite the few examples above, for most of our participants value was placed on those with high status while the value of their own voice was diminished. This is not inevitable, as both should be able to coexist. Summing up his take on Sina Weibo, Bill, who worked in a marketing firm, stated:

Weibo gives an opportunity for speaking. . . . You can speak out but it's fake freedom of speech. You can say what you want but no one will hear you. You can express negativity. It's good for society. You can speak out, but it actually keeps the stability of society. . . . It's sad but healthy.

Social Differentiation and the Denial of Voice

The divide between ordinary users' feelings about the efficacy and value of their own voice on Sina Weibo and that of celebrities and online public opinion leaders was also echoed in another form of differentiation. Although at the time of our research microblogging was done primarily by an urban, educated, relatively elite group of young adult users, China's urban areas are home to over 200 million rural labor migrants. As mentioned earlier, none of our interviewees who were rural-to-urban migrant workers used microblogs. Furthermore, during research in the Chinese countryside by one of the authors in 2013, most rural residents did not know what Weibo was. Even those who were younger and university educated and had heard of Sina Weibo did not use it because they felt it was not relevant to their lives. If they used a microblogging platform at all, they used Tencent Weibo, since it was connected to QQ, a social networking platform favored by migrant workers and rural residents. In this regard, voice as a process for these disenfranchised groups is quite limited on Sina Weibo.

In China, the small number of migrant workers who use microblogs are likely to be involved with NGOs that advocate for migrant workers' rights, as mentioned earlier (Svensson 2014). At the same time, several NGOs that serve the migrant community have Sina Weibo accounts that disseminate news about migrant workers and try to amplify their voices. However, although some of these accounts include posts written by migrant workers, others that seem to be the voice of migrant workers are actually the work of NGO staff. In at least one NGO where we conducted interviews, migrant workers' stories are edited before they are posted in order to make them more "interesting" and "humorous" for an urban audience. The rationale given for this was that urbanites do not want to read sad stories about migrant workers' exploitation or hardship. This claim might indeed be true, and one could argue that voice as a process is still being valued in this case because migrant workers create these initial narratives that are then polished. However, voice as a value is clearly devalued, just as migrant workers' lives are devalued in Chinese society.

Social stratification in China often emerges in government and popular discourse that has focused on building a "civilized" (*wenming*) society. People, residences, neighborhoods, hospitals, industries—just about everything can be the target for civilizing. Offline, being *wenming* serves as a form of differentiation and distinction from those people, places, or things that are *buwenming* (not civilized)—often the rural, the migrant, and the uneducated. Not surprisingly, the government has also sought to target online speech and behavior for civilizing. Many scoff at such efforts, yet these discourses nonetheless are often revealed in people's perceptions of their Internet use. For example, in their research on gamers, Lindtner and Szablewicz (2011, 94) found that those in relatively elite game clubs distinguished themselves from gamers in Internet cafés through invoking the language of *suzhi*, or quality.

Such language about civility and quality emerged in our research as well. Even though our migrant worker interviewees did not use Weibo, rural migrants were not absent from some of our informants' discourse about Sina Weibo. As mentioned earlier, a problem for several informants was the amount of rumors and false news that circulated through microblogs. Some of our informants, particularly students (both graduate and undergraduate), called this "uncivilized" usage. In contrast, sharing information, socializing, and using microblogs for social good were considered "civilized" usage (hence, the emphasis on positivity by some of our informants). Moreover, the "uncivilized" behavior was often blamed on those with low socio-economic status, in particular migrant workers, despite the fact that they make up a minute proportion of Weibo users.

Interestingly, such a critique took distinctly gendered forms. For example, male migrant workers, especially those who do manual labor, were blamed for using microblogs to stir up trouble and to incite "disorderly" behavior. Rural residents were also accused of rioting without just cause—it seemed their struggles for land rights were not viewed in the same manner as urban residents' protests against chemical plants. On the other hand, young migrant women were left out of this conversation altogether, with the assumption that they did not use Weibo. Instead, they were disparaged for having one-night stands through using the "shake" function on WeChat, which allows users to meet strangers in close physical proximity. In reality, our research suggested that all kinds of people, especially undergraduate students, use this function.

It is well documented that people take their offline prejudices with them online. When thinking about discursive constructions of microblogging in relation to migrant workers, we see one more instance of this phenomenon. In the process, voice as process and voice as value are both constrained and minimized for a population that needs these far more than others.

Conclusion

Microblogging in China has clearly shifted the discursive terrain by providing an alternative means of expression in a highly regulated media environment. For this reason, much prior scholarship on microblogs has utilized big data to analyze the connection between microblogging and shifts in state–society relations. In this chapter, we have looked instead at how ordinary people understand Sina Weibo as a mechanism for voice in their everyday lives. Studying users' perceptions and expression of voice on Weibo and how this voice is amplified, constrained, diffused, and sometimes completely diminished is a way to shed light on an understudied area of social media and social change in China.

Building on Couldry's (2010) work on voice, we examined how perceptions of voice online manifest in an authoritarian context that nonetheless has embraced certain neo-liberal imperatives. In this neo/non-liberal context, a focus on celebrity, consumption, and wealth co-exists with intense social stratification and digital inequality. Drawing upon interviews, participant observation, and analysis of Sina Weibo posts, we found that our informants who are Sina Weibo users enthusiastically embrace it as "our media," and they utilize microblogging to narrate their lives through posting and forwarding news and information and to a lesser extent photos and personal commentary. On one hand, the public nature of microblogs (as opposed to a closed social network such as WeChat) encourages such usage. On the other hand, Sina Weibo's hierarchical pattern of emphasizing the voices of celebrities and public opinion leaders also leads to a discursive environment in which many users feel their voice is unimportant and devalued. Even worse, rural-to-urban migrant workers, who do not use microblogs, are nonetheless blamed by some for "uncivilized" behavior online in the same way that they are socially constructed as "backward" and lacking "quality" offline.

Our findings regarding the emphasis on celebrity as leading at least partially to a microblogging atmosphere that constrains voice as a value has been confirmed by CNNIC's most recent survey, which found that with the rising influence of celebrity VIPs, VIPs in topical niches, and official government accounts, users are increasingly considering microblogs as a mass medium channel to seek "news topics," "content of interest," "professional knowledge," and "public opinions" (CNNIC 2016, 57). Government censorship and the greater migration to WeChat, a social network that reinstantiates the social as opposed to the public nature of Sina Weibo, are also presumably factors in this transition. However, even in the early stages of our research, at the peak of Sina Weibo's popularity (July 2013), the constraints and devaluing of voice were quite apparent. Thus, despite the belief in microblogging as "grassroots" or "our" media, practices and processes that promote voice as a value remain elusive in China's microblogosphere.

Acknowledgments

An early version of this paper was presented at the 11th Chinese Internet Research Conference, Oxford University, June 15, 2013. The first author is thankful for the insightful comments of participants both during and long after the conference, especially Elaine Yuan and Marina Svensson. We also thank Shaohai Jiang for help with some of the research for this chapter.

Notes

1 These two strains of scholarship can overlap, as in the volumes by Herold and Marolt (2011) and Marolt and Herold (2014).
2 Although China has a number of different microblogging platforms, Sina Weibo is the dominant platform and is also the focus of this chapter. On the development of microblogging in China, see Harwit (2014).
3 For an in-depth discussion of Sina Weibo's development and the BigVs, see Svensson (2014).
4 In her dissertation, *Talking to Strangers*, Tricia Wang interviewed and conducted participant observation among students and migrant workers. She focused on a range of social media, not just Sina Weibo.
5 Both authors also use Sina Weibo although one is more of a lurker and one is a more active poster.
6 For further detail on this incident, see www.theatlantic.com/china/archive/2013/03/did-cctv-hire-celebrities-to-bash-apple-on-weibo/274104/

References

Bondes, Maria, and Schucher, Guenter. 2014. "Derailed Emotions: The Transformation of Claims and Targets during the Wenzhou Online Incident." *Information, Communication & Society* 17(1): 45–65.
Couldry, Nick. 2010. *Why Voice Matters: Culture and Politics after Neoliberalism*. Thousand Oaks, CA: Sage.
CNNIC. 2014. The 34th Statistical Report on Internet Development in China. Beijing: China Internet Network Information Center (CNNIC).
——. 2016. The 37th Statistical Report on Internet Development in China. Beijing: China Internet Network Information Center (CNNIC).
Damm, Jens. 2007. "The Internet and the Fragmentation of Chinese Society." *Critical Asian Studies* 39(2): 273–94.
eMarketer. 2016. "Weibo Reaches 100 Million Daily Users." www.emarketer.com/Article/Weibo-Reaches-100-Million-Daily-Users/1013449. Accessed February 20, 2016.
Esarey, Ashley, and Qiang Xiao. 2011. "Digital Communication and Political Change in China." *International Journal of Communication* 5: 298–319.
Fu, King-wa, and Michael Chau. 2013. "Reality Check for the Chinese Microblog Space: A Random Sampling Approach." *PLoS ONE* 8(3).
Gao, Chong, and Boxu Yang. 2013. "Interest-Based Social Interactions: The Associational Logic among Fellow-Countrymen—The Associational Logic Based on the QQ Group of 'SZers' in Beijing." *Journalism and Communication Review of Peking University* 7: 94–111.

Giese, Kiese. 2004. "Speaker's Corner or Virtual Panopticon: Discursive Construction of Chinese Identities Online." In *Cyber China: Reshaping National Identity in the Age of Information*, edited by Francoise Mengin, 19–36. New York: Palgrave MacMillan.

Gleiss, Marielle Stigum. 2015. "Speaking Up for the Suffering (Br)other: Weibo Activism, Discursive Struggles, and Minimal Politics in China." *Media, Culture & Society* 37(4): 513–29.

Guo, Liang. 2007. *Surveying Internet Usage and Its Impact in Seven Chinese Cities (The CASS China Internet Project Survey Report 2007, November)*. Center for Social Development, Chinese Academy of Social Sciences.

Harwit, Eric. 2014. "The Rise and Influence of Weibo (Microblogs) in China." *Asian Survey* 54(6): 1059–87.

Hassid, Jonathan. 2012. "Safety Valve or Pressure Cooker? Blogs in Chinese Political Life." *Journal of Communication* 62(2): 212–30.

Herold, David Kurt, and Marolt, Peter, eds. 2011. *Online Society in China: Creating, Celebrating, and Instrumentalising the Online Carnival*. New York: Routledge.

Hine, Christine. 2015. *Ethnography for the Internet: Embedded, Embodied and Everyday*. London: Bloomsbury Academic.

Hjorth, Larissa, and Kay Gu. 2012. "The Place of Emplaced Visualities: A Case Study of Smartphone Visuality and Location-Based Social Media in Shanghai, China." *Continuum* 26(5): 699–713.

Horst, Heather A., and Daniel Miller. 2006. *The Cell Phone: An Anthropology of Communication*. New York: Berg.

Huang, Ronggui, and Xiaoyi Sun. 2014. "Weibo Network, Information Diffusion and Implications for Collective Action in China." *Information, Communication & Society* 17(1): 86–104.

Lagerkvist, Johan. 2006. *The Internet in China: Unlocking and Containing the Public Sphere*. Lund University.

Li, Li and Trisha T. C. Lin. 2015. "Examining Weibo Posting Anxiety among Well-Educated Youth in China: A Qualitative Approach." *Information Development*. 0266666915596057.

Lindtner, Silvia, and Marcella Szablewicz. 2011. "China's Many Internets: Participation and Digital Game Play across a Changing Technology Landscape." In *Online Society in China: Creating, Celebrating, and Instrumentalizing the Online Carnival*, edited by David Kurt Herold and Peter Marolt, 89–105. New York: Routledge.

Liu, Fengshu. 2011. *Urban Youth in China: Modernity, the Internet and the Self*. New York: Routledge.

Liu, Xiaoxuan and Tian Tan. 2007. "To What Extent Can Microblogs Grant Migrant Workers the Right to Express Themselves? A Case Study of SinaWeibo." *Journal of Guangdong University of Foreign Studies* 23(6): 55–59. [in Chinese]

MacKinnon, Rebecca. 2008. "Flatter World and Thicker Walls? Blogs, Censorship and Civic Discourse in China." *Public Choice* 134(1–2): 31–46.

Marolt, Peter and David Kurt Herold. 2014. *China Online: Locating Society in Online Spaces*. London: Routledge.

Miller, Daniel. 2011. *Tales from Facebook*. Malden, MA: Polity.

Peng, Yinni. 2012. "Internet use of Migrant Workers in the Pearl River Delta." *New Connectivities in China*, edited by Pui-lam Law, 95–104. Netherlands: Springer.

Qu, Yan, Chen Huang, Pengyi Zhang, and Jun Zhang. 2011. "Microblogging after a Major Disaster in China: A Case Study of the 2010 Yushu Earthquake." In *Proceedings of the ACM 2011 Conference on Computer Supported Cooperative Work*: 5–34. ACM.

Rauchfleisch, Adrian, and Mike S. Schäfer. 2015. "Multiple Public Spheres of Weibo: A Typology of Forms and Potentials of Online Public Spheres in China." *Information, Communication & Society* 18(2): 139–55.

Svensson, Marina. 2014. "Voice, Power and Connectivity in China's Microblogosphere: Digital Divides on SinaWeibo." *China Information* 28(2): 168–88.

Tai, Zixue. 20016. *The Internet in China: Cyberspace and Civil Society*. New York: Routledge.

Tong, Yanqi, and Shaohua Lei. 2013. "War of Position and Microblogging in China." *Journal of Contemporary China* 22(80): 292–311.

Wallis, Cara. 2013. *Technomobility in China: Young Migrant Women and Mobile Phones*. New York: NYU Press.

Wang, Tricia. 2013. "Talking to Strangers: Chinese Youth and Social Media." PhD diss. University of California, San Diego.

Wang, Weijia, and Lijuan Yang. 2012. "'Wu Ying Case' and the Party Principles of Intellectuals on Weibo." *Open Times* 5: 48–62. [in Chinese]

Yang, Guobin. 2009. *The Power of the Internet in China: Citizen Activism Online*. Columbia University Press.

——. 2013. "Contesting Food Safety in the Chinese Media: Between Hegemony and Counter-Hegemony." *The China Quarterly* 214: 337–55.

Zhang, Pengyi. 2013. "Social Inclusion or Exclusion? When *Weibo* (Microblogging) Meets the New Generation of Rural Migrant Workers." *Library Trends* 62(1): 63–80.

Zheng, Yongnian. 2008. *Technological Empowerment: The Internet, State, and Society in China*. Stanford, CA: Stanford University Press.

13

PARTICIPATORY COMPLICATIONS IN INTERACTIVE, VIDEO-SHARING ENVIRONMENTS

Patricia G. Lange

Making video has empowered many people. Sharing intimate ideas and feelings through video has spurred the formation of intense connections to other people who experience similar concerns, or who benefit from learning about experiences outside of their daily lives. Conversely, media sharing has prompted deeply emotional responses from critics, some of whom are concerned with media's role in creating a self-centered, narcissistic society. Whether hopeful or anxious, many discourses about media sharing in the United States share a "doxa" (Bourdieu 1977) or similar underlying assumption that video making begins and ends as an egocentric act. Ideas about online "participation" and "personally expressive media" (Lange 2014) imply an agentive centrality for media that does not always consider the parallel, intersecting, and contradictory forces that might influence how a video is made, or the interactive complications that participants face when trying to make and share mediated messages.

In this chapter I argue that the basic premise of interactivity in online, video-sharing sites interrupts a commonly accepted notion of the centrality of the video maker as a strictly independent force behind particular content. According to ethnographic research I conducted on YouTube and at video-themed events between 2006 and 2008—and continuing today—numerous factors influence how a video is created, shared, and viewed in participatory environments. Relevant issues include commercial pressures, asymmetrical demands from audiences, collaborative video making dynamics, and interactive participatory forces, all of which can yield tensions when media makers and participants share different ideas about how media should be created and distributed. Interactive dynamics create participatory conflicts when phenomena such as video deletions and parodies threaten video makers' reputations, or contribute to societal tensions.

Ideas about the effects of interactivity prompt a reconsideration of our rubrics on democratic access in online environments. Even if problems of participatory access based on class, gender, ethnicity, and ability are somehow adequately addressed, the dynamics of interactivity itself among multiple, heterogeneous participants means that tensions are likely to persist. Interactive conflict is therefore not a problem to be solved, but rather a dialogic tension that should be productively and respectfully managed. Ultimately, this chapter concludes that developing appropriate and meaningful distribution sites is as crucial to achieving equitable participatory access as is providing widespread Internet connectivity and ensuring access to content creation.

Participation and Sociality

When a video is created, the video creator often dominates media discourses and scholarly analysis. For example, early vloggers such as Paul Robinett (known as "renetto" on YouTube) and Bryony Matthewman ("Paperlilies") have rightly been profiled as instrumental for helping YouTube's early success. Their imaginative vlogs about their lives have sometimes received millions of views, and they were active in promoting community in YouTube's early years. Yet, when asked to reflect on their participation, they identify a range of video creation pressures they felt as YouTube became increasingly commercial. Google's acquisition of the site in 2006, the addition of YouTube's partner program, and increased advertising revenues from ads placed on videos were forces that they say complicated their individual video making process. Robinett was quoted as feeling uncomfortable about financially benefitting from the YouTube community that was forming in the site's early years (Tufnell 2013). Matthewman describes feeling "whorish" for subtly pushing products in her vlogs because she needed the money (Tufnell 2013). Their ideas about how to create a vlog were shaped by their interactions with other people as well as commercial entities. Although YouTube initially felt like a welcoming place for individual self-expression, vloggers faced numerous creative pressures.

For decades scholars have been exploring participatory challenges to creating media. Not surprisingly, these challenges often map to traditional sociological inequities related to class, social race, ethnicity and gender. More recent approaches are also considering how disability and lack of technical expertise may complicate individual, mediated self-actualization. For example, Paperlilies' economic hardships show how class issues play a role in complicating creative self-expression online. Much work is clearly needed to tackle these deeply entrenched problems that seem intractable in politicized environments. It has long been understood that simply having a computer and an Internet connection does not guarantee democratic online video participation. Although it is true that tools exist that greatly simplify video creation and global sharing, it is also the case that those with more training, adequate computer tools, and faster and more reliable Internet connections will quite likely have a substantial edge over someone struggling to participate with outdated hardware, software, Internet connection, and participatory skills.

Yet, even if such inequities—which are framed around sociological differences—could be adequately addressed, a range of additional issues related to the fundamentally interactive nature of socially oriented video demand attention. Interaction-driven environments may present challenges because of asymmetrical assumptions and dispositions people often bring to media-making activities. At root, conflicts often involve the basic assumption that a mediated work is the creator's sole property. However, commercialized entities, participants, and audiences do not always see vernacular media in this way. Videos are initially shaped by the parameters of an online site; once they are posted, participants other than the video maker might feel a stake in their continued presence online. In media research, videos are often analyzed as "texts" that exist in isolation from other factors—such as distribution platforms, other participants, and audiences—that also influence the resulting media artifact(s). Analyzing videos as texts privileges particular artifactual characteristics in ways that might ignore crucial forces that influence the media's creation and sharing. The more interactive an environment is, the more participants may conceptualize videos collectively in terms of how they are distributed, manipulated, and shared.

Participants might engage in "media skirmishes" (Lange 2014), in which different people express conflicting ideas about how media should be created and used. As discussed below, video deletions and remix have caused distress and, at times, social antagonism between participants. As long as media makers, distributors, and participants encourage *interactivity* with video, it is likely that commercial, emotional, and conceptual challenges over a video's ownership will remain. A single video artifact often represents a nexus of copacetic and conflicting agendas that not only present challenges for participants in video-sharing environments, but also invite reconsideration of the mythos of a singular, agentive media creator and its ramifications on future video making and sharing.

The Business of Sharing Video

Participants, audiences, and scholars often see a distribution site as merely a neutral platform or final step in the act of video creation and sharing. In this conceptualization, a person creates a personal statement apart from consideration of its distribution, and then a video creator uploads it to an online platform. However, even as a video is being made, ethnographic interviewees have reported thinking about how to shape its contents for a particular site. YouTube is said to have a special character or "YouTubeness" (Burgess and Green 2009) that creators consider when taking footage or even conceptualizing what kind of video they plan to make. In addition, online videos on sites such as YouTube are often linked to commercial forces that influence how a video is made and shared. People who wish to become famous obviously shape their content to attract audiences and advertisers to their videos. But even vernacular video makers who are not necessarily interested in making money or becoming famous are nevertheless ensconced in the commercial infrastructures and rules that undergird distribution sites.

People might believe that their work is their own, but can receive a rude awakening when their videos have been removed from a site due to financial or social concerns springing from the corporate entity of YouTube (which is owned by Google). YouTubers have complained in their videos, for example, that videos are removed for copyright reasons even when they use or quote other media under the terms of "fair use." The idea behind fair use under copyright law is that under particular circumstances media makers can create new works that depend on incorporating copyrighted material (Center for Social Media 2005). Under fair use, works can be integrated without permission from or payment to the author of the quoted material. If the new work transforms the incorporated material in a way that creates a new work and uses an appropriate amount that does not cause economic harm to the copyright holder of the quoted work, courts are likely to view this use as "fair use." The law is intentionally vague, which is seen as beneficial to vernacular media makers as technologies and practices change over time (Center for Social Media 2005, 2).

However, in cases of alleged violations of music copyrights, for example, the corporate entity of YouTube has reportedly manipulated videos by removing the audio sound track or including advertisements to pay royalties to the music's copyright holders (O'Neill

2010). Another option is to remove a video altogether. YouTubers often complain that such removals are made without warning or explanation. Others believe that the videos should not be removed, especially since in some cases, copyrighted material is being incorporated into videos that promote the artists and media makers whose work is being quoted. By virtue of the fact that a video is being posted to a particular site with specific terms and conditions, a video may be shaped from its conception, or manipulated after it has been uploaded according to a site's terms of service or audience. In a sense, terms of service and similar participatory obstacles may be characterized as "sandbar barriers," which are defined here as those that can theoretically be navigated, but might not be particularly easy to spot or practically parse. For example, people have physical access to a site's terms of service, but they might not actually read or understand them; in fact, participants often simply click through them (Singer 2014; Fiesler and Bruckman 2014).

Creators arguably take their chances by choosing YouTube, and they may certainly choose other distribution sites. However, other sites might not have adequate traffic, or they might exhibit similar commercial pressures and sandbar barriers. Finding a place of distributive purity online is, admittedly, difficult. Other sites have their own terms and conditions and commercial pressures that influence what remains online. For my digital ethnography on YouTube, I took a comparative approach and established two video blogs called *AnthroVlog*. One version still exists on YouTube; the other was created on a blogging site called WordPress. Video blogging purists at the time felt that one should exercise greater control over one's work by avoiding YouTube. I uploaded my videos to a video hosting site called blipTV and linked them to *AnthroVlog* on WordPress. Eventually blipTV removed videos that were not commercially profitable from their site. My videos were among those removed, making the video blog of *AnthroVlog* on WordPress a dead thing. To accurately revive it, the links would have to be restored in the dated postings in which they were uploaded. My video blog was not my own singular creation; I had to rely on the kindness of video hosting services to keep my work connected. Ironically, in an attempt to retain greater control over my work by maintaining a site off of YouTube, I actually experienced far less.

Of course as it becomes easier to upload video to one's own sites, instead of embedding or linking to them from third-party sites such as YouTube, perhaps video creators will experience more control in this dimension. However, as long as blog hosting services recommend linking to videos already uploaded onto video hosting sites—in part to gain audience traction from such popular sites—creators are subject to the structural parameters of those sites. Even if people do agree to them upon initially joining, terms of service tend to change, sometimes without warning or communication to creators who might continue to conceptualize their participation with respect to an outdated set of participatory rules (Verdi and Hodson 2006, 158).

Scholars have elsewhere argued that it is "dangerous" (Hess 2009, 426) for YouTubers to assume unlimited self-expression on sites such as YouTube because such an assumption leads to misconceptions about what participating on a video hosting site entails. In fact, YouTube adheres to corporate agendas that prioritize financial and copyright concerns. Although it is perhaps overstating the case to speak of "danger," the point is nevertheless well taken that many participants have learned the hard way that a site might not be the democratizing, vernacular-oriented platform that it was assumed to be upon joining. Such betrayals of trust become especially painful when YouTubers use video hosting sites as an alternate, personal storage method. I have discovered instances in which participants have become distraught when their video hard drive becomes corrupted and YouTube has removed their videos, which thus cannot be physically recovered.

YouTubers who I interviewed often saw their participation eventually decrease on the site as it became more commercial, and as advertisements and competition for commercial attention created tensions for participants interested in the social and community aspects of the site. In my ethnographic film, *Hey Watch This! Sharing the Self Through Media* (2013), one YouTuber named thetalesend reflected on his participation and stated that what was needed was a new platform through which people could share videos and maintain social connections. He stated:

> YouTube is still gonna go strong. But it's not going to be mainly from user-generated content. It's gotten more commercial, you've seen all the ads, pop up a lot more. As a community-based, kind of social media thing YouTube is pretty much done. But as a place for people to find interesting videos and videos that may be promoted by YouTube, it's not gone yet. But it may be. Someone is bound to make a service that is more user-friendly and whenever someone finds or adopts that area people will move on. It's like the rest of the Internet. We had MySpace and now we have Facebook. No one's on MySpace anymore and now we have Twitter, so. Whoever gives the next best step, that's who's going to go on. That's just the way the Internet is.

Thetalesend was optimistic that perhaps such a site could be created. Efforts to create non-commercial or separate environments do not always catch on. But it is worth engaging in collective efforts to capture the popular imagination by devising media-sharing platforms that are sensitive to participants' needs. All potential tensions will by no means be resolved, but at least participants may acknowledge and deal with interactive tensions.

Artifactual Commentary

Most discussions about obstacles to creating meaningful and open participatory environments focus on the particular challenges experienced by people according to sociological variables such as class and gender. Discussions about the challenges that people face within and across these categories are crucial and are extremely important for achieving democratic access to online spaces. However, even if these problems were solved, the fact is that having different people engage in media sharing can create complications when individuals express conflicting agendas about how to use media, including who ultimately "owns it." Such differing agendas are often rooted in "media ideologies" or "[sets] of beliefs about communicative technologies with which users and designers explain perceived media structure and meaning" (Gershon 2010, 3).

On YouTube, participatory media ideologies might include what constitutes appropriate material to share publicly, and whether a posted video becomes communal property or is the sole possession of the creator. Whether demographic groups share media ideologies can be empirically studied. Researchers might explore whether there are demonstrable intersections between sociological variables and particular media ideologies. For example, researchers might investigate whether people of a particular class or gender tend to share similar beliefs about media sharing. For the present discussion, however, it is important to acknowledge that merely having people with different agendas participate in the same video-sharing space might cause unpredictable forms of conflict.

Studying such spaces invites methodological questions about what exactly should be studied. In the past, the entity of the video has, not surprisingly, received the most attention in scholarly research on video-sharing sites. Yet, certain media ideologies challenge the boundaries of a video artifact as it is collectively created and shared. For instance, a video that is posted on an interactive site has the capability to receive comments and ratings. Once a video is posted, what constitutes the "artifact"? Is it merely the video that was posted, or is it the bundle of discourse and sociality that is now attached to the original video for others to see and experience? Of course many people watch a video and do not read comments, much less comment themselves. But the comments and ratings nevertheless become associated with the original video for those interested in interaction. For certain research questions, it is a logical and productive move to focus on videos. But for other research interests, it is important to examine how video artifacts morph within an interactive setting to include a larger mediated bundle.

The more people interact with a video, the more they may develop a stake in its existence. Tensions sometimes surfaced when YouTube participants became agitated to see videos deleted by their creators. Such tensions were described in a rant video called *A Rant Response for Renetto . . .* posted by OhCurt on August 16, 2009. In the video, OhCurt responds to another YouTuber's discussion about the importance of collaboration on the site. OhCurt expresses frustration that some people on YouTube are "delete happy" because they blithely delete their videos without considering the reverberations of their act on other participatory dimensions of YouTube. People state many reasons for deleting videos, including feeling embarrassed about the technical quality or emotional excess of old videos. In some cases, people take down videos that might violate copyright laws, or they might simply be bored and wish to freshen up their channel with new material.

Video deletions, although often quite justifiable, nevertheless can produce interactive ramifications. On YouTube, when a person deletes a video, all the comments and ratings that were posted along with the video are also permanently deleted. In addition, any video response that was posted remains on the site, but is no longer linked to the original video that was removed. The time and trouble that respondents took to make comments or provide suggestions are all removed along with the original video. OhCurt calls delinked video responses "orphan" videos because the material to which they respond is gone. In his emotional rant, OhCurt compares these orphaned video responses to the experience of hearing "half of a joke," which ultimately lacks context and is unintelligible. He vows to avoid posting video responses to video makers whom he calls "delete happy." OhCurt acknowledges that people have understandable personal reasons for deleting videos. Nevertheless, he is pained that people do not consider the ramifications of their choice on the collective artifact they are creating on YouTube. He states:

> But there's something that I think people are not taking into consideration here, is that, for the last, what two years, three years, four and a half years, however long you've been here, we have collectively been contributing to the creation of an ongoing, historical document.

OhCurt expresses a media disposition in which he feels more comfortable when others do not delete videos. Media disposition is defined as a preference for making certain kinds of media or engaging in particular media activities (Lange 2014, 35). To what extent personal media dispositions are rooted in collective media ideologies is an empirical question. In this case it would appear that his personal preferences could be traced to a media ideology in which YouTube participants are creating a collective "ongoing, historical document." What is created, therefore, is not necessarily solely owned by any individual creator to delete at their whim. His discomfort emerges from how he views the collective ownership of videos, responses, and comments on YouTube. Removing a video pulls an interactive thread from a complex tapestry in which deletions and omissions create mysterious ragged edges that impact the collective creation.

OhCurt issues a plea in his rant, not only to the person to whom he is responding (renetto) but to the YouTube collective, to refrain from deleting videos. He states:

> My plea I guess to myself and everyone who is within earshot of this, renetto yourself included, do not go back and delete old videos. It doesn't matter if it's a response video to something that's no longer on the site. Keep it there! Don't take it down because you just never know what is going to have some sort of value later on down the road.

The "artifact" that is created is not just a single video, and not even just a video along with its text description, text comments, and video responses, but rather is part of a collection of videos and all their associated discourse. He warns fellow YouTubers that even if a video appears modest, one cannot predict its future value. In his video rant, he cites the first video uploaded to YouTube, entitled *Me at the zoo*. The modest, 20-second video was uploaded by one of the founders, Jawed Karim, who comments on the elephants' trunks (Pham 2010). OhCurt's point is that the creation of this modest video eventually became a significant, historical moment in YouTube's trajectory. Even though someone might be tempted to delete modest videos, others may feel a stake in their online preservation.

Scholars studying linguistic ideologies advocate exploring "where" (Blommaert 2004) and "when" (Irvine 2004) evaluations of such ideologies take place. Similar intellectual questions can be applied to media ideologies, in terms of where and when different individuals come to understand what counts as appropriate participation in a video-sharing context. Do participants of sites outside of YouTube share ideas about the collective contribution of video creation? Do such ideologies persist over time?

In fact, practices do change. For example, YouTube eliminated the video response feature in 2013, claiming that only four out of every 1 million users actually clicked through to watch a video posted as a response to another video (Panzarino 2013). Viewers were encouraged to rechannel interactive impulses by using indexical hashtags, titles, and video descriptions to associate response videos to posted videos. Pundits argued that the move was commercial in nature, as modest videos targeted toward other videos exhibited low production values and did not assist in spurring commercialized advertising (Williams 2013). Certainly, the corporate entity of YouTube, which arguably began the video response feature as a way to increase interactivity with popular video makers, did not appear to share OhCurt's media ideology about the importance of collective video making.

The degree to which OhCurt's views about creating a collective historical document resonate with those of other participants would be interesting to explore. Either way, his rant video is instructive, because it provides a corrective to the assumption that videos exist in isolation as texts. Participants sometimes conceptualize a broader picture about what is being created and shared online, and these preferences do not always map to those of the corporate entities that run distribution sites.

Media ideologies about appropriate participatory competencies might vary across sites and over time. In addition, they might also be unevenly or idiosyncratically applied such that an injunction to participate in particular ways could conflict with a person's known behavior and media dispositions (Lange 2015). OhCurt, for example, admits that he himself has deleted videos and that he understands and appreciates why others are tempted to do so. However, he also feels deep frustration about how his contributions through video responses, as well as videos' historical importance may be minimized through deletions. He struggles with how to advocate for particular participatory behaviors, ultimately feeling a need to rant about the collective stake that people other than the video maker display for videos. Emotionally, videos can be viewed as part of a larger collective artifact whose social and interactive terrain reverberates far beyond a single video. OhCurt's own internal as well as external conflicts suggest that interactive issues are not problems to be definitively solved but rather dialogic tensions that need to be continually managed over time.

Video Alterations

Tensions have also ensued when posted videos are manipulated in unfortunate ways. Video parody is a popular genre, and forms such as mash-ups and remix have been used to great effect for important purposes such as political commentary. However, the power dynamic changes when a vernacular video is targeted in ways that malign individual creators. What happens when vernacular videos are used in ways that the original video maker considers disrespectful? One does not necessarily have control over one's media in these cases, and video makers may experience the painful effects of mean-spirited parodic appropriations.

One video maker named robtran who I interviewed at a meet-up in San Francisco illustrated the frustrations he experienced when his videos were remixed by "haters." Robtran told me he was initially very excited to post videos to YouTube but later became discouraged when haters remixed his video to make him appear to be making anti-Semitic remarks, when in fact, his videos had protested anti-Semitism. These poorly made, parodic, hater videos caused him great distress. He felt that they damaged his reputation, were inappropriate, and should be removed from the site. The multiplication of these videos renders criticism about individual video narcissism as rather flat and unconvincing. Many videos about him were made out of his control.

Robtran's frustration continued when his complaints to YouTube staff through private back channels remained unanswered. He was reportedly told that these were legitimate uses of his videos and they did not violate the site's terms of service. Complicating the situation was the fact that YouTube's viewing algorithm selected these videos to be featured next to robtran's own as "related content." He told me that the search algorithm even listed these hater mash-up videos first, before his original videos. He was distressed that the parodic videos were lewd and obscene. He felt anxious that family and friends searching for his videos would find these videos first, and innocently watch them, only to become exposed to their offensive content.

When a video is created and posted to YouTube, the "artifact" created may be read by participants as much more than a video—it becomes embedded in a media bundle that includes the video and the discourse that surrounds it. Intertwined with the video is the metadata associated with a video, such as the algorithmic assessment of its popularity and its position in listings such as search engine results, all of which are likely to be beyond the control of the video maker. Similarly, mash-ups that distort a video's original intent are also a product of interactively posting and sharing one's work online. Participants may not share ideas about who has control over the video and its legitimate interactive purposes. Robtran and others might espouse a media ideology that the videos are his and should be respected in terms of how they are viewed and displayed. YouTube's commercially driven parameters and participants who engage in mash-ups may treat the videos more as collective property that can be manipulated for other ends, such as to attract commercialized viewership. These problems might persist even if a media maker passes away, as heirs could be at odds with each other and the video maker in terms of which content should remain or be deleted.

Whether these differences in media ideologies diverge as a result of sociological indicators such as class or social race is worthy of investigation. I have observed, however, that even

people within similar socio-economic demographics can hold widely different media dispositions about their own personal comfort level with making specific kinds of media, and they
might display quite diverse media ideologies about who has the right to access and manipulate
videos. The fact that people with different media ideologies are encouraged to be interactive
within the paradigm of social media will likely continue to spur discomforting mediated discrepancies for the foreseeable future.

Conclusion

In many contexts, our media is not our own. In the tradition of individualized Western
media making and assumptions about copyright, a dominant media ideology that is embedded in many media makers is that one has the right to control who has access to one's media,
and to what purposes it should be applied. In many ways this is a logical assumption in that it
honors the wishes of the people who made an effort to use their insight, skills, and resources
to create media. Yet, today's heavily mediated, video-sharing idiom challenges the assumed
participatory limits of video makers' control over their own images. Once a video is posted
on a site with particular agendas, such as a drive toward monetization, design features that
facilitate sharing in commercial ways may dovetail or diverge from a media maker's ultimate wishes. Before media is even made, the parameters of its distribution destination can
influence its creation. Influences range from simple and obvious rules such as video length
limitations to assumptions about what makes an appropriate "YouTube video," with all of
its connotations of wackiness, marginal quality, monetization opportunities, and ever-present
potential for virality.

Examining tensions over ownership also prompts theoretical reconsiderations about what
constitutes the analytical boundaries of appropriate media "artifacts" to study. Analyzing
artifacts is an important facet of digital ethnography. Yet determining what constitutes a
coherently delineated artifact is a thorny question. The importance of questioning such analytical boundaries is made more visible when media artifacts travel through time and are
altered along the way. Many scholars of media treat a video as the only appropriate artifact for
study, but once a video is posted, it becomes linked to text commentary, and possibly video
responses, ratings, as well as certain features, structural parameters, metadata, and algorithms
associated with a distribution site.

People who I studied on YouTube were known to exhibit an emotional stake in many
forms of participatory media. For example, many people interviewed agreed that commenting on videos was as legitimate a form of participation on YouTube as was posting videos.
After all, they have taken the time and trouble to watch and respond to particular videos.
When videos are deleted their associated comments disappear, thus removing people's participatory, interactive, and personally expressive contributions. Although acknowledging that
these forms of participation do not constitute outright co-ownership of a video, frustration
nevertheless ensues for some participants when their contributions are removed. For some
participants, an "artifact" may even change in conceptual scale from a video or even video
page with comments to a larger view of the assemblage of YouTube videos as a "collective historical document" that deserves to continue for current and future participants to
experience. Although this might represent an extreme position, it is nevertheless important
for understanding the spectrum of possible emotional characterizations of what constitutes a
media artifact.

Interactivity in genres such as video remix presents challenges for media makers. New
literacy scholars are among the fiercest advocates of non-traditional vernacular genres such

as parody, which has accomplished much in areas such as civic engagement. However, the interactive dynamic changes when the person being parodied is a vernacular media maker, and their video is being distorted in ways that contribute to societal ills rather than exposing problems. Ideas about respecting terms of service and free speech offer precious little comfort during these antagonistic moments that feel like media skirmishes when the stakes are low, but become much more intense when public reputations and social justice are on the line.

As long as people are encouraged to interact, conflicts are bound to occur. Even if we were to miraculously solve problems of access to video sharing among traditionally under-represented groups online, clashing media dispositions and ideologies await. It is clear that future scholarly research will need to explore the roots of individual media dispositions and ideologies, and investigate ways to expose and deal with ongoing divisive discrepancies. It is no longer enough to say that media makers should simply accept the fact that a site that enables free circulation of videos can make all of the rules. Thetalesend argued that some day someone would devise a more "user-friendly" platform for sharing videos and media. Sadly, he passed away before this dream could materialize. Years ago discourse about achieving ade-quate Internet access moved from simply enabling online connection to having control over creating content. We can no longer simply be satisfied even to talk about content creation. The time is ripe for becoming more collectively active and creatively aggressive about craft-ing appropriate distribution platforms that anticipate and offer mechanisms for dealing with interactive tensions. We will probably never experience a perfectly egalitarian media-sharing environment, but that does not justify surrendering. Instead, we should work harder, as the yogis say, to move in that direction.

References

Blommaert, Jan. 2004. "Writing as a Problem: African Grassroots Writing, Economies of Literacy, and Globalization." *Language in Society* 33(5): 643–71.

Bourdieu, Pierre. 1977. *Outline of a Theory of Practice*. Cambridge, MA: Cambridge University Press.

Burgess, Jean and Joshua Green. 2009. *YouTube: Online Video and Participatory Culture*. Cambridge: Polity.

Center for Social Media. 2005. *Documentary Filmmakers' Statement of Best Practices in Fair Use*. Washington, DC: School of Communication, American University.

Fiesler, Casey and Amy Bruckman. 2014. "Copyright Terms in Online Creative Communities." Paper presented at CHI 2014, Conference on Human Factors in Computing Systems, April 26–May 1, Toronto, ON, Canada.

Gershon, Ilana. 2010. *The Breakup 2.0: Disconnecting over New Media*. Ithaca, NY: Cornell University Press.

Hess, Aaron. 2009. "Resistance Up in Smoke: Analyzing the Limitations of Deliberation on YouTube." *Critical Studies in Media Communication* 26(5): 411–34.

Irvine, Judith. 2004. "Say When: Temporalities in Language Ideology." *Journal of Linguistic Anthropology* 14(1): 99–109.

Lange, Patricia G. 2014. *Kids on YouTube: Technical Identities and Digital Literacies*. Walnut Creek, CA: Routledge/Left Coast Press.

——. 2015. "Typing Your Way to Technical Identity: Interpreting Participatory Ideologies Online." *Pragmatics* 25(4): 553–72.

O'Neill, Megan. 2010. "How YouTube Detects When You Upload Copyrighted Stuff . . . And Makes Money Off It!" *AdWeek*, December 8. www.adweek.com/socialtimes/youtube-make-money-off-your-videos/30526 (accessed September 22, 2015).

Panzarino, Matthew. 2013. "Google Dumps Video Responses from YouTube Due to Dismal .0004% Click-Through Rate." TechCrunch, August 27. http://techcrunch.com/2013/08/27/google-dumps-video-responses-from-youtube-due-to-dismal-0004-click-through-rate/ (accessed January 11, 2016).

Pham, Alex. 2010. "YouTube Turns 5, Can't Wait to Grow Up." *The Los Angeles Times*, May 17. http://articles.latimes.com/2010/may/17/entertainment/la-et-youtube-20100517 (accessed October 5, 2013).

Singer, Natasha. 2014. "Didn't Read Those Terms of Service? Here's What You Agreed to Give Up." *New York Times*, April 28. http://bits.blogs.nytimes.com/2014/04/28/didnt-read-those-terms-of-service-heres-what-you-agreed-to-give-up/ (accessed September 22, 2015).

Tufnell, Nicholas. 2013. "The Rise and Fall of YouTube's Celebrity Pioneers." *Wired.co.uk*, November 27. www.wired.co.uk/news/archive/2013-11/27/youtube-community (accessed January 11, 2016).

Verdi, Michael and Ryanne Hodson. 2006. *Secrets of Videoblogging*. Berkeley, CA: Peachpit Press.

Williams, David B. 2013. "Why YouTube Really Killed Video Responses." VideoInk, September 30. www.thevideoink.com/features/voices/why-youtube-really-killed-video-responses/#.VpPTqxEjGCo (accessed January 11, 2016).

14

INFLUENCER EXTRAVAGANZA

Commercial "Lifestyle" Microcelebrities in Singapore

Crystal Abidin

Winnie gets up in the morning, leisurely strolls to the bathroom, brushes her hair, puts on light concealer, draws her eyebrows and lines her eyelids, then gets back into bed. With an outstretched arm, she tilts her head towards her windowsill for natural lighting, and snaps a dozen selfies. In the next ten seconds, she carefully scrutinizes every shot, zooming into various body parts, and decides on one image. She then effortlessly processes the selfie through a series of photo-editing apps, and uploads the photo onto Instagram: "Good morning, guys! How is everyone doing today? #justgotoutofbed #nomakeup."

Within three minutes, her selfie has amassed over 5,000 "likes" and hundreds of comments. "I love you so much," writes one follower. "Your hair is #lifegoals. What do you use?" writes another. "I'm your biggest fan! From the US!" exclaims yet another. Winnie selects a few outstanding comments and rhythmically taps out quick responses: "Aww babe, you're the sweetest!"; "I use Sunsilk! Check out my hair tutorial on YouTube and my #SunsilkGoodTimes promo :)"; "<3 from Singapore!". Although she has never met them, Winnie broadcasts to hundreds of thousands of followers daily, reserving her coveted personal responses to a handful of followers at whim.

Winnie gets out of bed once more, completes her makeup regime, and gets dressed in an immaculately coordinated outfit with accessories, conscientiously styled the night before. She opens one of several packages addressed to her, personally couriered and customized in her favorite colors with compliments of yet another sponsor. This time, it's three pairs of high heels. Winnie puts them on in rotation, finally deciding on one pair to complete her outfit, and walks to the blank wall along the corridor of her apartment with a camera tripod. She sets up the self-timer, leans against the blank wall, and in an autopilot muscle memory, effortlessly displays ten poses in succession for the camera. She picks her favorite shot, makes a quick upload onto Instagram, and thinks up an inspirational caption: "Everyday is lived to the fullest when such gorgeous heels give you confidence #CharlesShoes, quote 'Winnie10' for a 10 percent discount from now till the end of this month!'" The "likes" and comments start streaming in again. #CharlesShoes' sales are on the rise. Winnie has earned another $1,000 for her advertorial. All in a morning's work.

Since their debut in 2005, commercial "lifestyle" bloggers in Singapore have progressed to become Southeast Asia's most lucrative, impactful, and longstanding microcelebrities. Having expanded their self-branding in "digital" spaces across integrated social media platforms, and in "physical" spaces across a range of different industries, this chapter examines how young women have transited from being lifestyle "bloggers" to "Influencers." In Singapore, Influencers are predominantly women between the ages of 15 and 35 who dominated in terms of numbers, impact, and earning power, catering to a market of regional consumers under the age of 35.[1] This chapter traces the growth of the microcelebrity and Influencer industry in Singapore. Drawing upon ethnographic research with Influencers in Singapore between 2011 and 2015, it illustrates how young women who began selling used clothes on the Internet developed into microcelebrity Influencers, and the role of supporting infrastructures, such as management agencies and followers, in their trade. Through an extrapolation of various digital methods grounded in anthropology and ethnographic practice, this chapter provides a brief overview of Influencers' communication norms, commercial activities, impact on mainstream industries, and self-branding concerns.

From Microcelebrity to Influencers

Senft (2008) first coined the term "microcelebrity" as a burgeoning online trend, wherein people attempt to gain popularity by employing digital media technologies, such as videos, blogs, and social media. Marwick (2013) further developed the concept of microcelebrities through her work in the San Francisco technology community focused on microcelebrity tech workers. Senft (2008, 16) describes microcelebrities as "non-actors as performers" whose narratives take place "without overt manipulation," and who are "more 'real' than television personalities with 'perfect hair, perfect friends and perfect lives.'" Drawing from Rojek's (2001) work on types of celebrity, Marwick (2013, 116–17) distinguishes between two types of microcelebrity: "ascribed microcelebrity" where the online personality is made recognizable through the "production of celebrity media" such as paparazzi shots and user-produced online memes, or "achieved microcelebrity" where users engage in "self-presentation strateg[ies]," such as fostering the illusion of intimacy with fans, maintaining a persona, and selective disclosure about oneself.

In contrast to microcelebrities, "Influencer(s)" is a vernacular industry term, inspired by Katz and Lazarsfeld's (2009) notion of "personal influence." I capitalize "Influencers" as a professional career focused on social media-based, multimedia microcelebrities in distinction from the term "influencer" in business studies used to describe a model of marketing and advertising that targets key individuals who exert influence over a large pool of potential customers. Although the original concept pre-dates the Internet, today Influencers can be defined as everyday Internet users who accumulate a relatively large following on blogs and social media through the textual and visual narration of their personal lives and lifestyles. Engaging with their followers in "digital" and "physical" spaces, Influencers monetize their following by integrating "advertorials" into their blog or social media posts and making physical appearances at events. A pastiche of "advertisement" and "editorial," advertorials in the Influencer industry are highly personalized promotions of products/services that Influencers personally experience and endorse for a fee (Abidin 2015a).

In Singapore, the development of Influencers can be traced back to the early beginnings of the "blogshop" industry from the mid-2000s and the "commercial blogging" industry. A Singaporean bricolage of the words "web blog" and "shop," blogshops were uniquely popular in Singapore, beginning as small home Internet-based businesses with low start-up costs that primarily market ladies' apparel and accessories such as shoes, bags, and jewelry, by sourcing products from "various regional countries" (Chung 2010a; Chung 2010b), including Thailand, Indonesia, Taiwan, and China (Greenhill and Fletcher 2011; Fletcher and Greenhill 2009). Abidin and Thompson (2012, 467), by contrast, argued that blogshops are "online sites in which young women model and sell apparel via social media" based on "commercial intimacies," "value (co-)creation," and "persona intimacy." Drawing on Roberts' (2004) concept of "lovemarks," wherein brands build positive feelings and loyalty with customers, Abidin and Thompson (2012, 468) identified a shift away from "product intimacy" towards "persona intimacy" through which blogshops "cultivat[e] an emotional attachment not to the products per se but to the online personas of the models via their blogs."

In a bid to interact with their customers, blogshop owners and models began crafting their own personae and depicted lifestyles through the use of personal blogs as a parallel commentary to their blogshops. Over the past ten years, Influencers have moved beyond a single platform and are no longer anchored in blogging as their main activity. Influencers now exhibit a command of social media platforms through depicting their personal lives and lifestyles as canvases for self-branding in which personal privacy is commodified (Abidin 2014a), and followers are persuaded to make purchasing decisions.

Management Agencies

With the Influencer industry in Singapore expanding so quickly, Influencer management agencies began launching in 2007 to aggregate Influencers across genres, and pitch them to clients seeking Internet personae for endorsements, sponsorships, and social media marketing campaigns. Signed Influencers are exclusive to the company and agree to relinquish advertising rights on all their social media platforms to the firm, save for a few exemptions such as blogshops, hair salons, and nail parlors, because these predate Influencer managements. Between 20–50 percent of advertising revenue is apportioned as the management's commission, which, in exchange, negotiates fair work conditions and timely payment for Influencers, and quality and timely work for clients. Unsigned Influencers are not exclusive to any management and are less likely to be pitched to clients unless they are sought after. Unsigned Influencers are usually those who are able to operate independently to attract and negotiate with clients because they are exceedingly popular and command strong bargaining power; whose daytime jobs do not allow them to be under other contractual agreements, such as women in civil service who instead attend exclusive events and receive products in kind; and who are fairly new and upcoming Influencers who have not yet garnered a sustainable following.

One of the key actors in such agencies is the "Influencer manager." As staff that work the most closely with Influencers, they play multiple roles (see Malefyt and Morais 2012, 20). Conceptually, Influencer managers curate the agency's portfolio of Influencers and keep them in line with clients' expectations. They are gatekeepers of the Influencer industry who maintain valuable connections with the public relations (PR) and marketing departments of several industries, thus providing access to highly sought-after events and exclusive networks. Operationally, Influencer managers identify potential Influencers, groom them, and pitch them to clients at face-to-face screening sessions or through an "Influencer deck"—a digital repository of available "assets" that is most commonly a PowerPoint presentation or online database featuring portfolios of available Influencers. They also chaperone Influencers at events, ensure Influencers deliver the work stipulated in the advertorial contract, and build unity and mediate conflict among contracted Influencers.

Followers

On the receiving end of the curated content are "followers" whom Influencers emically categorize as "readers" (neutral or supportive towards Influencers), "haters" (disavowing Influencers and have been known to denigrate their craft), and "bots" (dummy, purchased accounts that some Influencers have been accused of using to boost their numbers). Although a handful of Influencers do refer to some followers as "fans," this term is the least used, as it tends to imply a sense of distance and status elevation between Influencers and followers. Liew (2016) also conducted a case study on one prominent (and pioneering) Influencer's anti-fandom, whom she argues was motivated by "moral judgments" of the Influencer's "inauthentic presentation of self," "performance of femininity," and "nature of her celebrity." Additionally, the strong following of Influencers is reflected in the infocomm Development Authority's (iDA) 2012 report that "Reading blogs that are created by others" was documented the third most popular activity after "Social Networking" and "Instant Messaging" (iDA 2012).

Influencers often brand themselves as having "relatability," or the ability to persuade their followers to identify with them (Abidin 2015b). Although this concept is largely unarticulated and inarticulable among Influencers (i.e. "so that readers can relate to you"; "to make my posts relatable") and honed through "gut feeling" and "trial-and-error" (i.e. "it just feels right"; "the more you practice the more you will know"), relatability is comprised of the interrelated but distinct notions of "accessibility" (how easy it is to approach an Influencer in digital and physical spaces), "believability" (how convincing and realistic an Influencer's *depicted* lifestyle and sentiments are), "authenticity" (how genuine an Influencer's *actual* lifestyle and sentiments are), "emulatability" (how easy it is for followers to model themselves after an Influencer's lifestyle), and "intimacy" (how familiar and close followers feel to an Influencer).

A key feature of Influencers in Singapore is their extensive integration of face-to-face meet-ups with followers on a regular basis, in formal and informal settings. Formal events include those sponsored and organized by clients in conjunction with the launch of a new product or service, or parties organized by Influencers that are sponsored in kind by clients in exchange for advertorial publicity. Informal events include those casually organized by Influencers themselves, such as Christmas giveaways and lucky dips for selected followers, and impromptu coffee sessions in cafés where followers can take the opportunity to snap selfies with Influencers. These physical interactions usually incorporate the use of a dedicated event hashtag that followers are encouraged to use while they "live Tweet" or "live Instagram" their activities. Such practices are also commonly incentivized through competitions such as giveaways to selected users on the hashtag, or prizes awarded to the best Tweet or Instagram post. These physical space interactions complement digital space engagements because Influencers are expected to perform their personae in congruence with depictions they have displayed on their blogs and social media. As such, the intimacies fostered and negotiated in digital platforms are transferred to physical settings, in a feedback loop that amplifies the relatability followers feel towards Influencers.

Communication

Influencers have crafted their own unique language, drawing from Singlish (a creole of Singaporean colloquial English) and Internet conventions such as abbreviations, acronyms, bricolage, emoticons/emoji, keyboard symbols, leetspeak (Blashki and Nichol 2005), and onomatopoeic spellings. Singapore is a multicultural society whose citizens use a wide range of languages and dialects, such as Malay, Tamil, Mandarin, Cantonese, Hokkien, Teochew, and Hakka. As such, Influencers commonly intersperse English—the national business language that is dominantly used—with words from these other languages. Expressive interjections such as "*lah*," "*leh*," "*mah*," and "*meh*," among others, are also distinctive features of Singlish (Forbes 1993), and usually serve as conversation softeners or to convey emotions.

Influencers convey intimacy via text in a number of ways. Most often, they tended to heavily use terms of endearment in their conversations. My informants freely adopted personal referents (i.e. babe, dearie, sweetie, gal) in their exchanges. Such "girl talk" (Currie 1999) appears to be a strategy to stimulate a sense of closeness and friendship despite these women never having met in person, and at times even being complete strangers on the Internet. I (Abidin 2013a) have previously termed these intimate forms of communication "Perceived Interconnectedness," wherein Influencers use social media to produce a sense of familiarity. However, the tensions arising from expectations to cultivate familiarity include the needs for immediacy, constancy, exclusivity, intimacy, and a high quality of interactions (Abidin 2013a).

Emoticons/emoji also foster closeness among Influencers and followers. Emoticons are "graphological realizations of facial expressions" (Zappavigna 2012, 71) using keyboard characters, while emoji are small digital icons used to express ideas and emotion. Both feature prominently among Influencers. It is crucial to account for particular formations that emerge from social media-based/informed communication, particularly since paralinguistic indicators such as emoticons/emoji operate within networks of power and knowledge, as "linguistic currency" (Herring and Zelenkauskaite 2009, 3) that clearly differentiate members from outsiders. Emoticons/emoji were also used as euphemisms or mild substitutes for expressions that were otherwise offensive, or to water down or negate harsh comments, in a bid to diffuse tension (Abidin 2013b). Elsewhere, I (Abidin 2016a) had investigated how Influencers use emoticons/emoji, along with fonts, images, and vocabulary to convey a sense of cuteness that borrows from East Asian cute culture. The most frequently used emoticons were:

:) or :D	happy
:(or D:	sad
:'(	crying
>:(	frown, connoting anger
>.<	embarrassed
<3	heart, connoting love
</3	broken heart, connoting disappointment or sorrow
/★('___')/★	shaking a pompom, connoting celebrations
□_(ツ)_/ □	shrug, connoting "I don't know" or "whatever"
(╯°□°)╯ (┻━┻)	flipping a table, connoting frustration

In one memorable incident, an Influencer asked if I was upset with her because I had responded to her text message with a mere "k." She had found it difficult to situate my emotional state (i.e. "I didn't know if you were angry or if you just don't use smileys") because I had not included any emoticons to signal my mood. She also explained to me that "k." with a period appeared curt and less palatable than its variants, "ok," "okay," "ok.," and "okay." It would have been preferred if I had responded with an emoticon, such as in "okay :)," but better still if I had taken the effort to scroll through my keyboard to insert an emoji instead, as in "okay ☺." My texting faux pas underscored the tacit communicative norms Influencers seemed to collectively enact, but which I had to intentionally learn.

Through content analysis, Sinanan et al. (2014) later investigated "lifestyle blogs" through the lens of consumerism and citizenship, arguing that their aesthetic is both "parochial" for regional appeal and "global" in focusing on "particular globally circulated consumer products" (2014, 201). Focusing on visuality, the consumption Influencers express on their blogs embodies the normative aspirational consumerism prevalent in the country (2014, 209). This is primarily used to convey an impression that these Influencers "embody better-informed consumers who make good consumer choices as well as affluence," when directing followers towards products and services (2014, 209).

Commerce

In his study of consumerism in Singapore, Chua identifies "excessive materialism" (Chua 1998, 987) as one of the three ideological discourses of consumption in Singapore. He also posits that the period of youth allows for more unrestrained consumption and adornment of the self, as one has not yet inherited the financial responsibilities of "big ticket" items such as houses and cars and, thus, is more likely to have discretionary income. The body then naturally emerges as the primary locus of consumption (Chua 2002, 183) with bodily embellishments being most affordable.

In Singapore, Influencers market products and services from diverse industries, although the most popular have been fashion, beauty, F&B (food and beverage), travel, and electronics. There are an increasing number of young women who put tertiary education on hold (Gwynne and Abidin forthcoming) and quit their day jobs to pursue blogging full-time (Chiew 2009; Chung 2010a, 2010b; Aw Yeong 2013). In essence, Influencers display aspirational but accessible lifestyles to their followers, seemingly attainable through the goods and services marketed, thus driving "conspicuous consumption" (Veblen 1961). They earn revenue in four main ways:

1   through advertorials focused on facial and beauty products and services, plastic surgery and cosmetic enhancements, apparel and fashion, food and beverage, and travel;
2   through advertising space on their blogs and social media platforms in the form of banners and links;
3   through hawking "pre-loved" or used personal items on their blogs and on Instagram;
4   through guest appearances at events.

Owing to their capacity to shape public opinion and purchase decisions, the sponsorships and advertorials in which Influencers are engaged have progressed from small home business to blue-chip companies including Canon, Gucci, and KLM. Influencers' creative forms of commerce have been investigated through Instagram aesthetics (Abidin 2014b) and selfies (Abidin 2016b), and as social currency (Abidin 2013c) and digital labour (Abidin forthcoming b). More recently, industry stakeholders are discussing guidelines regarding the disclosure of their paid advertorials (Abidin and Ots 2015; Ots and Abidin 2015).

Impact

Published information pertaining to the Influencer industry in Singapore is located principally in mainstream media publications, such as newspapers and magazines, although these are only widely circulated locally. Articles written for a public audience are brief and usually angled to cover the economic success and beauty of Influencers—seemingly the two most appealing aspects of their activity. For instance, my coding of mainstream press coverage between January 2007 and June 2013 in the top six English-language newspapers revealed five major themes: DIY practice (Chiew 2009), entrepreneurship (Chung 2010a), affluence (Heng 2009), physical appearance (Ng 2009), and appearance enhancement (Chung 2010b), in addition to personal profiles on specific Influencers and their social impact, and miscellaneous articles on the blogshop trade.

The immense success and extensive popularity of the Influencer industry have garnered widespread attention from several other realms, including private and multinational corporations (MNCs), politics, social and humanitarian organizations, and mainstream media productions. I have also noted how Influencers use self-presentations known as "sex bait" as informal forms of sexuality education that counter state-authorized sentiments from the Ministry of Education (Abidin forthcoming a). Riding on their extensive popularity and consistent following, these sectors often invite Influencers to make special appearances to bring publicity to the project or special cause. Influencers are invited to events as special guests and VIPs in acknowledgment of their unique status and the social prestige they have earned.

In 2013, London-based social media analytics firm, Starcount, launched its inaugural Social Star Awards in Singapore at the Marina Bay Sands. The ceremony was streamed live on YouTube and honored the most popular personalities on the web from the sporting, gaming, music, film, and television industry. Over 280 winners were "decided by the activities of 1.7 billion Internet users around the world who use 11 major social media sites including Facebook, Twitter, YouTube, Sina and Weibo from China and VK from Russia" (STcommunities 2013). More recently, the international YouTube Fan Fest (YTFF), which celebrates and awards the most popular YouTubers in the region, was also held in Singapore in 2014 and 2015, where local Influencers were honored for their craft.

Self-Branding and the Self

To followers, many Influencers are interchangeably known by their social media monikers and their legal names. However, the Influencers themselves may personally distinguish between the two. Tammy uses her legal name, "Tammy Tay," on her personal Facebook page, but adopts her Influencer moniker "ohsofickle" for her monetized blog URL, and Twitter and Instagram handles. She also owns a blogshop by the same name, but hosts her shop's URL on a different domain to distinguish between her blog[2] and her shop.[3] The social media handles for her shop are a variant of her Influencer moniker, "@shopohsofickle." Tammy feels that it is important for her to "keep up [her] brand image" on her blog and social media feeds in order to "maintain the popularity of [her] blogshop." She believes that naming her blogshop and commercial Twitter and Instagram feeds after her popular blog easily signals to readers that these platforms are an extension of herself (Hopkins 2015, 10), and that the reputation she has built on one platform will have a halo effect (Dittmar 2008; Nisbett and Wilson 1977) on the others, thus giving her customers "security and trust."

In the same vein, Mae uses her legal name "Mae Tan" on her personal Facebook account, but her commercial persona "marxmae" on her monetized blog, Twitter, Instagram, and YouTube. However, unlike Tammy, who wants to be congruently known as "ohsofickle" so that her newer platforms can latch on to the repute of her more established ones, Mae prefers to separate herself from her social media enterprises:

> I feel that marxmae is a brand but not me . . . I actually don't like people to call me marx-mae . . . it's like so lame lah . . . I just got over it . . . like why should I become marxmae when my name is Mae Tan?

Mae implies that her master status is "Mae Tan," the legal name she was given at birth, whereas "marxmae" is the commercial persona she has developed on social media. What Mae's preference signposts is the emic distinction between the "commercial" and "personal" personae that Influencers adopt. However, her gripe over being called "marxmae" even when meeting with people in person emphasizes the undeniable connection between the personal and the commercial.

Although both Tammy and Mae refer to their Influencer monikers "ohsofickle" and "marxmae" as "brands," deeper conversations during our interviews clarify that what they emically mean is brand name, as opposed to brand identity or brand image. Brand identity comprises producers' constructions and encodings of meanings and values, while brand image comprises consumers' receptions and evaluations of these encoded meanings and values (Malefyt and Morais 2012, 100).

Brand name, however, refers to the trademark designation by which a product is known. That is, the Influencers were more concerned with the congruence and uniformity of their primary Internet handle, other web pseudonyms they might own, and their legal name. This is underscored by the fact that many Influencers who initially held varying user handles across their social media platforms eventually made them congruent. For example, jamietyj, who started off with a range of handles including "Jamie TYJ," "Jamie Tan," "Tan Yi Jing," and "Jamie Tan Yi Jing," is now uniformly known as "jamietyj" on all her commercial social media platforms.

Brand naming aside, Influencers are also concerned with the congruence of the types of products and services they advertise, as this remains one of their client's primary interests. An Influencer who is known for marketing "authentic replicas" or "knock-offs" is unlikely to be hired by clients selling the genuine product, although this does not mean an Influencer cannot simultaneously display counterfeit and genuine products when curating their personae. An Influencer who has recently advertised for a competitor is unlikely to be hired by other clients in the same industry. In other words, Influencers carry the baggage of past personae curations and advertorials whenever they are being considered for a new contract.

While fashion models are best promoted to clients as blank canvases with the allowance to embody the products advertised, Influencers differ slightly by projecting facets of their personae onto the advertised product. It has been noted that advertisers are shifting from promoting "rational public decision making" to marketing "personal sensations," using sentiment that is "more private, personal, and individually interpreted" (Malefyt and Morais 2012, 62). Being situated between advertisers and consumers, Influencers aptly become intermediaries of these "personal sensations" when they embed products for sale into their personal lives and depiction of lifestyles through the device of the advertorial. Their highly personalized approach makes ambiguous the distinction between private and public portrayals, such that they are able to harness the relatability they have established with followers to exercise impact upon purchasing decisions.

However, this not to say that Influencers have the freedom to take up any or as many engagement or sponsorship deals as they wish. Because the best Influencers are able to project their persona onto any product marketed, many brands include clauses in their contracts stipulating that an engaged Influencer is not to advertise for competitors within the same industry for a period of time. This usually varies between three months and a year, depending on the type of engagement. In the back-end, Influencer managers curate conscientious charts for their Influencers to prevent an overlap of competing engagements. Influencers who use more than one brand of a product will be careful not to reveal this incongruence in their candid—that is personal and non-sponsored—shots on social media. During my fieldwork, such slips occurred only very occasionally, and Influencer managers would quickly rectify the situation by calling upon Influencers to remove or edit their original social media posts. The testament to the effectiveness of Influencers' relatability is manifested in the ways countless brands and companies attempt to associate their product with Influencers in their advertising efforts. Overt promotional material tends to privilege an Influencer's endorsement of the product over its actual benefits and uses.

A Decade and Beyond

In the decade since its debut, Influencer commerce in Singapore has matured and expanded with the earliest cohorts moving into different life stages and monetizing several other aspects of their personal lives such as the "microcelebrity" (Abidin 2015a) of their young children, and "power coupling" of their romantic partners. Future research may focus on the expansion of their persona onto other areas of society (i.e. politics, housing), their commercial framings of proximate others (parents, partners, children, friends), appropriations of newer media (i.e. Snapchat, Weibo), emergent models of advertising (i.e. group YouTube channels), and their international impact.

Notes

1 Throughout this chapter I use feminine pronouns as the default for the lifestyle genre but also even feminized in praxis among the few prominent male Influencers.
2 ohsofickle.blogspot.com.
3 ohsofickle.com.sg.

References

Abidin, Crystal. 2013a. "Cyber-BFFs: Assessing women's 'Perceived Interconnectedness' in Singapore's commercial lifestyle blog industry." *Global Media Journal, Australian Edition* 7(1): 1–20.
———. 2013b. "'Cya IRL': Researching digital communities online and offline." *Limina* 18(2) Special Edition (2013): Humanising Collaboration.
———. 2013c. "#lifeisgood: Understanding social currency in the female commercial blog industry in Singapore." *ISA eSymposium for Sociology 2013*, isa.e-Forum.
———. 2014a. "Privacy for profit: Commodifying privacy in lifestyle blogging." *Selected Papers of Internet Research 15: The 15th Annual Meeting of the Association of Internet Researchers.* Accessed August 5, 2016 from www.academia.edu/15311632/Privacy_for_Profit_Commodifying_Privacy_in_Lifestyle_Blogging
———. 2014b. "#In$tagLam: Instagram as a repository of taste, a brimming marketplace, a war of eyeballs." In *Mobile Media Making in the Age of Smartphones*, edited by Marsha Berry and Max Schleser, 119–28. London: Palgrave Pivot.

———. 2015a. "Microcelebrity: Branding babies on the Internet." *M/C Journal* 18(5). Accessed October 27, 2015 from http://journal.media-culture.org.au/index.php/mcjournal/article/view Article/1022.

———. 2015b. "Communicative <3 Intimacies: Influencers and perceived interconnectedness." *Ada: A Journal of Gender, New Media, & Technology* 8. Accessed August 5, 2016 from http://adanewmedia. org/2015/11/issue8-abidin/

———. 2016a. "Agentic cute (^.^): (En)gendering cuteness in Singaporean commercial blogs." *East Asian Journal of Popular Culture* 2(1): 33–47.

———. 2016b. "Aren't these just young, rich women doing vain things online? Influencer selfies as subversive frivolity." *Social Media + Society* 2(2): 1–17.

———. (forthcoming a, 2016). "#sexbait: Sex talk on commercial blogs as informal sexuality education." In *Palgrave Handbook of Sexuality Education*, edited by Louisa Allen and Mary Lou Rasmussen. Basingstoke: Palgrave Macmillan. Accessed August 5, 2016 from www.palgrave.com/us/book/ 9781137400321#aboutAuthors

———. (forthcoming b, 2017). "Screens, streams, scenes, screams: Labouring sociality among young women Influencers." In [*Title TBC*], edited by Miriam Forman-Burnell and Diana Anselmo-Sequeira. Illinois: University of Illinois Press.

Abidin, Crystal, and Mart Ots. 2015. "The Influencer's dilemma: The shaping of new brand professions between credibility and commerce." *Association for Education in Journalism and Mass Communication (AEJMC)*, August. Accessed August 5, 2016 from www.academia.edu/16152220/The_Influencer_s_ dilemma_The_shaping_of_new_brand_professions_between_credibility_and_commerce

Abidin, Crystal, and Eric C. Thompson. 2012. "Buymylife.com: Cyber-femininities and commercial intimacy in blogshops." *Women's Studies International Forum* 35: 467–77.

Aw Yeong, Benita. 2013. "Instagram is fastest growing media application among mobile-savvy users here." *The New Paper*, September 1. Accessed August 5, 2016 from www2.tnp.sg/content/instagram-fastest-growing-media-application-among-mobile-savvy-users-here.

Blashki, Katherine, and Sophie Nichol. 2005. "Game Geek's Goss: Linguistic creativity in young males within an online university forum (94//3933k's 9055ONEONE)." *Australian Journal of Emerging Technologies and Society* 3(2): 77–86.

Chiew, Kristie. 2009. "From blog to riches." *Straits Times*, April 28, INS p. 8.

Chua, Beng-Huat. 1998. "World Cities, globalisation and the spread of consumerism: A view from Singapore." *Urban Studies* 35(5–6): 981–1000.

———. 2002. *Consumption in Asia: Lifestyle and identities.* New York: Routledge.

Chung, Gladys. 2010a. "Net worth." *Straits Times*, June 25, URBAN, pp. 13–14.

Chung, Gladys. 2010b. "Plastic fantastic." *Straits Times*, July 2, URBAN, p. 15.

Currie, Dawn. 1999. *Girl Talk: Adolescent magazines and their readers.* Toronto: University of Toronto Press Incorporated.

Dittmar, Helga. 2008. *Consumer Culture, Identity and Well-Being.* New York: Psychology Press.

Fletcher, Gordon, and Anita Greenhill. 2009. "Blog/shop: It is authentic so don't worry^^^." *Journal of Information, Communication and Ethics in Society* 7(1): 39–53.

Forbes, Duncan. 1993. "Singlish." *English Today* 9(2): 18–22.

Greenhill, Anita, and Gordon Fletcher. 2011. "Reframing online shopping through innovative and organic user-oriented design." In *Reframing Humans in Information Systems Development*, edited by H. Isomäki and S. Pekkola, 243–62. London: Springer.

Gwynne, Joel, and Crystal Abidin. (forthcoming). "Entrepreneurial selves, feminine corporeality, and lifestyle blogging in Singapore." *Asian Journal of Social Science.*

Heng, Edvarcl. 2009. "Social selling." *Straits Times*, October 7, DIGITAL LIFE, p. 8.

Herring, Susan C., and Asta Zelenkauskaite. 2009. "Symbolic capital in a virtual heterosexual market: Abbreviation and insertion in Italian iTV SMS." *Written Communication* 26(1): 5–31.

Hopkins, Julian. 2015. "Assembling blog affordances: Theorizing affordances and agency in new media." *Working paper for the EASA Media Anthropology Network's 51st e-Seminar.*

iDA. 2012. *Infocomm Usage: Households and Individuals.* Infocomm Development Authority of Singapore. Accessed April 10, 2013 from www.ida.gov.sg/Infocomm-Landscape/Facts-and-Figures/Infocomm-Usage-Households-and-Individuals.aspx#.UKyLS-3ajVJ (no longer available).

Katz, Elihu, and Paul F. Lazarsfeld. 2009. *Personal Influence: The part played by people in the flow of mass communications.* New Brunswick, NJ: Transaction Publishers.

Liew, Hattie. 2016. "Anti-fandom, moral panic and Singapore's celebrity blogger, Xiaxue." *Poster session presented at the 66th ICA Annual Conference,* Fukuoka, Japan, June 9–13.

Malefyt, Timothy de Waal, and Robert J. Morais. 2012. *Advertising and Anthropology: Ethnographic practice and cultural perspectives.* London: Berg.

Marwick, Alice E. 2013. *Status Update: Celebrity, publicity, & branding in the social media age.* New Haven, CT: Yale University Press.

Ng, Magdalen. 2009. "Model owners." *Straits Times,* September 27, LIFE, p. 6.

Nisbett, Richard, and Timothy Wilson. 1977. "The halo effect: Evidence for unconscious alteration of judgments." *Journal of Personality and Social Psychology* 35: 250–6.

Ots, Mart, and Crystal Abidin. 2015. "Commercialism, audience intimacy and brand credibility in fashion blogging." Paper presented at the conference *Communicative democracy: Protecting, promoting and developing free speech in the digital era,* October 6–7, University of Gothenburg. Accessed August 5, 2016 from http://law.handels.gu.se/forskning/forskningsprojekt/Marknadsdriven+yttrandefrihet/konferens—conference

Roberts, Kelvin. 2004. *Lovemarks: The future beyond brands.* New York: Powerhouse.

Rojek, Chris. 2001. *Celebrity.* London: Reaktion Books.

Senft, Theresa. M. 2008. *Camgirls: Celebrity & community in the age of social networks.* New York: Peter Lang.

Sinanan, Jolynna, Connor Graham, and Kua Zhong Jie. 2014. "Crafted assemblage: Young women's 'lifestyle' blogs, consumerism and citizenship in Singapore." *Visual Studies* 29(2): 201–13.

STcommunities. 2013. "Social Star Awards 2013: List of winners." *Straits Times,* May 23. Accessed January 2, 2014 from http://stcommunities.straitstimes.com/music/2013/05/23/social-star-awards-2013-list-winners

Veblen, Thorstein. 1961. *The Theory of the Leisure Class.* New York: Random House.

Zappavigna, Michele. 2012. *The Discourse of Twitter and Social Media.* London: Continuum.

15

NAH LEAVIN' TRINIDAD

The Place of Digital Music Production among Amateur Musicians in Trinidad and Tobago

Sheba Mohammid and Heather Horst

Introduction

Throughout the world digital media technologies have contributed to the transformation of music—especially its production, distribution, circulation and consumption—across different scales. At the micro-level, the experience of music sharing and listening has altered consumption. In contrast to the circulation of cassettes and CDs, music listeners now circulate MP3 files over Bluetooth networks via mobile and laptops, through the exchange of SD cards and flash drives and even through the increasing number of accessories that enable the sharing of music through multiple earbuds and small, portable speakers connected to smartphones and laptops (Sterne 2012; Bickford 2014). Designated music distribution sites such as iTunes and Spotify and video content aggregation sites such as YouTube or Vimeo are also shaping how, when and where people are able to listen to music (Gopinath and Stanyek 2014; Wasko and Erickson 2009).

While the proliferation of the channels of circulation is remarkable, for many musicians the increased accessibility and affordability of digital media technologies software to record, edit and remix music has shifted where music production occurs. Rather than requiring traveling and expensive fees to rent space in the centralized studio production of urban centers such as Los Angeles and London, music production can take place in homes via laptops and computers (Wikström 2013). It is no longer remarkable to see musicians across the world building home studios to create, edit and remix music (e.g. Crowdy 2007). Recent work focusing upon the implications of digital media technologies for the music industry, however, suggests that the places of music production and its consumption have changed. As Allington et al. suggest, "it is not important for the individual music-maker to be in any specific location," precisely because musicians continue to "orient to clearly located centers in the global cultural economy" (2015, 214). Within the dance music scene for example, Allington et al. argue these centers—which become "scenes" for music—continue to be locations such as London, New York and the San Francisco Bay area. Yet there remains little research on the implications of these changes and the significance of place in areas of the world that are often viewed as disconnected or marginal within the global system of music production. To what extent do digital media technologies provide access to new connections and audiences for musicians living in the historically defined margins? How might the centers and margins of music production be rethought or redefined?

This chapter explores the implications of the changing music landscape and the role of the place in music production and consumption through the lives of musicians based in Trinidad and Tobago (T&T). Drawing upon ethnographic research focused upon digital media technologies, informal learning and the knowledge society in urban T&T between 2015 and 2016, we consider the different ways in which musicians navigate this landscape and their exposure to new music, techniques and worlds through digital media technologies. We begin this chapter with a brief discussion of music in T&T before turning to three key trends in the uptake of digital media technologies by musicians currently based in T&T. We conclude by reflecting upon the consequences of these practices around digital music production for musicians' career aspirations.

Music Production in Trinidad and Tobago

Trinidad and Tobago is a significant site through which to understand how digital media technologies are shaping music production given the nation's long history of local music production. Genres such as soca and calypso continue to flourish through their connection to Trinidad's annual Carnival (Birth 1994; Dudley 2003; Warner 1982), and their scope is expanding through T&T's close connection to metropolitan sites such as London and New York through transnational migration (Scher 2003; Nurse 1999; Green and Scher 2007; Henry et al. 2001). In the lead up to Carnival from the December Christmas season until March, people search for popular musicians such as Machel Montano, Bunji Garlin, Fay Ann Lyons and others who have songs on the radio and are playing in *fetes* (large parties). They also share links to the videos with their friends on WhatsApp and talk about the songs that they think are the "hottest."

Many people in Belleton—a local community in Port-of-Spain where Mohammid carried out research—noted that their aunt, cousin, brother or friends from New York and London tune in during the Carnival season on YouTube or local sites such as TriniJungleJuice or TriniCarnivalDiary to locate calypso and soca tunes. Like other Caribbean countries, these transnational landscapes reflect the importance given to migration and "travel" (Horst 2006; Potter et al. 2005; Olwig 2007; Olwig and Sørenson 2002). It also represents an example of the importance of the diaspora's desire to connect with music during Carnival time (Tanikella 2009). This may be a prelude to their visit for Carnival or a way to nurse a feeling of heartache (*tabanca*), as it is known in T&T for not being at home.

At the same time engagement with gospel, pop, R&B, hip hop and other global genres sits alongside more locally produced music (Miller 1994; Rommen 2007). Exposure to global genres often occurs through local radio stations and through watching television music and entertainment channels such as MTV, VH1 and Black Entertainment Television (BET). Indeed, the popularity of Trinidadian-born Nikki Minaj and Barbadian Rihanna in the international music industry speaks to the Caribbean influence in these global genres. Increasingly, however, engagement with non-locally produced music is also occurring through YouTube (McDonald 2009). T&T musicians articulate the value of YouTube for music listening, exposure to new techniques and skills and promoting yourself and your music, and view YouTube as a space of experimentation and navigation as local musicians work to develop their craft and grapple with questions about their audience and reach. In the following section we begin by discussing how musicians use digital media technologies to build their skills in producing music and we then move on to explore the opportunities and tensions they face in extending their reach.

Making Music: Accessing, Learning and Production Resources Online

Aspiring musicians from the Belleton community use digital media technologies as online resources for skill development and music production. One of the participants in the research, Sarah (aged 26), believes that with new technology she now has tools and opportunities that she would never have had in Trinidad before. She works full time but is also part of a duo of DJs and a group that participates in Soundclashes, remixing tunes and adding electronic beats to transform their rhythms. She creates what she sees at Dance Anthems remixing mainly Caribbean tunes, many of which are from Jamaica. Sarah only studied music briefly in school in lower forms and did not pursue it for her O Levels (national examinations). She was not formally trained but has had a passion for music and started playing around with remixing music content that she found online. She learned how to use the majority of her software through YouTube tutorials and is enthusiastic about the prospect of being able to stay in the know and constantly upgrade her skills to become a better DJ.

Sarah's example of watching YouTube tutorials and adapting them in her own practice is typical of other aspiring musicians in T&T (Waldron 2012). Many musicians have not been formally trained but engage in informal learning that is situated in their everyday lives, and in processes of making and doing rather than via music theory (Lave and Wenger 1991). They actively engage in interest-driven learning that is production centered and peer supported (Ito et al. 2010) and often might not have had many opportunities for formal music education or lessons. For this reason, they actively seek and use resources online, applying and developing a range of media literacies from discovery to judgment to critical thinking and creation (Jenkins 2009; Hobbs 2010). Through these activities they orchestrate their own learning experiences, sifting through tutorials, practicing their craft and appropriating and remixing content. They also engage in experiential and experimental learning of software, instruments and techniques and these experiences are embedded in an interplay of online and offline communities.

Making Connections: Engaging in Communities of Practice

One of the most important dimensions of the online space for Trinidadian musicians is the ability to make new connections with other musicians who share expertise and information. Besides being a crucial part of her production process, DJ Sarah also uses the web to share the content she has created and to make connections. She is able to participate in communities of practice by gaining mastery and exchanging expertise with people who share her interest, which, in turn, helps to develop her identity as a musician (Lave and Wenger 1991; Wenger 1998). Her YouTube page is the most valuable to her but she also uses Facebook and SoundCloud. Her videos on YouTube include a mix of local gigs, jam sessions and visits abroad to music festivals, and have grown from a few hundred to a few thousand "likes." Some of the videos are of performances and the crowd while the group plays. Other videos detail journeys to music festivals and feature other bands, artists and DJs that are performing at these events. Yet what she raves about is not the number of hits on these sites, but the strategic connections she has been able to make.

By uploading videos on YouTube and liking and commenting on other musicians' sites she has made connections with other people who are interested in her genres of remixes. These have included fans as well as performers, promoters and people in the music industry who have invited her (and her partner and group) to music festivals, and sound clashes across the world (Baym 2007). To date, they have visited Toronto, Barbados and the Netherlands to play in music festivals and government ministries in T&T have also sponsored her performances abroad. Sarah is particularly enthused that they are getting such international exposure and people around the world are appreciating her music while she is able to stay in Trinidad with her family.

Making It on YouTube: Reaching Audiences and Increasing Fans

Local musicians perceive digital media technologies as an important part of music production and distribution. Some musicians are enthusiastic about digital media technologies as they believe they afford the opportunity to engage with their fan base, grow their audience and demonstrate success. Listening to music is an important part of life in T&T, emanating from cars, houses and commuters with earphones in their ears. Looking up music videos and playlists on YouTube is an everyday activity that often revolves around foreign genres and musicians and there is a widespread sense that in order to be a legitimate artist, you need a strong YouTube following marked by a substantial number of views. One example of this is a group of young people who attend a community church in Belleton and use YouTube to search for music for their worship sessions and youth groups. In addition to international gospel music stars such as Hillsong and Jesus Culture, many of the young people in the group are avid fans of a Trinidadian musician called Positive, a "rootsy" Christian singer from Port-of-Spain. Positive decided to share his music via the YouTube channel, PositiveTnt. He has over 7,000 subscribers and viewers who listen to his music and he has had views ranging from a few thousand to over 200,000 for one of his songs, "Mighty Healer." He received over 400,000 views for another song "Blessing after Blessing." Many people first heard of him on local radio stations and the Facebook page of the local radio station where Positive's fans talk about him, a practice that normally occurs with foreign musicians' videos, unusual for local musicians outside of the soca genre whose fans typically attend concerts as forms of support. People often describe Positive as an example of a local musician who has "got through" or made it. His popularity on YouTube is a testament to this and many amateur musicians in T&T attribute his success to his use of digital media technologies to achieve stardom.

Making It Big "Out There"

Many people across T&T cite Positive as an example of a local musician who has gained regional success while being based in Trinidad, and DJ Sarah feels she can reach and expand her fanbase and networks with fellow musicians through her online presence while living in T&T. Many other musicians, however, believe that the Internet and going online does not mitigate the need to migrate to the metropolis to "make it." Frank, for example, is an aspiring singer and bass player who works in business administration full time but performs ballads, sings cover songs and writes his own songs. He would ideally like to pursue his music professionally as a career but feels that T&T is too limited to offer him the opportunity to make a living through a creative career like music. Frank considers an online presence as linked to any chance of making it while he is still in T&T and believes there is the promise of being discovered on YouTube.

Burgess and Green (2009) argue that it is now common for individual stories to be used to mythologize success on YouTube. Frank acknowledges that it is a slim shot and posits he perhaps has a "one in a million" chance of being discovered, but he does not want to waste this chance so he uploads videos that are mainly covers of American songs with a couple of his originals. However, Frank is reluctant to upload originals in case someone steals his songs or lyrics. Instead, he uploads songs that he plays regularly at gigs which he is willing to "put out there," as he feels confident that people know that the songs belong to him. The songs themselves are performed in his bedroom, typically with Frank propped up against the bedpost, singing into the camera. He puts up a video every couple of months and currently has about 80 subscribers to his channel. His most popular videos have about 100 views. He feels that this is slow, but it is still progress. He is happy that his music is getting out there and is motivated by the idea that someone out there will hear his song and connect to it. He is particularly thrilled to receive feedback and comments on the music he uploads.

Alongside YouTube, Frank also established a SoundCloud page where he has put up 12 tracks, all covers of ballads. This is a site where musicians can put up music and people can listen for free. He only has eight followers here but is happy that he has started creating a presence online and feels that musicians should have a SoundCloud page as well as their YouTube one. A few of his local musician friends have also put up SoundCloud pages with music. He does worry a bit about issues of intellectual property and piracy online as one of the risks of exposing and marketing one's work, and does not believe he has yet found the right balance. Frank considers quite carefully how he constructs his online presence and what songs he uploads.

Although Frank has invested some time in his YouTube and SoundCloud pages and enjoys performing gigs and shows every few months in Trinidad, he feels that he must go abroad to "make it." He spent some time in New York when he was younger and feels that he must move back there if he is serious about a musical career. He works as an administrative clerk at a government ministry full time and is debating with his girlfriend whether they should leave their jobs and migrate to New York. There is a chance of acquiring citizenship because his mother lives there still. He feels that he is in a state of limbo where he feels unsatisfied with his job here and that he is getting older and his dreams of a professional musical career cannot, happen in T&T. His country is a limited place for Frank when it comes to achieving international success. While YouTube and SoundCloud are necessary marketing tools no matter where you are, he believes that you must leave the island and go abroad to a place with a more developed music industry if you want to have a serious career.

Place, Music and Mobility

The three examples reveal some of the realities of digital music and technologies for musicians in T&T. On the one hand, there has been a history of a music industry fraught with barriers to entry with respect to the ability to produce music. For many of the local musicians, albums and releasing songs were intermittent and they relied upon poor tools of production. Digital media technologies have in many ways changed and even reduced the entry barriers for production, providing access to production and editing software available internationally. Amateur and aspiring musicians use YouTube tutorials and online sites as skill development resources as they practice, experiment with and evolve their craft. Other musicians have created studios at home or in local contexts and hire out their studio in the same way that more formal music production practices do. They have expanded the scope through which they can reach people.

While production can now easily occur in T&T with, arguably, the same quality as what might occur in other locations, the distribution models should be viewed as complex. On the one hand, it is possible to both consolidate and expand one's fanbase online through sites such as YouTube or Facebook groups as we see in the case of local celebrities like Positive. Others, such as DJ Sarah, use digital media technologies to share the content created and to liaise with new and different communities of practice (Lave and Wenger 1991; Wenger 1998). However, for Frank, accessing music scenes through digital media technologies from Trinidad is limited, despite the fact that Frank and Sarah's practices and use of particular platforms and networks are very similar. Frank believes that creative industries in T&T are not adequately developed to offer him the exposure he needs.

What remains clear is that the extent to which musicians value digital media technologies is closely tied to their aspirations and notions of success. Although DJ Sarah's sphere of influence is more international, Sarah is content representing Trinidad and engaging in intermittent travel. Sarah lived abroad to pursue her university studies and feels that this opportunity to remain in Trinidad with her family and still stay in touch with the outside world through digital media technologies online is something that her generation enjoys in an unprecedented way. She notes that she feels lucky because she sees the Internet as affording her the opportunity to be based in T&T and still gain exposure to the outside world and "make it out there." In this sense, the scale at which Sarah seeks to operate is well served by the affordances of digital media technologies.

By contrast, Frank dreams of "making it," "making it big" and "making it away," interwoven concepts in the everyday lexicon of many Trinidadians who believe that international exposure or the idea of being a "world class" performer are the central markers of success. Being in Trinidad, to Frank, is limiting given the genres of music he writes and performs. Because he does not sing soca, calypso or anything else that may be regarded as "Trinidadian," he finds that the market is "too small" for what he would like to achieve. In this sense, and unlike Sarah, connecting to the "scene" through digital media technologies is not enough (Allington et al. 2015). Making it big, or taking things to the next level, requires immersing oneself in the established centers of music production, associated scenes, and face-to-face communities there.

Conclusion

The interplay of global and local content consumption and production has transformed everyday music practice. Musicians in T&T are enthusiastic about accessing music online. While the majority of the music is foreign in origin and production, aspiring musicians are increasingly able to access informal learning resources and production tools online that facilitate greater production development opportunities while staying "at home" in T&T. Yet there remains some ambivalence surrounding distribution and whether you can truly base your music career locally or whether you must migrate to the metropolis. On one level, musicians use the Internet to spread the word about local artists and their music, especially around Carnival or when tied to a community of shared interest such as a church youth group and local gospel singers. Local musicians feel that if they want to "make it big out there" they need to have an online presence. Some musicians complain that this is ultimately futile because the industry in Trinidad is too limited and they must go abroad to achieve success. Others, however, are realizing opportunities for their music to be promoted abroad through online channels while they are still in Trinidad. There is also a concern among amateur musicians who may see the value of marketing their music online to foreign markets but are reluctant to do so because of concerns that they do not feel they are at a professional standard.

The question of whether this popular allure of "making it away" is a criterion for success or if success can be redefined by developing the industry locally is fundamental to understanding if and how the supposed de-centering of the global music industry, spurred by digital media technologies, has changed musicians' practices. By focusing upon musicians' aspirations to increase their audience or fanbase, to gain skills and connections or "make it big," we can see how the kinds of aspirations musicians have for their craft—what can be described as attainment or expansive realization in seminal studies of the Internet in Trinidad (Miller and Sinanan 2013; Miller and Slater 2001)—determine the value of digital media technologies in their lives. One could suggest that these technologies have made a significant contribution to the expansion of the local industry, if only through the proliferation of DIY or amateur musicians and artists who can use digital media technologies to hone their craft. Yet, there are also perspectives that propose notions of success and "making it" still revolve around the same centers of music production and thus also suggest that these centers still hold despite changes to the margins. It is clear that there are complex negotiations within geographies of production as musicians in these spaces. This ethnographic research on the amateur music community in T&T therefore provides nuanced understanding of the conditions creative entrepreneurs are operating under, as well as the constraints and opportunities they face in the global and digital arena.

References

Allington, Daniel, Byron Dueck, and Anna Jordanous. 2015. "Networks of value in electronic music: SoundCloud, London, and the importance of place." *Cultural Trends* 24(3): 211–22.

Baym, Nancy K. 2007. "The new shape of online community: The example of Swedish independent music fandom." *First Monday*, 12(8).

Bickford, Tyler. 2014. "Earbuds are good for sharing: Children's headphones as social media at a Vermont school." In *The Oxford Handbook of Mobile Music Studies*, vol. 1, edited by Jason Stanyek and Sumanth Gopinath, 335–55. New York: Oxford University Press.

Birth, Kevin K. 1994. "Bakrnal: Coup, carnival, and calypso in Trinidad." *Ethnology* 33(2): 165–77.

Burgess, Jean, and Joshua Green, Eds. 2009. *YouTube: Online Video and Participatory Culture*. Cambridge: Polity.

Crowdy, Denis. 2007. "Studios at home in the Solomon Islands: A case study of Homesound Studios, Honiara." *The World of Music* 49(1): 143–54.

Dudley, Shannon. 2003. *Carnival Music in Trinidad: Experiencing Music, Expressing Culture*. New York: Oxford University Press.

——. 2007. *Music from Behind the Bridge: Steelband Aesthetics and Politics in Trinidad and Tobago*. Oxford: Oxford University Press.

Gopinath, Sumanth, and Jason Stanyek. 2014. "Introduction." *The Oxford Handbook of Mobile Music Studies*, 1: 1–36. Oxford: Oxford University Press.

Green, Garth L., and Philip W. Scher, Eds. 2007. *Trinidad Carnival: The Cultural Politics of a Transnational Festival*. Bloomington, IN: Indiana University Press.

Henry, Ralph, Alvin Daniell, and Stein Trotman. 2001. "The Music Industry in Trinidad and Tobago." *Report prepared for World Intellectual Property Organization* (2001).

Hobbs, Renee. 2010. *Digital and Media Literacy: A Plan of Action*. Washington, DC: The Aspen Institute.

Horst, Heather A. 2006. "The blessings and burdens of communication: Cell phones in Jamaican transnational social fields." *Global Networks* 6(2): 143–59.

Ito, Mizuko, et al. 2010. *Hanging Out, Messing Around and Geeking Out: Kids Living and Learning with New Media*. Cambridge, MA: MIT Press.

Jenkins, Henry. 2009. *Confronting the Challenges of Participatory Culture: Media Education for the 21st Century*. Cambridge, MA: MIT Press.

Lave, Jean, and Etienne Wenger. 1991. *Situated Learning: Legitimate Peripheral Participation*. Cambridge: Cambridge University Press.

McDonald, Paul. 2009. "Digital discords in the online media economy: Advertising versus content versus copyright." In *The YouTube Reader*, edited by P. Snickars and P. Vonderau, 387–405. Stockholm: National Library of Sweden.

Miller, Daniel. 1994. *Modernity: An Ethnographic Approach: Dualism and Mass Consumption in Trinidad*. Oxford: Berg.

Miller, Daniel, and Jolynna Sinanan. 2013. *Webcam*. Cambridge: Polity.

Miller, Daniel, and Don Slater. 2001. *The Internet: An Ethnographic Approach*. Oxford: Berg.

Nurse, Keith. 1999 "Globalization and Trinidad Carnival: Diaspora, hybridity and identity in global culture." *Cultural Studies* 13(4): 661–90.

Olwig, Karen Fog. 2007. *Caribbean Journeys: An Ethnography of Migration and Home in Three Family Networks*. Durham, NC: Duke University Press.

Olwig, Karen Fog, and Ninna Nyberg Sørensen. 2002. "Mobile livelihoods." In *Work and Migration: Life and Livelihoods in a Globalizing World*, edited by Karen Fog Olwig and Ninna Nyberg Sørensen, 1–19. London: Routledge.

Potter, Robert B., Dennis Conway, and Joan Phillips. 2005. *The Experience of Return Migration: Caribbean Perspectives*. London: Gower Publishing.

Rommen, Timothy. 2007 *"Mek some noise": Gospel Music and the Ethics of Style in Trinidad*. Berkeley, CA: University of California Press.

Scher, Philip W. 2003. *Carnival and the Formation of a Caribbean Transnation*. Gainsville, FL: University Press of Florida.

Sterne, Jonathan. 2012. *MP3: The Meaning of a Format*. Durham, NC: Duke University Press.

Tanikella, Leela. 2009. "Voices from home and abroad: New York City's Indo-Caribbean media." *International Journal of Cultural Studies* 12(2): 167–85.

Waldron, Janice. 2012. "Conceptual frameworks, theoretical models and the role of YouTube: Investigating informal music learning and teaching in online music community." *Journal of Music, Technology & Education* 4(2–3): 189–200.

Warner, Keith Q. 1982. *Kaiso! The Trinidad Calypso: A Study of the Calypso as Oral Literature*. Three Continents.

Wasko, Janet, and Mary Erickson. 2009. "The political economy of YouTube." In *The YouTube Reader*, edited by P. Snickars and P. Vonderau, 372–86. Stockholm: National Library of Sweden.

Wenger, Etienne. 1998. *Communities of Practice*. Cambridge: Cambridge University Press.

Wikström, Patrik. 2013. *The Music Industry: Music in the Cloud*. Cambridge: Polity.

Part IV

PLACE AND CO-PRESENCE

16

LOCATING EMERGING MEDIA

Ethnographic Reflections on Culture, Selfhood, and Place

Jordan Kraemer

Introduction: Space, Place, Media

Media have long shaped identities linked to place. Just as print media helped foster nationally imagined communities in the eighteenth and nineteenth centuries, emerging digital and social media are implicated in global and transnational networks in the twentieth. Yet new communication technologies, from mobile phones to the Internet, are not necessarily engendering the global world once predicted; instead, multiple social worlds and experiences of place proliferate. Ethnographic approaches provide insight into shifting configurations of identity, selfhood, and place through a critical empiricism that makes possible research across diverse sites and contexts, digital or otherwise.

In the early twenty-first century, for example, Berlin was transforming rapidly as a nexus of people, technologies, and new configurations of space and place. The once-divided city of Berlin was (and is) still being stitched together, the symbolic and geographic midpoint of post-Cold War Europe and Europe's ongoing cultural, political, and economic integration. By the late 2000s, many young adults moved to Berlin from Germany and elsewhere, part of a "knowledge" or creative class (Florida 2004), settling in the city's central districts.

Upon moving to Berlin, many joined social network sites for the first time, especially Facebook, and began using mobile devices more frequently. I conducted sustained ethnographic research over eleven months between 2007 and 2015, primarily in 2009–10, with small "friend circles" (*Freundeskreise*) and their extended networks online, to understand how emerging media are transforming urban European middle classes. In this chapter, I show how digital ethnography enables research across multiple sites and spaces, while inviting critical reflection on media, identity, and place making. One particular fieldwork incident illustrates an emerging European transnationalism, which I analyze as a form of geographic scale-making—that is, practices that produce the local, national, or global as spatial scales (Tsing 2005, 57–8; see also Brenner 1998; Marston 2000).

Many have explored what networked, digital communications entail for place and identity in a globalized, deterritorialized world. Thinking about place on transnationally circulating media, however, requires asking how identities come to be linked to place in the, well, first place. Cultural geographers contend that space and place are constructed culturally, suggesting that spatiality can form online. Anthropologists and Internet scholars, meanwhile, demonstrate that digital and online worlds exist as places in their own right where forms of social life flourish that cannot be predicted from their technological affordances (e.g., Boellstorff 2008; see also Baym 2010).

Online communities exist as legitimate places and, conversely, place-based communities exist online, such as national publics, regional networks, and local ways of living (Bernal 2006, 2014; Ellison et al. 2006). These accounts of place online, however, necessitate considering carefully what it means to talk about place; that is, what is a geographically based social formation when it takes place through the seemingly "placeless" Internet? I turn to ethnographic accounts of space and place to attend to the dimensions, temporalities, and scales of space and place, including non-representational registers of feeling and sensing. Non-representational approaches to place, for example, seek to account for how spatial experiences take shape through practice, interaction, and daily living in contingent ways (Anderson and Harrison 2010). Others reframe questions of scale and place making to rethink the connections, rhythms, and practices that constitute the "local" or "global" (e.g., Massey 1993; Marston et al. 2005; Lambek 2011).

The above inquiries all call attention to power and unevenness in the production of space and place, such as digital mapping, geotagging, and location services that render space uniform and homogeneous (e.g., DeNicola 2012). Considered broadly, emerging media, being simultaneously symbolic and material, provide an opportunity to rethink conceptual divides between matter and meaning in the ways they are engaged through daily, lived experience. In this view, emerging media shape experiences of place in ways that are always plural, heterogeneous, and uneven, stabilizing only temporarily.

"The Other Side of the Street Is a Bad Neighborhood"

In 2015, I returned to Berlin to reconnect with people and places from previous fieldwork. I found a city that had transformed rapidly, though many elements of life in Berlin endure.[1] Longstanding practices such as apartment sharing and subletting that were facilitated by web boards and Craigslist, for example, now increasingly take place through Airbnb and related "sharing economy" platforms. This coincided with demographic shifts ongoing since the *Wende*, or Turn, in 1989, and national German reunification in 1990. As my Airbnb host explained, he and his peers (having moved to this part of Berlin in the 1990s) could no longer afford hip districts like Kreuzberg (formerly in the West, bordering the Wall, and center of the lively German Turkish community; see Mandel 2008) or Friedrichshain in the former East. Remarking on the perceived divide between punk, edgy Kreuzberg and its shabbier, more residential neighbor Neukölln, home to numerous immigrant communities—the border of which ran past my rental apartment—he repeated what was clearly a familiar quip: "The other side of the street is a bad neighborhood."

These spatial and demographic changes cannot be separated from technological shifts. In a few short years, candybar-style "dumb" phones have disappeared, replaced by nearly ubiquitous smartphones, mostly touchscreen-based iPhones and their imitators. Airbnb did not exist in Berlin in 2010, but has since become immensely popular with "club tourists" (Rapp 2009) and other short-term visitors (including visiting researchers). These technologies have consequences for experiences of place, reshaping movements through urban space (think of restaurant recommendation apps or transit directions). But if emerging technologies do not necessarily replace local identities with global ones, nor simply reproduce geographically based communities online, what is happening? To investigate this, I want to lay out briefly ethnographic approaches to media and place.

Media have played a central role in fostering identities linked to place since at least the advent of print capitalism in the eighteenth and nineteenth centuries (e.g., Anderson 1991; Gellner 1983). By the twentieth century, electronic media such as cassettes, satellite television, and video games appeared poised to destabilize national boundaries and forms of selfhood linked to the nation. Anthropologists and others found, however, that national communities reassert themselves through new technological means, whether national television viewing in Egypt (Abu-Lughod 2005), or radio fostering a national speech community in Zambia through laterally circulating "public words" (Spitulnik 1996), among numerous examples (see also Mankekar 1999; Mazzarella 2004). In divided Germany, broadcast media contributed to the fall of the Berlin Wall, as many East Germans received West German radio and television. Through illicit consumption, many envisioned alternative lifeworlds, which incited growing political dissatisfaction (Hesse 1990).

Computer networks and mobile telephony were incipient when Germany reunified in 1990, but distributed unevenly—many West Germans had computers and video games, while most East Germans did not have household telephone lines. This divergent history shapes media practices still; for example, some young East Germans I knew shared their mobile phone handsets in ways that echo phone-sharing practices from the DDR[2] era (Schnöring and Szafran 1994). With the advent of the Internet and digital media, many predicted the realization of McLuhan's (2013 [1964]) "global village" or a global "space of flows" (Castells 1996). But digital media equally provide new means to articulate and enact local, national, and other place-based identities, as numerous examples of "virtual nationalism" attest (Bernal 2006, 2014; Lee 2007; Eriksen 2007), or of "geographically bound" communities such as college campus networks (e.g., Ellison et al. 2006).

If globally circulating media do not undermine place-based identities, nor replace parochial connections with cosmopolitan ones, how do emerging media reshape selfhood in relation to place? Anthropologists have contended since the 1980s and 1990s with increased mobility and deterritorialization under globalization (Appadurai 1996; Gupta and Ferguson 1992, 1997; Clifford 1992). Of course, human culture has long been predicated on circulation and exchange, from the Kula Ring of Papua New Guinea described by Bronislaw Malinowski (1922), Nancy Munn (1986), and others, to the interdependent "world-system" of Immanuel Wallerstein (1974; see also Wolf 1982). Arjun Appadurai (1996) proposed that mass media provide new imaginative resources for fashioning selfhood in a global, deterritorialized world, while David Harvey (1989) diagnosed the temporal and spatial effects of late modern capitalism in terms of "time-space compression," effectively making the world smaller.

Late modern reconfigurations of people, places, and identities challenge viewing culture as co-extensive with particular peoples or places, but what then does it mean to talk about identity or selfhood as place-based? Anthropologists and geographers address this by examining how space and place are constructed in uneven ways, pioneered by the work of Henri Lefebvre (1991). Anthropologist Setha Low, for example, calls attention to the political stakes of determining how spaces are produced and used (Low 2009, 2014; see also Munn 1986). Low argues that culture is "spatialized" in ways that mask ideological structures and inequalities: "both the production and the construction of space are mediated by social processes, especially being contested and fought over for economic and ideological reasons" (Low 2014, 35). How do we locate digital media in contingent cultural and historical processes that produce space and place?

Emerging Spatialities

Ethnographic accounts highlight the contingency of place making, offering a way to think about the production of space and place online. By this, however, I do not mean a singular, monolithic "cyberspace." As Daniel Miller and Don Slater (2000) noted, the Internet comprises an agglomerate of technologies, while online media practices always take place in specific, locatable instances: "what we were observing was not so much people's use of 'the Internet' but rather how they assembled various technical possibilities that added up to *their* Internet" (2000, 14). Cultural geographer Mark Graham similarly takes issue with spatial metaphors of the Internet that reduce a complex, relational networked space to a "distinct, immaterial, ethereal alternate dimension" (2013, 181). The metaphor of cyberspace evokes a separate dimension coterminous with physical space, everywhere yet nowhere. He advocates instead attending to multiple, complex spatialities that are always grounded, contingent, and material.

Spatial metaphors can make space and place appear natural and fixed, although this does not preclude online spaces and virtual worlds existing in their own right, as Tom Boellstorff (2008) and others have shown (e.g., Taylor 2006). In my work on social and mobile media, I find spatial terms like "local" or "global" inadequate to describing the multiplicity of spatial levels or scales that emerging media bring together—and reconfigure. Like print and broadcast, social and mobile platforms provide new means to enact relationships and worlds, bringing together lives and connections into the same spaces (Kraemer 2014). For those like Karoline, who moved to Berlin in 2007, Facebook brought together disparate parts of her life—friends from Magdeburg and from university, *Ausländer* (foreigners[3]) met in Berlin, and younger family members and work colleagues. Though this "context collapse" (cf. boyd 2014, 31–2) could spark tensions, Facebook did not necessarily homogenize social connections in a singular global space. Instead, it often became a nexus of conversations, communities, and interactions at multiple scales—not unlike cosmopolitan life in Berlin.

Conversely, the "local" scale of Berlin could also take place online. At a monthly *StrickenBar* (Knitting Bar), for example, one friend circle gathered to practice knitting over drinks. The event's Facebook page reflected aesthetics found in bars and cafés in Berlin,[4] and illustrated ways local life "offline" unfolded on Facebook (see Figure 16.1). The local here might be understood not as a scale, but as an affect or structure of feeling (Lambek 2011). Michael Lambek proposes rethinking the local as a tempo constituted through particular rhythms, activities, and feelings rather than an instance of some global phenomenon: "the site at which these multiple activities and temporalities . . . are lived simultaneously" (2011, 208). Local life in Berlin could be inhabited online through imagery, language practices, shared references, and shared affect specific to Berlin.

The notion of spatial scale, however, risks evoking a concentric circle that expands outward from the local to the national and the global. Cultural geographers and others contest this depiction, construing such levels instead as constellations of policy, infrastructure, circuits of capital, and so forth (Brenner 1998, 2001; Marston 2000; see also Massey 1993). Others question the utility of scale as an analytic and advocate doing away with vertical models of scale entirely. Marston et al. (2005), for example, propose a "flat ontology" that allows emergent spatialities to unfold by "accounting for socio-spatiality as it occurs throughout

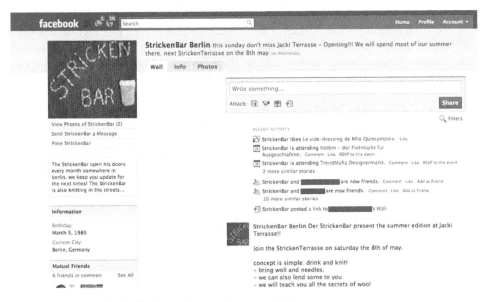

Figure 16.1   *StrickenBar* Berlin Event Page on Facebook, 2010

the Earth without requiring prior, static conceptual categories" (2005, 425). Such ontological and non-representational approaches (Anderson and Harrison 2010) attend to practices, enactments, affects, and material relationships rather than symbolic representations.

From my perspective as an anthropologist, media provoke pressing questions about space and place precisely because they are constituted materially *and* symbolically,[5] locatable yet circulating instantaneously. On returning to Berlin in 2015, I observed emerging media practices that link together people and places in an emerging European transnationalism: that is, a shared sense of Europeanness rarely articulated as such. Alongside anthropologists of affect such as Kathleen Stewart, I consider scenes of daily living to account for broader meanings and forces through embodied practice: "this is not to say that the forces these [totalized] systems try to name are not real and literally pressing. On the contrary, I am trying to bring into view as a scene of immanent force, rather than leave them looking like dead effects imposed on an innocent world" (Stewart 2007, 1).

European Transnationalism on Social Media

On January 7, 2015—one week into my stay in Berlin—two gunmen opened fire in the Paris offices of *Charlie Hebdo*, a French satirical publication featuring incendiary cartoons. Though the journal purports to target all religions equally, many find cartoons depicting Mohammed and Muslim themes exemplify widespread anti-Muslim sentiment in Europe. The attack by Arabic-speaking assailants (later identified as two French Algerian brothers) sent shockwaves through the Internet, and illustrated a European transnationalism forming in part through social media. News of the attack raced across my European Facebook and Twitter feeds,[6] provoking emotional, politically charged responses from many who avoided such topics otherwise.

Annette, who had friends and family in Paris, posted: "Sorry for the sad & political post. Anyone with an interest in the French political press know who these two persons are (were, sadly),"[7] with a link to the Twitter status of the French *LePoint*, showing photos of two murdered cartoonists. Comments piled up in French, German, and English, and Annette cut short one convoluted response, saying: "I don't want this post to turn into high-school political debate. Kthxbye." She posted frequently that afternoon, from a humorous image warning readers not to "discard brain," to a YouTube clip from a French children's show from the 1980s, featuring one of the cartoonists as an actor, writing:

> Second sad post today. Fuck everything about this. Non-French speakers: this is one of the victims of today's attack in Paris, a famous satirical cartoonist, who appeared in what was by far the best-known children TV show in this country in the 80s. He shouldn't have been murdered by idiots.

She moved between English and French, and in effect, between possible audiences. She also responded to a Facebook event page called "*Je Suis Charlie*," for a gathering in front of the French consulate in Berlin. The post was titled in French and German, and 209 people had also responded. A few hours later, that number had jumped to 1,136. In the comments, Annette added: "People not in Berlin," with a link to similar events across Europe. She moved back and forth between events in Berlin and conversations taking place in Paris and elsewhere, primarily engaging other French-speakers (and referring, indexically, to France as "this country").

Another person with many connections to France shared an image that read: "*Je Suis Charlie. Rassemblement citoyen à 19h, Place de la République à Paris pour la liberté de la presse, la démocratie, la République/SOLIDAIRES/CHARLIE HEBDO*" ["I am Charlie. Citizen gathering at 7pm, Place de la République in Paris for the freedom of the press, democracy, the Republic/Solidarity/CHARLIE HEBDO"]. He posted another that simply said, "COEXIST" in religious symbols,[8] with the tagline "*Triste attentat, évitons les raccourcis rapides svp—Coexistons*" ["Sad attack, let's avoid fast shortcuts please—let's Coexist"].

News of the attacks reverberated across Twitter, perhaps even more forcefully. #CharlieHebdo became a trending hashtag within hours (awkward besides others such as "Coachella" and "Justin Bieber"). By the next day, #JeSuisCharlie was trending in Berlin (according to Twitter's Near You search option) as well as "Everywhere." Plenty can and should be said about the cultural politics of #JeSuisCharlie, such as how universalizing discourses of freedom and secularism deny the legitimacy of Muslim cultural citizenship in Europe. In the broader postcolonial context, European supranationalism—the project of building shared European cultural identity at the supranational scale—depends on Islamaphobic views of Muslims as Europe's monolithic, nonwhite "Other" (Boyer 2005; Bunzl 2005). I want to focus, however, on two aspects of how these events encapsulated place making on social media.

Critiques soon erupted of #JeSuisCharlie, some coalescing around the counter-hashtag #JeNeSuisCharlie. This was less prevalent in my Europe-based newsfeeds than another curious combination, however: #JeSuisCharlie and a campaign protesting PEGIDA, a right-wing anti-Muslim group. PEGIDA[9] began demonstrating in Dresden in October 2014, a few months prior, accompanied by the hashtag #PEGIDA. Thousands had marched, recalling the protest movements of 1989 in Dresden and Leipzig, which helped trigger the *Wende*. Many appropriated the era's slogans, shouting "*Wir sind das Volk*."[10] But the contemporary context relates more to the rise in the numbers of asylum seekers in 2014, owing to conflicts such as civil war in Syria.[11] The demonstrations sparked a counter-protest and the hashtag #NOPEGIDA, attracting international headlines as thousands more marched under slogans such as "You are Cologne—no Nazis here." Notably,

Figure 16.2   COEXIST/#NOPEGIDA graphic that circulated on social media, January 2015 (by Jürgen Todenhöfer, https://www.facebook.com/JuergenTodenhoefer, http://juergentodenhoefer.de/?lang=en)

this slogan interpellates counter-protestors through a territorial identity as citizens of Cologne. Cologne's famed cathedral turned out its nighttime floodlights in silent protest, as did the Semperoper Opera House in Dresden and the Brandenburg Gate in Berlin (the site of the Berlin #JeSuisCharlie gathering).

That week in January 2015, the hashtags #JeSuisCharlie and #NOPEGIDA collided and became entwined in surprising ways. One person, Daniel, living in Cologne but connected to friends in Berlin, had previously protested PEGIDA on Twitter. The day after the *Charlie Hebdo* attacks, Daniel posted to Facebook saying: "The statements by PEGIDA about Charlie Hebdo make me ill, sad, angry. I'm speechless," and shared a version of the COEXIST graphic (Figure 16.2), on a blue background surrounded by yellow stars (evoking the European Union emblem), and reading: "*Der Terror von Paris und Die Pegida-Seuche/coexist #nopegida NEIN zu Terrorismus! Nein zu Fremdenhass!*" ["The terror in Paris and the PEGIDA epidemic/NO to Terrorism! NO to xenophobia!"].

It seems contradictory to espouse #JeSuisCharlie while decrying PEGIDA, which is not to say one cannot protest anti-Muslim activism and denounce violent attacks. But many argued (often through #JeNeSuisCharlie) that anti-Muslim sentiment in Europe revolves around liberal, Western logics of freedom, secularism, equality, and so forth, encapsulated by solidarity with *Charlie Hebdo*. Yet the same people, on social media, at protests, and elsewhere, expressed disgust with right-wing extremism and overt anti-Muslim, anti-immigration attitudes. Whether or not contradictory, these trends on Twitter and Facebook draw attention to something else: in addition to sentiments people articulated, images and hashtags circulated according to shared feelings of Europeanness. In this sense, I observed an emergent European transnationalism coalescing on social media, not necessarily through discourse or representations, but through shared ways of feeling at the supranational scale.

Annette, for example, had been living in Berlin for many years, but posted in English and French, addressing both a French-speaking audience (some living in France), and a broader audience imagined as international or transnational (especially in Berlin). She moved through communities at multiple scales—national French ones, local scenes in Berlin, and transnational networks of music fans across Germany, the UK, and elsewhere. When Daniel in Cologne posted in English about #NOPEGIDA, a German movement, he addressed, and imagined, a transnational audience—yet most of his friends on Facebook are German-speaking. A music producer in Berlin similarly posted in English, addressing translocal music fans across Berlin, Moscow, Copenhagen, and elsewhere: "I'm concerned. Frightened and speechless. Now is time to become a political person." All posted in emotion-laden registers of sadness and dismay, deeply affected by the violence, while circulating images of peace and pluralism. Social media helped engender this emergent European transnationalism by circulating through—and generating—multiple spatial scales. This transnational formation stabilizes only temporarily, however, coming into focus at particular moments, and then fading. It took shape, moreover, in and through Berlin, a city where life takes place at many scales.

Conclusion

Finally, I want to return to a plaza in Berlin, to show how ethnography can bring into focus the production of space through—and on—social media. The evening of the *Charlie Hebdo* attacks, I went to the site of the demonstration at the French consulate. Most demonstrators had already left, and the neighboring Mitte district, of wide boulevards and grand imperial buildings, was dark and desolate. As I walked down Under den Linden, the tree-lined boulevard leading to the Brandenburg Gate, I passed a woman carrying a sign that read "#JeSuisCharlie," and was impressed by how quickly the hashtag had become a printed sign. "Excuse me?" I tried, and then, "Pardon?" She turned, shaking her head until she responded, "*Deutsch*." She said she came from the assembly, but the police broke it up. A few people were still there lighting candles, and she offered me a tealight, saying, "You can light a candle too."

When I reached the French consulate, a concrete and glass building on Pariser Platz, I found the plaza mostly deserted. On the sidewalk, a small cluster of perhaps 30 people huddled around a shrine of candles, flowers, pictures—and signs that read "*Je Suis Charlie*" (Figure 16.3). I overheard a woman ask in English what it was about, and a younger woman, apparently her daughter, recounted the attack. Others photographed the memorial, some with professional-looking equipment. It was so windy, though, that I had trouble keeping my tealight lit.

I describe this final scene to give a sense of how the #JeSuisCharlie hashtag spiraled through multiple spaces, linking them together in emergent configurations. Digital and social media become agents in creating social spaces, whether persistent virtual worlds, transient conversations on Facebook, or digital publics at multiple scales. Media have long generated publics and scales; what's new here is how social and mobile media weave together lives in shifting configurations. My interlocutors in Berlin and elsewhere, for example, rarely posted political comments or strong affective sentiments—save for occasional posts about upcoming elections or censure of a musician for right-wing extremism. The #JeSuisCharlie hashtag, which dominated social media briefly, circulated through—and helped generate—this emergent European transnationalism.

Figure 16.3 The *Je Suis Charlie* gathering and shrine at the French consulate in Berlin, January 7, 2015. Photo by author

I offer this scale not as a stable geographic level between the national and the global,[12] but the product of ongoing processes, intersections, and practices. #JeSuisCharlie came into being temporarily, ricocheted across Twitter, Facebook, and public plazas, and then dissipated. Briefly, it fostered a shared European selfhood for a shifting urban middle class, at the supranational scale. The same people critiquing PEGIDA and racist, right-wing anti-Muslim extremism equally defended the liberal views of *Charlie Hebdo*, a contradiction that underpins cultural citizenship in Europe.

Place, then, comes into being through multiple means, including (but not limited to) media technologies. Online versus offline are not adequate in this sense to describe the role of emerging media in constituting social worlds. Social and mobile media, however, make possible experiences of place in novel ways, allowing the same people to move between addressing co-nationals on Facebook, organizing events in Berlin, and fostering shared European feeling and solidarity. Digital ethnography makes it possible to trace these place-making processes across contexts, calling attention to how space and place are virtually and materially constituted, inseparably, as Paul Dourish and Genevieve Bell (2007), Heather Horst and Daniel Miller (2012), Sarah Pink et al. (2016), and others explore.

Localness in Berlin can take place on Facebook event pages, through urban redevelopment projects, and through specific ways of living and being. Yet the same emerging media platforms equally generate social worlds at other levels, from national publics to shared Europeanness (predicated, as many have shown, on excluding Muslim Others). Common European feeling was articulated verbally and through imagery, in affective registers I rarely observed otherwise. These social worlds come into being not only through discourse, but also through shared feeling and sensing. Just as emerging social worlds unfold across media, means, and contexts, I contend that media practices are simultaneously meaningful and material, shaping lived worlds—and places—in singular yet iterative ways.

Notes

1 See Weszkalnys 2010 on urban redevelopment projects and the production of public space in Berlin.
2 Deutsche Demokratische Republik, or East Germany.
3 Often used to refer to Turkish Germans and other immigrants, but here primarily American, British, and other Europeans.
4 Similar to "Ostalgie," nostalgia for a (re)imagined East German past, especially consumer goods (see Berdahl 1999, 2000).
5 See Katherine Hayles' "media specific analysis" (2004).
6 Although I only maintain one account for both research and personal use, I create separate lists to view the posts of those whose practices I study.
7 Some written quotes have been slightly modified to protect confidentiality.
8 Long a favorite of US bumper stickers in the 1990s, mostly referring to religious pluralism.
9 *"Patriotische Europäer gegen die Islamisierung des Abendlandes"* [Patriotic Europeans against the Islamicization of the West].
10 "Anti-Islam 'Pegida' march in German city of Dresden," *BBC News*, December 16, 2014, www.bbc. com/news/world-europe-30478321 (accessed November 6, 2015); Deardon, Lizzie, "Germany anti-Islam protests: Biggest Pegida march ever in Dresden as rest of Germany shows disgust with lights-out," *The Independent*, January 6, 2015, www.independent.co.uk/news/world/europe/germany-anti-islam-protests-biggest-pegida-march-ever-in-dresden-as-rest-of-germany-shows-disgust-9959301.html (accessed November 6, 2015). In 1989 many had shouted *"Wir send ein Volk"* [We are one people], though many East Germans contested this sentiment.
11 Hudson, Alexandra and Hans-Edzard Busemann, "Cologne Cathedral to turn out the lights in protest at anti-Muslim march," *Reuters*, January 2, 2015, www.reuters.com/article/2015/01/02/us-germany-immigration-idUSKBN0KB0KU20150102 (accessed November 6, 2015).
12 See Mei Zhan on the translocal not as a scale but as a process (Zhan 2009).

References

Abu-Lughod, Lila. 2005. *Dramas of Nationhood: The Politics of Television in Egypt*. Chicago, IL: University of Chicago Press.

Anderson, Ben, and Paul Harrison. 2010. "The Promise of Non-representational Theories." In *Taking-Place: Non-Representational Theories and Geography*, edited by Ben Anderson and Paul Harrison, 1–36. Burlington, VT; Farnham, Surrey, England: Ashgate Farnham.

Anderson, Benedict. 1991. *Imagined Communities*. London; New York: Verso.

Appadurai, Arjun. 1996. *Modernity at Large: Cultural Dimensions of Globalization*. Minneapolis, MN: University of Minnesota Press.

Baym, Nancy. 2010. *Personal Connections in the Digital Age*. Malden, MA; Cambridge, UK: Polity.

Berdahl, Daphne. 1999. "'(N)Ostalgie' for the Present: Memory, Longing, and East German Things." *Ethnos* 64(2): 192–211.

——. 2000. "'Go, Trabi, Go!' Reflections on a Car and Its Symbolization Over Time." *Anthropology and Humanism* 25(2): 131–41.

Bernal, Victoria. 2006. "Diaspora, Cyberspace and Political Imagination: The Eritrean Diaspora Online." *Global Networks* 6(2): 161–79.

——. 2014. *Nation as Network: Diaspora, Cyberspace, and Citizenship*. Chicago, IL: University of Chicago Press.

Boellstorff, Tom. 2008. *Coming of Age in Second Life: An Anthropologist Explores the Virtually Human*. Princeton, NJ: Princeton University Press.

boyd, danah. 2014. *It's Complicated*. New Haven, CT: Yale University Press.

Boyer, Dominic. 2005. "Welcome to the New Europe." *American Ethnologist* 32(4): 521–3.

Brenner, Neil. 1998. "Between Fixity and Motion: Accumulation, Territorial Organization and the Historical Geography of Spatial Scales." *Environment and Planning D* 16: 459–81.

——. 2001. "The Limits to Scale? Methodological Reflections on Scalar Structuration." *Progress in Human Geography* 25(4): 591–614.

Bunzl, Matti. 2005. "Between Anti-Semitism and Islamophobia: Some Thoughts on the New Europe." *American Ethnologist* 32(4): 499–508.

DeNicola, Lane. 2012. "Geomedia: The Reassertion of Space within Digital Culture." In *Digital Anthropology*, edited by Heather A. Horst and Daniel Miller, 80–98. London, New York: Berg.

Dourish, Paul, and Genevieve Bell. 2007. "The Infrastructure of Experience and the Experience of Infrastructure: Meaning and Structure in Everyday Encounters with Space." *Environment and Planning B: Planning and Design* 34(3): 414–30.

Castells, Manuel. 1996. *The Rise of the Network Society*. Malden, MA: Blackwell.

Clifford, James. 1992. "Traveling Cultures." In *Cultural Studies*, edited by Lawrence Grossberg, Cary Nelson, and Paula A Treichler, 96–116. New York: Routledge.

Ellison, Nicole, Charles Steinfield, and Cliff Lampe. 2006. "Spatially Bounded Online Social Networks and Social Capital: The Role of Facebook." In *Proceedings of the Annual Conference of the International Communication Association*, June 19–23, Dresden, Germany.

Eriksen, Thomas Hylland. 2007. "Nationalism and the Internet." *Nations and Nationalism* 13(1): 1–17.

Florida, Richard. 2004. *The Rise of the Creative Class: And How It's Transforming Work, Leisure, Community and Everyday Life*. New York: Basic Books.

Gellner, Ernest. 1983. *Nations and Nationalism*. Ithaca, NY: Cornell University Press.

Graham, Mark. 2013. "Geography/Internet: Ethereal Alternate Dimensions of Cyberspace or Grounded Augmented Realities?" *The Geographical Journal* 179(2): 177–82.

Gupta, Akhil, and James Ferguson. 1992. "Beyond 'Culture': Space, Identity, and the Politics of Difference." *Cultural Anthropology* 7(1): 6–23.

——. 1997. "Ethnography at the End of an Era." In *Culture, Power, Place: Explorations in Critical Anthropology*, edited by Akhil Gupta and James Ferguson, 1–15. Durham, NC: Duke University Press.

Harvey, David. 1989. *The Condition of Postmodernity: An Enquiry into the Origins of Cultural Change*. Oxford: Blackwell.

Hayles, N. Katherine. 2004. "Print Is Flat, Code Is Deep: The Importance of Media-Specific Analysis." *Poetics Today* 25(1): 67–90.

Hesse, Kurt. 1990. "Cross-Border Mass Communication from West to East Germany." *European Journal of Communication* 5(2): 355–71.

Horst, Heather, and Daniel Miller. 2012. *Digital Anthropology*. New York, London: Borg.

Kraemer, Jordan. 2014. "Friend or Freund: Social Media and Transnational Connections in Berlin." *Human-Computer Interaction* 29(1): 53–77.

Lambek, Michael. 2011. "Catching the Local." *Anthropological Theory* 11(2): 197–221.

Lee, Helen. 2007. "Transforming Transnationalism: Second Generation Tongans Overseas." *Asian and Pacific Migration Journal* 16(2): 157–78.

Lefebvre, Henri. 1991. *The Production of Space*. Oxford, UK; Cambridge, MA: Blackwell.

Low, Setha. 2009. "Towards an Anthropological Theory of Space and Place." *Semiotica* 175: 21–37.

——. 2014. "Spatializing Culture: An Engaged Anthropological Approach to Space and Place." In *The People, Place, and Space Reader*, edited by Jen Jack Gieseking and William Mangold, 34–8. New York: Routledge.

Mandel, Ruth. 2008. *Cosmopolitan Anxieties: Turkish Challenges to Citizenship and Belonging in Germany*. Durham, NC: Duke University Press.

Mankekar, Purnima. 1999. *Screening Culture, Viewing Politics: An Ethnography of Television, Womanhood, and Nation in Postcolonial India*. Durham, NC: Duke University Press.

Marston, Sallie. 2000. "The Social Construction of Scale." *Progress in Human Geography* 24(2): 219–42.

Marston, Sallie A., John Paul Jones III, and Keith Woodward. 2005. "Human Geography Without Scale." *Transactions of the Institute of British Geographers* 30(4): 416–32.

Massey, Doreen. 1993. "Power Geometry and a Progressive Sense of Place." In *Mapping the Futures: Local Cultures, Global Change*, edited by Jon Bird, Barry Curtis, Tim Putnam, George Robertson, and Lisa Tickner, 59–69. Routledge.

Mazzarella, William. 2004. *Shoveling Smoke: Advertising and Globalization in Contemporary India*. Durham, NC and London: Duke University Press.

McLuhan, Marshall. 2013[1964]. *Understanding Media: The Extensions of Man.* Corte Madera, CA: Ginko Press.

Miller, Daniel, and Don Slater. 2000. *The Internet: An Ethnographic Approach.* Oxford, New York: Berg.

Munn, Nancy. 1986. *The Fame of Gawa: A Symbolic Study of Value Transformation in a Massim (Papua New Guinea) Society.* Cambridge; New York: Cambridge University Press.

Pink, Sarah, Elisenda Ardèvol, and Débora Lanzeni. 2016. *Digital Materialities: Design and Anthropology.* New York and London: Bloomsbury Academic.

Rapp, Tobias. 2009. *Lost and Sound.* Frankfurt am Main: Suhrkamp.

Schnöring, Thomas, and Uwe Szafran. 1994. "Telecommunications in Eastern Germany: A Success Story of East-West Integration." *Telecommunications Policy* 18(6): 453–69.

Spitulnik, Debra. 1996. "The Social Circulation of Media Discourse and the Mediation of Communities." *Journal of Linguistic Anthropology* 6(2): 161–87.

Stewart. Kathleen. 2007. *Ordinary Affects.* Durham, NC: Duke University Press.

Taylor, T. L. 2006. *Play Between Worlds.* Cambridge, MA: MIT Press.

Tsing, Anna. 2005. *Friction: An Ethnography of Global Connection.* Princeton, NJ: Princeton University Press.

Wallerstein, Immanuel. 1974. *The Modern World-System.* New York: Academic Press.

Weszkalnys, Gisa. 2010. *Berlin, Alexanderplatz.* New York: Berghahn Books.

Wolf, Eric. 1982. *Europe and the People Without History.* Berkeley, CA: University of California Press.

Zhan, Mei. 2009. *Other-Worldly: Making Chinese Medicine through Transnational Frames.* Durham, NC: Duke University Press.

17

MAKING "OURNET NOT THE INTERNET"

An Ethnography of Home-Brew High-Tech Practices in Suburban Australia

Kat Jungnickel

Stumbling for Digital Noise on a Suburban Rooftop

The afternoon is hot. It's about 30 degrees Celsius. The sky has turned thick with cloud as if a storm is brewing but the air is heavy and dry. From my experience of Adelaide summers, it is highly unlikely that relief will come in the form of rain. I'm sweating and my skin picks up dirt and dust from the roof tiles making my hands and feet red. Instead of making it easier to grip my bare feet slip on the tiles.

There are moments in every ethnographer's career when they wonder how it transpired that they came to be in a particular situation. For me there have been many, but one particularly memorable incident was located atop a vertiginous crest of an Australian suburban house in the height of summer:

> I am pleased I have my camera on a lanyard around my neck. I am less convinced by my decision to wear a long cotton dress, as my mobility feels compromised. I want to take lots of photos of the new vision of suburbia unfolding in front of me from this perspective. But both hands are already occupied; one is gripping the roof and the other a wireless dish with a split down the centre that is a "bit broken" and held together with black sticky tape.

I wasn't alone on the roof this sweltering Sunday afternoon. I was up there with a volunteer member of the local community wireless fidelity (Wi-Fi) digital networking group. I was dressed casually as the activity had not been framed as a complex technological event but rather a member

Figure 17.1 Stumbling for digital noise on a suburban rooftop

of the group had offered to "drop by" and "stumble for digital noise" in order to see whether I could and how it might be possible to join the network. "Stumbling" is a routine activity carried out by Wi-Fi makers to look for and represent digital "noise" in key sites as a precursor to, depending on the strength and direction of local wireless signals, the installation of a new—or upgrade of an existing—antenna.

> Watching Ben sweep the different aerials around in the sky I find myself thinking about the action of catching butterflies in nets or of whales filtering water for plankton. He is trying to net a material too small to see. His arms swoop and circle. He raises them up to the sky and sweeps them around in a horizontal direction. He then does it again vertically. He then crouches, his hands still holding equipment, and changes the position of his feet to sweep the other side.

Stumbling presents a very different vision of a new technology-in-the-making to that of a more stereotypical high-tech science setting. I was entranced by Ben's movements on the roof because they were not what I had anticipated when I had started my ethnographic study of this "new" digital technology. This is not a story of brightly lit fab labs, white-coated scientists or more conventional high-tech systematic processes. It is not about invisible things or abstract ideas. Instead, it reveals the making of a new sophisticated technology on suburban rooftops, on sunny weekends, with sticky-taped devices, barefoot and in cotton dresses, by volunteers who "drop by," using spare time and skills, along with improvised methods and at-hand adapted or re-appropriated materials. This high-tech home-brew version of Wi-Fi networking is made of a complex collection of things, people, skills and contingencies.

These fieldnotes come from a study using ethnographic methods that I was undertaking over an 18-month period with the largest volunteer community Wi-Fi group in Australia, located in Adelaide. I chose this group as they were at the time the most active community Wi-Fi group online with 70 members and 23 "backbone" nodes with a further 30 smaller "client" nodes spanning an area 70 km by 30 km. As a volunteer member I observed and participated in the making of a sophisticated digital communications network that spanned the largely suburban city by connecting homemade antennas, many of which were located in members' backyards.

What drew me to this group was their particular use and understanding of Wi-Fi. In Australia it operates on an unlicensed shared spectrum, which means individuals share the same rights to broadcast and receive wireless signals as corporate and governmental organizations. This enables volunteer Wi-Fi makers to use Wi-Fi to imagine and build alternate communications structures that circumnavigate conventional power structures of large-scale corporate telecom organizations. What is striking about this group is that it did not see Wi-Fi as simply a channel to the Internet but rather as a means of re-imagining the very structure of the Internet. They were using this technology to (re)build the architecture of a customised, deeply local communications network by linking together antennas in their backyards. In doing so, they were making what they called "ournet not the Internet."

Placing a Digital Ethnography

Stumbling is a routine technique employed by many community Wi-Fi networks all over the world as the first step to adding a new point in their technology infrastructure. Stumbling is a practice designed to detect and render visible the wireless spectrum or "digital noise" that inhabits the air around a particular site. More specifically, it measures the microwave signals that emit from wireless devices. This technique produces textual and graphic data of local wireless activity that members can use to see, understand and work with the digital landscape. It helps them determine the location, direction, strength and quality of local signals and, equipped with this knowledge, ascertain what kinds of wireless work is required to get new nodes connected to the network. This includes what type of antenna is appropriate and at what installation height and optimum direction it should point to join the community network. Stumbling is critical to the making of Wi-Fi because community networks operate via line-of-sight; each point needs to "see" another in order to make a connection.

Rooftops were key technological sites in the community Wi-Fi network. Roofs enclose, protect and surround space; rarely are they considered windows to new worlds. Yet, wireless group members consider them just that. The suburban rooftop is a central location for wireless work. In a densely populated suburban area, the roof delivers cost-free ample space, which is essential for volunteer unfunded community groups. Even more important, it provides proximity to the sky. Because Wi-Fi is a point-to-point technology the roof offers the highest location on which to locate a node and ensure an uncompromised connection. It is crucial for "stumbling" because it offers a way to secure access to narrow view corridors around and between tall trees and buildings, all of which have the tendency to block or seriously inhibit wireless signals. Although some nodes are installed in office buildings and decommissioned water towers, the majority of the volunteer community network nodes are located on top of members' suburban houses and sheds. The roof, however, aside from providing a key place from which to do wireless work, also offers a critical perspective on the sprawling suburbia in which it resides.

Looking beyond the physical nature of the city, Ben tells me that the sky is filled with streams of invisible data; from short wave radio signals used by ham radio operators, to cells that make our cordless home phones work, intermingled with bursts of microwaves when we reheat dinner to those emitting from baby and even heart monitors. All these and more contribute digital noise in the spectrum near 2.4 GHz. Since the advent of Wi-Fi in 1998, this spectrum has become ever more filled with 802.11b frequency signals that spill out of homes and businesses.

Within the edges of my house, I could see into my neighbors' lives. I could not see personal details but I could see the names they have given their wireless systems and the types of devices they owned, which pieced together provide insights into the technologies that augment their daily activities. Radio signals leached out of the houses. They seeped through walls, and slid through fences and into my yard. What Ben was documenting was a form of digital leakage. Although wireless devices can be "locked" to prevent unofficial use, they cannot be locked in place. And place matters as these digital traces changed in strength and weakness at different points in footprint. They overlapped and tangled. Operating on a shared spectrum meant signals can interfere with one another. They can even cancel each other out. Rather than being fixed and solid, these digital architectures are better considered permeable, malleable and transitory. The logic of space and place are reconfigured as a series of messy contingent entities.

Ben was hoping to locate the presence of a particular type of digital noise in the surrounds of the house that I could use to connect to the community network. To stumble therefore is not an accident but rather a deliberate and pre-meditated act. Vergunst (2008) writes about the routine happenstance of "trips," "mishaps" and "slips" in the experience of hill walking. Although an integral aspect of walking, he notes how no one ever plans to slip or trip, yet it regularly happens and because it is so mundane, it "can easily be passed over" (ibid.). The central tenet of his argument is not about deliberate accidents as such but about how, together, these incidents produce the "actuality of walking itself" (2008, 106). Ignoring or overlooking them has the effect of distancing the walker from the character of the environment and their place within it. Vergunst writes, "by a tiny movement or disjuncture, a slip between a boot and the shale, and the character of the walk changes radically" (2008, 105).

Focusing on these aspects of walking draws attention to the way the body accommodates changing conditions, and affords a new way of thinking about and understanding an otherwise taken-for-granted experience. Here, an awareness of (accidental) mishaps serves to bring the walker closer to the experience. While Vergunst (2008) concentrates on encounters between the body and the physical landscape, a focus on Wi-Fi makers opens up new ways of reconfiguring and participating in a digital landscape.

Critically, for a sociologist, what is interesting about stumbling is that it operates at a point where the design of the wireless network takes shape. Stumbling data is not always useful on its own but becomes valuable when it is imagined into a networked future. In a larger piece of this work I describe how members intertwine what is not seen (digital noise) with what can be seen (visual data) and what can be imagined (hope) and socially produced (Jungnickel 2014). What I want to draw attention to in this chapter is the place-ness of this wireless work, and in turn how this *placed* my digital ethnography.

Why Wi-Fi?

When I started this research in 2005, Wi-Fi was a technology that was rarely thought about in terms of place. In fact it signalled the opposite. The rhetoric surrounding its emergence at the turn of the century heralded the end of place. Wi-Fi is commonly known for facilitating the transfer of high-speed data, and is most often associated with provision of the Internet, multi-player gaming, file sharing and voice protocols. In place of wires, Wi-Fi operates via electromagnetic signals broadcast from a modem which means, equipped with a suitable device, access to the Internet is theoretically possible, anywhere, within a Wi-Fi zone. As a result it was largely seen as an Internet infrastructure, or rather, not seen at all. The media quickly became caught by the lure of the "freedom," "anytime" and "anywhere-ness" promised by this new wireless technology (Forlano 2008). No longer would a computer user be tethered to a desk and an Internet wire. Wireless-ness promised freedom from all of this.

In reality the location and visibility of Wi-Fi was brought to bear on Internet practices and behaviours even more than those of traditional fixed-line technologies (Goggin and Gregg 2007; Gregg 2007). As many have argued "places matter" (Wakeford 2003; Goggin 2004; Oudshoorn 2012) and Wi-Fi is not a placeless or disembodied technology, but rather is firmly embedded in distinctive material, social and cultural contexts. This is especially the case in Australia where the Internet is dominated and therefore shaped by commercial models of government and large-scale technology organizations. Here, as Goggin and Gregg have argued, wireless technology is most often represented in terms of "competitive discourse" and "nation building exercises such as railways and roads" and is "embedded in terms of responsibility and efficacy" (2007, 41). What is far less acknowledged is the possibility of other means of thinking about and getting connected. In other words, a study of a grassroots technology community presented an opportunity to re-imagine how Wi-Fi "might be otherwise" (Bijker and Law 1994, 3).

Broadly, I set out to examine the culture of a digital technology as it was made from the ground up, or in this case from the backyard out. The research was framed by the idea that the Internet is not universal or a one-size-fits-all system, and if we are to understand it we need to examine the many forms it takes in different contexts (Miller and Slater 2000; Goggin 2004; Goggin and Gregg 2007). Studying it ethnographically therefore makes sense. There are many good examples of the productivity of ethnographic studies of digital subjects. Miller and Slater's classic study, for instance, describes how national and cultural identity are central to understanding the Internet in Trinidad—it was simply part of "being Trini" (2000, 1). Here, the Internet was not viewed as a "monolithic" or "placeless" "cyberspace," somehow apart from everyday social worlds, but rather in terms of how Trinidadians "assembled various technical possibilities that added up to their Internet" (2000, 14).

Similarly Ito et al.'s (2005) study of Japanese mobile phone cultures explores the concept of *keitai* which translates as "something you carry with you." They explain it "is not so much about a new technical capability or freedom of motion, but about a snug and intimate techno-social tethering, a personal device supporting communications that are a constant, lightweight and mundane presence in everyday life" (2005, 1). These studies, amongst others, present valuable alternative versions and imaginings of the Internet in contexts outside Europe and the US.

Using ethnographic methods to study the making of Wi-Fi in suburban Australia involved a surprising network of actors. I was regularly struck by members' use of freely available or cheaply purchased materials and improvised methods as well as regular encounters with trees, thieves, birds, possums, neighbours, roof tops, technical complications, myriad materials and the weather in the daily practice of making Wi-Fi. Such heterogeneous assemblies of things can be explored from an STS perspective using Actor Network Theory or ANT (Callon 1986; Star 1999; Latour 1990, 2005). This approach involves taking seriously the power, positionality and connections of things to each other, regardless of whether they are human or not.

Fieldsites were equally diverse: residential houses, rooftops, garages and sheds, community centres, public schools, members' workplaces, cafés, libraries, websites, blogs and online forums. It quickly became obvious that Wi-Fi was certainly not "everywhere" or "anytime" but rather deeply local, highly social, made (and constantly remade) of a diverse assembly of stuff and contingent on myriad factors. How the group came to know, share and make sense of the network became a central concern in my research. More specifically, I began to ask about the role representations played in the making of a new digital technology.

The Visual Culture of Wi-Fi

To examine the place-ness of Wi-Fi involves considering the technology at the intersection of infrastructures, representations and in/visibility. Infrastructures are pivotal to the provision of many essential services, yet rarely do they garner intense scrutiny. The Internet is no different. Many studies in the past have tended to privilege experiences mediated by Information and Communication Technologies (ICTs) over the systems that support them. This is because infrastructures are, by their nature, hidden from view, hard to access or viewed as "singularly unexciting" (Star 1999). Conventionally they have taken the form of roads, water and sewerage pipes and cables that channel electricity and phone data. This means they are either embedded in the very architecture of the home or, if they are not concealed, they are rendered invisible by their sheer mundanity. Wi-Fi is not dissimilar. When many people think of wireless networks they think of how the Internet enters their home via a fixed cable router plugged in the wall and supplied by a commercial telecom giant. Much like electricity or water, with which it is often compared, it is seen as an essential service, often taken for granted, piped directly into the domestic footprint, that you pay for, switch on and off and consume. Although the idea of generating your own electricity or catching rainwater is possible and some people do it, it is a far stranger proposition to make your own domestic wireless connection and link your home computer with others across the city.

Community Wi-Fi networking provides an intriguing case in the study of representations of knowledge because it is often overlooked, rarely stable and impossible to see with the naked eye. The many ways people communicate and represent it become critical in locating and understanding how it operates. Axiomatic to media, commercial and community wireless organizations alike are a plethora of representations in the form of maps, diagrams, artefacts, websites, photos and drawings. However, because Wi-Fi relies on point-to-point connections, it can become easily disconnected when line-of-sight is broken, which is a particularly relevant issue for community wireless networks that operate across long distances. Interruptions can take many forms; from changing weather conditions, growing trees or local bird life to new buildings and even baby monitors that operate on the shared spectrum. As a result, it can seem unpredictable and temperamental, shifting from one place to another. If representing the presence of Wi-Fi in one place is not a guarantee that it will still be there in an hour, let alone in a week, how do Wi-Fi makers represent a technological network that constantly changes? How do they use what appear to be unreliable representations to share, communicate and expand their network?

Stumbling draws attention to the dynamics and dimensions of a technological infrastructure in its infancy, rather than accepting how it is already purposed and packaged for a specific use. It is a tactic for peering into the "black box" (Callon 1986; Latour 1999; Graham and Thrift 2007). STS scholars have argued that once paths of innovation become established they are harder to change than when they are fresh and new. It is not long before they appear as if they have always been there. Many advocate a close examination of mundane and easily overlooked heterogeneous assemblies that produce technological systems and practices in order to generate insights about taken-for-granted ways in which people make sense of and operate in everyday life (Star 1999; Michael 2006). Routinely overlooking artefacts and systems therefore serve as a catalyst for STS investigation.

Star (1999) has done much to advocate the study of infrastructure by pointing out that it is not the infrastructures themselves, but how we tend to look at them that is boring.

The problem in overlooking infrastructures such as Wi-Fi, and assuming they are simply a channel for more exciting content-based applications is why we neglect how they shape and are shaped by society and culture. As Garforth has argued: "[T]he boring work, the routines, the manipulation of machines, materials, and texts is often precisely what the STS researcher wants to see" (2011, 272).

One way of studying the cultural complexities of ICT infrastructure is to examine how it is rendered visible by the people who make and use it. Haring's (2007) study of male ham radio hobbyists in the US in the 1950s, for instance, focuses on a vast body of amateur publications such as club newsletters, technical handbooks and local media journalism. Her analysis illustrates how a marginal community infrastructure had direct implications in the shaping of social, technical and gendered encounters in the radio technology industry. The value of representational practice and visual knowledge is firmly established in STS in many disciplines, particularly science, engineering and architecture (Latour 1990; Lynch and Woolgar 1990; Cartwright 1995; Henderson 1999). Here, graphs, drawings and images are seen as pivotal in understanding how practitioners construct knowledge, design new technologies, organize action, and enrol allies. Broadly speaking, this literature holds that techniques of rendering are interlocked with particular ways of seeing the world. In other words, seeing is closely tied to local, social and cultural ways of knowing.

A visual culture is a distinct way of seeing the world through the experience of visual material. In seventeenth-century Dutch society Alpers observed how scientific and technological advances such as the camera obscura and microscope "confirmed pictures as the way to new and certain knowledge of the world" (1984, xxv). Dutch visual culture created a way of seeing the world in pictures rather than words and the power of this lay in the way this visual knowledge could be built upon and advanced with each new development in visual technology. Alpers' work describes the new experiences made possible through the intersection of new technologies, ways of seeing and rendering the world. It required a rethink and a re-imagining of social conventions for expression. What distinguishes Alpers' (1984) writing from other art historians and makes it interesting to STS scholars is her association between science and technology advancements and visual representations. She argues (1984, xxv) that seventeenth-century Dutch visual culture permeated all aspects of society, not just the world of science:

> In Holland the visual culture was central to the life of the society. One might say that the eye was a central means of self-representation and visual experience a central mode of self-consciousness. If the theatre was the arena in which the England of Elizabeth I most fully represented itself to itself, images played that role for the Dutch.

The way a society represents "itself to itself" is its visual culture. Alpers reveals the link between new ways of seeing and new ways of rendering the world in material form. Drawing on her work, Latour writes that visual culture contributes to "how a culture sees the world and makes it visible" (1990, 30). He argues that visual culture is often seen as a metaphorical "worldview," but in Alpers' writing it is given material form and presents both "what it is to see and what there is to see" (ibid.). The potential of representations to produce ways of knowing continues to influence STS scholars who pursue entanglements of seeing and knowing and also those who explore less certain and messier visual knowledge practices (Beaulieu 2002; Pauwels 2006; Latour and Yaneva 2008; Myers 2008; Garforth 2011; Street 2011; Coopmans et al. 2014).

Garforth, for instance, questions "unexamined assumptions that have tied together seeing and knowing" and argues that other forms of knowing emerge from private and solitary thinking practice in the science lab (2011, 265). Street's (2011) research in a Papua New Guinean hospital examines "artifacts of not-knowing" that emerge when multiplicity and ambiguity are embedded in medical records. She shows how instead of closing down ideas, not-knowing can open up alternate ways of considering actions and interactions, enabling new "open-ended" practices rather than negative consequences. This work paves the way for attending to the making of a form of visual knowledge and technological imagination that emerges from what can both be seen *and* not seen.

Making Sense of Digital Suburbia

Miller and Slater suggest "if you want to get to the Internet, don't start from there" (2000, 5). In the case of my study into Wi-Fi network makers, I did not start with Wi-Fi but rather attended to the kinds of technological work that took place on a residential rooftop. That sunny Sunday afternoon I discovered things in my suburban footprint about which I had not known or even thought to think about Wi-Fi digital networks.

Stumbling on the roof revealed a form of digital suburbia less bound by conventional notions of ownership; mortgages, buildings, locked doors, lawns and fences. This version has little to do with more conventional infrastructures and services that run in and out of the house. The digital traces Ben stumbled upon did not follow the roads or the lines of connecting fences. The Wi-Fi network is similarly unbounded—it operates via line-of-site and re-inscribes alternate techniques for connecting points. It cannot be understood in terms of traditional infrastructures and systems of knowledge. It also cannot be fixed in place. These traces shift and move, according to the digital composition of the spectrum at the time of stumble, dependent on the weather, the height of trees and location of buildings that interrupt line-of-sight and even the skill of the stumbler.

Stumbling is a method in which this invisible technological infrastructure is made visible, social and material while, at the same time, it presents an opportunity to explore the intersection of not/knowing and in/visibility. During my fieldwork I noted that the network crashed, and often. Far from unsettling or destabilizing the group, the inability to produce fixed representations served to strengthen the group, expand the network and grow membership. What I came to understand is that members did not make Wi-Fi in spite of these many interruptions but because of them. Rather than tidying up or smoothing out these disturbances, members built them into the network and it was the group's ability to deal with constant indeterminacy and multiple realities that affords it durability. Here, not-knowing was not only part of the everyday reality of using Wi-Fi but also purposely and deliberately built into the culture of the network.

References

Alpers, Svetlana. 1984. *The Art of Describing: Dutch Art in the Seventeenth Century*. London: Penguin Books.

Beaulieu, Anne. 2002. "Images Are Not the (Only) Truth: Brain Mapping, Visual Knowledge, and Iconoclasm." *Science Technology Human Values*, 27(1): 53–86.

Bijker, Wiebe. E and Law, John. 1994. *Shaping Technology/Building Society: Studies in Sociotechnical Change*. Cambridge, MA: MIT Press.

Callon, Michel. 1986. "The Sociology of an Actor-Network: The Case of the Electric Vehicle." In *Mapping the Dynamics of Science and Technology: Sociology of Science in the Real World*, edited by Michel Callon, John Law, and Arie Rip, 19–34. Hampshire and London: Sheridan House Inc.

Cartwright, Lisa. 1995. *Screening the Body: Tracing Medicine's Visual Culture*. Minneapolis, MN: University of Minnesota Press.

Coopmans, Catelijne, Vertesi, Janet, Lynch, Michael and Woolgar, Steve, eds. 2014. *Representation in Scientific Practice Revisted*. Cambridge, MA: MIT Press.

Forlano, Laura. 2008. "Anytime? Anywhere? Reframing Debates around Municipal Wireless Networking." *The Journal of Community Informatics, Special Issue: Wireless Networking for Communities, Citizens and The Public Interest*, 4(1). Available at: http://ci-journal.net (accessed October 12, 2008).

Garforth, Lisa. 2011. "In/Visibilities of Research: Seeing and Knowing in STS." *Science, Technology & Human Values*, 37(2): 264–85.

Goggin, Gerard, ed. 2004. *Virtual Nation: The Internet in Australia*. Sydney: University of New South Wales Press.

Goggin, Gerard and Gregg, Melissa, eds. 2007. "Wireless Cultures and Technologies." *Media International Australia*, vol. 125. University of Queensland.

Graham, Stephen and Thrift, Nigel. 2007. "Out of Order: Understanding Repair and Maintenance." *Theory, Culture & Society*, 24(1): 1–25.

Gregg, Melissa. 2007. "Freedom to Work: The Impact of Wireless on Labour Politics." In "Wireless Cultures and Technologies," edited by Gerard Goggin and Melissa Gregg. *Media International Australia*, vol. 125. University of Queensland.

Haring, Kristen. 2007. *Ham Radio's Technical Culture*. Cambridge, MA and London, England: MIT Press.

Henderson, Kathryn. 1999. *On Line and On Paper: Visual Representations, Visual Culture, and Computer Graphics in Design Engineering*. Cambridge, MA: MIT Press.

Ito, Mizuko, Matsua, Misa and Okabe, Daisuke, eds. 2005. *Personal, Portable, Pedestrian: Mobile Phones in Japanese Life*. Cambridge, MA: MIT Press.

Jungnickel, Katrina. 2014. *DiY WiFi: Re-imagining Connectivity*. Basingstoke: Palgrave Macmillan.

Latour, Bruno. 1990. "Drawing Things Together." In *Representation in Scientific Practice*, edited by Michael Lynch and Steve Woolgar, 19–68. Cambridge, MA: MIT Press.

——. 1999. *Pandora's Hope: Essays on the Reality of Science Studies*. Cambridge, MA: Harvard University Press.

——. 2005. *Reassembling the Social: An Introduction to Actor-Network-Theory*. Oxford: Oxford University Press.

Latour, Bruno and Yaneva, Albena. 2008. "Give Me a Gun and I Will Make All Buildings Move: An ANT's View of Architecture." In *Explorations in Architecture: Teaching, Design, Research*, edited by Reto Geiser, 80–9. Basel: Birkhäuser.

Lynch, Michael and Woolgar, Steve, eds. 1990. *Representation in Scientific Practice*. Cambridge, MA: MIT Press.

Michael, Mike. 2006. *Technoscience and Everyday Life: The Complex Simplicities of the Mundane*. London: Open University Press.

Miller, Daniel and Slater, Don. 2000. *The Internet: An Ethnographic Approach*. Oxford: Berg.

Myers, Natasha. 2008. "Molecular Embodiments and the Body-Work of Modeling in Protein Crystallography." *Social Studies of Science*, 38(2): 163–99.

Oudshoorn, Nelly. 2012. "How Places Matter: Telecare Technologies and the Changing Spatial Dimensions of Healthcare." *Social Studies of Science*, 42(1): 121–42.

Pauwels, Luc, ed. 2006. *Visual Cultures of Science: Rethinking Representational Practices in Knowledge Building and Science Communication*. Hanover and London: Dartmouth College Press.

Star, Susan, Leigh. 1999. "The Ethnography of Infrastructure." In *Analysing Virtual Societies: New Directions in Methodology*, edited by Peter Lyman and Nina Wakeford. *American Behavioural Scientist* 43(3): 377–91.

Street, Alice. 2011. "Artefacts of Not-Knowing: The Medial Record, the Diagnosis and the Production of Uncertainty in Papua New Guinean Medicine." *Social Studies of Science* 41(6): 815–34.

Vergunst, Jo Lee. 2008. "Taking a Trip and Taking Care in Everyday Life." In *Ways of Walking: Ethnography and Practice on Foot*, edited by Tim Ingold and Jo Lee Vergunst, 105–23. Hampshire, England: Ashgate.

Wakeford, Nina. 2003. "The Embedding of Local Culture in Global Communication: Independent Internet Cafés in London." *New Media & Society* 5(3): 379–99.

18

LOCATIVE MOBILE MEDIA AND THE DEVELOPMENT OF UNPLANNED, FLEETING ENCOUNTERS WITH PSEUDONYMOUS STRANGERS AND VIRTUAL ACQUAINTANCES IN URBAN PUBLIC PLACES

Christian Licoppe and Julien Morel

Introduction

According to Erving Goffman (1963, 22), "co-presence renders persons uniquely accessible, available, and subject to one another. Public order, in its face-to-face aspects, has to do with the normative regulation of this accessibility." In Goffman's public places—antedating the spread of digital technologies—people constantly monitored other people in their surroundings in both explicit and ambient modes of encounter. In these settings, the more *public* the place, the more it was *filled with strangers*. Goffman's metropolis—and more generally Western cities in the twentieth century—are places "for strangers" (Lofland 1998), whereby strangers pass one another in a civilly inattentive way.

However, what can also happen in such cities is that one meets acquaintanceships by chance in the course of one's mobilities and everyday activities. For Goffman, "acquaintance-ship" is an institution, and it has a lot to do with the way we might know and recognize another person's singularity. The preconditions for acquaintanceship "are satisfied when each of two individuals can personally identify the other by knowledge that distinguishes this other from everyone else, and when each acknowledges to the other that this state of mutual information exists" (Goffman 1963, 112). Crucially, co-present chance encounters between acquaintances entail and enact special rights and obligations which similar encounters with strangers do not, and particularly to initiate a more focused encounter than just civil inattention: when two acquaintances "come into the same social situation [which in Goffman's vocabulary involves being aware of their mutual presence], they are likely to possess a duty or right regarding face engagement" (ibid.). This normative power of the exchange of gazes between encounters in chance encounters makes meaningful some "body glosses," such as turning toward a shop window after seeing an acquaintance, so as to seem absorbed and minimize the chances for an exchange of gaze (Sudnow 1972).

In this zoology of twentieth-century public places as ecologies of interpersonal visibility and sites for chance encounters, the "familiar stranger" lies somewhere in between the complete stranger and the full acquaintance. The familiar stranger is that unknown person, whose face might become familiar in the course of repeated mobilities and encounters, but with whom interaction remains non-existent or minimal, precluding the sharing of personal information (Milgram 1974). We would argue that the kind of knowledge we have of the familiar strangers is mostly category-based as that "fellow passenger" who takes the same commuting train every morning, or some familiar face in my "neighborhood" with whom we cross paths repeatedly enough to have noticed them. Though the boundary between acquaintances and familiar strangers might be blurred, there is not the same duty to initiate a face encounter when one gets co-present with the familiar stranger in a social situation as there is with an acquaintance.

In the first section of this chapter we draw on one of Georges Perec's early works to get a sense of the lived experience of inhabiting the mid-twentieth century metropolis as a "city of strangers." Using this as a kind of baseline, what we want to discuss here is how such an analysis of sociability in public places should be elaborated to account for the contemporary experience of inhabiting public places augmented with mobile technologies, and particularly location-aware technologies (de Souza e Silva and Sutko 2009; Farman 2013). Though we can still retain Goffman's approach to the "public order," one has to reconceptualize the relevant features of the social situation. In Goffman's times, the social situation referred to a co-present ecology in which people could monitor one another's behavior through their naked senses, and mostly gaze.

When considering users of mobile technologies—and particularly location-aware social networking applications—the relevant "social situation" must also encompass those people who can monitor one another's presence through mobile technologies. Beyond those people we may discover with our eyes and ears in a given place there are all those figures who appear through the mediation of screens and location-aware technologies, who might be visible or not, under a guise which is also mediated by mobile interfaces. In a nutshell, one must include mediated mutual awareness as part and parcel of the normative regulation of mutual access in social situations. The sense of co-presence, which is characteristic of a social situation, has to be enlarged to take into account those who can monitor one another's behavior in a given place through their screens.

In previous work we have shown, for instance, that with respect to acquaintances, the special obligations to acknowledge and greet one another in chance encounters, which

Goffman had observed, were also relevant when such acquaintances would discover their mutual proximity through the mediation of mobile phone conversations or that of mobile location-aware applications (Licoppe 2009; Licoppe and Inada 2010). We explore here how the recent combination of location awareness with social networking applications and functionalities might make similar obligations relevant beyond the realm of acquaintances, and force us to refine our sense of which categories might be relevant in such augmented ecologies, beyond that of strangers, familiar strangers and acquaintances which Goffman and other researchers use to account for chance encounters in the non-augmented metropolis. To start to analyze this shift and some of its applications we will describe in more detail a few such mediated encounters in public places, based on some recent ethnographical studies of location-aware applications such as Foursquare, a mobile social network (Frith 2013; Licoppe and Legout 2014), and *Ingress*, a massive location-aware mobile game (Morel 2014).

Research Methods

Though our project in this chapter is not monographic, it involves a combination of "mobile methods" (Büscher et al. 2010) and ethnography to gain insight into the lived experience of such encounters. This requires in-depth interviews oriented toward the avoidance of generalizations and focused on the singularities and the contingencies of the situation. Mobile video-ethnographic methods are also highly relevant, such as close range methods of participant observations such as the shadowing of mobile users (Pink 2006), or equipping them with wearable cameras (Morel and Licoppe 2010; Brown and Laurier 2012; Licoppe and Figeac 2014). The latter, combined with smartphone screen video capture provides analysts with a chance to document how complex forms of encounters and social situations might unfold between screens and face-to-face, and we will give an example of such an ethnographic documenting of a multimedia encounter below in the case study section.

Meeting Strangers in the Street in Goffman's Metropolis: Georges Perec at the Terrace of a Parisian Café

In the late 1970s the French writer Georges Perec engaged in a literary project that seems to resonate deeply with Goffman's urban sociology of the time. He decided to sit at the terrace of a Parisian café three days in a row to attempt at "exhausting a place in Paris." His aim was to try to describe everything that would pass or happen in front of his eyes on the Place Saint-Sulpice from ordinary gestures to visual happenings:

> My intention in the pages that follow was to describe the rest instead: that which is generally not taken note of, that which is not noticed, that which has no importance: what happens when nothing happens other than the weather, people, cars and clouds.
>
> (Perec 2010, 3)

Perec's endeavor was framed as an attempt in exhaustivity—i.e. as a consciously self-defeating effort to encompass the whole of the fleeting urban experience and to account for it in writing. Perec as a writing observer did not delight in the spectacle he recanted, nor did he aestheticize his experience. Perec's inventories are written in a monotonous tone, mostly devoid of emotion. The force of his attempt is founded on the coherence of his stance as a neutral onlooker, both when gazing at the Saint-Sulpice square and when writing, and the framing of the reader as a similar onlooker, precisely achieved through the "neutral" and impersonal commonsensicality of his descriptions (Licoppe 2016). In that sense, Perec's literary project parallels Goffman's urban sociology in extolling the city as a place for anonymous crowds, the conduct of whom is designed to be open and meaningful to the neutral and disengaged onlooker. Both authors epitomized urban locales as lived public places, and highlighted the onlooker's stance as constitutive of their "public" character. Though he was obviously not a social scientist, as Howard Becker remarked, Perec's project has an affinity with the ethnographic mindset, in that it provides a literary description of the lived experience of inhabiting urban public places (Becker 2001).

In Perec's typical lists, all kinds of strangers are described as generic categories cued by their visual appearances:

> I again saw buses, taxis, cars, tourist buses, trucks and vans, bikes, mopeds, Vespas, motorcycles, a postal delivery tricycle, a motorcycle-school vehicle, a driving-school car, elegant women, aging beaus, old couples, groups of children, people with bags, satchels, suitcases, dogs, pipes, umbrellas, potbellies, old skins, old schmucks, young schmucks, idlers, deliverymen, scowlers, windbags. I also saw Jean-Paul Aron, and the owner of the "Trois Canettes" restaurant, whom I had already seen this morning.
>
> (Perec 2010, 18)

We may remark on the presence in this list of two very special kinds of strangers. First there is a "celebrity" (Jean-Paul Aron, a famous French political historian opposing Jean-Paul Sartre in the 1950s and 1960s), whose name and face is supposedly known to all (at least anybody in Perec's projected readership, without any need for further information). Second we have here an instance of someone framed as a familiar stranger, the owner of a restaurant nearby, the name of whom seems to escape Perec. Though he may be a familiar stranger, he still remains in a list alongside other, complete strangers, and one celebrity, sharing with them the fact that such mutual proximity and fleeting encounter does not project any kind of further involvement from the sitting Perec.

In the lists that account for his three days of observation, it only happened four times that Perec mentions seeing an acquaintance. This gives us a sense of the rarity of such chance encounters in Goffman's metropolis. First there is for instance a loose acquaintance of Perec:

> The café is packed
>
> A distant acquaintance (friend of a friend, friend of a friend of a friend) passed by in the street, came over to say hello, had a coffee.
>
> A Paris-Vision bus goes by. The tourists have headphones
>
> The sky is gray. Fleeting sunny spells.
>
> (Perec 2010, 33)

However weak their degree of acquaintance (not only is the acquaintance "a friend of a friend of a friend" but no name is provided), just the fact of passing in the street and the mutual acknowledgment of this co-proximity seem to make "naturally" relevant a focused encounter, that is engaging into greetings, and even sitting down to share a coffee, as if these actions were flowing from one into the other. The smooth flow of Perec's phrase embeds the institution of acquaintanceship as seen by Goffman: the enactment of special claims and obligations in chance co-proximities of which relevant parties are mutually aware, and visibly mutually aware because of the monitoring capacities with which the situation endows them, to acknowledge the fact of this and engage into focused encounters. Later on, he happens to see a probably closer acquaintance (this time she is described by her full name), who he already saw before in a way which led to a brief encounter, but this time he sees her from a distance:

Passage of a 63 bus

Geneviève Serreau passes by in front of the café (too far away for me to get her attention).

Project: a classification of umbrellas according to their forms, their means of functioning, their color, their material . . .

(Perec 2010, 42)

Admittedly they don't meet but such an interpretation is only a byproduct of a cursory reading. If indeed they do not meet, Perec still accounts for this with a justification: she was too far away, and hence could not get in a situation of mutual monitoring, that is a "social situation," where Goffman's point about acquaintanceship, and therefore the initiation of a focused encounter, would have become relevant. Because of such a "relevance rule," Perec's non-encounter with Geneviève Serreau is different from all the non-encounters with all the strangers he happens to see and list. In the latter case such encounters just did not happen. In the former, such a focused encounter is "missing" in a special sense, because of the special obligations that acquaintanceship entails with respect to encounters in public places.

What happens when participants are equipped with smartphone and location-aware mobile phone applications which allow them to "discover" on screen other people who might or might not be visible to them with the naked eye, and which are "known" in a certain way because of the way they are designed and profiled through mobile applications? Elsewhere we have tried to argue that it made untenable Perec's position as a neutral observer accounting for the people he sees as strangers in common sense categorical terms (Licoppe 2016). Here we would like to provide and discuss two different empirical examples of such encounters, which we might call mediated encounters.

A Foursquare Encounter: Re-specifying Strangers

Foursquare is a location-based mobile social network—sometimes called a Locational Mobile Social Network or LMSN (de Souza e Silva and Frith 2010)—in which users can choose to make their location known to others by posting it in the system. According to users' privacy settings, these "others" may be the whole set of users ("all"), a chosen list of friends, or no one at all. Moreover, all users who check into a venue see other users who have also checked into the location in the last three hours and can exchange messages with them, a feature that makes it possible for two unacquainted Foursquare users to discover their mutual proximity. Another particularity of Foursquare has to do with the "gamification" of such mobile social network-ing applications, in that users can compete for specific titles tied to these created places, such as "mayorships" and badges. This creates a playful and competitive environment for often checking into one's location; it is on the basis of the number of location checks in a given place that one might become the "mayor" of a particular place or lose the title (Lindqvist et al. 2011; Frith 2013). In our study of French Foursquare users (Licoppe and Legout 2014), one user reported this particular encounter:

This summer I was having a holiday in la Réunion, and I spent one afternoon with an Air France stewardess, precisely because she was checking in on Foursquare, and she came to look for me at the reception of the hotel, saying "Are you the Sandrine who just robbed me of my position of mayor for this hotel?" I said yes and we spent the afternoon talking about her job and many other things. And so these are real encounters I would not have made, she would not have talked to me if I had not been on Foursquare.

(Sandrine, 45 years old)

It transpires from this story that the narrator, known in her story as "Sandrine"—the pseudonym she uses in Foursquare—and the air stewardess (who remains unnamed in the story) she encounters are not acquainted in Goffman's sense. Neither have they previously interacted online. Nor are they involved in a social situation in Goffman's sense where the sense of mutual presence and mutual monitoring are crucial. The air stewardess was only in a position to infer "Sandrine's" potential presence in the hotel from her recent check on Foursquare, and Sandrine herself might have been unaware of the presence of the air stewardess. However, as the story tells, the discovery of the potential presence of the unknown narrator in the hotel seems to be enough to entitle the stewardess to look immediately for the narrator, and the latter will not apparently contest her rights to initiate such an encounter in any way.

This display of entitlement seems to rest on flimsy grounds. The discovery of their potential co-presence concerns someone the air stewardess has never met and only knows from a pseudonym. Actually meeting involves solving significant recognition issues (hence coming to the lobby and using the tag "Sandrine" and the categorical description "who just robbed me of my position of mayor"). Why was such an event involving a stranger not ignored and how could it be treated as making it possible and accountable to summon this almost stranger into an encounter? Precisely because in the Foursquare on-screen ecology this is not a complete stranger; it is someone who is identifiable (a) as a fellow Foursquare user, (b) with an individual pseudonym (Sandrine), and (c) whose previous behavior is known enough to support the categorization "who just robbed me of my position of mayor for this hotel." The narrator appears to the air stewardess as a kind of "virtually familiar stranger," someone who is a stranger in Goffman's sense, unknown, unmet in real life, but the Foursquare persona of whom has been fleetingly and repeatedly felt, without eliciting direct electronic interactions.

This is not enough to make relevant some obligation to meet, as would be the case with acquaintances, and much of the entitlement to initiate an encounter seems to rest here on the categorization "who just robbed me of my position of mayor for this hotel," the production of which actually does relational work. It frames both parties as members of what Harvey Sacks called a "membership categorization device," and more specifically here a "standard relational pair" (Sacks 1992; Hester and Eglin 1997). It enacts the narrator and the air stewardess as the pair of fellow Foursquare users that have been competing for the Foursquare mayorship of that particular hotel. The event (discovering she has just lost the title to the narrator) is made noticeable to the narrator within the design of the mobile social networking application. The event can be read as a cue for a possible co-presence in the hotel and as enacting an accountable category-bound affiliation of the two relevant persons; it can constitute reasonable and accountable grounds for further action under the form of initiating an encounter. Such a display of entitlement does not appear to be contested by the narrator. On the contrary it works as a kind of embedded and implicit driving agency in her tale, and it will be vindicated by the success of the encounter: the two virtually familiar strangers will meet in person and talk for hours, which provides a kind of justificatory coda to the whole thing.

An *Ingress* Encounter in the Street

In this second instance we move to the domain of location-aware games. The most sophisticated location-aware game played today is probably *Ingress*, a worldwide location-aware, massive online multiplayer game developed by Niantic-Google. It is an augmented reality game played on smartphones. Players worldwide are divided in two factions. The aim of each player is to capture virtual "portals" (which are localized and made visible as dots on digital map representations) by getting there, "hacking them" through the game interface, and linking the capture portals (by moving to each) into triangles ("control fields" in the game) which are then claimable by one's faction. According to the surface covered by the linked portals, each faction gets some points ("mind units") that are summed totally. Though players occasionally pay attention to such global scores, their individual behavior (linking portals on a large scale involves collaboration, even at an international level) is often local, aiming to capture and hack portals in their familiar haunts, or along their usual paths (with a significant number of game-induced detours) (Morel 2014). Portals are unequally distributed, with much higher concentration in urban areas.

In the ethnographic protocol we have developed, we video record the smartphone screens of the players (which is a normal smartphone, not a terminal dedicated to the game), and the player wears a portable camera and a microphone. In the encounter the user we observed, player K, is moving in the center of the provincial town where he lives, and is using his everyday mobility as an opportunity to capture portals in the vicinity without yet trying to link them (Figure 18.1a). As he does so new links between portals appear (Figure 18.1b) which provides him with evidence that another player (player C) nearby is actively engaged in the game. He can also anticipate that, for the same reason, that player is aware of his actions and their own proximity. Based on this mediated form of mutual monitoring, we can extend Goffman's concepts, and consider these players are in a (mediated) social situation, implying a sense of (mediated) presence. Indeed K checks directly the links recently created for a given place (Figure 18.1c) and a menu that displays

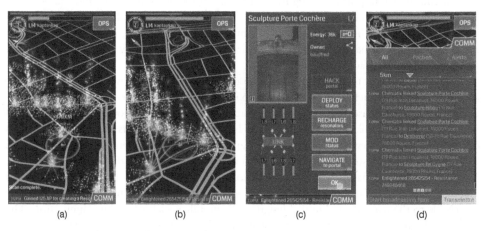

(a)　　　　　(b)　　　　　(c)　　　　　(d)

Figure 18.1　Discovering another *Ingress* player active nearby. (a) The position of player K is at the center of the orange circle; (b) Player K has moved a little to the left and to the top and, as he did, new lines appear on his left providing evidence for the presence of an active player nearby; (c) Alerted by this, player K checks the logs of the game and sees direct evidence of the actions of player C, described in written form in a kind of news feed (d) indicating the pseudonym of the close player, and the type and timing of his recent actions in the game

C's recent actions (Figure 18.1d). The sense of a social situation is here stronger than in the Foursquare example, for such monitoring is both mutual and the actions of the players are continuously and automatically updated by the system. However, like the Foursquare case it enacts the relevance of mutual access. Indeed a few seconds later player K initiates contact by sending player C the following text message (through the *Ingress* communication module): "lol quelle synchro" (Lol what a synchro).

Player K and player C are loose acquaintances in real life (they are on first-name terms but do not meet socially), and are what we could call here "virtual acquaintances" (they have occasionally interacted in the course of the game, under the guise of their game pseudonyms). K's message is nicely crafted. "quelle synchro" topicalizes the fact that they are performing actions within the game at the same time, and at about the same place, and it indexes their mutual awareness of this. So both the very action of the messaging and the content of the message acknowledge their both being participants in a social situation.

What is specific is that unlike Perec's example, this is not the case of two loose acquaintances suddenly seeing one another in a public place. Here the two acquaintances are mutually visible on the game maps, so the chance discovery of their being involved in a social situation is an online phenomenon. By its straightforwardness, the message displays a strong sense of entitlement: their awareness of mutual proximity and game behavior, coupled with existing channels of communication, seemed to enact a right to initiate electronic contact. A possible ground for such a display of entitlement is that the social situation enacts some categorical relevancies. It enacts the players as acquainted fellow players playing in the same area. Interestingly, player C will follow up by actually joining player K in the street. What follows is an audio transcript of their talk:

Extract 1

1	C:	uh [uh
2	K:	[ça va Romain
		how do you do Romain?
3	C:	uh uh uh salut=
		hi
4	K:	=excellent la synchro
		excellent the synchro
5	C:	ça va?
		how do you do?
6	K:	(0.3) pas mal
		not bad
7		(0.3)
8	C:	t'as pas une clé qui a disparu?
		haven't you got a key which disappeared?

After an exchange of greetings K provides a positive assessment "excellent la synchro" which echoes C's text message. However, now uttered in a co-present encounter, it extends the scope of their game-mediated mutual awareness as making relevant not only an electronic exchange but also a face-to-face encounter. It also displays K's alignment with this new development (it was C who joined K). At the anchor position (line 8), which marks a proper beginning, C provides a game-related turn, orienting their face-to-face conversation toward the game. After a short exchange on game resources nearby they go on:

Extract 1 (continued)

24 K: t'as un peu de temps? hhhhh
you got a little time?

25 C: (0.4) ouais::: un ptit peu ouais hhhh elle est par terre
yeah ::: a little yeah it's on the ground

26 (0.8)

27 K: je préfère
I prefer

28 (1.0)

29 C: j'ai vu que tu fermais les fields (.) je me suis dit l'enfoiré:::::
I saw that you were closing the fields I said to myself the fucke:::r

30 (0.8)

31 K: beh c'est ce que je voulais faire mais je ne m'attendais pas à ce que tu viennes
beh that's what I wanted to do but I was not expecting you to come

32 (0.3)

33 C: bah [en fait
actually

34 K: [bah/ (.) y en a un qui va faire le dessus et l'autre le dessous alors
there's one who will do the top and the other the bottom then

35 C: absolument
absolutely

K's question in line 24 can be heard as the first part of a pre-sequence, prefiguring an invitation or a proposal. It gets a limited "go-ahead" response (line 25), and then the interactional project surfaces in line 34, with K proposing to turn their encounter into a collaboration within the game, an offer which is accepted (line 35). The face-to-face encounter unfolds along the same categorical lines, which made it a relevant happenstance in the first place. The possibility of their unplanned face-to-face encounter in the street was grounded on their being enacted as acquainted fellow players, initially invisible to one another, but playing the game in the same place at the same time. The face-to-face encounter is initially given a game-related orientation before moving into an offer to collaborate in the game while together.

Conclusion

Goffman has highlighted social situations—defined as co-presence and mutual (often visual) capacities for participants to monitor one another—as a foundational unit for the organization of face-to-face interactions. Urban public places can then be described as the site of continuously happening, unplanned social situations involving strangers, and occasionally familiar strangers or acquaintances. In Goffman's public order, acquaintanceship is considered an institution, co-extensive to the enactment of particular obligations for relevant participants to engage in a focused encounter (an exchange of greetings at the minimum) when becoming mutually aware of one another, that is being involved together in a social situation. We then wondered how this particular aspect of the public order might be affected by the availability of smartphone and location-aware mobile applications endowing users with mediated monitoring capacities and allowing them to discover their mutual proximity and accessibility, thus augmenting co-present encounters and even turning configurations where participants are close but not co-present into screen-mediated "social situations," where they can monitor their mutual behavior on screen to some extent.

These considerations and our two empirical examples led us to three different types of observations. First, we were able to recognize that notions such as strangers, virtual familiar strangers and acquaintances, which were central to Goffman's sociology of the public order were relatively uni-dimensional, and that in the location-aware, smartphone-augmented public place, one had to take into account the multilayered character of these notions. Let us imagine a given *ego* who does not know the name of a given *alter* and would not be able to recognize them by sight, who are both users of the same location-aware mobile application.

Even if they are complete strangers "in the real world," they might still know one another on screen (through pseudonyms, profiles, observable traces of actions in the mobile application and even prior interaction in the case of virtual acquaintances), and they might happen to be able to discover their occasional co-proximity and therefore their joint involvement in a social situation (this is the point where location awareness plays a crucial role). The particular multilayered form that their mutual strangeness or acquaintanceship takes will then be consequential with respect to the way such an encounter might unfold, and the obligations that become relevant and toward which they would be expected to orient. It is useful to introduce here three special cases that are relevant to an understanding of the mediated public order:

1   The "pseudonymous stranger," who is a complete stranger in real life, and also in the mobile application, but who is available there when "discovered" as a pseudonym and a profile.
2   The "virtual familiar stranger," who is completely unknown in real life, made more or less familiar in the mobile application through repeated observation of prior behavior linked to a fixed pseudonym, as was the case with our two Foursquare users.
3   The virtual acquaintance, who is unknown in real life, but with whom one might have a history of prior interaction in the location-aware mobile application.

This typology can then be adjusted and refined according to varying degrees of strangeness or acquaintanceship in the real world, or even additional layers related to the relevance of other, interwoven location-aware platforms. Our two players in the *Ingress* example were, for instance, loose acquaintances in the real world and more closely acquainted within the *Ingress* game-world.

The gist of our argument is that the location-sensitive augmentation of public places, and the multilayered character of acquaintanceship it entails, transforms the interaction order in public places, though Goffman's general frame of analysis can still be applied. For instance, in the Foursquare case, we saw how two virtual familiar strangers, made aware of their mutual proximity on screen, oriented to such discovery as making "naturally" relevant an unplanned face-to-face encounter, on the basis of categorical affiliations (fellow competitors for the mayorship of a given hotel). So special obligations with respect to the initiation of focused encounters might also be relevant in the case of virtual familiar strangers, once they have overcome recognition issues (which derive from the fact they are strangers in real life, i.e. strangers in Goffman's initial meaning for the concept). In the case of virtual acquaintanceship, the *Ingress* example not only suggested special obligations to meet related to interwoven degrees of acquaintanceship, but also that the very trajectory of the encounter, particularly in its initial stages, might be framed by the characteristics of the mobile game and the design of the mobile application. Unlike Perec's loose acquaintance, the (mutual) sighting of which makes relevant greetings and coming to sit for a coffee and chat, the two *Ingress* players seem to remain attached to their online ongoing mobile game activities in the course of their face-to-face encounters. Though this does not work in a deterministic way, there might be a general orientation to the particular relevance of the virtual acquaintanceship and virtual activities, as if those were oozing into the face-to-face encounters and shaping to some extent the possibilities to interact in the latter. In any case our approach—a combination of mobile methods and ethnography—opens up the way into a more general consideration of the mediated public order, i.e. the way chance encounters in public places may unfold in specific ways for users of location-aware mobile applications.

References

Becker, Howard. 2001. "Georges Perec's experiments in social description." *Ethnography* 2(1): 63–76.

Brown, Barry and Eric Laurier. 2012. "The normal natural troubles of driving with GPS." In *Proceedings of the SIGCHI Conference on Human Factors in Computing Systems*, 1620–30. New York: ACM Press.

Büscher, Monika, John Urry and Katian Witschger. 2010. *Mobile Methods*. London: Routledge.

de Souza e Silva, Adriana and Daniel M. Sutko, eds. 2009. *Digital Cityscapes*. New York: Peter Lang.

de Souza e Silva, Adriana and Jordan Frith. 2010 "Locative mobile social networks: Mapping communication and location in urban spaces." In *Mobilities* 5(4): 485–505.

Farman, Jason, ed. 2013. *The Mobile Story: Narrative Practices with Locative Technologies*. New York: Routledge.

Frith, Jordan. 2013. "Turning life into a game: Foursquare, gamification and personal mobility." *Mobile Media and Communication* 1(2): 248–62.

Goffman, Erwing. 1963. *Behavior in Public Places*. New York: Free Press.

Hester, Stephen and Peter Eglin. 1997. "Membership categorization analysis: An introduction." In *Culture in Action: Studies in Membership Categorization Analysis*, edited by Stephen Hester and Peter Eglin, 1–23. Washington, DC: International Institute for Ethnomethodology and Conversation Analysis & University Press of America.

Licoppe, Christian. 2009. "Recognizing mutual 'proximity' at a distance: Weaving together mobility, sociality and technology." *Journal of Pragmatics* 41(10): 1924–37.

——. 2016 (forthcoming). "An attempt at exhausting an augmented place in Paris: Georges Perec, observer-writer of urban life, as a mobile locative media user." In *The Afterlives of Georges Perec*, edited by Rowan Wilken and Justin Clemens. Edinburgh: Edinburgh University Press.

Licoppe, Christian and Yoriko Inada. 2010. "Locative media and cultures of mediated proximity: The case of the Mogi game location-aware community." *Environment and Planning D: Society and Space* 28(4): 691–709.

Licoppe, Christian and Julien Figeac. 2014. "Direct video observation of the uses of smartphone on the move: Reconceptualizing mobile multi-activity." In *Mobility and Locative Media: Mobile Communication in Hybrid Space*, edited by Adriana de Souza e Silva and Mimi Sheller, 48–64. London: Routledge.

Licoppe, Christian and Marie-Christine Legout. 2014. "Living inside location-aware mobile social information: The pragmatics of Foursquare notifications." In *Living Inside Mobile Information*, edited by James E. Katz, 109–30. Dayton, OH: Greyden Press.

Lindqvist, Janne, et al. 2011. "I'm the mayor of my house: Examining why people use Foursquare—A social-driven location-sharing application." In *Proceedings of the SIGCHI Conference on Human Factors in Computing Systems*, edited by Desney Tan et al., 2409–18. New York: ACM Press.

Lofland, Lyn H. 1998. *The Public Realm: Exploring the City's Quintessential Social Territory*. New York: Aldine de Gruyter.

Milgram, Stanley. 1974. "The frozen world of the familiar stranger." In *Psychology Today* 17: 70–80.

Morel, Julien. 2014. "Ingress. Mobilités et sociabilités dans un jeu de réalité augmentée." *Interfaces Numériques* 3(3): 447–72.

Morel, Julien and Christian Licoppe. 2010. "Studying mobile video telephony." In *Mobile Methods*, edited by Monika Büscher, John Urry and Katian Witschger, 164–82. London: Routledge.

Perec, Georges. 2010. *An Attempt at Exhausting a Place in Paris*. Cambridge: Wakefield Press.

Pink, Sarah. 2006. *Doing Visual Ethnography*. London: Sage.

Sacks, Harvey. 1992. *Lectures on Conversation*. Cambridge: Cambridge University Press.

Sudnow, David. 1972. "Temporal parameters of interpersonal observation." In *Studies in Social Interaction*, edited by David Sudno, 259–79. New York: The Free Press.

19

MOBILE MEDIA MATTERS

The Ethnography and Phenomenology of Itinerant Interfaces

Ingrid Richardson and Brendan Keogh

Margaret, a 33-year-old accountant from Brisbane, Australia, is one of our participants in a three-year study of mobile media and play in the domestic context. When asked what games she regularly plays on her mobile phone, she answered, "Mostly free games. Little puzzle games as well." As she said the words "little puzzle games" she held her right hand in the air, index finger stretched out, and waved horizontal and vertical lines in the air. "Oh," we replied, "You mean those match-3 games like *Bejeweled* and *Candy Crush Saga*?" Margaret nodded, "Yes, exactly." In other interviews, we observed the same gesticulation. Multiple times, interviewees did not recall the names of the mobile games they had played, but were able to mimic the haptic and gestural movements required of them. These anecdotes point toward both the way mobile games and media interfaces are integral to our embodied ways of knowing, and the challenges posed to the mobile media researcher who wishes to capture, understand, and interpret this contemporary cultural and everyday practice.

Digital ethnography has emerged as one response to the study of digital, mobile, and networked media in everyday life. As proponents of the approach argue, there is no one method but rather such research is methodologically innovative or "mixed," transdisciplinary, empirical, contextual, and cross-cultural. Digital ethnography may include but is not limited to "virtual ethnography" (an approach that is adaptive to online environments as important sites of exploration), and more broadly focuses on how our engagement with digital media and technological interfaces configure the ways we attend to, communicate, and perceive the world. As we suggest (and as others have suggested), it need not always be media-centric in its analysis of the way digital interfaces are imbricated in and across everyday practices. Moreover, as Horst et al. (2012, 86–7) have noted:

[T]he pervasiveness of digital media and technology has spurred renewed attention to the particular capacities, or affordances—a concept that has its roots in the phenomenology of Merleau-Ponty and James Gibson (Norman 1988)—and the constraining and enabling material possibilities of media.

In this chapter we explore the material, sensory, corporeal aspects of digital ethnography, primarily in the context of mobile media. The mobility of mobile media and the need (espe-cially on more contemporary "smartphone" touchscreen devices) to literally "handle" screen objects with a corporeal body sees mobile media as both more implicitly integrated into users' everyday lives than other keyboard-based media and, at the same time, more intimately involved in the affordances, enablements, and constraints of the device. In what follows, we explore the "corporealization" of digital and mobile media—or the way our use of such interfaces is literally "realized" through the body—and identify the particular insights of a phenomenologically inflected digital ethnography. Our argument is broadly supported by our experience as digital ethnographers, and more specifically with qualitative data collected as part of an ongoing three-year multi-city research project into domestic practices around dig-ital media, mobiles, and games in Australian households. Our aim in this chapter is to convey how a digital ethnography of mobile media use can adeptly traverse and interweave material, corporeal, networked, online, and offline contexts.

Ethnographic Phenomenology, Phenomenological Ethnography

Ethnographers of online and digital media have argued that we need to acknowledge and explore the "ontological diversity" of online and mobile media, requiring the application of ethnography as an "adaptive methodology" (Hine 2015; Hand 2014; Evans 2015). Such an approach makes no distinction between online and offline engagement, or at least rec-ognizes and interprets the mutual imbrication of sense perception, materiality, and digital networks in the construction and articulation of space, place, identity, knowing, and being in the contemporary lifeworld. A number of our project participants, for example, described their engagement with digital games as multi-contextual, simultaneously involving online networks, the specificity of domestic spaces, the materiality of interfaces and their haptic demands, and communication with others both physically and virtually present. Clearly, eth-nographies of online, mobile, and digital media cannot attend solely to the online and the digital, but must also account for the material, social, and embodied experiences within and alongside which the online and digital are situated.

Phenomenology provides one solution to this quandary. As Horst et al. (2012) identify, both Gibson's ecological notion of affordance (as that which describes the physiological and material *relationality* between organism and environment) and phenomenology can be usefully applied to the study of body–technology relations in terms of their individual, collective, social, and cultural effects in everyday life contexts. The coupling of tools and humans is effectively articulated by Merleau-Ponty's term intercorporeality, a word that describes the irreduci-ble relation between technics, embodiment, knowledge, and perception. As Merleau-Ponty famously claimed, the body "applies itself to space like a hand to an instrument" (1964: 5), an application that depends as much on the specificities of perception and bodily movement as it does on the materiality of the tool-in-use.

From this perspective, it is our somatic *openness* to the "stuff" of our environment that allows us to incorporate technologies and equipment into our own corporeal organization. Thus, our being-in-the-world is rendered as always-already a *technosomatic* relation. More recently, cultural phenomenology and post-phenomenology (Ihde 2012; Csordas 2011) have considered how a palimpsest of cultural practices and collective habits always-already informs these body-technology relations. That is, our sensorium is "continually shifting and culturally variable . . . according to a society's rules or proscriptions as well as technological mediation and the physical environment" (Paterson 2009, 771). This affects the reflexivity of the ethnographer, along with the interpretation of participant language and idioms, and gesture, posture, and bodily habits.

The phenomenological approach, then, is particularly useful for interpreting both the haptic intimacy of wearable and handheld media in specific life contexts, and in the case of our research, for exploring how the routines of bodily movement and interaction within the home are modified by mobile media user-practices, affecting our experience of touch, immediacy, proximity, distance, and togetherness in domestic space. As de Brabandere argues in her discussion of the ways sensation and affect in everyday experience impact upon our research strategies, "the boundary of our physical extremities is constituted in the plastic dynamism of perceptive experience" (2014, 235). The practical application of phenomenological enquiry to ethnographic methods also turns our attention toward the multisensory and tactile nature of our being-in-the-world, countering the predominance of audiovisual approaches in the study of contemporary media.

In its focus on experience and perception, phenomenology is also concerned with the embodied everyday—that is, in Moores' (2014) terms, our "habitation," "at-homeness," or indwelling—by reflecting upon those mundane micro-practices that congeal into collective routines and processes just as they simultaneously rework and transform those patterns of perception and ways of knowing. Thus, although our quotidian being-in-the-world inevitably apprehends the broader processes of mediation, our interpretive and experiential access to these processes is via the concrete "fixings" of media use and perception.

As researchers such as Moores (2012) and Couldry (2012) argue, our empirical approach to digital media use is frequently colored by the media-centrism apparent in much media and communication theory, often influenced by McLuhan and Innis, and articulated through such terms as mediation, intermediality (Helles 2013), and mediality (Jäger et al. 2010). For example, for Kember and Zylinksa, our "originary technicity" is conflated unproblematically with the idea that "we are media" (2012, 13). Jäger et al. develop the field of mediality research, which is explicitly grounded upon the premise "that cultural artifacts and communicative processes are fundamentally organized by media," thus allowing for "the systematic analysis of inter- and multimedial constellations to supersede the monomedial study of individual media" (2010, 12). This expansive treatment of media processes—particularly dominated by screenic overdetermination—means that mediation and accompanying media tropes of connectivity and networking are often taken to describe our being-in-the-world *tout court*. Here, the most significant problem with attributing ontological and historical primacy to the process of mediation in the form of networks and platforms is that it privileges a quasi-universal system of mediatic relations and connections (e.g. the network) over the specific properties of objects and bodies, or instances of everyday use and habit. Indeed, we can see how connection—grounded in conduit and transmission metaphors—is now commonly understood as the condition of collective existence (where collective being and community become reified as a matter of connection), or how the network metaphor now indicates a fuzzy or "vague structure of interconnectedness" (van den Boomen 2014, 177).

Against these approaches, both Moores (2012) and Couldry (2012) argue for the positioning of media uses and forms alongside other non-media contexts. Couldry's strategy refocuses our attention onto everyday practices, actions, and habits without assuming that media is the most important thing going on in people's lives, while Moores' approach is to situate media as part of our embodied routines of dwelling and movement in daily life, and in terms of our habitual and orientational "familiarity with the world" (2009, 2013). In our research we have applied a phenomenological ethnography to our being-with-media, adopting what Moores refers to as a "know-as-we-go" approach alongside a realization of the sedimented histories of our originary technicity—both within and without media-centrism. *In situ* observation and "go-alongs" (following participants as they enact their everyday engagement with media), for example, means the researcher can literally be "at the interface" of user and technology, unlocking deeper knowledge about routines and movements and their affects. Elsewhere, recent work that has focused on the rising prominence of play, play culture, and an emerging "lusory sensibility" (Mäyrä 2012; Hjorth and Richardson 2014), while situating analyses in the embodiment of digital games and the phenomena of gameplay, also turn to the function and affordances of playfulness outside the rubric of media use (e.g. by referring to the ludic and paidiac play of animals).

In further support of the corporealization of research methods and strategies, van den Boomen argues that any definition of a medium implicitly or explicitly mobilizes a bodily metaphor or metonym: "There is no medium outside of metaphor" (2014, 102). Thus, for example, our use of screen interfaces is saturated with orientational, entity, and conduit metaphors (left and right arrows to go "back" or "forward" along a search trajectory, folders and trash bins, and application icons that contain files or "open" software programs). There is thus a fundamental and irreducible relation between bodily dexterity (knowledge in the hands and fingers) and our perceptual orientation and movement as we engage in the practices of online "wayfaring" (Moores 2013), and we use numerous and familiar somatic metaphors to conceptually and perceptually manage our engagement with screen media.

Significantly, such tropes are not neutral; as Van den Boomen asks, "What does the metaphor foreground and amplify—literally, materially, and discursively—and what does it nullify and ignore?" (2014, 189). For example, the metaphor of the screen as window-on-the-world, originating from Alberti's perspectival grid, is a visualist mode of imagining the world that generates an ontological boundary between observer and observed. This body-metaphor—one that is defined by a facial or frontal ontology—remains as one of the most tenacious interfacial tropes influencing our experience and understanding of contemporary media today, evidenced by the way that the user interface is commonly and metonymically taken to mean the screen interface, rendering invisible or trivial the myriad other aspects of use (such as the haptics and function of input devices, the complex synaesthesia involved in our engagement with touch-screens, or the proprioceptive and locative aspects of mobile media use) (Richardson 2010).

Indeed, we might argue that frontal and visualist metaphors of mediation can often work to occlude the perceptual specificities of concrete body–medium couplings, suggesting that we must be critically aware of the way both participants, and ourselves as researchers, deploy them. In the analysis of haptic media such as mobile touchscreens, for example, researchers have identified the way that hands and fingers take on a metonymic function as they "stand in" for the perceptual body (Pink et al. 2015; Bratton 2014). For Elo, mobile media is complexly multisensual and synaesthesic—the "taps, pushes and sweeps" quite literally "challenge the familiar concretia of the world" (Elo 2012, 5), evidenced by the way we apprise media objects with skeuomorphic real-world effects. Van den Boomen writes: "Metaphors such as virtual community, Web 2.0, Facebook friend, following, phishing, and liking all tap from other resources. They translate and transform conventions, acts, habits, and desires into digital-material entities that subsequently become mediatized" (2014, 191).

If our quotidian modes of being-in-the-world are situated, contingent, and enacted, for those of us who seek "deep" interpretations of such experience, analysis must be ethnographically and contextually informed. For Jacucci et al. (2007), since emergent practices cannot be "known in advance" they must be explored and evidenced through empirical interpretive work. The unintentional, creative, ad-hoc usage of media can only be gleaned from the critical observation of actual practices. As Wiley et al. point out:

> The increasing complexity of social relations, mobility and mediated connectivity in late modernity requires a new approach to the study of social space—one which does not start with a sweeping, metahistorical narrative about the transformation of space and place . . . but begins, instead, with what is happening on the ground: with empirical fieldwork that will allow us to *discover* the realities of spatial transformation that people are (or *may* be) actually experiencing.
>
> (2012, 185)

Shifts in the relational ontology between body and technology are of crucial importance to the digital ethnographer. Such shifts can only properly be grasped through *enactive* observation. Body habits, gestures, micro movements, and practices reveal our being-toward the lifeworld—in short, they reveal self–world relations. Pink et al., for example, describe their observation and interpretation of mobile media use as a kind of "researching through hands" (2015, 2), while Bratton (2014) shows how the hand embodies cognition and reveals a corporealized attitude about the world and toward others.

In our own research, we frequently observed the way participants managed their mobile device as a material interface, such as habitually placing the screen face down in between showing us what was on their screens and how they used it. When questioned, participants described how this seemingly trivial gesture actually embodied a wealth of "deep" attitudes about privacy, social etiquette, and care for the device. Other participants expressed an explicit preference for mobile games that require the phone to be held in different ways. Games played in an upright "portrait" position were preferred for their convenience (typically only requiring a single hand to both hold the phone and to play the game) and inconspicuousness.

Matthew, a 24-year-old from Brisbane, played mobile games on the train to work, and would sometimes want to finish a game level once getting off at a station, albeit surreptitiously. As he described, with games playable one-handed in portrait mode, one could conceal, through a particular hand-device arrangement commonly and habitually adopted for other non-game applications, that a game was being played: "You can just look like you are doing whatever and it's like 'I'm not playing a game on the way to work!'" Others preferred games played in a "landscape" orientation that required both hands, as these were "handily" familiar to the more traditional console gamepad configuration, using two thumbs to control the game. In each of these examples, the bodily methods of interfacing *with* the materiality of the screen are of paramount importance to the participants' engagement. In our study of mobile media, then, these new "techniques of the body" at play must be accounted for if we are to interpret the complexities and intentionalities of use.

The Materiality and Embodiment of (Mobile) Media

The intimate, haptic, social, and playful nature of mobile interfaces has become a key focus of media research, yet to date there has been limited ethnographic analysis of the way such devices are deeply embedded within the communicative and spatial organization of the home. As Hand (2014, 4) notes:

[W]hile the role of networks and platforms in constituting contemporary media culture or ecology has been usefully highlighted, significantly less attention has been paid to the related dynamics of devices and their uses as material and mediating objects in daily life.

Like ourselves, a number of ethnographic researchers such as Hand, Pink, Hjorth, Moores, and Couldry are now focusing on how mobile media are "articulated and *domesticated* within the rhythms of everyday life" through sedimented and emergent routines and habits (Hand 2014, 5). Our three-year study, based on a multi-city qualitative evaluation of mobile media and mobile play practices in Australian households, seeks to analyze mobile media practices as part of the dynamics of domesticity, and further contribute to "haptic" or "multisensory" ethnographic approaches (Pink 2009; Bates 2015) that can effectively be applied to the study of touchscreen interfaces. In this context, by taking a (post)phenomenological approach as described above, we are equipped to explore the ways that mobile touchscreens are transforming our embodied experience of sociality and material culture within domestic environments (i.e. our ways of "being-with-others" and "being-with-media" at home).

Over the past decade, too, we have seen significant developments in the experimental and creative use of mobile and wearable media devices as data-collection tools in ethnographic research. Such innovative modes of data collection are deployed as a means to more authentically disclose people's lived experience in everyday life, their *in situ* sensory encounters with place, and affective engagement with others, both situated and mediated. In our ethnography of mobile media use in the home, we are exploring a range of participant activities as a means of capturing habitudes of embodiment, including technology "walkthroughs," dynamic "day-in-the-life" recordings of gameplay using wearable GoPro cameras, media diaries (both mobile and web-based), and video re-enactments of media use and interaction. Our study reveals how mobile media touchscreens work to reconfigure the space of the home, affording new patterns of haptic and collaborative play, new ways of perceiving and experiencing intimacy and "touchability" (of others and things), and hybrid varieties of co-presence (see Licoppe and Morel's chapter in this volume) and emplacement (proximal, networked, alone, and together).

These ethnographic methods enable us to capture the physical movement of bodies and objects, to record participants' use of media *in situ*, to follow participant pathways of intention and action, and the longitudinal span of the project allows us to observe and ask questions about changes in sensory experience, emplacement, and to document how objects, spaces, and people in domestic environments are configured and reconfigured (Hine 2015, 63). As Srnicek (2014, 75) comments:

[H]umans are materially constructed in such a way as to be open to technological augmentation and one of the primary media for this extension today is the mobile phone and its associated apps. . . . The mobile phone is already one of the most subtly disruptive technologies of the past few decades. Everyday behaviors have been widely modified by the introduction of smartphones.

Quite literally, mobile media interfaces and apps connect us to the environment in particular ways, altering the way we engage with and are affected by the lifeworld. In other work Hjorth and Richardson (2014) have documented how mobile media instantiate new assemblages and orders of attention and distraction, and identified the way mobile apps and games work "ambiently"—both fitting into the patterns and interstices of everyday life, and at the same time modifying spaces and bodies to their particular demands.

One example of this can be seen in our observations of the Whitlam family in Brisbane, who shared a family iPad. The three girls (aged nine, four, and two) would play a number of games on this device including *Minecraft*, *Angry Birds*, and the various playful apps produced by studio Toca Boca such as *Toca Band* and *Toca Hair Studio*. More telling than *what* games the Whitlam children played, however, was *how* they went about playing them. During our observation, the four-year-old would take the iPad and sit on the couch to begin playing *Minecraft* (a game that would be physically arduous for a four-year-old's hands to manage on either a desktop computer or home console). Almost immediately, her siblings, who would sit on each side of her, leaning over so as to be able to see the screen, would join her. Occasionally, each would reach over to touch and interact with the screen (sometimes to the four-year-old's frustration). At another time, the two-year-old sat on her mother's lap, opened the *Toca Tea Party* application, and they proceeded to play the game together, each of them tapping and interfacing with the screen simultaneously. We observed this kind of adaptable screen-sharing often, highlighting the intimate and communal ways that mobile screens become an integral part of our being-with-others, challenging the more typical apprehension of such screens as deeply private and personal.

Mobile media thus both follows and departs from sedimented and evolving trajectories of mediation, body-media tropes, and collective habits. Some of these might include, for example: the familiarity of touching and seeing and perceptual synaesthesia we bring to the experience; the sensorial and metaphoric legacies of screen-based interfaces and the more recent transformative effects of networked and locative media; social mores relating to image-capture and sharing, privacy, and personal communication; the long, long histories of navigational, peripatetic and place-making practices that diverge along new paths formed in part by our uptake of location-based and mobile media, and so on (by no means a comprehensive list).

These situated, intercorporeal, evolving, and dynamic ontologies clearly show the irreducible relation between specificity and broader media and material histories out of which the mobile interface has emerged. As illustrated by Moores, Couldry, van den Boomen, and others, a non-media-centric approach allows us to critically interpret the ways our media metaphors inform and are informed by myriad extra-medial experiences in the everyday lifeworld. In our corporeal apprehension of the mobile screen there is clearly a complex assortment of habits, conventions and affects, some of which are related to media and screen engagement, but many others which originate from a broad spectrum of body–world relations. As always, these relations must be considered in terms of both their situatedness (i.e. as instances of body–tool couplings) and their more enduring effects on our collective habitudes and practices.

Thus, for example, Hjorth and Richardson (2014) have explored the way that users of *Foursquare* and *Jiepang* (China's Foursquare-like social networking service) creatively incorporate and embody image-sharing practices specific to gender, culture, and generation. In their study, the way that users playfully exceed the spectra of intended use is revealed through ethnographic work that then apprises a broader understanding of the way mobile media are modifying visual cultures through the complex entanglements of place making, co-presence, intimacy, affect, and mobility (Hjorth and Richardson 2014). Our current project participants have also disclosed, through the deliberate placement of their devices and bodies, specific configurations of domestic space and networked communication in which mobile devices are integral. As described above, iPads and tablets are frequently shared devices—both asynchronously, and in the form of co-watching or collaborative play—that commonly reside in shared spaces (such as the kitchen and lounge room).

In this way, mobile devices work to alter the dynamics of cohabitation, which can also have ongoing effects on our experience of social presence. Several of our participants described the way one member of the household would appropriate the primary role of social networking across shared devices. Kelly and John, for example, are an Adelaide couple who share Kelly's Facebook page, as John is reluctant to take on the material and communicative labor of managing his own, and happy to engage (often vicariously) in their friend groups online. They would frequently sit cosily on the couch or in bed, share the laptop or mobile screen, to see what comments had been added or images uploaded, and Kelly would sometimes comment or add content on behalf of both of them. In a sense, John says, "she *is* my social network."

Through a phenomenological ethnography of the micro-practices surrounding our experience of contemporary screens, then, we can effectively interpret the way mobile devices modify our ways of being-in-the-world. The mobile media device, to a degree at least as significant as the cinematic, televisual, and computer screen, presents a significant shift in the relational ontology of body and technology, and thus of the process of mediation. Our coupling with mobile screens is exceedingly intimate, ever-present and affective, involving the peripatetic, ambulatory, and motile body in ways that counter the frontal ontology of other face–screen relations. In a very fundamental way the mobile interface modifies what we pay attention to, what we "turn to" and face (and turn away from) in the everyday lifeworld, and the modalities and *durée* of that attentiveness. While our collective screen-based habitudes are in part preconfigured by established or sedimented processes of mediation—with all the historical, cultural, and tropological specificity that entails—it is also clear that emergent and *in situ* media–body couplings are in themselves generative and originary.

Conclusion

When Margaret waved her finger around to signify a particular genre of mobile puzzle game in the anecdote at the start of this chapter, she did not simply forget the name of a game but drew attention to the fundamentally intercorporeal ways in which we engage with digital media generally, and mobile media specifically. In this chapter we have used the example of mobile media to demonstrate the significance and challenges of accounting for the phenomenological relation between body and technology in digital and network ethnography. When accounting for the everyday, domestic, and playful experiences of mobile media in our own ethnographic study, the vast range of haptic and kinaesthetic modes of intercorporeally engaging with mobile screens demanded we deploy a range of ethnographic methods that are not necessarily digital. Participant activities such as media walkthroughs, day-in-the-life observations, interviews, and video recorded play sessions allowed us to account for the fundamentally embodied ways in which digital media are not only engaged with, but literally handled and entwined with.

As researchers of mobile media, then, we would claim that a conceptual and theoretical grasp of the processes of mobile and social mediation compels us to devise and realize productive methods of data collection and analysis with the aim of effectively capturing the fixings, concretizations, routines, and habits of everyday practice (Pink and Leder Mackley 2013). In this way, we can see how theoretical perspective, methodological approach, and *in situ* observation are co-constitutive; that is, a concurrent and non-hierarchical consideration of both big-picture processes and contingent and material micro-practices is what is required.

Acknowledgment

This chapter is part of an Australian Research Council grant, *Games of Being Mobile* (DP140104295).

References
Bates, Charlotte, ed. 2015. *Video Methods: Social Science Research in Motion*. New York: Routledge.

Bratton, Benjamin H. 2014. "On Apps and Elementary Forms of Interfacial Life: Object, Image, Superimposition." In *The Imaginary App*, edited by Paul D. Miller and Svitlana Matviyenko, 1–16. Cambridge, MA: MIT Press.

Couldry, Nick. 2012. *Media, Society, World: Social Theory and Digital Media Practice*. Cambridge: Polity Press.

Csordas, Thomas J. 2011. "Cultural Phenomenology." In *A Companion to the Anthropology of Embodiment*, edited by Frances E. Mascia-Lees, 137–56. Blackwell Publishing. doi: 10.1002/9781444340488 (accessed November 22, 2015).

de Brabandere, Nicole. 2014. "Performing Surfaces: Designing Research-Creation for Agentive Embodiment." *Cultural Studies Review* 20(2): 223–49.

Elo, Mika. 2012. "Formatting the Senses of Touch." *Transformations*, no. 22. www.transformationsjournal.org/issues/22/article_07.shtml (accessed November 9, 2015).

Evans, Leighton. 2015. *Locative Social Media: Place in the Digital Age*. Basingstoke: Palgrave Macmillan.

Hand, Martin. 2014. "Persistent Traces, Potential Memories: Smartphones and the Negotiation of the Visual, Locative, and Textual Data in Personal Life." *Convergence* 2014: 1–18. doi: 10.1177/1354856514546094 (accessed November 14, 2015).

Helles, Rasmus. 2013. "Mobile Communication and Intermediality." *Mobile Media & Communication* 1(1): 14–19.

Hine, Christine. 2015. *Ethnography for the Internet: Embedded, Embodied, Everyday*. London: Bloomsbury.

Hjorth, Larissa and Ingrid Richardson. 2014. *Gaming in Social, Locative and Mobile Media*. London: Palgrave Macmillan.

Horst, Heather, Larissa Hjorth and Jo Tacchi. 2012. "Rethinking Ethnography: An Introduction." *Media International Australia* 145: 86–93.

Ihde, Don. 2012. *Experimental Phenomenology: Multistabilities*, 2nd edition. Albany, NY: SUNY Press.

Jacucci, Giulio, Antti Oulasvirta and Antti Salovaara. 2007. "Active Construction of Experience through Mobile Media: A Field Study with Implications for Recording and Sharing." *Personal and Ubiquitous Computing* 11(4): 215–34.

Jäger, Ludwig, Erika Linz and Irmela Schneider, eds. 2010. *Media, Culture, and Mediality: New Insights into the Current State of Research*. Bielefeld: Transcript Verlag.

Kember, Sarah and Joanna Zylinska. 2012. *Life After New Media: Mediation as a Vital Process*. Cambridge, MA: MIT Press.

Mäyrä, Frans. 2012. "Playful Mobile Communication: Services Supporting the Culture of Play." *Interactions: Studies in Communication and Culture* 3(1): 55–70.

Merleau-Ponty, Maurice. 1964. *The Primacy of Perception, and Other Essays on Phenomenological Psychology, the Philosophy of Art, History and Politics*. Evanston, IL: Northwestern University Press.

Moores, Shaun. 2009. "That Familiarity with the World Born of Habit: A Phenomenological Approach to the Study of Media Uses in Daily Living." *Interactions: Studies in Communication and Culture* 1(3): 301–12.

——. 2012. *Media, Place and Mobility*. Basingstoke: Palgrave Macmillan.

——. 2013. "We Find Our Way About: Everyday Media Use and 'Inhabitant Knowledge.'" *Mobilities* 10(1): 17–35. doi: http://dx.doi.org/10.1080/17450101.2013.819624 (accessed September 8, 2014).

——. 2014. "Digital Orientations: 'Ways of the Hand' and Practical Knowing in Media Uses and Other Manual Activities." *Mobile Media & Communication* 2(2): 196–208.

Paterson, Mark. 2009. "Haptic Geographies: Ethnography, Haptic Knowledges and Sensuous Dispositions." *Progress in Human Geography* 33(6): 766–88.

Pink, Sarah. 2009. *Doing Sensory Ethnography*. London: Sage.

Pink, Sarah and Kerstin Leder Mackley. 2013. "Saturated and Situated: Expanding the Meaning of Media in the Routines of Everyday Life." *Media, Culture and Society* 35(6): 677–91.

Pink, Sarah, Jolynna Sinanan, Larissa Hjorth and Heather Horst. 2015. "Tactile Digital Ethnography: Researching Mobile Media through the Hand." *Mobile Media & Communication*: 1–15. doi: 10.1177/2050157915619958 (accessed February 6, 2016).

Richardson, Ingrid. 2010. "Faces, Interfaces, Screens: Relational Ontologies of Attention and Distraction." *Transformations*, no. 18. www.transformationsjournal.org/journal/issues/18/article_05.shtml (accessed March 8, 2012).

Srnicek, Nick. 2014. "Auxiliary Organs: An Ethics of the Extended Mind." In *The Imaginary App*, edited by Paul D. Miller and Svitlana Matviyenko, 69–82. Cambridge, MA: MIT Press.

Van den Boomen, Marianne. 2014. *Transcoding the Digital: How Metaphors Matter in New Media.* Amsterdam: Institute of Network Cultures.

Wiley, Stephen B. Crofts, Tabita Moreno Becerra and Daniel M. Sutko. 2012. "Subjects, Networks, Assemblages: A Materialist Approach to the Production of Social Space." In *Communication Matters: Materialist Approaches to Media, Mobility and Networks*, edited by Jeremy Packer and Steve B. Crofts Wiley, 183–95. London: Routledge.

20

PLACING MOBILE ETHNOGRAPHY

Mobile Communication as a Practice of Place Making

Didem Özkul

On a busy Saturday afternoon in London, I'm out with a friend, Emma, and her son, Charlie, who is just about 18 months old. Charlie needs a new pair of shoes, and the closest place we can get some shoes is the disturbingly crowded Carnaby Street. The plan is to find the closest shop that sells kids' shoes, and while I keep an eye on Charlie and entertain him for a few minutes, Emma will go into the shop, buy the shoes, and meet us outside. Once we agree on the plan, I quickly run a Google search on my phone, find the closest shop, see how to get there on the Google Maps, and in no time Emma starts walking there while I start following her with Charlie. Charlie, sitting in his buggy disoriented and confused about what is going on, starts looking at me as if he is going to cry. "Mommy is right *there*," I say, to calm him down pointing my finger to the shop, "She will be *here* very soon." Charlie looks at my hand pointing at the shop, and says "Daddy!" I get confused. I start looking around trying to see if Tim (Charlie's father who is in Tokyo at that time) miraculously happens to be in London with us at exactly that moment. Realizing that I am a bit puzzled, Charlie quickly grabs my hand, which is holding my phone, and again says "Daddy!"—shaking the phone.

This was one of the many moments that once again reminded me of the role of mobile communication technologies not only in our daily lives, but also in our kids' imaginary worlds. There is no doubt that these mobile technologies are powerful tools in bringing the distant ones closer to us even on an imaginative level. Tim can be there with Charlie in Carnaby Street on FaceTime (when actually he is in Tokyo), and Tim's (online) presence (on my smartphone screen) can calm Charlie down while his mom is away in the shop around the corner. That moment I was also fascinated with how Charlie associates the phone with "daddy." He knows that he can see him and talk to him any time anywhere (as long as the mobile connection allows). Having witnessed a toddler's reaction to cope with an unfamiliar situation and the anxiety that absence (and disconnection) can cause, I also realized how (perceived) distances can feel as shrinking (or expanding) with the touch of a button. As I have argued elsewhere, mobility and location matter a lot to us and mobile communication technologies enable us to be mobile *and* located at the same time (Özkul 2015a). Either celebrated, or approached with anxiety and worry, mobile communication technologies can have an effect on our everyday lives, our interactions with people and places, our perception of distance, nearness and closeness, and our experiences of absence and presence. It is sometimes difficult to believe how such a (relatively) tiny piece of technology has such a significant role in our daily lives.

Studying that important role of mobile communication technologies, especially, mobile phones in contemporary societies, can sometimes be challenging because such ethnographic fieldwork requires the researcher to "elicit empirically interesting results from a familiar everyday setting" (Oksman 2006, 106). On the other hand, as a mobile phone user for almost two decades, and as a researcher working on mobile communication practices and mobile media since 2010, I am still amazed by various meaning-making processes, routines, and social contexts associated with the use of these technologies. Research of an ethnographic nature, argue Höflich and Hartmann, "constantly asks the researcher not to be satisfied with what he/she has already understood, but to be repeatedly amazed instead" (2006, 12). As Pink (2012, 12) noted, "the developments in digital, mobile and locative media challenge us to rethink ways in which media(ted) research and the ethnographic encounter is understood." In this chapter, following the traces of (mobile) transformations in everyday life in relation to mobile communication practices, I present a framework through which our everyday uses of mobile communication technologies and their relationship to place, presence, and meaning-making can be understood and analyzed.

Mobile Communication: From "Spatial Turn" to "Locational Turn"

Social sciences, starting particularly during the 1980s, witnessed a "spatial turn" (Urry 2007). "This involved theory and research, which demonstrated that social relations are spatially organized, and such spatial structuring makes a significant difference to social relations" (Urry 2007, 34). This turn can also be described through reflecting on the global transformations of the 1980s and 1990s (Massey and Thrift 2003), and it is no surprise that analogies can be found between the political and economic conjuncture of the 1980s and 1990s, and the corresponding spatial turn in social sciences. Graham (2004), on the other hand, argues that research into spatial relations attracted more attention from the mid-1990s onwards, focusing more on the links between Information and Communication Technologies (ICTs) and urban life. As Graham notes, "[s]ince the mid-1990s, high quality theoretical, empirical and policy research on the links between ICTs and the changing nature of cities and urban life has rapidly emerged in many disciplines across the world" (2004, 3). However, the social sciences have largely ignored the importance of movement in their analysis of spatial relations, and hence have been accused of being "a-mobile" (Sheller and Urry 2006a).

In time, the increasing use of ICTs stirred up questions relating to space, everyday life, and social relations, including media and sense of place (Meyrowitz 1985), global networks and political economy (Castells 1989, 1996), mobility (Sheller and Urry 2006b), interpersonal communication (Ling 2008), and mobile communication technologies (Ling and Campbell 2009; de Souza e Silva 2004, 2006; Gordon and de Souza e Silva 2011). This rising interest occurred especially in the fields of media and communications studies and sociology and proliferated the attention drawn to these notions in relation to modernity, everyday life, and urbanity. As mobility and mobile communications began to take center stage, the existing interest in urban space in understanding was expanded even further to take into account how these technologies are used and adopted in everyday life.

As Urry argues, "social life involves a continual process of shifting between being present with others and being distant from others" (2007, 47). In other words, in a mobile world, where social life revolves around one's presence or absence, communication technologies, especially mobile modes of communication, gain fundamental importance in everyday life. "[Social] presence is thus intermittent, achieved, performed and always interdependent with other processes of connection and communication" (Urry 2007, 47). As a result, mobility studies have expanded into the field of mobile communications, along with other modes of communication, in their discussions of space and place. This focus on mobility and modes of communication that has arisen in social sciences can be explained also by the "new mobilities paradigm" and the "mobility turn" in everyday life.

> And partly as an effect a "mobility turn" is spreading into and transforming the social sciences, transcending the dichotomy between transport research and social research, putting social relations into travel and connecting different forms of transport with complex patterns of social experience conducted through communications at-a-distance. It seems that a new paradigm is being formed within the social sciences, the "new mobilities paradigm."
>
> (Sheller and Urry 2006a, 208)

Sheller and Urry launched their discussion of the mobilities turn with the important global fact that "all the world seems to be on the move" (2006a, 207). One can argue that the world being on the move is closely associated with physical mobility (i.e. transportation), however by looking at these statistics, it can also be argued that "new forms of 'virtual' and 'imaginative' travel are emerging, and being combined in unexpected ways with physical travel" (Sheller and Urry 2006a, 207) aided by advances in communication technologies (especially the Internet and wireless communication technologies) and fast diffusion rates of these technologies.

In particular, smartphones offer new means of interaction while on the move, or of "being in a sense of present while apparently absent" (Sheller and Urry 2006a, 207), which is conceptualized as "absent presence" (Gergen 2002). The use of mobile media has significantly changed both how we perceive distance on a physical level as well as how we experience it as nearness or closeness on an emotional level (Özkul and Gauntlett 2014). Accordingly, our perceptions and definitions of physical or social space, and our representations of those spaces (such as maps or in the form of geo-tagging a photo) have also changed.

Mobile communication and the ubiquity of the Internet have opened up new ways of accessing media content while on the move. There has been a notable growth in the use of mobile Internet and location data as part of daily activities such as using a mobile location-based app such as Yelp to find nearby restaurants with good reviews. Worldwide, hundreds of millions of people are using location-based services (LBS) and mobile apps on their smartphones. It is predicted that at least 50 percent of all mobile subscribers in Europe will be using LBS by 2018 (Malm nd. Berg Insight report). According to PEW 2013 research findings, in the US, 74 percent of mobile subscribers use at least one LBS on their smartphones (Zickuhr 2013).

These locative media apps include the ones developed by Internet companies such as the mobile mapping apps Google Maps and Google Earth, social media apps Facebook and Foursquare, and local search apps such as Yelp. They collect location data not only through their own services, but also through joint efforts such as aggregating data from other LBS and apps as well as other location Application Programming Interfaces (APIs). Users of these services are encouraged to share their locations through the promise of meeting new people in close proximity (e.g. Glympse), receiving discounts from various places they visit frequently (e.g. Foursquare), finding the "closest and best" restaurants and events (e.g. Yelp), or sometimes even for avoiding certain people in their social network (e.g. Cloak). Also, types of information with which we interact have started to heavily rely on our physical location (such as receiving "local" news based on one's current location, or receiving weather or travel updates based on one's future location).

Parallel to these changes in communication and everyday life practices, today, a paradigm shift is taking place in mobile communication and Internet studies. This shift, which may be classified as an extension of the spatial turn in social sciences (Urry 2007), focuses on the importance and role of location data in everyday life. Goggin conceptualizes this paradigm shift as the "locational turn," which he defines as the new direction in "the works of making place that has been occurring with mobile technologies" (2012, 198). There is also a shift in the way we interact with the Internet (de Souza e Silva and Sheller 2015; Gordon and de Souza e Silva 2011) and "imagine and navigate the online in conjunction with physical spaces" (Hjorth and Arnold 2013, 7). Locative media have become "the harbinger of the emergent media of our time, from big data to drones, from Internet of Things to logistics, all with their urgent cultural, social, and political implications" (Wilken and Goggin 2015, 2). Increasingly, the kinds of information we access online depend on our physical location (de Souza e Silva and Sheller 2015). Hence, location is now the organizational logic and the "currency of networked interactions" (Gordon and de Souza e Silva 2011).

Mobility

"In a mobile world there are extensive and intricate connections between physical travel and modes of communication and these form new fluidities and are often difficult to stabilise" (Urry 2007, 5). In such an unstable world (of fluidities), the terms "mobile" and "mobility" can take various meanings. As Urry (2007, 7) depicts, the term "mobile" is a property of things and of people, referring to something or someone that moves or is capable of moving, which is mainly understood as a positive category. On the other hand, something that is mobile can also be thought of as being disorderly, and hence untraceable and harder to regulate socially.

Building on these four different understandings of the terms "mobile" and "mobility," and analyzing them within the context of social interactions and communication activities of everyday life, Elliott and Urry (2010, 15–16) suggest the existence of five interdependent mobilities in the production of social life: corporeal movement, physical movement of objects, imaginative travel, virtual travel, and communicative travel. Imaginative travel is "effected through the images of places and peoples appearing on, and moving across, multiple print and visual media" (Elliott and Urry 2010, 16), which is also referred to as "co-presence," affecting the act of mediation and communication in simultaneous contexts. On the other hand, virtual travel is "often in realtime and thus transcending geographical and social distance," while communicative travel is "through person-to-person messages via messages, texts, letters, telegraph, telephone, fax and mobile" (Elliott and Urry 2010, 16).

Accordingly, mobile and locative media, their *being technically mobile*, and also the mobilities that they bring with them into everyday life, such as imaginative, virtual, and communicative travel, should be taken into consideration when defining mobility. The concept of mobility and its relationship with space and place, as well as presence, is therefore important while discussing perceptions of space and identity formation alongside and within that space.

From Space to Location through Mobile Media

The concepts of space and place are sometimes a source of confusion. As Casey (1997, x) argues, *place* started to be assimilated into *space* in the sixth century AD, and as a result, while the former has started to be considered simply as a modification of space, the latter has come to be regarded as an infinite extension. Place and space have many generic qualities. According to Harvey, place can be understood as, and used to refer to, milieu, locality, location, locale, neighborhood, region, and territory, while also reflecting on the wide range of its metaphorical meanings, emphasizing that "we internalize such notions psychologically in terms of knowing our place, or feeling we have a place in the affections or esteem of others" (1993, 4).

On the other hand, as Heidegger argues, "place is the locale of the truth of Being" (Heidegger quoted in Harvey 1993, 9), according to which, it is a source of existence, identity, and experience. Following this Heideggerian approach, Relph (1976) also conceptualizes the understanding of place as an integral part of our existence. Place has been taken for granted, given our existence within in it, which Casey defines as "a priori of our existence on earth" (1997, x). The importance of place "leaves place itself an unclarified notion" (Casey 1997, xii). Following this phenomenological tradition, Tuan (1975, 165) conceptualizes space as an abstraction. Both Tuan and Relph define place as the center of meaning in human life. Every single individual perceives and experiences space differently, which, in turn, helps them to assign meanings to places and build their own sense of place.

In Augé's definition of "anthropological place," it is clearly stated that place is in fact a "concrete and symbolic construction of space" (1995, 42), which somehow strengthens the argument of place's assimilation into space. However, critical theorists such as Michel de Certeau (1984, 65) argue that as places can transform into spaces, so can spaces also transform into places, with the help of narratives and language. Space, for de Certeau, is a "frequented place," "an intersection of moving bodies," and he claims that, "it is the pedestrians who transform a street (geometrically defined as a place by town planners) into a space" (de Certeau 1984, 64).

The relationship between "location" and "place" is also important in understanding the impacts of mobile communication technologies and LBS in everyday life. Relph (1976) and Cresswell (2004) argue that places are meaningful locations. However, "this line of thought degrades the importance of locational information in place making, while prioritizing other aspects of place attachment, such as cultural and emotional meanings" (Özkul 2015b, 104). Another line of thought which degrades the importance of mobile communication technologies in place making is concerned with physical proximity and time. ICTs are usually regarded as tools for minimizing time, and in achieving this, also annihilating space constraints (Graham 2004). Although there are many arguments suggesting that communication technologies and media have changed the perception of space and time, these changes are not necessarily always negative. Accordingly, it is necessary to look at different theories (in relation to the sociological, philosophical, and anthropological theories) of space and place, and how they can be related to electronic and mobile communication technologies, with the intention to come up with a different conceptualization of space.

In the new mobilities paradigm, places themselves are considered mobile and dynamic (Sheller and Urry 2006a), and "places are about relationships, about the placing of peoples, materials, images, and the systems of difference that they perform" (Sheller and Urry 2006a, 214). Accordingly, uncertainty about a physical location, which is supplemented by mobility in urban interactions, can be a reason for the raising of monitoring/locating questions (Townsend 2001, 62), and as a consequence, this is still the first thing that comes into mind when talking to someone on the phone—"Where are you?" (Laurier 2001;

Ferraris 2006). Hjorth (2005) discusses the relationship between presence, mobile communication, and place, and she argues that mobile media expands different dimensions of place whether social, psychological, geographical, lived, or imagined.

Kopomaa (2000) describes this attribute of mobility and transformation in the time/space distinction with a metaphor, referring to this new *mobile society* as a new "nomadic tribe," which, with the elimination of distance, has made an appearance on the urban landscape. "To the new nomads, no place is entirely foreign, because they can always contact their telefriends and acquaintances wherever they are" (Kopomaa 2000, 6). In other words, the more physically mobile we become, the more we feel the need for newer ways of communication and an ability to be somewhere else virtually. Within this dialectical relationship, mobile media started to be seen as a significant component of everyday life, but the opposite is also possible: after checking-in at a random place with your smartphone, your friends, who might not have been aware initially of your whereabouts, can come and say "Hi" if they are nearby. As such, this relationship between physical mobility and mobile communication serves to transform space.

Mobile media have always been intimately tied to place (Hjorth 2005, 2013). As argued by Hjorth and Arnold (2013, 19), "place, in all its complexity, has always mattered to mobile media. And through mobile media we see the ways place is shaped, and is shaping, practices of mobility, intimacy and a sense of belonging." The popularity of communication technologies, especially smartphones, can be argued to contribute to the loss of significance of distance and location, and has eased our detachment from places as complementing physical mobility. Some scholars, such as Meyrowitz (1985) and Casey (1997), understand ICTs as causes of displacement. However, "being mobile and being in a place can be complementary" (Hjorth and Arnold 2013, 4), and "mobile communication can increase our chances to attach to new places, while maintaining old ones" (Özkul 2015b, 103).

"Place" in the Ethnographic Approaches to Mobile Communication

Starting from the early 2000s social scientists tried to differentiate and understand various uses of mobile communication technologies in everyday life. The mobile phone as "a medium of public space" (Höflich and Hartmann 2006) has immediately attracted the attention of researchers. Methodologically, such a medium, with its public nature, "allows access to media use that used to be difficult to observe" (Höflich and Hartmann 2006, 13). Additionally, as Höflich (2006, 47) argues, "a study of mobile phone use offers an excellent opportunity to obtain detailed insight into communicative behaviour and the constitution of social life." Hence the ethnographic approaches to mobile communication have extensively focused on mobile phones and looked at the changing practices of face-to-face communication in public spaces, in relation to the notions of public and private space (Katz and Aakhus 2002; Gergen 2002; Höflich 2006; Okabe and Ito 2005) and mobile phone appropriation among teens and their families, including the practice of texting (Haddon and Vincent 2009; Matsuda 2009). On the other hand, the public nature of mobile phones is also argued to be limiting the ethnographic observation (Höflich and Hartmann 2006, 14). As Okabe and Ito (2006, 83) argue, "it is not realistic for an ethnographer to directly observe all of the interstitial communications and information access that mobile phone users engage with."

With the introduction of the camera function to the mobile phones, the focus of ethnographic research of mobile communication shifted toward the everyday contexts of cameraphone use (Hjorth 2007; Okabe and Ito 2006), and then from cameraphones to mobile social networking (Humphreys 2008). Mobile social media introduced another challenge to conduct research on mobile phones. As Pink argues, "online place is an online locality" (Pink 2012, 118). Hence, mobile social media "requires us to consider the relationality between the online and offline localities" (Hjorth and Pink 2014, 43) and one needs to understand social media "as a fieldwork environment that is social, experiential and mobile" (Postill and Pink 2012, 125).

This very brief overview of the ethnographic approaches to mobile communications actually reveals how an ethnographic view of mobile phones is "extremely shaped by—or even clouded through—its object" (Höflich and Hartmann 2006, 13). Although the aim of any ethnographic research is not to come up with findings that could be generalized, there are some commonalities between diverse research on mobile communications (ibid., 11). However, as Höflich and Hartmann (2006, 11) argue, "the question arises whether such commonalities appear only on the surface structure and are actually deeply engrained in rather different cultural structures underneath." One of those commonalities in various daily uses of mobile communication technologies and ethnographic approaches to understanding such uses is about their entanglement with place and presence.

Place and presence are at the intersection of research on mobile communication and ethnography. Mobile communication (and media) has always been linked to place. "Place is an obvious feature of mobile communication," argue Wilken and Goggin, referring to the "micro" practices of mobile media use; "most obviously because communications is occurring in different locales" (2012, 3). The mobile ontology of mobile communication practices constructs one of the first understandings of mobiles' relationship to place. "The mobile is that which moves; mobility is the capacity to move" (Malpas 2012, 26). Consequently, mobile communication technologies are not only themselves mobile and carried anywhere we may roam, but they also enable us to do so by freeing us from fixed lines and cables, and therefore from places. On the other hand, as I argued elsewhere, mobile communication technologies also foster attachment to places by creating a renewed interest in location, and they have the potential to influence what a place represents and embodies for its inhabitants (Özkul 2015b, 101). Hence, they have the potential to affect not only our perception of place, but also presence.

Conclusion

It is almost impossible to think of social practices without space since one supplements the other—space is a social construct (Lefebvre 1991). Today we are witnessing a new level of co-construction of space and sociality, triggered and enabled by the coming together of mobile communication, location-determination technologies, and the Internet. As in the Carnaby Street scene I described in the introduction to this chapter, the relationship between physical distance and physical presence can be pretty straightforward; if something/someone is physically distant, then that thing/person is not physically present in a given place at a given time. Hence, physical distance can be (or at least, used to be) a barrier against presence. Interestingly, although it is argued that the act of mediation itself and electronic media enable people to overcome distances, mobile media and mobile communication technologies are usually associated more with opening up and founding new spaces in which people can connect to each other and be (or feel) co-present.

Mobile communication technologies alter our experience of a place, not only because they are portable, but also because they provide a connected form of presence that can help their users establish new relationships and maintain old ones. It has always been the promise of mobile communication technologies and mobile media to connect people, things, and places to each other that are deemed to be mobile. On the other hand, due to the increased pace of modern life, mobile communication technologies started to serve as interfaces that allow people to explore new ways of experiencing a place (social space), while also acting as tools that assist us in avoiding the people around us.

Today, just by checking-in at a train station we can convey a message that we are returning home; by sharing a photo of a cup of coffee we may be conveying the message "wish you were here"; or by calling our loved ones on their mobile phones no matter where we (or they) are located, we might feel a lot more connected despite being physically apart. Accordingly, location-awareness should not be thought of as specific only to a particular type of technology, but in relation to the social space and how we maintain our social relationships. Whether one owns a smartphone or not, it is apparent that in order to acquire a sense of place (especially in a new place) users of mobile technologies have begun to rely on mobile communications and their location-aware features.

As Richardson and Wilken argue, "mobile media use occurs across a spectrum of 'placing' and 'presencing'" (2012, 185). Referring back to the symbiosis between Charlie and his father's "placing and presencing" (as defined in Richardson and Wilken 2012) and the use of mobile communication technologies, not only such *uses* of those technologies, but most importantly, such *experiences* are common in daily lives. Hence, these experiences could be normalized and it might not be a surprising observation for an ethnographer. On the other hand, each of those individual experiences is unique, and understanding those experiences requires the researcher to delve deeper into the mundane of everyday life and participate, or even become a part of those stories and be *present* when and where they take *place*. As Ardèvol and Gómez-Cruz (2014, 10) noted, what characterizes the ethnographic method "is the participatory approach: the social presence of the ethnographer 'in the field.'"

Everyday *uses* of mobile communication technologies and their relationship to place, presence, and meaning-making can be understood and analyzed through various research methods such as collecting geo-coded data, finding patterns and relationships among what people share (e.g. a photo of Charlie and his new pair of shoes), with whom (e.g. with Charlie's dad, Tim), when and where (e.g. on a Saturday in the early afternoon because that is when Emma does not work and so she can spend the entire day with Charlie); but they can be limited in understanding and explaining (not *uses* of those technologies but) individual *experiences* (e.g. why Charlie shouted "Daddy!" when he saw my phone while Emma was in the shop). On the other hand, interviewing users of these technologies or navigating with them in public spaces while they are using their mobile phones, or asking them to keep user diaries can be effective methods, but at times they can also be limiting the scope and our understanding of mobile experiences. Hence research into mobile communication and media can benefit from creative research methods which can "provide the participants with a platform to tell their stories and the researchers with a tool to better understand the *inner worlds* of the participants" (Özkul and Gauntlett 2014, 125) as well as innovative methods which can be borrowed from other disciplines and adapted to the field of media and communications. Although ethnography is defined as a "*slow science* methodology" (Ardèvol and Gómez-Cruz 2014, 10), ethnographic approaches such as "applied multi-method ethnography" (e.g. Oksman 2006) are proven to be effective ways to conduct research into mobile communication.

References

Ardèvol, Elisenda and Edgar Gómez-Cruz. 2014. "Digital Ethnography and Media Practices." In *The International Encyclopedia of Media Studies Volume VII: Research Methods in Media Studies*, edited by Fabienne Darling-Wolf, 1–21. London: John Wiley & Sons.

Augé, Mark. 1995. *Non-Places: Introduction to an Anthropology of Supermodernity*. Translated by J. Howe. London: Verso.

Casey, Edward. 1997. *The Fate of Place: A Philosophical History*. Berkeley, CA: University of California Press.

Castells, Manuel. 1989. *The Informational City: Information Technology, Economic Restructuring and the Urban-Regional Process*. Oxford: Blackwell Publishing.

———. 1996. *The Rise of the Network Society Vol. I: The Information Age, Economy, Society and Culture*. Oxford: Blackwell Publishing.

Cresswell, Tim. 2004. *Place: A Short Introduction*. Malden: Blackwell.

de Certeau, Michel. 1984. *The Practice of Everyday Life*. Translated by S.F. Rendall. San Francisco, Berkeley: Regents of the University of California.

de Souza e Silva, Adriana. 2004. "Mobile Networks and Public Spaces: Bringing Multiuser Environments into the Physical Space." *Convergence: International Journal of Research into New Media Technologies* 10(2): 15–25.

———. 2006. "Mobile Technologies as Interfaces of Hybrid Spaces." *Space and Culture* 9(3): 261–78.

de Souza e Silva, Adriana and Mimi Sheller. 2015. "Introduction: Moving Towards Adjacent Possibles." In *Mobility and Locative Media: Mobile Communication in Hybrid Spaces*, edited by Adriana de Souza e Silva and Mimi Sheller, 1–16. New York: Routledge.

Elliott, Anthony and John Urry. 2010. *Mobile Lives*. London: Routledge.

Ferraris, Maurizio. 2006. "Where Are You? Mobile Ontology." In *Mobile Understanding: The Epistemology of Ubiquitous Communication*, edited by Kristof Nyíri, 41–52. Vienna: Passagen Verlag.

Gergen, Kenneth J. 2002. "The Challenge of Absent Presence." In *Perpetual Contact*, edited by James Everett Katz and Mark Aakhus, 227–41. Cambridge: Cambridge University Press.

Goggin, Gerard. 2012. "Encoding Place: The Politics of Mobile Location Technologies." In *Mobile Technology and Place*, edited by Rowan Wilken and Gerard Goggin, 198–212. New York: Routledge.

Graham, Stephen. 2004. "Introduction: From Dreams of Transcendence to the Remediation of Urban Life." In *The Cybercities Reader*, edited by Stephen Graham, 1–29. London: Routledge.

Gordon, Eric and Adriana de Souza e Silva. 2011. *Net Locality: Why Location Matters in a Networked World*. London: Wiley-Blackwell.

Haddon, Leslie and Jane Vincent. 2009. "Childrens' Broadening Use of Mobile Phones." In *Mobile Technologies: From Telecommunications to Media*, edited by Gerard Goggin and Larissa Hjorth, 37–49. New York: Routledge.

Harvey, David. 1993. "From Space to Place and Back Again: Reflections on the Condition of Postmodernity." In *Mapping the Futures: Local Cultures, Global Change*, edited by Jon Bird, Barry Curtis, Tim Putnam, George Robertson and Lisa Tickner, 2–29. London: Routledge.

Hjorth, Larissa. 2005. "Locating Mobility: Practices of Co-presence and the Persistence of the Postal Metaphor in SMS/MMS Mobile Phone Customization in Melbourne." *The Fibreculture Journal* 6. http://journal.fibreculture.org/issue6/issue6_hjorth.html (accessed April 15, 2016).

———. 2007. "Snapshots of Almost Contact: The Rise of Camera Phone Practices and a Case Study in Seoul, Korea." *Continuum: Journal of Media and Cultural Studies* 21(2): 227–38.

———. 2013. "The Place of the Urban: Intersections between Mobile and Game Cultures." In *Re-Imagining the City: Art, Globalization and Urban Spaces*, edited by Kristen Sharp and Elizabeth M. Grierson, 55–69. Bristol: Intellect.

Hjorth, Larissa and Michael Arnold. 2013. *Online@AsiaPacific: Mobile, Social and Locative in the Asia–Pacific Region*. London: Routledge.

Hjorth, Larissa and Sarah Pink. 2014. "New Visualities and the Digital Wayfarer: Reconceptualizing Camera Phone Photography and Locative Media." *Mobile Media & Communication* 2(1): 40–57.

Höflich, Joachim R. 2006. "Places of Life—Places of Communication: Observations of Mobile Phone Usage in Public Places." In *Mobile Communication in Everyday Life: Ethnographic Views, Observations and Reflections*, edited by Joachim R. Höflich and Maren Hartmann, 19–51. Berlin: Frank & Timme GmbH.

Höflich, Joachim R. and Maren Hartmann. 2006. "Introduction." In *Mobile Communication in Everyday Life: Ethnographic Views, Observations and Reflections*, edited by Joachim R. Höflich and Maren Hartmann, 11–17. Berlin: Frank & Timme GmbH.

Humphreys, Lee. 2008. "Mobile Devices and Social Networking." In *After the Mobile Phone? Social Changes and the Development of Mobile Communication*, edited by Maren Hartmann, Patrick Rössler and Joachim R. Höflich, 115–30. Berlin: Frank & Timme GmbH.

Katz, James E. and Mark Aakhus, eds. 2002. *Perpetual Contact: Mobile Communication, Private Talk, Public Performance*. Cambridge: Cambridge University Press.

Kopomaa, Timo. 2000. *The City in Your Pocket: Birth of the Mobile Information Society*. Helsinki: Gaudeamus.

Laurier, Eric. 2001. "Why People Say Where They Are During Mobile Phone Calls." *Environment and Planning D: Society and Space* 19(4): 485–504.

Lefebvre, Henri. 1991. *The Production of Space*. Translated by D. Nicholson-Smith. Malden, MA: Blackwell.

Ling, Rich. 2008. *New Tech, New Ties: How Mobile Communication Is Reshaping Social Cohesion*. Cambridge, MA: MIT Press.

Ling, Rich and Scott W. Campbell, eds. 2009. *The Reconstruction of Space and Time: Mobile Communication Practices*. New Brunswick, NJ: Transaction Publishers.

Malm, André. nd. "Mobile Location-Based Services." *LBS Research Series*. www.berginsight.com/reportpdf/productsheet/bi-lbs8-ps.pdf (accessed February 15, 2016).

Malpas, Jeff. 2012. "The Place of Mobility: Technology, Connectivity, and Individualization". In *Mobile Technology and Place*, edited by Rowan Wilken and Gerard Goggin, 26–38. New York: Routledge.

Massey, Doreen and Nigel Thrift. 2003. "The Passion of Place." In *Century of British Geography*, edited by Ron Johnston and Michael Williams, 275–99. Oxford: University of Oxford Press.

Matsuda, Misa. 2009. "Mobile Media and the Transformation of Family." In *Mobile Technology and Place*, edited by Gerard Goggin and Larissa Hjorth, 62–72. New York: Routledge.

Meyrowitz, Joshua. 1985. *No Sense of Place: The Impact of Electronic Media on Social Behavior*. Oxford: Oxford University Press.

Okabe, Daisuke and Mizuko Ito. 2005. "Keitai in Public Transportation." In *Personal, Portable, Pedestrian: Mobile Phones in Japanese Life*, edited by Mizuko Ito, Daisuke Okabe and Misa Matsuda, 205–18. Cambridge, MA: MIT Press.

——. 2006. "Everyday Contexts of Camera Phone Use: Steps Toward Techno-Social Ethnographic Frameworks." In *Mobile Communication in Everyday Life: Ethnographic Views, Observations and Reflections*, edited by Joachim R. Höflich and Maren Hartmann, 79–102. Berlin: Frank & Timme GmbH.

Oksman, Virpi. 2006. "Mobile Visuality and Everyday Life in Finland: An Ethnographic Approach to Social Uses of Mobile Image." In *Mobile Communication in Everyday Life: Ethnographic Views, Observations and Reflections*, edited by Joachim R. Höflich and Maren Hartmann, 103–19. Berlin: Frank & Timme GmbH.

Özkul, Didem. 2015a. "Mobile Communication Technologies and Spatial Perception: Mapping London." In *Locative Media*, edited by Rowan Wilken and Gerard Goggin, 39–51. New York: Routledge.

——. 2015b. "Location as a Sense of Place: Everyday Life, Mobile, and Spatial Practices in Urban Spaces." In *Mobility and Locative Media: Mobile Communication in Hybrid Spaces*, edited by Adriana de Souza e Silva and Mimi Sheller, 101–16. New York: Routledge.

Özkul, Didem and David Gauntlett. 2014. "Locative Media in the City: Drawing Maps and Telling Stories." In *The Mobile Story: Narrative Practices with Locative Technologies*, edited by Jason Farman, 113–27. New York: Routledge.

Pink, Sarah. 2012. "Advances in Visual Methodology: An Introduction." In *Advances in Visual Methodology*, edited by Sarah Pink, 3–16. London: Sage.

Postill, John and Sarah Pink. 2012. "Social Media Ethnography: The Digital Researcher in a Messy Web." *Media International Australia* 145(1): 123–43.

Relph, Edward. 1976. *Place and Placelessness*. London: Pion.

Richardson, Ingrid and Rowan Wilken. 2012. "Parerga of the Third Screen: Mobile Media, Place, and Presence." In *Mobile Technology and Place*, edited by Rowan Wilken and Gerard Goggin, 181–97. New York: Routledge.

Sheller, Mimi and John Urry. 2006a. "The New Mobilities Paradigm." *Environment and Planning A* 38(2): 207–26.

——. 2006b. *Mobile Technologies of the City*. London: Routledge.

Townsend, Anthony M. 2001. "Mobile Communications in the Twenty-First Century City." In *Wireless World: Social and Interactional Aspects of the Mobile Age*, edited by Barry Brown, Nicola Green and Richard Harper, 62–77. London: Springer-Verlag.

Tuan, Yi Fu. 1975. "Place: An Experiential Perspective." *The Geographical Review*, LXV (2).

Urry, John. 2007. *Mobilities*. Cambridge: Polity Press.

Wilken, Rowan and Gerard Goggin. 2012. "Mobilizing Place: Conceptual Currents and Controversies." In *Mobile Technology and Place*, edited by Rowan Wilken and Gerard Goggin, 3–25. New York: Routledge.

——. 2015. "Locative Media: Definitions, Histories, Theories." In *Locative Media*, edited by Rowan Wilken and Gerard Goggin, 1–19. New York: Routledge.

Zickuhr, Kathryn. 2013. "Location-Based Services." *PEW Research Report*. www.pewinternet.org/2013/09/12/location-based-services/ (accessed April 10, 2015).

Part V

PLAY

21

DIGITAL GAMING, SOCIAL INCLUSION, AND THE RIGHT TO PLAY

A Case Study of a Venezuelan Cybercafé

Tom Apperley

Introduction

While digital games and gaming have recently received some attention from anthropologists (e.g. Boellstorff 2008; Nardi 2010; Taylor 2006), the focus has often been on interactions in virtual worlds (Boellstorff et al. 2012, 61–4). This chapter reports on a "situated" digital ethnography that took place in a cybercafé in Caracas, Venezuela, during early 2005. This ethnography involved daily observations of digital games being played in the cybercafé over a period of four months, and was conducted in order to observe the integration of digital gaming with everyday activities. The goal was to gather observational data that supported a detailed understanding of the "cultures of use" of digital gaming technologies in Venezuela (Sassen 2006, 347–8).

In particular, I was interested in the role that such a peripheral context of game play might contribute to creative social practices of digital games. Creativity, in the sense of the practices of everyday meaning-making that Paul Willis outlines in *The Ethnographic Imagination* (2000), which are "embodied and embedded" (27), and "sensual and material" (20). The virtual networks of gaming were connected in an embodied and material manner to the locality of the cybercafé, making it a key location for considering how everyday creativity figured in the enactment of this connection.

There is already a considerable body of research that examines creative practices in digital games and gaming communities, through discussion of practices such as the design of paratexts

(Consalvo 2007), modding (Banks and Potts 2010), and creative forms of play (Meades 2015; Parker 2008), as well as the extensive literature that connects digital gaming with new, emergent literacy practices (e.g. Zimmerman 2009). The dominant trends of this research, however, have addressed the North American and European contexts, with very little material exploring the cultures of use around digital games in the global South. The exception to this has been the recent collections examining the cultures of digital games on global (Aslinger and Huntemann 2012; Wolf 2015) and regional (Hjorth and Chan 2009) scales, which have usefully highlighted unique creative practices of geopolitically subaltern gaming cultures.

This chapter examines the creative practices of digital game players against the backdrop of these asymmetries in experience, caused by the digital divide, through discussing the cultures of use in a location that is peripheral to global entertainment networks. Digital game players in Venezuela represent a particular configuration of digital inclusion that is precarious and partial; somewhere in-between being fully connected and absolutely excluded. This has important consequences for creative practice with digital games and gaming technologies that suggest the need to revalue digital play as a right of citizenship, along the lines of the Latin America Cultural Studies scholar Néstor García Canclini's (2001) argument that the eighteenth-century values of citizenship need to be rethought in relation to contemporary technologies.

In contrast to other gaming ethnographies that focus on online interactions, this chapter first presents a discussion of the embodied and material sociality of the cybercafé. The chapter then moves on to discuss how the creative practices that are enacted in this location connect digital literacy and piracy with notions of RIGHTS and citizenship. This highlights the inequitable and asymmetrical stakes of digital gaming between the North and South.

Cybercafé Avila

Cybercafés are popular, social locations in Venezuela. For many they provide access to the Internet, as well as other important digital services, such as printing. The phenomenon of cybercafés providing grassroots community access to the Internet in Latin America is described as *cibercafezinhozación* (Horst 2011, 45–6), and many Venezuelans rely on privately owned, semi-public cybercafés for access to computers, software, and the Internet. From late March through to mid-July 2005 I conducted an ethnographic study of digital game play in Cybercafé Avila in the suburb of San Bernardino in the Libertador district of Caracas.

Like most cybercafés in Venezuela, Cybercafé Avila operated in the country's large "grey" economy (Lugo and Sampson 2008). Consequently, they were subject to very little official regulation. This was significantly different from the kinds of controls and restrictions placed on other methods of accessing information. In Venezuela under the United Socialist Party of Venezuela—the party of Hugo Chávez (1954–2013), now led by Nicolás Maduro (1964–)—newspapers, radio, and particularly television are strictly regulated. However, while the activities that take place in cybercafés are largely unregulated, digital games have been subjected to draconian and practically unenforceable regulation, which I have discussed elsewhere (Apperley 2010, 2015).

Cybercafé Avila catered to both commercial and community interests and fulfilled an important role for the locals and businesses of the neighborhood. Small business owners, including the neighboring garage and a nearby McDonald's, used the computers and other services as part of their day-to-day work practices. Teachers from local schools used the café's computers to prepare classes and do their administration; university students studied and did their assignments there, occasionally begging the owner to lock them in overnight so that they could make an important deadline.

Students from the local high school were crucial for the business. The high school students were easily identified by their nation-wide uniforms, with white (junior), blue (middle), or brown (senior) identifying their grade. They attended school in shifts, some in the morning, and others in the afternoon. Students used the café as a meeting place, to gather on their way to and from school, as well as to crossover and socialize with students from the other shift.

In addition to the owner, one full-time staff member and up to three part-timers were employed at the café. The employees provided customer support for the operation of any requested software and also to do maintenance and repairs on computers customers had brought into the café, or even at people's homes or places of business. Occasionally, Xavier (pseudonym) would agree to forego a cash payment in favor of the rendering of a reciprocal service, which worked well when he got maintenance for his car. In contrast, the time that he negotiated a week's worth of lunch from the canteen of the local elementary school for him and his employees in return for conducting maintenance on their computers was not considered to be a success.

This cybercafé was characterized by sociality. It was used by a remarkable cross-section of locals, and a large number of visitors to the district, particularly through the large number of hospitals and medical specialists, and the military bases in adjacent streets. The play of digital games contributed a great deal to this sociality as it formed a mutual interest between many of the predominantly younger customers. This social environment was also characterized by the relatively free exchange of information and knowledge about digital games between friends, acquaintances, and strangers. Playing digital games and sharing information about digital games was entangled, moving between the activities was fluid, and it often occurred simultaneously.

In some cases these activities would not involve much verbal communication, and players would simply observe the screens of other parties to learn about unfamiliar titles or new tactics. Sometimes the information shared was based on prior research on the Internet. For example the hotkeys, cheats, and shortcuts used in a particular digital game were often shared between players of *Counter-Strike* (Valve 2000), as this was considered "fairer" than allowing this knowledge to just be in the hands of experienced players.

In the space of the cybercafé there was an easy transition between playing digital games and discussing them. This social element of gaming usually focused on the sharing of information about "how" to play digital games, a negotiation of skill and expertise that involved knowledge sharing. This knowledge sharing was often in the form of competitive one-upping, however, sometimes more expert players shared information in order to support the development of their team members and opponents and thus get a better challenge from playing with them. One older patron of the café, Johnny Lima (pseudonym), often mentored younger players in games that he was interested in, such as *Age of Mythology: The Titans* (Ensemble Studios 2003).

Johnny was popular, and would arrive with much fanfare as he was extensively greeted by the other regulars and hustled by the café staff to be next in the queue for one of their fastest computers. When Johnny started to play he conducted a terse commentary of his in-game activities, which often attracted the attention of other clients, particularly because he would often bring and install new games to the café. On one occasion he played a lengthy session of *Age of Mythology: The Titans*, while Gabriel—a teenaged male from a Portuguese immigrant family that lived on the same block as the café—watched him play, occasionally interrupting Johnny's commentary to respectfully ask a question. Over the days following, Gabriel disseminated what he had learnt about the unique tactics required to succeed as the Atlantean faction among some of the other players his age that also frequented the café.

General research into digital games was also shared between the patrons and staff, with the staff occasionally installing new games suggested by the patrons. They would allow a new game to be uploaded to one or two computers by its owner, in order to "market test" the game with other patrons. New games were common in this environment, because they were pirated. Pirated commercial games were available in street markets around San Bernardino, next to stalls that sold pirated music, films, and pornography. Consequently, digital games were affordable and came in a wide variety including relatively niche titles like *Mount & Blade* (TaleWorlds 2007). Piracy both permitted and multiplied access to digital games, thus becoming a crucial element to the experience of digital play in Cybercafé Avila (Apperley 2010).

Patrons of Cybercafé Avila described how they would pay careful attention to the street stalls' digital games when they passed in order to find out if there was anything new which sparked their interest. Kermit (pseudonym)—a Colombian immigrant who had just finished high school and was close friends with the staff of the café—also often made a point of asking the stallholders if they had any new games. Although this was not always helpful, he explained, as only a few of the stalls in the neighborhood were run by people who knew anything about computers or digital gaming. Some stalls were stocked in a manner that seemed random, while others—the ones that he preferred—had carefully curated collections of recent releases as well as many of the older "classics." These stallholders often sourced the games' instructions from file-sharing networks. Kermit's understanding of digital games involved integrating online research about new release digital games with a more streetwise knowledge of what was available in the neighborhood, along with a discerning knowledge that made informed distinctions between neighborhood locations.

Other cybercafé patrons, such as Gabriel, preferred to use pirated games, because digital games were so expensive, and expense was not necessarily an indicator of quality. The young people engaging in digital play, knowledge sharing, and piracy at Cybercafé Avila demonstrate how cybercafés in places like Venezuela—that are peripheral to global entertainment networks—are a crucial site for informal pedagogies with digital technology, that can position people in relation to the knowledge economy in situations where formal training is not available. This suggests that digital play in such cases has qualitatively different stakes and might well be worth considering within a different rubric: as a right of citizenship.

Digital Play as a Right

In *Citizens and Consumers: Globalization and Multicultural Conflicts* (2001), originally published in Spanish in 1997, Néstor García Canclini argues for a radical reformulation of the notion of citizenship in relation to contemporary forms of media use. Cultural consumption, including the consumption and production of media, is "an ensemble of practices that shape the sphere of citizenship" (2001, 22). Access to information through media is a civic right because it is crucial for individuals to have access to information in order to make informed decisions (ibid., 45). Such a level of access would be important to a society because it would allow individuals to "act autonomously and creatively" (ibid., 130–1). Since the notion of citizenship was formed in the eighteenth century, the creation, circulation, and storage of information have shifted to no longer be the exclusive role of the government. Market forces now play a large and important role in providing access to information. García Canclini argues that this requires a re-evaluation of the role of consumption in civic life. As a consequence of consumption becoming imbricated with citizenship rights, that the *rights themselves* should be redefined in terms of contemporary consumption rather than enduring as abstract ideals (ibid., 5, 21). García Canclini's argument has strong resonance with more recent discussions of digital citizenship (Mossberger et al. 2007) and digital rights (see Postigo 2012), although it is tailored more specifically to the issues facing the global South.

The stakes of digital play are not derived just from how the activity allows access to a form of community. What is crucial for supporting access to information is how through the processes of participation in these communities, the development of research and technical skills were fostered. The situation in Cybercafé Avila illustrates how access to key productive and creative skills and literacies that allow the collating, editing, and remixing of existing content may be substantially precarious in some contexts. Furthermore, it suggests that there is scope for shifting discussion of media piracy away from one of *absolute criminality* in order to also consider how it may provide a gateway to otherwise inaccessible networks.

An appreciation of the new forms of literacy that are emerging with digital forms of communication is extremely important for digital inclusion in Latin America (Martín Barbero 2011, 59). To have access to information no longer means to receive information; rather it requires that people are able to receive and produce information (ibid., 57). In light of the shifting exigencies of contemporary literacy Latin American communications scholar Jésus Martín Barbero has called for an examination and understanding of "*virtual literacy*" (ibid., 58; original emphasis). Paralleling many discussions of digital or new literacies, he argues that virtual literacies are more than just skills, but are also capacity-building habits and dispositions developed through the use of digital technologies (ibid., 58). Emerging forms of digital or virtual literacy are particularly important for changing patterns of global labor. They are essential for inclusion in the knowledge economy (Drucker 1969), that is characterized by the growing economic importance of intellectual and creative labor augmented by information and communication technologies. In these changing circumstances, digital games offer a smooth transition that links informal literacies developed through childhood forms of play to wider literacies that are relevant in other spheres of economic and civic activity.

Recent discussions have emphasized the potential that digital games have to contribute to education. Not simply in the sense of using "educational" digital games to teach curriculum—often called games-based learning—but rather that digital games designed for entertainment encapsulate a key informal encounter with developing a "literate" command over new digital, interactive media (Apperley 2014). Other scholars argue for an acknowledgment of "game literacy" or "gaming literacy" (Beavis et al. 2015; Buckingham and Burn 2007; Salen 2007, 2008; Zimmerman 2009). Zimmerman argues that "gaming literacy" is a paradigm for new digital literacy that engenders a playful understanding of the various—virtual, physical, social—structures that individuals inhabit; and an approach to design that is about "creating a set of possibilities" (2009, 29).

An area where gaming literacies are palpably demonstrated is in the creation of digital game paratexts. The term paratext was introduced to the study of digital games through Mia Consalvo's book *Cheating: Gaining Advantage in Video Games* (2007), which refers to the various texts used and developed by game players that circulate within digital gaming cultures. While the authoring of paratexts is rarely a requisite for playing a digital game, they are often accessed before, during, and after play. This occurs in order to clarify some technical detail such as the cheat codes for *Grand Theft Auto: Vice City* (Rockstar North 2003), or a particular strategy or approach, for example information on how to complete the helicopter mission in the same game. Not all engagement with paratexts is instrumental; other subgenres are more playful, whimsical, and artistic: for example fiction or artwork involving the character from a game, or animations (*mechanime*) made using a game engine.

Other paratextual productions might involve the production and distribution of new scenarios or levels for the game, as is common in *Counter-Strike*. These latter paratexts have more explicit links to practices of game design. The relationship between digital games and paratexts exemplifies how the Internet is used to coordinate, collaborate, and conduct research, and, in the process, build communities (Banks and Potts 2010). Furthermore, the multiple and versatile paratextual practices of game cultures demonstrate the new modes of audience participation that support engagement in the production and sharing of user-generated content.

To return to Cybercafé Avila, the community engaged with paratexts primarily to research elements of games being played in the café. As a result, there was a distinctly different relationship between digital gaming and new digital or virtual literacies within the café's gaming circles. The precarious context of the cybercafé, where people play for just a few short periods of time during the week dissuades cultural production; although paratexts made by others are used, they are used in a way that manages the small amounts of time that they have with the computers. For example, the cheat codes for *Grand Theft Auto: Vice City* were widely distributed by the staff, and were widely used by patrons to shape their own experience of the game. But while the cybercafé provided access to digital games, it did not provide access to the spectrum of engagement available to people with more flexibility around when, and for how long, they could use the computers.

At stake in the uneven levels of access to digital games and gaming communities is the extent to which they can foster the relevant knowledges, literacies, and skills. Gaming literacies' strongest advocate, Eric Zimmerman, argues: "While we are not all going to be game designers, game design and gaming literacy offer a valuable model for what it will mean to become literate, educated and successful in this playful world" (2009, 30).

Playing digital games and participation in global gaming networks provides a palpable opportunity for an informal engagement with contemporary literacy practices that are considered essential for fostering wider participation in cultural and economic activities. They are informal in the sense that, while potentially educative, they are not connected to a curriculum or institution. Yet these readily available engagements with popular culture contribute to informal literacies that many individuals in the developing world might not have the opportunity to develop through more formal means.

The context of the cybercafé reveals another creative practice that thrives in Venezuela and in some respects provides the opportunity to develop a different set of skills. Digital game piracy is a creative practice that is embedded in the local practices of digital gaming. It requires an understanding of global gaming cultures that have to be gleaned from the Internet, as players have to purchase any new games they want to play without the assistance of the videogame industry (who produce magazines and other promotional materials), expert staff, or even the information found on the cover or box of the game. This means that, through trial and error, patrons discover which computers have DVD drives and which only have CD-ROMs, and the various minimum specifications of the computers in the café. Installing the games involves relatively easy steps, but includes the manual reorganization of files after installation in order to activate the No-CD Crack which allows the copyright protection to be circumvented. The No-CD Cracks are usually on the pirated discs with the games, however, occasionally it would be necessary for the patron installing the game to locate and download the correct file from the Internet.

It has already been established that piracy is essential for the sustainability and profitability of cybercafés in Venezuela (Lugo and Sampson 2008), and Latin America more generally (Mattelart 2010). Piracy gives business owners a way to surmount the "technological, financial and political obstacles to the importing of this media technology and its content" (Mattelart 2010, 313). Piracy has a similar role in digital game play. While it is clearly not a part of play, piracy is essential for digital play to occur as it establishes the possibility for it to take place at all. At Cybercafé Avila creative practices of piracy shared among staff and patrons provided material access to networks that would otherwise be unavailable. This provided a fuller experience of inclusion in global networked culture, than would otherwise be available. Thus, in situations such as that of Cybercafé Avila, piracy has a significant role in mitigating exclusion; however, as reliance on piracy for inclusion is extremely precarious, this makes the stakes of inclusion extremely "risky."

In the decade since this initial fieldwork was conducted, the digital distribution of games has become more commonplace. Infrastructures such as Steam and the PlayStation Network now allow the digital distribution of PC and PlayStation games in Venezuela. These new models of distribution are less vulnerable to technologies like the No-CD Crack. Furthermore, any change in how the local laws are applied by the Federal government could effectively end the flexible conditions under which cybercafés in Venezuela operate. It is the combination of this threat, along with these constant technical changes that are, in part, developed to prevent and limit piracy that make access to digital gaming ever more precarious. In the developing world digital gameplay is widely understood as a creative practice that engenders collaboration, literacy, and computing skills, which in the developing world is considered to have *unambiguous segues* into working in the knowledge economy; it appears that excluding people in the developing world from digital gameplay could have particularly serious repercussions.

Conclusion

The culture of use of digital games at Cybercafé Avila is not one of deprivation. The practices of digital gaming and gaming cultures connect people to skills and literacies that support creative and productive use of global networks. These skills and literacies involve emergent communicative, productive, and connective elements of networked technology; to lack full access to such services curtails the development of literacies and skills that are essential to function in the global economy and contribute to global culture. Is it acceptable that because digital games are entertainment media, that their role in social and economic inclusion in the developing world is overlooked? In the lively and embodied context of the cybercafé, digital games are central to building basic technological efficacy with computers, as well as supporting the development of key informal knowledges, literacies, and skills, both through play and by participating in online game communities.

García Canclini's reconfiguration of citizenship to include the right to consume information offers scope to reconsider how we think about playing digital games. One has only to turn to how scholarship that examines the impact that digital gaming has on digital skills and literacies in the developed world widely concludes that they contribute autonomous participation in civic and economic life in the global network society, to recognize that those with different levels of access consequently suffer. The uneven experiences that characterize local gaming cultures globally may have grave implications for inclusion, but also demonstrate the potential for diversity in gaming cultures. A considered application of the notion of the right to play could make digital play less precarious and asymmetrical, and protect, even expand this diversity.

Acknowledgments

The travel and fieldwork expenses for this project were funded by the School of Culture and Communication, School of Graduate Studies, and the Faculty of Arts at the University of Melbourne, Australia.

References

Apperley, Thomas. 2010. *Gaming Rhythms: Play and Counterplay from the Situated to the Global.* Amsterdam: Institute of Network Cultures.

——. 2014. "Understanding digital games as education technologies: Capitalizing on popular culture." In *Popular Culture, Pedagogy and Teacher Education: International Perspectives*, edited by Phillip Benson and Alice Chik, 66–82. New York: Routledge.

——. 2015. "Venezuela." In *Videogames Around the World*, edited by Mark J. P. Wolf, 613–28. Cambridge, MA: MIT Press.

Aslinger, Ben and Nina Huntemann, eds. 2012. *Gaming Globally: Production, Play, and Place.* New York: Palgrave.

Banks, John and Jason Potts. 2010. "Co-creating games: An evolutionary analysis." *New Media & Society* 12(2): 253–70.

Beavis, Catherine, Chris S. Walsh, Clare Bradford, Joanne O'Mara, Thomas Apperley and Amanda Gutierrez. 2015. "'Turning around' to the affordances of digital games: English curriculum and students' lifeworlds." *English in Australia* 50(2): 30–40.

Boellstorff, Tom. 2008. *Coming of Age in Second Life: An Anthropologist Explores the Virtually Human.* Princeton, NJ: Princeton University Press.

Boellstorff, Tom, Bonnie Nardi, Celia Pearce and T.L. Taylor. 2012. *Ethnography and Virtual Worlds: A Handbook of Method.* Princeton, NJ: Princeton University Press.

Buckingham, David and Andrew Burn. 2007. "Game literacy in theory and practice." *Journal of Educational Multimedia and Hypermedia* 18(3): 323–49.

Consalvo, Mia. 2007. *Cheating: Gaining Advantage in Videogames.* Cambridge, MA: MIT Press.

Drucker, Paul. 1969. *The Age of Discontinuity.* New York: Harper & Row.

Ensemble Studios. 2003. *Age of Mythology: The Titans.* Microsoft Game Studios [PC]. Redmond, WA.

García Canclini, Néstor. 2001. *Consumers and Citizens: Globalization and Multicultural Conflicts.* Minneapolis: University of Minnesota Press.

Hjorth, Larissa and Dean Chan, eds. 2009. *Gaming Cultures and Place in the Asia-Pacific.* New York: Routledge.

Horst, Heather A. 2011. "Free, social, and inclusive: The appropriation and resistance to new media technologies in Brazil." *International Journal of Communication* 5: 437–62.

Lugo, Jairo and Tony Sampson. 2008. "E-informality in Venezuela: The 'other path' of technology." *Bulletin of Latin American Research* 27(1): 102–18.

Martín Barbero, Jesús. 2011. "From Latin America: Diversity, globalization, convergence." *Westminster Papers in Communication and Culture* 8(1): 39–64.

Mattelart, Tristan. 2010. "Audio-visual piracy: Towards a study of the underground networks of cultural production." *Global Media and Communication* 5(3): 308–26.

Meades, Alan F. 2015. *Understanding Counterplay in Videogames.* London: Routledge.

Mossberger, Karen, Caroline J. Tolbert and Ramona S. McNeal. 2007. *Digital Citizenship: The Internet, Society and Participation.* Cambridge, MA: MIT Press.

Nardi, Bonnie. 2010. *My Life as a Night Elf Priest: An Anthropological Account of World of Warcraft.* Ann Arbor: The University of Michigan Press and the University of Michigan Library.

Parker, Felan. 2008. "The significance of Jeep Tag: On player-imposed rules in video games." In *Loading . . .: the Journal of the Canadian Game Studies Association* 2(3). http://journals.sfu.ca/loading/index.php/loading/article/view/44/41 (accessed February 20, 2016).

Postigo, Hector. 2012. "Cultural production and the digital rights movement." *Information, Communication & Society* 15(8): 1165–85.

Rockstar North. 2003. *Grand Theft Auto: Vice City.* Rockstar Games [PC]. New York.

Salen, Katie. 2007. "Gaming literacies: A game design study in action." *Journal of Educational Multimedia and Hypermedia* 18(3): 301–32.

——. 2008. "Towards an ecology of gaming." In *The Ecology of Games: Connecting Youth, Games and Learning*, edited by Katie Salen, 1–17. Cambridge, MA: MIT Press.

Sassen, Saskia. 2006. *Territory, Authority, Rights: Global Assemblages*. Princeton, NJ: Princeton University Press.

TaleWorlds. 2007. *Mount & Blade*. Paradox Interactive [PC]. Stockholm.

Taylor, T. L. 2006. *Play between Worlds: Exploring Online Gaming Culture*. Cambridge, MA: MIT Press.

Valve. 2000. *Counter-Strike*. Sierra Studios [PC]. Fresno, CA.

Willis, Paul. 2000. *The Ethnographic Imagination*. Cambridge: Polity.

Wolf, Mark. J. P., ed. 2015. *Videogames around the World*. Cambridge, MA: MIT Press.

Zimmerman, Eric. 2009. "Gaming literacy: Game design as a model for literacy in the twenty-first century." In *The Video Game Theory Reader 2*, edited by Bernard Perron and Mark J. P. Wolf, 23–32. New York: Routledge.

22

/KAYFABE[1]

An In-Depth Look at World Wrestling Entertainment (WWE) and Its Fandom Using Digital Ethnography

Crystle Martin

Introduction

People who do not watch professional wrestling always have the same question for fans—Do you think it's *real*? However, this question of "reality" doesn't really engage with the underlying reasons fans find the sport so pleasurable. It has a long and storied history—moving from a more traditional version of Greco-Roman wrestling to the theatrical spectacle of sports entertainment that it is today. Professional wrestling offers its fans a complex form of entertainment with its own genre conventions and insider language. The complexity of this fan culture is often surprising to those who are not initiated.

Fans of professional wrestling knowingly participate in a collective fantasy (Fine 1983); they know what they are watching is not real but they buy into the fantasy and therefore make it authentic. Professional wrestling has often been compared to soap operas. Jenkins (2005) calls it "masculine melodrama." The competitive elements are secondary compared to the drama before and after each match (Ball 1990). It is that drama that makes professional wrestling so enticing for its fans. Mazer (2005) describes professional wrestling as being made up of a set of dichotomies. It is at once real and fake, spontaneous and rehearsed, genuinely felt and staged for effect, prodigious and reductive, profoundly transgressive and essentially conservative. The wrestlers constantly read the audience and adjust their performances to match the mood of the crowd.

A prominent promoter from the 1940s described professional wrestling's staged nature as a benefit: "You never know beforehand when you're gonna see a lousy prizefight. In wrestling, we give you guaranteed entertainment" ("Guaranteed Entertainment" 1948, 51–2). Contemporary professional wrestling fans appreciate the nuance—they are educated consumers who use social media and online communities to more deeply participate in their interest. The chapter provides a brief history of professional wrestling, and then offers descriptions of the culture of fan education, the participation of fans in online contexts, and what digital ethnography has and can offer in terms of creating deeper understanding of the community.

Brief History of Wrestling

American professional wrestling as a popular performance genre can trace its roots back to vaudeville and burlesque (Sammond 2005). Professional wrestling is a mixture of choreography and improvised athletics, where the performers actively participate in creating the illusion of real violence and real mayhem (Wrenn 2007, 150). Professional wrestling is born out of the Greco-Roman wrestling tradition, but over time it transitioned into its modern equivalent. By the mid-1910s wrestling had been completely reworked—that is, it became choreographed. This shift was a response to the fans becoming bored of long matches and the increased need by fans for more excitement, entertainment, and charismatic wrestlers (Beekman 2006).

During the 1920s, professional wrestling realized the importance of wrestlers developing a persona, with good guys "faces" versus the bad guys "heels." Tag-team matches, that is, two teams of wrestlers wrestling against each other with one wrestler from each team active in the ring at a time, became popular in the 1930s, and were found to be useful because the match became slower as wrestlers became winded. The tag-team aspect changed up the rhythm and added excitement. There was no organization to wrestling as a whole, no overarching governing body. So this often created strife between wrestling promoters.

Between roughly 1916 and the late 1920s, wrestling promotions started to coalesce and consolidate power. A "trust" of East Coast wrestling promoters formed to control the wrestlers and the venues, not terribly different than with big wrestling promotions of the late twentieth century (Beekman 2006, 60). The trust controlled who wrestled, what matches they were booked in, and who won. When a professional wrestler who had dominated the competition in the 1930s retired while still holding the championship belt, a gigantic power vacuum was created and several wrestling promotions at once claimed to have the world champion. This created turmoil that took several years to shake out.

Wrestling promoters realized early on that television could be harnessed, which spurred professional wrestling's popularity in the 1950s. However, they overexposed wrestling, having too many televised matches too often, and caused a downturn in its popularity that nearly drove it off the air and lasted for almost 30 years. Professional wrestling struggled to regain popularity as more sports and entertainment moved to television, capturing the attention of professional wrestling's former fans. It really wasn't until the late 1980s that professional wrestling began to make a comeback. The feud between World Championship Wrestling (WCW), owned by Ted Turner, and the World Wrestling Federation (WWF now WWE), owned by Vince McMahon—which lasted until the WCW's acquisition by the WWF in 2001—was what sparked the rekindling of professional wrestling and the love of modern fans for "sports entertainment."

The process of becoming a professional wrestler changed over time, just as wrestling had. Originally, when professional wrestling was broken into regional territories, novices would hang around arenas until they were selected as an apprentice by an established wrestler. However, as wrestling evolved and consolidated, this path to wrestling ended and wrestling camps and training schools became the way into professional wrestling for aspiring wrestlers (Hackett 2006). Learning the game is more than just learning the athletic and performative moves; wrestlers must also learn the intricacies of performance and professional wrestling as a genre. This process of continuous learning is similar for fans.

Making of a "Smark"

Professional wrestling fans are in a continual process of becoming insiders (Mazer 1998). There is a delicate balance between "buying into" the fantasy and knowing the reality of the situation. Fans' "penchant for 'authentic inauthenticity' is key to the logic, spirit, and practice" (Wrenn 2007, 149) of professional wrestling. The wrestlers strike a balance between sport and theater in order to pull off the authentic inauthenticity that the fans crave. Wrestlers, to be successful, need to manipulate both their opponents and their audience. The way the game is played is more important than winning or losing, or even rules.

For wrestling fans, at least those who started watching wrestling as children in the pre-Internet age, they would first view the wrestlers as superhuman, and once they "smartened up" they would stay with wrestling because of wrestling's mystique and the feeling of being part of an in-crowd (Hackett 2006, 109). There is an educational process that professional wrestling fans go through, starting from a naive state and then developing expertise. Those who do not "smarten up" are referred to as "marks." Marks are spectators who believe in the legitimacy of the match. They do not recognize that the matches are choreographed and scripted. Once fans begin to understand that wrestling is choreographed and scripted, they then become "smart" fans. The transition to becoming a smart fan begins by seeking insider information. These fans transform into critical consumers looking for performances that are authentic to professional wrestling as a genre.

Fans can also be referred to as "smarks." A smark is a term specific to professional wrestling. It denotes a "smart" fan who wants to be taken in by the spectacle of professional wrestling (Mazer 1998). That is, the fans want the spectacle to be so well done that they will be drawn in and believe that it is "real." In these cases, "what is at stake is not winning or losing per se. Rather it is, literally, the way in which the game is played" (Mazer 1998, 8). This trajectory of learning, enculturation, and growth is a development track that professional wrestling fans embark on not in isolation but, rather, with the support of fellow fans. This type of peer mentorship originally only took place in person, and for many finding another fan to share the experience and enjoyment of professional wrestling, let alone a mentor, was difficult, especially as fans passed out of their early teen years. The Internet changed this for professional wrestling fans, connecting them across the globe.

Professional Wrestling Fandom Goes Digital

Being digitally savvy might not be the first thing that comes to people's minds when they think of professional wrestling fans; but the whole genre, from the professional wrestling franchises like WWE to the individual fans, uses a variety of digital media to deepen their engagement. Wrestlers use Twitter, Facebook, YouTube, and Tout to continue their feuds between the televised matches, which allows fans to both have access to far more content than they had previous to the Internet, as well as to participate in the conversation and share the parts they like easily with their friends and the world. There are also a multitude of websites, wikis, and news sites dedicated to professional wrestling, where fans can find current and historical information about specific wrestlers or storylines, as well as leaks about upcoming plot twists. By far the most interactive place for professional wrestling fans online are the fan-run forums. These forums are where the most intensive fan discussions take place.

I conducted an eight-month ethnography of a professional wrestling fan community called the Wrestling Boards, from October 2012 to May 2013. Interviewees varied by age (ranging from 16 to 36); gender (24 males and 1 female); and geography (North America,

South America, Europe, and Asia). The community also ran a fantasy wrestling federation called Over the Ropes. Interview questions were informed by observations in the forum. The interviews were semi-structured, allowing for probing of emergent themes.

Professional wrestling fans are often isolated by their fandom. As interviewees from my ethnography of professional wrestling fans described, once they passed the age of middle school the number of people around them that were also interested in professional wrestling decreased significantly, many times leaving them with no one. Professional wrestling is considered "uncool" for older teens and adults often see it as juvenile. Zach (17) said, "Personally, I tend to keep [my professional wrestling interest] to myself." Rhashan (19) had a more pointedly negative view: "WWE is not something that's like amazing to show around, it's just something I like."

For those who were alone in their interest, it did not take them long to discover that there were other fans online. However, finding a group of fans that shared similar interests and were actually supportive of other fans was a more challenging undertaking. Not every community offers emotional and educational support. Jonathan (16) noted, "The only time I really talk to anyone about WWE is on Wrestling Boards." In the Wrestling Boards (Martin 2014a) many members participated in this particular community because it was extremely supportive.

Another benefit of online activities for professional wrestling fans is that each fan has access to large numbers of other fans rather than only having access to those in their local area, which usually number in the few. The Wrestling Boards welcome newcomers on a subforum named "The Ramp." New participants are invited to introduce themselves with a tagline that reads: "The music has hit. The spotlight is on you. The crowd is cheering. Make your impact here and tell us who you are!" To help foster a strong sense of community the administrator of the forum created a template to help people feel comfortable, along with this note: "Just in case you're stuck on what to say on your big introduction to Wrestling Boards, I've come up with a template. It's just something to give you a helping hand if needed." As members of the community get comfortable they begin to participate across the forum. For these online communities, participants form strong bonds with each other. They originally find the community because they are looking for others with whom they can discuss professional wrestling. However, over time, the community becomes one where they come to discuss other interests, and even personal problems. Similar interactions can be seen in other online communities, like fan fiction and video games (Black 2007; Rafalow 2015; Martin 2014b).

Participating in an online professional wrestling community offers participants more than just community—it becomes a place for building identity. Those who participated in the Wrestling Boards develop a sense of themselves in the contrasting social situations of this supportive community and in the larger, and often unsupportive world (Holland et al. 1998), using multiple identities to navigate the complex landscape (Weber and Mitchell 2008). The participants express identity through their digital production for the online professional wrestling community. As sourced directly from my fieldwork, Rhashan expresses his identity through his participation in the fantasy wrestling, "No one else really does Over the Ropes like I do, to the extent of shooting real promos." Rhashan actually role-plays his wrestling character for the fantasy wrestling federation and records video promos in character as part of this participation in Over the Ropes. For Rhashan, participating in fantasy wrestling means more than just creating the character and feuding with others. Jonathan also produces videos for the site: "I upload short WWE clips for members, often like 'best of' videos and such." He does this to enhance other participants' enjoyment of professional wrestling, making it easier for fans with limited time to be able to keep up with WWE shows and storylines. Keeping up can be a major time commitment, with more than three hours of WWE television programming per week.

For fans once isolated by physical distance, online communities offer a space to come together and explore their fandom. The Internet offers professional wrestling fans connection to each other, as well as access to more content—both fan-produced and official. Online communities are asynchronous, which means that no matter the time of day or night, wrestling fans can join conversations and read others' opinions about what is going on in professional wrestling. This record of asynchronous conversation also offers an opportunity for ethnographers.

Impact of Digital Ethnography on Professional Wrestling

Online communities offer a place for ethnographers to explore the intricacies of a community. Ethnographers can view a record of conversation, from a large community and over long periods of time. Prior to the Internet, access to something like this would not have been possible, but now it offers uncommon insights into the daily workings of individual interest-driven communities. Examples of these communities range from video games to fan fiction to knitting communities and beyond (Black 2007; Rafalow 2015; Cody Pfister 2014).

In online fan fiction communities, the record of comments and conversations between members gives researchers a unique insight into how peers support developing writing skills. As Black (2007) illustrated, the learning opportunities in these online affinity spaces gives the affordance of learning outside of the classroom in ways that "will facilitate student knowledge of multiple modes of meaning making, access, participation, affiliation, learning, and success in a globalized, networked society" (Black 2007, 395). Black (2007) stated that Fanfiction.net has participants using a variety of skills, including digital literacies that allow them to explore and problem solve writing and reading difficulties. The participants in these affinity spaces vary drastically in age and education levels. Sites like Fanfiction.net also allow for a user to have some control over their experience, asking for specific types of feedback and offering their work in a specific manner that is not always readily accessible in other spaces. Black (2007) also demonstrated that participants have many opportunities to contribute knowledge and content, which for students is not an opportunity that happens often in K-12 classrooms. The younger affinity space participants also have the opportunity to be experts, which is a rare occurrence in student–teacher relationships of formal educational settings.

Similar affordances for ethnography have been seen in videogame communities (Consalvo 2009; Jensen and de Castell 2011; Martin 2014b; Nardi 2010; Taylor 2009). In the online community of *Little Big Planet 2*, digital ethnographers used the record of conversation to understand how reputation functioned within the community (Rafalow 2015). The online conversations are supplemented by interviews to create a multi-faceted description of how reputation works within the community and how individuals feel that they are impacted by it. As members of the community cultivate more notoriety and a higher status reputation, they become idolized within the community, holding a position of reverence among participants.

In *World of Warcraft*, conversation is a main activity between players. Even though a player might be concerned with game play, social interaction is the main activity between the player and the affinity space (Martin 2014b). Conversation is important for the enculturation of new participants, for players who need assistance, and for maintaining and changing social norms over time. Because massively multiplayer online (MMOs) games are persistent worlds, they are accessible to players at all times, allowing players to log on and off at will, as well as being accessible from anywhere in which the player has an Internet connection.

For many, an MMO becomes a home away from "home," where the player plays regularly and their absence is noted and remarked upon by others. Players can become regulars, especially in relation to a guild or clan, and their fellow players might always expect to see them playing when they log in (Steinkuehler 2005). In a game like *World of Warcraft* there could be other people whom you always expect to see in trade chat when you are in town. This is just one of the many routes to participation offered in the affinity space. At the other end of the spectrum, a player could remain completely anonymous and have no one recognize that they have come and gone, depending on their choice. Martin (2014b, 2012, 2011) took this research further by exploring the information literacy of participants in the *World of Warcraft* community. Martin's study explored the development of information literacy as well as how information literacy functioned at a community level. This research demonstrated that information literacy is a collective process that happens within the interactions of those participating in the community, not an individual process.

Exploring the nuances of practices of these communities is facilitated by the structure of the online community studied and the ability to do a digital ethnography on the record of conversations. For professional wrestling communities, very few digital ethnographies have taken place up to this point with the exception of Martin (2015, 2014a). Looking at digital ethnography in other online communities demonstrates what can be gained from digital ethnography in understanding the professional wrestling community.

The study of professional wrestling described in the section "Professional Wrestling Goes Digital" is currently the only study of online professional wrestling fan communities. This study differs from previous studies of professional wrestling, as it focuses on the fans and how they develop in the community, instead of starting at professional wrestling as a media that people take in and interact with. Through a sociocultural learning approach to the research, this study highlights the importance of having other participants to interact with regarding professional wrestling.

The Wrestling Boards not only support participants' enjoyment of professional wrestling but also support expertise development and learning. As Jonathan said:

> I give and get feedback often about what I do. I often help/mentor new members of the forum to the best of my ability. At the end of the day, we're all alike and we're like a family on Wrestling Boards.

Cloud, a 28-year-old from the UK, felt much the same:

> We all try and help each other on here it's a friendly community and we constantly give feedback and advice to each other and I know a lot of us give feedback and advice to Crayo about the site and things we would like to see.

Zach, who participates in the fantasy wrestling federation Over the Ropes, describes his feedback for the writers as such, "I really look into Over the Ropes and try to help them improve it by writing reviews of their work so they can improve." The members of the fantasy wrestling federation offer fine grain feedback to help others improve their writing. For example, here is a snippet of Zach's feedback to a match:

3. Yet another well written match. Loved, loved, loved the mosquito reference. I like how Heavy Jones just came off as an absolute monster in this match. Not sure if I like how he pretty much dominated the whole match, I would like to have seen all 3 wrestlers have a moment in the match where they were dominating. By the way, this line made me cringe: "Sid: Oh-Oh, Clash's head, he has definitely lossed a few IQ points after that" Lossed. Lossed. Lossed. Lossed. *facepalm* It's okay though, every match had some errors. This one had a lot though. For the last quarter of the match all the commentary said: Standard Commentary and there was only one person commentating. You have to start reading the whole thing before you post it. Still a great match though. Rating: 7/10

This is just one section of Zach's detailed analysis of one week's match. He both comments on the structural qualities of the writing as well as the genre conventions selected by the writers. Zach through his participation was not only able to help those writing the matches to improve their writing, but he also develops his own skills at giving high-quality feedback. Participants in this community also developed a variety of digital media skills like website design, Photoshop, video and audio editing. Through this digital ethnography, I found that the Wrestling Boards was a vibrant learning community that allowed participants to develop both their interest, their fandom, as well as learning opportunities.

Digital Ethnography and Professional Wrestling Going Forward

Digital ethnography allows researchers to investigate the nuances of online communities such as those around professional wrestling. It understands the digital as entangled within the everyday. Each online community offers a digital record of interaction between participants. It not only shows the conversation but also the development of expertise of individuals and the development of relationships between participants. This confirms what Martin (2014a, 2015) has found regarding the professional wrestling community as a site for various forms of learning and support that can influence the career trajectories of young participants. Through digital ethnography we can understand the complex value of communities and their various forms of literacies and practices that influence disciplines such as education, sociology, and communications. Digital ethnography opens new realms for understanding the depth and value of fandom and community for professional wrestling fans.

Note

1 Kayfabe is a portrayal in professional wrestling of staged events as real. In terms of the Wrestling Boards it is when participants speak as their wrestling characters as part of Over the Ropes, the fantasy wrestling federation. /Kayfabe is used on the Wrestling Boards to indicate when the players are entering and leaving the portrayal of their character, so as not to have their wrestling character's words misconstrued as their own.

References

Ball, Michael R. 1990. *Professional Wrestling as Ritual Drama in American Popular Culture*. Lewiston, NY: Edwin Mellen Press.

Beekman, S. M. 2006. *Ringside: A History of Professional Wrestling in America*. Westport, CT: Praeger.

Black, Rebecca W. 2007. "Fanfiction Writing and the Construction of Space." *e-Learning* 4(4): 384–97.

Cody Pfister, Rachel. 2014. *Hats for House Elves: Connected Learning and Civic Engagement in Hogwarts at Ravelry*. Irvine, CA: Digital Media and Learning Research Hub. http://clrn.dmlhub.net/wp-content/uploads/2014/05/hatsforhouseelves.pdf (accessed February 13, 2016).

Consalvo, Mia. 2009. *Cheating: Gaining Advantage in Videogames*. Cambridge, MA: MIT Press.

Editorial. 1948. "Guaranteed Entertainment." In *Time*, 51–2. May 31.

Fine, Gary Alan. 1983. *Shared Fantasy: Role Playing Games As Social Worlds*. Chicago, IL: University of Chicago Press.

Hackett, Thomas. 2006. *Slaphappy: Pride, Prejudice, and Professional Wrestling*. New York: HarperCollins.

Holland, Dorothy, William Lachicotte Jr, Debra Skinner, and Carole Cain. 1998. *Identity and Agency in Cultural Worlds*. Cambridge, MA: Harvard University Press.

Jenkins, Henry. 2005. "Never Trust a Snake: WWF Wrestling as Masculine Melodrama." In *Steel Chair to the Head: The Pleasure and Pain of Professional Wrestling*, edited by Nicholas Sammond, 33–66. Durham, NC: Duke University Press.

Jenson, Jennifer and Suzanne de Castell. 2011. "Girls@ Play: An Ethnographic Study of Gender and Digital Gameplay." *Feminist Media Studies* 11(2): 167–79.

Martin, Crystle. 2011. "An Information Literacy Perspective on Learning and New Media." *On the Horizon* 19(4): 268–75.

———. 2012. "Video Games, Identity, and the Constellation of Information." *Bulletin of Science, Technology, and Society. Special issue, Game On: The Challenges and Benefits of Video Games, Part I* 32(5): 384–92.

———. 2014a. *Learning the Ropes: Connected Learning in a WWE Fan Community*. Irvine, CA: Digital Media and Learning Research Hub. http://clrn.dmlhub.net/wp-content/uploads/2014/05/learning-the-ropes-final-2.pdf (accessed May 15, 2015).

———. 2014b. *Voyage across a Constellation of Information: Information Literacy in Interest-Driven Learning Communities*. New York: Peter Lang.

———. 2015. "Connected Learning, Libraries, and Bridging Youth Interest." *Journal of Research on Young Adults and Libraries*. www.yalsa.ala.org/jrlya/2015/03/connected-learning-librarians-and-connecting-youth-interest/ (accessed May 15, 2015).

Mazer, Sharon. 1998. *Professional Wrestling: Sport and Spectacle*. Jackson, MS: University of Mississippi Press.

———. 2005. "'Real' Wrestling/'Real' Life." In *Steel Chair to the Head: The Pleasure and Pain of Professional Wrestling*, edited by Nicholas Sammond, 67–87. Durham, NC: Duke University Press.

Nardi, Bonnie. 2010. *My Life as a Night Elf Priest: An Anthropological Account of World of Warcraft*. Ann Arbor, MI: University of Michigan Press.

Rafalow, Matthew. 2015. "n00bs, Trolls, and Idols: Boundary-Making among Digital Youth." In *Technology and Youth: Growing Up in a Digital World (Sociological Studies of Children and Youth, Volume 19)*, edited by Sampson Lee Blair, Patricia Neff Claster, and Samuel M. Claster, 243–66. Bradford: Emerald Group Publishing Limited.

Sammond, Nicholas. 2005. "A Brief and Unnecessary Defense of Professional Wrestling." In *Steel Chair to the Head: The Pleasure and Pain of Professional Wrestling*, edited by Nicholas Sammond, 1–22. Durham, NC: Duke University Press.

Steinkuehler, Constance. 2005. "The New Third Place: Massively Multiplayer Online Gaming in American Youth Culture." *Journal of Research in Teacher Education* 3: 16–33.

Taylor, T. L. 2009. *Play Between Worlds: Exploring Online Game Culture*. Cambridge, MA: MIT Press.

Weber, Sandra and Claudia Mitchell. 2008. "Imaging, Keyboarding, and Posting Identities: Young People and New Media Technologies." In *Youth, Identity, and Digital Media*, edited by David Buckingham, 25–47. Cambridge, MA: MIT Press.

Wrenn, Marion. 2007. "Managing Doubt: Professional Wrestling Jargon and the Making of 'Smart Fans.'" In *Practice Culture*, edited by Craig Calhoun and Richard Sennett, 147–70. New York: Routledge.

23

RUNNING, GENDER, AND PLAY WITH *ZOMBIES, RUN!*

Emma Witkowski

In this chapter I reflect on digital ethnography and play through a one-year study with women who both work out using the mobile audio-adventure running game app, *Zombies, Run!* (Six to Start and Naomi Alderman 2012), and post about their running on Instagram. This study highlights how a multi-sited, mixed methods and sensory digital ethnography can contribute to a complex representation of how play intersects with and impacts on people's everyday lives. Looking at personal configurations of playing *Zombies, Run!* (ZR henceforth), which are rendered here as playful and identity building lifestyle activities, this research produces a sociophenomenological account on women's embodied knowledge in what is a commonplace networked leisure activity. The sensorial dimensions of running with zombies emerged as vital early in this study as participants denoted the sensorium of ZR running as a core motivation for continuing in this form of networked play.

In addition, distinctive multimodal pleasures were harnessed through processes of "wayfinding"—where travelers "'feel their way' through a world that is itself in motion, continually coming into being through the combined action of human and non-human agencies" (Ingold 2000, 155)—intensified aural awareness, proprioception, as well as fear (or lack thereof) experienced while running. The centrality of these sensory dimensions starts to highlight some of the sociophenomenological tensions associated with women who run, such as the balance of risk to agency while playing in public space (Allen-Collinson 2010), as well as signifying what is really at stake in having the freedom of movement to play games.

ZR is a location-based game dependent on networked technologies such as a smartphone, stable global positioning system (GPS), and compatible software in order to deliver a smooth framework for play. Sarah Pink notes the importance of such socio-technical figurations in her sensory ethnographic approach to research:

The algorithmic architectures and digital interfaces of these environments shape both everyday life and research practices. They form part of the context and the subject matter of what I would define as "digital ethnography": meaning a way of doing ethnography that is part of and participates in a digital-material-sensory environment rather than simply ethnography about the digital.

(Pink 2014, 420)

The configurations and processes involved in running with ZR, and sharing/doing of such experiences via digital services are, as such, articulated as digital-material-sensory processes of running; they are practices from situated and historical bodies with specific socio-technical running competencies and ways of doing ZR. The new relationships that emerged most strongly in this exploration are as diverse as: the dynamic and often playful negotiation of risk-space on the run; increased awareness of body-technology competencies and location awareness in play; along with realizing personal body rhythms, but also rhythms of local space through running with ZR. As such, the colliding themes of risk-space, embodiment, and playfulness are central to this chapter, and considered here through the lens of phenomenologically inspired sociology, which is "a phenomenological form that also acknowledges the myriad effects of culture, of the historical 'moment' and of social-structural elements upon lived-body experience" (Allen-Collinson and Leledaki 2014, 3).

The everyday experiences of sensory running practices are well documented in the extensive research of Jacquelyn Allen-Collinson (2010, 2011, 2013), however sociophenomenological considerations on running practice taper considerably when looking at networked runners and play (Kan et al. 2013), and are diluted further still when concentrating on women's experiences of such everyday leisure (Witkowski 2013). As such, this research contributes to accounts of women "on the run" in their networked play, and how these participants push at gendered norms through play and games (de Souza e Silva and Hjorth 2009). The chapter explores three areas. First, it reflects upon a mixed-methods sensuous digital ethnography, followed by a discussion of embodiment and networked play in the context of ZR. Finally it considers women, risk, and playing in public space with ZR.

Entering the Digital Apocalypse

Research on the experiential qualities of the running body extends across fields of sports philosophy (Martin 2007), human–computer interaction (Rooksby et al. 2014), and phenomenology (Allen-Collinson 2010, 2013). The latter provides the implications for this running research with attention to the senses—where the body-world experience is expanded (including visual, haptic, aural, and proprioceptive senses), in order to recognize lived bodies in terms of "possibilities and constraints" (Sparkes and Smith 2012, 107). The sensuous turn of this study started from running itself. As a practiced runner, I was using various sports-tracking apps when ZR came to my attention. ZR is a mobile phone application that supports runners by quantitatively documenting their run (including time splits, speed profile graphs, and distance markers—features common to most running apps). Its main point of difference from other running apps is its story-based missions (standard missions are set at 30- or 60-minutes); during a mission, runners hear a fictional zombie-apocalypse story line, and at times are "chased" by the living dead. Chases are a central agent in cultivating this playful attitude toward running space, and toward a running practice that extends beyond a rationalized focus.

Accordingly, the following exploration refers specifically to ZR with "Chases on" (here-on called "Chases"). Technically, Chases involve toggling-on the option in the app, which is available to runners with smartphones, and their GPS functionality. Adrian Hon and Naomi Alderman (CEO and lead writer, respectively) highlight that this key design element presented participants with an alternative incentive to run, by motivating runners to live in a story, and through smooth story-technical integration Chases can be seen to drive that as a playful game mechanic (pers. comm., email to author, October 7, 2013). Each time a Chase drops into the storyline (3–4 times per run), a session of interval running or "speed play" begins. Speed play is a practice that joins a run with multiple speed play interludes—shorter sprints weaved into a workout.

For example, on the start of a Chase in ZR, a runner needs to increase their speed by approximately 20 percent in order to evade the zombies. During the Chase, the runner is also traversing the terrain, sensing and navigating obstacles, and thinking of or moving toward foreseeable movement space. When combined, these elements make the Chase a period of time where the runner is pressed *out of equilibrium* (Martin 2007). The struggle against the local space heightens the awareness of "the doing of running" itself, which brings about transient moments of panic and disequilibrium. And that playful imbalance—both unpredictable and challenging—can be pleasurable to pursue, especially in its full sensorial engagement required to successfully evade the walking dead. As ZR has speed play available from "Mission One," it could be argued that some of the running excitement voiced about the Chase sits with this alternative experience of movement, an experience unique for novice runners in particular.

My own altered running practice was perceptible by my seventh outing with ZR: less oriented toward time and distance, and more toward running as play, where straight roads and regular running paths were switched out for escape trails and lonely atmospheres. Despite ZR's commercial casing, movement with ZR is a clear reflection of The Situationist International's method of the *dérive* (French term meaning drift), a chance-led practice of wandering through the city, and "A mode of experimental behavior linked to the conditions of urban society: a technique of rapid passage through varied ambiances" (Knabb 1981, 45). As my running lines "drifted" in and out of an environment in a less linear way, my attention to the process of running was altered from "just doing it" to "being there." Being there moved beyond just getting one's feet on the road by extending to other sensorial details of moving through space, as highlighted in this early fieldnote (Copenhagen, Tuesday morning, June 4, 2013):

> The smell "on the inside" of the public cemetery (where I run), away from the outer ring, is fresher, denser, and more strange—we are mid-city after all. And Sunday's run and today's were the first runs through this space where I had moments of complete disorientation, lost amongst the trees and many small dirt pathways. Lost in a run— mid-city! It was beautiful, safe, and something I hadn't felt for a long time. I took photos today. I wanted to get back to places—the winding tree, the rhododendron path, the place I got lost.

The locational attention, highlighted in this run, was made on the move but with several other key changes involved. Body movement and technological attention were retuned— focused strides, attention to cadence during Chases, choosing specific earbuds for speed play, and steady awareness of networked functionality. And a shift in a running habitus was recognized, as new ambiances were taken in as I ran into the same geographical region. Tim Ingold describes this keen awareness of a region as one made in the process of "wayfinding," where the traveler "'feels his way' towards his goal, continually adjusting his movements in response to an ongoing perceptual monitoring of his surroundings" (2000, 220). Ingold continues, "Our perception of the environment as a whole, in short, is forged . . . in the passage from place to place, and in histories of movement and changing horizons along the way" (2000, 227). This expression of wayfinding encapsulates running movement with ZR, where a different feel and perception is borne from a body *en route*, which hints toward how a playful change might extend one's very reach into the world by way of running.

As an experienced runner, the qualitative shifts in my own running signaled the requirement of a mixed-methods approach, starting with a form of autobiographical research exploring my multi-sited running practice. Following Woodward and Woodward (2009, 138), "Embodiment is central to being in the world, yet in many instances and situations this embodiment is routine and therefore becomes taken for granted"; accordingly, by starting from the focused researcher body as participant, the sensorial aspects and tacit knowledge of a running aesthetic are illuminated (however partial) from a specific body in action, and offer a point of reflection to the new worlds expressed by other ZR runners with some of the taken-for-granted mundanities of running revealed (Sparkes and Smith 2012).

Sensuous Digital Ethnography

This exploration started out by documenting a situated running aesthetic from the runner/researcher (see Witkowski 2013) in order to gain a particular corporeal awareness attuned to the phenomenological features associated to running with ZR. Established under multiple names, from autoethnography, case study, to life story (Gruppetta 2004), the researcher as a key informant is explored in this study by way of autophenomenography. Well established in research on sporting embodiment within sports and physical culture studies, autophenomenography is

> an autobiographical genre in which the phenomenological researcher is both researcher and participant in her/his study of a particular phenomenon or phenomena, rather than of a particular ethnós (social group that shares a common culture) subjecting her/his own lived experience to a sustained and rigorous phenomenological analysis.
>
> (Allen-Collinson 2011, 53)

The autophenomenographical exploration of this study offers a prop to think with, attention to the sensuous frenzy of the activity, and a technique "to 'live' the experience rather than merely to analyze it" (Allen-Collinson and Hockey 2009, 77). That is, to animate what a culturally situated and practiced running body goes through in their running aesthetic, however incomplete that exploration might be. By starting from a situated body, the research acquires a contextual frame and fine-tuned dialogic partner to reflect on other (interviewed) runners who participated on ZR-related Instagram threads.

During the main body of fieldwork, I ran consistently with ZR for a year totaling over 40 runs or 180 kilometers/18 hours. Fieldnotes were typed up immediately during cool down or post-shower with attention to my researcher/running positionality, changing body, technologies, and wayfaring involvements. My smartphone images were cataloged in the fieldnote diary with running notes referenced. Many images were distributed post-run (via ZR-related Instagram hashtags) as records to both revisit and contribute to experiential dialogs with other ZR runners. The images of running experiences were a key sensory touchstone for participants, as highlighted in a dialog that followed my posting of an injury (a bruised toenail) on an Instagram ZR-hashtag. My "toe shot" prompted a collaborator to mention her personal experiences of losing toenails from running. Her reflection illustrates how phenomenological experiences can be stimulated and shared, where the visual is just a starting point which kindles a body memory, and a tacit piece of knowledge on the everyday running body in practice (Pink 2007). My photograph of a specific running practice was not a "tool to obtain knowledge," but rather a part of a conversation which is situated as "a visual object through which people reference aspects of their experience and knowledge" (Pink 2007, 82). In this sense, the multi-sited locations and expressions of modern running move far beyond the pavement, and one would be remiss not to look toward the various ways and places in which individuals "do running" and to consider how to connect to such subtle, tacit involvements.

Doing digital ethnography around ZR practices brought together an assemblage of runs, fieldnotes, personal photos, collected public domain image/text Instagram posts (with permission), games developer interviews, and seven runner interviews (five interviews conducted with regular Instagram ZR contributors and two interviews held with novice runners). In engaging with mixed-methods research, a detailed sense of running with ZR from a particular kind of engagement and position was produced. Qualitative interviews carried out with ZR runners highlight the multi-sited aspects of participating in this particular way of running. And runner/interviewees, snowballed from near-networks and approached on ZR-related Instagram hashtags, revealed how completing a run was a much longer and involved process than just stepping outside with trainers on. "Anji," a 44-year-old runner (with a few thousand Instagram followers), expresses this well in the networked nature of her broader running practice:

> Posting on Instagram keeps me motivated . . . people drop by and comment and share their own stories and sometimes let me know that I've motivated them too. Knowing that ive [sic] helped someone else on their journey is a nice boost and im grateful to all the people that have helped me along. It builds a sense of community and shared purpose, which is very supportive and motivating.

In this manner, running with zombies is not played alone. Participants extend this notion through their personal configurations of running play—from references to their phone technology (older smartphones and choppy net connections were often blamed for choking on heavy data processing), to comments on taking in the running environment with a sensitivity to time/space (hills contra flat pathways, tempo tied to weather conditions, urban rhythms in contrast to the pace and pressures of rural running), running partners, and peripherals (family members, babies in prams—earbuds, new or painful footwear).

Through the text/image assemblage of Instagram, ZR runners also performed their sociocultural situations, and posts were often used as a starting point for dialog with runners directly speaking from their own Instagram entries and expanding on their running life-world. Themes drawn from visually prompted conversations included nascent corporeal experiences, as well as the harder side of running which comprised of images of bloodied socks, and bruised or scuffed body parts that were posted as satisfying achievements with high social capital. The constant stream of such images, tied to positive conversations and comments, make an argument that these presentations of flawed bodies moves beyond any story of a silly stumble on the road; rather, these presentations present a fleshier self. As one runner expressed it, it is about

> letting people know that although it [running and injuries that follow] may not be easy or plain sailing—its [sic] ok! Its not as bad or scary as it seems and again its about saying—yep im not perfect or highly skilled—im just determined and ready to have a go.

Painful failings are front and center in this woman's running lifestyle. And in our con-versation, which started from her visualized experiences, she revealed how she confronts gender and age stereotypes in her own practical way. By reflecting on her injury shots, she portrays herself as someone accurately partaking in public life, without editing away the failures. Her expression highlights how many women (using ZR on Instagram) are engaging with other kinds of sensuous experiences of running, and celebrating them in their net-worked public narratives and visuals as a part of their pleasurable leisure practice. Within this exploration, the sense making of this mundane leisure practice is revealed as multifaceted, personal, sensuously attentive, and made on a field that is always in flux. Runners express the sensory-work that goes into their running as a consistent part of their everyday movement practices which, following Pink (2011, 344), is central to the analysis and understanding of running play performances.

In particular, the sensory performances of those women who run with ZR reorient expres-sions around "risks" (body-time-space burdens) experienced by many women who move into public space alone (Allen-Collinson 2010). The playfulness prompted in ZR is a process of movement that assists in attuning runners to the deeper rhythms of their own body in motion; the rhythms of a local space, urban or otherwise; and the body habitation and perception of such spatialities. By working with mixed methods and multiple "embodied methodologies" and productions of self (Sparkes and Smith 2012), the sensuous experiences of running are illuminated in the involvements of networked runners who play with zombies.

Moving with Networked Play

Roger Caillois' foundational text *Man, Play and Games* references a core rubric of play in the following: "[I]t is a question of surrendering to a kind of spasm, seizure, or shock that destroys reality with sovereign brusqueness. The disturbance that provokes vertigo is com-monly sought for its own sake" (1961, 23).

Vertigo, or *ilinx*, is a feel of play that resonates deeply with the corporeal excitements voiced by ZR runners. These excitements are somewhat remarkable experiential pleasures—not straightforwardly accessible in the everyday—that are readily yoked in a zombie chase by combining fear, intense body effort, and a deep attentiveness to locational movement. @NurseKate expresses these experiential layers in action:

> [D]ecided to do a quick mission since it was 50 degrees out. I tried to keep up the pace wihout slidi [*sic*] too much. . . . [suddenly] there were zoms chasing me, and I panicked! . . . And of course it was on the iciest, slushiest bit of back road possible. Managed to evade and not fall and break a leg.

NurseKate accentuates her multimodal attention, where running play unfolds as a complex process of movement with multiple actors and attentions involved in producing the tracked results. She offers a clear expression of the ongoing location-making contributing to the experience of movement. Sensorial pleasures and pains involved in play, such as NurseKate's navigation of the "voluptuous panic" of vertigo (Caillois 1961, 23), which are seldom unpacked and located sociologically, leaving our knowledge base unquestionably trim around these mainstream leisure activities.

Speaking on fell-running from a physical-culture studies perspective, Atkinson (2011) also finds this absence in scholarship, stating: "Intersections between panic, play, and gritty aspects of athletic movement are today heavily undertheorized" (119). That intersection might be complicated further from a games and play research perspective, adding the nexus of gendered perceptions of movement and mobility throughout co-present space (simultaneously online/offline—see excellent qualitative examples in the work of Dovey and Kennedy (2006) and Taylor (2012)). As indicated in early work on gender and computer games by Bryce and Rutter, the importance of such knowledge is clear, for: "As with traditional sport, computer gaming may represent a leisure context in which resistance and renegotiation of gender stereotypes can occur" (2003, 14). Expressions of the sensorial pleasures of runners contribute to a nuanced understanding of how gendered involvements, technologies, and wayfaring in public space are entangled and negotiated in this characteristic play experience: the voluptuous panic of being chased.

For ZR players, the Chase is a compelling movement experience, not only for the unique game-app functionality of "Chases on," but also for the core characteristics of play, which it engages. These characteristics are established within the work of Caillois (1961), where chance-based play (*alea*) is located alongside three other play-forms: *mimicry* (play-acting), *agôn* (competition), and *ilinx* (vertigo-inducing play). Each of these characteristics of play is intelligible at some point during a Chase, but it is the synthesis of chance-based play (*alea*) and vertigo-inducing play (*ilinx*) that draws many runners' attention. Thousands of running apps are available on the smartphone market, everything from free run-mapping trackers to more complex and costly self-monitoring software. Many of these products position data and instrumental engagement as the staple of their design. Runners are placed in charge of the program minutiae (and subsequent process of a run) with every detail rationalized in the system before moving into the world. Runners' movements frequently mirror the topographical coding of the application itself—straight lines, forefronting distance over process, "doing it" rather than "being there."

However, ZR's use of *alea* prompts runners to playfully engage in the process of running, as runners drift through local space and produce new attentiveness toward it, as exemplified by @LNboo, who found that her run unexpectedly took her to a different place: "My Zombie Run took me here (image outside of a prison)." @LNboo expressed her journey as a surprising encounter, and in her running dérive she highlights how this playful turn enabled her to be "drawn by the attractions of the terrain and the encounters they find there" (Knabb 1981, 50). Alongside new orientations to a neighborhood or the locations of the run, the chance-based experience of speed play produces a luscious quality in the body, a tension in being kept on your toes. "Landing" a Chase at the perfect spot on a running route is revealed as rapturous for a runner, and I have laughed out loud (while running full speed) at my good fortune in being just at the right place at the right time to escape the horde. This chance experience of *alea* is, however, only a part of a specific assemblage of playful involvement, and perhaps via speed play it can be better understood how Caillois' categories have multidimensional distinctions when revealed in their combined spatial/temporal conditions.

A particular spatio-temporal configuration of play is highlighted in ZR, where *alea* is revealed as a momentary sensation followed by a string of overlapping play-forms. The random start of a Chase profoundly affects the execution and outcome of a run, but the moment the surprise start is on a runner, it has also departed. And as *alea* transitions into the dizzying panic of *ilinx*—that destruction of "the stability of perception" (Caillois 1961, 23)—the Chase increases its intensity in a rush of information, action, and location overload, orienting the runner to engage in a multi-sensorial construction of movement. In very few words, @Queenbee highlights how this works in terms of her affected sense of proprioception (the experience of movement, acceleration, and body position) and interoception (internal sense, thirst, pain, respiratory pressure): "@Queenbee: 'I've never run so fast or so hard in my life!!! I knew it [the zombies] wasn't real, but the sense of urgency took over.'"

Running "fast" and "hard" are new experiences, completely fresh corporeal involvements for many runners experiencing speed play for the first time. The following post-run commentaries illuminate the various affecting experiences in similarly shallow fashion, referencing thirst (interoception), fear, environmental pressures, and urban rhythms:

@looloobee: "Run for 1 minute? OMG I DYING [*sic*] MUST DRINK ALL THE WATER"

@Secretsafe: "got mob attacked once. The zombie sounds rly [*sic*] freaked me out and I nearly ran into [emojis used in message] 'bike', 'dizzy face'. I can still feel my heart beating in my chest 'crying' [emoji]."

@kim88: "My run today, hills suck, but having to wait to cross streets because of traffic sucks worse."

Such lackluster communication is not surprising in clarifications on body knowledge, as digging deep into this playfully driven running sensorium involves comprehending a tacit cacophony of corporeal impressions, many of them new. However, @Queenbee does turn us toward her visceral feel of this configuration of play, in that "urgency took over": quick action, and having to do it fast and hard. This is a part of the joy of the Chase, the playful tension of urgency and uncertainty, which is transported by the game mechanic ("Zombies detected!"), and tied to the locations made on the run, and one's nascent awareness of being-in-the-world as a practiced runner.

Both *alea* and *ilinx* hint to other layers of embodied experience, notably those strong feelings of surprise and disorder and how to manage them, which are threaded into moving with a ZR running aesthetic (a personal running practice). By unpacking Caillios' play categories of *alea* and *ilinx* through the lived, sensorial experiences of women who play ZR, a fuller bodied familiarity around the embodied aspects of play is grasped, which includes proprioception (knowing the body in movement, and playfully exploring that), and the significant aspects of visceral play—where play includes darker but pleasurable aspects of play such as the tightening of uncertainty and fear in the body, not playing well (falling during the Chase), and even a loss of orientation or equilibrium in the world.

Having a ZR running corporeality brings together an assemblage of specific humans/non-humans, categorized game/play elements, histories of running, and personal perceptions of moving through the world. By way of running as play, a digital-material-sensory awareness is prompted, indicating the mutable struggles that can be involved in this simplest of things—a body moving forward under a pretext of (speed) play. But in these playful situations, ZR runners' dynamic movement does other important work than that of engaging in embodied pleasures. While playing in local space, environments are often navigated in new ways and with new orientations to them, and in such wanderings women who run with zombies both play and move into those spaces often designated as risk-space.

Women Who Play with Running

Running is often called the most autonomous of sports; all you need is to get outside and go (Baker 2012). While running cultures are entangled with various gateway leisure issues (body ability, local running environments, and their aged and gendered tangents), interviewees also endorsed that autonomy is reflected in their freedom of movement, or as "Nat" words it: "I can run anytime, anywhere I feel like it." A Danish citizen running in "small-city" Copenhagen, Nat is representative of many women who run with zombies. She is located in a country where

ZR is popular—Western and industrialized nations—where the network is widespread and accessible, and where smartphone penetration is most thorough (Google 2013).

Women who use ZR are frequently located along the lines of cohesive and affordable technological infrastructures, which dovetail for many into familiarity and practice with data-dense social media services such as Instagram. Running, data tracking, and data sharing are becoming steady companions through the tacit work of particular networked infrastructures, and the interconnectedness of footsteps, national broadband plans, and followers all play into enactments of running leisure. This final look at ZR running practices attends to a most dynamic and networked performance realized by such women on the run: namely, their productive resistance to (perceived and recognized) gendered risk-space, which is achieved by regularly running into it, often alone, while also documenting their playful expeditions on Instagram.

In Allen-Collinson's work on "embodied vulnerability," she highlights the balance of risk to agency as a woman running alone in public space (2010, 15). Her own experiences express an embodied paradox:

> On the one hand I found . . . the dangers of, and bodily vulnerability to harassment (verbal and physical), threat and attack. On the other hand, the positive elements, which for me predominate, include narrative experiences of empowerment, social agency, resistance, bodily power, strength and sensory pleasure.
>
> (Allen-Collinson 2013, 44)

Knowing vulnerability as a female running alone is an oft heard reflection made by runners, which is only complicated by Nat's assertion that "a lot of running is also about being alone with your experience." Risk-space is a social production, a reified current of socially produced orientations around gendered "wellbeing" in public space (Chisholm 2008), honed specifically on the lone woman embarking outdoors—the same silhouette of women who love to run. Risk-spaces are accounted for as unoccupied spaces: parks, canals, countryside, or closed and unlit spaces such as dark-alleyways or tunnels with limited exits (Valentine 1989, 386). And runners often speak to the pressures around traversing "running risk-space," as space that is both perceived as risky (by body) and preserved as such via social institutions (mass media and family in particular). The following jogger's announcement illuminates what attentiveness is for many women who run: "I like to think I'm quite aware when I'm running. I obviously know as a female running on my own, you're vulnerable" (Lillebuen 2014).

While Allen-Collinson's positive experiences dominate her running practice, the lingering presence of embodied vulnerability impresses on the everyday sensuous involvement of running. And I would suggest that such implicit pressures can orient one's sensuous connection with the environment, where multimodal sensations are at times directly pursued as a requirement of safety, rather than for the pleasures found in the freedom of movement in public space. Teasing out the complexity of the expressions and experiences of women's vulnerability in public space, feminist geographer Gillian Rose (citing from Marilyn Frye's 1983 text *The Politics of Reality*) articulates how the risk–agency balance can tip quite destructively: "Being in space is not easy. Indeed, at its worst this feeling results in a desire to make ourselves absent from space; it can mean that 'we acquiesce in being made invisible, in our occupying no space. We participate in our own erasure'" (Rose 1993, 151).

Women who run are frequently confronted by warnings on how to navigate public space ("not at night," "not with music/headphones," and "not alone") which makes ZR runners all the more compelling, as they often embrace all three caveats at once, and with visibly expressed pleasure in doing so as their runs drift down "eerie pathways" and into "creepy tunnels." ZR runners represent a transportation away from Valentine's (1989) "geography of fear" in a celebration of the experience of fictional-fear, and the pleasures therein, which supports them to move deeper into public space and generate other kinds of sensuous orientations toward it.

Conclusion

This digital ethnographic approach to studying running as play started from my own footsteps, and branched out to contain other voices and orientations toward digital-material-sensory practices of running. The multi-sited field was drawn together along routine lines of running participation, including relationships between social network sites, followers, friends and family, hashtags, smartphones, earbuds, weather, nationwide data packages, access to local space, and the very human knowledge of running. These connected actors, from flesh to code, each play a role in the sociophenomenological outcomes of running with zombies. Namely, new sensuous orientations and understandings of self and (running) environments, often in a runner's own neighborhood, produced through playful prompts to moving through the world.

And, just as significantly, women's dynamic drifting through public space via running is produced in the homespun markers (images and texts) of ZR Instagram users. Their documented performances and everyday movements illuminate how "risk-space" is regularly entered alone by women on their running routes, where they run toward public space as keen explorers and playful participants, rather than as vulnerable objects, and reap the rewards of other kinds of sensuous knowledge by way of the freedom of movement shored up by play.

References

Allen-Collinson, Jacquelyn. 2010. "Running embodiment, power and vulnerability: Notes towards a feminist phenomenology of female running." In *Women and Exercise: The Body, Health and Consumerism*, edited by Eileen Kennedy and Pirkko Markula, 280–98. London: Routledge.

———. 2011. "Intention and epoch in tension: Autophenomenography, bracketing and a novel approach to researching sporting embodiment." *Qualitative Research in Sport, Exercise and Health* 3(1): 48–62.

———. 2013. "Narratives of and from a running-woman's body: Feminist phenomenological perspectives on running embodiment." *Leisure Studies Association Newsletter* 95: 41–8.

Allen-Collinson, Jacquelyn, and John Hockey. 2009. "The essence of sporting embodiment: Phenomenological analyses of the sporting body." *The International Journal of Interdisciplinary Social Sciences* 4(4): 71–81.

Allen-Collinson, Jacquelyn, and Aspasia Leledaki. 2014. "Sensing the outdoors: A visual and haptic phenomenology of outdoor exercise embodiment." *Leisure Studies* 34(4): 457–70.

Atkinson, Michael. 2011. "Fell running and voluptuous panic: On Caillois and post-sport physical culture." *American Journal of Play* 4(1): 100–20.

Baker, Katie. 2012. "Women on the run." *Grantland Quarterly* 2: 134–41.

Bryce, Jo, and Jason Rutter. 2003. "The gendering of computer gaming: Experience and space." In *Leisure Cultures: Investigations in Sport, Media and Technology*, edited by Scott Fleming and Ian Jones, 3–22. Leisure Studies Association.

Caillois, Roger. 1961. *Man, Play, and Games*. Translated by Meyer Barash. Urbana: University of Illinois Press.

Chisholm, Dianne. 2008. "Climbing like a girl: An exemplary adventure in feminist phenomenology." *Hypatia* 23(1): 9–40.

de Souza e Silva, Adriana, and Larissa Hjorth. 2009. "Playful urban spaces: A historical approach to mobile games." *Simulation and Gaming* 40(5): 602–25.

Dovey, John, and Helen Kennedy. 2006. *Game Cultures: Computer Games as New Media*. Berkshire, UK: Open University Press.

Google. 2013. "Our Mobile Planet." http://think.withgoogle.com/mobileplanet/en/downloads/ (accessed November 23, 2014).

Gruppetta, Maree. 2004. "Autophenomenography? Alternative uses of autobiographically based research." Paper presented at Association for Active Researchers in Education, Melbourne. www.aare.edu.au/data/publications/2004/gru04228.pdf (accessed February 5, 2016).

Ingold, Tim. 2000. *The Perception of the Environment*. New York: Harper Perennial.

Kan, Alexander, Martin Gibbs, and Bernd Ploderer. 2013. "Being chased by zombies! Understanding the experience of mixed reality quests." In *OzCHI '13: Augmentation, Application, Innovation, Collaboration*, Adelaide, 207–16.

Knabb, Ken. 1981. *Situationist International Anthology*. Berkeley, CA: Bureau of Public Secrets.

Lillebuen, Steve. 2014. "Sex attacks on joggers linked to western suburbs incidents." *The Age*, May 30. www.theage.com.au/victoria/sex-attacks-on-joggers-linked-to-western-suburbs-incidents-20140530-397wh.html#ixzz39718gV00 (accessed July 3, 2014).

Martin, Christopher. 2007. "John Dewey and the beautiful stride: Running as aesthetic experience." In *Running & Philosophy: A Marathon for the Mind*, edited by Michael W. Austin, 171–9. Malden, MA: Blackwell Publishing.

Pink, Sarah. 2007. *Doing Visual Ethnography*. London: Sage.

——. 2011. "From embodiment to emplacement: Re-thinking competing bodies, senses and spatialities." *Sport, Education and Society* 16(3): 343–55.

——. 2014. "Digital–visual–sensory design anthropology: Ethnography, imagination and intervention." *Arts & Humanities in Higher Education* 13(4): 412–27.

Rooksby, John, Mattias Rost, Alistair Morrison, and Matthew Chalmers. 2014. "Personal Tracking as Lived Informatics." In *CHI '14: SIGCHI Conference on Human Factors in Computing Systems*, Toronto, 1163–72.

Rose, Gillian. 1993. *Feminism and Geography: The Limits of Geographical Knowledge*. Cambridge: Polity Press.

Sparkes, Andrew, and Brett Smith. 2012. "Embodied research methodologies and seeking the senses in sports and physical culture: A fleshing out of problems and possibilities." In *Qualitative Research on Sport and Physical Culture*, edited by Kevin Young and Michael Atkinson, 167–90. Bingley: Emerald.

Taylor, T. L. 2012. *Raising the Stakes: The Rise of Professional Computer Gaming*. Cambridge, MA: MIT Press.

Valentine, Gill. 1989. "The geography of women's fear." *Area* 21(4): 385–90.

Witkowski, Emma. 2013. "Running from Zombies." In *Proceedings of the 9th Australasian Conference on Interactive Entertainment: Matters of Life and Death*, September 30–October 1, Melbourne, 1–8.

Woodward, Kath, and Sophie Woodward. 2009. "Material bodies: Bodies as situations." In *Why Feminism Matters: Feminism Lost and Found*, edited by Kath Woodward, 136–60. New York: Palgrave Macmillan.

24

HANDS BETWEEN THE WORLDS

Isabel Fróes and Susana Tosca

Introduction

"I have been there before."

So said by "M," a five year old to his two peers to communicate that he had used an application on a tablet before.[1] Through language "M" highlights his understanding of the digital as interwoven with the physical world. This is best illustrated by "M"'s deployment of the physical situation referral of "been there" to describe his digital experience of the application. The expression was striking—a digital interface within a device was being described as a location—or, as we are proposing here—to parallel universes contained within a screen. Instead of a wood forest with pools or wardrobes, we have glass and metal devices to transport us into multiple dimensions. Tablets are portals.

Digital media, as the name suggests, happens through the digits, but expands the fingers and the perception. Young children's interactions with touch-sensitive digital technologies happen when their hands communicate their intention to the device. However, hands are more than just tools in this case—they demonstrate intention, hesitation as well as action. As Keogh has described in relation to videogames: "Input devices—gamepads, joysticks, keyboards, mice, motion sensors, touchscreens—are the umbilical through which the player's senses, intent, and identity are transported (or more accurately, translated) into the virtual world" (2015, 118).

Such aspects of hand communication became apparent when analyzing the video data collected during a transnational study with young children aged between four and seven years while interacting and playing with tablets. A number of aspects emerged due to the choice of data collection format and setup, including the hand intention illustrating the communication that sets the play in motion.

Hand movement complemented spatial perceptions either by reinforcing or contradicting them. In some cases, while hands were touching a specific location on the device, children still described the pointed location as "there" and not here. This could be explained by the fact that some game interfaces present a 3D spatial dimension and children incorporate this spatial perception while playing, imposing the digital aspect over the physical one informed by their immediate touch.

When using and playing on digital devices, keeping the hands on the side of the device or floating above the device can indicate intentions and possible choices through minimal and fast finger movements; observing hands also shows "hand slips" or when hands or arms touch the screen by accident, choosing something by chance. Besides intent and chance, hands also indicate engagement and, one could argue, even stubbornness, as when the children add force to their touch or try selecting the same symbol multiple times as if trying to force the device into a response. Even when hands refrained from touching, they indicated something; sometimes it seemed to be uncertainty, fear or insecurity about not knowing how to act in an "unknown ground."

During the observations there were some children who did not choose any application (apps). Even though they had turned the device on and had browsed through, they did not dare; just like one is not supposed to talk to strangers, maybe playing in "strange" arenas is also not okay. In some cases this no-choice could be understood as a lack of interest for what they saw. Because they did not know the applications, they did not necessarily become interested in trying. Obviously some of these points can be considered to be speculation over the gestures observed, nevertheless they could point to some curious questions regarding digital playing and digital playgrounds.

As others have noted, observing hands (Pink et al. 2015b) proved to be the ideal entry point for collecting empirical data about children's perception of their own interaction with technology. Observing hands also provided a way to overcome the language challenges of using very young children as research subjects, as they "digitally" communicated things that they were not able to verbalize, or as their hands complemented their semiotic perceptions expressed through language.

Methodological Approach

This chapter is based on a tablet interaction transnational study between Denmark and Japan with the aim of exploring the field of young children's play and tablets. In order to contribute to existing research looking at children and emerging technologies (Livingstone 2009; Drotner and Livingstone 2008; Holloway et al. 2013; Marsh 2014; Ito et al. 2013; Chaudron 2015), some of the initial points that were of interest to the study related to types of skills young children might develop and acquire through playing with tablets, besides also mapping how existing definitions of media literacy (Marsh 2004; Buckingham 2006, 2007) cover young children's tablet play. Therefore, a grounded theory (Charmaz 2014; Thornberg 2012; Glaser and Strauss 1999) approach was chosen as it did not require an initial review of a set field, but instead it suggests the empirical data should inform the questions leading to theories that are relevant to research. Consequently, the study initiated by setting up a pilot study where the first observations informed the rest of the data collection.

There are some methodological challenges to observing how young children freely play on tablets. The first one is discrepancy among devices and environments, which could compromise the data analysis, so limiting the number of variables was a key step in the setup process. Therefore, new devices were bought and customized for the observations with the same applications for all sessions, which allowed for consistency in the digital content offered. These devices would also present an unfamiliar layout and possibly unknown applications to the children, thus giving the possibility to assess their tablet use knowledge.

Another variable to limit was the location. Although many children studies reinforce the importance of the home environment (Ogan et al. 2012; Chaudron 2015), and by being at home one could see how the devices are placed and used within an everyday routine, unique physical and family settings (siblings, parental layouts, etc.) could interfere with the observations. Thus we opted for doing the observations at educational institutions, where the environment could be more neutral and controlled. Finally, we chose to remain with the children while they played on the devices, which allowed us to further investigate unexpected modes of use. This choice also provided the opportunity to see and hear children's own ways of playing and describing their play while also taking ethnographical notes. A further consideration when setting up the room was where the camera should be placed and what it should focus upon. As this study is concerned with children's digital play, the decision to focus on children's hands and their use of the device instead of the whole setting—including the location and children's faces or expressions—was deliberate and it aided the observations and the data collection in important ways. This decision about the camera focusing upon the context in and around the hands has been further supported by the fields of digital ethnography and tactile digital ethnography (Pink et al. 2015a, 2015b), where researchers are invited to rethink ways of capturing data related to the digital domain, including that of the hand.

> Visualizations on the touch screen are not just seen but they are part of both *what* the hand incrementally learns and knows, part of *how* the hand knows and are inextricable from our sensory perception of the wider environments we are in.
>
> (Pink et al. 2015b, 5)

Being able to follow children's intentions through their hand gestures and movements (moving their hand over some apps before selecting one—as a way of "thinking" with the hands) could inform modes of interaction, and tacit knowledges when interacting with touch-sensitive interfaces. Even though focusing on the hands removes the environment information (where children are located and what is happening around them while they play), this did not compromise the observations. In addition to these modes of documentation, some "contextual" pictures were taken before or after the sessions. By focusing on the hands using the devices, we were able to focus upon children as immersed within the digital environment—a process that involved a partial disconnection from their surroundings. In addition to this practice, focusing on the hands on the device also helped preserve the anonymity of our participants' identities—a sensitive aspect when dealing with children.

With these decisions in place, we contacted a couple of institutions. One of them was keen on participating as they already owned tablet devices and were considering how to involve them in their daily activities with the preschool children. The pilot study took place in spring 2014, followed by the coding and analysis of the data. For the pilot study, 19 children were observed individually at their care institution. A room with a table and chairs was set up with a camera positioned over the children's heads, to focus on the tablet play instead of children's faces or full torsos. Two devices were available, and the children were offered the use of both. The observations lasted a maximum of 20 minutes, with a few children using less of that time and some trying to extend it. All the video material captured during the pilot study sessions was watched several times and fully transcribed.

The initial coding took place after all the transcriptions were done and read through multiple times. The relationship among the initial codes was then identified, generating the focused codes, which provided the final data for the theoretical coding (Charmaz 2014). This process was followed by the main data collection, which was divided into two phases—one in Denmark and the other in Japan. The data collection took place between February 1 and May 29, 2015, and involved three institutions in metropolitan areas of both countries.[2] A total of 84 children were observed, 41 in Denmark and 43 in Japan.

In the first phase of the data collection, the children were invited individually to a room that contained a table and chairs, a video camera set up and the digital devices placed on the table. In the second phase, the children were in groups in one of the classrooms, where they could engage with either the devices or drawing materials in different areas of the room. Some of the activities happened in parallel, with some children playing on tablets, while others were drawing. Thus the observation was "divided," as at times one researcher had to be going back and forth between the two groups. As the rooms were not very large, this was not a big issue, but obviously represented that a few points might have been missed. However, when this second phase took place in Japan, two student assistants were present helping with both the language and the recording. Moreover, in Japan we had two video cameras available instead of one, which during the analysis proved to be more helpful than having just one camera.

Overall, it became clear that the earlier decisions about devices, setup and camera focus still allowed for a collection with a rich data set. In addition, having the focus on the hands using the device proved in itself to be invaluable, as it helped shape questions and guide the analysis towards unforeseen but appreciated directions. The method choices, together with some of the results we present, contribute to the field of digital ethnography by bringing the value of having focus on hands when studying digital media and children.

Hands of Perception

Hands are not a new topic in anthropological studies, with scholars from distinct disciplines drawing their attention to the importance of the hands beyond tools for interacting with the world around us (Merleau-Ponty 2002; Ingold 2013; Pink et al. 2015b; Keogh 2015). Merleau-Ponty has described habit through the example of using a typewriter—as while one types one does not necessarily describe the location of the keys, however the hands "acquire" such knowledge through practice.

> If habit is neither a form of knowledge nor an involuntary action, what then is it? It is knowledge in the hands, which is forthcoming only when bodily effort is made, and cannot be formulated in detachment from that effort. The subject knows where the letters are on the typewriter as we know where one of our limbs is, through a knowledge bred through familiarity which does not give us a position in objective space.
>
> (Merleau-Ponty 2002, 166)

Merleau-Ponty's example above resonates with Brendan Keogh's observations about gamepad interaction, where he suggests that the hands know better than one can verbalize:

> When I first explained to my housemate how to approach this challenge, I thought I "knew" what to do. Looking at my hands as I re-enacted the scene, however, it became apparent that "I", consciously, did not know what to do at all. The knowledge was in my hands.
>
> (Keogh 2015, 118)

Ingold (1994, 2009, 2013) explores the knowledge embodied within the hands in his work debating the field of art and technologies. He points out that creations emerge and feed on the encounter between the medium and the practitioner, affording the knowledge in what he describes as the "weaving." In his words, some disciplines are characterized for the "thinking through making" (2013, xi). More recently, in their essay about tactile digital ethnography,

Pink et al. (2015b, 3) present an extensive review of how hands have gained attention in related fields of studies. Among these theories, they bring up Ingold's perspective and apply it to digital interfaces, exemplifying with smartphones: "The tactile screen implicates the knowing hand as well as the eyes in how we make narratives with and through the (audio) visual content of smartphones" (Pink et al. 2015b, 5).

We are aligned with Ingold's (2013) and Pink et al.'s (2015a, 2015b) emphasis on the key value of the encounter between hands and medium when dealing with artifacts. We consider that this perception can be expanded to devices—such as tablets—as they afford similar properties in their touch-based interaction. Tablets require the practitioner, in our case the child, to create knowledge about using and playing on digital touch-sensitive interfaces in the making of the interaction. In this chapter we are concentrating on this making of the interaction and breaking it down into distinct aspects, proposing an emergent typology of the hands' movements.

Hands On

It is undeniable that children are gaining "knowledge in the hands" when interacting and playing with tablets. Tablet interfaces provide a unique possibility; that of many visual activities designed in diverse ways requiring distinct interactions for each application, all in one device. The multimodal interfaces of tablet devices require that children apply a range of hand movements and actions together with other inputs such as voice commands to use and play with the device. Besides this, each application might carry its own arrangement of how the touch and/or movement is to occur, having their own "hand language" or "hand code."

To illustrate the hand learning process, or how by handling one acquires the hand knowledge required to interact with such devices, we bring an example from the study. One of the subjects, who was five years old and had never used a device with a touch interface, acted differently from those who had experienced such interfaces before. He had seen other people use tablets or smartphones, but he had never done it himself. This example is further described below with some adapted excerpts from the fieldnotes:

> Turning on the device, J. asked what he had to do. It was suggested he tried "interacting with it." He tried hand movements, such as moving the finger vertically, as well as horizontally on the screen (the device had no password or code to enter) with none of the actions being successful. He then asked how he had to do it, and this time the researcher made the sliding movement "in the air" while suggesting he "pushed" with the finger. He tried again, this time successfully . . .
>
> When he was then presented with a set of applications, he "armed" the hand with a stiff pointy finger, trying to select one icon with a fast touch. Without success, he tried to exchange fingers, also using force upon touching the screen this time, leading all the applications to go on "delete" mode . . .
>
> After a few trial and error attempts, he managed to use and play on the device, gaining more and more hand control as he used them, although he kept exchanging the fingers when the application or symbol did not initially respond (as that seemed to him to do the trick initially).[3]

Throughout the session previously described—together with the rest of the observations— many aspects of hand knowledge emerged. It became apparent that even something as simple and popularly recognized as "intuitive," such as moving a finger across the screen, did not seem to be so, but was instead an *acquired* hand knowledge. The hands also revealed some of the thinking behind the children's action, as in the case of switching a finger to a different finger if the first finger "did not do the trick." It was as if the child had thought: "Maybe the problem is the finger." The acquired perception regarding force and pressure when interacting with glass and metal surfaces and materials, something one brings from their physical experiences, needs adjustments in the case of touch-sensitive screens.

The hand also changed from tense to more relaxed as it "learned"—in many cases we witnessed children transitioning from unfamiliarity to familiarity in their movement in and around the interface. This practice was supported by other examples of children who were familiar with similar devices and did not "arm the hand" or appear tense. Instead, these familiar practitioners would either play with their hands near their body while looking at the device or just keep the hands near or over the device while choosing an application, bringing the hand to touch the screen on their icon of choice, but the motion seemed natural and their hands relaxed. When the first attempt at the interaction did not work, these children simply tried again without necessarily asking for help—knowing that this type of tacit and tactile play was also a characteristic of tablets.

The aspect of immersion became apparent on many occasions, as the children's hands took them into the play. For example, two children were playing a game where one has to be the worker at a Lego ice cream shop. When they were asked how one plays that game they answered "we have to make ice cream for people" while touching the pieces needed to build the Lego ice cream. This action was followed by the child pointing at a character approaching the screen saying "That's me, that's me!"—then enthusiastically fulfilling the ice cream order requested by the character. Until this point the children had ignored all previous orders from other characters, instead creating and "delivering" their own ice cream combinations.

Through looking at the hands, it became apparent that young children bring with them their physical knowledge of buttons to their digital experience, so when a symbol did not respond upon their fast touch motion, their following hand movement would either be to apply pressure, to touch the screen for a longer period or to tap consecutively, just as when pressing a physical doorbell or lift button. As in the case of a lift, if there is no sound feedback, or no one opens the door or a light does not come up and the lift does not move, one would try again to press that button slightly tweaking one's first attempt by pressing it harder or longer. Although this process can be observed both with children and adults, one aspect appears to be inherent in young children, that of consecutively touching the screen. This movement was observed numerous times during the study. We are not able to define specifically why this movement was so prominent; nevertheless it represented knowledge of both the device logic (I am doing something, something should happen), as well as clear intention of choice (I want this).

The observed variety of actions, aligned with differences in hand movements and intentions, led us to classify the touch inputs observed into a preliminary typology[4] that can be of use to those observing children–screen interaction, and which we summarize here:

1 Hovering:
   1.1 *Action*: moving with the hands or just one finger over the interface;
   1.2 *Suggested intention*: still in doubt and exploring the possibilities, making a choice, deciding what to do.
2 Tapping:
   2.1 *Action*: fast touch with one finger (or by chance with an arm or another hand);
   2.2 *Suggested intention*: to play, child had made a choice regarding an app and decided to interact with it.

3 Swiping:
  3.1 *Action*: while touching, moving one finger across a small area on the screen;
  3.2 *Suggested intention*: to enter the device, to browse device, to go forward pages in a book, to go forward inside of an app.
4 Dragging:
  4.1 *Action*: tap and without leaving the contact interface, move the finger/hand across the screen;
  4.2 *Suggested intention*: to move a character or icon around the interface, to move apps across the screens/areas of the device.
5 Continuous tapping:
  5.1 *Action*: a series of consecutive short taps;
  5.2 *Suggested intention*: to try to get an icon to respond (even in cases when it is not necessarily interactive), insistence.
6 Force tapping:
  6.1 *Action*: tapping with pressure (can be related to using force when drawing on paper);
  6.2 *Suggested intention*: to try to force an icon to respond, persistence.
7 Long tapping:
  7.1 *Action*: tapping for a bit longer than a short tap (observed when either trying to choose something for a second time, or trying a non-interactive symbol);
  7.2 *Suggested intention*: also persistence as if the device had not obeyed.
8 Tilting:
  8.1 *Action*: moving the device sideways, vertically or horizontally;
  8.2 *Suggested intention*: to control icons within an app, e.g. to pour liquids, to drive, to make things fall, etc.
9 Divergent dragging:
  9.1 *Action*: moving two fingers in opposite directions;
  9.2 *Suggested intention*: to see things "closer," zoom in.
10 Convergent dragging:
  10.1 *Action*: moving two fingers towards each other;
  10.2 *Suggested intention*: to bring it back to original size, zoom out.
11 Simultaneous holding:
  11.1 *Action*: tapping and holding simultaneously with both fingers;
  11.2 *Suggested intention*: to move the orientation of the space in the case of 3D environments.
12 Reach:
  12.1 *Action*: pointing closely as tapping or "touching" an icon;
  12.2 *Suggested intention*: showing something related as "far," using words that indicate physical distance despite device proximity.

Some of these terms, such as tapping and swiping, already belong to an everyday vocabulary when referring to touch screen interfaces. However, even though some of them are associated with digital devices, they are not necessarily defined beyond their precise physical actions. The typology proposed defines some of the actions a bit further, together with matching them to intentions of use, for example while playing a game where one needs to drag a boat across the screen, the dragging action was accompanied by the child saying "you have to take him there" (Figure 24.1). The actions identified in the analysis and classified in the typology helped frame the hand language vocabulary, which seems to have been learned through interacting with tablet devices. It is noticeable that other aspects, such as that of game narrative, general functionalities, etc. also come into play in this learning process, however, they would be outside the focus in this article.

Figure 24.1   Hand gesture showing that the one playing has to take the boat "there"

Hands in Motion

Besides the requirement for interaction from each application that a mobile device (in this case tablets) might contain, the device itself "listens" for a general set of designed interactions. These are combinations of both the use of the physical button as well as the touch input. Some of the children in the study were aware of those possibilities, while others just stumbled upon them, for example bringing up the delete function through *long tapping*. Another example was trying to get an application to open by *tapping*, or *tapping* by chance with the side of the hand touching the overview application function in one of the platforms. These unintended interactions, or hiccups, are also part of the making, consequently also creating hand knowledge.

Another methodology point worth noting involves how the device is held, as it will affect some of the hand language. In the case of the study, there were two phases: in the first phase the devices were lying flat on a table, and although some of the subjects chose to hold the device closer to their body or upright, it was still requested that they did not take the device from the table. In the second round of the study, when the children were in groups, this option was open and children chose to use the device differently, sometimes holding it on their lap, sometimes laying it flat on a surface (table or floor). However, as they played in groups, the holding aspect was significant, not only because it affected the hands' movements, but also as it was a way of exerting control of the play; since it becomes physically more challenging for others to collaborate if one holds the device with both hands, therefore preventing certain movements. On these occasions, hands also played a very defining part by demonstrating ways of avoiding or inviting a peer to play according to how they were positioning themselves on the device, with hands raised on the side avoiding the other to play, or holding the device further below as an invitation for playing together—allowing the other to enter the play. Although these welcoming or avoidance actions were also done with the hand, they are not exclusive to digital devices, as such attitudes also occur when children play with physical toys, so we kept them out of the typology.

After young children have attained hand knowledge through their playful encounters with touch-sensitive devices, this knowledge informs even non-digital interactions, guiding their expectations towards other interfaces present in random places in the environment. One example we recently witnessed was that of a child *tapping* a physical billboard encased in glass at a local bus stop or *swiping* non-interactive platforms (there are online videos showing very young children—even younger than the target group—trying to *swipe* random objects).[5] The hand is also responsible for enacting the child's notions of digital space, exemplified at the beginning of this chapter, but also when the hand touches the devices, pointing at specific icons or locations and this action is accompanied by words such as "there" instead of "here." This *reach*, as described in the typology, indicates a positioning of the child in relation to that specific icon as if they are distant (separated by a screen), however reachable through the "magic touch." At the same time, this reach shows the immersive aspect with the notion of "being there" or "taking him there." The hand vocabulary created by the actions children perform allows them into the other worlds that the portal-tablet contains.

Due to the speed with which digital technologies are being developed, the hand vocabulary, besides being fast incorporated in children's play, will also evolve together with the technologies and it might extend beyond their physical artifact, such as the tablet. As in this digital *weaving* (Ingold 2013), the digital (and to some extent also the physical) materials are under constant adaptation, the hands will follow, transforming this into an everlasting *making* process (Ingold 2013), requiring scholars to observe and learn accordingly.

Conclusion

Directing focus on the hands of young children while they interact and play with digital devices offers an insight into the process of emergence of their digital knowledge; which by no means is "natural" or "intuitive." The typology proposed here presented the vocabulary of hands on tablets, and hopes to aid studies of young children's learning in the making with digital interfaces. Having the focus on the hands, together with a common vocabulary of actions linked to children's intentions of use, this chapter hopes to facilitate how we develop and engage in future studies in related fields.

The *making of knowledge in the hands* with digital platforms can widen beyond the embodied hand–eye relationship (Pink et al. 2015b), with the hand–screen relationship being also able to defy how we understand aspects of intuition and physical perceptions of digital spaces, enlarging the field of interaction to another dimension and placing the hands as the holders of the key.

Notes

1 All names are pseudonyms.
2 While both phases were carried out in Japan between April and May 2015, in Denmark only the group phase was carried out in February 2015, as the pilot data proved sufficient for the individual observations and it could be re-used in the analysis.
3 Adapted fieldnotes, J, five years old, April 2014.
4 Crescenzi et al. (2014) have presented a set of touch-based codes in their research with nursery school kids, aged one and a half to three years old, while doing finger painting activities on iPads and paper. Merchant (2015) similarly presents a set of touch interactions in a research with young children, aged 14–22 months, when using story apps on an iPad together with an adult. Despite identifying a couple of similar touch behaviors, our research foci differ in both the age group as well as type of analysis. For example, although the authors identify some of the same hand movements, such as *tapping*, they do not associate that behavior with any type of specific intention. Nevertheless, the studies are related as all three look into young children interacting with digital technologies.
5 www.youtube.com/watch?v=aXV-yaFmQNk, www.youtube.com/watch?v=qGO8zgqNEbA

References

Buckingham, David. 2006. "Defining Digital Literacy: What Do Young People Need to Know about Digital Media?" *Nordic Journal of Digital Literacy* 4: 263–76. www.idunn.no/ts/dk/2006/04 (accessed August 26, 2014).

———. 2007. *Beyond Technology*. Cambridge: Polity Press.

Charmaz, Kathy. 2014. *Constructing Grounded Theory*, Second Edition. London: Sage.

Chaudron, Stéphane. 2015. "Young Children (0–8) and Digital Technology: A Qualitative Exploratory Study across Seven Countries." Luxembourg: Publications Office of the European Union. http://publications. jrc.ec.europa.eu/repository/handle/JRC93239. (accessed August 14, 2015). doi:10.2788/00749

Crescenzi, Lucrezia, Carey Jewitt, and Sara Price. 2014. "The Role of Touch in Preschool Children's Learning Using iPad Versus Paper Interaction." *Australian Journal of Language & Literacy*, 37(2): 86–95. http://eprints.ncrm.ac.uk/3372/1/Crescenzi_Jewitt_and_Price_2014_The_role_of_touch_in_pre-school_ch's_learning_using_iPads_vs_Paper.pdf (accessed February 13, 2016).

Drotner, Kirsten, and Sonia Livingstone, eds. 2008. *International Handbook of Children, Media and Culture*. London: Sage.

Glaser, Barney G., and Anselm L. Strauss. 1999. *The Discovery of Grounded Theory: Strategies for Qualitative Research*. New Jersey: Aldine Transaction.

Holloway, Donell, Lelia Green, and Sonia Livingstone. 2013. "Zero to Eight: Young Children and Their Internet Use." London: EU Kids Online. http://eprints.lse.ac.uk/52630/1/Zero_to_eight. pdf (accessed August 14, 2015).

Ingold, Tim. 1994. "Tool-Use, Sociality and Intelligence." In *Tools, Language and Cognition in Human Evolution*, edited by Kathleen R. Gibson and Tim Ingold, 429–45. Cambridge: Cambridge University Press.

———. 2009. "The Textility of Making." *Cambridge Journal of Economics* 34(1): 91–102. doi:10.1093/cje/bep042 (accessed September 13, 2010).

———. 2013. *Making: Anthropology, Archaeology, Art and Architecture*. London: Routledge.

Ito, Mizuko, Kris Gutiérrez, Sonia Livingstone, Bill Penuel, Jean Rhodes, Katie Salen, et al. 2013. "Connected Learning: An Agenda for Research and Design." Irvine, CA: Digital Media and Learning Research Hub. www.lse.ac.uk/media@lse/WhosWho/AcademicStaff/SoniaLivingstone/pdf/Connected-Learning-report.pdf (accessed August 14, 2015).

Keogh, Brendan. 2015. "A Play of Bodies: A Phenomenology of Videogame Experience." PhD thesis. RMIT University.

Livingstone, Sonia. 2009. *Children and the Internet*. Cambridge: Polity Press.

Marsh, Jackie. 2004. "The Techno-Literacy Practices of Young Children." *Journal of Early Childhood Research* 2(1): 51–66. doi:10.1177/1476718X0421003 (accessed May 6, 2015).

———. 2014. "Media, Popular Culture and Play." In *Sage Handbook of Play and Learning in Early Childhood*, edited by Susan Edwards, Mindy Blaise, and Liz Brooker, 403–14. London: Sage.

Merchant, Guy. 2015. "Keep Taking the Tablets : iPads, Story Apps and Early Literacy." *Australian Journal of Language and Literacy* 38(1): 3–11. http://shura.shu.ac.uk/9100/ (accessed March 26, 2016).

Merleau-Ponty, Maurice. 2002. *Phenomenology of Perception*. London: Routledge.

Ogan, Christine, Türkan Karakuş, and Engin Kurşun. 2012. "Methodological Issues in a Survey of Children's Online Risk-Taking and Other Behaviours in Europe." *Journal of Children and Media* 7(1): 133–50. doi:10.1080/17482798.2012.739812 (accessed January 18, 2016).

Pink, Sarah, Heather Horst, John Postill, Larissa Hjorth, Tania Lewis, and Jo Tacchi. 2015a. *Digital Ethnography: Principles and Practice*. London: Sage.

Pink, Sarah, Jolynna Sinanan, Larissa Hjorth, and Heather Horst. 2015b. "Tactile Digital Ethnography: Researching Mobile Media through the Hand." *Mobile Media & Communication* (December): 1–15. doi:10.1177/2050157915619958. http://mmc.sagepub.com/content/early/2015/12/15/2050157915619958.full.pdf+html. (accessed January 19, 2016).

Thornberg, Robert. 2012. "Informed Grounded Theory." *Scandinavian Journal of Educational Research* 56(3): 243–59. http://liu.diva-portal.org/smash/get/diva2:433790/FULLTEXT01.pdf (accessed May 27, 2014).

Part VI

ARTS

25

CURATING AND EXHIBITING ETHNOGRAPHIC EVIDENCE

Reflections on Teaching and Displaying with the Help of Emerging Technologies[1]

Paolo Favero

The scope of the image-maker, documentarist or artist today is no longer that of showing what was previously unseen given that today this, with the present spread of new imaging technologies, can be done by anyone. Rather her duty is to create a space in which viewers can share their own experiences and reflections around topics characterizing their everyday life.

(Shuddha Sengupta, Raqs Media Collective, interview April 2013, n.p.)

This is a particularly challenging moment to work with images. Thanks to the entanglements of the visual with digital technologies, images are today constantly entering new territories, morphing their nature and appearances. They are, as those of us living in digitized environments discover every day, networks, relations and communities made visible (think of the textual dialogues, the "@" and the hashtags on the timelines of Facebook and Instagram); they are geographies (think of the incorporation of GPS metadata in the images we produce with our cameras); and they are also things (think about the popularity of 3D printing which, through the mediation of images, converts abstract ideas into material items, or about interactive documentaries (iDocs) and their constant invitations to engage with the world surrounding the viewers).

Today we are accustomed to the idea that digital images are intrinsically different from analog ones with their supposed anchorage in the "real" (cf. Sontag 1979; Barthes 1993). Their open-ended, performative, incomplete character shows that digital images are not only ontologically different; they also seem to ask viewers and users to engage with them in new ways. They seem to be constantly inviting us to interact with them, to do something with and to view them with the help of cursors (on computers) or fingers (on smartphone and smart-pads); to inscribe metadata in them (with the help of hashtags, @s, comments and geotags); to save them and resize them; and to morph them with the help of the manifold editing pro-grams at our disposal today. We still need to figure out the extent to which all such changes correspond to an actual revolution in the field of visual culture or to the birth of a new model of vision (as Crary (1990) argued long ago). However, as social scientists, we can already notice today the extent to which such changes have entered our multiple ways of engaging with images. The instances of serendipitous ethnographies made possible by smartphones are probably the most evident example of this change but such traces can also be found in the new venues made available to us for displaying our works online.

With the present chapter I wish to reflect upon the extent to which such changes are and can be incorporated in our attempts at both conducting and communicating image-based ethnographic work. I will suggest that images today, more than ever, ask us to approach them beyond representation and indexicality.[2] Images are not just containers of traces of the mate-rial past that they portray but are, as digital images concretely highlight, multimodal, material and relational items. Contemporary images do also seem to cry out loud their desire to do more than "illustrate," "underline" or "decorate" our texts. They want to become constitu-tive of new relations, engagements and knowledge, of new ways of not only presenting but also of producing ethnographic evidence.

This chapter explores the latter transformation and will focus on some concrete expe-riences with the act of communicating and teaching ethnography through contemporary audio-visual technologies. I begin by tracing a brief background of my (practice-based) eth-nographic engagement with visual technologies in order to explain the subsequent focus on interactive documentaries, a practice that capitalizes upon the use of non-linearity and rela-tionality. I will share with the readers a series of teaching experiences that I have conducted in this terrain in India and Belgium, reflecting upon the extent to which "interactive"[3] platforms can function as a tool for generating new multimodal and participatory ways for both display-ing (and producing) ethnography. I conclude by offering glimpses into future venues for a digital practice-based visual ethnography.

Background: Performing the Documentary

In 2004, right after the completion of my documentary film on young middle-class people in New Delhi,[4] I was left with a sense of frustration. I had collected somewhere around 45 hours of footage, out of which my audiences could see only 53 minutes, the standard running time for a one-hour televised documentary film. The editing process, and the adaptation to the particular viewing format requested by television channels and festivals, had led me, as is the case for most filmmakers, to be very selective. As I went further and further into the process of editing the film I had to exclude all materials dealing with Mumbai (which I had originally considered to edit as a parenthesis to the Delhi material). I also had to exclude a large number of interviews and interactions with interesting characters in Delhi as well as several hours of open-ended explorations of the visual and material culture of the city. It felt like violence to do this but it was, indeed, a necessary gesture in order to construct a coherent filmic narrative. This is something that most filmmakers experience and it is nothing but the "natural" evolution of a film. As *Flyoverdelhi* was finalized and screened on television and festivals I very much enjoyed listening to the questions, reflections and doubts it generated for the viewers. I increasingly felt the desire to incorporate those audience-generated ruptures in the narrative coherence of the film in the film itself and to produce a document capable of progressively building itself up through a set of interactions with the viewer. The leftovers of the film—those 44 hours of material that no one would ever see—could indeed have been a useful tool for achieving this epistemological openness.

In 2004, interactive documentaries and similar platforms were really incipient and I had neither the skills nor the budget to even attempt at building some alternative display format for my work. However, I did understand that this was the space in which I should have ideally moved in order to achieve the above-mentioned result. I therefore tried to conceptualize an online platform on which to host such materials. I had started designing a map of the city of Delhi in which I could "place" the video materials so that they could be viewed on the basis of the location in which they had been shot. As I progressed into the development of this idea I realized that such a platform could allow me to also host all those other materials that had been conducive to the creation of the film, such as photographs, fieldnotes, newspaper clips, street sounds, etc. According to this model it would be the job of the viewer to build a narrative from and within this archive. Indeed, as I anticipated, this project was never realized. What I managed to do, however, was to bring out some of the above-mentioned materials to the public with the help of a series of exhibitions and live video installations in which I ended up using the physical space of a variety of venues and a multiplicity of projectors as an alternative to the hypertextual links provided by the Internet.[5]

In the years since, I have increasingly incorporated such ideas in a dialogue with emerging digital technologies and practices as tools for teaching and conducting visual ethnography. At the core of my practice has been the engagement with interactive documentary; a visual form that has really been booming in the past decade and that is today attracting a growing amount of scholarly attention (Ashton and Gaudenzi 2012; Nash 2012; Favero 2013). As an avant-garde visual language that blends the tradition of documentary film with the principles of interaction that characterize Internet-based communication (cf. O'Reilly 2005; Quiggin 2006; Goggin 2009; Shirky 2008; Leadbeater 2009) iDocs provide a generative, complex, non-linear viewing experience centered on the users' own choices. Building on a re-definition of the meaning of narrative, on the activation of the viewers and on the creation of a set of connections between the material displayed, the viewers and their everyday lives, iDocs offer, I suggest elsewhere (Favero 2014), a mirror onto the changing meaning of images in a digital landscape. They highlight questions of relationality, multimodality and materiality remanding us also to a set of debates, practices and technologies that are external to this particular visual form. The following section explores the possible significance of this practice as a tool for teaching and conducting visual ethnography.

Mixing Technologies: Exploring the Streets in Delhi, Antwerp and Mumbai

My first experiences with teaching a combination of ethnography, image-making and interactive practices took place in Lisbon. In 2011 at the Lisbon University Institute (IUL-ISCTE) I launched my first intensive summer course in "Interactive ethnographic documentary filmmaking" which catered to a wide crowd of anthropology students but also to teachers, journalists and artists. Aiming at combining the principles of ethnographic research and filmmaking with the possibilities for non-linear image-based communication made possible by interactive documentary, this course built on the adoption of an open source program, called Korsakow. Based on the principle that the construction of the narrative of the "film" depends upon the choices of the viewer, Korsakow forces the filmmakers to lose control of the film. No longer directors, they have to learn to identify with the role of the curator, the coordinator of a generative archive of images. For most students, and especially those coming from an anthropological background, this was a big challenge. They resented losing the opportunity to offer an explanation and constantly attempted to subjugate the software to their linear needs.

The Lisbon summer courses were indeed strongly connected to the idea of "making a film." In the following years my interest shifted toward the incorporation of such non-linear practices into a broader ethnographic scenario, one where emerging technologies and techniques dialogue with questions of production and communication of ethnography. The workshops I have organized in Antwerp, Delhi and Mumbai during the last four years speak of this attempt and will be the object of the following pages. Conventionally beginning with the selection of a particular, well-delimited, space to work on, these workshops generally translated into the exploration of a square, a stretch of street, etc. Alternatively, inspired by psycho-geography, I have on some occasions drawn a circle around the campus or a particular place in the city and made the students explore that space by following the map while at the same time collecting/producing audio-visual materials.[6]

The selection and exploration of a specific social and physical space have, in these workshops, always moved in parallel with the exposure of the students to a set of emerging tools/ technologies. I must admit that I have always been—at the very opening of these courses— twisted between the option of inviting students to first engage with the selected space without the help of technological mediations or, instead, to let the technologies adopted reveal to them new angles to explore that which would have been unavailable to them in the absence of that particular tool. The result of this twist is that I end up selecting the path to follow step by step, carefully monitoring the skills and experiences of the students and the characteristics of the habitat they aim at working on (I will describe this further case by case in the following discussion). The core idea behind all these different workshops, however, is always to let the choice of form (for the display) grow hand in hand with the actual exploration of the space (and hence with the content) and with the choice of technology to employ.

The central dynamic of the workshops I have held in Antwerp, Delhi and Mumbai is also that of a group mission. With the help of the first explorations, indeed under supervision, the students identify the particular technology and angle of observation that will characterize their own engagement. Someone will, for instance, focus on sound, while someone else will focus on photography; someone will make short video-diaries while someone else will be mapping the space, etc. At times small groups are created where several students collaborate on the same topic. The material hence produced is therefore always the result of the progressive dialogue between the space explored (the object of the research) and the various individual engagements of the participants (the subjects and their media). Eventually this dialogue will make an overall form for the presentation emerge (a map, a gallery of videos, etc.). Let me now discuss these various experiences one by one.[7]

For the 2015 IVMS workshop in Antwerp[8] the group working with me (made up of lecturers and PhD students) selected a particular square, De Coninckplein, as venue for the study. Known for being an arena of multicultural encounter De Coninckplein attracted my students also because of the large number of topics it seemed to bring to their attention. The work was divided into moments of individual or group exploration with alternating brainstorming workshops. During these sessions I would progressively pin down topics, forms, insights, technologies, etc. by writing or drawing them on the blackboard. The students would then comment back and so we went on. On these occasions an old-fashioned blackboard with chalks (better if colored) is still the best tool for progressively drafting a structure of a possible online platform (Figure 25.1).

After having debated topics, forms and tools, a possible map would start materializing itself. We identified the places in which the various materials gathered by the members of the team could be positioned and, thanks to the presence of one PhD student[9] who had skills in web-design, we started developing the idea of transforming the map into an immersive 3D space into which the viewers could enter. With the help of a 360-degree camera, our web-designer colleague managed to create an immersive photogrammetry-produced environment within which we placed the various media that the group had collected (Figure 25.2).[10]

In fact, for the purpose of the IVMS workshop we ended up activating only a limited number of paths (see the thick line designed with chalk on the blackboard). Along this line we positioned the materials collected by the members of the group. We then placed a series of interviews with the people encountered on the square (supported by one or more photographs), video explorations of the movements of people and vehicles in various corners of the square (we called these videos the "rhythms" of the square), found historical material (grabbed online) representing this space in earlier epochs, and drawings representing the various symbols found on the walls of the square presented as a card game (aimed at helping viewers to learn more about the politics of the square). The variety of audio-visual technologies deployed (ranging from GoPro cameras, to smartphones and regular cameras, drawings, etc.) helped us generate a multilayered representation of the square.

We decided that the final interface should also contain a side menu allowing the viewer to choose whether to explore the contents by moving within the 3D environment or by searching for specific media and topics. In the menu we also added a brief introduction to the history of the square, as well as a lengthy reflection on the methodology and on the ethical issues we

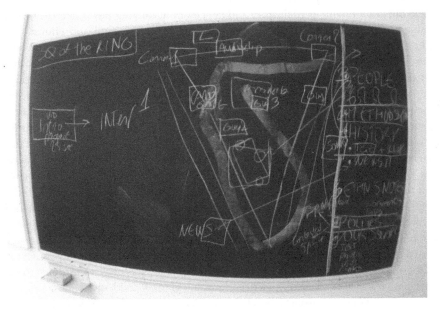

Figure 25.1 Blackboard scheme of an emerging interactive platform. Photo and drawing by Paolo Favero

Figure 25.2 Screenshot of the interactive platform "The King's Square." Design and screenshot by Ryan Pescatore Frisk

encountered during the research. Finally, we also envisioned, similarly to most iDocs, a space where viewers could upload their own images or stories about the square or comment on what they had found within this platform. Entitled "your square" this area would allow the users to link such materials through conventional social media.[11]

Constituting a platform capable of both activating the viewers in the construction of a narrative but also of being participatory and hence of outsourcing new materials from them, this project ended up raising so-called conventional epistemological and ethical questions regarding ethnography (when and where to make images, how to create rapport with the subjects, permissions, etc.). It also stimulated discussions regarding the nature of collaborative knowledge production. In producing the materials the students had in fact ventured out on a series of individual missions, yet united by common intent. Each individual would focus on one particular slice or aspect of the square. This material would then be negotiated with that found by the other participants. A final understanding of the place or community under study would then emerge from this multiplicity of voices. I found these moments of dialogue particularly enriching. I must admit that I was a bit puzzled when I discovered that visual sociologist Jon Wagner, who headed the structuring of the schedule for the IVMS, had chosen to present my iDoc session under the rubric "collaborative ethnography."

Until that point I had never really reflected much on this label but from that moment onwards I realized how this is probably one of the most successful ways to describe the contribution of iDocs to social science research. The collaboration between different researchers generated during the workshop could make us travel back in time, to the days in which ethnography was carried out by a team of researchers. While we are today accustomed to think of ethnographic research as a solitary practice ("imagine yourself suddenly set down surrounded by all your gear, alone on a tropical beach," wrote Malinowksi), fieldwork has long been, and in many places still is, a group endeavor. Just think of the Torres Straits expedition where a large number of researchers were engaged, each with their own task.

The workshops in Delhi and Mumbai employed a similar approach yet further exploring the possibility of using emerging technologies for enacting sensorial explorations of space. At the School of Arts and Creative Expressions, Ambedkar University, Delhi, India I organized a workshop in January 2015 where the goal was to push the students to explore the different ways in which audio-visual technologies can be used for gaining understanding of urban space. On this occasion I activated the students to explore the area surrounding the campus, with the help of a map. I drew a circle around the campus and invited them to attempt to follow it while documenting everything they encountered on their path. The circle brought them mainly to three key streets that became the actual focus of the workshop. On this occasion I asked the students to each select a particular technology and/or focus before starting the walk. Then, we all walked out together, each with a well-defined task: low-angle and high-angle photographs; black and white and negative photography; someone produced video clips and someone focused on the activities taking place on the street; sounds were collected in the places where photographs were being taken and one student produced, starting from an observation of the bus lines crossing the area, a series of drawings of the space in which we would walk. My duty during the walk was to document the students' work, something that I must admit I found very difficult to do in a coherent manner.

After the walk we gathered in the classroom and started developing ideas, first around what the material collected was telling us about the nature of the spaces visited. Then we started discussing how to display such materials. A large number of topics emerged by doing this and we all discovered we had learned something new about a place that we all believed we knew pretty well. Among the key topics emerging, for instance, was an interesting dialogue between high-angle and low-angle photographs. The high-angle photographs revealed the material culture of waste and hence directed our attention to the relation between social class and cleanliness. The quantity and quality of dirt on the streets changed, for instance, once we turned one corner and entered what is a residential area. The low-angle photographs instead revealed the layered, stratified character of the history of neighborhood. The student covering this particular aspect managed to identify the epoch in which the various extensions to the buildings had been constructed. Another interesting experiment, directing our attention toward questions of materiality, was conducted by a student who took negative color shots. With inverted colors all conventional references were cut out. Portraits ceased to offer clear references to people's social and ethnic backgrounds. Also, these photographs revealed with clarity the materiality of the street pavements, the cracks in the walls of the buildings and, to our surprise, also the large quantity of nature surrounding the campus. The defamiliarizing effect generated by viewing images in negative really helped us reveal what our eyes, guided by habit and preconceptions, no longer managed to see. Along similar lines, the student recording sounds played with the idea—by shifting between diegetic to extra diegetic sounds accompanying the photographs—of exploring the extent to which our visual experience of space morphs on the basis of sound. This, he suggested, could be incorporated into a homepage becoming a kind of participatory experience, possibly a game, that viewers could actively engage with.

During the workshops we ended up discussing—at quite some length—the various modalities through which the local dwellers reacted to our presence. Inviting the students to reflect on how such reactions offer precious insight into the visual culture of the photographed/filmed subjects, these debates also unleashed a set of discussions on gender. The girls of the group felt that they had had great difficulty in getting men to accept being portrayed by them. Also they felt observed as they walked around taking pictures in this largely male-dominated environment. The workshop at AUD finished with a discussion regarding how to present such diverse materials within the same interface. Due to time constraints, we never managed to get much further than the idea of positioning the various materials gathered during the research phase within the drawing of one of the students, which beautifully compressed space and time.

A following workshop held in Mumbai at the Tata Institute of Social Sciences (TISS) during January 2016 allowed me to take the workshop format further. This time, on the basis of the experiences gathered from Delhi, I decided to focus more on the mimetic aspects of image-making, inserting also from the very beginning concrete discussions regarding the final format for the presentation of the materials. At TISS the students selected a small street located behind the campus. Using their own smartphone cameras, a couple of DSLRs, a sound recorder, a GPS tracking app, a life-logging camera and a GoPro camera (the last two I had put at their disposal) they managed to produce within a few days a wide archive of sensorial experiences that characterize human and material life in that small stretch of space where a couple of popular eateries catering to the college's students are located side by side with a tea shop, a shop and a temple. During their work the students identified a series of interesting topics. Two young men jointly photographing the walls of the street in an alternation between wide-angle, close ups and macro managed to offer a first visual experience of the material culture of the street. The group immediately felt that the walls could also function as a useful interface for the final platform and, with the help of a couple of examples, I invited them to reflect on the possibility of playing with the idea of horizontal expansion. I showed them "Mainstreet,"[12] an iDocs produced by the National Film Board of Canada that exploits a large horizontal image made up of the stitching together of a variety of stills. The viewers can zoom in and out of these images which function as the visual impulse for a series of reflections on the ideological uses that authorities make of main streets in American small towns. Another example I used was Rodrick Coover's "Unknown Territories," a series aiming to allow the exploration of "spatial representation, narratives of exploration and land use."[13] Some of the works contained in this series, "Voyage into the Unknown"[14] and "Canyonlands: Edward Abbey and the Great American Desert," use again a horizontal format. The users are asked to scroll sideways along a document that could be read as a map or a timeline in which various materials recomposing a story are placed. While the first example really dialogued explicitly (given the visualization of a street) with the project we were conducting, the latter constituted more a kind of symbolic reference that we could have applied for incorporating different kinds of materials within the same space.

Another workshop participant decided to investigate an area that also led to some important insights. Attracted by the presence, on the opposite side of the street to where the shops were located, of peaceful residential buildings she decided to explore the soundscapes that characterized these various environments. Rather than moving horizontally, however, she decided to question verticality, recording sound at different heights: at an average human being's height, at 50 centimeters from the floor and, by mounting the sound recorder on a bar, at 2–3 meters height. Three different aural environments corresponding roughly to that of the by-passers, that of the inhabitants of the residential complex and that of the street dwellers (the clients of the eatery, the *dhaba*, and the people sitting on the stairs of the Hindu temple located in a small street in between the shops) were thus identified, which added to the sensorial complexity of the space under scrutiny. The question of heights, which would become a key topic in the discussions regarding possible display formats, was noticed also by another student who, with the help of drawings, showed how the clients of the *dhaba* and other street dwellers actually lived at different heights, hence having access to entirely different sound (and smell) impressions.

With these first exchanges, questions regarding social class and the different uses of the street became the focus of our attention. A blend of functionality and social class was also addressed by another student who picked up on my reflections on the meaning of color in public places in postcolonial societies. Producing out-of-focus wide-angle photographs of the street this participant managed to show how commercial and residential spaces were marked out by the presence/absence of color. The students also became progressively fascinated by what was happening inside the *dhaba* and one of the shops. One of them decided to use the GoPro for exploring the work of the *dhaba* owner from his perspective, his own rhythms in preparing the food, etc. Mounting the camera on the *dhaba whalla*'s (the food vendor) arm with the help of a set of rubber bands, she managed to generate a series of images that, albeit difficult to use, offered us a unique degree of proximity to the material culture characterizing this particular environment. The GoPro helped to heighten the haptic qualities of these images hence allowing us to start making sense of the various textures and smells present in the *dhaba*. This also inevitably brought to the fore questions of hygiene. In a dialogue between the macrophotographic shots and GoPro clips, the discussion moved toward an understanding of the varying, culturally situated notions regarding cleanliness and hygiene that were at stake in his space. One student took the question of the use of new technologies into the *dhaba* further and mounted my life-logging camera on a shelf in order to produce a time-lapse that would hopefully give us a sense of the various passages of activities taking place. Alas, the material got lost in the importation (a problem that occurs at times with such technologies) but we still considered that a time-lapse series would surely be important for identifying the various rhythms and time-based changes happening on the street. Also, the use of this particular camera raised a series of ethical debates, as some of the by-passers protested over having to be in the images.

In addition to the materials I have discussed so far, the exploration also led to the production of more "conventional" materials, such as photo and video portraits of by-passers, of the activities taking place on the street and surrounds. The first insights collected by the participants of the workshop revealed, however, primarily how the sensorium of this street was to be addressed; not only through a horizontal spanning but also through a vertical one and also in an on-going alternation between external surfaces and internal environments. This entailed a challenge into how to present the collected materials. Neither a simple image of the surface of the walls nor a 2D map of the area—one student created a map based on GPS-tracked movements of the students—was capable of rendering the depth of the materials that had been so far gathered. A 3D space was needed to do this, a space justifying the questions of verticality addressed by some of the students and allowing the possibility of moving in and out of the buildings. Our interface, we realized, should allow us to move from an aerial to a 3D perspective, enabling us to zoom in and out of the spaces in question. This would enable viewers to make sense of all the various sensorial engagements that characterize the social and material life of this street. Our interface would also have to contain a menu quickly bringing us to "people," "things," "nature" and "maps." We also contemplated the possibility of constructing a timeline reconstructing a walk in the neighborhood. One student suggested that the interface could be a stylized drawing of the *chai whalla* (the tea vendor) whose body would become the repository for all the different media we had produced. Indeed, within the scope of this workshop we did not have the time to delve deeper with this. However, the possibility of a simulated 3D environment containing the materials collected became the connecting point for all the participants at the workshop.

Conclusions: Toward a Serendipitous Multimodal Ethnography

The practices that I have described above do indeed leave us with a number of questions regarding the present and future possibilities for conducting visual ethnographic research in a digital habitat. In the first place, the examples I have discussed here indicate that images' changing ontology (their changing "imageness"; see Rancière (2008)) does indeed seem to constitute an invitation to conduct more multimodal work. Today, the ethnographer has the opportunity to bring different media into dialogue with each other, hence blurring the distinction between textual and visual (sensory) information. An important step for contemporary visual social science research, this possibility is nicely embodied by the smartphone as a tool granting us an on-going opportunity for conducting serendipitous instances of multimodal ethnography. As witnessed also by the possibilities of using emerging technologies such as wearable cameras, apps, etc. this change might also prove functional for reclaiming a more central role to audio-visual and sensory practices in the social sciences.

A second aspect worth mentioning concerns the changing role of the viewers in relation to the materials shared. In the context of contemporary image-viewing practices, viewers are increasingly immersed and brought into a direct dialogue with the images displayed. Within this context they are often asked to actively intervene upon the narrative displayed, constructing their own meaning as they proceed in the exploration of the materials of display. Materializing the forms of active spectatorship implied in Rancière's notion of the "emancipated spectator" (2009) as well as in Bourriaud's "relational aesthetics" (1998), such practices can constitute a unique opportunity for the ethnographer to close the gap between the ethnographic material they put on display and their viewers. While not representing a proper revolution in our ways of communicating ethnography (we do after all, as Barthes already suggested long ago, construct our own narratives even when consuming a linear story), this change may indeed help us bring to the fore the nature of knowledge as a "processual aspect of human social relations" (Banks 2001, 112) rather than as a static thing "out there" waiting to be discovered and "documented." We must also acknowledge that the dialectic with the viewers includes another possibility, i.e. that of generating, with the help of this very same platform used for communicating, new ethnographic materials. Viewers can today, as we have seen, actively interact with online materials, generating not only new interpretations but also actively adding new materials capable of opening up new interpretations. Transforming a space of display into a space of on-going production of ethnographic evidence, this practice might not be easy to manage and interpret; yet it carries the potential of offering an on-going form of participatory (crowd-sourced) data production.

The changes mentioned above do, indeed, call for the need to address another and more all-encompassing question, that is, the change in how to visualize the role of the ethnographer in relation to audio-visual materials. In today's digital landscapes, where multimodality and the incorporation of the viewing and co-authoring strategies of the spectators generate a set of innovative relations object-to-object, object-to-viewer and viewer-to-viewer, the role, intentions and authoriality of the ethnographer assume new meaning. No longer directors or authors, ethnographers must start viewing themselves as curators of ethnographic content. Their main task is that of creating a space within which viewers can engender their own searches, interpretations and narratives, to facilitate their path of meaning-making (see the opening quote). As my students in the interactive ethnographic documentary film course in Lisbon already experienced, this is indeed a difficult shift, a great challenge whose consequences we need to carefully evaluate. It is, however, a necessity to contemplate such possibility given the complexity of the data that we are collecting about the surrounding world and also the growing literacy in media production of our viewers and research subjects. Perhaps one of the greatest characteristics of this epoch is that the tools for producing audio-visual materials (at high definition too) are, today, no longer in the hands of the elected few but also of most of the subjects (research participants, students, colleagues) that inhabit the wired parts of the world.

Contemporary and emerging image-making technologies are therefore posing a threat to conventional ways of addressing the field of audio-visual ethnography. They force us to go beyond conventional explanatory models, opening up the space for more interactive and participatory strategies of knowledge communication. Such strategies, as I have suggested, amount also to just as many opportunities for not only exhibiting ethnography but also for producing new ethnographic evidence. I believe that this challenge may help us highlight again images' intrinsic polysemy[15] and open-endedness (cf. Barthes 1977; Berger 1972) while helping us to bring to the fore images' capacity to open us up to the sensorial and emotional dimension of everyday life (MacDougall 1997; Pink 2006; Edwards 2006). In this scenario, ethnographers might be asked to move beyond their obsession with text and with what, paraphrasing Chris Wright (1998), we could call "scientific relevance" (or more simply "content"). Rather than approaching photographs and film primarily as "documents" "capturing" what is "out there," and as illustrations of textual explanations, they must dare to play with their potential to generate stories and interpretations.

Such a challenge might ultimately bring the ethnographers to question the role (and limitations) of narrative and of the story. Gathering inspiration from philosopher Krishnamurti, we must today reflect upon the extent to which consolidated interpretations (which root themselves often nicely in verbalized narratives) can have the side-effect of limiting the scope of our observations. The Indian philosopher wrote:

> [T]he moment you have a conclusion or start examining from knowledge, you are finished, for then you are translating every living thing in terms of the old. Whereas if you have no foothold, if there is no certainty, no achievement, there is freedom to look, to achieve.
>
> (Krishnamurti 2010, 19)

Facing an archive made up of a variety of multilayered and perhaps even contradictory materials (perhaps generated with mimetic wearable tools such as life-logging cameras) may allow contemporary viewers to engage a fairly open-ended exploration centered on their own "knowledge-seeking strategies" (Färber 2007). Indeed, with this call I do not intend to suggest that iDocs or similar platforms constitute a hymn to the freedom of the viewers. Nor is it my goal to celebrate them as the only available future for ethnography. The limits of software, of the materials presented and of the links generated between them are, indeed, present. I want, however, to suggest that such practices and technologies might represent tools that offer a concrete step in the direction of a more participatory and inclusive ethnography, one more attentive to the establishment of a dialogue with the viewers. Through this interaction, the ethnographers will receive newer insights and possibly new materials dialoguing with their own interpretations. While posing a threat to the construction of epistemological authority in the voice of the ethnographer, the new practices that I have described in this chapter seem to open up the space for the progressive incorporation of a multiplicity of voices. In a way, they manage to represent the truth as something living and moving, hence creating a correspondence between life and images that reminds us of Rancière's (2006, 2) observations about cinema, which, according to him, just like life, is "not about stories, about actions oriented towards an end, but about situations open in every direction. Life has nothing to do with dramatic progression, but is instead a long and continuous movement made up of an infinity of micromovements."

Notes

1 This chapter builds on a series of experiences that have been made possible thanks to the help and collaboration of my colleagues of: the International Visual Methods Seminar (Antwerp) Luc Pauwels, Jon Wagner, Richard Chalfen and John Grady; the School of Culture and Creative

Expressions, Ambedkar University (Delhi) and in particular to Shivaji K Panikkar, Rajan Krishnan, Santhosh Sadanandan and Benil Biswas; the School of Media and Cultural Studies, Tata Institute of Social Sciences (Mumbai) and in particular Anjali Monteiro and K.P. Jayasankar. I am particularly indebted to all the participants of my workshops who have provided me with the materials and insights that I am hereby sharing with the readers. Whenever possible I will mention their specific contributions in the text.

2 This is indeed a point that was already made by scholars devoted to the study of analogic practices such as Elisabeth Edwards and Christopher Pinney. My point is, however, that digital images make this shift more evident and necessary.

3 In this text I will stick to the term interactive even though I find it at times abused. Many of the online projects that we conventionally place under this label do not, in fact, contain proper instances of interactivity but rather only of "activity." They do not allow viewers to change the materials displayed (the essence of interactivity) but only to view them more dynamically.

4 Entitled *Flyoverdelhi*, the film was directed by Angelo Fontana and myself and edited by Luca Gianfrancesco. It was produced thanks to funding received from the Swedish Bank of State's Tercentenary Fund and the Helge Ax:son Johnsons Foundation, Stockholm. It was broadcasted by Kusnskapskanalen (Swedish National Television Educational Channel) and Italian National Television Channel RAI News24.

5 One such project was called *Indica Mistica Mediatica*, a dialogue between images and music enacted by a DJ (Fabrizio de Piccoli) and myself with the help, regarding my interventions, of various video sources and a video mixer.

6 I am grateful to Andrew Irving who inspired me to use this particular mapping during a lab held at the 2014 EASA conference in Ljubljana.

7 Let me point out that all these short-term workshops focus more on the process than on the final outcome. My wish is always to make them become showcases of what could possibly be a larger project in the future.

8 The IVMS is a summer school organized by Luc Pauwels and taught by himself and Richard Chalfen, John Grady and Jon Wagner. For the 2015 edition I was invited to join the group of teachers focusing in particular on emerging technologies.

9 Thank you Ryan Frisk for your valuable help during this workshop.

10 Inspiration for this particular format came from one of the works that I showed to the students during the first sessions of the workshop in order to give them inspiration. "Pregoneros De Mellin" is an iDoc exploring the voices and songs of street vendors within a structure reproducing a walk in Medellin. www.pregonerosdemedellin.com/#en

11 Questions remain indeed as to how to curate this process and how to generate and stir a possible flow of information.

12 http://mainstreet.nfb.ca/#/mainstreet

13 www.roderickcoover.com

14 http://astro.temple.edu/~rcoover/UnknownTerritories/VoyageIntoTheUnknown/index.html

15 With "polysemy" Volosinov indicated that signs and representations carry varied layers of meaning (cf. Cubitt 2001).

References

Ashton, Judith and Sandra Gaudenzi. 2012. "Interactive Documentary: Setting the field." *Studies in Documentary Film* 6(2): 125–39.

Banks, Marcus. 2001. *Visual Methods in Social Research*. London: Sage.

Barthes. Roland. 1977. *Image Music Text*. London: Fontana Press.

——. 1993. *Camera Lucida*. London: Vintage.

Berger, John. 1972. *Ways of Seeing*, chs 1 and 2, 7–44. London: Penguin.

——. 2014. *Understanding a Photograph*. London: Penguin.

Bourriaud, Nicholas. 1998. *Relational Aesthetics*. Dijon: Les Presses du Réel.

Crary, Jonathan. 1990. *Techniques of the Observer: On Vision and Modernity in the Nineteenth Century*. Cambridge, MA: MIT Press.

Cubitt, Sean. 2001. *Simulation and Social Theory*. London: Sage.

Edwards, Elisabeth. 2006. "Photographs and the Sound of History." *Visual Anthropology Review* 1(2): 27–46.

Färber, Alexa. 2007. "Exposing Expo: Exhibition entrepreneurship and experimental reflexivity in late modernity." In *Exhibition Experiments*, edited by Paul Basu and Sharon MacDonald, 219–38. London: Blackwells.

Favero, Paolo. 2013. "Getting Our Hands Dirty (Again): Interactive documentaries and the meaning of images in the digital age." *Journal of Material Culture* 18(3): 259–77.

——. 2014. "Learning to Look Beyond the Frame: Reflections on the changing meaning of images in the age of digital media practices." *Visual Studies* 29(2): 166–79.

Goggin, Gerard. 2009. "Adapting the Mobile Phone: The iPhone and its consumption." *Continuum: Journal of Media & Cultural Studies* 23(2): 231–44.

Krishnamurti, Jiddu. 2010. *Freedom from the Known*. London: Rider.

Leadbeater, Charles. 2009. *We-Think: Mass Innovation, Not Mass Production*. London: Profile Books.

MacDougall, David. 1997. "The Visual in Anthropology." In *Rethinking Visual Anthropology*, edited by Marcus Banks and Howard Morphy, 276–95. New Haven, CT: Yale University Press.

Nash, Kate. 2012. "Modes of Interactivity: Analysing the webdoc." *Media, Culture & Society* 34(2): 195–210.

O'Reilly, T. 2005. "What Is Web 2.0? Design Patterns and Business Models for the Next Generation of Software." http://oreilly.com/web2/archive/what-is-web-20.html (accessed March 21, 2016).

Pink, Sarah. 2006. *The Future of Visual Anthropology: Engaging the Senses*. London: Routledge.

Quiggin, John. 2006. "Blogs, Wikis and Creative Innovation." *International Journal of Cultural Studies* 9(4): 481–96.

Rancière, Jacques. 2008. *The Future of the Image*, ch. 1, 1–31. London: Verso.

——. 2009. *The Emancipated Spectator*, ch. 1, 1–23. London: Verso.

Shirky, Charles. 2008. *Here Comes Everybody*. London: Penguin Books.

Sontag, Susan. 1979. *On Photography*. London: Penguin.

Wright, Christopher. 1998. "The Third Subject: Perspectives on visual anthropology." *Anthropology Today* 14(4): 16–22.

26

THE ART OF PLAY
Ethnography and Playful Interventions with Young People

Larissa Hjorth, William Balmford,
Sharon Greenfield, luke gaspard,
Amani Naseem, and Tom Penney

Introduction

Ethnography, as the writing up of cultural practice, has, much like culture itself, taken on various manifestations. Once a method used by sociologists and anthropologists, ethnography is now a widely deployed approach and conceptual framework in contemporary media research. Throughout this evolution, the reflexive negotiation of self, power, labor and participation have remained central to ethnographic practice. Given ethnography's commitments, it is not surprising that ethnography—as a way in which to frame cultural practice—has been embraced within the visual arts. In particular, the significant increase of the socially engaged practices in late twentieth-century art—identified in the 1990s by Hal Foster in "The Artist as Ethnographer" (1996) and Nicolas Bourriaud's "Relational Aesthetics" (1998 [2002])—foregrounds art as a social/cultural encounter (Hjorth and Sharp 2014, 128).

The importance of ethnography within art practice has expanded throughout the twentieth century—especially as art moves toward socially engaged interventions. Central to this ethnographic—or what Singaporean art theorist Lee Wong Choy (Lee and Hjorth 2011) calls "ethno-geographic"—movement have been the critiques of Bourriaud's "relational aesthetics" (1998). As Claire Bishop (2004) observes, "relational aesthetics" operates as a "curatorial modus operandi" within the social and political confines of the gallery and thus does not challenge notions of power and participation in the real world.

More recently, art has taken to more rigorous unpacking of participatory practices through analysis of collaboration and moving outside the sanctuary of the gallery space (Jenkins 2006; Kester 2011). This focus upon participation also marks the shift of the participatory role of digital and networked media as an integral part of everyday life whereby new media/visual art divides are no longer applicable (Bishop 2012). As Grant Kester suggests, there is a need to canvas techniques, tools and frameworks for art practice that reimagine the socially engaged dimensions beyond just the "aesthetic playfield" (2010) in order to shape different forms of inter-subjective affect, identification and agency (2011, 68).

In this chapter we explore the collaboration between ethnography and art. Through a series of workshops with young people focused on play and well-being, we consider how participatory art can inform ethnographic methods and modes of transmission. These workshops were part of an exhibition at the Centre for Contemporary Photography (CCP) called *The Art of Play*, part of a broader project that takes an ethnographic approach to games in everyday Australian households.[1] This chapter begins by framing debates in and around art, media and ethnography especially in terms of participation through a consideration of young people's relationship to media practice and participation. It then reflects upon debates at the intersection of games, play and the everyday, followed by a discussion of the increasing importance of play.

Art Meets Ethnography Meets Play

In a recent article in *Visual Studies*, Jungnickel and Hjorth (2014) argue that one of the key sites in need of examination is the role of transmission or translation—that is, the ways in which the entanglement between art and ethnography is contextualized and articulated into broader public cultures. One of the obvious vehicles for transmission is context, which means moving the projects outside the gallery.[2] This tactic has a long history in twentieth-century art through movements such as the Situationist International, which sought to intervene in everyday urban environments. As Jungnickel and Hjorth contend, contemporary forms of transmission need to reconsider the relationship between method and final outcome—a process that requires art practice to draw on various interdisciplinary tropes such as sociological and anthropological inquiry.

They also point to the interdisciplinary practice of ethnography whereby the process of making and thinking through art-based methods is an integral part of doing research. Both art and ethnography involve processes of transmission and translation from the fieldwork or studio to the reader/gallery. As they note, "although some are reluctant to embrace changes borne of the affordances of digital media, many others favor the transformative potential of new forms of attentiveness to understanding, evoking and provoking the social world" (Jungnickel and Hjorth 2014, 137). As Lury and Wakeford argue, we need to understand how the subject and content also transform methods. These "methods in the making" are "methods or means by which the social world is not only investigated, but may also be engaged" (Lury and Wakeford 2012, 6). Taking a "methods in the making" approach requires engaging with play.

Play is central to contemporary media (Sicart 2014; Raessens 2006). Play is also a useful way for understanding the process of adaption and transmission. For Sutton-Smith (1997), understanding play can provide insight into cultural practice. Play is local and contextual. While the nuance of context can often seem overlooked in global digital games, the practice of playing is unquestionably informed by the local. This phenomenon can be witnessed in the uneven uptake of massively multiplayer online (MMO) games by different cultures (Hjorth 2008).

In the CCP exhibition, a non-digital version of *Minecraft* was installed. *Minecraft*, often called "the digital version of Lego," is a great example of a sandbox game that affords many different types of play and context. From its different modes—creative or survival, single or multiplayer—*Minecraft* deploys creativity as much as it does play. This has led to key media scholars such as Katie Salen and Mizuko Ito establishing *Minecraft* boot-camps to harness play and creativity for e-learning (also see Cipollone et al. 2014; Hooper and de Byl 2014; Hill 2015). With its retro, highly pixelated aesthetics, *Minecraft* affords different types of play that draws from both digital and non-digital (Lego) experiences. Digital ethnography allows for ways in which to understand the interrelationship and entanglement between the digital and non-digital play (Pink et al. 2016).

Noel Dyck combines well over ten years of ethnographic exploration into his work *Fields of Play* (2012). He explores how people of all types become entangled in children's sports—from the children to the parents, the helpers, coaches and officials—and the complex fields of play that result out of such meshing. Extrapolating this exploration of play, he is able to intelligently probe wider debates on community, family and the shaping of everyday life. It is his use of ethnographic methods to explore play and its associated scenarios that enables such rich exploration. Laurence Goldman (1998) also explores physical-based children's play, using detailed ethnographic description of games and imaginative genres in Huli, Papua New Guinea. Rather than Dyck's focus on the communities formed through play, Goldman's work examines the relationships between play, storytelling and identity. Through this context, Goldman frames play as an informative tool for building Huli knowledge and cultural traditions, while also using his ethnographic data to reveal much about the everyday lives of the Huli people. Beyond this, Goldman makes important note of how the structures formed through play can reveal the complex and nuanced ways children invoke lived experiences, reimagining and using them as types of "virtual reality."

Where digital ethnographers such as Malaby (2009), Boellstorff (2008) or Bonnie Nardi (2010) discuss the growing field of digital play and billion dollar sales of downloadable content, Dyck's (2012) work captures the notion of "child's play" and reveals it as a much more complex social field, underpinned with its own array of social roles and responsibilities. Steinkuehler (2006) argues that the games we play are not always the ones that were designed, but instead become the result of a back and forth dialectic between player, context and game. In the exhibition, *Minecraft* aesthetics were used to activate audiences to become players.

Introducing *The Art of Play*

Hjorth's art exhibition, *The Art of Play*, consisted of a *Minecraft*-inspired imagery adapted into a physical gallery space (Figure 26.1). There were *Minecraft* vinyl clouds on the wall and artificial grass cut-outs on the ground. In the space were wooden cubes mimicking the pixelated space of *Minecraft*. Lego pieces could be found in and around the boxes. Audiences could move the cubes and Lego pieces to make their own worlds. Then audiences could photograph their world and send to the CCP Instagram account. The Instagram images were then printed and exhibited on the wall. As the exhibition went on, the wall filled with the audience-as-artist's playful expressions and interventions. Their images went up alongside the images from the ethnographic images inside people's homes. The audience-as-artist images went from the sanctuary of the gallery space to social media and back to the gallery again—a journey that took various forms of adaption, translation and transmission.

This relationship between the making and the maker being transformed informs *The Art of Play* exhibition. Part of the ethnographic techniques involved scenarios of use, interviews, playing maps and video re-enactments. From this research it became clear that the best context for transmission might not be academic publications, but actually putting it back into

Figure 26.1   CCP Gallery installation: *Minecraft* cubes filled with Lego and *Minecraft* wall clouds. Photo: J. Forsyth

the context of the community it came from and allowing them to further reflect upon these playful interventions as themselves, not just "audiences" but active makers (of art, of ethnography). It was this idea that informed the conceptual and material dimensions of *The Art of Play*. They are not subjects of the ethnography but become the ethnographers themselves as they perform and document their playful interventions. They are not the audience—rather, they become the artists.

Another dimension of the exhibition was the play intervention workshops. During the workshops we reflected upon how young people can be empowered with art/ethnographic tools to not only develop creative solutions (i.e. games) but also be proactive in building feelings of well-being among peers. This mode of ethnography deployed elements of the "ethno-geographic" (Lee and Hjorth 2011) by considering the way in which the gallery space informs limits and restrictions upon game play. In the workshops, young people were empowered as play masters who needed to collaborate with their peer play masters. The workshops asked the participants to adapt, design and test their own favorite digital games into physical games that then became part of the exhibition's transmission, and images of the workshop were then presented on the exhibition wall as the artwork.

Play Intervention Workshops

One of the key dimensions of the exhibit that pushed the relationship between art and ethnography were the play intervention workshops. The workshops were held at the CCP as part of *The Art of Play* exhibition from July to September 2015 in Melbourne, Australia. The workshop ran for two hours. Participants were shown examples of face-to-face games that reflect upon digital gaming and transform or intervene spaces in creative ways. For example, *PacManhattan, Flash Mob Freeze/Starwars, Big Urban Games (B.U.G.), Multiple Massively Thumb*

Wrestling, Chocomel Experiment, Hovergarden, to name a few. To warm up they played *Multiple Massively Thumb Wrestling* (by monochrom).

Participants first reflected upon the digital games they liked and why. They then worked in teams to TEST, PLAY and PERFECT a site-specific game. They had to reflect upon the gallery space and what elements (such as Lego) they could deploy. Participants worked together in groups to problem solve and make a PLAYABLE game. They moved between designer, tester and player modes. This required students to consider what skills and experiences are involved in playing and how it can reflect a sense of well-being, place or community. Each group had a designated photographer/documentary maker. They made stop-motion animation videos (my create app) of the play activities.

Through a series of five workshops conducted over two weeks at CCP, various primary (8–11 years old) and high school (13–15 years old) students (from three diverse schools, totaling 250) participated in the workshops. The authors of this chapter operated as facilitators—or "play masters." As play masters they helped participants respond to the workshop's exercises as well as time keep. The workshops required participants to adapt, redesign and test a digital game that is translated into the physical space of the gallery. Participants needed to work collaboratively and adapt to the physical and rule restrictions. In the workshop they had to negotiate each other's preferred game play and work together in the designing and testing of the game. For example, adapting the digital game of *Crossy Roads* (by Hipster Whale 2014, see Figure 26.2) to the gallery space. Restrictions of the space included typical gallery etiquette such as being quiet and not running. Participants had to reflect upon the restrictions of the game space and try to use it as part of game play.

The workshop sought not only to make students active participants in the designing and testing of adapted digital games but also to reflect upon the experiences, pleasures, connections and disconnections between non-digital games (i.e. Lego) and digital games like *Minecraft.* Throughout the workshop, participants moved between occupying a role of

Figure 26.2 Students attempt to adapt the digital game *Crossy Roads* to the gallery space

game designer, game player and ethnographer. They reflected narratives of place and power in and around the gallery space and tried to reflexively adapt the games. The participants both talked, and kinesthetically engaged with, notions of play, place and collaboration. They also collaborated with peers to understand different pleasures and forms of engagement with game play. Through connecting with peers in new ways they considered play and well-being (see Figures 26.3–26.5).

Figure 26.3   Participants testing their games and the limits of the gallery space

Figure 26.4 Part of the game play involved players being immobilized in the space

Figure 26.5 A participant attempts to push the boundaries of game and gallery limitation

Playful Interventions

Play is one of the most significant concepts informing contemporary media culture and practice (Sicart 2014). And yet, play has a long and culturally specific genealogy (Sutton-Smith 1997). Play throughout history has had a broad application to different cultural activities. Children's playground games, board games and digital games are some that obviously fall under the banner of "play." Importantly, Johan Huizinga, in his work *Homo Ludens* (1955), articulated that play is a cultural phenomenon, and that it precedes culture. As an archaic activity, evident even in animals, play precedes culture but ultimately has some role in shaping and producing it. Play, with its ability to produce a separate temporary reality, is a space to simulate and test relationships and rules prior to their application in society.

One of Huizinga's five characteristics of play is that "play creates order" (Huizinga 1938[1949], 10), that is, play creates rules out of an activity that is seemingly free-form. When we play, we are not just being children, free or having fun (although play is fun!), we are creating scenarios with clear rules that have set boundaries. These boundaries make the consequences of the game "safe" from real-world pressures, but interestingly allow us to isolate and "play-out" relationships, rules and behaviors that might occur within the real world. *The Art of Play* workshops, in association with Young and Well CRC, engaged young people from diverse backgrounds in the process of game design. The idea of using games to gain ownership of students' everyday scenarios was important in these workshops, through the playing, production and testing of games that reflected their own everyday situation.

Mary Flanagan's notion of *Critical Play* (2009)—and the critical play method of designing games—informs us that ownership of societal rules and conventions can be achieved through the simulation of everyday settings in play environments. Flanagan's notion of "critical play" as a theory or game design paradigm calls not just for making play as a critique of the status quo, but making play for political, social and cultural change. Activities such as cooking, getting dressed, working out, and planning how to fit such activities into a day, reflect the "operations"

Figure 26.6 A "bird's-eye" view of the participatory workshops in action

of their respective real-world processes. The performativity of play becomes important here, as players of dollhouses or computer game simulations such as *The Sims* must pretend, or "play," each member of the household. Through role-play players must embody or empathize with their different characters' scenarios, and acknowledge the perspectives of others. For this reason, role-play has been often used in therapy to help individuals understand and empathize with each other's perspectives within the safe boundary of a play space (Corsini 1975).

The "critical" element of *Critical Play* refers to cognitive engagement and the potential that can arise from altering the rules of the "real" within play scenarios. Flanagan's assertion is that play not only reflects reality but produces something new when it critically engages with it. Because play environments are, here, simulations representing everyday scenarios and their operation, designers of play (who can be anyone) can exaggerate and change these represented scenarios. Play makers can suggest changes and alternatives to the rules without concern for such ideas being shut down in real life.

Flanagan (2009) suggests "re-skinning" (changing the appearance of game characters and their role), "un-playing" (playing the game the way it is not supposed to be played) and "re-writing" (altering the narrative and story of a game) as strategies to reveal critical potential. Such changes, or subversions, come to bear on the reception of their respective simulated real-world processes by understanding them in a new light, by having had control over systems one otherwise might not have, or by having the space to discover new possibilities in the simulation that one might not have had the chance to in the "real" otherwise.

As designers, the young participants in *The Art of Play* workshops were encouraged to reflect on design choices and think about rules and the positions they would put each other in as players. They were asked to consider how the rules of their games interacted with social and physical "rules." This request on our part required some sensitivity in assessing the ethical implications of designing for play with young people. In particular, one of our considerations was the notion of a physical/digital divide as many of our young participants experienced games or conceived of them primarily as digital experiences.

Figure 26.7 Students move between being designers, players and testers of their adapted games in the gallery space

When writing about the ethics of computer games, Sicart (2009) posits that games are morally accountable as objects and play artifacts. A game is seen as a moral object, with ethical implications inherent in the design and imprinted on the way the game is shaped, its content and expected interactions. A general concern with digital games is that they can be procedural, often rigidly requiring players to follow tight control schemes and a deterministic set of interactions. As such, they can "play the player," forcing players to submit and carry out actions adhering to the moral choices imprinted in the game (Sicart 2009). Such processual limitations can restrict the notion of "freedom" in play and, as such, have an impact on who can be represented or included in a play activity. We opted for more traditional "hands-on" approaches with our participants, giving them primarily non-digital tools (but allowing them to document using digital tools) in order to create socially engaged, spatial and physical games suiting a more "playground" style.

In consideration of the above ideas, for *The Art of Play* workshops, we asked the participants to consider play (as games) as having a set of key ingredients that would reflect the ideas of role-playing, representing everyday scenarios, simulating rules and operations, and critically playing (play-testing) in order to change, gain ownership over, or improve such rules. They were as follows. Play involves roles, characters, personalities; it involves places, environments, settings; it has rules that set boundaries for the play activity; it can be both digital and non-digital.

As such, participants were asked to brainstorm what roles (and therefore characters) were involved in their chosen real-world scenarios, what environments their chosen scenario would take place in, what rules govern and limit their behavior in such spaces, and especially how they could realize their game in a physical space, not just a digital one. Participants then had to come up with a game, and iterate it through play-testing.

Figure 26.8 Players in action

Conclusion

We need to move on from the convention in sociology to assimilate other practices on its own terms and within its own image (i.e. a "sociology of art" for a "sociology of computing") for a more collaborative practice that is mutually transformative (i.e. sociology with art or sociology with computing). As a consequence I am not suggesting that the boundary between sociology or ethnography can be collapsed with art but I am implying that research practice can be more artful (Back 2012, 33).

In the workshop, the young participants were not only designers and players but also became artists and ethnographers. Just as the exhibition sought to transmit the ethnography from three years of fieldwork into games in everyday Australian life into the hands of the active audience through play and social media (Instagram), the workshop sought to make the participants not just subjects of ethnography but also become ethnographers themselves as they moved from designer–tester–player and back again. Just like the exhibition, the workshop participants are not the audience—rather, they become the artists, designers and players.

This workshop sought to provide a different context for transmission and impact. Indeed, rather than doing studies of young people playing games in their homes, these workshops afforded young people with the space to collaborate and reflect upon normalized play practices and to rethink what makes games great/pleasurable/fascinating. Through collaboration the participants took on different roles and became reflexive to the numerous power relations in and around game making, testing and playing. It makes unfamiliar their familiar everyday game practices. It stretches the capacity of art into the ethnographic. It makes ethnography more artful while making art more socially engaged.

Notes

1 This project was funded by the Australian Research Council Discovery program. *Games of Being Mobile* (DP140104295) is also part of the "connected and creative" stream of the Young and Well CRC.
2 Art and creative research within the academy have moved toward the umbrella of "practice-led" or "practice-based" research (Candy 2006; Sullivan 2010). However, these rubrics do not capture all of the different practices. In particular, interdisciplinary practices that sit outside the conventional visual arts but "deploy art-related methods and techniques" can find it hard to be located within the academy's increased focus on accountability and impact.

References

Back, Les. 2012. "Live sociology: Social research and its futures." In *Live Methods*, edited by Les Back and Nirman Puwar, 18–39. Oxford: Blackwell Publishing.

Bishop, Claire. 2004. "Antagonism and relational aesthetics." *October* 110: 51–79.

———. 2012. "Digital divide: Contemporary art and new media." *Artforum.* https://artforum.com/inprint/issue=201207&id=31944&pagenum=0 (accessed February 10, 2016).

Boellstorff, Tom. 2008. *Coming of Age in Second Life: An Anthropologist Explores the Virtually Human.* Princeton, NJ: Princeton University Press.

Bourriaud, Nicolas. 1998 [2002]. *Relational Aesthetics.* Dijon: Les Presses du Réel.

Candy, Linda. 2006. "Practice based research: A guide." *Creativity & Cognition Studios (CCS).* www.creativityandcognition.com/resources/PBR%20Guide-1.1-2006.pdf (accessed August 10, 2016).

Cipollone, Maria, Catherine C. Schifter, and Rick A. Moffat. 2014. "Minecraft as a creative tool: A case study." *International Journal of Game-Based Learning (IJGBL)* 4(2): 1–14.

Corsini, Raymond. 1975. *Role Playing in Psychotherapy.* London: Transaction Publishers.

Dyck, Noel. 2012. *Fields of Play: An Ethnography of Children's Sports.* Toronto: University of Toronto Press.

Flanagan, Mary. 2009. *Critical Play*. Cambridge, MA: MIT Press.

Foster, Hal. 1996. "The artist as ethnographer." In *The Return of the Real*. Cambridge, MA: MIT Press.

Goldman, Laurence R. 1998. *Child's Play: Myth, Mimesis and Make-Believe*. London: Bloomsbury.

Hill, Valerie. 2015. "Digital citizenship through game design in Minecraft." *New Library World* 116(7/8): 369–82.

Hjorth, Larissa. 2008. "The game of being mobile: One media history of gaming and mobile technologies in Asia-Pacific." *Convergence: The International Journal of Research into New Media Technologies*. Games issue edited by Jason Wilson and Helen Kennedy, 13(4): 369–81.

Hjorth, Larissa and Kristen Sharp. 2014. "The art of ethnography." *Visual Studies Journal* 29(2): 128–35.

Hooper, James and Penny de Byl. 2014. "Towards a unified theory of play: A case study of Minecraft." *2014 DiGRA Australia Symposium—What Is Game Studies in Australia?* June 17. Melbourne, Australia. Online.

Huizinga, Johan. 1938[1949]. *Homo Ludens*. London: Routledge.

———. 1955. *Homo Ludens: A Study of the Play Element in Culture*. Boston, MA: The Beacon Press.

Jenkins, Henry. 2006. *Convergence Culture: Where Old and New Media Collide*. New York University Press.

Jungnickel, Katrina and Larissa Hjorth. 2014. "Playing with methodological entanglements: Messiness, machines, research probes and intangibilities." *Visual Studies Journal* 29(2): 136–45.

Kester, Grant. 2010. www.greenmuseum.org (accessed May 10, 2016).

———. 2011. *The One and the Many: Contemporary Collaborative Art in a Global Context*. Durham, NC: Duke University Press.

Lee, Weng Choy and Larissa Hjorth. 2011. "Nostalgia for the dial-up modem: Cultures in transition." *Broadsheet*. December: 256–8.

Lury, Celia and Nina Wakeford, eds. 2012. *Inventive Methods: The Happening of the Social*. London: Routledge.

Malaby, Thomas. M. 2009. "Anthropology and play: The contours of playful experience." *New Literary History* 40(1): 205–18.

Nardi, Bonnie. 2010. *My Life as a Night Elf Priest*. Ann Arbor, MI: University of Michigan Press.

Pink, Sarah, Jolynna Sinanan, Larissa Hjorth, and Heather Horst. 2016. "Tactile digital ethnography: Researching mobile media through the hand." *Mobile Media & Communication* 4(2): 237–51.

Raessens, Joost. 2006. "Playful identities, or the ludification of culture." *Games & Culture* 1(1): 52–7.

Sicart, Miguel. 2009. *The Ethics of Computer Games*. Cambridge, MA: MIT Press.

———. 2014. *Play Matters*. Cambridge, MA: MIT Press.

Steinkuehler, Constance. 2006. "The mangle of play." *Games & Culture* 1(3): 199–213.

Sullivan, Graeme. 2010. *Art Practice as Research: Inquiry in Visual Arts*. Los Angeles, CA: Sage.

Sutton-Smith, Brian. 1997. *The Ambiguity of Play*. London: Routledge.

THE (BE)COMING
OF SELFIES

Revisiting an *Onlife* Ethnography on Digital Photography Practices[1]

Edgar Gómez Cruz

This chapter focuses upon a central digital and visual phenomenon of contemporary culture: selfies. The main premise for my argument is that the conditions that configured the development of imagery as a core element in online interactions were shaped in early text-based practices and therefore represent a distinct trajectory from the tradition of self-portraiture in painting and photography. Building upon a previous account on the topic (Gómez Cruz and Thornham 2015), I suggest that selfies represent the latest stage of an evolution and convergence between technologically mediated practices of communication and visual cultures. This convergence has been refined through mass adoption, technical innovation, corporate and media discourses and the rise of algorithmic culture (Striphas 2015). Digital photography practices, and specifically selfies, represent an interesting case study to characterize some of the virtues and possibilities of digital ethnography. At the same time, the digital, as an object of inquiry "makes us aware and newly self-conscious about those taken-for-granted frames" (Miller and Horst 2012, 12) and photography (traditional, familiar, vernacular) was one of them (see Gómez Cruz 2016; Hand 2012).

By bringing together digital ethnography and the study of contemporary digital and visual practices such as selfies, I illustrate how digital ethnography represents a powerful tool to envision early emergent phenomena in digital culture (Hand 2008) while it is taking place. In particular, I explore how use of previous fieldwork, as a historical archive, could help us rethink current phenomena in alternative ways and via alternative, even non-linear, genealogies, while attempting to avoid focusing merely on new technological platforms or iterations. I close with three elements that I consider fundamental to understanding digital ethnography as an epistemic intervention in the era of Big Data.

Introduction to an Ethnography of Photography Practices

After years of studying early systems of online interaction on BBC, IRC and Chats as a Master's/PhD student, I was profoundly disenchanted with the speed with which platforms appeared and disappeared. I realized that following the latest technology was probably a mistake since all the claims and findings seemed (mistakenly) to be unavoidably attached to a single platform. I decided, then, to change my approach; instead of chasing the latest flashy technology, I started focusing my attention on an "old" technology, one that has been widely studied and researched in the past but that was experiencing profound changes with the convergence of digital technologies.

Photography, as an object of study, invited me to ask a different set of questions, where the importance was not so much on how this technology "revolutionizes" society but, instead, on the relationship between what was understood as photography and discourses, and practices of photography being shaped by the increasing presence of digital technologies. Photography was present in the everyday life of almost everyone everywhere. It was not an elitist technology and, although not everyone had a digital camera let alone a cameraphone at the time, almost everyone had, one way or another, seen, taken or appeared in a photo. At the same time, it seemed that the affordances of the digital were creating different practices and opening new ecologies. In fact, an important factor in my decision to study photography was that images were increasingly becoming present in online interactions (especially since the emergence of the World Wide Web).

Some scholars actually observed, very early on, the importance of exchanging images online (Slater 1995, 1998), the banal use of images in mediated mobile communication (Koskinen et al. 2002) or the epistemological challenge that technology would bring to the photographic field (Mitchell 1992; Lister 1995). In addition, I was in a position to witness and document a series of emergent practices in the field that could be useful for understanding how derivations and nuances of actual mainstream phenomena were unfolding;[2] not so much in terms of the fetishization of the new, but in how different assemblages (of practices, discourses, affordances, etc.) collide into a single assemblage that could be regarded as selfies. Moreover, some of the practices that I observed could also be useful to understand future uses of camera technologies that go beyond images (see Gómez Cruz 2016). Within this context, digital ethnography became a useful tool to detect emergent practices with technologies but, more importantly, to enrich the milieu where these take place and therefore reposition them within a complex and nuanced context. In the following section I will be focusing on one of these practices.

From Kodak Culture to Networked Image

The main findings of my ethnography on photographic practices were synthetized in a theoretical concept: "Networked Image."[3] Drawing upon 18 months of fieldwork, I argued that our relationship to photography was changing to the extent that current photographic practices in everyday life were radically different to those founded in classic studies on vernacular photography (Bourdieu 1996[1964]; Schwartz 1986; Chalfen 1987). At the same time, I suggested thinking about *photo-graphy* in alternative ways since the representational and semiotic approaches to images did not seem to capture the complexity of emplaced, located, malleability and multiplicity of the digital photography practices observed (see Gómez Cruz 2012).

My ethnographic research and fieldwork was neither about a group of people, nor a technological platform, but about sociotechnical practices that crossed several platforms and used different technologies. I carried out participant observation mostly with a series of Flickr and Instagram groups in Barcelona, Madrid, Granada and Oxford, but then I moved my observations, following participants' traces, to Facebook, Twitter, Skype and blogs. In this way, by following practices, my results were not limited to one platform or a single group of people but to the way photography was adopted, adapted and affiliated in everyday life. The key was that my object was constructed when a series of technologies, different people and certain discourses set specific assemblages of action/thinking, or practices (see Gómez Cruz and Ardèvol 2013b; Bräuchler and Postill 2010).

Participant observation took place *online* (using Flickr, Instagram, email, Skype, Twitter and Facebook), *onsite* (in different towns, pubs, at picnics and on walks in Catalunya, Spain and England) and *offline* (interviewing people face-to-face, visiting their houses and studios and watching them downloading, processing and uploading photos while sitting next to them). Inspired by Luciano Floridi's work (2009), I called my study an "Onlife Ethnography"[4] of how different people use, learn, exchange, talk, think and integrate photography into their everyday lives. These practices were, to use Hine's (2015) terminology, embedded, embodied and part of the everyday, but also emplaced, experienced and connected both online, offline and somewhere in between. Many of the situations that arose during the photo-walks and encounters could not be explained without the base online interactions, and vice versa: ways of talking, common references, jokes, challenges, etc., were started online or offline and continued in both seamlessly.

My fieldwork was packed with moments when informants said things like: "What you said on Twitter" or "As I told you on Facebook," "I can see you right now, taking photos" (in an SMS) or "Let me show you this video on YouTube," all of these while having a beer in a bar that was being photographed and uploaded to different platforms for various reasons. At the same time, I chatted with participants while they were shooting or while they posted questions on the forums, if in doubt about something they were doing. The digital practices I observed were very much situated in the body, in specific places, and constantly posted on social media. Internet platforms and cultural settings were of equal importance in my fieldwork because all of them were part of a complex assemblage that shaped specific practices, specific forms of mediations.

Constantly living "onlife" is the result of years of practices of mediation that have become cemented in the way we experience everyday life. This is the perfect ground for certain phenomena to emerge from, spread and become mainstream. Indeed, while I write this, we are witnessing the boom of the selfies phenomenon in Western scholarship. Selfies could be regarded as one of the most explosive, ubiquitous and studied occurrences in the history of the digital world. The word of the year in 2013, hundreds of articles and media coverage, special issues in journals (Senft and Baym 2015), groups of academics devoted to its study with hundreds of members,[5] dozens of published papers on the subject and scholarly courses, seminars and MOOCs represent just a few illustrations of the importance of the selfie as a cultural object. Within just a few months, the selfie, as a practice, was positioned as one of the most important and studied manifestations of digital culture. In the context of my ethnographic work on photography practices, selfies could be regarded as the paradigmatic example of how these networked images are different to analog photography. In the following section I will try to explain why.

Self-Portraits: The Paradigmatic Practice of Digital Photography—An Ethnographic Finding

My fieldwork started in Flickr following two strategies: on the one hand I chose a "Flickr group" where I could develop a participant observation of practices that were shared by a number of people. The intention of this first strategy was to have a comprehensive view of the relationship between photo-practices and online and offline socialization.[6] Doing participant observation with a group as a "base" was helpful in order to develop a rapport and get a deep understanding of these practices from within a group.

The second strategy I employed was to detect specific practices that were common to Flickr as a whole. I spent hours and hours taking notes, navigating groups and talking to people, individually and in groups, about their practices. This second strategy had a twofold goal: to detect spreading practices that were not necessarily present in the group that I was observing and, at the same time, to use the group's expertise to discuss practices that I was finding inside and outside the group. Of all the different practices I documented, there was one that was subtly but ubiquitously present on Flickr and by far the most important in other sites such as Fotolog. This was the practice of self-portraits. As one long entry in my fieldnotes highlights:

> Emma arrived home from work at around six. Her role as a manager in a hotel takes up most of her time. It is precisely because of her role that she has to be online constantly. Emma is young and attractive and she lives in a country where physical beauty is an important form of social capital. She arrives home, puts some music on her sound system and undresses herself. Completely naked, she dances playfully around the living room while she prepares the camera. In today's session she will take around 50 or 60 images of herself posing in ways that resemble Greek sculptures. Always using the self-shooter, always in black and white, and always looking for forms and angles to create classy images that are intended to be both erotic and artistic. Emma is both her favorite model and her only photographer. After revising the shots, she gets dressed and sits in front of the computer, downloading, organizing and processing the images with Photoshop. Finally, she will choose one or two images to be uploaded to her Flickr account where she will get several comments and "favorites" from her thousands of contacts.[7] She will keep the rest of the unpublished images to upload them "when I'm too lazy to shoot new ones." This way, she will always have "new images" ready to be uploaded.

In my fieldwork I have several notes like these. I found the use of self-portraiture by different people (but mainly by women) that developed the practice in a careful, resourceful and reflexive way. For many of these women, self-portraiture became their main photographic motif and it was a practice that allowed them to create an online persona; to experiment with themselves; to create a visual diary and to use it as a self-reinforcement, self-caring practice (see Gómez Cruz 2012, chapter VI). What most of these women had in common was that they understood self-portraiture mainly as a reassuring and positive practice to see and experience their body in a different way, by connecting technological affordances, visual tropes and social interactions (see Tiidenberg and Gómez Cruz 2015).

This focus on the self was a finding that was not "held" or "represented" in the image itself. Indeed, an aesthetic or semiotic reading of the images would not only "read" differently, they would also *counter* this initial reading. An aesthetic reading of the images would highlight (for example) issues of to-be-looked-at-ness, narcissism, display, and more broadly issues of representation, performance, posing. Second, by focusing on the practice as the initial and central phenomenon, the images have to be read through a different lens and the experiences of the photographer-models acquire a different meaning that actually works to challenge representational approaches.[8]

Although widespread, this was indeed a very specific use of self-portraits that I fully documented and wrote about because of its power and importance. Nevertheless, coming back to my ethnographic notes as an archive (see Marcus 1998), I found several records, in both fieldnotes and images, which were coded in different ways to self-portraits (for example, in ways of socializing). Here are two examples:

Today D. couldn't come on the photo-walk because he was sick. He is a very well regarded member of the group and everybody felt his absence dearly commenting on how much they wanted him to get well. They started a playful activity: since D. is well known as a plane spotter, some members of the group started taking self-portraits with a toy plane that one of the member's son brought with him. They took these photos in order to post them later in the group pool, as a collective "get well" or "we missed you" message.

While this phatic and communicative use of images is very common with cameraphones, to perform it with SLRs and without instant Internet connection required a series of processes that were necessarily planned and required different amounts of time and effort. At the time, I read this record as a way for the group to solidify and create a sense of community (they did these kinds of things all the time, with images and without them). However, a new reading of my records led me to a conclusion about the increasing use of self-images to convey and send messages where the presence of the photographer, in the picture, meant something along the lines of: "I," "here," "doing this," but more importantly, and this cannot be read necessarily from the image itself: photographers position themselves in the image for a very specific reason and that reason was always contextual to both the sender and the receiver. This means that people were positioning (and posing) themselves in their pictures as an explicit way to send a message, to someone in mind and for specific purposes. It was more a personal message or statement than a narcissistic pose. It was to include the "I" in the act of showing and telling something.

The second example of how self-portraits were used was in relation to camera affordances themselves. It was very common for the members of the groups to photograph each other (especially in the act of photographing, see Gómez Cruz and Ardèvol 2013b). Nevertheless, when they were alone (and the light, scenery or equipment available "required" a model), or when they were bored and/or wanted to experiment with a technique or develop an idea right away, they used to take self-portraits. As one of my informants told me: "you yourself are the most available and diligent model you can find." The other side of this argument was the common suggestion, by the photographers, that their equipment (both cameras and/ or lenses, software, computers or platforms) constantly "push them" to keep shooting (see Cohen 2005). This was either because of their investment in equipment (that was understood as a waste if not fully used), or because their presence was "needed" on social media, because they wanted to learn more techniques (to "fully dominate the functions") or because they wanted "to be ready for when the important photos come."

This practice opens up another important stream of thinking. On the one hand, it suggests the co-dependence (and importance, in different moments) between the elements in the sociotechnical network of digital photography (camera affordances, discourses about what photography is and photographers are, social media affordances, etc.). This co-dependence shaped a practice that acquired its full meaning when it was performed over and over again. The constant practice, in return, generated more "obligations" (as in connections, reciprocations, status in the platforms, etc.) to the extent that more photos generated more communication and increasing communication needed more visual elements for the exchange. It was an iterative and repetitive practice. All of this was happening while the iPhone (as the first cameraphone that required a data plan to be purchased as a prerequisite) burst onto the market, creating a new category for mobiles: smartphones.

But let us get back to the three examples mentioned before. If we read into the images of these three different examples, we could observe three different forms of self-portraits, the first more aesthetically traditional, the second more candid and the third depicting the photographer as the main element of the image. While it could be argued that the images are three different forms of the same genre, the meanings that different people understood were radically different (and, even for the same people, the practice changed depending on the context). Given this, I argue that, as in Emma's case, the reflexive practice of self-portraiture was indeed a rearticulation of traditional self-portraiture in painting and photography and its politics (see, for example, Jones 2014). Nevertheless, the second and third are examples of how photographers shoot self-portraits in order to show themselves in a specific context, out of boredom or to visually share a message. These last two, I suggest, had their roots, as an action, in practices of mediated communication already present in the text-based era, and therefore represent a different genealogy of what constitutes a selfie (see Gómez Cruz and Thornham 2015). Selfies, as a series of sociotechnical practices, are more complex than what can be inferred from the images. Digital ethnography helps us to account for those complexities.

By using the phenomenon of selfies as an example of the nuances that digital ethnography can find, I revisited an ethnographic fieldwork, using it as an archive. I did this to convey two main arguments: on the one hand, the potential of ethnography to find the nuances in digital practices instead of reinforcing concepts to deploy digital phenomena—by focusing too much attention on traceable and easy-to-collect data, we are probably missing several points on how people feel, think, use, perceive and adopt digital media in their lives. This is the main strength of ethnography and its potential to intervene in the discussions regarding digital culture. The second argument has to do with how an ethnographic digital fieldwork is never entirely over, nor dead, and this challenges our understanding of ethnography (see Pink et al. 2016). The possibility of coming back, revisiting, recoding and reinterpreting raw observations is there and it opens its potential as an archive,[9] especially in order to give historical context to current phenomena (or current context to the history; see Miller and Horst 2012).

Conclusion

In this brief chapter I revisited my past fieldwork to argue that some conditions that configured the development (and success) of selfies as a core element in online interactions were developed and shaped in early text-based practices. Selfies, I suggested, represent the convergence of distinct trajectories, from the tradition of self-portraiture in painting and photography to the use of SMS and textual online practices. It is through a careful observation of photographic practices that different genealogies are revealed, turning past fieldwork into a useful tool for contextualizing the emergence of present phenomena. This has important implications for the relationship between methods and objects. Digital ethnography does not necessarily mean ethnography of the new. What seems to be relevant is not (only) what new assemblages are formed with the digital but how the digital reminds us, by showing these transformations, that what we considered immobile was indeed only one assemblage of the many possible (Miller and Horst 2012; Pink et al. 2016).

In this sense, and returning to selfies as an example, the selfie—as a practice—has its roots in several mediated forms of communication and it is obvious that it has ramifications in many others. Selfie, as a concept, is an oversimplification of a very complex set of practices and materialities. A scholar following the history of self-portraiture could probably reach selfies as a topic as much as an engineer doing work in optical sensors and an anthropologist studying forms of online communication. It is not the new that needs to be studied but using the new to ask better questions about what has always been there. Moreover, ethnography, digital or not, is an essential tool to think through the relationship between people and algorithms, from the people's point of view. In this way, ethnography can also be understood as an epistemic intervention into how knowledge is constructed, going beyond representational approaches that claim to read and infer from a single element (i.e. pictures).

Notes

1 I thank Helen Thornham for her comments and suggestions on this text.
2 I was, by no means, the first one to think about digital or mobile photography. Texts like those of Lister (1995) or Mitchell (1992) had already signaled these changes a decade before I became interested in the topic, and in both Scandinavia and Japan there were pioneer scholars actively researching mobile images at the beginning of the century. Nevertheless, the co-constitution between photography and Internet practices was at its peak, at least in Spain and the UK where I did the majority of my fieldwork.
3 Although originally coined by the studies of Human-Computer Interaction and first used in the context of digital photography by Rubinstein and Sluis (2008), I used the concept as a "theoretical scaffold" to signal the changes in the field of photography, from a "Kodak Culture" to a "Networked Image" (see Gómez Cruz 2012).
4 Onlife ethnography has two different meanings, both useful and necessary for digital ethnographies. On the one hand, it tries to bridge, by following the practices, the online and the offline. However, a second meaning emerges as well; onlife also accounts for the relationship between the researcher's own life and their role as an ethnographer, not only as part of the ethnographic reflexivity but also as a way to engage and make a personal commitment to the others.
5 See www.selfieresearchers.com/
6 For a comprehensive description of how the fieldwork was carried out and the decisions made, see Gómez Cruz and Ardèvol (2013a, 2013b).
7 It is important to notice the nomenclature: on Facebook there are "friends," "followers" and "likes," in Flickr there are "contacts" and "favorites." These names, constructed along with algorithmic decisions, shape specific forms of interaction and, ultimately, of use of the system.
8 Images, of course, as circulating documents that are untethered to the practices also *do* mean in particular aesthetic ways. However, for me, this reveals a key paradox and one that relates to selfies as phenomena.
9 I want to thank Adolfo Estalella for pointing me in this direction and for the reference to Marcus' text.

References

Bourdieu, Pierre. 1996[1964]. *Photography: A Middle-Brow Art*. Stanford, CA: Stanford University Press.
Bräuchler, Birgit, and John Postill. 2010. *Theorising Media and Practice*. Oxford: Berghahn Books.
Chalfen, Richard. 1987. *Snapshot Versions of Life*. Bowling Green, OH: Bowling Green State University Popular Press.
Cohen, Kris R. 2005. "What does the photoblog want?" *Media, Culture & Society* 27(6): 883–901.
Floridi, Luciano. 2009. "Web 2.0 vs. the Semantic Web: A philosophical assessment." *Episteme* 6(1): 25–37.
Gómez Cruz, Edgar. 2012. *De la Cultura Kodak a la Imagen en Red. Una etnografía de fotografía digital*. Barcelona: Editorial UOC.
—— 2016. "Photo-genic assemblages: Photography as a connective interface." In *Digital Photography in Everyday Life: Empirical Studies on Material Visual Practices*, edited by Edgar Gómez Cruz and Asko Lehmuskallio, 228–42. London: Routledge.
Gómez Cruz, Edgar, and Elisenda Ardèvol. 2013a. "Ethnography and the field in media(ted) settings: A practice theory approach." *Westminster Papers in Communication and Culture* 9(3): 27–46.
——. 2013b. "Performing photography practices in everyday life: Some ethnographic notes on a Flickr group." *Photographies* 6(1): 35–44.
Gómez Cruz Edgar, and Helen Thornham. 2015. "Selfies beyond self-representation: The (theoretical) f(r)ictions of a practice." *Journal of Aesthetics & Culture* 7.

Hand, Martin. 2008. *Making Digital Cultures: Access, Interactivity, and Authenticity*. Aldershot: Ashgate Publishing, Ltd.

———. 2012. *Ubiquitous Photography*. Cambridge: Polity.

Hine, Christine. 2015. *Ethnography for the Internet: Embedded, Embodied and Everyday*. London: Bloomsbury Publishing.

Jones, Amelia. 2014. "The 'eternal return': Self-portrait photography as a technology of embodiment." *Signs* 40(1): 947–78.

Koskinen, Ilpo, Esko Kurvinen, Turo-Kimmo Lehtonen, Juha Kaski, Nely Keinänen, and Kimmo Absetz. 2002. *Mobile Image*. Helsinki: Edita, IT Press.

Lister, Martin. 1995. *The Photographic Image in Digital Culture*. London: Routledge.

Marcus, George E. 1998. "The once and future ethnographic archive." *History of the Human Sciences* 11(4): 49–63.

Miller, Daniel, and Heather Horst. 2012. "The digital and the human: A prospectus for digital anthropology." In *Digital Anthropology*, edited by Heather Horst and Daniel Miller, 3–35. London: Berg.

Mitchell, William J. 1992. *The Reconfigured Eye: Visual Truth in the Post-photographic Era*. Cambridge, MA: MIT Press.

Pink, Sarah, Heather Horst, John Postill, Larissa Hjorth, Tania Lewis, and Jo Tacchi. 2016. *Digital Ethnography: Principles and Practice*. London: Sage.

Rubinstein, Daniel, and Katrina Sluis. 2008. "A life more photographic: Mapping the networked image." *Photographies* 1(1): 9–28.

Shwartz, Dona. 1986. "Camera clubs and fine art photography: The social construction of an elite code." *Journal of Contemporary Ethnography* 15(2): 165–95.

Senft, Theresa M., and Nancy Baym. 2015. "Selfies introduction—What does the selfie say? Investigating a global phenomenon." *International Journal of Communication* 9: 1–19.

Slater, Don. 1995. "Domestic photography and digital culture." In *The Photographic Image in Digital Culture*, edited by Martin Lister, 129–46. London: Routledge.

———. 1998. "Trading sexpics on IRC: Embodiment and authenticity on the Internet." *Body & Society* 4(4): 91–117.

Striphas, Ted. 2015. "Algorithmic culture." *European Journal of Cultural Studies* 18(4–5): 395–412.

Tiidenberg, Katrin, and Edgar Gómez Cruz. 2015. "Selfies, image and the re-making of the body." *Body & Society* 21(4): 77–102.

28

MOBILE FILMMAKING

Marsha Berry

Introduction

Imagine a world without smartphones. It is as hard as imagining a world without cars, without electricity, and indeed without movies. Yet smartphones have been around for only a little over a decade. A Gallup poll in July 2015 reported that nearly half of smartphone users in the USA could not imagine life without it according to Lydia Saad (2015, n.p.). Over the past decade, mobile media has completely changed our emotional and social cartographies in ways that we now take for granted. Mobile media has also pushed filmmaking and photography into new terrains where old ways of working are being profoundly challenged. In his review of a decade of mobile phone filmmaking, Schleser argues that the accessibility to filmmaking technology has clearly increased through the ubiquity of mobile phones and smartphones and that this, in turn, is "shaping not only new modes of film production but also modes of consumption, distribution, and exhibition, by embedding these digital stories in network media" (Schleser 2014b, 155). Schleser concludes his review of mobile moving-image practice to claim that smartphones "provide prospects for the twenty-first century citizen to develop innovative and imaginative cultural competencies" (2014b, 167).

The proliferation of smartphone camera applications means that tools and editing techniques once only available to professionals are now readily accessible. We can all be mobile filmmakers now, provided we have smartphones, video-editing applications, and are prepared to play in mobile media ecologies. This has had a substantial impact on what it means to be a filmmaker and on the art of filmmaking itself. Felipe Cardona observes that ready access to filmmaking technology has the potential to disrupt more traditional aesthetics:

> Today, when YouTube allows any user to upload and exhibit his or her videos to the world, there is the possibility that uninitiated users and producers of video material can dare to take montage to its limits . . . New technology and workflow democratisation allows end users, now prosumers, to teach television channels, film studios, and even mainstream record labels, the future course of music, film, and television.
>
> (Cardona 2014, n.p.)

Not only has the smartphone disrupted traditional ways of making films, but also there are some indications that mobile filmmaking is starting to become more and more mainstream.

Indicators of this wider acceptance include the rise of film festivals and participatory art projects dedicated to films and video art made with mobile devices (see, for example, Disposable Film Festival, Cinephone International Smartphone Shortfilm Festival, iPhone Film Festival, Mobile Innovation Network Australasia Film Festival); the fact that films made on mobile devices are now included in prominent film festivals such as Sundance (for example, *Tangerine* was a hit at Sundance in 2015 and was shot on an iPhone 5S); and that films professionally made on smartphones now feature in advertising campaigns such as the Bentley *Intelligent Details* advertisement. This is occurring contemporaneously with the emergence of participatory media cultures fueled by social media.

In this chapter I locate mobile filmmaking practices using mobile media ecologies as a working concept to unpack some key implications of these for creative practice. I use digital ethnography as a way to uncover some of the dynamics of mobile media ecologies and the materiality of filmmaking practices within and for these ecologies.

The chapter has four sections. The first section provides a brief overview of how the idea of co-presence shapes mobile media environments and forms; the second section focuses on five mobile filmmakers whose works engage with some of these ethnographic aspects; the third section explores the new opportunities afforded by participatory cultures; and the final section provides some concluding remarks.

Being Co-present in Mobile Media Ecologies

The word ecology implies an environment or ecosystem in which we live, that surrounds and affects what we do in our everyday lives, and that it also affected and shaped by our actions. Postman and McLuhan both regarded media as environments "in which individuals live like fish do in water" (Scolari 2012, 206). In 2000, Postman put forward the idea that the term media ecology also suggests "we were not simply interested in media, but in the ways in which the interaction between media and human beings give a culture its character and, one might say, help a culture to maintain symbolic balance" (Postman 2000, 11). So how does this metaphor contribute toward a better understanding of contemporary mobile filmmaking practices and opportunities?

A relational approach to mobile filmmaking, which considers the significance of emergent socialities and visualities rather than one focused primarily on the technology itself, can offer different perspectives to think about opportunities for practice. In order to better understand mobile filmmaking practices it is important to acknowledge the ways that smartphones also shape and inform our day-to-day social practices and facilitate new modes of self-expression. Social practices and communications are adapted in order to fit within the parameters of constantly changing networked media ecologies.

Mobile media ecologies contain complex social contexts where time zones and diverse cultures converge and these may well disrupt symbolic balances. Networked socialities across time zones and between people of diverse backgrounds are commonplace. The lines between online and offline can be difficult to distinguish through the ubiquity of both smartphones and mobile media. According to Postill and Pink, the distinction between online and offline is problematic, so they advocate that to understand the impacts of social media we need to look at how "research participants navigate their wider social, material and technological worlds" (2012, 123). Their insight from the field of digital ethnography is of benefit to a clearer understanding of how relationships between people and social media platforms affect the production and consumption of mobile video.

Mobile filmmaking inhabits messy media ecologies that are constantly shifting and changing where the circulation of creative expressions is overlaid with social relations. Another valuable insight into mobile media ecologies for mobile filmmaking that can be drawn from research and theories in digital ethnography is that of networked co-presence.

Networked co-presence is a theoretical concept building upon the centrality of co-presence to the analysis of social interaction. In his seminal text *Behavior in Public Places* (1963), Goffman analyzed contexts of co-presence. An awareness of being in the physical presence of other people is essential to understanding how co-presence influences our behavior because "persons must sense that they are close enough to be perceived in whatever they are doing, including their experiencing of others, and close enough to be perceived in this sensing of being perceived" (Goffman 1963, 17). According to Goffman, all face-to-face interactions and encounters have physical co-presence as a given. However, definitions of co-presence have been expanded beyond physical face-to-face contexts since the proliferation of mobile phones.

New kinds of co-presence have been observed by ethnographers and media scholars (see, for example, Ito 2005; Horst and Miller 2012; Pink and Hjorth 2012; Postill and Pink 2012; Jenkins 2009) in mobile media ecologies where physical co-presence is no longer a given because online and offline cartographies are clustered together. In a groundbreaking study in 2005, Ito demonstrated the importance of co-presence to sociality through her ethnography into how Japanese youth used mobile phones to include physically absent friends in social gatherings. For example, a group of girls shopping for clothes would include a physically absent friend by asking her opinion of a particular item through text messages and photos. Co-presence here is not predicated on face-to-face presence but, rather, it is created through networked communication including visual images between the interlocutors.

People share moments as they are out and about with their social circles using social media to engage in a networked sociality (Wittel 2001). Banal and routine details such as the weather, and what they are eating or drinking are shared in social media on a habitual or routine basis. Such practices can be regarded as examples of "emplaced visuality" (Pink and Hjorth 2012). Anyone can easily observe examples of networked and emplaced visualities that assume networked or electronic co-presence on social media timelines where people post, share, "like," and comment on each other's photographs and videos. Networked co-present situations and gatherings do provide a powerful impetus for the evolution of social interactions and new visualities and this impetus also plays an important part in the evolution of mobile filmmaking beyond considerations of semiotics and representation within mobile media ecologies.

Co-presence can be viewed as an underlying attribute of mobile media ecologies that motivates social and communicative needs for new forms of phatic communication and creative visual vernaculars. Non-representational dimensions of visual images and video in mobile media ecologies often include phatic functions as well as phenomenological aspects to acknowledge that these ecologies are shared by people who may co-present with each other. Phatic communication can be conceived of as "a type of speech in which ties of union are created by a mere exchange of words" (Malinowski 1923, 151). Its main purpose is to create a rapport between interlocutors and can be seen as a sort of social glue. Numerous studies analyze the role of phatic communication in social media (see, for example, Radovanovic and Ragnedda 2012; Marwick and boyd 2010; Horst and Miller 2012).

A detailed review of these studies is beyond the scope of this chapter but to underscore the significance of phatic communication for mobile filmmaking practices, I turn to Radovanovic and Ragnedda who observe "the relevance of the phatic function of microposts is emerging as a form of online intimacy and of social connections in social networks" (2012, 13). The desire for intimacy and social connection where the presence of others is acknowledged also gives rise to the formation of vernaculars that are not only creative expressions but also serve to strengthen social ties between people.

We can see this operating in social media timelines through visual vernaculars and cultural memes such as "lol cats." Burgess (2008, 215) describes vernacular creativity as "both an ideal and an heuristic device, to describe and illuminate creative practices that emerge from highly particular and non-elite social contexts and communicative conventions." Through emplaced visuality and networked sociality, visual images and video can function as an idiomatic visual language or creative vernacular to enhance a sense of social connection and intimacy.

Playing in Mobile Media Ecologies

We might think about filmmaking in and for mobile media ecologies simply from a perspective that focuses on representational dimensions. However, such perspective fails to account for the dynamic richness and materiality of mobile media ecologies and the ever-changing media practices they enable. So what do mobile media ecologies and smartphone cameras offer filmmakers? To better understand both the potentials and challenges for playing creatively with smartphone video in complex media environments, we should consider the implications of mobility itself along with networked co-presence. Cresswell (2010), a cultural geographer, proposes that we look at mobility as three elements or threads that are bound together—movement through the physical world, representations of movement, and practice as an embodied phenomenon. Mobility as defined by Cresswell (2010) provides a useful frame for conceptualizing filmmaking practices in environments overlaid with mobile media and where access to cameras might be taken for granted.

To elaborate further, in mobile media ecologies, people are often moving through physical environments that are separated by time zones and geography yet at the same time they are connected with each other through networked technologies in material ways. Mobility, then, is fundamental to mobile media ecologies along with co-presence and can offer filmmakers novel and playful ways to think about how the "parameters of the camera phone" (Berry and Schleser 2014, 5) can inspire new creative practices.

If we look at the community of practice of mobile filmmakers we can observe that many of these play on Cresswell's (2010) three aspects of mobility. The ability to experiment with smartphone camera apps and share any resulting moving images through social media with location-based overlays has given rise to new ways of communicating visually using smartphones and other networked mobile devices in our everyday social interactions. In this section, I look at the work of four mobile filmmakers to see how they play out their practices in mobile media ecologies. While the mobile films produced by these four filmmakers are diverse and engage with different subject matters, they share concerns with the materiality of everyday practices with mobile phone cameras and can be viewed as having some qualities of digital ethnography, in that they engage with cultural dimensions of what it means to be mobile with a camera phone.

Dean Keep, a mobile media artist who has been making short evocative films about his lived experiences with camera phones for the past decade, like Palmer (2012), has argued that in the decade 2004–2014, the camera phone has reconfigured our relationship to photography so that narratives of everyday life can be collected and shared "promoting a 'liquid aesthetic' whereby changes in technology, as well as our relationship with personal computing, may be understood as key drivers which shape image making practices" (Keep 2014, 23).

Experimentation with mobile media aesthetics also permeates the work of Max Schleser, a filmmaker who has also studied mobile devices as creative tools over the past decade.

He has explored the *keitai* (Japanese for mobile phone) aesthetic in his work (see Schleser 2014a, 2014b) and has recently turned his attention to the selfie phenomenon and its implications for mobile filmmaking. He proposes that selfies are all about the present tense whereby they are not taken for posterity but rather their function is to engage in conversations in social media timelines. He argues that selfies and documentaries made on smartphones not only produce new filmmaking genres but also extend autobiography and life writing as creative practices. He submits that

> as a narrative strategy mobile media can enable personal and intimate storytelling in a self-reflexive and self-representational style utilizing the mobility and pocket format of mobile devices. This adds a quality to the contemporary mediascape, which can be positioned on the opposite spectrum of 4K digital cinematography and contemporary broadcast cameras.

> (Schleser 2014b, 155)

To put it another way, mobile filmmaking moves beyond the purely representational aspects of filmmaking techniques and practices into phenomenological domains, where the implications of having constant access to the means of filmmaking and image capture are manifested through tangible creative expressions and works that engage with and reflect local and personal conditions. Mobile filmmaking then takes on elements of autoethnography, which Ellis et al. have defined as a combination of autobiography and ethnography that seeks "to produce aesthetic and evocative thick descriptions of personal and interpersonal experience" (Ellis et al. 2010, n.p.). It provides a way to move beyond more traditional forms of biographical writing and documentary filmmaking to embrace the opportunities afforded by social media.

Themes of local and the personal experience are also evident in Patrick Kelly's films and creative practice research. He argues that the "development and rapid uptake of platforms and applications to capture and share video are generating emergent practices associated with social media, presenting new opportunities for filmmakers to explore different contexts" (Kelly 2014b, n.p.). His creative practice research expands on debates about the apparently ever-increasing space taken up by mobile media in everyday life. In his autoethnographic film *North*, screened at the MINA 3rd International Mobile Innovation Screening, Kelly acknowledges traditional filmmaking genres and forms and uses these as playful, and sometimes ironic counterpoints to the new creative vernaculars associated with emplaced visuality and sociality. He used the mobile video-sharing platform Instagram to reflexively engage with his experiences while moving through Melbourne as a juxtaposition of moments. Kelly suggests mobile filmmakers "might discover the emergence of even more contexts and auratic experiences" (2014a, 136) because of the inherent "juxtapositioning nature" (2014a, 136) of contemporary mobile media platforms. *North* focuses on the mobility of the self as both the subject and object of enquiry to provide a fruitful interrogation of selfies as a contemporary social phenomenon.

Kossoff, an artist filmmaker, suggests that the mobile phone "allows us to imagine that we are part of the flow of everyday life" and argues that mobile phones may now be seen as an "inherent part of the event, as theorized by Alain Badiou" (Kossoff 2014, 40), where the event is tied to a zeitgeist and some kind of unpredictable and major social, political, or personal disruption (Badiou and Žižek 2010). He sees mobile phones as double edged where they are both "an object of desire" (Kossoff 2014, 43) that can give us a type of agency in the world, yet at the same time they are "a fetish that obscures us from the world" (Kossoff 2014, 43). In his film, *Moscow Diary* (2011), Kossoff revisits the streets and buildings in Moscow, which

Benjamin mentions in his famous diary from his visit to Moscow in 1926–27. The film, shot on a mobile phone camera, engages with the modernist notion of a *flâneur* as an "urban wanderer who individualizes time and space by remaining outside of the metropolitan crowds and the cut and thrust of the city" (Kossoff 2014, 39). This work has elements of evocative autoethnography as explicated by Ellis et al. as he entwines his lived experience with Benjamin's diary entries "to produce aesthetic and evocative thick descriptions of personal and interpersonal experience" (Ellis et al. 2010, n.p.). The three aspects of mobility here play out through an intricate braided narrative to bring in a fourth aspect of collapsed time that both obscures and enhances his movements through contemporary Moscow.

Mobility as theorized by Cresswell (2010) along with networked co-presence operates within mobile media ecologies where practices that could be described as emplaced visuality are becoming increasingly taken for granted. Mobility has become a dominant theme in contemporary mobile filmmaking as filmmakers grapple with the extreme accessibility of cameras and the implications of playing with their practice in mobile media ecologies. In the next section, I examine some of the implications of the emergence of cultures of participation and illustrate how social media has expanded forms of mobile filmmaking into new directions.

Participating in Mobile Media Ecologies

In 2008, Jenkins proposed that a new form of culture with participation as its hallmark was emerging through the use of social media and Web 2.0 technologies. Such cultural phenomena have had a profound influence on both the production and consumption of media including film and photography. Vickers puts it this way: "Online and social media platforms offer a means for participation, collaboration and distribution or dissemination that was unimaginable even a decade ago" (Vickers 2013, 139).

Emergent visualities and socialities (Pink and Hjorth 2012) in social media encourage people to participate actively with new and remediated (Bolter and Grusin 1999) forms of video and photography, in complex media ecologies where people can move seamlessly between physical and social media environments. Through our routine entanglements with mobile computing and social media, participatory cultures have arisen where anyone with a smartphone can make, geotag, and share photographs and films that, in turn, can shape creative vernaculars.

In the introductory chapter to *The Mobile Story*, Farman (2014) notes that mobile locative media disrupt the ways in which we think about the production and distribution of narratives because "emerging mobile stories are multivoiced, layered, situated and tell important (and often contradictory) narratives about a place and what it means to live in that space" (Farman 2014, 15). They also engage with Bauman's paradox of contemporary social interactions where "Distance is no obstacle to getting in touch, but getting in touch is no obstacle to staying apart" (Bauman 2003, 62).

While Bauman claims that the "advent of virtual proximity renders human connections simultaneously more frequent and more shallow, more intense and more brief" (Bauman 2003, 61), I would argue that it is this very paradox that makes social media so rich in opportunities for creative practice. It is easy to join and to leave collaborative projects that occur within mobile media ecologies. The participatory mobile media film projects I present in this section show locative media overlays combined with physical places to create polyphonic narrative collages that traverse both time zones and geography.

The following extract taken from my Facebook timeline in May 2013 is an invitation from Iceberg Fernandez for mobile filmmakers to participate in a collaborative project, *NOW&HERE = EVERYWHERE.*

NOW&HERE = EVERYWHERE is a Quantum Filmmaking project, participatory mobile phone cinema, celebrating cultural diversity, in which you can collaborate with your mobile phone.[1]

The project is part of Fernandez's PhD study at the University College of the Arts, London and is an excellent example of how research can be disseminated and integrated into the everyday life of people other than the candidate or researcher. While this project is not explicitly ethnography, it does show how creative practice research can contribute to the emerging and growing field of digital ethnography because it does engage with, and is dependent on, digital co-presence (Hjorth and Pink 2014) and virtual proximity (Bauman 2003).

We can see Bauman's paradox of virtual proximity at play in this creative project, and in this case exploited by an artist to create a new work through emplaced visuality. Participation is low risk in the sense that it can end "without leftovers and lasting sediments" because it relies on a virtual proximity, which can "both substantively and metaphorically, be ended with nothing more than the push of a button" (Bauman 2003, 62). While Bauman laments virtual proximity as being a cause of weakening social bonds, within the context of participatory art projects it provides a condition to enable greater access for those who would like to become involved with global locative media projects to express a point of view within predefined parameters.

The *NOW&HERE = EVERYWHERE* project has strong resonances with Schleser's (2013) *24 Frames 24 Hours* project as well with Vicker's (2013) interactive documentary project *24-hours.in*. Schleser's *24 Frames 24 Hours* project (see Schleser and Turnbridge 2013) aimed to capture life and a perception of place in different cities over a 24-hour period, and has developed into a dynamic website)[2] where visitors are encouraged to contribute their work and are provided with tutorial so they can access clips from parts of the world that interest them. The collaboration was between students at Te Papa Museum, Massey University, New Zealand and the University of Padeborn in Germany. Forty-three filmmakers working only with mobile phone cameras created 23 two-minute videos. Online videoconferences were used to workshop ideas and provide feedback. The videos produced were pinned to a Google map so that viewers can see exactly where they were shot. Location-based technology provided the film producers with an innovative way to present their work that moves away from more traditional linear show reels and where the viewers can order the films according to geographic location. In this way, the project invites viewers to become digital wayfarers (Hjorth and Pink 2014) who can trace paths to create their own journeys through *24 Frames 24 Hours*.

The idea of gathering together filmed expressions of mobility over a 24-hour time frame across global time zones using location-based technology is emerging as a dominant trope in contemporary mobile filmmaking. Vickers's *24-hours.in*[3] is another example. *24-hours.in* is inspired and underpinned by Vertovian ideas of the camera lens standing in for the biological eyes offering new perspectives on commonplace sights and is inspired by Baudelaire's *flâneur*. The project exploits the assemblages of smartphones and networked technology to pick up the threads left by Vertov's montage techniques to offer contemporary insights into life in our cities where montages can be created from "fleeting moments of existence of the 'I' and the 'non-I' with an immediacy and scale never before possible" (Vickers 2013, 142). Like Schleser, Vickers also uses a map to show the film locations.

Participatory art and digital storytelling projects such as the three examples cited above are extending the field of documentary filmmaking into new areas. In these projects, "we see an emplaced visuality that creates and reflects, unique forms of geospatial sociality" (Hjorth and

Pink 2014, 54) through a kind of no strings attached virtual proximity and co-presence. The three participatory mobile filmmaking projects chosen as illustrative examples in this section also connect with the idea of digital wayfaring as theorized by Hjorth and Pink:

> [T]the digital wayfarer as we conceptualize her or him does not simply weave her or his way around the material physical world. Rather, their trajectory entangles online and offline as they move through the weather and the air, with the ground underfoot and surrounded by people and things, while also traversing digital maps, social·networking sites, and other online elements.
>
> (2014, 45–6)

Concluding Remarks

To better understand how mobile filmmaking fits within the broader ecologies of mobile media, we need analytic scaffolds and methods that can address the non-representational aspects of filmmaking to focus on filmmaking practices as well as the ecologies within which mobile films and photographs circulate. Digital ethnography—with its anthropological and sociological underpinnings—provides strong conceptual frames through which mobile media ecologies might be viewed and understood. Wayfaring, co-presence, and mobility are concepts drawn from digital ethnography through which filmmaking can be reimagined. Through these ethnographic frames we can see that photography and filmmaking are a way of participating in networked socialities and emplaced visualities. We can observe how ecosystems may form around a collaborative and participatory media project exploiting the Internet's inherent logics of participation, sociability, and replicability (Shifman 2007) to generate new visual vernaculars that are in constant flux.

Our ability to document our movements through everyday life has shifted how we think about film and photography. Mobile media has disrupted traditional media distribution power relationships to open up new expressive potentials as we collectively grapple with the everyday realities of networked co-presence, virtual proximity, and what these can mean for our everyday social activities and rituals. According to Bauman we live in a world of uncertainties, flux, and change, a world that he terms as a "liquid" modernity where "the conditions under which its members act change faster than it takes the ways of acting to consolidate into habits and routines" (Bauman 2005, 1). I started this chapter with a challenge to imagine a world without smartphones. The difficulty of doing this is a testament to the fact that social practices are agile and adaptable. As new technologies emerge, we evolve our practices and aesthetics to embrace them. Digital ethnography provides a useful lens through which these emerging everyday creative practices and evolving aesthetics might be understood.

Notes

1 See www.now-here-everywhere.org.uk
2 See www.24frames24hours.org
3 See www.24hours-in.lincoln.ac.uk/

References

Badiou, Alain and Slavoj Žižek. *Philosophy in the Present*. Cambridge: Polity Press.
Bauman, Zigmund. 2003. *Liquid Love: On the Frailty of Human Bonds*. Cambridge: Polity Press.
——. 2005. *Liquid Life*. Cambridge: Polity Press.

Berry, Marsha and Max Schleser. 2014. "Creative Mobile Media: The State of Play." In *Mobile Media Making in an Age of Smartphones*, edited by Marsha Berry and Max Schleser, 1–9. New York: Palgrave Macmillan.

Bolter, J. David and Richard A. Grusin. 1999. *Remediation*. Cambridge, MA: MIT Press.

Burgess, Jean. 2008. "'All Your Chocolate Rain Are Belong to Us?' Viral Video, Youtube and the Dynamics of Participatory Culture." In *The Video Vortex Reader*, edited by Geert Lovink and Sabine Niederer, 101–11. Amsterdam: Institute of Network Cultures.

Cardona, Felipe. 2014. "Videoloop: A New Edition Form." *Journal of Creative Technologies*. Special Issue 4, https://ctechjournal.aut.ac.nz/paper/videoloop-new-edition-form/ (accessed November 20, 2015).

Cresswell, Tim. 2010. "Towards a Politics of Mobility." *Environment and Planning D: Society and Space* 28(1): 17–31.

Ellis, Carolyn, Tony E. Adams and Arthur P. Bochner. 2010. "Autoethnography: An Overview [40 paragraphs]." *Forum Qualitative Sozialforschung/Forum: Qualitative Social Research* 12(1), Art. 10. http://nbn-resolving.de/urn:nbn:de:0114-fqs1101108 (accessed January 28, 2016).

Farman, Jason. 2014. "Site-Specificity, Pervasive Computing, and the Reading Interface." In *The Mobile Story: Narrative Practices with Locative Technologies*, edited by Jason Farman, 3–16. New York: Routledge.

Fernandez, Iceberg. 2015. "Now&Here = Everywhere." www.now-here-everywhere.org.uk/ (accessed July 20, 2015).

Goffman, Erving. 1963. *Behavior in Public Places: Notes on the Social Organization of Gatherings*. New York: The Free Press.

Hjorth, Larissa and Sarah Pink. 2014. "New Visualities and the Digital Wayfarer: Reconceptualizing Camera Phone Photography and Locative Media." *Mobile Media & Communication* 2(1): 40–57.

Horst, Heather A. and Daniel Miller. 2012. "The Digital and the Human: A Prospectus for Digital Anthropology." In *Digital Anthropology*, edited by Heather Horst and Daniel Miller, 3–35. London: Bloomsbury.

Ito, Mizuko. 2005. "Introduction: Personal, Portable, Pedestrian." In *Personal, Portable, Pedestrian: Mobile Phones in Japanese Life*, edited by Mizuko Ito, Daisuke Okabe and Misa Matsuda, 1–16. Cambridge, MA: MIT Press.

Jenkins, Henry. 2009. *Confronting the Challenges of Participatory Culture: Media Education for the 21st Century*. Cambridge, MA: The MIT Press.

Keep, Dean. 2014. "Artist with a Camera-Phone: A Decade of Mobile Photography." In *Mobile Media Making in an Age of Smartphones*, edited by Marsha Berry and Max Schleser, 14–24. New York: Palgrave Macmillan.

Kelly, Patrick. 2013. *North*. Directed by Patrick Kelly. Australia: Patrick Kelly. MINA 3rd International Mobile Innovation Screening. DVD.

——. 2014a. "Slow Media Creation and the Rise of Instagram." In *Mobile Media Making in an Age of Smartphones*, edited by Marsha Berry and Max Schleser, 129–38. New York: Palgrave Macmillan.

——. 2014b. "Mobile Video Platforms and the Presence of Aura." *Journal of Creative Technologies*, Special Issue 4. https://ctechjournal.aut.ac.nz/paper/mobile-video-platforms-presence-aura/ (accessed November 21, 2015).

Kossoff, Adam. 2014. "The Mobile Phone and the Flow of Things." In *Mobile Media Making in an Age of Smartphones*, edited by Marsha Berry and Max Schleser, 35–44. New York: Palgrave Macmillan.

Malinowski, Bronislaw. 1923. "The Problem of Meaning in Primitive Languages." In *The Meaning of Meaning*, edited by Charles K. Ogden and Ivor A. Richards, 146–52. London: Routledge and Kegan Paul.

Marwick, Alice E. and danah boyd. 2010. "I Tweet Honestly, I Tweet Passionately: Twitter Users, Context Collapse, and the Imagined Audience." New Media Society, online, July 7, 2010. doi: 10.1177/1461444810365313.

Palmer, D. S. V. 2012. "iPhone Photography: Mediating Visions of Social Space." In *Studying Mobile Media: Cultural Technologies, Mobile Communication, and the iPhone*, edited by Larissa Hjorth, Jean Burgess and Ingrid Richardson, 85–97. New York: Routledge.

Pink, Sarah and Larissa Hjorth. 2012. "Emplaced Cartographies: Reconceptualising Camera Phone Practices in an Age of Locative Media." *Media International Australia* 145: 145–56.

Postill, John and Sarah Pink. 2012. "Social Media Ethnography: The Digital Researcher in a Messy Web." *Media International Australia* 145: 123–34.

Postman, Neil. 2000. "The Humanism of Media Ecology." *Proceedings of the Media Ecology Association* 1: 10–16. http://w.media-ecology.org/publications/MEA_proceedings/v1/postman01.pdf (accessed October 10, 2015).

Radovanovic, Danica and Massimo Ragnedda. 2012. "Small Talk in the Digital Age: Making Sense of Phatic Posts." Published as part of the #MSM2012 Workshop proceedings, available online as CEUR Vol-838. http://ceur-ws.org/Vol-838.

Saad, Lydia. 2015. "Nearly Half of Smartphone Users Can't Imagine Life Without It." www.gallup.com/poll/184085/nearly-half-smartphone-users-imagine-life-without.aspx?utm_source=Economy&utm_medium=newsfeed&utm_campaign=tiles (accessed October 10, 2015).

Schleser, Max. 2014a. "Connecting through Mobile Autobiographies: Self-Reflexive Mobile Filmmaking, Self Representation, and Selfies." In *Mobile Media Making in an Age of Smartphones*, edited by Marsha Berry and Max Schleser, 148–58. New York: Palgrave Pivot.

——. 2014b. "A Decade of Mobile Moving-Image Practice." In *The Routledge Companion to Mobile Media*, edited by Gerard Goggin and Larissa Hjorth, 157–70. New York and London: Routledge.

Schleser, Max and Tim Turnbridge. 2013. "24 Frames 24 Hours." *Ubiquity: The Journal of Pervasive Media* 2(1&2): 205–13.

Scolari, Carlos Alberto. 2012. "Media Ecology: Exploring the Metaphor to Expand the Theory." *Communication Theory* 22(2): 204–25.

Shifman, Limor. 2007. "Humor in the Age of Digital Reproduction: Continuity and Change in Internet-Based Comic Texts." *International Journal of Communication* 1: 187–209. http://ijoc.org/index.php/ijoc/article/viewFile/11/34 (accessed November 20, 2015).

Vickers, Richard. 2013. "Mobile Media, Participation Culture and the Digital Vernacular: 24-hours.in and the Democratization of Documentary." In *Ubiquity: The Journal of Pervasive Media*, 2(1&2): 132–45.

Wittel, Andreas. 2001. "Toward a Network Sociality." In *Theory, Culture & Society* 8(6): 51–76.

29

CURATING DIGITAL RESONANCE

Jennifer Deger

A composer is a dead man unless he composes for all the media and for his world.
(Dick Higgins, Statement on Intermedia 1966)

What if, rather than creating an archive of the already gone, digital media were used to orchestrate a renewal of life? To thicken and deepen time beyond the present? To fill the world not with data, but with a mutisensory pulse of poetry and possibility? How to extend such worlds of sensuous kinship to others? How to use digital light and colored pixels not just to draw strangers close, but to disrupt categories and easy assumptions and so to clear the way for new affinities?

The above questions refract a set of ideas that have become central to my ambitions as a practice-led anthropologist working on film and exhibition projects with Aboriginal people in north Australia. Drawing inspiration from my Yolngu collaborators—although the above is my formulation, not theirs—it is an agenda assembled from slow-gathered insights, many of which predate my practical or disciplinary affiliation to something that might be labeled digital ethnography.[1] These questions locate my epistemological concerns with the digital at the intersection of the aesthetic, ethical and ontological. By claiming the digital as much more than discrete data, or something somehow separable from the "real" or the analog, they position digital processes, and indeed digital materiality, as intensely social and potentially transformative.[2] They also signal a concern with the performative potential of digital anthropology.

In my research the study of digital media entails finding ways to appreciate, and respond to, emergent forms of Aboriginal digital audio-visual culture on something resembling the terms of their creation and circulation. Digital technologies do not just create new areas for anthropological study, they provide the means by which to extend and remix our methods: to creatively refigure the grounds of ethnographic encounter and, in the process, to recast what counts as academic knowledge.[3] Our digital films and installations do not simply *record* or *exhibit* the new media, they actively work to remediate digital images in ways that both participate with, and comment on, the cultural-historical-technological dynamics from which they arise.

In order to explore these possibilities I undertake my research as part of the new media collective called Miyarrka Media, based in the community Gapuwiyak in Australia's northeast Arnhem Land. We are a group of Yolngu and non-Indigenous filmmakers and artists (with membership varying according to the requirements of the project) who came together in 2009 specifically as a means of enabling Yolngu to use new media technologies in projects directed from a community level. Miyarrka's goal is to use media to respond to contemporary Yolngu concerns and, in the process, open up new possibilities and spaces for cultural reflection and creativity. For Miyarrka Media the digital is not only the means by which to express contemporary Yolngu social values, it is its impetus: as a life lived increasingly via screens and data networks makes available new dynamics of intermediality and relational sociality to people already attuned to poetics as creative—and participatory—acts of worldmaking.

And yet our projects are not digital by definition. Far from it. The forms of generative resonance that we pursue are of quite different order to digital poetics of remix elaborated by theorist/practitioners such as Mark Amerika (2015). While a certain recombinatorial potential enables and energizes new forms of digital media in the communities in which we work, it is not the digital *per se* that determines the underlying poetics—or the politics—that enliven these shared creative projects: the creative potentiality, and historical social urgencies, that lie at the heart of this work cannot be stripped back to code.

Over the years, as Miyarrka Media have made films and installations for local, national and international audiences, the terms that we use to describe our work to others has shifted, often in response to institutional contexts. Sometimes we say we are making art, other times we talk about a shared project of anthropology. This unstable relation to categories is productive, I think. It leads me to conclude that we are actually doing neither: as our work both challenges and extends the fields of anthropology and art, we are making up something new, something born of specifics and particularities but which opens outwards with a radically encompassing agenda informed by an approach—adapted from Yolngu ritual—to exhibition making as a mode of worldmaking.

Working under the guidance of senior community members, while at the same time consciously creating works that are distinctly new in terms of both form and content, our projects harness digital media as technologies of enlivenment and relationality, rather than as the means of cultural documentation or archiving. We use photography, video and installation as a means to renew relationships between kin and country, giving life to ancestral connections, while simultaneously generating new relationships with people and places far from home. This sense of digital media as both a profoundly connective and invigorating technology gives a defining focus, not to mention a sharpened sense of urgency, to the new forms of art and public anthropology we develop together.[4] This work is not concerned with achieving empowerment through strategies of self-representation, but rather with materializing concepts, possibilities and, indeed, a certain quality of life itself, by generating an encompassing field of resonance. (The digital's generous capacity for assemblage, remix and plain old repetition has been most accommodating in this regard.) Working with a keen awareness of the attractions of light, color and movement, our work also focuses equally on affects beyond the screen as we harness digital media to enact small, but ambitious gestures toward an ethics of affinity. In our projects difference matters, but it is never incommensurable.

While Aboriginal people are well known for their conception of an ancestrally animated world, a particular historical urgency shapes this embracing of new media—and the possibility of a shared anthropology mediated through the digital. These projects arise from a society in which poverty, welfare dependency, ill health, premature death and neo-assimilationist government policies combine to wear people down, stripping meaning and purpose from their daily lives. As clan leaders articulate the stakes of the Miyarrka Media projects in terms of life and death, both literal and otherwise—"Make everything alive" is one of the Miyarrka refrains—it allows us to understand something more about the particular stakes of contemporary Yolngu life.

In considering these stakes in relation to contemporary anthropology I appreciate what anthropologist and curator Tarek Elhaik says about the need for anthropology to find new ways forward:

> We ought to cultivate another logic: I study Y not to enact a cultural critique of X where I am from, but to do something with Y, yet to be formulated, that will be named Z. X is not bracketed, mourned, and a source of colonial guilt. Self and Other, and their blurring, are not longer useful points of departure. We are monads living in assemblages, more than subjects living in nation or region X.
>
> (Elhaik 2013, 792)

This Deleuzian formulation chimes with what I think we have been doing, at least to a point. A crucial difference is that Yolngu refuse to surrender the primacy of place as central to modes of belonging and relating. In Elhaik's formulation this would seem to make them stubbornly old-fashioned in their attachment to place as enduring cultural logic. But in this chapter, as I elaborate one version of our attempt to do something named Z (or P or W), I will argue to the contrary.

This chapter describes a Miyarrka Media exhibition called *Gapuwiyak Calling: Phone-Made Media from Aboriginal Australia* (Figure 29.1). It was conceived as an experiment in activating a Yolngu poetics of digital connection in a museum context. From the outset we knew that, in order to succeed, the exhibition had to do more than simply classify and display phone-made media as contemporary cultural artifacts from a once-remote Australian Aboriginal community. It needed also to do something more than maneuver *against* established museum practices in relation to Indigenous culture. We sought to strike a different chord to that of the postcolonial. For us, the art of curation lies in finding ways to remediate a collection of phone-made photographs and video files in ways that might give them a new life and meaning appropriate to the broader context of the American Museum of Natural History in New York. To this end, we approached this media not as individual images or films, but as exemplars of a specifically Yolngu relational dynamic.

Figure 29.1 Miyarrka Media's Paul Gurrumuruwuy introduces the exhibition. Video stills (Miyarrka Media 2014a)

We wondered if these might also serve as the means by which to generate new relations beyond Arnhem Land. Or, at least, to gesture toward this possibility. With an emphasis on material processes and aesthetic effects, we approached the exhibition as an opportunity to use mobile phones, as well as the media created with it, to instantiate new sensuous cartographies of connection.

Phone–Made Media from Arnhem Land

In 2008 the introduction of Telstra's 3G mobile networks generated a wave of creative energy across the bush communities of Australia's northeast Arnhem Land. New genres of video, photography and performance flourished. Traveling lightning-speed via satellite and Bluetooth, this digital culture rode the energy of the new and the cheeky. Moving hand-to-hand, kin-to-kin, community-to-community, it drew inspiration from both the Internet and the ancestral. It was made to be watched, to be shared, and then deleted to make way for the next.[5] So began a new era in Australian Indigenous media, a period of intensified communication and creativity in which Yolngu took up mobile phones as devices readymade to plug into networks of multi-sensuous connection that extend well beyond the signal range of talk or text.

As someone who had been working on Yolngu media projects since the days of VHS, I found myself captivated by these early photos and movies. I loved them for their wit, pixelated vitality, and garish beauty. I loved them even more for the sheer confidence and audacity with which they appeared. They had a refreshing lack of earnestness, not only because they were made *by* Yolngu *for* Yolngu, but also because they were made for fun, or out of deep affection, without the need for budgets and bureaucratic rationales. I saw these new media forms as a great example of the verve and imagination of the residents of communities so often portrayed in the national arena as sites of social dysfunction, places defined exactly by their geographic and cultural remove from metropolitan centers. And so I began storing away these tiny files, nurturing the idea of an exhibition.

From time to time I worried about this new acquisitive impulse, concerned that this was a retrogressive move compared to the practice-led methods I had been cultivating precisely against the collecting and conserving imperatives of an older anthropology. I worried too that there was something inherently disfiguring about wrenching these works out of the specific, kin-based networks through which they were made to move. But when Paul Gurrumuruwuy and his late wife Fiona Yangathu enthusiastically agreed to lead the curatorial process, the exhibition project took on a sense of shared purpose, focused around ideas distilled in the name *Gapuwiyak Calling*.

From the outset, we conceived this project as an experiment in activating a Yolngu poetics of digital connection in a museum context, knowing that in order to succeed, we had to do more than simply classify and display phone-made media as contemporary cultural artifacts or twenty-first century digital curios.[6] For the purposes of this chapter I will not discuss the various components of the exhibition (but see Deger 2016). Rather I will focus on the ways in which we designed the show to create a performative intermediality that invited visitors to experientially contemplate new trajectories of social connection.

I use the term intermedial to signal a fundamental concern with the generative spaces of betweenness: the space of poetics. As Irina Rajewsky defines the term, it designates

> those configurations which have to do with a crossing of borders between media, and which thereby can be differentiated from intra medial phenomena as well as from trans medial phenomena (i.e., the appearance of a certain motif, aesthetic, or discourse across a variety of different media).

(2005, 46)

This betweenness provides the grounds for the kinds of resonance that concern me here; and—together with the back and forth dynamics that it enables—it is this betweenness that provides the grounds for appreciating Yolngu political and social investment in digital media, in ways that challenge those who would presume that the participatory worldmaking I mentioned above should be driven by a free-for-all flow of information, endlessly remixed in intensified temporality of the now and the flattened, de-territorialized and avowedly democratic world of open access that many digital artists and theorists embrace (cf. Markham 2013; Irvine 2014).

The creation of relationships between specific people and places through acts of call-and-response is a strong organizing principle of Yolngu sociality. Ancestral stories about the creation of relations between various Yolngu clans are often figured through such performative dynamics. There are many variations on the theme in which ancestral beings signal their identity to others from specific places, thereby establishing a set of relationships between these places and the people belonging to them. For instance, in Dhuwalkitj, a Marrawungu homeland near Gapuwiyak, an ancestral hunter signaled his identity to other places and hunters by lifting up the turtle meat he had caught and showing it to other lands. In return, other ancestral hunters, standing in their own country, demonstrated their own identities in response by holding up a different kind of meat such as fish, or shark. Clans belonging to these places understand that their identities became united through the actions of these hunters and the same-but-different relationships produced through this call-and-response dynamic.

In curating *Gapuwiyak Calling* we set out to locate mobile phones within this more encompassing relational dynamic of call-and-response. After consulting with representatives of the clan responsible for the land on which Gapuwiyak was settled, we drew on the figure of Murayana, a *mokuy* ancestral trickster figure, who lives in the forest surrounding the community. Murayana is known for his special didgeridoo known as *dhadhalal* with which he called other clans to ceremony.[7]

Our first idea for the exhibition was to create a forest of phones. Visitors, attracted by the sound of ringing phones, would enter a fairly dense forest (constructed from what, we were not sure) to find, and then answer, mobile phones hanging among the trees. The act of answering the phone would trigger a series of collated media files that visitors would watch before being drawn away by the sound of another phone. It was a very literal idea. But we liked it. We liked especially that it would not be obvious from outside the forest what exactly was going on and that people would be called to enter by a curiosity and openness triggered by the sonic field produced by phones.

It was only when we found an experienced video artist-programmer to collaborate with that we discovered how difficult this would be, both in terms of setting up a network to control the very basic model flip phones that people were using in 2009 and in terms of the occupational health and safety regulations that govern museum exhibitions and public spaces.

Initially it had seemed vital to exhibit the media on the very technologies that had given rise to them. The phones made materially manifest the new vectors of connection that this media both moved through and aesthetically consolidated. These little videos and photographs after all were made to move and connect. But as it turned out, the moment we gave up on the phones as the sites of display, we found a different way to create our forest of phones.

It took us almost six years to realize the project. Over that time new genres of phone-based performance and art emerged, and sometimes also disappeared, as in the case of the "musical slideshows" produced on the now obsolete 2010 Nokia 6700, as the phones themselves have changed, and with them various media features. In 2011 Miyarrka's co-founder, Yangathu, died unexpectedly, which led to the project being set aside for several years. Then in 2013, as a new wave of photo art made possible through the cut-and-paste functions of touch phones and on-line templates and decorative functions began circulating, we started work again, this time with the help of a new generation of phone-savvy Yolngu including two of Gurrumuruwuy and Yangathu's daughters.

In the final months of preparing the show we started thinking more closely about how to address the potential for this highly contemporary media to confuse non-Yolngu audiences. We worried that the work might be taken as meaningless cultural mishmash by audiences accustomed to the somber ochres and magisterial presence of bark paintings. As a senior man with international experience as a dancer and leader of a performance troupe, Gurrumuruwuy became more determined to locate this new media within a continuum of visual and performative traditions that have their roots in *rom* (ancestral law and precedent). If the exhibition was to succeed, he said, we had to leave viewers in no doubt about the enduring significance of *rom* in contemporary Yolngu life. They needed to understand that the deliberate mixing of cultural forms on display was not to be taken as evidence of cultural decline, but rather a playful mixing of the here and the there into a new unity located in and through Yolngu bodies and imaginations. These concerns led to the inclusion of the "video call" features in the exhibition, whereby Yolngu curators would speak directly to these issues via a network accessed via the visitors' own phones.

Gapuwiyak Calling at the American Museum of Natural History

In October 2014 *Gapuwiyak Calling* was installed as a special event within Margaret Mead Film Festival at the American Museum of Natural History in New York (AMNH).[8] The show attracted over 8,000 visitors in four days and generated high levels of interest and enthusiasm from New York audiences. Whether or not they took the time to appreciate what we were trying to show and share doing is, of course, another question. There was quite a lot going on beneath the surface of digital resemblance.

The exhibition featured a range of Yolngu phone-made videos collected over the previous six years, together with a series of HD video projections, large-scale assemblages of phone-made photo collage mounted on a series of plywood panels, and a two-channel installation of our film *Ringtone* made especially as part of this project.[9]

We designed the show at the AMNH to work in the large, and often busy, spaces of the Grand Gallery. As visitors approached from the front, the most prominent image was a large-scale HD projection of forest scenes that intermittently cut to footage of young men dancing the *mokuy* to the sound of the *dhadalal*. This sound of the didgeridoo and the boys' yiiii-yiiii called out across the hall intermittently, before the speakers fell back to the low-level audio buzz of forest, leaves, water and wind.

In front of that wall sat a series of tall black plinths housing pico projectors that back-projected the phone-made videos onto small screens made of drafting paper. (The paper, while effective in budgetary terms, proved to be an error of judgment. Too many of our visitors were children—digital natives who expectantly prodded the screen, disappointed, if not confused by the simplicity of paper and projection and the lack of interactivity at this level.) Each projection used a retro phone handset as a speaker: a means, as I have said, of symbolically enacting the "answering" of Gapuwiyak's call. While for some these retro-handsets were a confusing addition to the show, for us it added another playful dimension to the "old"–"new" technology remix vibe. As the plinths visually echoed the

Figure 29.2 *Gapuwiyak Calling* at the American Museum of Natural History, New York, October 2014

trees and forest projected behind them, a *mokuy* sculpture with his own *yidaki* sat on a plinth flecked with the projected video, so casting his own shadow into the forest.

A low plinth displayed a range of favorite mobile phones valued over the years for their multimedia capacities. In this metropolitan context they looked very basic and outmoded. Nearby sat an arrangement of two monitors in a plywood structure. Visitors could settle onto benches covered with the patterned blankets from Yolngu homes to watch the two-channel version of *Ringtone*, a film we made for the exhibition about the poetics of connection enacted by one's choice of personalized ringtones.

A series of large plywood panels featured a collage of the phone-made family collages to mimetically invoke the bark paintings for which the region is known. The resemblance was not accidental. A small text on one of the boards explained that these Yolngu see these elaborate digitally decorated photographs as just the same as bark paintings.

On the back of a series of large, heavy cardboard postcards (made like this to mediate against a sense of disposability) we printed the address of the exhibition website where we had included a number of videos of the Yolngu curators explaining the processes of making the media and describing the aims of the exhibition.[10] One main explanatory text was mounted on the back of one of the plywood television cabinets:

GAPUWIYAK CALLING: phone-made media from Aboriginal Australia

A long time ago in the stringybark forests around Gapuwiyak a *mokuy* (ancestral trickster spirit) named Murayana Ganbulapula Yangbulu Burrulurrpulu made a special sound with his *dhadhalal* (didgeridoo). Echoing across the land, signalling back and forth, this sound moved the people. It reached all the clans, drawing everyone together for ceremony.

In this exhibition the *dhadhalal* calls to people and places far beyond Arnhem Land. No matter if you're American, European, Chinese, Tahitian, African, Indian, Aboriginal … this sound can connect us all together. Just like mobile phones!

Figure 29.3 Enid Gurungumi and Warren Balpatji with the "digital bark painting." American Museum of Natural History, October 2015

Modern Yolngu live in a very different world to that of the old people. Phones are everywhere. We use them out hunting, even to make video calls in ceremonies. We watch YouTube, search Google, share videos, texts and MMS; we do banking and plan rituals, all through the phone. With the phones we also create new kinds of *gamunungu* (art) and *bungul* (dance).

We curated this exhibition to share Yolngu life. We want to show that our young people are smart. They can use phones to make us laugh—and also to strengthen kinship and culture.

We named our show *Gapuwiyak Calling* because now we're calling you through our phones, calling so you can connect to us. We're grabbing hold of new possibilities using these little things. Maybe you'll answer us?

Miyarrka Media

Maybe You'll Answer?

Throughout the curatorial process we played with ideas of how we might design into the show the possibility of a formally structured response adequate to the organizing conceit. My concern, in particular, was that if there was no way for visitors to formally respond—whether through recording their spontaneous own video performance, or photography, uploaded back to a screen in Gapuwiyak—then we risked producing an inherently "one-way" call, one that short-circuited the very potentiality for relationship that we sought to highlight. I worried further that if we did not provide a means by which visitors could overtly "answer" the call, we risked the exhibition re-enacting forms of disregard and refusal symptomatic of the ongoing history of colonialism and racism that continues to shape many Yolngu encounters with people from elsewhere.

We considered a photo-booth where visitors might record a message or even a little performance to send back to Gapuwiyak via a webpage. We even considered the possibility of a two-way link to Gapuwiyak with a screen set up in the Culture and Arts Centre. Ultimately, however, all our ideas for staging a performative response to the call from Gapuwiyak felt forced and gimmicky. Gurrumuruwuy's question—maybe you'll answer?—worked better as a rhetorical gesture. Leaving the question hanging left more space for the *maybe*—and, indeed, the *maybe not*—in all of this: it enabled the show to claim both the possibility for new connection without denying the inherent economic, geographic and cultural gaps that, at other levels, so profoundly define and delimit relationships between Gapuwiyak and New York, new technologies notwithstanding.

And so *Gapuwiyak Calling* set up a field of intermedial resonance that worked on many levels. The "forest of phones" made manifest by the tall black plinths with little screens and black handsets visually echoed the forest footage projected on the back wall. As the Murayana sculpture cast a shadow back into the forest, the video played across his painted chest and a reverberating syncopation of the *yidaki* filled the space; as the ancestral call to connection sounded out in concert with the calls of mobile phones, time becomes thickened, made less linear. The resulting play of "old" and "new" media simultaneously disrupted categorical distinctions between "Yolngu" and "foreign technologies" allowing something else to come into view.

At the same time the exhibition implicitly sets up a relationship between the phones and phone media on display and the phones and phone-made media carried in the pockets and purses of museum visitors. While many visitors approached the exhibition with the

Figure 29.4 Murayana in his video forest

presumption that our message to them was that *Yolngu are just like you*, those that stayed for a while were far more likely to recognize a more complex field of sameness-difference being put in play. From our perspective, visitors answered this call each time they stopped to look, listen and, hopefully, recognize the possibilities of relationships being constituted out of a play of sameness-difference and the encompassing aesthetics of resonance they set up.

As Dick Higgins puts it in the epigraph to this chapter: "a composer is a dead man unless he is composing for all media and for his world" (1967). *Gapuwiyak Calling* is an intermedial project composed for *worlds-coming-into-relationship*. It is an ode to the possibility of new forms of located connectedness, and marks a specific moment in which Yolngu use mobile phone technologies to engage with people and practices well beyond their ancestral homelands. As the exhibition claims the possibility of new outward directed relationships extending past Arnhem Land, Yolngu remain located within a very specific geography of a data networked global. Place remains the grounds of difference—the location from which to generate connections to other people and places that Yolngu also identify as belonging to somewhere specific, i.e. Japan, the US, Australia, etc.

For the members of our collective, *Gapuwiyak Calling* worked as an exhibition because we found a way to assemble individual media files into a performative work that simultaneously claimed ancestral authority *and* the possibility of contemporary global connection. We found a curatorial tone that we felt suited the *mokuy*—at once cheeky and serious—and an overarching design that situated this work not in the endless recombinatorial potential of digital remix, but in the particularities of a world made and marked by ancestral action. In this exhibition the old energized the new; and vice versa. As a result the show claimed the enduring particularities of place infused with a temporality far more complex than the very particular, and rapidly outdated historical moment materialized by the phones themselves, or the pixelated projections that jumped and flickered as they called into being an emergent, and participatory global, made resonant, alive and meaningful through an ongoing, creative interplay of sameness and difference.

By offering museum goers an alternative perspective on the globalizing forces of the digital, the show insisted local ontologies and perspectives as an enduring source of creative friction and particularized insistence. In this way the show made specific demands on the participatory, and highly aestheticized, forms of sociality increasingly made, and mediated, via hand-held mobile devices.

Notes

1 In the spirit of remix—and with thanks—this title is adapted from Jacqueline Hazen's perceptive review "Curated Resonance: A review of *Gapuwiyak Calling: Phone-made media from Aboriginal Australia*" (n.d.).

2 This project was supported by the Australian Research Council with additional funds from Arts NT, New York University, The University of Queensland, The Cairns Institute, James Cook University, The Pratt Foundation and the Fox Family Foundation. The development of the first iteration of *Gapuwiyak Calling* was supported also by the Anthropology Museum at the University of Queensland. I owe a great deal to Diana Young, Jane Willcock, Charla Strelan, Kiri Chan and Camella Hardjo. Faye Ginsburg provided invaluable support in the curation of the New York show in collaboration with the Margaret Mead Film Festival. Thanks also to Fred Myers and the NYU Graduate students who helped out with the show. Santiago Carrasquilla and Wade Jeffree did an amazing job on the design of the NY show. Special thanks also to Jacqueline Hazen whose review entitled "Curated Resonance: A review of *Gapuwiyak Calling: Phone-made media from Aboriginal Australia*" (n.d.) confirmed that at least some visitors appreciated the show on the terms we intended. The title of her piece has been remixed for this chapter. Thanks also to Matthew Gingold who helped us develop our original ideas and shot the forest and dancing sequences that were projected. Most of all thanks are due to the Miyarrka Media team who keep it interesting at so many levels: Meredith Balanydjarrk,

James Bangaliwuy, Paul Gurrumuruwuy, Warren Balpatji, Enid Gurunulmiwuy, Kayleen Djingawuy Wanamb, Oliver Wadawarda Lanzenberg and Evan Birrbirr Wyatt.

3 Several sections of this text first appeared in the catalogue essay "Call-and-Response" (Deger 2014; Miyarrka Media 2014b).

4 See Miyarrka Media 2012, 2014a, 2014b and Deger 2013.

5 Since those early days people have begun keeping multiple memory cards in order not to have to constantly delete.

6 The first iteration of the exhibition was installed at the University of Queensland Anthropology Museum in collaboration with Dr Diana Young, March–July 2014, and was called *Gapuwiyak Calling: Phone-made media from Arnhem Land*. The second iteration of the exhibition, substantially re-designed for the space and context was entitled *Gapuwiyak Calling: Phone-made media from Aboriginal Australia*.

7 From a Yolngu perspective Gapuwiyak is not a single "community," as it might be imaged from the perspective of Google Earth or local government policies. Rather it is lived as a site of socially situated inter-connectivity, a place in which the structures and authorities of ancestral kinship networks continue to shape both everyday relationships and creative possibilities. As we selected the media, rather than attempting to represent every clan in the community (and thereby turning the show into a complex and always potentially fraught project mired in the inevitably of inter-clan politics), we made a strategic decision to feature media already circulating the Yolngu curators' own family networks. This made it significantly easier to gather the necessary permissions and authority to show the images in the museum context.

8 *Gapuwiyak Calling* was first exhibited at the University of Queensland Anthropology Museum, March 15–August 15, 2014 (www.anthropologymuseum.uq.edu.au/gapuwiyak-calling) under a slightly different name; a re-designed version of this show featured at the American Museum of Natural History as part of the Margaret Mead Film Festival 2014 (www.amnh.org/explore/margaret-mead-film-festival/history-archives/margaret-mead-film-festival-20142/events); a third exhibition was held at the Cairns Institute, James Cook University, September 16–October 16, 2015. See also the exhibition website (http://gapuwiyakcalling.com/).

9 Ringtone (Miyarrka Media 2014a) has also been released as a stand-alone film distributed by Ronin Films.

10 http://gapuwiyakcalling.com

References

Amerika, Mark. 2015. "remixthecontext (A Theoretical Fiction)." In *The Routledge Companion to Remix Studies*, edited by Eduardo Navas, Owen Gallagher and xtine burrough, 310–20. New York: Routledge.

Deger, Jennifer. 2013. "In-Between." In *Anthropology and Art Practice*, edited by A. Schneider and C. Wright, 105–14. Oxford: Berg.

——. 2014. "Call-and-Response" in *Gapuwiyak Calling*, 2–6. St Lucia: University of Queensland.

——. 2016. "Thick Photography." *Journal of Material Culture* 21(1): 111–32.

Elhaik, Tarek. 2013. "What Is Contemporary Anthropology?" *Critical Arts* 27(6): 784–98.

Higgins, Dick. 1967. "Statement on Intermediality." In *Dé-coll/age (décollage) * 6, Typos Verlag, Frankfurt*, edited by Wolf Vostell, n.p. New York: Something Else Press. Reproduced at www.walkerart.org/collections/publications/art-expanded/crux-of-fluxus/

Irvine, Martin. 2014. "Remix and the Dialogic Engine of Culture: A Model for Generative Combinatoriality." In *The Routledge Companion to Remix Studies*, edited by Eduardo Navas et al., 15–42. New York: Routledge.

Markham, Annette. (2013). "Remix Culture, Remix Methods: Reframing Qualitative Inquiry for Social Media Contexts." In *Global Dimensions of Qualitative Inquiry*, edited by N. Denzin and M. Giardina, 63–81. Walnut Creek, CA: Routledge/Left Coast Press.

Miyarrka Media. 2012. *Manapanmirr, in Christmas Spirit*. Gurrumuruwuy dir.

——. 2014a. *Ringtone*. Paul Gurrumuruwuy and Jennifer Deger dir. Australia: Ronin Films.

——. 2014b. *Christmas Birrimbirr*. Moesgaard Museum.

Rajewsky, Irina O. 2005. "Intermediality, Intertextuality, and Remediation: A Literary Perspective on Intermediality." *Intermediality: History and Theory of the Arts, Literature and Technologies*, 6(autumn): 43–64.

Part VII

INFRASTRUCTURES

30

INSTANT ARCHIVES?

Haidy Geismar

Since its launch in San Francisco in October 2010, Instagram—a social media photography application for smartphones—has garnered over 100,000 million monthly active users. By March 2014 over 20 billion photographs had been shared on the platform, with roughly 60 million images being uploaded each day, and 1.6 billion expressions of "like."[1] No wonder the platform was purchased by Facebook for approximately $300 million in 2012. The overwhelming scale of Instagram seems to prevent, even resist, many kinds of analysis. How can we talk about style, genre, aesthetics, or even meaning, in the context of millions of users and billions of photographs? How can such a global phenomenon be inflected with an aesthetics or politics of the local? With the conundrum of scale interfering with our usual analytic categories, what frameworks can we use to make sense of Instagram, and what are the implications for the methodologies of digital ethnography? While Big Data has become a seductive frame within which to develop new theories of scale, and more specifically to develop new techniques of visualization to analyze social media images (e.g. Manovich et al. 2012), in this chapter I argue that thinking of Instagram using the language and frame of the archive enables us to develop an analytic perspective that might make sense of either a single image or the multitude, understanding this proliferation of images through a new institutional lens.

The archive is a particularly evocative image to think about social media, which seems to have obsolescence built into its technical form, and fickleness built into its user base. While social media might seem to resist many archival processes and practices (such as preservation, the imagination of a specific future, and often state-centralized control), the archive is also increasingly recognized as an interpretive form, and metaphor, par excellence for the digital age (Featherstone 2006). In developing a perspective on social media photography that draws upon the rich literature that has emerged about the sociality, politics, materiality, and governance of archives I argue that we may better draw out the epistemologies and values that underpin social media photography, in turn constituting new visible, and visual, publics, but ultimately arguing that we need to take seriously how social media has become a new institutional framework for social life and visual expression. By asking what kind of an archive Instagram is, and by comparing Instagram to other contemporary archiving projects, I open up social media platforms to a new analytic, which I hope can assist us in understanding the implications of these structures and frameworks of organizing images for the future, whether that be intentional or not. Here I deliberately position my analysis as counter, and complementary, to ethnographic perspectives that would focus more on the substance and content of individual images. Rather, I work to explore how we might make sense of aggregates of images in social, cultural, economic, and political terms, unpacking the blackbox of corporate infrastructures that, alongside user-generated content, constitute social media.

Understanding Archives

At first glance, Instagram seems to be a user-generated anti-archive, one that frustrates efforts at systematic searching and analysis, resisting historicization and any archival research beyond the momentary event of looking.[2] For the viewer, images emerge momentarily, in feeds, and are almost instantly lost again, to be replaced with yet more images. The experience of time is compressed by volume, provoking a perpetual sense of contemporaneity—no two searches in this archive will ever be the same and recovering an image is not always possible as users delete and manage the privacy settings of their accounts. If, as is often argued, there is a mutual constitution of the archive and the public, Instagram exposes a public culture that is contingent, in flux, and enduringly momentary. The act of looking, or searching, through Instagram is therefore as much one of trying to find what you already know is there, as it is an active process of engagement with an image world, encapsulated in the platform as "liking."

While the sheer scale and daily proliferation of images has a marked effect on how we may even see Instagram as an archive, understanding Instagram in archival terms not only has the potential to inform us about contemporary visual strategies of self-presentation, visual economies, and the classificatory systems that frame and narrate popular photographic practices. It also allows us to rethink the nature of the archive itself. Rao argues for an understanding of the Indian city as archive suggesting that:

> archives can be treated as anchors in the reconstitution of social relations rather than as reflections of an already existing set of underlying conditions. Further, if we can treat density as a reflection of a network of information and relationships rather than as a demographic indicator of the quality and nature of the experience of place, then I suggest that these newly mobile forms of density can themselves be positioned as a form of archive.
>
> (2009, 380)

Rao's vision of the city as archive dovetails with my proposal to read Instagram in archival terms. As she observes, "We need to rethink the notion of archive to encompass a dynamic sense of ordering and interpretation, unmoored from the politics of preservation and evidence creation for historical understanding" (ibid., 381).

Thinking about Instagram as a massive archive, simultaneously user-generated and structured by a largely unseen corporation, allows us to move away from analytics such as style and genre, and away from an analytic gleaned from external cultural worlds, to understand more broadly how the platform is used to create value and constitute new publics. Simultaneously bringing into being, and archiving, what seems to be understood as a new visual commons, Instagram is also a corporate archive, gradually sedimenting a massive database of user information, now owned by Facebook, gleaned from both the images uploaded and the people who interact with them. Photographs on Instagram are, in classically archival terms, more than just representations of their makers and users; they recursively reflect the epistemologies, classifications, and political economy of this archival infrastructure which itself plays a constituent role in Instagram's dominant aesthetic conventions.

Many analyses of social media simultaneously present such platforms as a priori to their use and users, and as "always already new" (see Gitelman (2006) for an incisive expansion to the historicity of "new" media). It might seem anathema to think of Instagram users as self-consciously producing an archive. Certainly, images are generated and collated in a non-centralized way (although the platform itself plays host and manages content in particular ways, including censoring images it considers inappropriate). Equally, most users have not developed any common or explicit discourse about the future of their images, or about preservation, and the resulting temporality of user accounts is remarkably shallow (although many are in fact engaged with the question of intellectual property rights, which became clear when Instagram changed their terms and conditions in 2012). Instagram, like Rao's city, is an unruly and instant archive; it is centralized by corporate interest; and its classificatory system is emergent and fluid, based upon a relatively new communicative artifact, the hashtag.

Archival Models

Many discussions tend to understand digital archives as either Foucauldian instruments of governmental control and surveillance, or tools of decentralized "choreography" within the network society (Castells 2012; Gerbaudo 2012). Media archaeology (e.g. Ernst 2012) exemplifies a growing tendency to reify form over content and by developing analytic modes that privilege the aggregate over the individual in terms of understanding the meaning and utility of archival information. Such accounts suggest: "The content of archives, in fact all content, has become largely irrelevant. What matters is not what is gathered, arranged, and transmitted, but how such gathering, arranging, and transmitting works" (Smith 2013, 385). However, such analytic sacrifice of content for structure undermines a more ethnographic perspective of the ways in which archives are in fact constituted, utilized, and experienced.

A burgeoning literature emphasizes the recursivity and reflexivity of many contemporary archival projects, in which the collection and collation of information is structured within a self-aware commentary on the nature of archival forms and methods (e.g. Edwards 2001; Zeitlyn 2012; Povinelli 2011). The practice of reading "against the archival grain" (Stoler 2009) in order to draw our attention to epistemic anxieties of users within the archive is in fact increasingly a characteristic of the practice and process of archiving itself. For instance, archival projects have emerged in Argentina, Chile, and Spain to confront the legacies of fascist dictatorship and materialize those who were "disappeared" (Taylor 2003) or to visually reconstitute a sense of territory for homeless and marginalized peoples (e.g. Susan Meiselas' AKA Kurdistan project).[3] These projects highlight the complicity of the archive in state operations of disappearance, genocide, oppression, and in turn formulate the archive as a site of resistance. The practice and technology of archiving has also become a strategy for linked political activism and artistic production, for instance in the Atlas Group's (artist Walid Raad) fictional archive of contemporary Lebanon.[4] Such projects subvert the ways in which archives are used as tools of power, social control, and centralization, and develop the archive as an aesthetic platform for the emotional exploration of place, politics, and personal experience.

"Indigenous" archiving platforms such as Mukurtu (Christen 2011) or Ara Irititja in Australia (Thorner 2010) have emerged to manage colonial collections of Aboriginal images, texts, music, song, dance, and knowledge in the context of Indigenous protocols and knowledge-management systems (see also Povinelli 2011).[5] Ara Irititja, for instance, allows Aboriginal users to manage images of the dead, blacking out individuals from group photographs, limiting access to images with ritual content, and requiring passwords to access family- or territory-specific archives. These archives insist on developing a relationship between these collections and "the public" in which the users must identify themselves in order to achieve appropriate degrees and levels of access. These Indigenous projects, often state funded, sit in tension with state ideals of public access, constituting a newly differentiated public sphere which, while similarly resisting the privatization or archival material, runs parallel to the open access movement, in fact challenging key tenets of openness and accessibility (Christen 2011; Geismar 2013).

Instagram as Archive

It is not usually the case that relatively small-scale Indigenous archiving projects are linked analytically to mass-produced social media. Yet, in the light of the growing trend to include a critique and commentary about the archive within the constitution of the archive itself, I wish to locate the organizational logic of Instagram within these kinds of analog and digital precedents that in fact might help us to better understand the unsettling scale and screen-effects of this proliferation of digital images. These projects highlight the reflexivity that digital technologies bring to the process of archiving in which the archive increasingly preserves a commentary or documents the process of archiving alongside the "original" material it contains. Such self-consciousness, or metadata, alters our understanding of what the archive is—not just a machine or system for documenting and preserving, but an epistemology forever in motion. All archives are responsive systems in which user experience or subjectivity is built into the usability of the archive.

The ways in which some Indigenous digital archives utilize generic database systems to challenge the political sensibilities of the archive mirrors a broader tension within the anthropology of digital infrastructures that explores the relationship between local cultural imperatives and the global forms that increasingly co-opt them into recognizable generic forms, and raises questions about whether these digital frameworks either incorporate meaningful cultural differences or eradicate them (see Geismar and Mohns 2011). Larkin describes infrastructures as:

> built networks that facilitate the flow of goods, people, or ideas and allow for their exchange over space. As physical forms they shape the nature of a network, the speed and direction of its movement, its temporalities, and its vulnerability to breakdown. They comprise the architecture for circulation, literally providing the undergirding of modern societies, and they generate the ambient environment of everyday life.
>
> (2013, 328)

While Larkin is referring to built environments such as electricity grids and roads, it is productive to think of social networking platforms as aggregates of hardware and software that create "architectural" infrastructures for the archival appreciation and exploitation of data.

So what kind of an archive is Instagram? If the "visual image is an archive in its own right" (Mirzoeff 2011, xv), how do we analyze structure, epistemology, and meaning in the terms of a single Instagram image? What methods do we use? Big Data has become a dominant epistemology for understanding mass digital media, creating new ethical frames, new claims to objectivity, and new conflations of scale with significance (boyd and Crawford 2012). For instance, a recent project focused on Instagram by Hochmann and Manovich (2013) converts the image-archive into "Big Data" within which they can undertake what they describe as "data ethnography" (2013, 14) or analysis of aggregated clusters of visual information (see Figure 30.1).

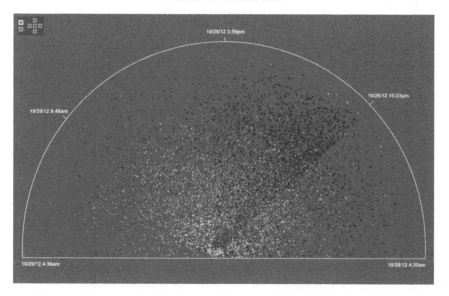

Figure 30.1 A detail from radial plot visualization of 24 hours from the Brooklyn area during Hurricane Sandy by Manovich and Hochman. Source: http://phototrails.net/radial_sandy_hue_created/. Permission to reproduce courtesy of Nadav Hochman

Hochman and Manovich draw on massive numbers of Instagram images to create visualizations that they argue "can lead to cultural, social, and political insights about particular local places during particular time periods" (ibid.). They correlate computer-generated visualizations of these aggregated images onto already existing knowledge about history, culture, society, and politics. For instance, in Figure 30.1 you can see the moment when night falls and the power cuts out during Hurricane Sandy, New York, 2012. However, this visualization tells us little we did not already know either about Instagram or of the role that social media might, or might not, play within these events. Nor does it really provide us with a useful methodology for understanding images as meaningful data in and of themselves (rather than visualizations which then need to be interpreted). Hochman and Manovich's visualization gives us no understanding of how we might understand aggregated Instagram images to have meaning—as geolocated marks, as potentially legal evidence of political activity, or as indices of social opinion and commentary. The computational power behind their visualization might make distinctions that allow us to speak of the cognitive processes of image-making at a level that might be imperceptible to the human eye or unimportant to the human mind. In our current moment, in which "Big Data" itself is an increasingly fetishized artifact of study, what are the implications of sheer volume in developing tool-kits to understand visual practices such as Instagram? Manovich et al.'s (2012) visualization of style or form across a million images brings a new definition of style into being but cannot help us in understanding how style and genre are socially constructed.

A very different account of popular photographic practices and their engagement with Instagram is emerging from fieldwork based within specific communities, or with specific users, and these are currently being undertaken in numerous locations (Costa et al. 2016). Here I deliberately side-step a more traditional anthropological form of enquiry yet build on basic anthropological principles of locating these images in context to consider how a focus on the archive might help us to grapple with the issues of scale, categorization, and value that underpin Instagram.

The Unruly Archive

We might think of Instagram as a "very messy kind of archive" (Jimenez and Estalella 2014). Reading Instagram as an archive allows us to analyze the ways in which people work with the fixed format of the screen, the limitations of the software and photo-processing filters (which reference past photographic technologies as well as corporate virtual environments) and generate remarkably generic yet personal image collections, organized by epistemologies that emerge from specific users and yet also, through key words, feeds, and comments, are shared across global communities.

Instagram is a platform and network that is forged from three primary practices: the production and presentation of images, their aesthetic evaluation (the appreciation, enjoyment, and judgment of images), and their classification (the constitution of textual frames for image using tags and captions that creates an infrastructure of aestheticized categorization). Instagram accounts present a stream of images, in chronological order simultaneously embedded in a new archival chronology delineated by tags and by user-defined searches. The capacity of smartphones to geolocate also places images within a searchable global map.

For the first year of its existence, Instagram users simply uploaded photographs directly from their smartphone cameras into the signature square format (nostalgically referencing Kodak instamatic and polaroid images), undertook some basic photo editing (including the application of a number of different filter options which similarly referenced older styles and processes of photography), and shared their images with other users. Users could follow other users and have the options to "like" and briefly comment on images. In January 2011 Instagram introduced hashtags to increase lateral connections across user accounts. Hashtags are essentially user-defined captions prefaced by the symbol # creating a searchable cross-referencing system, connecting all images that share the same tag. In the summer of 2013, having acquired Instagram, Facebook added the hashtag facility to its own platform promising even greater integration between the two applications.[6]

Classification

Since its introduction, the hashtag has become an archival tool that underpins the organizational logic of Instagram from the perspective of its users. Aside from following images through an individual account, numerous web-based search engines have been developed to access and browse this massive photographic collection. The hashtag is the device that collects and collates images bringing a second dimension to user accounts, and facilitating the social networking and image-networking component.

The tag is the lynch pin of Instagram's archival stability and instability and links it definitively to the other archival projects mentioned above. Collections of images develop unsystematically, randomly, in a decentralized way. Yet, visual codes within Instagram are hung together by a user-generated classificatory system we might want to think of as a folksonomy, in which user-generated classifications are connected via the hashtag as textual artifact of access. Hashtags can be used to generate images for specific purposes, such as in daily competitions and themes that invite users to cluster images around tags or to promote events or commodities. Users cluster around hashtags to share their communal experience both with their friends and others. The clustering of images around hashtags also generates a shared visual sensibility around events, as the mobile nature of the platform ensures that people are able to take photos and look at other people's photographs from the same place simultaneously creating global events, such as #tourdefrance.

Figure 30.2   #xxxxthedog (via findagram.com) screengrab from September 2, 2013

Hashtags are also selected to generate more personal communities of practice or of friendship, for instance in the generation of a tag #xxxxthedog, clustering intimate images of a household pet and those close to her (Figure 30.2).

Unlike folksonomy projects in museums in which crowd-sourced categories float on top of museum catalogs yet rarely, if ever, enter a dialog with the formal key words of museum collection management systems, the Instagram tagging system both constitutes the archival qualities of the platform and demonstrates the ways in which classificatory systems are in fact not a priori, but created out of a networked infrastructure of images. Alongside the smartphone application itself, various search engines that allow one to search Instagram images depend heavily on their tags which can vary between the selective, small, and the wildly generic: from the ten images clustered around the tag #brunolatour, to the 184,519,839 images linked to #love on September 2, 2013, or the 82,825,375 images tagged #likeforlike on July 7, 2014.

There is a tension between the truly liberated and unruly power of the hashtag, which powerfully organizes communication across platforms, and the shallow temporality of belonging within the community of Instagram images, in which searches render images that are temporarily linked and generate clusters that continually change. Hashtags are recursive in that they reflect user-generated categories at the same time as bringing those categories into being for users to connect to. Instagram exists as a series of images presented by users or clustered under the categorical imperatives of the tag. Most importantly, hashtags are the interface through which images are connected through the experience of "liking": a discursive form of tastemaking that underpins the Instagram community. Users are able to search through tags for images that align with their own classificatory manifestation of interests, and express this by liking and commenting on images. In this way, the combination of hashtag search and user account(ability) comes together to forge networks of appreciation for specific images. In the following short sections I focus on three ways in which these qualities of the platform structure and mould particular archival logics which, in turn, account for some of the most interesting phenomena on Instagram—the mass production of genres, the user-led classification of images, and the development of networks of appreciation that are increasingly loaded with commodity value.

Regulation

Regulation is a key quality of the archive, yet social media is famously governed by both a dispersed normativity, and by a motley assortment of trolls (Coleman 2011). The promise of broad circulation seems to underpin the social media image. The conflict between Joy Garnett, a New York-based artist, and Magnum photojournalist Susan Meiselas over Garnett's painting of, via an internet search, a cropped, yet copyrighted, photograph taken by Meiselas of a Nicaraguan Sandanista throwing a Molotov cocktail, exemplifies the irrepressibility of the digital image and the ethics of its circulation. Garnett eventually removed the image from her website after receiving a cease and desist letter from Meiselas' lawyers, but the image of her work was rapidly recirculated and remixed by a broad community of artists and supporters (Garnett and Meiselas 2007). Yet despite controversies sparked within "JoyWar," Instagram images circulate primarily within a network of intense normativity.

Most accounts of ubiquitous photographic practices within social media (e.g. Hand 2012; van Dijk 2007) argue that digital photography facilitates a continuation of the basic nature of popular photography to produce and publicly circulate identities and constitute memory practices. Miller's account of Facebook profile photographs (2015) focuses on the ways in which these image practices extend and embody social networks, being the visual vehicles by which users enter into the process of self-making and the process of relationship building (and unbuilding, see Gershon 2010) through the image as a communicative practice. Miller and Sinanan (2013) argue in their discussion of webcam that image-making through social media represents a retrospective "attainment" of latent capacities to understand the self and develop new forms of self-consciousness.

Yet it is the very sociality of Instagram and the ways in which it forges networks of images that is also the most profound regulator of the production of normative images. The archival logic of Instagram revolves around an infrastructure of value forged by the formation of classificatory systems based on user appreciations, underpinned by the epistemological logic of the hashtag. Not only does this have a practical application, in the exploitation of these circuits of appreciation in the form of commercial interest, it also in part might explain the emergence of particular genres within the platform.

The use of hashtags demonstrates the emergence of visual genres, in which images (understood as composites of symbols, framed tableaus, and visual conventions) emerge in relation to key categories and simultaneously constitute those categories, creating communities of taste and distinction (following Bourdieu 1984). The power of the hashtag is demonstrated by its conflation with whole categories of image, and the way in which it has been incorporated into everyday speech ("I can't find a wireless connection . . . hashtag First world problem"). At first glance the genre of #selfie that moulds self-portraiture in Instagram demonstrates how much the genre is circumscribed here by the form of the smartphone and the affordances of Instagram: selfies present selves in squares, seen from the distance of an arm's length (although this is changing with the advent of the selfie stick), and through the frequent presence of mirrors often include the camera itself. At second glance we can see how the interplay between classificatory tags and the visual conventions molded by the platform's software (used on smartphones) interact together to constitute genres within Instagram. In a mocking web article,[7] one pundit lampoons the emergent popular genres: "photographs of legs from above, photographs of legs standing, photographs of lips, photographs of fingernails, photographs of meals, photographs of pets and children, self-portraits taken in mirrors or by holding the phone away from the body" and so forth. These genres—singular categories characterized by a shared style, which seemingly reproduce themselves (Neale 1987)—are global, and they are each constituted by millions of images. It is the consensual recognition of these genres of photographic practice that reinforces the values that are marked by the processes of liking and the forging of classificatory connections between images. Hashtags such as #selfie, or #maori, expose not just a convention of portraiture, but the emergence of broader kinds of subject position specifically formed within the archive.

Corporate

The archival recursivity of image circulation on Instagram can be seen most clearly in the ways in which value and self-expression are mutually constituted in the platform itself. Alongside the ways in which people use tagging to both perpetuate and develop existing visual codes and paradigms, the act of liking images is fundamental to the social networking of the platform. While liking and commenting form the basis of large numbers of community, even larger numbers of Instagram images are in fact not instantiations of self-making or identity in relation to culture, practice, politics, or sociality. Rather, they are vehicles expressly designed for the interconnection between aesthetic contemplation and taste making, uploaded specifically to engender social networks of appreciation. Images that focus primarily on achieving likes and followers are therefore hyper-recursive images, in that they refer to Instagram and the process of engagement with Instagram (which in turn may provide commercial benefits and other forms of value). The use of the tags #likeforlikes, #tagforlikes, #followme, #instalike, and #instafollow, for instance, are oriented toward attracting maximum numbers of followers and appreciative comments and user references which create a sense of success in terms of the capacities of Instagram, and create a form of capital that is increasingly attractive to publicists and marketing organizations seeking to generate visible proof networks of appreciative consumers (Figure 30.3).

This practice indicates the ways in which Instagram is perceived by many of its users as a kind of visual "trap" (Miller 2000) in which the process of appreciation is a form of visual and cognitive stickiness that creates strategic networks used in order to maximize various forms of capital. Here, the archive is an infrastructure of appreciation, often exploited for profit. The unsettlement of this kind of practice, particularly through the presence of fake Instagram accounts that exist solely to create links, likes, and tags, and present a visible appreciative community around specific events or objects, demonstrates the malleability of this archive and unmoors it from existing models of the archive, which at heart presume a moral perspective on collection, organization, and preservation ultimately aimed at generating knowledge, history, and memory.

Figure 30.3 Images to gain likes and friends are images of that relationship between friends and likes

Social Media Archives as a Form of "Civil Imagination"

I have briefly discussed the affordances of Instagram as a particular kind of archive in order to argue how it is useful to consider these platforms to be archives despite the seemingly anti-archival, even explicitly corporate, nature of these popular photographic practices. There is a tension between understanding social media as generic, reproducing normative genres that are informed largely by market-driven concerns; and understanding social media as the ultimate form of self-expression. I have emphasized that we might see convergences between user-led aesthetic practices and the intentions coded into the platforms and collated in more corporately inflected archival tendencies. Both types of use focus on the production of value for images and forge communities of taste. Azoulay (2008) has posited that the practice of making and viewing photographs instantiates a civil or social contract—a relationship between viewer and viewed that demands an ethical engagement and facilitates a framework of what she terms "civil imagination" (as opposed to state domination of our visual capacities to empathize and connect through images). If this civil contract is found in the very material form of photography then this could and should extend into some of our perceptions of popular photography outlets such as Instagram as a new institutional form of image consumption. Bassett (2013) suggests that one might be able to intervene in the cacophony of social media by producing a "silent commons": a re-appropriation of the space of social media and a use of communicative media that does not necessarily only produce data that conforms to the use-value of corporate social media platforms and which subverts our usual expectations.

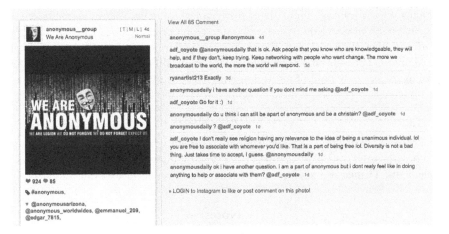

Figure 30.4 Discussion about being part of Anonymous. Screenshot on January 31, 2014 through Web.stagram.com

A silent commons could be understood as an archive that can be created inadvertently and without intention yet still be mobilized as a form of public culture with resonance far beyond the marketplace. Can we understand Instagram as a space in which the crowd-sourced classificatory system is truly utilized at cross-purposes to an institutional archival logic that constitutes hegemonic epistemologies and values for companies such as Facebook? If we understand social media sites in the same way we do state archives, we might see them as massive centralizations of information and data that colonize our taste, and even our sociality, to benefit a small number (of shareholders). However, if we follow other accounts that posit social media to be the remedy for archival centralization can we still use the frame of the archive in order to unravel the centralizing tendencies of social media? I have suggested here that the radical or recursive archives of artists or indigenous groups work against centralization and surveillance in exactly this way. The user experience of Instagram is one of a shallow temporality in which images are continuously replacing each other in terms of immediate access. This is more a problem of scale than of the archive itself which successfully maintains images and organizes them chronologically. Yet we cannot allow ourselves to be defeated by scale—rather we have to analyze scale itself as an aesthetic convention and visual effect and locate it as a particular phenomenon for the archive.

Historically there have been numerous failed attempts at total archiving projects from Warburg's iconographic Mnemosyne project to the Mundaneum. These projects, like that of Google's book project or even its search engine, might be understood as a kind of imperial hubris, like the mapping project described by Borges in his short story "On the Exactitude of Science." However, platforms such as Instagram can be seen as new forms of archives of the everyday, constructing a predetermined and emergent infrastructure through which persons circulate in the digital world as assemblages of taste and, by extension, work collectively to construct new forms of value.

It is the archival logic that produces the qualities of Instagram that are of such interest to analysts—the classificatory system of the hashtag, the normativity of genre production, and the self-identification of users within this new normative and visible public sphere. Instagram opens up the possibility of registering or archiving a slice of reality that was absent in the traditional archive, and in so doing makes it possible to incorporate that into circuits of value and the production of meaning. Thinking of Instagram as an archive allows us to make sense of the ongoing tensions about the visual economy, the monetization of user data, the corporate structure of the interface, alongside the analysis and understanding of user-generated content. We need this kind of archival perspective to make sense of the growing place and proliferation of social media as a new kind of institution within our everyday lives.

Acknowledgments

I am indebted to Fernando Dominguez Rubio for inviting me to write this paper for a conference he organized on Infrastructures at the Open University and for his astute reading of multiple drafts. Thanks also to Hannah Knox and Zachary Hecht for critical input.

Notes

1 Source: http://instagram.com/press.
2 Snapchat, which is replacing Instagram in popularity with many young people, takes this immediacy of experience to the logical conclusion of deleting the image after a set, and short, period of time. Perhaps for this reason, witnessing, rather than looking is a better verb to use in discussing how we experience social media images.
3 www.susanmeiselas.com/akakurdistan.
4 www.masumiyetmuzesi.org/?Language=ENG; www.theatlasgroup.org.
5 See www.mukurtu.org, http://irititja.com.
6 Instagram, like Facebook, censors tags that are perceived to be pornographic or otherwise overtly problematic. They also block the use of tags such as #iphone and #photography claiming that they are too generic to be functional.
7 http://photodoto.com/15-reasons-why-your-instagram-followers-hate-you.

References

Azoulay, Ariella. 2008. *The Civil Contract of Photography*. New York: Zone Books.
Bassett, Caroline. 2013. "Silence, Delirium, Lies?" *First Monday* 18(3).
Bourdieu, Pierre. 1984. *Distinction: A Social Critique of the Judgement of Taste*. London: Routledge & Kegan Paul.
boyd, danah, and Kate Crawford. 2012. "Critical Questions for Big Data." *Information, Communication & Society* 15(5): 662–79.
Castells, Manuel. 2012. *Networks of Outrage and Hope: Social Movements in the Internet Age*. Cambridge, UK; Malden, MA: Polity.
Christen, Kimberly. 2011. "Opening Archives: Respectful Repatriation." *American Archivist* 74(1): 185–210.
Coleman, E. Gabriella. 2011. "Hacker Politics and Publics." *Public Culture* 23(3): 511–16.
Costa, Elisabetta, Nell Haynes, Tom McDonald, Daniel Miller, Razvan Nicolescu, Jolynna Sinanan, et al. 2016. *How the World Changed Social Media*. London: UCL Press.
Edwards, Elizabeth. 2001. *Raw Histories: Photographs, Anthropology and Museums*. Oxford; New York: Berg.
Ernst, Wolfgang. 2012. *Digital Memory and the Archive*. Minneapolis, MN; London: University of Minnesota Press.
Featherstone, Mike. 2006. "Archive." *Theory, Culture & Society* 23(2–3): 591–96.
Garnett, Joy, and Susan Meiselas. 2007. "On the Rights of Molotov Man." *Harper's Magazine*, February. http://harpers.org/archive/2007/02/on-the-rights-of-molotov-man/ (accessed January 21, 2016).
Geismar, Haidy. 2013. *Treasured Possessions: Indigenous Interventions into Cultural and Intellectual Property*. Durham, NC: Duke University Press.

Geismar, Haidy, and William Mohns. 2011. "Database Relations: Rethinking the Database in the Vanuatu Cultural Centre and National Museum." *Journal of the Royal Anthropological Institute* 17(s1): 2126–48.

Gerbaudo, Paolo. 2012. *Tweets and the Streets: Social Media and Contemporary Activism*. London: Pluto Press.

Gershon, Ilana. 2010. *The Breakup 2.0: Disconnecting Over New Media*. Ithaca, NY: Cornell University Press.

Gitelman, Lisa. 2006. *Always Already New: Media, History, and the Data of Culture*. Cambridge, MA: MIT Press.

Hand, Martin. 2012. *Ubiquitous Photography*. Cambridge, UK; Malden, MA: Polity Press.

Hochman, Nadav, and Lev Manovich. 2013. "Zooming into an Instagram City: Reading the Local through Social Media." *First Monday* 18(7).

Jimenez, Alberto C., and Adolfo Estalella. 2014. "Assembling Neighbors: The City as Hardware, Method, and 'a Very Messy Kind of Archive.'" *Common Knowledge* 20(1): 150–71.

Larkin, Brian. 2013. "The Politics and Poetics of Infrastructure." *Annual Review of Anthropology* 42(1): 327–43.

Manovich, Lev, Jeremy Douglass, and Tara Zepel. 2012. "How to Compare One Million Images." In *Understanding Digital Humanities*, edited by David Berry, 249–78. London: Palgrave.

Miller, Daniel. 2000. "The Fame of Trinis: Websites as Traps." *Journal of Material Culture* 5(1): 5–24.

——. 2015. "Photography in the Age of Snapchat." *Royal Anthropological Institute Photography and Anthropology Series 1*.

Miller, Daniel, and Jolynna Sinanan. 2013. *Webcam*. Cambridge, UK: Polity Press.

Mirzoeff, Nicholas. 2011. *The Right to Look: A Counterhistory of Visuality*. Durham, NC: Duke University Press.

Neale, Stephen. 1987. *Genre*. London: BFI Books.

Povinelli, Elizabeth A. 2011. "The Woman on the Other Side of the Wall: Archiving the Otherwise in Postcolonial Digital Archives." *Differences* 22(1): 146–71.

Rao, Vyjayanthi. 2009. "Embracing Urbanism: The City as Archive." *New Literary History* 40(2): 371–83.

Smith, Marquard. 2013. "Theses on the Philosophy of History: The Work of Research in the Age of Digital Searchability and Distributability." *Journal of Visual Culture* 12(3): 375–403.

Stoler, Ann Laura. 2009. *Along the Archival Grain: Epistemic Anxieties and Colonial Common Sense*. Princeton, NJ: Princeton University Press.

Taylor, Diana. 2003. *The Archive and the Repertoire: Performing Cultural Memory in the Americas*. Durham, NC: Duke University Press.

Thorner, Sabra. 2010. "Imagining an Indigital Interface: Ara Irititja Indigenizes the Technologies of Knowledge Management." *Collections: A Journal for Museums and Archives Professionals* 6(3): 125–47.

van Dijk, José. 2007. *Mediated Memories in the Digital Age*. Stanford, CA: Stanford University Press.

Zeitlyn, David. 2012. "Anthropology in and of the Archives: Possible Futures and Contingent Pasts. Archives as Anthropological Surrogates." *Annual Review of Anthropology* 41(1): 461–80.

31

THE FORTUNE OF SCARCITY

Digital Music Circulation in Cuba

Alexandrine Boudreault-Fournier

From the cassette tape distribution networks in the 1990s, to CDs, VCDs, DVDs in the 1990s and 2000s, and more recently MP3s shared through transportable devices and Bluetooth connection, the consumption of music in Cuba is catalyzing the emergence of systems of digital media circulation. The distribution of music has promoted the strengthening of circulation networks, some receiving full support from state authorities, and others involving elicit practices. Yet all of the new networks of circulation contribute to the development of an effective model of digital music distribution that is based on the hand-to-hand transfer of musical content.

This chapter provides an overview of the networks of music circulation and distribution in Cuba, and concludes with a parallel between these networks and my presence as an anthropologist also participating in the circulation of digital music while conducting fieldwork. Drawing upon ethnographic research in Cuba conducted in 2012, I introduce the concepts of luck and fortune (*lo fortuito*) to explain how a discourse based on serendipity is commonly articulated by Cuban music aficionados to refer to the luck of discovering and acquiring new music. Material shortage and scarcity is recurrent in Cuba and music aficionados have historically struggled to access music. Periods of limited access to goods and the lack of diversity on the official market reflect the widespread perception of socialist systems as representing "economies of shortage" (Verdery 1996, 21). Extensive social networks, based on barter, bribes, exchanges, and obligations, further help resolve everyday problems. I conclude by reflecting upon these practices for understanding the networks of music consumption and circulation in Cuba before and during the digital age.

MusDig Research Project

The ethnographic research discussed in this chapter was carried out as part of the "Music, Digitisation, Mediation: Towards Interdisciplinary Music Studies" (MusDig) research program, which began in 2010 and ended in December 2015, led by Georgina Born.[1] The objective of the MusDig project was to map, analyze, and compare ethnographically how, in different cultural and geopolitical contexts, digitization and digital media are transforming music and musical practices. Born, four post-doctoral associate researchers, and one doctoral researcher took part in the main comparative stage of the program, which involved approximately one year of ethnographic fieldwork in one or two main locality(ies) for each researcher, with several projects also pursuing multisite fieldwork as well as fieldwork online. Together, the ethnographies encompassed the digital mediation of popular, folk, and "art" music cultures in the developing and developed worlds. Some studies focused on the creation of digital music and the development of new institutions and industries, others on music's collection and sale, circulation and distribution, curation, and consumption. Additional ethnographies focused on dominant software packages, online music platforms, and the emergence of Internet-mediated music genres (see the chapter by Born and Haworth, this volume). Crossing all of the studies were a series of research themes, manifest differently in the distinctive studies, and underpinning the comparative analysis: consumption, circulation, aesthetics and genre, materialities and literacies, mediation, industry and institutions, intellectual property, creativity, subjectification, and historical transition—notably, the emergence of digital music cultures, economies, and regulatory apparatuses in the specific locality under investigation.

Among the six main ethnographies, Aditi Deo conducted fieldwork in North India on the digital recording, curating, and archiving of folk music; Geoff Baker addressed the conditions for the emergence and circulation of a series of digital music genres, among them digital *cumbia*, in Buenos Aires, Argentina; Andrew Eisenberg focused on the birth of a new, "born digital" music recording industry and copyright regulatory regime in Nairobi, Kenya in a context of national media effervescence and liberalization; Patrick Valiquet examined the novel materialities and aesthetics of digital art music both within and without the university system in Montreal, Canada; and Georgina Born investigated the evolving aesthetics and ideologies, materialities, and institutional forms of the burgeoning university-based digital art music and sound art scenes in the United Kingdom and in Montreal.[2] Rather than focusing upon an individualized approach to the digital, we adopted Born's (2011, 2012, 2013) model of the social mediation of music, which posits a cross-scalar approach to understanding the social dimensions of digital music experience. This model acknowledges the distinctive socialities that music (including digitally mediated music) can generate—whether in its creation, circulation, or consumption.

As I highlight below, my own comparative ethnographic research on digital music consumption in Montreal and Cuba highlighted the distinctive modes of sociality in which digital music consumption and circulation are entangled. The ethnographic and comparative approach developed during my data collection takes full account of the encultured or culturalized environments in which such musical practices take place (see for instance Bull 2006; DeNora 2000). Furthermore, my research departs from previous work that takes for granted the association between the digital, on the one hand, and the increase in individualized and privatized practices, on the other. The circulation of digital music in Cuba, which is based on the movement of people with their storage devices (on mobility and music, see Gopinath and Stanyek 2014), creates new social relations that are in continuation with already existing networks of consumption and distribution (also Stern (2014) in Vanuatu).

My contribution to the MusDig program involved five months of fieldwork in Montreal and six months in Havana and Santiago de Cuba between 2011 and 2012. My research was intended to highlight, comparatively, how the circulation and consumption of digital music and other data differed between the North American and the Cuban contexts; it also took in the existence of vibrant grey economies in these three cities. As expected, the circulation of digital music in Canada and Cuba took very different shapes (see Born and

Boudreault-Fournier forthcoming, for an in-depth comparative discussion of the field sites). In Montreal, my focus was on trends of digital music consumption based on illegal downloads, streaming, online radio, ripping programs, and sharing practices online which rely heavily on the presence of the protagonists on the web, as well as in concerts, festivals, and other musical venues. The research on heavy music consumers in Montreal explored the relationship between the strategies that consumers adopt to acquire large amounts of music, preferably for free or at very low cost, as well as the responses of musicians, labels, producers, distributors, and consumers to such trends. I also conducted ethnographic research among a group of beat makers and fans associated with a Montreal-based beat movement referred to as Piu Piu, a kind of electronic-futurist beat music. Piu Piu represents an emerging scene that effectively relies on various networks of connection, circulation, and distribution. It moves fast and does not have a specific common aesthetic; yet it does have an ambivalent, on-off identification with the hip hop tradition (see Boudreault-Fournier and Blais 2015, 2016, forthcoming; Born and Boudreault-Fournier, forthcoming, for more details about the Piu Piu movement).

In Cuba, I also followed heavy consumers of music and producers of electronic music (including beat makers, electro-acoustic musicians, and hip hop DJs). But what captured my attention most was the physical distribution of digital data through an effective hand-to-hand network of circulation. The non-availability of the Internet for most Cubans at the time of fieldwork meant that digital data was not shared or downloaded online; instead it was passed on through various types of networks based on the physical co-presence of or connection between the participants. Some of these networks were based on friendship and proximity; others on being connoisseurs and fans for certain key music genres; and others grew around the official street sellers of CDs and DVDs. In this complex set up, in which the different networks intermingled, the circulation of music depended upon the circulation of distinctive formats and commodity forms, from vinyl records and cassette tapes to CDs, VCDs, and DVDs later in the 1990s and 2000s. More recently, however, the distribution of digital music and other data occurs through complex networks of circulation based on external hard drives and memory sticks. The *paquete* refers to the weekly (and semi-weekly) package of digital material sold in bulk and transferred from one's hard drive to someone else's memory stick, or any other digital portable device. While the Montreal case illustrated coeval forms of digital music consumption and effervescent sharing both online and offline, the Cuban case exhibited a particular sense of discontinuous forms of togetherness that emerged from a sequential chain of physical contacts. In the remainder of the chapter I focus on this Cuban ethnography.

Accessing Digital Music in Cuba

Growing public access to international Internet[3] since the year 2010 suggests that Cubans increasingly have the opportunity to access digital data, including music, films, and other texts, outside the official media channels. However, Cuba still has one of the world's lowest Internet penetration rates.[4] At the time of fieldwork, access to the Internet was extremely limited and slow for the majority of the population. Only a few Cubans—primarily artists and university students—had access to the Internet. Other Cubans had access to email accounts and national and international networks. In May 2013, the Cuban government set up 118 Internet stations within the ETECSA[5] national telecommunication company offices located all over the island. For the equivalent of US$4.50 per hour and provided that they had ID cards registered by their local ETECSA office, Cubans could legally browse the Internet, and at a higher speed than what was encountered on the island at the time of fieldwork.[6] On July 1, 2015, Cubans had, for the first time, access to legal Wi–Fi Internet connections as 33 Wi–Fi access points, all located in public spaces, became available throughout the country. For instance, in Santiago de Cuba, Wi–Fi antennas were installed in four main areas of the city: three in parks and one in a popular back alley. As most residents connect to the Internet in order to get in touch with their family and friends living abroad, parks at night become public spaces where people can not only catch a rare breeze in a damp summer, but also communicate with relatives. Cubans can get access to a Wi–Fi connection card at US$2 for a one-hour high-speed connection. Given that the official average Cuban salary for a professional in the public sector stands at approximately US$28 to $30 per month, Internet access still remains limited for a large segment of the population.

The difficulty of accessing the Internet easily, or at a reasonable cost, encourages Cubans to create alternative ways of coping with digital scarcity, including hidden Wi–Fi antennas and ethernet cables strung over streets and rooftops. The *intranet callejera* (the intranet of the street) or the SNET (Street Net)[7] have emerged to counter the inefficiency and unreliability of the official media infrastructures by providing large networks of people with access not only to digital media and games, but also to data circulating in the present time outside of Cuba. Yet, because of political and technical limitations on the nation's available bandwidth, access to the Internet was—and still is—a key concern (Venegas 2010, 58; also see Recio Silva 2014). Legal connections in hotels and universities were slow when conducting fieldwork for the MusDig project and they relied exclusively on dial-up access. The speed of the connection never exceeded 52kbps, what Ignacio Ramonet labeled a "prehistoric Internet" (Ramonet in Recio Silva 2014, 335).

Despite this growing access to the Internet, the most accessible way to share digital data, including music, remains physical networks of digital media circulation that rely on the hand-to-hand passage of data through memory sticks and other portable devices. In Cuba, people visit each other to share music and other digital data, and networks are temporarily created and recreated thanks to the resulting exchanges. The different models of exchange create social relationships in their own modes (Humphrey and Hugh-Jones 1992, 8) and the sharing of music in physical settings also influences the nature of the microsocialities that emerge in the act of sharing music. Lino, a young DJ who lives in Havana, clearly illustrates this idea of socialities when he compares the Internet to the physical network that evolved with the hand-to-hand sharing of digital data:

> In a place where Internet is easily accessible, there is a kind of relationship that arises between the network [red] and the users. In the Cuban system, people create *links and relationships with each other*; the information that they pass on to each other physically represents the network [red]. It is a less centralized type of network than the Internet but it is just as effective. [my emphasis]

The use of portable storage devices is not limited to memory sticks but encompasses a whole series of devices that also serve to store music. Cubans use *reproductores* ("reproducers" such as iPods and memory sticks with headphone plugs), external drives, SD cards, micro-SD cards,[8] and of course, CDs, VCDs, and DVDs in order to acquire, consume, transport, and share digital music (among other data).[9] Hand-to-hand sharing of digital data based on mobile storage devices has rapidly become an effective network of dissemination in Cuba (see also Pertierra 2012). As one young Cuban told me, "The memory stick is *our* Internet"; another told me, "It is our weapon," suggesting that these devices allowed the circulation of material that is not available in Cuba's official media.

There are no music stores in Cuba that allow Cubans to buy original CD albums at an accessible price. Official music stores such as ARTEX S.A. sell Cuban music, but they are mainly targeting a tourist clientele. Cubans can hardly afford an original album by the popular Cuban timba group Los Van Van, sold in these stores for approximately US$15. To further complicate matters, there are no stores in Cuba that sell original international albums. In other words, there is no official—and legal—way to buy Beyoncé's latest physical album (whether in-store or online). The large majority of Cubans do not own credit cards and because of their restricted access to the Internet, the embargo, and the unreliability of the postal system, it is impossible for Cubans to buy official albums (in digital or physical format) on the Internet, or to buy any equipment or objects sold on sites such as Amazon.[10] There is no domestic online music market in Cuba analogous to what iTunes offers outside the island.[11] Therefore, because of infrastructural restrictions, it is extremely difficult for Cubans to consume music legally.

Official buyers and vendors of copied CDs and DVDs sell copies of albums, or fill up memory cards with music, in exchange for money in what seems to be a legalized system of copied music distribution (Boudreault-Fournier, forthcoming). These vendors, officially known as the "disc buyers and sellers," can be found throughout Havana and they represent a cheap and accessible option for acquiring digital media, including music. In addition to copying CDs and DVDs, the vendors also sell digital data in bulk, transferred on memory sticks priced according to the size of their digital content (1G for CUC$1; 2G for CUC$1.50, etc.). The weekly packages are sold directly from the package vendor's portable hard drive to the vendor's computer who, in turn, sells it to his clients. These exchanges take place through the physical presence of all parties.

Chance and the Digital

The idea of *fortuito*, or fortune, to refer to chance, luck, contingency, serendipity, and something that was unplanned, surfaced on many occasions when conducting interviews and meeting music aficionados in Cuba. The chance narrative is also commonly articulated in various spheres of Cuban life; it is a kind of "happy-go-lucky aesthetic of 'the Cuban,'" a character that is often referred to as a standard of Cubans' idiosyncrasy (Holbraad 2010, 72). Until the 1990s, Cubans had little access to music produced outside the island. At the time, cassette tapes and later CDs left behind by the rare tourists visiting the island and by the foreign students from South America and Africa were the only way to get access to foreign music. To a certain extent, this has changed since the 2000s as visitors and travelers transport digital music to the island. The growth of the tourist industry and Cubans' increased propensity to travel internationally has enabled more access to music produced outside Cuba. Many music aficionados I met in Cuba argue that the chance factor (*lo fortuito*) is in large part responsible for getting to know a specific type of music, a musician, or a group that was previously unknown to them. It is also, by extension, a way to connect with people through music. In relation to digital music circulation and consumption, chance constitutes new forms of sociality and relationality, and in this sense, flows of luck create "interlaced spheres of exchange" (da Col 2012, 17). What one listens to is deeply entrenched in a series of fortuitous events.

During my fieldwork in Montreal, I never noticed a discourse based on serendipity or chance when referring to the process of finding digital data online or offline, or of meeting people with common musical interests. It does not mean that a narrative based on chance is not articulated in the digital world though. For instance, the presence of the now obsolete "I'm Feeling Lucky" button on Google echoes a narrative based on the idea of chance.

Yet, it was estimated that only 1 percent of Google searches were going through the "I'm Feeling Lucky" button.[12] Since 2010, with the new "Google Instant" platform, the "I'm Feeling Lucky" button still appears on the main page of the search engine, but it is not accessible any more to the navigators. In contrast, in Cuba, chance was a strong topic that kept coming back when people were telling me about how they get access to music, how they get to learn about a specific group, and how they find people who share common musical interests.

For Ricardo, a music aficionado living in Havana, chance is the main reason why he acquired the reputation of being an electronic music connoisseur in addition to being known as a music "server" in the capital. In every music scene (at the local and national level), there are people who act as *servidores* (servers). These people are known among the local population to share music and information about musicians and groups often associated with a specific music genre. They are all music aficionados and they share music for free through an efficient network created through the hand-to-hand passage of data—with the use of memory sticks and other portable devices. The server is often at the source of the spread of emerging groups and genres (i.e. they are often among the first to access what's new and what can be accessed on the island).

The narrative of chance in relation to music follows a common narrative which is articulated around a chain of fortuitous events, connected to one another, and that explains a present situation. For Ricardo, *lo fortuito* began in 1993 when a foreigner gave a Sony discman to his sister. It was an exceptional thing, something that he would never have dreamed of. He remembers listening first to his sister's classical music CDs. He had connections with a few people who lived outside of Cuba and a few years later thanks to them he acquired his first CDs of electronic music. Ricardo is convinced that without his sister's Sony discman, he would not have had the chance of listening to all of this music and would never have become an electronic music specialist.

Lo fortuito kept coming back when Ricardo told me about a friend who came to his house to acquire new music on his iPod. Unfortunately, Ricardo mistakenly erased all of his friend's music when he connected the iPod to his computer. His friend was sad because he had a lot of music on his iPod that he had accumulated through a lot of effort. But Ricardo told him: "You have to take this accidental event and make the best of it." He then filled up the iPod with music his friend would probably never have listened to (according to Ricardo). As a consequence, Ricardo explained, his friend opened himself to new genres, new styles of music. Without this "unfortunate" event, he would probably never have had the interest to listen to the music Ricardo gave him on his iPod. Losing digital music files is painful for Cubans who struggle to acquire music through hand-to-hand music sharing practices. On the other side, losing digital files is expected and part of the game; the question is not if it will happen, but rather when. Music collections are precious but at the same time they are precarious, unstable, and of limited duration. Cubans acquire digital music files in a context of space storage scarcity. There is no easy turning around when one loses digital data. This is why the situation was so desperate and in many ways, *lo fortuito* was Ricardo's only remaining redemption.

I also found many people explaining the acquisition of their large music collection according to the same discourse of luck, both in Havana and Santiago de Cuba. For instance, Ivan, who likes metal music, remembers that in the 1980s and 1990s, in order to get access to this kind of music, he had to rely on his contacts with foreigners. It was the only way for him to gain access to this music. He says that many *jineteros* (prostitutes, dealers with foreigners) used to come to him with cassette tapes tourists had left behind. Ivan used to buy those tapes and he discovered a lot of groups in that way. He says that this happened to him many times and that by chance, he discovered groups that he still listens to today. His cassette tape collection is then the result of a series of fortuitous encounters with people who gave him or sold him music. A similar discourse occurred when music collectors began in the 2000s to look everywhere to find the digital versions of their cassette tape collection.

The difficulty involved in building up a music collection in Cuba is associated with the *qualitative valorization* of what one owns—and this is in contrast with most music aficionados I met in Montreal who tended to express a pride in the *amount* of what they own (usually measured in terms of quantity, "gigs") rather than valuing the quality of their collection. Accessing and owning music in Cuba is not a simple task; it implies resolving a series of challenges that include problems of access, transportation, storage, and reproducibility. Consumption of music and other audio-visual data is, therefore, far from a straightforward enterprise.

According to many music aficionados, the articulation of a discourse based on chance is not as strong today as it was in the 1990s, but it still remains a key factor to explain how someone can acquire a music collection and music knowledge. Better access to digital music would explain the decrease of the chance factor narrative. Yet, nostalgia for *lo fortuito* remains strong among the older generation of music aficionados. Therefore, scarcity—of foreign music, both non-digital and digital—encouraged the articulation of a discourse based on chance. With an increase in access to digital materials and technologies, it is reported that the chance factor narrative began to decline.

An Anthropologist in the Network

As part of my fieldwork, I soon became involved in the passage of digital music with the Cubans I met throughout the research project: I too became a *circulateur*, a human intermediary, someone assisting circulation. As a foreigner on a funded project, I had the ability to travel, to bring music to Cuba, and aid in its transport and circulation. Indeed, acquiring music became an incentive for many participants to spend time with me and explain how they consume and share music. Music aficionados strongly valued the acquisition of new digital music files and folders and they all wanted to learn more about what were the new musical tendencies outside Cuba. Therefore, it was common after an interview with a music aficionado to exchange music files. For instance, after an interview, Ivan asked me to fill his memory stick with all of the music I had on my computer without any discrimination of genre. I was rapidly involved in sharing not only music from outside Cuba, but also local music to Cubans who had not had the chance to access the musical files I owned. I was also interested in knowing what Cubans listened to and what they kept on their memory sticks. Interviews converted themselves into opportunities to exchange music between the interviewees and the interviewer. The process of directly exchanging music proved to be an effective method for understanding how Cubans access certain types of music, and what is difficult to access and why.

Similarly to Cubans—who always carry a memory stick in their pocket, around their neck, in their bra, or in their purse when they leave their home—I began to rely on my memory stick as a means to connect to other people and to exchange music and information. Alejandro, a 30-year-old autodidact R&B and soul singer and composer living in Havana, told me that memory sticks are part of the Cuban person: "we depend on it, it's our ID card." This takes on much more significance in a context like Cuba, where it is illegal to leave home without one's official ID card and police have the right to request identification documents at any time. Leaving home for a meeting or an interview without my memory stick felt like I was missing a key tool of data collection; in fact, my memory stick became "the" most important device to conduct research in Cuba among music aficionados. The process of conducting fieldwork, therefore, involved a replication of the ways in which music is shared and circulated in Cuba. In bringing the memory stick back home, I was not only transporting random digital information, but more importantly, digital materials that were entrenched in the discussions and meetings I had the same day. Wearing the memory stick at all times also implied, and made visible, symbolically that I was ready to catch any fortuitous opportunity to fill up my memory stick with digital data. This is a reminder that serendipity, which involves both chance and sagacity, is a key strength of the ethnographic method (Rivoal and Salazar 2013, 178); indeed, it is even "the essence of ethnographic research" (Pieke in Rivoal and Salazar 2013).

Conclusion

The hand-to-hand sharing practices of digital music files through transportable storage devices and Bluetooth connection in Cuba are inherently social, and rely on various levels of socialities. Born's (2011, 2012, 2013) model of sociality speaks to the various forms of socialities that are assembled by musical experiences and practices, and by music's circulation, in Cuba. In particular, the circulation of digital music brings together individuals who temporarily meet and connect to listen to, share, and consume music. The role of the server, a music aficionado who attracts friends and contacts to meet so as to access and share music files, as well as the CD and DVD vendors who act as nodal points around which people aggregate to buy, consume, and discuss music, are examples of how microsocialities take shape momentarily in the processes of music's circulation and consumption.

The discourse of chance among music aficionados might have declined with the increase of access to digital music files. Yet, the circulation of digital data on physical storage devices has definitely contributed to strengthening the offline and physical networks of exchanges and socialities in a context where access to the Internet is limited. The proliferation of nodes of encounter between those who own and seek music has boosted the spread of the digital, providing more accessible means to consume and share digital music. Music aficionados' nostalgic discourse about chance highlights their ironic and reflexive awareness of the way that fortune is linked to scarcity in Cuba, and the exquisite sense of privilege in such a context of owning something rare and difficult to obtain. The increasing access to the digital and to the Internet in the present conjuncture will certainly contribute further to the ongoing transformation of what fortune means in Cuba.

Notes

1 The MusDig research program, including the research on which this article is based, was funded by the European Research Council's Advanced Grants scheme, project number 249598, based at the University of Oxford, UK.

2 More information about this large-scale research program can be found on the MusDig research webpage (http://musdig.music.ox.ac.uk/) and through a series of publications also listed on the website.

3 Cubans also have a national Internet called "Intranet."

4 BBC news, May 31, 2013 (www.bbc.co.uk/news/world-latin-america-22696637, accessed September 28, 2016). As for the Caribbean region, according to the most recent data available, only Haiti has a lower Internet penetration rate: 8.5 percent in Haiti (2011) compared to 23.2 percent in Cuba (2012) (www.internetworldstats.com, accessed September 28, 2016). Yet, the Cuban rate is biased because it includes the use of Intranet (national Internet with no international access) and public Internet stations.

5 ETECSA stands for Empresa de Telecomunicaciones de Cuba S.A.

6 Two other Internet services were also offered at ETECSA: US$1.50/hour for international email, and US$0.60/hour for national Internet.

7 For instance, see "SNet, la intranet callejera tolerada por el regimen," published in *Diario de Cuba* on January 27, 2015.

8 SD cards are storage devices that are used in photo and video cameras, and in sound recording machines. The micro-SD cards are used in cell phones.

9 Friends might use Bluetooth connection to exchange a limited number of music files.

10 On February 9, 2015, Netflix launched its services in Cuba, suggesting that online market services might rapidly be headed for rapid expansion on the island.

11 The new license agreement between Sony and EGREM signed on September 15, 2015, which will allow the distribution of EGREM's catalog of Cuban music at the global level, might create new dynamics in the availability of Cuban music worldwide. However, this licensing will primarily have effects on the consumption of Cuban music outside Cuba.

12 Carlson, Nicholas, September 8, 2010, "Google Just Killed the 'I'm Feeling Lucky Button.'" Business Insider, www.businessinsider.com/google-just-effectively-killed-the-im-feeling-lucky-button-2010-9 (accessed December 7, 2015).

References

Born, Georgina. 2011. "Music and the Materialization of Identities." *Journal of Material Culture* 16(4): 376–88.

——. 2012. "Music and the Social." In *The Cultural Study of Music: A Critical Introduction*, edited by Martin Clayton, Trevor Herbert and Richard Middleton, 261–74. London: Routledge.

——. 2013. "Introduction—Music, Sound and Space: Transformations of Public and Private Experience." In *Music, Sound and Space: Transformations of Public and Private Experience*, edited by Georgina Born, 1–70. Cambridge: Cambridge University Press.

Born, Georgina, and Alexandrine Boudreault-Fournier. Forthcoming. "Consumption and Circulation in Two Musical Digital Cultures: Montreal and Cuba." In *Digital Musics: A Global Anthropology*, edited by Georgina Born.

Boudreault-Fournier, Alexandrine. Forthcoming. "Pirates of the Caribbean: Digital Music Circulation and Author's Rights in Cuba." In *Music, Digitization, and Intellectual Property: Sounds, Culture, and Law in Global Remix*, edited by Georgina Born. Durham, NC: Duke University Press.

Boudreault-Fournier, Alexandrine, and Laurent K. Blais. 2015. "Nous sommes le future. Afro-futurisme et images Piu Piu." In *Images, sons et récits des Afro-Amériques*, edited by Francine Saillant and Jorge P. Santiago, 81–108. Paris: Éditions des archives contemporaines.

——. 2016. "La comète Piu Piu: Nouveaux médias et nationalisme en mutation." *Anthropologie et sociétés* 39(3): 103–23.

——. Forthcoming. "Post-Nationalist Hip Hop: Beatmaking and the Emergence of the Piu Piu Scene." In *Hip Hop North of the 49th Parallel: Hip Hop in Canada and Canadian Hip Hop*, edited by Charity Marsh and Mark Campbell. Montreal: McGill-Queen's University Press.

Bull, Michael. 2006. "Investigating the Culture of Mobile Listening: from Walkman to iPod." In *Consuming Music Together: Social and Collaborative Aspects of Music Consumption Technologies*, edited by Kenton O'Hara and Barry Brown, 131–49. Netherlands: Springer.

da Col, Giovanni. 2012. "Introduction: Natural Philosophies of Fortune—Luck, Vitality, and Uncontrolled Relatedness." *Social Analysis* 56(1): 1–23.

DeNora, Tia. 2000. *Music in Everyday Life*. Cambridge: Cambridge University Press.

Gopinath, Sumanth, and Jason Stanyek. 2014. "Anytime, Anywhere? An Introduction to the Devices, Markets, and Theories of Mobile Music." In *The Oxford Handbook of Mobile Music Studies*, edited by Sumanth Gopinath and Jason Stanyek, 1–34. Oxford: Oxford University Press.

Holbraad, Martin. 2010. "The Whole Beyond Holism: Gambling, Divination, and Ethnography in Cuba." In *Experiments in Holism Theory and Practice in Contemporary Anthropology*, edited by Ton Otto and Nils Bubandt, 67–85. Oxford: Wiley-Blackwell.

Humphrey, Caroline, and Stephen Hugh-Jones. 1992. "Introduction: Barter, Exchange and Value." In *Barter, Exchange and Value: An Anthropological Approach*, edited by Caroline Humphrey and Stephen Hugh-Jones, 1–20. Cambridge: Cambridge University Press.

Pertierra, Anna Cristina. 2012. "If They Show Prison Break in the United States on a Wednesday, by Thursday It Is Here: Mobile Media Networks in Twenty-First-Century Cuba." *Television & New Media* 13(5): 399–414.

Recio Silva, Milena. 2014. "La hora de los desconectados. Evaluación del diseño de la política de 'acceso social' a Internet en Cuba en un contexto de cambios Milena." *Crítica y Emancipación* 11: 291–378.

Rivoal, Isabelle and Noel B. Salazar. 2013. "Contemporary Ethnographic Practice and the Value of Serendipity." *Social Anthropology* 21(2): 178–85.

Stern, Monika. 2014. "'Mi wantem music blong mi hemi blong evriwan' ["I want my music to be for everyone"]: Digital Developments, Copyright and Music Circulation in Port Vila, Vanuatu." *First Monday* 19(10). http://firstmonday.org/ojs/index.php/fm/article/view/5551

Venegas, Cristina. 2010. *Digital Dilemmas: The State, the Individual, and Digital Media in Cuba*. New Brunswick, NJ: Rutgers University.

Verdery, Katherine. 1996. *What was Socialism, and What Comes Next?* Princeton, NJ: Princeton University Press.

32

AN INFRASTRUCTURAL APPROACH TO DIGITAL ETHNOGRAPHY

Lessons from the Manchester Infrastructures of Social Change Project

Hannah Knox

In this chapter I outline how recent work on the anthropology of infrastructure can provide a particularly fruitful set of resources for framing and designing ethnographic analyses of digital technologies. This chapter aims to go beyond work that focuses on digital media practices and the way in which digital devices are given meaning and used by different social groups in order to draw attention to the material, ontological and relational qualities that are built into digital devices. Building on the work of the Infrastructures of Social Change group at the Economic and Social Research Council (ESRC) funded Centre for Research on Socio-Cultural Change (CRESC) at the University of Manchester, the chapter outlines the potential for developing an ethnographic approach to understanding the formation, circulation and use of digital infrastructural systems and their implications for social life.

Researching the Infrastructure of Social Change

The material discussed in this chapter emerged largely from discussions that I had with an interdisciplinary group of colleagues at the University of Manchester who worked together from 2004 to 2014 at the ESRC Centre for Research on Socio-Cultural Change (CRESC). In the final three years of the center, the group agreed to work under the heading "infrastructures of social change" and a concerted effort was made to explore the benefits that might accrue from researching social processes in terms of their manifestation as infrastructure, broadly defined. People in the group[1] came from a variety of different social science and humanities backgrounds and were researching topics ranging from airports to roads, genomics to sport, urban redevelopment, migration and transformations in work. Many of us had worked at one time or another on issues associated with technologies of different kinds, from the role of information systems in framing business and management as a problem of knowledge, to the role of digital technologies in undoing the textual form of the book. In each of the projects that people had worked on, technological systems figured large. Members of the group were grappling with questions about how to analyze, ethnographically, databases of genetic information, to questions about how to study the technologies used to manage an airport, model a city or imagine future environmental change.

One of the reasons why technologies were so present in our discussions is that we were working to find a way of describing social change. A key preoccupation of the group was how to analyze social change through the deployment of qualitative, and in particular ethnographic methods and, importantly, to see change as inhering not just in social practices but also in the interplay between human and non-human forms. Although coming from diverse disciplinary backgrounds, the group was held together through a commitment to the insights that could be provided by ethnographically informed, deconstructive analyses of how change was generated in differentiated and technologized social worlds. To answer this question we collectively read and explored the work of Henri Bergson, Gilles Deleuze, Felix Guattari and Bruno Latour[2]—thinkers whose project of understanding social processes chimed with our own.

A turn to infrastructure was an attempt to concretize this set of discussions that had circled around the relative role of knowledge, information, technology, culture, materiality and embodiment in processes of social change. Thinking of the relationships we had been interrogating and tracing in our different research settings in terms of infrastructure seemed to provide us with a means of tracking and tracing resonances, affinities and disjunctures across our different fieldsites. It offered the possibility of generating a description of contemporary social processes that kept open the possibility of difference. We tried hard not to resort to evoking the sweeping categories of more epochal accounts of social transformation: capitalism, neoliberalism, and modernity. We were wary of the silencing effect of analyses that emphasized broad historical claims about the nature and scale of social transformation and found that the question of what kind of infrastructures were at play in these different research sites seemed to offer a more nuanced, less prescriptive way of describing social change.

While we initially evoked the concept of infrastructure to describe a quality or form of relating that might be social, material or technological, another reason for using the language of infrastructure was its concreteness. Infrastructure offered not just an analytic device but also a presence in the world that was raising its own challenges for experts: the engineers, policy makers, scientists and architects, charged with bringing infrastructures into being and making them work. Part of our turn to infrastructure was an attempt to open up a conversation with those who were producing concrete infrastructural forms—roads, airports, pipelines, borders—in order to both learn from them how infrastructure operated as a site of social change, and to contribute to current political discussions through a comparative analysis of infrastructural relations ethnographically described. It was from both our internal discussions and our engagement with these practitioners and other scholars who had begun to analyze similar infrastructural projects[3] that there emerged for us three key dynamics at play in the anthropology of infrastructure, which I draw attention to and unpack in this chapter as a means of informing digital ethnography: Infrastructure Relations and Politics, Infrastructure and Scale, and Infrastructural Analytics.

Infrastructural Relations and Politics

Ethnographies of digital technologies are often put forward as an antidote to more explicitly political analyses of digital devices and their implications. Technology is a powerful cultural imaginary (Marx 2010) and both the fear and the promise of digital technologies in particular risk stifling analysis, so caught up are they in political projects of different kinds. Much early enthusiasm for the Internet, for example, was driven by libertarian promises of an emancipatory future that would be able to circumvent institutional structures and untether individuals from the controls of government by creating a new frontier where information could circulate and communities could form (Rheingold 1993). As with all frontiers, hot on the heels of this promise of freedom came the threat that this space would be colonized by capital and delimited by institutions of regulatory control. The initial freedoms of the Internet have been increasingly curtailed by the securitization of online space by corporations and by governments in the name of protecting the customer from fraud, and shielding the citizen from both digital and non-digital forms of violence (Coleman and Golub 2008).

While this oscillation between libertarian ideals and the colonizing tendencies of capital might be understood as a battle over competing ideologies, many scholars have asked whether there might be something particular to the relational principles of the digital that lends itself to mobilization by these particular political imaginaries. As Dominic Boyer (2013) points out in his work on the digital transformations of journalism, political ideologies are not divorced from the particular circumstances in which they arise. While the libertarian promise of new digital frontiers has precedent in prior political movements, it is not insignificant that it re-emerges and is refigured through the affordances of digital technological forms.

This is where ethnographic approaches to infrastructure offer some resources. Anthropological studies of infrastructure look at the way in which political relations emerge out of struggles with mundane matters of concern. Nikhil Anand's (2011) work on the politics of water supply in Mumbai is a wonderful example of the way in which a close anthropological attention to situated battles for access to material resources can reveal how distributions of responsibility between different kinds of social actors are established. Here the citizen and the state are shown to be remade through techniques of political negotiation that include technical practices of measurement, the normativity of appropriate forms of political participation, and the appearance (or not) of water as a material agent effecting possibilities for social and political life in Mumbai. Similarly the work that Penny Harvey and I (Harvey and Knox 2015) conducted on road construction in Peru took roads as a distributed object through which we could study the historical and contemporary formation and deformation of political relations. We found politics to inhere not only in ideological positions but also in expert practices, spatial imaginaries and issues of social responsibility that appeared when matter—mud, asphalt, sand and stones—was transformed and relocated.

What then would this look like when brought into the digital arena? Recent work on the sociology and anthropology of "big" data provides a good example of how an infrastructural approach to digital politics might proceed. One of the capacities of digital technologies identified by anthropologists of the digital is their ability to produce, replicate and circulate data in ways that are qualitatively different to prior methods of information collection, distribution and retrieval (boyd and Crawford 2012). Struggles over the appropriate uses of this data have opened up deeply contentious discussions about what data is, to whom it belongs and how it should be used (Gitelman 2013). From concerns over copyright and piracy (patent), to questions of privacy and international security (Amoore 2011), the issue of who or what produces data, how this data circulates, and to what uses it is put constitute important sites of politics.

An ethnographic approach deriving from the anthropology of infrastructure aims to trace these issues, debates and controversies by investigating how they become manifest in relation to specific material configurations. A concern with international security would take, as Louise Amoore (2011) has done, a specific database being developed, with a view to tracing, tracking and analyzing the activities of citizens. It would explore the tensions around the practice of trying to derive, algorithmically, the probabilities of someone constituting a security risk. Approaching this politics through an ethnography of infrastructure would entail an investigation into the institutional, political and regulatory issues that are confronted in the formation of such a database, and the unforeseen consequences of such a database as it is put into use. It would look at how these unforeseen consequences are known and dealt with, the classificatory principles that are materialized in the structure and form of such an information system, and the means by which such a system is itself imbued with infrastructural qualities that allow it to "stand for itself" (Wagner 1986).

This act of tracing politics as it inheres in infrastructural forms poses, however, some important challenges to ethnography. First is the sense of where the ethnographic field lies (Amit 2000). The focus on infrastructure rather than social group or community has the effect of siting an ethnography in a concrete set of material relations that are demarcated by specific institutional, technological, material, regulatory and social contours. At the same time these relationships are often internationally distributed, historically embedded and, at the same time, located in particular places. The anthropology of infrastructure thus adds a nuance to Marcus' (1995) call for multi-sited ethnography, emphasizing less the multi-sited quality of ethnographic research on infrastructural forms than the tendency of studies of infrastructure to force a reconsideration of what constitutes the "sit-uatedness" of any fieldsite. It is to this quality of sitedness and to the capacity of infrastructure to disrupt the anthropological concept of the fieldsite that the next section turns.

Infrastructure and Scale: Beyond Structure and Agency

By virtue of their systemic, distributed and networked relationality, infrastructures necessarily exceed that which is materially present and draw attention to that which is not immediately visible. The very idea of infrastructure implies an inherently networked, distributed or systemic form of social and material organization. While infrastructures are encountered in day-to-day living, their systemic qualities always posit an extension beyond their tangible form, or indeed their diagrammatic representation. Once again the road is a good example of this. Roads are simultaneously things that are made, repaired and traveled, and things that open up routes of imaginative connection to other places, from the village to the nation state to the transnational flows of goods and people from elsewhere.

Given that this extendable quality of infrastructural form seems central to its contemporary manifestation as a social and political technology, this raises the question of just how and when material arrangements manifest this sense of extendibility. In order to consider the practices by which particular arrangements are able to flip into and out of an infrastructural mode, our group at CRESC invoked the idea that infrastructures are material arrangements that are not just tacking between the visible and the invisible, but which manifest themselves in "vanishing points."

The vanishing point is a concept used in geometry to refer to a particular effect in perspectival representation where lines converge into a point of disappearance. Historians of art have located the vanishing point as the invention of the enlightenment, a technical advance that enabled the development of perspectival drawing (Jay 1988). With infrastructures often graphically represented in the perspectival style, the vanishing point seemed a particularly apt metaphor for thinking about the relationship between the immediacy and extendibility of infrastructure. Certain infrastructural forms such as roads, railways and electricity networks very literally produce the vanishing point as an ocular effect, with parallel lines disappearing into an indiscernible spot at the horizon. Moreover, infrastructures are often discussed in terms of their invisibility (Star and Ruhleder 1996). On the one hand infrastructures are frequently located underground or otherwise out of sight, something that is particularly the case with digital technologies whose material infrastructural basis is so obscured we have no difficulty imagining information as "floating" in an ungrounded cloud (Starosielski 2015). At other times infrastructures exist as quite visible structures but remain unseen in that they are taken for granted. At other times they are only partially visible, accessible only from a particular vantage point or via a diagrammatic abstraction. This is particularly relevant when it comes to thinking about digital infrastructures because although the wires and cables that allow information transmission to occur are often invisible, the information they transmit is valuable precisely because it can be made visible in some kind of representational form. The promise of information depends on the capacity of digital devices to leave readable material traces that allow information to be captured, analyzed and visualized in ways that were not previously possible. Information infrastructures are thus strangely invisible and hypervisible at the same time.

To understand this tension, the vanishing point is a useful notion. It allows us to pay attention to the particular way in which certain material formations—whether objects such as a computer, a faucet, a telephone, or an airport, a supermarket or a road work—operate on the basis of systems of interconnectivity and technical operation that are rendered invisible by casings, containers, sockets and standards that work to hold them in place, and at the same time open up to new images that remake the imagination in their unfolding.

In this respect, the vanishing point of infrastructural formations operates rather like what Sassen (2001) has called an "analytic borderland," giving "discontinuities a terrain" and preventing them from "being seen as mutually exclusive" (Sassen 2001, 17). Here in the concept of the vanishing point, the apparent discontinuities between matter and the imagination or the immediate and the extended are held together in a single moment. It is the vanishing points of infrastructural formations that draw forth questions about their extendibility, about what it is that holds them together, what we need to better visualize, and what kinds of relations are needed to effect their transformation.

To stay with the ocular metaphor, the concept of vanishing points also allows us to consider the relationship between infrastructure and positionality. Vanishing points are not simply a quality of a material arrangement itself, but are tied to the position of a viewer, altering as the subject position moves in relation to the infrastructural object. Travel along the road or the rail line and the vanishing point recedes into the distance. Dig up the ground where fiber-optic cables penetrate, or unpack their institutional affiliations and the vanishing points of these relations also shift. In this respect, the concept of the vanishing point can help us move beyond an overly fixed opposition between the seen and the unseen, the visible and the invisible, the located and the extensive (see also Vertesi 2014). Instead, an attention to the vanishing points of digital infrastructure forces us to focus on the particular technologies, techniques and relations that enable an infrastructural imagination at any particular moment.

A final advantage of the notion of the vanishing point is that it allows us to move beyond a common trope that infrastructures only become visible when they fail (Star and Ruhleder 1996). While the breakdown of infrastructural systems is certainly a key political preoccupation, it is not strictly true that the infrastructure only becomes visible at this moment of failure. Questions about the make-up of infrastructure might become that much more pertinent when they fail or when the specter of their potential failure is put on the table, but what the work of the CRESC group has shown is that the appearance of infrastructure is not only a function of failure, but the manifestation of an attentiveness to the extendibility of the present and the immediate into broader systemic configurations (see also Knox, forthcoming 2017).

By drawing attention not to the breakdown of infrastructures but to their vanishing points, it becomes possible then to point to the way in which infrastructures appear as infrastructure via a particular mode of attention, that is both indicative and formative of contemporary social relations. This raises questions about whether the ethnography of infrastructure does something more than simply expand the fieldsites that anthropologists pay attention to, and actually changes the nature of anthropological analysis itself. It is to this possibility of a transformation, not only of the sites of anthropology but also of the analytic resources and theoretical assumptions that we as ethnographers deploy in our analysis of social relations, that I turn in the final section.

Infrastructural Analytics

One of the implications of the discussion so far is that infrastructures are more than a historical or contemporary phenomena to which social scientists should attend if we are to understand the worlds in which we live. The qualities of infrastructure that I have touched on—their capacity to act as technologies of mediation, as sites for differentiation and as vanishing points—all point to the possibility that there might be a distinctive analytic stance that could derive from this attention to infrastructure. To suggest this is not entirely surprising in light of the history of infrastructural thinking in relation to digital technologies.

Susan Leigh-Star, a stalwart of analyses of systems of information, classification and technological organization, wrote a joint-authored piece with Karen Ruhleder—one of the first and still one of the most influential systematic analyses of infrastructures and their social function (Star and Ruhleder 1996). In the article they set out a rationale for why an attention to infrastructure might provide a specific kind of analytic viewpoint on modern forms of social organization. The central argument of this piece was that what was specific, unique and challenging about these information technologies was that they performed an *infrastructural* way of being in the world. These technologies were not self-evidently infrastructures, but rather they performed infrastructural capacities that drew attention to a broader set of questions for social research about the qualities that rendered particular arrangements of people and things "infrastructural." For Star and Ruhleder, infrastructure was not so much a thing to be defined—a particular set of relationships that fulfilled certain conditions. The question the ethnographer was encouraged to ask was not *what* is an infrastructure, but "*when* is an infrastructure?" (Star and Ruhleder 1996, 112).

This offers an instructive starting point for thinking about how the focus on infrastructure that we developed at CRESC might re-inflect an anthropological attention to digital technologies. Much of the discussion that has taken place regarding what might constitute the field of digital anthropology has centered on the question of how to define the digital as an object of study, with questions like what is the difference between online and offline (Turkle 1997), what is the digital (Horst and Miller 2012), and what is the difference between the virtual and the actual framing the debate? For infrastructure studies to begin with the question not what is a digital infrastructure but *when* is a digital infrastructure immediately expands the ambition of digital anthropology from one of dividing the world up into a series of discrete sub-specialisms or multiple fieldsites, to the question of the power of relational assumptions that inhere in decisions about how to construct the world in which we live. The question "when is an infrastructure?" draws attention to the work that the appeal to infrastructure does, and requires not that we go out looking for concrete infrastructures to study, but that we attend to the operations through which digital devices, technologies and material arrangements become "infrastructural."

Let us consider this through the concrete example of smart meters, those digital devices that enable energy companies to continuously monitor energy use in people's homes.[4] In what sense might these devices be understood to be infrastructural? Taking Star and Ruhleder's definition of the infrastructure we might argue that it is only when a smart meter is installed, when the Internet connection through which information from the smart meter is sent is up and running, when the databases and servers that collect information at the energy company are functioning and correctly configured, when the correct email address is used to contact the consumer about what their energy usage is and when the consumer reads and understands their bill that we can say that this set of relationships is operating in terms that fulfill Star and Ruhleder's definition of the infrastructural. On the other hand, at the moment when the engineer who installs the meter is concentrating on getting it attached to the wall, when the customer finds the glow from the energy display irritating and turns it around to face the wall, or when the heating engineer has to master the manual that describes how the digital rather than analog meter works, the infrastructural qualities of the technology fall away.

This approach to the "when" of infrastructure has implications both for how we understand the intellectual project of digital anthropology, and for how we might conceive of digital ethnography as a method that is capable of getting at both the experiential and the distributed, socio-technical dimensions of human social worlds. Methodologically then, attending to infrastructure in Star and Ruhleder's terms is not about finding something that is or is not an infrastructure to study, but attending to how particular arrangements of things can move in and out of an infrastructural mode of being. Digital technologies are not the only technologies that can perform this infrastructural move, but as their benefits are frequently associated with their capacity for networked connectivity and the transformative social, economic and political effects that this connectivity affords, these infrastructural qualities often come to the fore in evaluations of their functional success or failure. An infrastructural analytic, then, is not just something that we can deploy as scholars, but something that we need to be aware of as a particular aspect of being in the world that characterizes contemporary social relations.

Conclusion: Ethnographic Challenges in the Anthropology of Digital Infrastructure

In this chapter I have outlined how a broadly infrastructural approach might be useful when conducting an ethnography of digital technologies. I end the chapter with two reflections on the challenges of such an approach. The first is about boundaries. All ethnographic research requires that some kind of boundaries become established around the object being studied. However, the extendibility of infrastructural relations can create problems for this kind of boundary work, making it at times difficult to design a project that has a logical set of limits. More work needs to be done in thinking methodologically about how, as ethnographers, we deal with the infrastructural relations described in this chapter. Is George Marcus' idea of multi-sited ethnography enough? What happens to the promise of ethnographic comparison in light of ethnographies of infrastructure? Do we move from comparative ethnography to an ethnography of global connectivity, and if we do then how do we retain openness to difference in ways that do not just locate difference in the local, and universality in the techniques and forms of infrastructure itself. And last, how do we manage the boundaries between ethnography of and ethnography through infrastructure? What kind of collaborative relationships might we need to forge as we work with interlocutors to co-produce understandings of more-than-human relationalities? Are there methods we can learn from the engineers and bricoleurs that develop infrastructural systems in order to develop new methods of infrastructural inversion—prototyping, experimentation, diagnostic tests—through which the project of ethnography might be expanded?

The second issue that this kind of approach raises is one of analytic distance. If infrastructure is the term that is deployed to describe the relational qualities inherent to technical systems, then does the deployment of the same terminology in framing an analytical stance close down the possibility of seeing the practices entailed in relation to any particular infrastructure in self-similar rather than self-differing ways? That is, does approaching roads, databases, oil pipelines, sewage systems and communications networks as infrastructure open up or close down the possibility of gaining a fresh anthropological perspective on the way in which these material formations participate in social worlds? (See Horst (2013) for further reflections on these issues.) I would caution that a turn to infrastructure should be deployed only insofar as it is analytically and conceptually generative. It might be that alternative concepts—ferality (Tsing 2015), recursivity (Kelty 2008), friction (Tsing 2005), algorithmicity (Kockelman 2013), pre-emption (Anderson 2010)—will emerge from the study of infrastructure to create new resonances and lines of association and affinity through which we can continue to approach the social implications of distributed material processes.

Notes

1 The group was led by Penny Harvey and myself and during the time of discussions about infrastructure included Eleanor Casella, Adolfo Estalella, Jeanette Edwards, Gillian Evans, Gemma John, Yannis Kallianos, Christine Maclean, Damian O'Doherty, Annabel Pinker, Madeleine Reeves, Elizabeth Silva, Nick Thoburn, Kath Woodward and Peter Wade.

2 Books that we collectively read included *Matter and Memory* (Bergson 1912), *A Thousand Plateaus* (Deleuze and Guattari 1988), *Difference and Repetition* (Deleuze 1968), *Francis Bacon* (Deleuze 2003), *Cinema 1 and 2* (Deleuze 1986, 1989), *The Fold* (Deleuze 1993), *Reassembling the Social* (Latour 2005) and *An Enquiry into Modes of Existence* (Latour 2013).

3 For example, Nikhil Anand (2011) on water infrastructure, Brian Larkin (2008) on media infrastructure; Cymene Howe and Dominic Boyer (2016), Andrew Barry (2013) and Timothy Mitchell (2011) on energy infrastructures; Stephen Collier (2011) on cities and housing; and Casper Bruun Jensen (2015) on environmental infrastructures.

4 Noortje Marres (2013) has also looked at the smart meter as an example of digital technologies that participate in the formation of contemporary social life.

References

Amit, Vered. 2000. *Constructing the Field: Ethnographic fieldwork in the contemporary world*. London: Routledge.

Amoore, Louise. 2011. "Data derivatives." *Theory, Culture & Society*. 28(6): 24–43.

Anand, Nikhil. 2011. "PRESSURE: The PoliTechnics of Water Supply in Mumbai." *Cultural Anthropology*. 26(4): 542–64.

Anderson, Ben. 2010. "Preemption, precaution, preparedness: Anticipatory action and future geographies." *Progress in Human Geography*. 34(6): 777–98.

Barry, Andrew. 2013. *Material Politics: Disputes along the pipeline*. Malden, MA: Wiley Blackwell.

Bergson, Henri. 1912. *Matter and Memory*. London: C & Allen Co.

boyd, danah and Kate Crawford. 2012. "Critical questions for Big Data." *Information, Communication & Society*. 15(5): 662–79.

Boyer, Dominic. 2013. *The Life Informatic: Newsmaking in the digital era*. Ithaca, NY: Cornell University Press.

Coleman, E. Gabriella and Alex Golub. 2008. "Hacker practice." *Anthropological Theory*. 8(3): 255–77.

Collier, Stephen J. 2011. *Post-Soviet Social Neoliberalism, Social Modernity, Biopolitics*. Princeton, NJ: Princeton University Press.

Deleuze, Gilles. 1968. *Difference and Repetition*. London: The Athlone Press.

——. 1986. *Cinema 1: The movement image*. London: The Athlone Press.

——. 1989. *Cinema II: The time image*. London: The Athlone Press.

——. 1993. *The Fold*. London: The Athlone Press.

——. 2003. *Francis Bacon: The logic of sensation*. London: Continuum.

Deleuze, Gilles and Felix Guattari. 1988. *A Thousand Plateaus: Capitalism and schizophrenia*. London: The Athlone Press.

Gitelman, Lisa, ed. 2013. *Raw Data is an Oxymoron*. Cambridge, MA: MIT Press.

Harvey, Penny and Hannah Knox. 2015. *Roads: An anthropology of infrastructure and expertise*. Ithaca, NY: Cornell University Press.

Horst, Heather. 2013. "The infrastructures of mobile media: Towards a future research agenda." *Mobile, Media and Communication*. 1(1): 147–52.

Horst, Heather and Daniel Miller. 2012. *Digital Anthropology*. London: Berg.

Howe, Cymene and Dominic Boyer. 2016. "Aeolian extractivism and community wind in Southern Mexico." *Public Culture*. 28(2 79): 215–35.

Jay, Martin. 1988. "Scopic Regimes of Modernity." In *Vision and Visuality*, edited by Hal Foster, 3–23. New York: The New Press.

Jensen, Casper Bruun. 2015. "Experimenting with political materials: Environmental infrastructures and ontological transformations." *Distinktion: Scandinavian Journal of Social Theory*. 16(1): 17–30.

Kelty, Chris M. 2008. *Two Bits: The cultural significance of free software*. Durham, NC: Duke University Press.

Knox, Hannah. Forthcoming 2017. "Affective infrastructures and the political imagination." *Public Culture*.

Kockelman, Paul. 2013. "The anthropology of an equation: Sieves, spam filters, agentive algorithms, and ontologies of transformation." *Hau: Journal of Ethnographic Theory* 3(3). http://dx.doi.org/10.14318/hau3.3.003 (accessed August 10, 2016).

Larkin, Brian. 2008. *Signal and noise: Media, infrastructure, and urban culture in Nigeria*. Durham, NC: Duke University Press.

Latour, Bruno. 2005. *Reassembling the Social*. Oxford: Oxford University Press.

——. 2013. *An Inquiry into Modes of Existence: An anthropology of the moderns*. Cambridge, MA: Harvard University Press.

Marcus, George E. 1995. "Ethnography in/of the world system: The emergence of multi-sited ethnography." *Annual Review of Anthropology*, 95–117.

Marres, Noortje. 2013. *Material Participation: Technology, the environment and everyday publics*. London: Palgrave MacMillan.

Marx, Leo. 2010. "Technology: The emergence of a hazardous concept." *Technology and Culture*. 51(3): 561–77.

Mitchell, Timothy. 2011. *Carbon Democracy: Political power in the age of oil*. London: Verso.

Rheingold, Howard. 1993. *The Virtual Community: Homesteading on the electronic frontier* (revised edition). Boston, MA: Addison Wesley.

Sassen, Saskia. 2001. "The city: Between topographic representation practices and spatialized power projects." *The Art Journal*. 60(2): 12–20.

Star, Susan Leigh and Karen Ruhleder. 1996. "Steps toward an ecology of infrastructure: Design and access for large information spaces." *Information Systems Research* 7(1): 111–34.

Starosielski, Nicole. 2015. *The Undersea Network*. Durham, NC: Duke University Press.

Tsing, Anna. 2005. *Friction: An ethnography of global connection*. Princeton, NJ: Princeton University Press.

——. 2015. "Feral Biologies." Paper for Anthropological Visions of Sustainable Futures Conference, University College London, February 2015.

Turkle, Sherry. 1997. *Life on the Screen: Identity in the age of the Internet*. New York: Simon and Schuster.

Vertesi, Janet. 2014. "Seamful spaces: Heterogenous infrastructures in interaction." *Science, Technology and Human Values*. 39(2): 264–84.

Wagner, R. 1986. *Symbols that Stand for Themselves*. Chicago, IL: University of Chicago Press.

33

RIDING THE RAILS OF MOBILE PAYMENTS

Financial Inclusion, Mobile Phones, and Infrastructure

Stephen C. Rea, Ursula Dalinghaus, Taylor C. Nelms, and Bill Maurer

Introduction

Since the early 2000s, mobile phone carriers, device manufacturers, and the mobile industry's trade associations have promoted the use of the mobile network as a digital payment network. In doing so, they are attempting to use the networks they have built to carry financial data, muscling into banks' territory, posing challenges to how states regulate money flows, and potentially "disrupting" the payments industry itself. Such disruption invites opportunities for ethnographic study of the rapidly changing landscape of digital and mobile payment. Much traditional ethnographic fieldwork took place in areas that are now, in the early twenty-first century, at the forefront of new mobile payment technologies. Alternately, ethnographers may find opportunities for working laterally with payments industry professionals, many of whom have enlisted ethnographers in their work and experience, once they get into the business of payment, the denaturalization of money familiar to anthropologists (Maurer 2016).[1]

This chapter analyzes payments as a set of technical and social infrastructures for "financial inclusion"—political, business, and philanthropic projects designed to extend formal financial services to un- and underbanked populations around the world. Specifically, we are concerned with mobile payments—the use of mobile phones and networks to exchange electronic value—as the "rails" upon which a broad range of financial products and services (insurance, credit, savings) ride, and the social and political consequences of new payments infrastructures that become platforms for services far from their intended uses. Platforms are political—they create, sunder, extend, and transform relationships—and infrastructures are settled political claims. Mobile payments provide an example of what happens when such claims get unsettled; their ethnographic study offers a window into infrastructural change, the displacement of legacy systems, and the layering of new functionality onto existing systems. Different strategies for deploying mobile payments reveal, in short, the political and social entailments of financial infrastructures.

MNOs and Digital Payments

As mobile network operators (MNOs) got into digital payments, they realized they would need to make a case to governments about why they should be allowed into the business of value transfer. Initially, some business leaders promoted the idea that mobile phone transaction records—stored on MNO servers—could be useful in assessing and monitoring taxes. But around the same time, the United Nations released its Millennium Development Goals, the first of which focuses on poverty reduction. Working with state-based aid agencies, new philanthropic organizations with roots in Silicon Valley, the World Bank, and other international organizations, MNOs hit on mobile phone-based money transfer and payment as a means of "financial inclusion" (Schwittay 2011). They would leverage the mobile network, which, unlike bank branches, was "everywhere," to bring the un- and underbanked into the formal financial sector. In the developing world, where less than 50 percent of people have access to formal financial institutions, yet over 90 percent have access to mobile phones, the hope was that mobile payments services would be vehicles for poverty alleviation by furnishing poor or historically marginalized populations with tools to help them secure, manage, and *mobilize* their money, both literally and figuratively.

Early MNO-led mobile payments deployments like Globe's GCASH in the Philippines and Safaricom's M-Pesa in Kenya (launched in 2004 and 2007, respectively) were primarily used for person-to-person (P2P) value transfers such as remittances, and to a lesser extent for bill pay and wage disbursement. The relative successes of these deployments encouraged MNOs to develop more complex financial services and products, such as savings, loans/credit, social welfare benefits, and insurance. When mobile payment services become platforms for still other services, they become more contested: it's well and good for an MNO to offer a P2P micropayment service, but when it starts offering savings or insurance products, banks—and their regulators—start to worry about competition, oversight, and the politics of platforms (Gillespie 2010). The transformation of the mobile network into a payment rail and platform (Kendall et al. 2012) is thus ripe for ethnographic attention.

In the following sections, we introduce payments and their infrastructures and discuss three recent approaches to designing and implementing financial inclusion schemes that ride the rails of mobile payments: the M-Shwari savings and loans product in Kenya, which rides on top of Safaricom's M-Pesa mobile money transfer service; India's "payments banks," a new category of financial institution that enables non-bank entities to provide their clients with value transfer, savings, and remittance services; and the Central Bank of Ecuador's (BCE) new mobile money system, "the first ever publicly mandated and central bank-administered mobile payments scheme to be implemented in the world" (Félix 2014). Each example showcases a different conversation about the role of MNOs, states, and banks in payments, with different stakes, players, and assumptions about the public good. We conclude that mobile money as an emerging platform is surfacing questions about the role of payments in the public interest. Payment rails determine where your money can go, how fast it can get there, and how much it will cost you to do so. Absent a kind of "network neutrality" for payments, payment platforms will necessarily present political problems.

What Is Payment?

Payment is not money itself, but the infrastructures that facilitate its movement, whether hand-to-hand, over a proprietary network, or through the Internet. People make payments for various reasons: buying a cup of coffee, paying a utility bill, sending money to friends or family. Governments pay people social benefits and tax refunds. Businesses pay wages to their workers, and pay each other for inventory or services. Businesses and people pay governments taxes. The payments industry consists of public and private entities that facilitate these transfers of value.[2] Payments professionals refer to their infrastructures as sets of "rails." The metaphor comes from the nineteenth-century extension of the railroads in the United States, and, with them, the first telecommunications lines; wires on poles alongside the rails (Swartz 2015).

From an anthropological perspective, payments are significant because they are implicated in creating, maintaining, and dissolving social relationships with others that stretch across space and time. In terms of infrastructure, payments are significant because of how they bring together people, technologies, and regulations in different sociotechnical systems that make transactions possible. Today's increasingly complex payments ecosystems frequently introduce new ways of paying for things, and with them new ways of using infrastructures and relating to others (see Maurer 2016).

All payments systems share some common features: they must (1) be able to move value from one party to another, including processing and settling the payment, (2) have rules to which all participants in the system agree, and (3) afford participants means of communicating with one another about which system they agree to use for a given transaction. Often, payment systems and their infrastructures only become apparent at points of transaction— handing over cash for goods, using a debit card at a point-of-sale terminal, entering credit card information into an online retail form—or in times of breakdown—when a card-reader machine stops working, when a bank customer finds her account has been hacked. Most of the time, however, people remain unaware of the infrastructural arrangements that support payments activities. They think about the money; the rails that it rides are incidental.

Core payments systems since the mid-twentieth century have been the preserve of banks and states. Cash, checks, and interbank clearinghouses derive from the operations involved in the state issuance of currency, as well as the chartering and regulation of banks and government-mandated interbank settlement systems. Credit and debit systems linked mainly to plastic cards derive from consortia of banks building their own private networks to facilitate electronic value transfer (Stearns 2011). With the Internet, businesses created new payment services that made using credit, debit, and interbank infrastructures possible online. PayPal, for example, is said to "ride the rails" of the credit, debit, and Automated Clearing House (ACH) systems, providing an online user interface into these existing systems. While state-mandated and private payments systems have remained relatively stable, mobile payments systems complicate institutional and infrastructural arrangements by blurring the lines between currency issuance and value transfer. Debates around mobile payments signal the inherently political character of payment systems, especially when they are (re)configured as platforms for other services.

M-Shwari's Alternative Credit

M-Shwari is a savings account product offered by the Commercial Bank of Africa (CBA) that can only be accessed through the mobile money service M-Pesa, itself a product of Safaricom, Kenya's near-monopoly mobile telecommunications company. M-Pesa is the archetypal mobile money transfer service. Designed as a microfinance loan repayment product, M-Pesa took off after its launch in 2007 and as of 2015 was being used by over 40 percent of Kenya's population, or 61 percent of its mobile phone users (Ipsita 2015). M-Pesa allows Safaricom customers to convert physical cash into electronic credits ("e-money," according to regulators) at any Safaricom location and then send those credits via text message to another Safaricom customer. Users "cash in" at a kiosk, where they might also purchase airtime or a new phone, and "cash out" at another such facility after they receive a text message indicating that money has been sent to them. A number of other companies have sought to create products and services, such as health insurance or savings tools, that would ride M-Pesa's rails (Kendall et al. 2012).

Importantly, M-Pesa does not allow customers to earn interest on the funds held in their accounts. It is essentially a prepaid value storage and transfer service. Were it to offer interest or credit, it would fall under Kenya's banking regulations. Most MNOs are loath to become, or be regulated as, banks. Doing so would require adherence to stricter "Know Your Customer" (KYC) rules around verifying the identities of their clients and compliance with national and global anti-money laundering regulations, not to mention capital adequacy rules.

M-Shwari appears to be the most successful of the services that ride the M-Pesa rails. Not only a savings account at a bank linked to one's M-Pesa account, accessible primarily via one's phone, M-Shwari also uses M-Pesa payment data to create an alternative credit score, a potential boon to unbanked customers, who have no formal credit history. This allows CBA to do the risk assessment necessary to offer small loans to M-Shwari customers. In our conversations with mobile money experts and regulators, we have found some skepticism about M-Shwari's algorithm for determining credit risk, which the company claims is done through a combination of "telecommunication variables from Safaricom's data related to airtime, airtime credit, M-Pesa, and length of time as a customer" (Cook and McKay 2015, 6). Leveraging payment data—its regularity, its amounts—provides a way of gauging how much the bank might lend the client and the likelihood of its repayment. The loan, in turn, then builds that traditional credit history (Kiiti 2014, 2015; Mas 2013).

M-Shwari exemplifies the goal of using mobile payments to provide access to finance. Because the CBA is a bank, Kenya's banking regulators can rest assured that it complies with prudential requirements like KYC. In fact, CBA uses a novel "tiered" method for verifying customer identity: different levels of verification are required for different deposit thresholds (the higher the amount saved, the more identity documentation is required). This alleviates one of the key barriers to financial inclusion for the poor: the frequent lack of extensive identity documentation. With M-Shwari, a customer can begin with only their Safaricom phone, and the CBA cross-references data in their phone's SIM card with the national ID database.

M-Shwari also allows Safaricom to maintain its near monopoly in Kenyan mobile money service provision. Providing another service on the M-Pesa rails makes those rails more indispensable to people. It also underscores the boundaries between Safaricom's network and those of its competitors. One competitor, Bharti Airtel, has been seeking government intervention into the mobile money market because M-Pesa charges high fees on transfers between M-Pesa and Airtel accounts—double the fee for in-network transfers. This points to a concern that regulators and others in the mobile money space often express: mobile money services are generally non-interoperable. That is, MNOs offering mobile money services do not always permit transfers from their service to competitor MNO services. Consortia of banks working together developed bank-based payment rails; some, like check-clearing and the ACH, were developed under government mandate. MNOs beginning to operate in the payments industry are not similarly coordinating with one another—nor are they often compelled to do so by government regulators, though there are exceptions.

India's Payments Banks

M-Shwari exemplifies how mobile payments can become the rails upon which other financial products ride in regulatory contexts where MNOs are prohibited from offering banking services. But what if MNOs *could* act more like banks? What might this entail for payments infrastructures and financial inclusion? The creation of "payments banks," a new category of Indian financial institution introduced by the Reserve Bank of India (RBI), raises such questions. In effect, payments banks permit non-bank entities such as MNOs to offer their customers some of the same financial products and services that banks do.

Payments banks are part of a larger financial inclusion agenda known as the *Pradhan Mantri Jan-Dhan Yojana* (PMJDY)—"Prime Minister's People Money Scheme"—launched by Prime Minister Narendra Modi's Bharatiya Janata Party (BJP) government in 2014. The PMJDY was founded on the principle that India's poor and unbanked need both secure and reliable mechanisms for sending and receiving payments and "universal access to savings" (RBI 2014). When the RBI announced the creation of payments banks in July 2014, it invited non-banking finance companies, corporate business correspondents, MNOs, supermarket chains, and cooperatives to apply for payments bank licenses. By the application deadline in February 2015, it had received 41 applications, including from Bharti Airtel (India's largest mobile phone carrier) and India Post, the country's publicly operated postal system.

Indian payments banks are restricted to the "acceptance of demand deposits and provision of payments and remittance services" (RBI 2014). These restrictions differentiate payments banks from other types of banks, which can offer their customers credit and savings in addition to value transfer and deposit taking. However, a key provision in the RBI regulation guarantees that deposits held in payments banks will be covered by deposit insurance and will earn interest for account holders, formal banking service features that financial inclusion experts have advocated for mobile money services (Ehrbeck and Tarazi 2011). In this respect, payments banks advance the project of financial inclusion that also motivates products like M-Shwari.

It is difficult to imagine payments banks without the earlier experience of mobile payments in India. The Indian financial services firm Eko launched the country's first dedicated mobile payments service in 2007 (Chen 2012). Other services, such as Bharti Airtel's Airtel Money and Vodafone India's M-Pesa followed, making the case for the mobile network infrastructure as a means of delivering financial services to India's unbanked. These providers also learned that a successful mobile payments service needs a network of human agents who can receive deposits and remit payments to clients (Banerjee 2012; Wright et al. 2013). This lesson has been crucial for understanding the infrastructural requirements of mobile payments, especially in rural contexts: payments depend on social infrastructures as well as technical ones (Eijkman et al. 2010; Maurer et al. 2013).

Despite the proliferation of bank—and non-bank—led options and efforts to build out agent networks, uptake of mobile payments in India has remained low (Tiwari and K.C. 2013). The RBI and others hope that payments banks could solve the uptake dilemma by freeing non-bank entities such as MNOs from regulatory restrictions preventing customers from holding money in mobile accounts (Mirani 2014). Payments banks complement rather than replace previous financial inclusion deployments, encouraging the development of new payment infrastructures while also riding the mobile payments rails and eliminating regulatory obstacles these services have encountered.

Payments banks may best complement existing mobile payments schemes in their scalability. The RBI's reforms allow entry into the financial services industry by organizations such as MNOs that have the "distribution muscle to provide payment and deposit services at scale in India" (Kumar and Radcliffe 2015b). Moreover, MNOs have historically done better at managing customer service than banks because their business models depend on creating and maintaining robust social infrastructures to handle customer complaints and needs. Operating in a regulatory environment where formal financial services can ride mobile payments' social and technical rails, payments banks have the potential to be "the engine that helps PMJDY get over the finish line" (Kumar and Radcliffe 2015a).

Of course, PMJDY's success means securing a victory for the Modi government. Critics have pointed out that the majority of accounts (63 percent) still show a zero balance (Singh et al. 2015) while describing the PMJDY as "populism gone berserk" (Perumal 2014). This new payments platform might also be a political platform, promoting the agenda not just of financial inclusion, but also a particular political party. Can such legacies be extracted from an infrastructure once in place? The fact that we still use railroad metaphors to describe the payments industry—and still fight over payments' monopolistic tendencies (see Levitin 2005)—would argue against the proposition. Still, this is a question for further ethnographic and historical investigation.

Ecuador's E-money

Many in the mobile money industry argue that the government-to-person (G2P) channel can be leveraged to jumpstart mobile payments adoption. They look to the experience of card-based state social assistance disbursements and tax refunds provided through prepaid cards in the US and elsewhere. Similarly, in India, G2P payments like these may ultimately determine the success or failure of payments banks. The ability of payment banks to deliver social benefits—particularly to people in rural areas—while remaining competitive with credit-issuing banks would help demonstrate the utility of mobile payments infrastructures for unbanked clients (Kumar and Radcliffe 2015a). Moreover, since G2P payments are typically disbursed on regular schedules, they establish reliable channels between the parties in a payments transaction that endure over time, creating and cementing relationships. But what kind of relationships? The idea that G2P payments delivered over corporate rails might generate brand loyalty to a private payment provider might be farfetched. If the service works and is invisible because it works seamlessly, it is the money, after all, not the payment infrastructure *per se*, that recipients really care about. At the same time, the provision of government payments over private rails might trap the recipient into certain relations with which she would otherwise not have to contend. In the US, the disbursement of tax refunds over prepaid cards has been controversial because of the large number of fees associated with the use of prepaid debit cards (Fox 2007). G2P payments might also foster or reinforce relationships with state institutions or even the national community; in some contexts, these might be similarly problematic—again, a question for ethnographic study.

The Central Bank of Ecuador (BCE) is banking on G2P payments with the 2014 launch of a new public mobile payment system, the first of its kind in the world. The BCE's plan makes the central bank the sole emitter of e-money as legal tender, although regulations require that e-money issuance be anchored to liquid deposits denominated in US dollars, Ecuador's official currency. As with other mobile money schemes, the BCE's explicit aim is to facilitate the financial inclusion of those traditionally excluded from access to the formal financial system, while also redistributing national economic surplus more equally throughout the economy.[3] Indeed, M-Pesa served as a model for the BCE, demonstrating the effectiveness of mobile payments as a way of reaching a large unbanked population, especially in rural areas.

The BCE's plan is unique in several regards. The system will accommodate a full range of transactions, including bill payments, remittance transfers, G2P social benefits, and P2P and B2P (business-to-person) transactions. The BCE subsidizes the cost of use under a non-profit model. Furthermore, the platform is designed to be interoperable with all national platforms and providers—as with India's payments banks, accounts are intended to complement commercial banks, credit unions, cooperatives, and other institutions. To ensure the system's interoperability, the BCE has reached agreements with each of the country's MNOs and is requiring the participation of financial institutions. This is to ensure that different carriers do not assess fees for moving money between clients of different mobile carriers, avoiding disputes like the one between Safaricom and Bharti Airtel in Kenya. Importantly, the design, management, and regulation of e-money and its platforms reside with the authority of the central bank. Individual bank accounts for Ecuadorian citizens are held directly with the central bank.

Internet access and formal bank accounts are not requirements, and the primary goal is not the inclusion of everyone in the formal banking system *per se*. Rather, the aim is to provide people with a viable additional mobile option, while preserving choice of payment. Having multiple places where BCE-issued mobile money will be accepted cuts down cash transactions, both enhancing safety in places where robbery is common and eliminating the need to make change, which poses problems in a dollarized economy where fractional currency can be scarce. National ID numbers and password security are built in to ensure privacy and protection of user data. To address money laundering and consumer protection concerns, an upper limit is imposed on transaction amounts, with the emphasis on small amounts necessary for daily consumer needs and basic necessities such as food and transportation.

Ecuador's e-currency is still in its early stages, with around 50,000 accounts opened since its initial launch. It remains to be seen how people will embrace e-money in their daily transactions, as well as how "oversight and compliance mechanisms [will be] put in place for an e-money issuer that is also a regulator and financial authority" (Almazán and Frydrych 2015, 18). That is, the system is both operated and regulated by the same entity, the central bank, which could generate potential conflicts of interest. The project has already provoked controversy in Ecuador for other reasons, too. The dollarization of the economy was supposed to insulate economics, specifically the emission of money, from politics. Since the BCE project promotes the state's broader financial inclusion goals, many see it as reintroducing politics through the state's development agenda. Critics worry that it could be used to increase the national money supply and undermine the dollar's official status there (Nelms 2015). The hope, however, is that other services will eventually be built on top of its rails, like the services riding the rails of M-Pesa. Scalability and an enabling ecosystem will be essential to building trust in the system among its various agents, institutional stakeholders, and the public. These are just as important as the BCE's legal guarantee that e-money be backed by equivalent value in dollar assets—a concession intended to quell anxieties over the impact of e-money on dollarization.[4]

The BCE's project thus envisions not only money, but also its infrastructures as a "public good" (Nelms 2015). Ensuring the stability of this national monetary platform will require its own communications rails—customer service and technical support—among other supports. Trust in the system and cultivating acceptance will depend on how well the technical platform works with mobile and electronic transactions, on the reliability of cashing in/out, and on a critical mass of end-users who benefit from the system. Electronic, central bank-issued currency will perhaps engender greater public awareness of the infrastructural arrangements that support their payments activities; these will "back" the system as much as dollars and other liquid assets.

What counts as a public good, and to whose and what ends it is used, will differ historically and culturally. Typically, central banks and states constitute a political framework crucial for ensuring, among other things, that the unit of account will settle at par. This political achievement foments the perception that money is a neutral medium of exchange and that payment infrastructures are incidental to economies. Yet most private electronic value transfer systems do not settle at par. There are fees and tolls, albeit often limited by state regulation (Maurer 2012, 285). The Ecuadorian project of state-issued mobile e-money will contribute to debates about the role of such regulation, the mandate of monetary policy, the capacity for electronic money and mobile money payment platforms to contribute to financial inclusion, and the digital means of value transfer generally. It remains to be seen whether this project will make payment public, but it is already publicizing payment, making visible both money's infrastructures and its politics.

Conclusion

Consider the contrasts among M-Shwari, India's payment banks, and Ecuador's e-money. M-Shwari rides the rails of what was essentially a P2P money transfer service, provided by a private network infrastructure. Its relational paradigm is individualist, capitalist, one might say economically liberal insofar as it disentangles the user from government regulations around bank supervision and the constraints of banks that favor elites. Indian payment banks are part of a particular political agenda. In opening payment provision to multiple providers while disallowing other banking functions to ride those rails, it creates the potential for profusion of new digital payment providers—but with some important restraints. This is a kind of controlled capitalism. The Ecuadorian example is state-controlled and -animated, seeking to make an explicit political statement by preserving the state's regulatory position and legal authority while suturing relationships between citizens and a specific vision of the nation. Dollarization complicates these efforts, but for the BCE, e-money is a political project. It is meant to be a publicly accessible and negotiable collective good. But it is also fueling debates over the hierarchy of digital forms of inclusion relative to cash and other forms of payment. In so doing, it spotlights what had been implicit in M-Pesa and made somewhat more explicit in India's payment banks: payments are not neutral.

Payments systems can shunt people and transactions in one direction or another—they can charge different amounts for their services, subtly pushing someone toward the use of one network over another; they can be completely opaque to end-users and thereby charge even more; or they can set hidden rules that trap unsuspecting consumers when something goes wrong. As different corporate systems vie for market share, they might simply not work everywhere, cutting off the possibility of a transaction if the user does not have the "correct" means of payment available.[5] In southern California at the time of our writing, private toll roads only accept payment via an electronic transponder that must be linked to a credit or debit card, effectively excluding drivers without them from using the road. In December 2010, PayPal, VISA, MasterCard, and Western Union blocked donations to the whistle-blower website, Wikileaks, demonstrating the political power that comes with control over the payment rails (Worstall 2011). As infrastructures, payments systems can channel and block relationships and flows of all kinds.

These differences have implications for the points of entry to the ethnographic study of digital payments. They also have implications for whether or not we think about payment infrastructures—and payments themselves—as public utilities. We note that G2P mobile payment programs such as conditional cash transfers or salary and bill payment are currently clustered regionally in Latin America, with a scattering of deployments elsewhere. Mobile money services on the M-Pesa model exist in most countries of the former British Empire in Africa. India's payments banks are, for now, unique hybrids. This would suggest that payment also rides other rails, legacy infrastructures going back centuries laid in the heyday of colonialism and imperialism. If new digital payment systems are reopening questions of infrastructure and politics settled in the mid-twentieth century, while exposing tracks laid down hundreds of years ago, what new rails are they building now that will channel and route our relations in the next hundred years? And how can ethnography anticipate and respond to the call and challenge they pose?

Notes

1 Some trace the mobile payments industry's origin to the ethnographic observation by Jan Chipchase, formerly of Nokia, that people in Uganda were informally trading mobile airtime credits (Chipchase and Tulusan 2007).
2 We use the term "private" to refer to non-state-controlled corporate entities—business enterprises or corporations, whether or not they are publicly traded or privately held. By "public," we refer to state entities.
3 Unless otherwise noted, discussion of the BCE financial architecture is drawn from Javier Félix (2014, 2015).
4 See BCE information in English at: www.bce.fin.ec/en/index.php/electronic-money-system.
5 VISA famously ran ads in the 1990s that stressed the limited reach of its rival, American Express, e.g. "In Fog City Diner, they take things easy. But they don't take American Express" (1990).

References

Almazán, Mireya, and Jennifer Frydrych. 2015. "Mobile Financial Services in Latin America & the Caribbean: State of Play, Commercial Models, and Regulatory Approaches." *GSMA*. www.gsma.com/mobilefordevelopment/wp-content/uploads/2015/09/2015_GSMA_Mobile-financial-services-in-Latin-America-the-Caribbean.pdf (accessed October 23, 2015).

Banerjee, Shweta S. 2012. "Building India's Model of Agent Banking." *CGAP*, June 6. www.cgap.org/blog/building-india's-model-agent-banking (accessed August 9, 2016).

Central Bank of Ecuador. 2015. "Electronic Money." www.bce.fin.ec/en/index.php/electronic-money-system (accessed October 23, 2015).

Chen, Greg. 2012. "Eko's Mobile Banking: A Basic Payments Product." *CGAP*, March 13. www.cgap.org/blog/eko's-mobile-banking-basic-payments-product (accessed August 9, 2016).

Chipchase, Jan, and Indri Tulusan. 2007. "Shared Phone Practices: Exploratory Field Research from Uganda and Beyond." *Future Perfect*. www.janchipchase.com/sharedphoneuse (site discontinued).

Cook, Tamara, and Claudia McKay. 2015. "How M-Shwari Works: The Story so Far." *Access to Finance Forum Report*. Washington, DC: CGAP and FSD. www.cgap.org/sites/default/files/Forum-How-M-Shwari-Works-Apr-2015.pdf (accessed October 23, 2015).

Ehrbeck, Tilman, and Michael Tarazi. 2011. "Putting the Banking in Branchless Banking: Regulation and the Case for Interest-Bearing and Insured E-money Savings Accounts." In *The Mobile Financial Services Development Report*, edited by James Bilodeau, William Hoffman, and Sjoerd Nikkelen, 37–41. New York: World Economic Forum USA Inc.

Eijkman, Frederik, Jake Kendall, and Ignacio Mas. 2010. "Bridges to Cash: The Retail End of M-PESA." *Savings & Development* 34(2): 219–52.

Félix, Javier. 2014. "El Contexto Socio-Político de la Nueva Arquitectura Financiera y el Sistema Público de Dinero Electrónico en Ecuador." Irvine, CA: IMTFI. www.imtfi.uci.edu/files/JavierFelix_ReporteFinal%20_Spanish.pdf (accessed October 23, 2015).

———. 2015. "The New Financial Architecture and the Public Mobile Money System in Ecuador." *IMTFI Executive Summary*. Irvine, CA. www.imtfi.uci.edu/Ecuador2pager-FINAL.pdf (accessed October 23, 2015).

Fox, Jean Ann. 2007. "Fringe Bankers: Economic Predators or a New Financial Services Model?" *Western New England Law Review* 30: 135–49.

Gillespie, Tarleton. 2010. "The Politics of Platforms." *New Media and Society* 12(3): 347–64.

Ipsita. 2015. "Kenyan Mobile Transfer Business to See a Major Shift, with Government Regulators Stepping in to Check Dominance of Safaricom's M-Pesa." *Let's Talk Payments, July* 7. http://letstalkpayments.com/kenyan-mobile-transfer-business-to-see-a-major-shift-with-government-regulators-stepping-into-check-dominance-of-safaricoms-m-pesa (accessed August 9, 2016).

Kendall, Jake, Philip Machoka, Clara Veniard, and Bill Maurer. 2012. "An Emerging Platform: From Money Transfer System to Mobile Money Ecosystem." *Innovations* 6(4): 49–64.

Kiiti, Ndunge. 2014. "Lessons from the Field: M-Shwari and the Jua Kali in Kenya." *IMTFI* (blog), November 20. http://blog.imtfi.uci.edu/2014/11/lessons-from-field-m-shwari-and-jua.html (accessed August 9, 2016).

———. 2015. "IMTFI at UNCTAD's Expert Meeting on the Impact of Access to Financial Services (Part 2)." *IMTFI*, March 23. http://blog.imtfi.uci.edu/2015/03/imtfi-at-unctads-expert-meeting-on_23.html (accessed August 9, 2016).

Kumar, Kubir, and Dan Radcliffe. 2015a. "Can India Achieve Universal Digital Financial Inclusion?" *CGAP*, January 20. www.cgap.org/blog/can-india-achieve-universal-digital-financial-inclusion (accessed August 9, 2016).

———. 2015b. "What Will It Take for Payments Banks to Succeed in India?" *CGAP*, January 27. www.cgap.org/blog/what-will-it-take-payments-banks-succeed-india (accessed August 9, 2016).

Levitin, Adam J. 2005. "The Anti-Trust Super Bowl: America's Payment System, No-Surcharge Rules, and the Hidden Costs of Credit." *Berkeley Business Law Journal* 3(1): 265–336.

Mas, Ignacio. 2013. "Founding Myths of Mobile Money." *IMTFI*, October 21. http://blog.imtfi.uci.edu/2013/10/founding-myths-of-mobile-money.html (accessed August 9, 2016).

Maurer, Bill. 2012. "Credit Slips (But Should Not Fall)." *Distinktion: Scandinavian Journal of Social Theory* 13(3): 283–94.

———. 2016. *How Would You Like to Pay? How Technology Is Changing the Future of Money.* Durham, NC: Duke University Press.

Maurer, Bill, Taylor C. Nelms, and Stephen C. Rea. 2013. "Bridges to Cash: Channelling Agency in Mobile Money." *Journal of the Royal Anthropological Institute* 19(1): 52–74.

Mirani, Leo. 2014. "A New Kind of No-Frills Bank Could Kickstart India's Long-Awaited Mobile Money Revolution." *Quartz*, July 21. http://qz.com/237847/a-new-kind-of-no-frills-bank-could-kickstart-indias-long-awaited-mobile-money-revolution (accessed August 9, 2016).

Nelms, Taylor. 2015. "'Ecuador Bans Bitcoin'! A Monetary Mix-Up." *King's Review*, October 20. http://kingsreview.co.uk/magazine/blog/2015/10/20/ecuador-bans-bitcoin-a-monetary-mix-up (accessed August 9, 2016).

Perumal, Prashanth. 2014. "Jan Dhan Yojana: Populism Gone Beserk." *Live Mint*, September 1. www.livemint.com/Opinion/9huedGeHxU770Gq7vvi13M/Jan-Dhan-Yojana-populism-gone-berserk.html (accessed October 23, 2015).

Reserve Bank of India (RBI). 2014. "Committee on Comprehensive Financial Services for Small Businesses and Low Income Households." *Reserve Bank of India*, January 7. https://rbi.org.in/scripts/PublicationReportDetails.aspx?UrlPage=&ID=732 (accessed October 23, 2015).

Schwittay, Anke F. 2011. "The Financial Inclusion Assemblage: Subjects, Technics, Rationalities." *Critique of Anthropology* 31(4): 381–401.

Singh, Aishwarya, Lokesh Kr. Singh, and Mukesh Sadana. 2015. "PMJDY: Improved Financial Inclusion, but Roadblocks Remain." *CGAP*, March 26. www.cgap.org/blog/pmjdy-improved-financial-inclusion-roadblocks-remain (accessed August 9, 2016).

Stearns, David L. 2011. *Electronic Value Exchange: Origins of the VISA Electronic Payment System.* London: Springer-Verlag.

Swartz, Lana. 2015. "Token, Ledgers, and Rails: The Communication of Money." PhD dissertation. University of Southern California.

Tiwari, Mudita, and Deepti K.C. 2013. "Mobile Payment Systems: What Can India Adopt from Kenya's Success?" *CGAP*, April 2. www.cgap.org/blog/mobile-payment-systemswhat-can-india-adopt-kenya's-success (accessed August 9, 2016).

VISA. 1990. "Fog City Diner (San Francisco)." YouTube video, 00:29. Posted October 2011. www.youtube.com/watch?v=Mqy2l6m9s_U.

Worstall, Tim. 2011. "Wikileaks to Close Over Funding Blockade?" *Forbes*, October 25. www.forbes.com/sites/timworstall/2011/10/25/wikileaks-to-close-over-funding-blockade (accessed August 9, 2016).

Wright, Graham A.N., Manoj K. Sharma, and Puneet Chopra. 2013. *Behind the Big Numbers: Improving the Reach and Quality of Agent Networks in India*. Lucknow: MicroSave. www.microsave.net/files/pdf/1377583661_PB_9_Behind_the_Big_Numbers.pdf (accessed October 23, 2015).

34

POLAR INFRASTRUCTURES

Juan Francisco Salazar

Introduction

Antarctica is undeniably different to the rest of the planet. As the driest, coldest, highest, and most remote land on the planet, it is quasi-extraterrestrial in its extreme ecology and lack of sustenance for human life. Despite being anything but lifeless, sterile, or still, as it was often historically constructed, Antarctica's off-limit condition still entails—as Elena Glasberg observes—that the "status of humanity on Antarctic ice is at once highly assumed and under-theorized" (2012, xxii). Australian environmental historian Tom Griffiths, echoing the words of US nature writer Barry Lopez, once observed that Antarctica is "a place from which to take the measure of the planet" (Griffiths 2008). Griffiths goes on to forewarn that Antarctica is

> not only a region of elemental majesty; it is also a global archive, a window on outer space and a scientific laboratory. It is not only a wondrous world of ice; it is also a political frontier, a social microcosm and a humbling human experiment.
>
> (Griffiths 2008, 4)

This chapter draws from recent anthropological literature on the politics and poetics of infrastructure (Larkin 2013) and my ongoing ethnographic research in the Antarctic Peninsula, to argue that both infrastructures—as built networks that facilitate circulation of goods, people and data, and logistics; as the coordination and control of movement of people and things along and within global supply chains—are crucial to the establishment and subsistence of semi-permanent settlements, and, as such, they are deeply implicated in the making and unmaking of experiences of community, solidarity, and peculiar modes of belonging in extreme polar environments.

Polar Infrastructures: General Remarks

When writing about polar infrastructures it is necessary to make a distinction between the Arctic and the Antarctic (the "Anti-Arctic"). The polar regions have a very different political, juridical, and ecological history and hence the deployment of infrastructure is often quite dissimilar. In the Arctic, Ruiz (2014) has observed how the emergence of satellites, fiber optic cables, and intranets enact modes of social infrastructure in constant processes of rene-gotiation and re-design across civic, governmental, and corporate interests. But Antarctica has taken a very different trajectory, perhaps more akin to the exploration and future colonization of outer space and other global commons such as the high seas. One point of distinction with Arctic polar infrastructures—among many—is that Antarctica, unlike the Arctic, remains one of a handful of areas of the planet that lies outside of the undersea cable network. The closest undersea cable from Amundsen-Scott South Pole Station for instance is in New Zealand, more than 3,000 kilometers away. The closest one from King George Island—in the tip of the Antarctic Peninsula—is near Valparaiso, in central Chile, also more than 3,000 kilometers north.

In Antarctica, infrastructures enact particular modes of state governance, where civic and corporate interests play a much more minor role compared to the Arctic. On the other hand, I argue that infrastructures in the Antarctic are essential in the assembling of a new political frontier, a social microcosm and humbling human experiment (in reference to Griffiths 2008) where infrastructures enact particular ways of being on "the Ice." As built networks that facilitate circulation of goods, people, and data, they are crucial to the establishment and sub-sistence of semi-permanent settlements, and as such, they are deeply implicated in the making and unmaking of experiences of community, solidarity, and new modes of belonging in this extreme environment.

Antarctica has been a sphere of human endeavor for well over a century. Humans are now physically present in Antarctica year round by 1,000 temporary scientists, engineers, and logistics personnel, a figure that expands—like Antarctic ice expands in winter—to 5,000 in summer. On top of this, thousands of tourists visit the fringes of the Antarctic continent every year. In some exceptional cases in the Antarctic Peninsula there is one permanent civilian settlement with a transient population of families and children.

An important part of my ongoing research in Antarctica since 2011 has aimed to under-stand how humans are learning to live on the ice, looking at social practices of inhabiting the extreme, the cultural dynamics of intercultural dialog among international scientific research stations, and concomitant processes of "making Antarctica familiar" (Bureaud 2012). These new forms of sociality are subjected "to a bracing and disjunctive seasonal rhythm. The human generations are annual. It is a peculiar civilization where the workings of history might be laid bare" (Griffiths 2008, 4). As I have observed and described ethnographically (Salazar 2013) this consciousness of a peculiar community to come, which resonates with Bloch's *Spirit of Utopia*, is akin to how outer space is also becoming a site for human sociality (Valentine et al. 2012). Temporary, recurring, and semi-permanent dwelling in these extra-extreme spaces are also indicative of new forms of subjectivity which are, in turn, also shaped by the ways through which infrastructural systems create and sustain dynamic political and moral spaces (Harvey 2012; Salazar 2013).

The Field Site: King George Island and the Fildes Peninsula Network

King George Island is one of the South Shetland Islands located in the Antarctic Peninsula and is roughly 900 km south of Cape Horn in the southernmost tip of South America. This is one of the areas experiencing the most rapid and pervasive global warming on the planet. King George Island has been pictured as a "mesocosm of the change that is occurring in response to climate warming and a test-bed for predicting future responses to climate change"

(Kennicutt 2009). The island is dominated by a pervasive ice cap with more than 90 percent of the island being glaciated. However, the Fildes Peninsula, on the southern end of the island, is in fact one of the largest ice-free areas in the maritime Antarctic, and together with adjacent coastal zones of the island, has high levels of biodiversity. Over the past 50 years, 87 percent of the island's glaciers have retreated.

The island is host to 15 international research stations as well as a military-civilian permanent village with families and a school. The area is home to about 200 inhabitants all year round and up to 2,500 people in summer including scientists, visitors, and tourists. King George Island and the South Shetlands are arguably becoming "a hotspot of land-based tourism development" (Liggett et al. 2011, 357). As some estimates suggest, the South Shetland Islands and other areas in the Antarctic Peninsula experience approximately 98 percent of the over 46,000 tourist visits (2007–2008 figure) and over 220,000 individual landings per year. Scientific, logistic, and tourist activities are concentrated here and frequently overlap in space and time along with those contested territorial claims.

Most importantly, the South Shetlands and the northern part of the Peninsula is today the most accessible Antarctic region, accounting for one of the highest levels of seasonal occupation by scientific parties in Antarctica. This occupation includes summer-only refuges, field camps as well as ship-based landings and is most intensive in the 16 permanent stations that are occupied by 13 states. King George Island is the site with the largest concentration of national research activities in Antarctica, and arguably the world. Human activities on the island are based on nine permanent stations (six in Fildes Peninsula built between 1968 and 1994, plus the Teniente Marsh airstrip built by the Chilean Air Force in 1980).

The airfield has effectively turned the area into a major logistical hub for the Antarctic Peninsula and is capable of handling intercontinental and intra-continental flights for transporting cargo, station personnel, and visitors between stations in the South Shetland Islands and to and from South America. For all its dullness, the airfield acts as a crucial interface in the regulation of mobility to and from Antarctica. The Marsh Airfield operates close to 2,000 flights in a single year, moving several thousand travelers (civilian and military) to and from King George Island (to South America and other bases in Antarctica). It is a site of circulating knowledge connecting Antarctica with the outside, as well as with several national field stations in King George Island and further inland.

As I have discussed elsewhere (Salazar 2013), Fildes Peninsula can be conceptualized as a zone that must be understood as both a social and a technical arrangement; as a "zone of entanglement," to use Ingold's notion of a zone in which earthly substances and aerial media are brought together in the constitution of beings which, in their activity, participate in weaving the textures of the land (Ingold 2008). In Ingold's view, organisms figure not as externally bounded entities but as bundles of interwoven lines of growth and movement, together constituting a meshwork in fluid space. This zone becomes a meshwork traversed by a number of geographies: a territorial geography of networked autonomous national field stations; a non-human geography of bio-geophysical things, entities, processes, events, force-fields, and phenomena; a material geography of international logistical cooperation; a social geography that includes labor geographies of daily scientific practices and logistic personnel involved in field science support; and the leisure geographies of international tourists.

Digital Ethnographies in King George Island

The first phase of the research involved a strategy of co-presence (Beaulieu 2010), deployed as a platform to construct a field site before physically traveling to Antarctica in which mediated settings (including face-to-face situations via Skype) allowed for a starting point to enable preliminary forms of interaction with people living in Antarctica. While the phase also included participant observation on Facebook sites with people living in the Antarctic Peninsula or who have lived there, the focus was on digitally interacting via Skype with a co-researcher who was in situ for three months. Google Earth was a complementary technology of choice to "travel" to the Antarctic Peninsula as part of this ethnographic experiment of co-presence. Google Earth became that "digital peep-box" (Kingsbury and Jones 2009, 502) creating mashups of Antarctica by weaving data from different sources to generate visualizations of the features of the Fildes Peninsula (King George Island, South Shetlands, Antarctic Peninsula). I was able to get a "street view" of where I would be staying which immediately made visible the institutional points of view embedded in these layers of information.

The second phase of the research involved a digital storytelling project *Digital Storytelling Antarctica* that was implemented in the Antarctic Peninsula in 2012 and 2013 with young Chilean students (Salazar and Barticevic 2015) participating in the annual School Antarctic Fair organized by the Chilean Antarctic Institute. The project examined cultural production processes at play in the configuration of a contemporary Antarctic national imaginary in Chile, arguing that such processes operate through a set of overlapping symbolic and material arrangements. It was an instance to reflect on how a performative focus on the experiences of young people doing science in Antarctica provides an innovative shift for understanding digital storytelling not only in terms of media democracy, but also rethinking its expediency as a novel mode of science diplomacy and democratization of science.

Digital Storytelling Antarctica was a pioneering initiative and the first, and possibly still the only, digital storytelling project to date produced entirely in situ in Antarctica. It was implemented as part of the annual School Antarctic Fair to try out a mode of digital media engagement and to capture first-person narratives of young people's experiences during an educational trip to Antarctica.

More than 100 Chilean children under 16 years old have lived in Villa Las Estrellas—a civilian settlement in Fildes Peninsula—and attended the F-50 public school there since the village was erected in 1984 at the height of the geopolitical tensions between Chile and Argentina in the South Atlantic. In 1984 and 1985 three children were born there. While residents tend to stay for a maximum period of two to three years, there is an observable, immanent, and ongoing arrangement of human material traces that goes back almost 50 years since the adjacent Chilean President Eduardo Frei base and Russian Bellingshausen base were constructed in 1969 and 1968, respectively. Villa Las Estrellas was inaugurated on April 9, 1984, within the complex formed by the Chilean Air Force Base Presidente Eduardo Frei Montalva on Fildes Peninsula, King George Island, South Shetlands. It is located roughly 900 kilometers south of Punta Arenas on latitude 62° 12□S; 58° 58□W. The Chilean government began construction of the complex in 1969, with the inauguration of Presidente Eduardo Frei Montalva Base that today also encompasses a meteorological center, an airstrip, and Julio Escudero Base (managed by the Chilean Antarctic Institute, INACH). The base has a school, bank, church, gym, hostel (for 80 people), and post office.

It is interesting to note that the two major infrastructural developments implemented by Chile during this period (President Eduardo Frei Base in 1969 and Villa Las Estrellas in 1984) coincided with the building of the Russian (former Soviet) Bellingshausen Base (1968) and China's Great Wall Research Station in 1983. Villa Las Estrellas is a dynamic place where over a thousand people have resided in the past 25 years. These configurations include human and non-human traces that affect each other.

Like the Chilean school with its two teachers and around ten primary school students, the Russian Orthodox Church built in 2004 to commemorate Russian and Soviet endeavors in the Antarctic, or the telecommunications antenna built by Chilean company ENTEL in 2005 to provide mobile telephony and location services to the residents of Villa Las Estrellas and Presidente Eduardo Frei Station, infrastructure becomes that liminal space that enables people "to reach toward or withdraw from each other . . . to be held in place, to be witnessed, touched, avoided, scrutinized or secured" (Simone 2012).

One of the important outcomes of using digital storytelling as a digital ethnographic method was to turn around the perception of human dwelling in the Antarctic by revealing that despite the rotation of residents every few years, the new modes of sociality and subjectivity emerging in these Antarctic places are far from ephemeral (Salazar 2013). Hence, an ethnographic focus on the study of infrastructures becomes critical in shifting the attention from the study of Antarctica as ideational form subject to particular politics of representation, to the materiality of lived experience, to the ontological and epistemological diversity of science and of the meaning of technology (Beaulieu 2010), and to emergent socialities and subjectivities of and in an Antarctica in the making. Through this short-term digital ethnography, it was possible to develop deep, contextual, and contingent understandings of what everyday life in Antarctica might mean, and the process of creating digital stories took place through "intensive and collaborative sensory, embodied engagements" of knowledge co-production (Pink 2009; Postill and Pink 2012).

My ethnographic work in the Antarctic Peninsula began in 2011 and aims to develop an account of temporary, recurring, and semi-permanent dwelling in these places that is indicative of new forms of sociality and subjectivity, perhaps more akin to what Spivak (2003, 72) calls "planetary subjects" where these new socialities are emerging in an extreme space that, to a significant extent, is shaped by the ways through which infrastructural systems create and sustain dynamic political and moral spaces (Harvey 2012). A critical quality of these—or any—ethnographic fieldworks was that particular modes of immersion in "the materialities, sounds and weather-worlds here and there" (Hastrup 2012) are used to address questions of scaling by investigating life processes—human and more than human in this entangled zone.

An important part of this work in Antarctica—and a form of immersion and atmospheric attunement (Stewart 2011)—involved the production of the 92-minute speculative ethnographic film *Nightfall on Gaia*, which I wrote, produced, and directed (2015). An example of a kind of generative ethnography that materializes a speculative future, the film aims to work as a diffractive method to account for how Antarctic futures might look and feel like. I will come back to this later in the chapter, but for the time being I would like to say that the film is a form of speculative fabulation (Haraway 2013; Salazar 2017, forthcoming) that shows how people in Antarctica, many of whom called themselves Antarcticans, are, as David Valentine et al. say, "by necessity ontologically agile" (2009, 11), not unlike those people and publics of outer space, cyber, and virtual worlds.

This "ontological liveliness" also extends to infrastructure. Antarctic infrastructures—digital and physical—are essential in assembling this new political frontier, this social microcosm and humbling human experiment that Griffiths speaks about and with which I started this chapter. As built networks that facilitate circulation of goods, people, and data, and drawing on Ash Amin's (2004) notion of "lively infrastructure" as a way of acknowledging the liveliness of socio-technical systems, I argue that polar infrastructures enact particular modes of governance and are also crucial to the establishment and subsistence of semi-permanent human settlements. As such, they are deeply implicated in the making and unmaking of experiences of community, solidarity, and new modes of belonging in this extreme environment.

A third phase within this digital ethnographic approach involved an experiment in "inventive methods" (Lury and Wakeford 2012) again using the speculative film *Nightfall on Gaia* (2015). The film as method and as outcome of research is an account of this Antarctic community to come, still formless but forming at a moment in time where Antarctica is becoming a keystone in an unstable world of shifting global geopolitics, environmental crises, and resource scarcities.

The film zooms into the infrastructural spaces of Fildes Peninsula to provide an account of how multiple material, technical, political, multinatural, and social relations are bundled together into "the irreducible plurality" (Harvey 2012, 78) of Antarctic infrastructural spaces. The film as device also attempts to open up into a lively world of relations between humans and the non-human or more than human, and reveals the multispecies stories about relationships of life in anthropocenic environments.

As an experiment in digital ethnography the film opens up a digital ethnographic science fiction narrative which is simultaneously factual, fictional, and fabulated in the sense suggested by Donna Haraway (2013), as well as a multi-form worlding practice to evoke a defining question: how are we learning to live in the Anthropocene? In this way the film shifts registers from opting for a creative treatment of actuality to a "creative treatment of possibility" (Salazar 2015) and outlines the contours of an anticipatory ethnography of life in [future] extreme environments.

Heterogeneous, Multinatural, Lively Infrastructures

These three digital ethnographic research strategies (from Google Earth and Skype, through digital storytelling, to a feature-length digital film) entail a constant movement from co-presence to co-location and back again. On the one hand, and in different intensities, they reveal how life for human groups in Antarctica can be distinctly isolated and intensely hazardous, especially if something goes wrong with the infrastructure. A satellite glitch can mean no off-continent connectivity; a malfunction in any of the life support systems can mean trouble with the water purification system or problems with the heating system that powers the research station that you call home; and extreme weather conditions can signpost the nature of logistics dependency of this place; determining when people, food, fuel, cargo, or supplies can go in and when they can come out, including export of human biological and physical waste from the continent.

But on the other hand, they reveal the agential work of infrastructures. The process of creating digital stories, observing interactions on Facebook, designing a speculative ethnographic film, forced me as a researcher/media producer to engage with or focus on what Casper Bruun Jensen calls "the unstable, emergent interrelations between infrastructures, their human developers and numerous other entities" (Jensen 2016). In this case the array of entities ranges from microorganisms, water pipes, oil containers, icebergs, seals, petrels and penguins, telecommunication antennas, and the ice itself. In this sense, the symbols and imaginaries of infrastructure in King George Island, together with their organizational and technical dimensions, also elicit another feature of polar infrastructures: what Casper Bruun Jensen calls the multinatural characteristics of infrastructure (Jensen 2016). Acknowledging the "multi-naturalness" of infrastructure is also a way of recognizing the liveliness of socio-technical systems, or what Ash Amin calls "lively infrastructures." In the case of Fildes Peninsula on King George Island, infrastructures are fully implicated in the human experience of the ice and in shaping a sense of identity and belonging to place. Public sentiments of nationalism and globalism, innovation, scientific discovery, and safety become attached to iconic buildings such as the Russian Orthodox Church, or the airfield, the housing complex of Villa Las Estrellas with its school, shops, bank, post office, gym; or the ENTEL telecom antenna.

In other words, infrastructures not only form the material basis for the provision of basic services to the international research stations and civilian settlement of Villa Las Estrellas— the airfield, the zodiac, drinking water, waste management, mobile telephony, Internet. Infrastructures become crucial to the establishment and subsistence of semi-permanent settlements, and as such, they are deeply implicated in the making and unmaking of experiences of community, solidarity, and new modes of belonging in extreme polar environments. What is so evident in this place is how ferocious is the process through which infrastructure sinks into nature, as human footprint, as anthropogenic pollution. Antarctic wilderness, the sublime, becomes "covered over" by infrastructure. In Antarctica infrastructures are most notably invested with broader geopolitical significance and do not always maintain transparency in their use (Starosielski 2012). Infrastructures in human settlements in Antarctica like the entangled zone in Fildes Peninsula I have described—whether a research station, a water pipe, an antenna, a church—are so pervasive, visible, even ubiquitous, that it is difficult to conceive them as "below surface," and probably what we need is a new conceptual vocabulary to account for the intricate and specific ways in which Antarctic polar infrastructures present their own politics, standards, ways of knowing, ontologies, temporal rhythms, and interactional possibilities (Vertesi 2014).

As Glasberg (2012) has noted, the material structure of science is the center of Antarctica's contemporary culture. However, while science practices continue to be the centerpiece of activities in the Antarctic and the Southern Ocean, the substantive weight of scientific research is dwarfed by logistic support activities. Infrastructure and logistics in support of science represent nine times the amount devoted to research activity. This ratio could increase as the implanting and maintaining of long-term observing and remote-sensing systems require additional data storage, communications capacity, transportation reach, and autonomous operation.

So the question that arises is to what extent are these places more than sites for organizing logistical operations in support of science? It is still unclear the extent to which these sites put pressure on the relation of territory to sovereignty in this extra-territorial space or the nature of potential to generate new forms of polity. In other words, how can the design of technological infrastructure be used to afford certain forms of behavior and cultural practices while preventing others, especially considering the topological qualities of social relations in the Antarctic?

As Nicole Starosielski (2015) argues in her study of the "undersea network," the environments that undersea cables occupy are historical and political realms, where the network and the connections it enables are made possible by the deliberate negotiation and manipulation of technology, culture, politics, and geography. In this zone, the analytical challenge becomes how to account for diverse notions of relationality and connectivity, and the ways they are mobilized in the production of infrastructural systems that sustain the capacity of "state-space" to simultaneously emerge as closed territorial entity and as open, networked form. This is particularly the case of the Chilean state, which has over the years assembled an infrastructural system that operates in effect as an interface that conjures both topological and topographical space.

One significant example can be seen in the way telecom companies from Chile and Uruguay have built new antennas in Fildes Peninsula. In the case of Chile, ENTEL installed in 2005 a 24-meter-high antenna weighing 2.2 tons on King George Island, which now complements satellite telephony based on GSM networks with mobile telephony services by ENTEL using the Chilean code +56. Scientists and logistics personnel at the Russian Bellingshausen station, as well as thousands of tourists visiting the place each summer, also used the service. On the other hand, the Chinese and Korean bases located within a five-kilometer radius are serviced by their own satellite infrastructures that provide Internet and location services, which in the case of the Chinese station allow it to restrict access to Facebook and other sites.

One consequence of this investment in infrastructure, as Horst (2013) observes in relation to her work on the infrastructures of mobile media, is that corporate telecommunications companies (both national and transnational) are playing an increasingly prominent role in domains once considered the focus of state governance, such as Antarctica. What Horst shows in her work is how efforts by telecom companies to develop markets on a regional and national scale "both interpret and influence the regulatory environments, technical infrastructures, language and state currencies" (Horst 2013, 149). But how is this played out in Antarctica? Understanding the consequences of such infrastructures and how telecommunications companies operate in extra-territorial spaces is a core question for future research. As Horst rightly argues, "the broader political economy and the reconfigured relationships between states and corporations constitutes one of the core infrastructure issues" (Horst 2013, 149). What are strikingly distinctive in the case of Antarctica are the ways in which infrastructures determine physical access and forms of formal connectivity to an off-limit, extra-territorial space. In the case of ENTEL, it becomes a de-facto national carrier where scientists, logistical personnel and families do not have the luxury to subvert, resist, and reconfigure mobile media infrastructures. What this analysis shows is that in order to have a more nuanced understanding of the complex and changing dimensions of governance in Antarctica, more careful attention needs to be paid to the institutional dynamics between states undertaking activities in the Antarctic and corporate companies such as ENTEL, or other private service providers such as DAP Antarctic Airways for instance, another Chilean company providing the only commercial air service between Punta Arenas and the Antarctic.

Conclusions

A digital ethnographic approach during fieldwork and analysis is a persuasive way of opening up and extending understandings of how worldmaking in extreme polar environments occurs. The digital stories and speculative film taken together form a disciplined preoccupation with how material practices and social imaginaries enact and articulate a new society in the making in the southern polar region.

Drawing on contemporary anthropological perspectives for conceptualizing infrastructures, I have provided a glimpse into the lively and multinatural heterogeneous infrastructural spaces of the Fildes Peninsula, King George Island, Antarctic Peninsula, to reveal how this area, as an entangled zone of territorial and relational geographies, is an intricate aspect of the friction that emanates from state practice, the flows of scientific capital, the circuits of transnational Antarctic logistics, and new modes of belonging in an extreme off-limit environment.

The ethnographic approach mobilized here hopes to be able to trace these movements as a way to contribute to upset prevalent visions of an Antarctica "out there" divided into discrete territorial claims, by setting out to investigate the worlding capacity of infrastructures in these new ecological and political zones for permanent human habitation in the near future.

References

Amin, Ash. 2014. "Lively infrastructure." *Theory, Culture & Society* 31(7–8): 137–61.

Beaulieu, Anne. 2010. "From co-location to co-presence: Shifts in the use of ethnography for the study of knowledge." *Social Studies of Science* 40(3): 453–70.

Bureaud, Annick. 2012. "Inhabiting the extreme or making Antarctica familiar." In *Far Field: Digital Culture, Climate Change, and the Poles*, edited by Jane D. Marsching and Andrea Polli, 187–97. Bristol: Intellect.

Glasberg, Elena. 2012. *Antarctica as Cultural Critique: The Gendered Politics of Scientific Exploration and Climate Change*. New York: Palgrave Macmillan.

Griffiths, Tom. 2008. "The cultural challenge of Antarctica: The 2007 Stephen-Murray Smith Memorial Lecture." *The La Trobe Journal* 82: 4–14.

Haraway, Donna. 2013. "SF: Science fiction, speculative fabulation, string figures, so far. *Ada: A Journal of Gender, New Media, and Technology* (3).

Harvey, Penelope. 2012. "The topological quality of infrastructural relation: An ethnographic approach." *Theory, Culture & Society* 29(4–5): 76–95.

Hastrup, Kirsten. 2012. "Scales of attention in fieldwork: Global connections and local concerns in the Arctic." *Ethnography* 14(2): 145–64.

Horst, Heather. 2013. "The infrastructures of mobile media: Towards a future research agenda." *Mobile Media & Communication* 1(1): 147–52.

Ingold, Tim. 2008. "Bindings against boundaries: Entanglements of life in an open world." *Environment and Planning A* 40(8): 1796–810.

Jensen, Casper Bruun. 2016. "Multinatural infrastructure and Phnom Penh sewage." In *Infrastructures and Social Complexity: A Routledge Companion*, edited by Penny Harvey, Casper Bruun Jensen, and Atsuro Morita. London and New York: Routledge.

Kennicutt, Mahlon C. 2009. "King George Island and SCAR science." Invited paper for COMNAP meeting, Punta Arenas, www.scar.org/scar_media/documents/publications/King_George_Island_Science_Kennicutt.pdf (accessed August 10, 2016).

Kingsbury, Paul and John Paul Jones. 2009. "Walter Benjamin's Dionysian adventures on Google Earth." *Geoforum* 40(4): 502–13.

Larkin, Brian. 2013. "The politics and poetics of infrastructure." *Annual Review of Anthropology* 42(1): 327–43.

Liggett, Daniela, Alison McIntosh, Anna Thompson, Neil Gilbert, and Brian Storey. 2011. "From frozen continent to tourism hotspot? Five decades of Antarctic tourism development and management, and a glimpse into the future." *Tourism Management* 32(2): 357–66.

Lury, Celia and Nina Wakeford. 2012. *Inventive Methods: The Happening of the Social*. New York/London: Routledge.

Nightfall on Gaia. 2015. Video. Australia/Chile: Juan Francisco Salazar.

Pink, Sarah. 2009. *Doing Sensory Ethnography*. London: Sage.

Postill, John and Sarah Pink. 2012. "Social media ethnography: The digital researcher in a messy web." *Media International Australia, Incorporating Culture and Policy* 145: 123–32.

Ruiz, Rafico. 2014. "Arctic infrastructures: Tele field notes." *communication +1*. Vol. 3, Article 3. http://scholarworks.umass.edu/cpo/vol3/iss1/3 (accessed January 25, 2016).

Salazar, Juan Francisco. 2013. "Geographies of place-making in Antarctica: An ethnographic perspective." *The Polar Journal* 3(1): 1–19.

——. 2015. "Anticipatory modes of futuring planetary change in documentary film." In *A Companion to Contemporary Documentary Film*, edited by Alisa Lebow and Alexandra Juhasz, 43–60. Chichester, West Sussex: John Wiley and Sons Ltd.

——. Forthcoming, 2017. "Speculative fabulation as ethnographic method: Researching worlds to come in Antarctica." In *Anthropology and Futures: Researching Emerging and Uncertain Worlds*, edited by Juan Francisco Salazar, Sarah Pink, Andrew Irving, and Johanes Sjoberg. London: Bloomsbury.

Salazar, Juan Francisco and Elias Barticevic. 2015. "Digital Storytelling Antarctica." *Critical Arts: South-North Cultural and Media Studies* 29(5): 576–90.

Simone, AbdouMaliq. 2012. "Infrastructure: Introductory commentary." *Cultural Anthropology – Curated Collections*. www.culanth.org/curated_collections/11-infrastructure (accessed January 25, 2016).

Spivak, Gayatri Chakravorty. 2003. *Death of a Discipline*. New York: Columbia University Press.

Starosielski, Nicole. 2012. "'Warning: Do not dig': Negotiating the visibility of critical infrastructures." *Journal of Visual Culture* 11(1): 38–57.

——. 2015. *The Undersea Network*. Durham, NC: Duke University Press.

Stewart, Kathleen. 2011. "Atmospheric attunements." *Environment and Planning D: Society and Space* 29(3): 445–53.

Valentine, David, Valerie Olson, and Deborah Battaglia. 2009. "Encountering the future: Anthropology and outer space." *Anthropology News* 50(9): 11–15.

——. 2012. "Extreme: Limits and horizons in the once and future cosmos." *Anthropological Quarterly* 85(4): 1007–26.

Vertesi, Janet. 2014. "Seamful spaces: Heterogeneous infrastructures in interaction." *Science, Technology & Human Values* 39(2): 264–84.

Part VIII

POLITICS

35

DIGITAL ETHNOGRAPHY OF MOBILES FOR DEVELOPMENT

Sirpa Tenhunen

At the turn of the millennium, the ICT4D (information and communication technologies for development) discourse had envisaged that access to the Internet and computers would induce development in the Global South. Ideas about the empowering capacities of both computers and mobile telephony echo media and communication scholars' debate on the digital divide. The digital divide concept emerged in the 1990s to refer to the unequal access and usage of digital technologies. Castells' (2001, 269) argument that not having access to the Internet is tantamount to marginalization in the global, networked system summarized the digital divide idea well.

India's National e-Governance Plan, NeGP, which in 2006 endeavored to provide all government services at computer kiosks, is an example of the kind of influence ICT4D discourses have had on the national development strategies. However, as Sreekumar and Rivera-Sánchez (2008) conclude, most of the computer-based ICT experiments failed dismally in poverty reduction. Cecchini and Raina's (2002) research on a pilot project in rural India exemplifies some of the challenges of inducing development through giving people access to computers: in the Maharastra village they studied in India it was mostly the rural elite who used the public computer services.

In comparison to computers, mobile phones are more affordable, require fewer infrastructures, do not require the user to have much technological knowledge, or to be able to read and write. Mobile phones have emerged as the first extensive electronic communication system during the past two decades in most parts of the developing world. Ninety-two percent of people in developing countries had mobile phone subscriptions in 2015, whereas only 34 percent of households in developing countries had Internet access at that time (International Telecommunication Union, 2015). The rapid spread of mobile telephony revived many of the hopes for development that the ICT4D had raised; consequently, Mobiles for Development (M4D) discourse emerged to address the use of mobile technologies in global development strategies.

In this chapter I begin by providing an overview of the key issues of the scholarly debate on mobile telephony and development within social sciences. My main focus will be on how the use of mobile phones for developmental purposes in India relates to state initiatives and policies. Drawing upon my research on the appropriation of mobile telephony in rural India, I then highlight how ethnographic research can contribute to this debate by exploring how the appropriation of mobile telephony in rural West Bengal influenced economy and health-care as well as governance and politics. I argue that digital ethnography—which explores the appropriation of phones as part of everyday life over a time-span—can play a role in helping us understand both the possibilities and limitations of digital innovations, as well as the need for multiple solutions to problems due to complex social processes.

The Promise of M-development

In India, the rapid growth in phone density coincided with broader economic reforms. Similar telecommunications sector deregulation, which opened up telephony for private operators, has accompanied mobile telephony growth in most parts of the Global South. The expansion of mobile telephony is thus often celebrated as a showcase example of how neoliberal globali-zation can promote development and reduce poverty. Indeed, transnational companies have emerged as builders of infrastructures and, hence, as initiators of development policies—a role which was earlier considered to fall under the purview of states (Horst 2013). As Horst (ibid.) argues, this change, in turn, necessitates a new research agenda to explore the changing roles of transnational companies and states as well as mobile phone users' agency. In his review of mobile telephony and development literature, Donner (2008) distinguishes three strands of the discussion: scholarly works on the factors that determine the diffusion of mobile phones in developing countries; studies on the impact of mobile phones on development; and on how users actively choose to use their phones—of these, I discuss the two latter ones.

Most social scientists are critical of technological determinism, which views technical innovations, or technology in general, as the sole or prime causes of changes in society. Nevertheless, economists have been interested in exploring the role of mobile telephony in economic development. Using data from 92 countries between 1980 and 2003, Waverman et al. (2005) found that an increase of ten mobile subscriptions per 100 people increased a country's GDP growth by 0.6 percent. Donner's (2009) study on mobile phone use by micro-entrepreneurs in Rwanda revealed some of the everyday practices through which phones improve the efficiency of economic activities: phones helped entrepreneurs to extend their market, stay in touch with their customers, collect stock, and deliver products effi-ciently. He found that most of the productivity gains arose from the phones affording people, who are beyond a convenient traveling distance—even if the distance is just a matter of a kilometer or two—the possibility to exchange information rapidly. Jensen's (2007) longitu-dinal study of sardine prices at various landing ports in northern Kerala, India over five years has become one of the most cited examples of the economic benefits of mobile phones. Jensen (ibid.) found that the arrival of mobiles brought significant and immediate reductions in the price variability and in the amount of waste in Kerala's fishing system. His findings have not only been generalized to other contexts, but they have also resulted in the devel-opment of myriad mobile technology-based applications that convey price information to small-scale entrepreneurs in the Global South. However, Srinivasan and Burrell (2016), who returned to the site of Jensen's work to explore the generalizability of his findings, argue that the fish trade in northern Kerala is a special case: the coastal geography and prevalent credit relationships there enable the fishermen to optimize their profits by using their mobile phones to sell to different markets. Conditions are different, for instance, on Kerala's south-ern coast where—unlike in the North—the steep ocean floor and rough surf prevent the use of large boats. Srinivasan and Burrell (2016) also maintain that Kerala fish markets cannot be regarded as archetypical free markets, because fishermen collectives and government regulation have crucially influenced them. Moreover, there is a great difference in how fishermen profit from their mobile phone use even in northern Kerala. The use of mobile phones to access price information is most important for affluent fish market actors, who can afford to invest in their trade and, consequently, catch higher volumes of fish.

Interest in the economic impacts initially dominated the M-development debate. However, most ethnographic studies on mobile telephony in the Global South indicate that people largely tend to use their phones for other purposes than mere narrow economic ones (Donner 2009; Horst and Miller 2006; Sey 2011; Archambault 2011). Crentsil (2013) has showed how mobile technology can be harnessed to increase the well-being of the most vulnerable part of the population in Ghana—HIV positive women who can currently simply phone in, determine their next counseling date, and discuss their treatment with hospital counselors. Nevertheless, only one third of the patients Crentsil (ibid.) interviewed possessed a phone. The calling costs are another major challenge for patients and local health workers. In Indonesia, the government gave mobile phones to midwives in order to improve health services in the rural province of Aceh, which was recovering from the devastating impact of the 2004 tsunami. Chib and Hsueh-Hua Chen (2011) describe that the possibility to get advice over the phone gave midwives the courage to handle difficult pregnancy cases. Midwives also benefited from the community's increased trust. However, Chib (2013) argues that despite ample evidence of successful MHealth projects utilizing mobile telephony to improve communication, coordination, and access to healthcare (Fjeldsoe et al. 2009; Cole-Lewis and Kershaw 2010; Krishna et al. 2009), there is still inadequate proof of mobile phone adaption for mass healthcare.

Ethnographic studies of mobile telephony have vigorously challenged the technological determinism and optimism inherent in the M-development discourse. Horst and Miller (2006) observed that phones rarely helped people in Jamaica start new businesses; instead, they use phones to solicit economic help, which puts a burden on the welfare of those from whom assistance is frequently sought. Archambault (2011) found that, in Mozambique, young people's opportunities to use phones for development purposes were limited due to a lack of jobs and business opportunities. She hence broached the idea that the link between ICTs and development might be based on wishful thinking. By studying phone users' positionality in various contexts in urban China, Wallis (2013) shed light on why marginalized workers' use of mobile phones will not necessarily lead to greater income, a better job, or more autonomy. Phone use might also turn out to be detrimental for phone users' welfare as in a Dar es Salam slum, where minors conceal their sexual behavior with the help of mobile phones which contributes to the intergenerational transmission of female poverty through early pregnancy and marriage (Stark 2013). The abovementioned ethnographic studies demonstrate that impact studies have tended not to take into account the many factors which, beside mobile telephony, influence phone users' well-being. The SCOT (Social Construction of Technology) paradigm, which has revealed technologies as socially constructed, also helps us understand that mobile telephony's consequences depend on how users choose to use phones and on the terms on which they are offered mobile services. As Wajcman (2002) argues, ICTs do not offer simple technological fixes for social problems, but are part of social changes through the ways technologies are socially produced and used.

Recent research has sought to develop a more nuanced understanding of the role of mobile technology for development by paying attention to mobile phones' range of benefits for users. Oreglia (2014) discovered unlikely ICT users from rural China where older women, helped by their children and peers, maintain relationships and access entertainment online. Among market women in Ghana, the phone's utility rested in enlivening trade networks instead of impersonally acquiring or exchanging information (Oreglia 2014). As Burrell and Oreglia (2015) argue, based on their research among farmers in China and fishermen in Uganda, in addition to price such variables as long-term relationships with trade partners and attitudes towards risk influence economic decision-making. Ling et al. (2015) found how, among the trishaw (rickshaw) pullers in Myanmar, mobile phones have strengthened ties with important clients, meaning a more stable income, but also an enhanced power for these customers.

Ethnography of Phone Use in an Indian Village

I have observed the appropriation of mobile telephony in Janta, a village in rural West Bengal, India, ever since people started to use phones there. I subsequently take stock of how mobile telephony influenced development in this village, based on my ethnographic research from 1999 to 2013. Drawing on Nussbaum (2000) and Sen (1999) whose definitions of development take capabilities into consideration, i.e. what people are effectively able to do, instead of merely measuring wealth and poverty levels, I broadly understand development as improved well-being and capabilities.

Janta is a multi-caste village with 2,441 inhabitants (Census of India 2011) in the Bankura district of West Bengal in the eastern part of India. By 2013 all households had phones and most households possessed a smartphone. As phones had become ubiquitous, differences in usage emerged. Low-income families share an understanding that phones need to be used sparingly, whereas the upper classes can spend generously on phone calls. Wealthier people can make and receive tens of calls a day, whereas low-income families only receive and make a few calls weekly. The villagers' monthly phone expenses varied between INR 30 and INR 1,000.

Most phone owners use the Internet indirectly on their phones. They buy music, videos, and pictures, which are downloaded on their phone's memory chip in shops selling chips, and content downloaded from the Internet. Although this practice differs crucially from the autonomous use of smartphones to browse the Internet, it offers easy and affordable access to Internet contents. The few people in the village who have used their personal phones to browse the Internet belong to a small college-educated minority (around 1 percent of the village population)—accessing the Internet's textual content requires an even higher level of literacy than operating the phone for calling. The few who had tried the Internet had found many uses for it: Facebook, downloading music and movies, finding out about prices, products, jobs, and exam results, as well as sending e-mail and accessing study sources, such as literature and dictionaries.

Mobile Telephony's Shifting Economic Influence

People mostly used their phones for calling their relatives and friends, and I have demonstrated how these calls contribute to changes in gender and kinship relations (Tenhunen 2014). However, occasional calls for specific instrumental purposes were also of great importance to villagers. When I asked mobile phone owners how they benefit from their phones, the prevalent answer was that a mobile phone enabled them to do more in less time: they could now manage various errands within a fraction of the cost and time that they previously required. My initial research on the mobile phone use of the early adapters in Janta supported earlier research findings on the economic benefits of phones for small-scale businesses. It did not take the local entrepreneurs in Janta long to realize that mobile phones could help them extend their clientele. Mobile phones allow micro-entrepreneurs to keep in touch with their customers, even when they are on the road. Phones are also used to check product availability, order stock, and compare wholesale prices in different markets. Phones helped people in diverse fields increase their income and their businesses' efficiency (Tenhunen 2008). Nevertheless, the picture of mobile phones' economic benefits became more complicated after I had a chance to observe phone use in diverse economic fields over time.

Most of the small-scale entrepreneurs concentrate on selling their services to the villagers. While the villagers do call stores to inquire about a product's availability, phones have not increased storekeepers' business margins considerably. Instead, storekeepers maintain that they use phones for the convenience and not to increase their income. Depending on their ability to obtain credit from wholesale sellers, storeowners can order stock for their village store from the nearby town. Consequently, they now spend less time commuting. If they need to travel to make the purchase themselves, they can first call and check the product's availability before they travel to do so. However, the convenience of doing business that phones offer has helped more people start stores, which has led to increased competition.

Local entrepreneurs who have benefited economically from phones are: insurance and investment agents, carpenters, mechanics, a chicken farmer, and artisans who build wooden structures and other constructions for celebrations. They not only use their phones to communicate with wholesale markets and customers in the village, but also to extend their clientele to people outside the village. Carpenters and insurance agents report modest economic gains, while the chicken farmer prospered remarkably. The latter was among the first persons in the village to obtain a mobile phone and, shortly after, he also bought a three-wheeler, which helped him extend his clientele as he can receive orders even when he is out making deliveries. These further investments caused a five-fold increase in his monthly sales. He soon invested in the village's first refrigerator to store chickens. In addition to the new logistical efficiency that phones enable, this business has benefited from the growing demand for chicken meat, which in turn was enabled by the growth in agriculture and economic prosperity since the 1980s.

Competition has not increased fiercely in the chicken business, because chicken farming requires large investments to raise the chickens and transport them to customers. Most other businesses that successfully use mobile phones to increase their profitability have had to deal with growing competition. For instance, an agent who trades agricultural products explained that his mobile phone allows him to carry out more business transactions than before. However, the ease of doing such business has increased competition, which, in turn, has lowered his profit margin. Mobile phones have been more instrumental in increasing the number of economic activities in Janta and the surrounding region than in helping individual entrepreneurs earn better incomes.

Whereas deals concerning the selling of agricultural produce were previously closed by signing a written contract well in advance of the products' delivery, sellers can now continue haggling with various buyers until it is time to deliver the products. The prices can be settled by phone at the very last moment, which has decreased the middlemen's profit and benefited the farmers. There is, however, a great variation in how farmers have benefited from phones. Middle-size and large farmers regularly ascertain the vegetable prices in the nearby towns of Bishnupur, Bankura, Asansol, and Durgapur. Nevertheless, it is unprofitable to transport large crops, such as paddy and potatoes, far. Most people therefore prefer to sell them in the markets close by. Even middle and large farmers often rely on a dealer who has provided them with credit to invest in farming, as many such dealers also act as moneylenders. Small-scale farmers do not benefit from comparing prices between different markets by phone, because they do not have much to sell at a market. A farmer might travel daily to sell just a few vegetables at the Vishnupur open market, using the day's income to buy groceries there.

The biggest economic change in the village since the turn of the century was not due to the use of mobile phones, but to the agricultural policies, which have led to small farmers' decreasing profits. The price of fertilizers and gasoline has increased, while income from the sale of agricultural products has dwindled. Since farming small plots of land has become increasingly unprofitable, young men from small farms use their phones to find paid employment outside the village.

Mobiles for Healthcare: Opportunities and Limitations

Villagers perceive the ability to call for help as one of mobile phones' most crucial benefits. I met people who had been motivated to purchase their first phone due to a family member's illness. Phones allow seriously ill patients in the village to be transported to a doctor, or to hospital, as it is possible to hire a car by phone. However, phones have not made it possible to summon trained medical help to the village in times of emergencies. Public health centers do not have sufficient staff to attend patients outside the center, and trained medical doctors in towns do not leave their clinics to attend patients in villages. The self-taught doctor who lives in the adjacent village is the only person family members can call if a villager is too sick to travel.

People do not trust either the public or private healthcare systems in the region, or those in West Bengal state. Faced with serious illnesses, the villagers prefer to spend large sums of money to travel to southern India to obtain proper treatment at the few hospitals with a good reputation for fair pricing and reliable care. Traveling to South India to obtain care in a foreign language environment is an arduous task for the villagers. People who have acquired an understanding of the medical organizations in the few popular South Indian hospitals, offer their services as medical agents for payment, traveling with patients and helping them to obtain treatment. Recently, many of my friends and acquaintances have traveled alone from Janta to South India after other people had phoned them to relate their experiences and told them how to cope with and obtain treatment at these hospitals. Phones also help raise money for medical treatment from relatives and help patients stay in touch with the healthcare personnel outside the village, or with previous patients who have traveled to other states to obtain medical treatment.

Two public health workers in the village have phones, but do not use them to stay in frequent touch with the villagers, because the government's small remuneration does not cover their phone costs. They had two weeks' medical training and their duties are to collect information about the health situation in the village, to advise people about child nutrition, and to encourage women to give birth in hospitals. The worker responsible for getting pregnant women to give birth in hospitals phones pregnant mothers occasionally, because her remuneration is based on the number of women she can persuade to do so. She has, however, not benefited economically, as she now spends the major part of her remuneration on phone costs. A worker in charge of child welfare in the village does not use her phone to communicate with the villagers due to these costs. Instead, she uses her phone to communicate with the health administration. Health workers regularly report on the people they have advised, including providing the administration with their phone numbers, so that their superiors can check that the reported cases actually exist.

Mobile Phones and Political Agency

While the state in West Bengal is not using mobile technology to deliver services, mobile phones, nevertheless, proved influential for the direction of state politics in West Bengal (Tenhunen 2011). Mobile telephony was a crucial factor in the rise of the opposition in West Bengal, where the Communist Party (CPI(M)) had been in power from 1977 until 2011, when the Trinamul party gained power. In 2010 opposition activists related to me how mobile phones help them secretly mobilize against the ruling party, and party activists are among the heaviest phone users in rural West Bengal. Although phones helped both the opposition and the ruling party act more efficiently, opposition activists used phones for spontaneous activities, such as organizing wildcat strikes and reporting the ruling party's misdeeds, more than the ruling party. Opposition activists emphasized that phones help them react faster to events. News about local political disputes can be communicated upward in the party hierarchy, and party leaders can, in turn, coordinate political action and request that news about such action be spread horizontally through the party hierarchy's lower levels and among other potential supporters.

CPI(M) rule was not solely based on violence, but coercive means have repeatedly been crucial for its electoral success (Gupta 2010). Where the CPI(M) sought to overpower the opposition through violent means, Trinamul organized protection through phones, sending its cadres to protect its supporters even if an attack was merely anticipated. Nevertheless, political activists use phones more to organize party meetings and offer political patronage than to organize spontaneous demonstrations and support. The parties' power is largely derived from their role as arbitrators of disputes—any person who feels that he or she has suffered an injustice can call a village meeting, led by local political leaders, during which a solution will be negotiated between the disputing parties. Political activists and leaders receive calls from people in different types of trouble, and phones have made it possible to react faster and to accomplish more in a shorter time-span than previously. As a result, patronage is now increasingly sought from other sources in addition to local leaders.

Conclusion

This article has exemplified how the developmental impacts of mobile telephony relate to state policies in rural India. The use of mobile telephony in local politics improved the possibilities to safeguard the transparency of public fund usage. At the same time, there were power shifts that transferred power from village leaders to translocal political organizations. However, changes in local politics induced by mobile telephony had little influence over policies of the central government, nor did they translate into immediate improvements in healthcare or agricultural policies, which mostly fall under the purview of state governments in India. The market rationality and cost efficiency enabled by phones did not guarantee economic growth for all stakeholders. In addition to the ability to communicate, the level of the competition, the market size and its growth rate as well as governmental economic and agricultural policies influence the profitability of small-scale businesses crucially. Nor could the efficiency provided by phones compensate for the shortcomings of the public healthcare systems. Identification of mobile telephony as belonging to the realm of the market hampers its use for developmental purposes. Service provider companies have not been able to provide affordable healthcare solutions or useful information for the low-income people as part of their business practices in a sustainable way while the state has not introduced initiatives for harnessing the potential of mobile technology for development in India.

My ethnographic research shows that despite their many benefits for users, mobile phones alone do not solve developmental problems: there is a need for multiple solutions due to the complexity of social processes. As Donner (2015) notes, ICT4D discourses have emerged as heterogeneous: they now stretch from shallow technologically deterministic approaches to views, which capture complexities, as well as potentialities (Donner 2015). An overarching interest in a few success cases and successful pilot projects at the expense of sustainable development has dominated M4D discourses. Long-term holistic ethnographic research can improve our understanding of how to better encourage digital inclusion through policy and design. Communication between different stakeholders—states, service providers, handset manufacturers, and NGOs—is challenging but M4D conversation provides possibilities for such a dialog.

References

Archambault, Julie Soleil. 2011. "Breaking up 'because of the phone' and the transformative potential of information in Southern Mozambique." *New Media & Society* 13: 444–56.

Burrell, Jenna and Elisa Oreglia. 2015. "The myth of market price information: Mobile phones and the application of economic knowledge in ICTD." *Economy and Society* 44(2): 271–92.

Castells, Manuel. 2001. *The Internet Galaxy: Reflections on the Internet, Business and Society*. Oxford: Oxford University Press.

Cecchini, Simone and Monica Raina. 2002. "Village information kiosks for the Warana Cooperatives in India." *E-Government*. World Bank. http://casesimportal.newark.rutgers.edu/storage/documents/technology/public/case/Village_Information_Kiosks_for_the_Warana_Cooperatives_in_India.pdf (accessed October 15, 2015).

Chib, Arul. 2013. "The promise and peril of mHealth in developing countries." *Mobile Media and Communication* 1(1): 69–75.

Chib, Arul and Vivian Hsueh-Hua Chen. 2011. "Midwives with mobiles: A dialectical perspective on gender arising from technology introduction in rural Indonesia." *New Media & Society* 13: 486–501.

Cole-Lewis, Heather and Trace Kershaw. 2010. "Text messaging as a tool for behavior change in disease prevention and management." *Epidemiologic Reviews* 32(1): 56–69.

Crentsil, Perpetual. 2013. "From personal to public use: Mobile telephony as potential mass educational media in HIV/AIDS strategies in Ghana." *Journal of the Finnish Anthropological Society* 38(1): 83–103.

Donner, Jonathan. 2008. "Research approaches to mobile use in the developing world: A review of the literature." *The Information Society* 24(3): 140–59.

———. 2009. "Blurring livelihoods and lives: The social uses of mobile phones and socioeconomic development." *Innovations. Technology, Governance, Globalization* 4(1): 91–101.

———. 2015. *After Access: Inclusion, Development, and a More Mobile Internet*. Cambridge, MA: The MIT Press.

Fjeldsoe, Brianna S., Alison L. Marshall, and Yvette D. Miller. 2009. "Behavior change interventions delivered by mobile telephone short-message service." *American Journal of Preventive Medicine* 36(2): 165–73.

Gupta, Monobina. 2010. *Left Politics in Bengal: Time Travels among Bhadralok Marxists*. Delhi: Orient Blackswan.

Horst, Heather. 2013. "The infrastructures of mobile media: Towards a future research agenda." *Mobile Media and Communication* 1(1): 147–52.

Horst, Heather and Daniel Miller. 2006. *The Cell Phone: An Anthropology of Communication*. Oxford: Berg.

International Telecommunication Union. 2015. *The World in Figures: ICT Fact and Figures*. www.itu.int/en/ITU-D/Statistics/Documents/facts/ICTFactsFigures2015.pdf (accessed October 15, 2015).

Jensen, Robert. 2007. "The digital provide: Information (technology), market performance, and welfare in the South Indian fisheries sector." *Quarterly Journal of Economics* 122(3): 879–924.

Krishna, Santosh, Suzanne A.Boren, and E. Andrew Balas. 2009. "Healthcare via cell phones: A systematic review." *Journal of Telemedicine and e-Health* 15(3): 231–40.

Ling, Rich, Elisa Oreglia, Rajiv George Aricat, Chitra Panchapakesan, and May O. Lwin. 2015. "The use of mobile phones among trishaw operators in Myanmar." *International Journal of Communication* 9: 3583–600.

Nussbaum, Martha C. 2000. *Women and Human Development: The Capabilities Approach.* Cambridge: Cambridge University Press.

Oreglia, Elisa. 2014. "ICT and (personal) development in rural China." *Information Technologies & International Development* 10(3): 19–30.

Sen, Amartya. 1999. *Development as Freedom.* New York: Alfred A. Knopf.

Sey, Araba. 2011. "'We use it different', making sense of mobile phone use in Ghana." *New Media and Society* 13: 375–90.

Sreekumar, T. T. and Milagros Rivera-Sánchez. 2008. "ICTs and development: re-visiting the Asian experience." *Science, Technology and Society Journal* 13(2): 159–74.

Srinivasan, Janaki and Jenna Burrell. 2016. "Revisiting the fishers of Kerala, India." ICTD '13 *Proceedings of the Sixth International Conference on Information and Communication Technologies and Development* 1: 56–66.

Stark, Laura. 2013. "Transactional sex and mobile phones in a Tanzanian slum." *Journal of the Finnish Anthropological Society* 38(1): 12–36.

Tenhunen, Sirpa. 2008. "Mobile technology in the village: ICTs, culture, and social logistics in India." *Journal of the Royal Anthropological Institute* 14(3): 515–34.

———. 2011. "Culture, conflict, and translocal communication: Mobile technology and politics in rural West Bengal, India." *Ethnos* 76(3): 398–420.

———. 2014. "Mobile technology, mediation and gender in rural India." *Contemporary South Asia* 22(2): 157–70.

Wajcman, Judy. 2002. "Addressing technological change: The challenge to social theory." *Current Sociology* 50: 347–63.

Wallis, Cara. 2013. *Technomobility in China: Young Migrant Women and Mobile Phones.* New York and London: New York University Press.

Waverman, Leonard, Meloria Meschi, and Melvyn Fuss. 2007. "The impact of telecoms on economic growth in developing nations: An economic analysis of the impact of mobile." *India: The impact of mobile phones. Moving the debate forward.* The Policy Paper Series, no. 9. Vodafone Group Plc.

36

MEDIATED POLITICAL AGENCY IN CONTESTED AFRICA

Mirjam de Bruijn

In Figure 36.1, A, an illiterate herder living in the desert region of Central Mali, shows a short film on his son's smartphone of the arrival of the Tuareg liberation movement (MNLA) in Boni. It is 2012 and Northern Mali is at war. The region where A lives was occupied by the MNLA and later, the same year, by a Jihadist movement MUJAO. It is a mediated war (de Bruijn et al. 2015). We are observing profound changes in the experience of war and conflict in West and Central Africa.

Figure 36.1   A with his son's new telephone

Introduction

This chapter scrutinizes the role of small media, Information and Communication Technologies (ICTs) such as mobile phones, tablets, and smartphones (Spitulnik 1999), in recent political developments in Africa, as is exemplified by the (youth) movements such as "Y'en marre" in Senegal, "Balai Citoyen" in Burkina Faso, and "Trop c'est Trop" in Chad. It seems that a new political agency (Chabal 2009) is emerging that can be understood in relation to the increase in use of small media (see e.g. Rheingold 2002; Postill 2012; Jeffrey and Doron 2013). Small media influence communication in networks and the flows of information, leading to actions that inform political change and the appearance of movements.[1]

Discussions on the Arab Spring (Stepanova 2011; Rennick 2013; Lim 2012) and sub-Saharan Africa (Bouhdiba 2013; Ekine 2010) have analyzed the role of new ICTs in uprisings and new social movements. These discussions show that the role of new ICTs can only be a partial explanation. Other factors, such as social and economic inequality, people's anger and frustrations, the presence of youth, and the increasing living standards that make inequality more visible, should be taken into consideration. Nevertheless, in this chapter I show that small media might, in fact, be the main agent in the movements that have occurred in West and Central Africa in recent years. I follow Castells' (2009) main thesis in his book *Communication Power*, which shows how new ICTs carried by small media are a new incentive to move power to ordinary people, who increasingly have access to these new communication tools. Small media are discerned from mass media (such as TV, radio, journals) in order to shift the analysis to the agency of "ordinary" people. Fahlenbrach et al. (2014), Hands (2011), and Miller (2013) also direct our attention to how the use of small media changes the ways access to information is achieved, by linking people to the outside world through social networks of communication.

In this chapter, I focus on mediated information and communication circles/networks in circumstances of conflict, war, and oppressive regimes in Africa. Drawing on research on ICTs and political change in 2012–2016 in Central and West Africa, I reflect upon various protests—the "revolution" in Burkina Faso; the protests in Kinshasa; the less well-known protests in Chad; and movements that are generally judged in a negative light, i.e. the liberation movement in Mali (2012); several Jihadist movements, including Boko Haram in Nigeria and MUJAO in Mali—and how they are being shaped by the increasing presence of small media. Illustrating this through two case studies, I reveal how, in such contexts, mediated communication is guided by specific codes of communication, often informed by fear, avoidance, or, in contrast, forms of protest and resistance. The messages and information that are carried by a variety of small media, and which inform people about political developments and about the often unjust situations in their countries, are different from those in times before accessing small media. This can influence political agency, i.e. more engagement and participation, but also decision-making in political developments. It can also facilitate the organization of new (political, protest, liberation) movements, with the help of small media and by increasing adherence; that is to say, as people acquire new ideas, they are more inclined to take their destiny into their own hands and hence join movements, comment on them, and search for alternatives. This raises the question, whose political agency counts?

Small Media and Political Agency across Africa

The ICT revolution in Africa is widely discussed and, indeed, hailed for the new opportunities it offers in economic, social, and political life. New ICTs entered Africa via the urban gateway at the end of the last century, marked by the liberation of the mobile phone market. Although it took a few years to enter more remote areas, statistics show a rapidly increasing percentage, which means that, today, the majority of the population in Africa has access to this means of communication (see Castells et al. 2007; de Bruijn et al. 2009, 2013).[2] Over the past decade, smartphones with an in-built light version of Facebook are available on the market. Their source is the Chinese production for African (poor) markets. The development has been rapid and is depicted as leapfrogging as it landed in a very poorly developed communication infrastructure. Prior to this development, phones were only for the few: landlines were almost non-existent or access was limited to elites (Nkwi 2010). The mobile phone has been depicted as a democratization tool, and, indeed, those in Africa who have no voice do have a phone today (Gegen 2008).

The cases I will present are part of on-going research within the project Connecting in Times of Duress (CTD)[3] that started in September 2012 as a follow-up to research that I started in 2006 on mobile telephony in Africa. The year 2006 can be depicted as the moment that mobile telephony made serious inroads on the continent. Expectations were high and our research showed that, indeed, the new technology did have the potential to change society, but probably not as radically as some of the early publications suggested. Socio-economic dynamics, especially in mobile communities, are affected.[4]

In 2012, at the end of the research project, a transformation of mobile phones to smartphones took place, raising the question of whether this would mean a new wave of change. Then, social media such as Facebook appeared as a medium for (political) change. For instance, in Chad it offered a platform for young people to discuss politics without being "seen" (Seli 2014, chapter 9). People who hitherto did not really have a voice, or were not well informed, were finding a new platform to express their political choices and quest for identity, and were able to comment on decisions taken by the government, etc. Facebook use has been rising in recent years. Such developments became the core of the research project CTD.

How do we research the interaction between socio-political actors in Africa and ICTs and change in political agency? The CTD research project adopted an ethnographic approach. Following actors' political actions and use of (new) ICTs or small media over time is at the core of such an approach. Hence, I will present two persons and their central actions in political events. Their stories have been part of other publications (de Bruijn 2016; de Bruijn et al. 2015), but not in the same detail as I present them here.

Mali 2012

Northern Mali acquired wireless connectivity from 2009 onwards. Earlier, connectivity was available in small towns (2005) and some rural areas could receive wireless signals, but only by chance. From 2009 onwards, the rural areas gradually became connected (Keita 2015). Although large parts of the desert are still without coverage, it is clear that almost everybody can, if they have the means, make a (mobile) phone call and access the Internet. Of course, not everybody has a phone yet, but sharing of phones is common and there are phone booths in towns where one can make calls.

Hence, the occupation of the Northern part of Mali that followed the Tuareg/Tamacheck "rebellion" found the Hayre (in the southern part of North Mali) "connected." At this time, government services had fled the region and disorder ruled. It is interesting to note the stories of how people encountered the MUJAO, who took control of the Hayre from the MNLA. MUJAO members integrated mobile phones into their practice to establish themselves in the region. They exchanged phone numbers and asked people to call if they encountered problems. They also used film and photos as means of disseminating their messages. However, the most effective method of spreading their force and convincing people of their power, has been their training camps in the desert, where young men from the Hayre went to learn how to fight and to be able to defend themselves (auto defense groups).

The region, and especially the nomads from this region, is very mobile. So, many people have left and relocated to Southern Mali, for instance, after the droughts of the 1970s and 1980s. But people also migrated to town for economic reasons. In short, the Hayre is connected to a wide mobile community. The situation in the Hayre was being communicated by phones and Facebook, and soon people living outside the Hayre were organizing food transportation and healthcare. Such things were mainly in the hands of the richer elites, but even for them the conflict was very real and they could not ignore it. They were connected to events by calls from family and friends, but also by activities on Facebook, and they were inspired to act. Mobile phones and Facebook functioned as glue[5] for this society, which became more connected during 2012.

Another effect of Facebook pages and other online exchanges has been that news about the region became international. The conflict in Mali received a lot of attention from the international media who could not send their journalists to the area for security reasons. Spokespeople in Paris, messages from people in the region and from Mali's capital, Bamako, formed a backbone for the news. This circuit, however, comprised information that could not be verified.

Associations have gained new dimensions in the time of social media and the Internet. This is the case for the worldwide association Taabital Pulaaku, which has an important office in Bamako. This association also entered into communication about and with the people in the Hayre. They posted about the situation on their Internet pages and some members of this association have become spokespersons for the nomads in the region. These illiterate nomads were confronted with atrocities and hardship as a result of the occupation, as the story of A presents (see Figure 36.1).

A[6] and his son's smartphone symbolize how illiterate people can also be part of these developments, in which communicating the war has become central. A has appropriated the mobile phone for his own needs. He was, in fact, the first in his group to buy a phone, which he used to connect with Dutch researchers and with the researcher Boukary Sangare, but also to link to political actors, as he became increasingly politicized and interested in representing his group. A became used to the phone; it gave him access to people, and it helped enhance his position in his group. During 2012, the phone became even more important for A. He communicated the war and events to me and to Boukary, and was able to link to the outside world to signal various injustices. He also received information in the form of films that were sent through the connected community by Bluetooth. In short, information was very accessible and it did influence his reasoning. Boukary and I (to a lesser extent, due to security concerns) were able to follow A and do some interviews. His ideas about the war and his group's situation clearly developed in another direction.

A new phase in this connectivity war occurred when a Marabout nomad from a village close to the border of Burkina Faso decided to mobilize the nomads to organize and claim their rights. He is a well-traveled man who was active in the MUJAO camps and had been involved in different spheres of exchange. He managed to convince A to join him in this mobilization effort. They were able to organize a big meeting in November 2013, where the discussion about the marginal position of the nomads and the difficulties they have with the Malian state were central. The uniting of the nomads would not have been possible without mobile phones since, in addition to traveling to face-to-face meetings, recruitment was done through mobile telephony.

2012 was a turning point for the Hayre and, more specifically, for the nomadic population who had never had a real voice, but instead was led by their elites, who maintained good relations with the state, but did not negotiate very well for the nomads. The MUJAO discourse on marginality, the contact with politicians in Bamako, the possibility of finding support in associative circles and among researchers connected to UN missions, EU circles, and other possible "protagonists" of the nomadic cause, opened their eyes. The role of small media is clear. The illiterate A could access a wider world through his mobile phone and voice communication in the form of film and audio speeches from Muslim religious leaders, etc. This interaction ultimately led him to travel to Bamako and frequently to Mopti, where he would meet with people. Another world became visible in which he could situate himself and his people as a marginalized group, but also with the possibility of claiming their rights. A problematic turn in the story of A, however, is that although their claims are heard by international instances, no action is undertaken. So far, they feel they have only had genuine support from the MUJAO, and although they do not share their ideology they can sympathize with their cause. Many young Fulani nomads have joined the MUJAO in recent years, or are, at least, sympathetic to their ideas.

The context in which A's moves are situated is a largely mediated context. The information that is disseminated to the wider public comes through journalists who often do not visit the region and have only second-hand information, or information from Facebook pages, interviews with outsiders, etc. In this circuit, there has been a recent development— an accusation that the nomads are joining Jihadist movements and becoming radicalized. Whatever this means, it does define the attitude and decisions of those who have to deal with the nomad case and their movement in the Hayre.

Chad, March 2015

The protest march of March 9, 2015 in Ndjaména, the capital city of Chad, ended in bloodshed. Three students were killed. Students were arrested and tortured. Usually, this would go unnoticed by the majority of Chadians (or they would hear about it much later). This time it was different and a Facebook exchange followed. A short video of this event was watched by Chadians all over the world and all those interested in Chad. There are no limits here in terms of accessing social media. It alerted the president and finally the head of police was removed and the families of the dead students compensated, but their immediate reaction was, "We do not want their money."

Z was in Ndjaména at this time, and participated in the peaceful march to bury his fellow student, who died during the protest. The march was announced on Facebook and people committed to attending. This march, too, was violated by the police and many discussions on the Internet, mainly Facebook, ensued.

These serious incidents were followed by (terrorist) attacks on the central market in Ndjaména, a few months later, at the beginning of July 2015. Other attacks in various parts of the country would soon follow. The government and international media present these incidents as attacks against the Chadian state, which is fighting (successfully) against Boko Haram in Nigeria and Cameroon and against Jihadist groups in Northern Mali.

The first protest march was against the imposition of helmets for motorcycle drivers, who are mainly students and pupils at secondary school. Nobody can really be against such a measure, but the incredible rise in helmet prices and the exaggerated response of the police were a catalyst for the protest. The protest was organized from gatherings at schools and then spread via SMS. The aftermath was organized entirely through Facebook Messenger, SMS, etc. An interesting detail is that the march and helmet-wearing law were translated by a Chadian Slammer in a song in which he discussed what this helmet stood for. The song spread through Ndjaména and later also other cities via Bluetooth. Later, it was posted on YouTube and has been viewed up to 500 times, which means it has been shared many times more. He now performs this song during concerts, which generally attract many people.

Z participated in these events and shared the information with me. He is in his mid-twenties, a law student, calls himself an activist, is a blogger, and feels marginalized in his own society. He is angry, based on all the injustice that he faces in his country. There is little he can do about it, other than being angry and participating in these protests, making his voice heard (against the advice of his family, but he is an orphan and does not respect their authority). He hesitated before publishing his blog. To become a blogger Z did a course in Yaounde in 2014 (November–December). Being a blogger in Chad is not without risk. He postponed his start and decided to begin by posting on Facebook instead, where his audience is growing. He commented furiously on the attacks, accusing the government of being behind them. He felt that he probably went too far with his comments and was getting nervous. After being intimidated by two police officers, he decided to flee the country for a few months. His fear was real. How does fear affect accessing information and being active on social media, or the organization of protest?

Facebook, used as a platform for expression, might not be so open and liberal after all. Chad has a long history of civil war. The memories of the repressive regime of Habré (1984–1990) are vivid (but not spoken of) and practices of suppression, albeit in a less severe form, continue under President Deby. Z grew up mainly under Deby's rule, and experienced only a few years under Habré, but his parents' generation lived during this period and certainly transmitted some of their feelings of fear to their children. The fear that people feel today is often a self-proclaimed fear. However, like Z, other bloggers have been sent into exile, making this fear a reality.

The youth participating in these uprisings are probably all relatively well connected—they have phones, are literate, read newspapers, etc. They are also well informed and keep up with the news via the Internet, reading newspapers online and radio-frequency interference (RFI) radio. Z was eager to access the Internet when the first connections were possible in Ndjaména, despite the fact that being connected remained very expensive. Today, despite difficult Internet connectivity, Z is often connected and surfs the web in hotel lobbies, where he has access through their Wi-Fi networks. I first met Z in a hotel, where he had gone to get connected. He needs to know; it is like food for him. He has two phones, including his all-important smartphone. Little wonder, then, that he has become a self-made web designer.

Discussion: Political Agency and Small Media

The two regions that are the focus of this chapter are either conflict- or even war-torn, or there is (and sometimes these go together) an authoritarian regime where freedom of speech is contested. These conditions influence the way people access ICTs (cf. Mutsvairo 2006, for Zimbabwe; Seli 2014, for Chad). Their emotions and experiences of the conflicts and repression can be labeled duress. It is a hardship that influences their decisions and, at the same time, limits their room for maneuver (see blog Mirjam: mirjamdebruijn.wordpress.com; de Bruijn and Both forthcoming; Schlee 2004). The two case studies explore the role of small media in the changes in political agency in contested Africa. In both cases, a rapid increase in wireless technology changed the communication landscape profoundly, and in both cases it led to an opening for actors to relate differently to politics and reinforce their political agency. The case studies have shown that there is an explicit relation between ICTs, carried by small media, and political agency under conditions of stress and duress.

The two case studies show that, indeed, a new political agency is taking shape. We are witnessing the creative new ways of *politique par le bas* with the advancement of wireless connectivity and development of communication technologies/gadgets. The young people in Chad have a space on Facebook, but also communicate via SMS exchanges. There are new initiatives to make one's voice heard, including blogging. However, the Chadian case also shows how difficult it is to be really free in one's expression, because of an ever-present fear of censorship and control. To what extent is this also a question of self-censorship, based on the internalized fears from former times?

In the case of Mali, the shaping of political agency (*par le bas*) gained momentum in the tumultuous circumstances of 2012. Different changes came together and formed a vital conjunction for people like A and, in fact, for his whole group.

In both cases, the question is, do these new political actors really control communication? Are they really in power? We have to follow both developments further to be able to assess the sustainability of these changes. However, both cases do show a change in who the power holders of communication technologies are. In the Chadian case, Facebook posts were able to force the government to take pro-population measures; does that make Facebook the agent here? In Mali, the uniting of nomads in using different forms of communication transformed them into power holders: their voices are now heard and they will no longer be silenced! Here, the mobile phone could be seen as the agent. From these cases and the discussed literature, we can tentatively conclude that small media have changed the power relations in societies where power inequalities, such as in Authoritarian Africa, reign in everyday life.

In both cases, various small media converge and open up new ways for expression and organization. Madianou and Miller (2012) call this polymedia: a combination of Facebook, Twitter, SMS, Facebook Messenger, voice calls, and WhatsApp (which now has a voice function) interfere in people's lives and create new political spaces that interact with old spaces, and together merge into an innovative socio-political space where new forms of political agency are produced. These observations are in line with the work of Rheingold (2002), who, in his book *Smart Mobs* (2002), described how political movements organized increasingly with the help of these new media.

In conflict studies there is relatively little attention for people's experiences (emic) of wars/ conflicts/authoritarian regimes (cf. Schlee 2004). In this chapter, I focused on the agency of people whose experience of their environment relates to their actions and reactions, which, in turn, influence the environment. This approach emphasizes the possibilities a person has, rather than the limitations to his or her actions; duress, the experience of conflict and authoritarian regimes, is therefore a crucial element in understanding political agency. However, these creativities and possibilities are different depending on whether it is a time of peace and calm or a time of conflict and war. They are also different under democratic regimes or authoritarian regimes.

As the two case studies have shown, this emic of conflict, war, and repressive regimes is influenced by information accessibility. Information/knowledge about one's environment is important for the interpretation of conflict and war and for the decisions and directions in one's itinerary. Changes are not linear and people decide to act differently, making decisions that change their itinerary, at different times. As Johnson-Hanks (2002) infers, with her notion of vital conjunction, the spread of information—be it propaganda or information about where and how troops move, about security in town, or the position of loved ones, but also about the causes of the conflict—is important for people to be able to position themselves, to understand their situation, and hence to be able to (formulate) protest. Access to information is, therefore, part of political agency. New ICTs, or small media, give people in different parts of Authoritarian Africa access to new/other information that helps them to develop their opinions and to formulate a political position; in short, it influences their political agency. Apparently, small media do play a role in the appearance of "new" movements, both on the side of the movement and on the side of the population who decide to join or not.

Reflection on Methodology and Ethics

This chapter is based on a qualitative methodology, the ethnographic approach. An innovative element is the "Information Biography," as exemplified by the stories of Z and A. They did not become communication hubs (in fact, they themselves have become ICTs, as they have become central in the dissemination of information) by coincidence. Their life histories show a particular interest in information and communication; they have always been eager to embrace technologies, to use them to further their and their people's cause. They also share a deep feeling of injustice and inequality, which is one of the driving forces behind who they are and why they play these (political) roles.

Writing about the situations of Z and A, people living in authoritarian states where politics is a violent arena, is a tricky endeavor. The protection of informants is very important. On the other hand, A is a public figure and already ventilates his ideas in the public space. In his case, our writings can also liberate him from the Jihadist image that the Malian media have reserved for him. Z's situation is different. He is not a well-known public figure and he has been very explicit about his position as an activist. His actions feed his fear. It would, in fact, help Z to become a public figure, in order to be protected. Not only because it is more difficult to arrest and torture public figures, because of the international attention that it would provoke, but also because being more international gives the person in question a feeling of power over his situation and, in turn, a feeling of protection.

Why are we witnessing a wave of youth movements in Africa? Part of the answer certainly lies in the advancement of wireless technologies and the appropriation of small media by the population. We should further this research and follow more itineraries/information biographies of people to confirm these first and rather preliminary conclusions.

Notes

1 I will not further develop the forms of movements that we discuss here: the uprisings we witness are sometimes related to more traditional social movements, or they are hybrid movements (see, among others, De Waal and Ibreck 2013).
2 www.itu.int/en/ITU-D/Statistics/Pages/stat/default.aspx (accessed December 2015); ITU keeps records of statistics for all countries in the world about mobile phone coverage, Internet coverage, etc. These are, of course, aggregate data and do not show differences between regions. The research project Mobile Africa Revisited gathered data on these differences (see mobileafricarevisited.wordpress.com, accessed December 2015).
3 See project at www.connecting-in-times-of-duress.nl (accessed December 2015).
4 See de Bruijn et al. (2009, 2013), de Bruijn (2014) and Chéneau-Loquay (2000). https://mobileafricarevisited. wordpress.com (accessed December 2015).
5 I refer here to the famous glue of society as stated by Vertovec (2004).
6 The story of A is described at length in my blog: mirjamdebruijn.wordpress.com, two texts entitled: "Nomads unite" and "A nomad leader."

References

Bouhdiba, Sofiane. 2013. "Will Sub-Saharan Africa Follow North Africa? Backgrounds and Preconditions of Popular Revolt in the Light of the 'Arab Spring.'" African Studies Centre, Leiden ASC working paper; 109.

Castells, Manuel. 2009. *Communication Power*. Oxford: Oxford University Press.

Castells, Manuel, Mireia Fernandez-Ardèvol, Jack Linchuan Qiu and Araba Sey. 2007. *Mobile Communication and Society: A Global Perspective*. Cambridge, MA: MIT University Press.

Chabal, Patrick. 2009. *Africa: The Politics of Suffering and Smiling*. London and New York: Zed Books.

Chéneau-Loquay, Annie, ed. 2000. *Enjeux des technologies de la communication en Afrique: du téléphone à internet*. Paris: Karthala.

De Bruijn, Mirjam. 2014. "Connecting in Mobile Communities: An African Case Study." *Media, Culture & Society* 36(3): 319–35.

———. 2016. "Citizen Journalism at Crossroads: Mediated Political Agency and Duress in Central Africa." In *Participatory Politics and Citizen Journalism in a Networked Africa: A Connected Continent*, edited by Bruce Mutsvairo, 90–104. London: Palgrave Macmillan.

De Bruijn, Mirjam and Jonna Both. Forthcoming. "Introduction: Duress: Exploration of a Concept to Grasp Agency in Situations of Hardship." In *Realities of Duress: Responding to Situations of Enduring Hardship*, edited by Jonna Both and Mirjam de Bruijn (to be published in 2017).

De Bruijn, Mirjam, Inge Brinkman and Francis Beng Nyamnjoh, eds. 2009. "Mobile Phones: The New Talking Drums of Everyday Africa." Leiden/Bamenda: ASC/Langaa.

———, eds. 2013. *Side@Ways: Mobile Margins and the Dynamics of Communication in Africa*. Leiden/Bamenda: ASC/Langaa.

De Bruijn, Mirjam, Boukary Sangaré and Lotte Pelckmans. 2015. "Communicating War in Mali, 2012: On-Offline Networked Political Agency in Times of Conflict." *Journal of Africa Media Studies* 7(2): 109–28.

De Waal, Alex and Rachel Ibreck. 2013. "Hybrid Social Movements in Africa." *Journal of Contemporary African Studies* 31(2): 303–24.

Ekine, Sokari, ed. 2010. *SMS Uprising: Mobile Activism in Africa*. Oxford: Pambazuka Press.

Fahlenbrach, Kathrin, Sivertsen Erling and Rolf Werenskjold, eds. 2014. "Introduction: Media and Protest Movements." In *Media and Revolt, Strategies and Performances from the 1960s to the Present*, 1–19. New York, Oxford: Berghahn Books.

Gegen, Kenneth J. 2008. "Mobile Communication and the Transformation of the Democratic Process." In *Handbook of Mobile Communication Studies*, edited by J. E. Katz, 297–309. Cambridge, MA: The MIT Press.

Hands, Joss. 2011. *@ Is For Activism: Dissent, Resistance and Rebellion in a Digital Culture*. New York: Pluto Press.

Jeffrey, Robin and Assa Doron. 2013. *The Great Indian Phone Book: How Cheap Mobile Phones Change Business, Politics and Daily Life*. London: Hurst & Company.

Johnson-Hanks, Jennifer. 2002. "On the Limits of Life Stages in Ethnography: Toward a Theory of Vital Conjunctures." *American Anthropologist* 104(3): 865–80.

Keita, Naffet. 2015. *Téléphonie et Mobilité au Mali*. Bamenda/Leiden: Langaa/ASC.

Lim, Merlyna 2012. "Clicks, Cabs and Coffee Houses: Social Media and Oppositional Movements in Egypt, 2014–2011." *Journal of Communication* 62(2): 231–54.

Madianou, Mirca and Daniel Miller, 2012. *Migration and New Media: Transnational Families and Polymedia*. London: Routledge.

Miller, Danny. 2013. *Tales from Facebook*. Cambridge: Polity Press.

Mutsvairo, Bruce. 2006. *Power and Participatory Politics in the Digital Age, Probing the Use of New Media Technologies in Railroading Political Changes in Zimbabwe*. PhD Dissertation, Twente University.

Nkwi, Walter Gam. 2010. *Voicing the Voiceless: Contributions to Closing Gaps in Cameroon History, 1958–2009*. Mankon, Bamenda: Langaa Research and Publishing Initiative Group.

Postill, John. 2012. "Digital Politics and Political Engagement." In *Digital Anthropology*, edited by Heather Horst and Daniel Miller, 165–84. Oxford: Berg.

Rennick, Sarah Anne. 2013. "Personal Grievance Sharing, Frame Alignment, and Hybrid Organisational Structures: The Role of Social Media in North Africa's 2011 Uprisings." *Journal of Contemporary African Studies* 31(2): 156–74.

Rheingold, Howard, 2002. *Smart Mobs: The Next Social Revolutions, Transforming Cultures and Communities in the Age of Instant Access.* Cambridge: Basic Books.

Schlee, Gunther. 2004. "Taking Sides and Constructing Identities: Reflections on Conflict Theory." *Journal of Royal Anthropological Institute* (N.S.) (10): 135–56.

Seli, Djimet. 2014. *(Dé)connexions Identitaires Hadjeray: Les enjeux des technologies de la communication au Tchad.* Leiden/Bamenda: ASC/Langaa.

Spitulnik, Debra, 1999. "Media." *Journal of Linguistic Anthropology* 9 (1/2): 148–51. www.jstor.org/stable/43102451 (accessed December 2015).

Stepanova, Ekaterina. 2011. "The Role of Information Communication Technologies in the 'Arab Spring.'" *Ponars Eurasia* 15: 1–6.

Vertovec, Steven. 2004. "Cheap Calls: The Social Glue of Migrant Transnationalism." *Global Networks* 4: 219–24. doi: 10.1111/j.1471-0374.2004.00088.x.

37

ETHNOGRAPHY BEYOND AND WITHIN DIGITAL STRUCTURES AND THE STUDY OF SOCIAL MEDIA ACTIVISM

Veronica Barassi

Introduction

On April 21, 2011, I was carrying out participant observation on one of the mailing lists of the Corsari Collective, an autonomous collective that I had been following for over a year as part of a comparative ethnographic research on social media activism. That day I started following an email exchange between Franz, one of the key members of the group, and other activists. Writing from Lampedusa—where he was organizing actions in solidarity with refugees and migrants arriving to Europe—Franz wanted to know how he could share some videos on Facebook so that everyone in Milan could "witness at a distance." His simple question initiated a group discussion among the collective as different members were skeptical of his use of Facebook, given the fact that Facebook was a corporate platform, and was going to appropriate the copyright of their videos. Armed with pen and paper to dutifully write my fieldnotes on the piece of digital ethnography I was carrying out, I started to remember all the different instances during my fieldwork in which activists raised similar questions. My fieldwork revealed that, in the study of social media activism, we need to appreciate how activists understand and negotiate with the corporate nature of social media platforms.

This chapter was inspired by this finding, and argues that in the study of social media activism we need to develop a digital ethnographic approach that simultaneously challenges deterministic understandings of technological impacts while taking into consideration how technological structures matter in the everyday life of social movements. It is clear that this approach finds its roots in Hine's earlier definition of "virtual ethnography" (Hine 2000), which was based on the understanding that ethnographers of the Internet need to consider both technological development on one side and technological appropriation on the other.

However, this chapter brings the argument a bit further. By using the concept of "digital ethnography," I locate myself among the recent literature in the field that has shown that, today, we need a much more complex definition of the relationship between ethnographic practice and the Internet. Such a definition needs to take into account how Web 2.0 platforms combined with the extension of mobile and wireless technologies have created a "messy" situation (Postill and Pink 2012) whereby the understanding of the digital should be influenced by ideas of openness, complexity, and multiplicity (Pink et al. 2015) and should take into account new ideas of everyday interactions, embodiedness, and embeddedness (Hine 2015).

Moreover, with this chapter I wish to add to existing debates in the field by arguing that digital ethnographers often do not engage with critical questions about the political economy of the Internet and digital media (Barassi 2015a). This is particularly true if we consider the context of social media activism, where these questions are at the very heart of social movements' everyday interactions with Web platforms. By rethinking the concept of "digital capitalism" as a methodological and theoretical tool, the chapter will argue that such a concept enables us to explore the complex and multi-faceted ethnographic tensions that emerge in the cultural encounter between activist cultures and the political economy of the Web.

The Study of Social Media Activism and the Problem of Techno-determinism

In the last five years, the emergence and survival of large-scale movements that relied on social media in order to mobilize and organize collective action has prompted a series of questions on the way in which these mediated platforms are transforming the experience of political mobilization and action, and what possibilities for bringing about social change do they really offer. These questions are at the heart of current research that seeks to analyze and understand the "revolutions" that have affected the North African and the Middle Eastern regions, the mass protests of the 15M movements in Spain, or the development and emergence of the Occupy movements in the US (Sreberney and Khiabany 2010; Postill 2014; Barassi 2015a; Gerbaudo 2012; Castells 2012; Juris 2012). What *is* becoming clear is that social media technologies have become a new repertoire of political action, and that the study of "social media activism" is an urgent topic of inquiry in the social sciences because it could shed light on the social complexities of contemporary forms of political participation.

The study of social media activism finds its roots in the earlier literature on digital activism. The theoretical frameworks on digital activism, which emerged at the end of the 1990s and beginning of the 2000s, highlighted how Internet technologies were enabling new forms of political imagination and organization. Particularly influential in this regard was the work of Castells (1996, 1997) who argued that the Internet has created a situation for which the *network* became a privileged and more flexible mode of social organization and, in doing so, it created new political possibilities for social movements. These "new" political possibilities according to Castells (1997) could be seen in the political repertoires of the global justice movements, which strongly relied on networked affinities. Influenced by the Zapatista teachings and Deleuze and Guattari's (2004)—and in a similar line to the classical anarchists of the nineteenth century, such as Kropotkin and Laundauer—the movements at the end of the 1990s represented a rupture with the "identity politics" of the 1960s, 1970s, and 1980s, and argued that state relationships "capture" and "control" minorities (Day 2005). Hence they organized themselves collectively and non-hierarchically by relying on the concept of "network" (Graeber 2002; Juris 2008).

In understanding these new political imaginations that have affected the movements for global justice, scholars such as Hardt and Negri (2000) have thus emphasized the "power of networks," and contended that we were witnessing the rise of a new form of net-worked struggle, which did not rely on discipline, but on creativity, communication, and self-organized cooperation (2000, 83). While the Italian autonomists talked about "multi-tude" (Hardt and Negri 2000; Virno 2004), others emphasized generalized concepts such as "mobs" (Rheingold 2002) or "networked individualism"/creative autonomy (Castells 2001, 2009). The overall assumption was that new information technologies had radically transformed older forms of political participation and action, and that if we wanted to understand the relationship between digital activism and social change we needed to look at the more flexible and networked forms of political belonging and participation that these technologies have enabled.

Influenced by these works, the study of digital activism in the last decade has been highly dominated by the understanding that the relationship between media technologies and social movements needed to be theorized by focusing on the concept of "network." Social move-ments scholars argued that the logic of networks, which was triggered and facilitated by Internet technologies, was radically transforming the ways in which social movements under-stood and acted political participation.

With the development of social media technologies, we have seen the emergence of much scholarship which—influenced by the literature in the 1990s—claimed that social media technologies "determined" the emergence of new forms of political organization. Castells (2012), for instance, argued that the mass uprising of 2011 was determined by the use of social networking sites. He argued that social media created a "space of autonomy" where activists could express their feelings of collective outrage and hope, and enable a form of mass emotional contagion. It was by looking at the grassroots forms of emotional expression and organizing that Castells concluded that social media technologies have become the material support of a new type of political participation based on horizontal networks and leaderless organization. In contrast to Castells, Gerbaudo argued that far from being "horizontal" and "leaderless" these movements often have their leaders and reference points and social media technologies, in fact, enable the creation of a "soft" type of leadership (Gerbaudo 2012). According to him, social media enabled the choreography of participation bringing people together in the streets and the squares.

Like Gerbaudo (2012), other scholars have tried to move beyond the concept of "network" by introducing new conceptual terms such as "commons" (Hands 2010) or "connective action" (Bennett and Segerberg 2012) to address the new "logic" of political participation that is fostered by social media activism. All of these contributions have been important to the emergence of the field of social media activism as they mapped the changing repertoires of political action, and the role social media technologies played in the development of new forms of protest cultures.

Although insightful, the works in the field of social media activism of the last decade have been marked by a profound techno-determinism. Scholars focused on how technologies have determined the rise of new forms of political organization. This is to the detriment of a careful appreciation of the fact that the relationship between political activists and social media technologies involves open-ended and complex processes of social construction and human negotiation, which change from context to context, from group to group. This lack of engagement with the cultural specificity of movements on the ground can be found in the work of Castells (2012) or Gerbaudo (2012) who focused on the example of different movements, from Egypt to Europe and the US without providing us with a thick analysis of the different cultural and political contexts in which these movements emerged and without exploring the different types of social media activism they engage with. As the next part of the chapter will show, this techno-determinism has been challenged by the emergence of the work of those scholars who have focused on the analysis of movements' media practices and who have employed the digital ethnographic method.

A Critique of Techno-determinism: The "Media as Practice" Approach and the Importance of Digital Ethnography

In contrast to the implicit techno-determinism of scholars such as Castells (2012), in recent years we have seen the emergence of a variety of studies that, drawing from the understanding of "media as practice" (Couldry 2004; Brauchler and Postill 2010), have provided us with a variety of scholarship on activists' uses of Web technologies (McCurdy 2011; Mattoni 2012; Barassi and Treré 2012; Cammaerts et al. 2013; Feigenbaum et al. 2013; Barassi 2015a; Dencik and Leistert 2015). In a well-known article, Couldry (2004) argued for the importance of moving beyond functionalist approaches in the study of media and analyzing *media as practice*. For Couldry (2004), the emphasis on practice as theoretical paradigm presupposes an openness to the variable and complex organization of practice, and a concern with the principle and beliefs whereby practices are ordered, both of which are pivotal if scholars want to avoid functionalist approaches. Prior to Couldry, the concept of practice has often been central to the anthropology of media. However, as Postill (2010) has noticed, one problematic aspect of the media anthropology literature is represented by the fact that the concept of practice has not been properly defined or problematized. Together with Bräuchler, Postill (2010) has therefore collected in recent years important contributions, which thoroughly engage with practice theory and propose a more nuanced and thorough understanding of *media as practice* (Bräuchler and Postill 2010).

In the understanding of social media activism, the practice approach is perceived as fundamental because it enables us to analyze the different forms of media practices that define the everyday life of social movements without being constrained by techno-centric perspectives. This body of work focuses on the tension between old and new media technologies (Mattoni 2012; Treré 2012; Cammaerts et al. 2013), on the relationship between digital practices and beliefs (Barassi and Treré 2012; Postill 2014), on the connection between digital environments and offline spaces (Juris 2012; Feigenbaum et al. 2013), or on the emergence of new temporalities (Barassi 2015b; Kaun 2015). Current research on social movements' practices is insightful and necessary especially in the study of social media activism. This is because it challenges techno-deterministic assumptions on the pervasiveness and agency of social media technologies, and provides us with more nuanced and context-specific understandings.

It is within this body of literature that we generally find the employment of the digital ethnographic approach and we can fully appreciate its importance (Juris 2012; Postill and Pink 2012; Postill 2014; Treré 2015; Barassi 2015a; Bonilla and Rosa 2015). Within this body of literature the digital ethnographic approach has been developed mostly by combining field research among activists with online participant observation. The overall understanding is that there is a deep interconnection and integration between online and offline ethnographic contexts (Miller and Slater 2001; Hine 2000), and therefore we can only gain an ethnographically thick analysis of social media activism if we appreciate how online practices, texts, and personal choices are based on the real-life dynamics, beliefs, power relationships, and political imaginations that define the everyday life of the groups studied.

By developing digital ethnographic accounts that look at the interconnection between social media platforms and everyday life, these works in social media activism are important because they challenge contemporary communication research in the field. They do so by showing that focusing merely on the online dimension can lead scholars to overlook how online information and practices relate to activists' political cultures (Barassi 2015a) and produce quantitative data (e.g. number of tweets) that do not really talk about the lived experience of social media activism (Bonilla and Rosa 2015). Yet they are also important because they provide the field with subjectively thick understandings of the complexity involved in the encounter between political participation and social media technologies.

One of the advantages of digital ethnography is represented by the fact that, as Hine (2000) and Markham (1998) have argued, this method enables scholars to learn through direct experience. The richness of the ethnographic method in general lies in the fact that the ethnographer finds him/herself immersed in a different world and proceeds to explore it through the self. Dealing with social injustice, and becoming politically engaged through social media use is a very subjective and personal process, and the digital ethnographic method is thus essential in the study of social media activism, not only because it can challenge techno-deterministic perspectives on the democratic potential of social media technologies but also because it can shed light on this level of social experience. This latter point is evident if we consider the edited collection by Juris and Khasnabish (2013) where they argue that activist ethnographers, through their subjective political engagement, produce new meanings and understandings of collective action. It is for this reason that digital ethnographers at present are struggling with the personal traces that they leave behind within the online contexts (Postill and Pink 2012) and with the fact that they may become political agents only by defining the particular site of their research (Bonilla and Rosa 2015). The challenges encountered by digital ethnographers are not to be understood as deterrents but rather as opening up new possibilities for social research in the study of social media activism.

Although important for developing a new way in which we can understand social media activism today, digital ethnographers are faced by a theoretical and methodological conundrum. On the one hand, they are rightly aware of the fact that their method is essential in order to avoid techno-centric and deterministic perspectives. On the other hand, they need to come to terms with the fact that—in the study of social media activism—technological structures matter. This is especially true if, as emerged from my field research, not only do we realize that social media platforms are shaped by corporate discourses and practices, but we also take into account the fact that political activists whose values are rooted in anti-capitalist political cultures perceive the use of these platforms as challenges. In the final part of the chapter, I will therefore draw on my own research to discuss how I dealt with this conundrum in the field.

Digital Ethnography beyond and within Technological Structures and the Question of Digital Capitalism

In the last five years I have been conducting ethnographic fieldwork among three collectives of activists in the UK, Italy, and Spain. My ethnographic research focused on activists' "social media practices," and questioned how social media activism impacted on the political strategies of the groups studied, on their political imaginations, and on their internal politics. As argued elsewhere (Barassi 2015a), one of the main findings of my research had to do with the tensions activists faced as they tried to come to terms with the corporate nature of social media technologies. Not only were activists aware of the fact that social media technologies exploited personal data for corporate purposes, but they also thought—as Javier, a Spanish environmental activist once explained to me—that social media were "privately owned spaces," which were structured in a particular way that guaranteed the "standardization of profiles" and the commodification of human relationships.

This understanding shares many lines of similarities with current communication research on the political economy of Web 2.0. However, while political economic scholars argue that social media corporations have a remarkable advantage over users, whose creative content and free labor is systematically exploited (Fuchs 2007, 2013; Terranova 2000, 2013), the activists I worked with believed that this advantage is not that granted, and that they can negotiate with the corporate structure of social media, and use these technologies in instrumental ways. In fact, in the same chat with Javier, he argued for the importance of using social media technologies in tactical ways to build different types of values, and different types of social relationships that escaped the logic of capitalism.

During my fieldwork, therefore, it became clear that I needed to address the issue of technological structure when studying social media activism, and tackle critical questions on the corporate logic of social media technologies. Within "practice theory" scholars have often considered questions of technological structure by relying on a non-techno-deterministic perspective. In fact they have explored not only how structural models are internalized—as Bourdieu (1977) and Giddens (1986) pointed out—but also how human actors simultaneously reproduce technological structures while circumventing them and creating new possibilities for social organization (Orlikowski 2000). The approaches of virtual and digital ethnography, as mentioned in the introduction, have been dominated by such understandings (see Hine 2000, 2015) regarding the importance of simultaneous considerations of technological design and structures as well as issues of adaptation and appropriation. However, as argued elsewhere (Barassi 2015a), what is missing from contemporary digital ethnographic approaches is an engagement with the literature on the political economy of the Web and digital technologies (Fisher 2010; Fuchs 2007; Curran 2012; McChesney 2013). The two fields remain separated and defined by a specific research position. On the one hand, political economic approaches neglect a careful consideration of everyday social practices and of how people negotiate with and resist the political economy of the Web. On the other hand, digital ethnographic approaches often do not take into consideration the broader political economic factors that shape digital environments.

It is for this reason that, during my fieldwork, I decided to analyze activists' everyday negotiation with the corporate structure of social media technologies by rethinking and reframing the concept of *digital capitalism*. Schiller (2000) demonstrated that in the 1990s—under pressure of the neoliberal logic of Western governments (and in particular the US)—the Internet began a political economic transition in order to support "an ever growing range of intracorporate and intercorporate business processes" (2000: 1). This process led to the establishment of a communication infrastructure network that is highly shaped by neoliberal logic. Such an understanding is broadly shared among critical communication scholars (Curran 2012; McChesney 2013) who have argued that the establishment and strengthening of digital capitalism was tightly linked to the refashioning of the World Wide Web as a consumer medium (Schiller 2000, 89–142). With the development of Web 2.0 technologies, and especially corporate social media, such critical approaches have become particularly important. This is because it became clear that, as mentioned above, Web 2.0 technologies were in fact consumer media that were designed to exploit user data for profit, and hence were largely shaped by corporate discourses and practices (Fisher 2010; Fuchs 2007; Curran 2012; McChesney 2013).

Despite being insightful in raising critical questions on the political economy of the Web, the concept of digital capitalism as used in communication research is grounded on a monolithic perspective (Wheeler 2000) and does not consider the cultural tensions of digital capitalism, and how people are understanding and experiencing the political economy of the Web. In contrast to these approaches, during my research I decided to use the concept of digital capitalism as an analytical and methodological tool that enabled me to explore the corporatization of Web platforms, by looking at how technological structures are often shaped by *cultural processes* that are rooted in the history of capitalism, such as individualism, time regimes, or the exploitation of free labor (Barassi 2015a). At the same time the concept has also enabled me to explore the ethnographic tensions that arise in activists' *encounter with digital capitalism* through their everyday Web uses, and I have focused on three different tensions: networked individualism, the temporal context of immediacy, and the exploitation of digital labor.

Although my own ethnographic research focused on the concept of digital capitalism, and on the social and cultural tensions that digital capitalism creates, especially in the context of political activism, I certainly believe that "cultural experiences witnessed on Web platforms" cannot be "simply dismissed as yet another form of corporate control over culture, or Orwellian dataveillant machine" (Langlois et al. 2009, 1). However, I wanted to focus on the cultural experiences created by digital capitalism, because I feel that we have little data available on how activist cultures—that have been fighting for years against capitalism—are dealing and negotiating with the corporate nature of social media. This understanding, I believe, is essential to critically reflect on the advantages and challenges of social media activism for political activists, and to rethink the importance of the digital ethnographic method beyond and within technological structures.

Conclusion

In order to understand the way in which social media technologies are transforming political participation and action, it is important to maintain a critical perspective that challenges the techno-determinism implicit to current research. In this framework the ethnographic method is essential. The understanding of the way in which social media is transforming political participation and action can only be really achieved on the ground; by looking at activists' everyday experiences, and by considering the cultural and context-specific issues that emerge on the field. The extension of the digital ethnographic method within the study of social media activism has been crucial precisely for this reason: it has highlighted the cultural nuances of social media activism and the unpredictability of activists' experiences of these technologies. Furthermore, the digital ethnography of social media activism, as different scholars have shown, is also important because it sheds light on the fact that political participation on social media technologies is a very subjective process.

Digital ethnographic approaches in the study of social media activism, therefore, shed light on how Web 2.0 technologies are impacting on political participation and imagination, by moving away from techno-centric and deterministic perspectives. However, as this chapter has argued, digital ethnographers are challenged by a theoretical and methodological conundrum. Although it is clear that in the study of social media activism we have much to gain if we move away from techno-determinism, it is also clear that in the everyday life of political activists, technological structures matter. This is particularly true if we consider the fact that activists are aware that social media technologies are highly shaped and defined by corporate discourses and practices. By reframing the concept of digital capitalism, therefore, this chapter aimed at discussing this conundrum and at taking a first, tentative step in the development of a digital ethnographic approach that enables us to appreciate the impact of technological structures while understanding how people actively negotiate with them.

References

Barassi, Veronica. 2015a. *Activism on the Web: Everyday Struggles against Digital Capitalism*. New York: Routledge.

———. 2015b. "Social Media, Immediacy and the Time for Democracy: Critical Reflections on Social Media as 'Temporalizing Practices.'" In *Critical Perspectives on Social Media and Protest: Between Control and Emancipation*, edited by Lina Dencik and Oliver Leistert, 73–89. New York: Rowman & Littlefield International.

Barassi, Veronica, and Emiliano Treré. 2012. "Does Web 3.0 Come after Web 2.0? Deconstructing Theoretical Assumptions through Practice." *New Media & Society* 14(8): 1269–85. doi: 10.1177/1461444812445878.

Bennett, W. Lance, and Alexandra Segerberg. 2012. "The Logic of Connective Action." *Information, Communication & Society* 15(5): 739–68. doi: 10.1080/1369118X.2012.670661.

Bonilla, Yarimar, and Jonathan Rosa. 2015. "#Ferguson: Digital Protest, Hashtag Ethnography, and the Racial Politics of Social Media in the United States." *American Ethnologist* 42(1): 4–17. doi: 10.1111/amet.12112.

Bourdieu, Pierre. 1977. *Outline of a Theory of Practice*. Edited by Jack Goody. Translated by Richard Nice. Cambridge, UK; New York: Cambridge University Press.

Bräuchler, Birgit, and John Postill. 2010. *Theorising Media and Practice*. Oxford; New York: Berghahn Books.

Cammaerts, Bart, Alice Mattoni, and Patrick McCurdy. 2013. *Mediation and Protest Movements*. Bristol, UK; Wilmington, NC: Intellect.

Castells, Manuel. 1996. *The Rise of the Network Society: Information Age: Economy, Society, and Culture*, vol. 1. Chichester, West Sussex; Malden, MA: Wiley-Blackwell.

———. 1997. *The Power of Identity: The Information Age: Economy, Society, and Culture*, vol. 2. Malden, MA: Wiley-Blackwell.

———. 2001. *The Internet Galaxy: Reflections on the Internet, Business, and Society*. Oxford: Oxford University Press.

———. 2009. *Communication Power*. Oxford: Oxford University Press.

———. 2012. *Networks of Outrage and Hope: Social Movements in the Internet Age*. First edition. Cambridge, UK; Malden, MA: Polity Press.

Couldry, Nick. 2004. "Theorising Media as Practice." *Social Semiotics* 14(2): 115–32. doi: 10.1080/1035033042000238295.

Curran, James. 2012. "Rethinking Internet History." In *Misunderstanding the Internet*, edited by James Curran, Natalie Fenton, and Des Freedman, 34–67. London; New York: Routledge.

Day, Richard J. F. 2005. *Gramsci Is Dead: Anarchist Currents in the Newest Social Movements*. London; Ann Arbor, MI; Toronto: Pluto Press.

Deleuze, Gilles, and Félix Guattari. 2004. *A Thousand Plateaus: Capitalism and Schizophrenia*. New edition. London: Continuum International Publishing Group Ltd.

Dencik, Lina. 2015. "The Struggle Within: Discord, Conflict and Paranoia in Social Media Protest." In *Critical Perspectives on Social Media and Protest: Between Control and Emancipation*, edited by Oliver Leistert and Emiliano Treré, 163–81. New York: Rowman & Littlefield International.

Dencik, Lina, and Oliver Leistert, eds. 2015. *Critical Perspectives on Social Media and Protest: Between Control and Emancipation*. New York: Rowman & Littlefield International.

Feigenbaum, Anna, Fabian Frenzel, and Patrick McCurdy. 2013. *Protest Camps*. London: Zed Books.

Fisher, Eran. 2010. *Media and New Capitalism in the Digital Age: The Spirit of Networks*. Basingstoke, UK; New York: Palgrave Macmillan.

Fuchs, Christian. 2007. *Internet and Society: Social Theory in the Information Age*. London; New York: Routledge.

——. 2013. "Class and Exploitation on the Internet." In *Digital Labor: The Internet as Playground and Factory*, edited by Trebor Scholz, 211–25. New York: Routledge.

Gerbaudo, Paolo. 2012. *Tweets and the Streets: Social Media and Contemporary Activism*. London: Pluto Press.

Giddens, Anthony. 1986. *The Constitution of Society: Outline of the Theory of Structuration*. Berkeley, CA: University of California Press.

Graeber, David. 2002. "The New Anarchists." *New Left Review* II(13)(Feb): 61–73.

Hands, Joss. 2010. @ *Is for Activism: Dissent, Resistance and Rebellion in a Digital Culture*. London and New York: Pluto Press.

Hardt, Michael, and Antonio Negri. 2000. *Multitude: War and Democracy in the Age of Empire*. New York: Penguin.

Hine, Christine. 2000. *Virtual Ethnography*. London: Sage.

——. 2015. *Ethnography for the Internet: Embedded, Embodied, Everyday*. London: Bloomsbury Publishing.

Juris, Jeffrey S. 2008. *Networking Futures: The Movements against Corporate Globalization*. Durham, NC: Duke University Press.

——. 2012. "Reflections on #Occupy Everywhere: Social Media, Public Space, and Emerging Logics of Aggregation." *American Ethnologist* 39(2): 259–79. doi:10.1111/j.1548-1425.2012.01362.x.

Juris, Jeffrey S., and Alexander Khasnabish, eds. 2013. *Insurgent Encounters: Transnational Activism, Ethnography, and the Political*. Durham, NC: Duke University Press.

Kaun, Anne. 2015. "'This Space Belongs to Us!' Protest Spaces in Times of Accelerating Capitalism." In *Critical Perspectives on Social Media and Protest: Between Control and Emancipation*, edited by Lina Dencik and Oliver Leistert, 89–109. New York: Rowman & Littlefield International.

Langlois, Ganaele, Fenwick McKelvey, Greg Elmer, and Kenneth Werbin. 2009. "FCJ-095 Mapping Commercial Web 2.0 Worlds: Towards a New Critical Ontogenesis." http://fourteen.fibreculture-journal.org/fcj-095-mapping-commercial-Web-2-0-worlds-towards-a-new-critical-ontogenesis/.

Markham, Annette N. 1998. *Life Online: Researching Real Experience in Virtual Space*. Lanham, MD: Rowman Altamira.

Mattoni, Alice. 2012. *Media Practices and Protest Politics: How Precarious Workers Mobilise*. Farnham, UK: Ashgate.

McChesney, Robert W. 2013. *Digital Disconnect*. New York: The New Press.

McCurdy, Patrick. 2011. "Theorizing 'Lay Theories of Media': A Case Study of the Dissent! Network at the 2005 Gleneagles G8 Summit." *International Journal of Communication* 5: 20.

Miller, Daniel, and Don Slater. 2001. *The Internet: An Ethnographic Approach*. Oxford; New York: Berg.

Orlikowski, Wanda J. 2000. "Using Technology and Constituting Structures: A Practice Lens for Studying Technology in Organizations." *Organization Science* 11(4): 404–28. doi: 10.1287/orsc.11.4.404.14600.

Pink, Sarah, Heather Horst, John Postill, Larissa Hjorth, Tania Lewis, and Jo Tacchi. 2015. *Digital Ethnography: Principles and Practices*. London: Sage.

Postill, John. 2010. "Introduction: Theorising Media and Practice." In *Theorising Media and Practice*, edited by Birgit Bräuchler and John Postill, 1–32. Oxford and New York: Berghahn.

——. 2014. "Democracy in an Age of Viral Reality: A Media Epidemiography of Spain's Indignados Movement." *Ethnography* 15(1): 51–69. doi: 10.1177/1466138113502513.

Postill, John, and Sarah Pink. 2012. "Social Media Ethnography: The Digital Researcher in a Messy Web." *Media International Australia, Incorporating Culture & Policy*, 145(Nov.): 123.

Rheingold, Howard. 2002. *Smart Mobs: The Next Social Revolution*. New edition. Cambridge, MA: Perseus Books.

Schiller, Dan. 2000. *Digital Capitalism: Networking the Global Market System*. New edition. Cambridge, MA: MIT Press.

Sreberny, Annabelle, and Gholam Khiabany. 2010. *Blogistan: The Internet and Politics in Iran*. London; New York: I.B. Tauris.

Terranova, Titziana. 2013. "Free Labor." In *Digital Labor: The Internet as Playground and Factory*, edited by Trebor Scholz, 33–54. New York: Routledge.

Treré, Emiliano. 2012. "Social Movements as Information Ecologies: Exploring the Coevolution of Multiple Internet Technologies for Activism." *International Journal of Communication* 6: 2359–77.

——. 2015. "The Struggle Within: Discord, Conflict and Paranoia in Social Media Protest." In *Critical Perspectives on Social Media and Protest: Between Control and Emancipation*, edited by Lina Dencik and Oliver Leistert, 163–81. New York: Rowman & Littlefield International.

Virno, Paolo. 2004. *A Grammar of the Multitude*. Cambridge, MA; London: Semiotext[e].

Wheeler, Mark. 2000. "Dan Schiller, Digital Capitalism: Networking the Global Market System." *Convergence: The International Journal of Research into New Media Technologies* 6(2): 126–8. doi: 10.1177/135485650000600211.

38

THE SEARCH FOR
WIKIPEDIA'S EDGES

Heather Ford

Fanfare around the Internet's potential as a platform for speech by all still echoes around us. Heralded as the site in which geographic, social and political barriers were being overturned, early rhetoric around the impact of networked technologies positioned platforms as the means by which users were able to take back the means of production and publish news and information without the need for media power brokers and intermediaries of the past.

The 2006 *Time Magazine* Person of the Year Award perhaps best illustrates this zeitgeist. In December 2006, *Time Magazine* declared that its person of the year was "you." The cover of the magazine featured a computer screen with the words, "You. Yes, you. You control the Information Age. Welcome to your world" (Grossman 2006). The editorial argued that ordinary people now controlled the means of producing information and media because they dissolved the power of the gatekeepers who had previously controlled the public's access to information.

> [2006 is] a story about community and collaboration on a scale never seen before. It's about the cosmic compendium of knowledge Wikipedia and the million-channel people's network YouTube and the online metropolis MySpace. It's about the many wresting power from the few and helping one another for nothing and how that will not only change the world, but also change the way the world changes.
>
> (Grossman 2006, n.p.)

The idea that the "many" were "wresting power from the few" was shared by a host of commentators and scholars at the time. It was inspired by the evidence that many more people were now doing work that had previously been done by credentialed individuals within large institutions. Now, non-academics were writing encyclopedia articles, laypeople producing films, and concerned citizens producing news articles. A decrease in the costs of the means of production meant that millions of ordinary people were now connected to a network of potential audience members, co-producers, employees and publishers. Now anyone could be a journalist, an engineer or a scientist (Gillmor 2004; Leadbeater and Miller 2004; Shirky 2009); anyone could be an expert in something (Weinberger 2011). We had moved from a "read only" culture to a "read write" culture (Lessig 2011) that was characterized by active cultures of participation (Jenkins 2006) instead of passive consumption of a culture that had previously been presented to the public ready-made.

Cracks have, however, begun to appear in this revolutionary picture in which the user reigns triumphant. In this chapter, I outline the current debates and research relevant to this more complicated picture in the area of Wikipedia studies, and argue that what is missing from Wikipedia research is a deeper analysis of what is missing from Wikipedia. I argue that the ethnographic tradition is vital for studying Wikipedia's edges, its silences, its lacunae and that instead of more ethnographic work that considers only those who are highly active and visible on Wikipedia, there is a need to also study those who remain on the edges of Wikipedia because of disappointment, rejection or invisibility. By highlighting Wikipedia's widening multiplicity, ethnography has the potential to focus attention on the platform as a significant global, political arena in which there are emerging power configurations and new landscapes of inequality. Such research is necessary in order to continue struggling toward greater global democratic decision-making within the world's critical representative platforms.

Wikipedia as a Dominant Platform

The dominant position of platforms including Facebook, Google and YouTube in the Western world have led some to question the opportunities afforded by participatory sites to enable democratic debate. Commentators have highlighted the role of such platforms in the surveillance of users—either in the interests of capitalism (Lovink 2012) or autocratic regimes (Morozov 2011). Wikipedia has, however, remained largely unsullied in such debates. Christian Fuchs (2013) in his critique of social media, for example, holds up Wikipedia as an example of info-communism as opposed to the likes of capitalist Facebook and Google. A closer analysis of the politics of Wikipedia, however, starts to complicate the notion of Wikipedia as the model for global democratic production. Although Wikipedia's structure and values might be the best opportunity that we have for envisioning a global democratic online public sphere at the present moment, it is important to understand that it, too, suffers from tensions relating to its position as the dominant reference work on the Internet.

Wikipedia promises to be working towards reflecting "the sum of all human knowledge" (Wikimedia Foundation 2016) in 288 languages. Every day, however, thousands of contributions to Wikipedia are rejected. In a study that I conducted with Stuart Geiger (Ford and Geiger 2012) of Wikipedia articles for deletion, for example, we learned that the majority of articles in English Wikipedia are deleted under the category of "no indication of importance." Understanding the power dynamics behind such decision-making is a critical task for scholars of knowledge and the media. Wikipedia has become the site of significant power to represent. This power stems from its identity not as a platform in which thousands of editors participate in the construction of articles, but as an authoritative source for facts about the world.

Understanding who (or what) governs Wikipedia and which users and uses such configurations empower is important for two key reasons. First, Wikipedia is often used as a model for the participatory development of public information goods. Wikipedia has become an important model for answering questions about whether the Internet can and should be regulated, who should ideally regulate it, as well as how regulation should occur.

Second, Wikipedia has become an authoritative source for facts about the world, used not only by the millions of individual users who visit the site every day, but by other platforms (especially search engines such as Google, Yahoo! and Bing) as a source of public information displayed as fact to the user. With the advent of Google's Knowledge Graph, a search for "What is the capital of Israel?" on Google, for example, will result not only in a list of possible sites that might provide answers to our query, but also a fact box presented as *the* answer. Wikipedia is one of the core sources from which search engines are drawing data for these answers. Understanding Wikipedia as a site of power and politics is therefore critical to analyzing the ways in which the power to represent is being reconfigured in today's mediated environment (see, for example, Ford and Graham 2016).

Researching Wikipedia

Wikipedia has been the subject of a rich and varied array of research over its 15-year history. Because the site makes data about every edit available to the public under open data licenses, the majority of research on Wikipedia consists of quantitative studies in computer science and information systems (Okoli et al. 2012). Some of the most influential studies on Wikipedia are, however, derived from qualitative or mixed methods research approaches. Studies in this arena benefit from the rich open data that Wikipedia provides about editing behavior, but complement such research with interviews and participant observation.

As the rhetoric about the revolutionary potential of the Internet, and peer production in particular, to enable particular freedoms and values has waxed and waned, so too have responses to the stock of evidence that has been built up around how platforms like Wikipedia are both unique but also extend historical trends. Taken as a whole, Wikipedia research can be summarized as attempting to answer three core questions over time: (1) Does Wikipedia work? (2) How does it work? (3) For whom does it work?

1 Does Wikipedia Work?

Wikipedia reached its growth peak in early 2007 (Suh et al. 2009). In six years, Wikipedia's editor numbers had reached over 300,000 and English Wikipedia moved over the one-million-article milestone. In this first phase of Wikipedia's development the key question driving research and commentary was whether Wikipedia was as good as its commercial counterparts. A breakthrough study by *Nature* in 2005 started off this slew of research, comparing the accuracy of Wikipedia with that of *Encyclopaedia Britannica* and finding that *Britannica* contained only marginally fewer errors of fact (Giles 2005).[1] Since the *Nature* study, others have investigated Wikipedia's quality according to topics that include famous Americans (Rosenzweig 2006) and Western philosophers (Bragues 2007).

Theoretically, Yochai Benkler's *Wealth of Networks* (2006) made an important contribution to debates about the validity of Wikipedia's production model. According to Benkler, there have been significant changes in the organization of information production catalyzed by the Internet that have resulted in the rise of non-market and non-proprietary production, where unaffiliated individuals are able to take a more active role in the production of information than was previously possible. Benkler argued that the rise of individual agency leads to an inevitable clash with previous hierarchical market-driven industries, the result of which will ultimately decide the fate of each of these models. Wikipedia is used as a key example of non-market, non-proprietary and non-hierarchical peer production where incentives to create cultural goods are based not on price signals but on pro-social goals. According to Benkler, Wikipedia works because it is a natural outcome of a network in which the costs of connecting and producing information products together is undergoing a radical decline.

2 How Does Wikipedia Work?

The question of Wikipedia's comparative quality was followed by empirical research into *how* the site works, with a number of research projects laying the foundations for understanding the social and processional dynamics behind Wikipedia's everyday functioning. One of the most popular research questions in this topic area concerns the motivations for contribution to Wikipedia. Why, the question was asked, would anyone write for Wikipedia for free?

In response to this question, Forte and Bruckman (2005) found that Wikipedia resembles the scientific community in their cycles of credit and that Wikipedia editors are motivated to "collaboratively identify and publish true facts about the world" (Forte and Bruckman 2005, 1). Despite the potential for anarchy, researchers found that there is a strong focus on group coordination mechanisms within the architecture and norms of Wikipedia that enable users to rapidly respond to vandalism (Viegas et al. 2007). Wikipedia policies, also developed by community members, are considered an important element of social interaction on Wikipedia because they provide a common resource for new users to learn about editing and behavioral conventions (Viegas et al. 2007). One such policy or principle, that of "assum(ing) good faith," is the subject of Joseph Reagle's (2010) ethnographic study of Wikipedia. Reagle considers the history and rhetoric employed by the Wikipedia community on mailing lists, talk pages and a host of other forums in order to argue that the principle of good faith shaped the success of Wikipedia in its early years.

Another strand to research around questions of how Wikipedia works is to pay attention to the significant role of automated software agents in the everyday functioning of Wikipedia. Geiger and Ribes (2010), for example, demonstrate the role of non-human actors in the process of vandal banning, arguing that the decentralized activity enabled by automated and semi-automated tools on Wikipedia is a type of "distributed cognition" (2010, 117). Similarly, Niederer and van Dijck (2010) investigate the increasingly important role of bots in the rise of Wikipedia, arguing that it is impossible to understand Wikipedia's response to vandalism without an appreciation of the encyclopedia as a sociotechnical system driven by collaboration between users and bots. The authors provide a schematic overview of Wikipedia users according to their technical permission levels, and note that the permission level of bots is below that of administrators but well above the authority of registered users (2010, 1373). Wikipedia's content management system, argue Niederer and van Dijck, allows for "protocological control, a mode of control that is at once social and technological—one cannot exist without the other" (2010, 1373).

In my own research, I have discovered that addiction to responses from other editors as well as other negative social and psychological influences can catalyze increased participation (Ford 2013). Following an editor who began his work with Wikipedia as a model editor and ended it by being banned from English Wikipedia enabled me to discover the dark side of Wikipedia editing and the driving forces behind it. More work is needed, however, in order to fully understand motivations (both positive and negative, automated and human) for contributing to Wikipedia if we are to gain a fuller perspective of how Wikipedia works.

3 For Whom Does Wikipedia Work?

In response to the early democratic rhetoric espoused by researchers and pundits of Wikipedia and the Internet in general, a number of researchers have started to expose inequalities in Wikipedia's representation of the world and to ask questions about the source of these inequalities. Such questions are an inevitable step from the recognition that, whether we like it or not, Wikipedia is an important feature of the global information environment for many countries around the world and, as such, Wikipedia needs now to be seen not as an anomaly but as a feature of our public information infrastructure.

A number of valuable studies into Wikipedia's representational scope and coverage have highlighted significant sources of inequality on the platform. The first group of studies investigates Wikipedia's representation along the lines of social stratification including gender and geography. Demographic studies in this area indicate that between 84 and 90 percent of Wikipedia editors are men (Glott and Ghosh 2010; Hill and Shaw 2013; Lam et al. 2011), the majority have tertiary education and a significant number of editors across language versions speak English (Wikimedia Foundation 2011). Lam et al. (2011) find that the low proportion of females participating in English Wikipedia has resulted in measurable imbalances relating to content quality so that articles relevant to women are significantly shorter and have lower assessment ratings than those interesting to men (Lam et al. 2011, 6).

Similarly, mapping geotagged articles in English Wikipedia, Mark Graham finds that "almost all of Africa is poorly represented in Wikipedia" (Graham 2011, 275) thus mirroring existing inequalities online. Analyzing accounts of Singaporean and Philippine history on Wikipedia, Luyt (2011) argues that, despite the potential of new media for making visible previously marginalized voices, a more likely outcome is a reproduction of the status quo in historical representation. According to Graham et al. (2014), it is not only issues of connectivity or lack of Internet access that prevent people in developing countries from contributing to Wikipedia. Representation is a vicious cycle for those with strong editing cultures in local languages, while those on the peripheries of these countries fail to reach critical mass.

Other studies have indicated that Wikipedia's representations not only mirror existing asymmetries but can actually exacerbate those asymmetries. Reagle and Rhue (2011) find that, although Wikipedia biographies on women are longer and more numerous than *Encyclopaedia Britannica* in absolute terms, "Wikipedia articles on women are more likely to be missing than are articles on men relative to Britannica" (1138). Reagle (2013) extended these findings with a qualitative study in which he argues that low female participation in free culture communities, particularly within Wikipedia, is the product of a culture that is alienating towards women and that gender disparities are even worse in Wikipedia than in the computing culture from which it arose. Reasons for this include that geek stereotypes can be alienating, open communities are especially susceptible to difficult people, and the ideas of freedom and openness can be used to dismiss concerns and rationalize the gender gap as a matter of preference and choice.

Although the aforementioned studies are useful in highlighting Wikipedia as a source of inequality in opposition to the rhetoric it espouses, studies tend not to fully consider the systematic sources of bias inherent in Wikipedia's processes, policies and technologies. Wikipedia's infrastructure is unique in that it is mediated almost entirely by software and because the policies that stand in for editorial authority number in the hundreds. Instead of a small group of editors making site-wide decisions on what to include or exclude, there is instead an array of policies, templates, guidelines and tools that aim towards standardization. The growing stratification of users along the lines of their ability to deploy such objects has begun.

A handful of researchers have started to investigate the peculiarities of the Wikipedia system and how it is affecting power configurations on the site. Wikipedia policy is an important feature in defining the rules by which editors "delimit the sayable, define legitimate perspectives and fix the norms for the elaboration of concepts" (Pentzold and Seidenglanz 2006, 65). Although policy provides a common language for action, their ambiguity leads to power play among participants who may interpret policies differently according to their editorial interests (Kriplean et al. 2007).

Apart from complex policy debates applied to editorial decision-making, effective Wikipedia editors also demonstrate a sophisticated "trace literacy" (Ford and Geiger 2012) that results in power imbalances among users. The ability to both read and write according to the rules of Wikipedia's complex site-specific vocabulary has a significant impact on who is able to have their edits sustained. Along similar lines, Hargittai and Shaw (2015) note that inequalities in the representation of women on Wikipedia are exacerbated by a similarly significant Internet skills gap. They find that the most likely contributors are "high-skilled males" and that, actually, among low-skilled Internet users no gender gap exists.

Such research is beginning to shed light on questions relating not only to how peer production platforms such as Wikipedia may serve to exacerbate certain inequalities, but also how Wikipedia is resulting in the reconfiguration of the power to represent knowledge. Those who are able to master Wikipedia's technocratic system of representation with an emphasis on facts and other modular pieces of verifiable information are consequently able to emerge as power brokers within this environment. Those who fail to master this system, either because their knowledge of the world does not fit with what Wikipedia recognizes as knowledge (see, for example, Gallert and Van der Velden 2013) or because negative social interactions on the platform have led to their leaving the platform (Halfaker et al. 2013), will remain on Wikipedia's edges, unable to contribute to having their knowledge represented.

Situating Ethnography

Although the aforementioned studies are a useful starting point for future research into Wikipedia's shadows, there is a significant gap in research that investigates Wikipedia's edges according to the perspectives of those whose knowledge remains unrepresented. Ethnography can play a significant role in highlighting such knowledges, but ethnographers need to find innovative ways of seeking out actors who are largely invisible to Wikipedia's system—actors whose traces are feint or isolated if they exist in digital form at all.

There have been at least three previous ethnographic studies of Wikipedia including *Good Faith Collaboration: The Culture of Wikipedia* by Joseph Reagle (2010), *Janitors of Knowledge: Constructing Knowledge in the Everyday Life of Wikipedia Editors* by Olof Sundin (2011) and *Common Knowledge? An Ethnography of Wikipedia* by Dariusz Jemielniak (2014). Each of these ethnographies provides a rich source of understanding about Wikipedia laws, norms and dynamics but all of them are filtered through the perspectives of Wikipedia's most active contributors—that is, through the lens of those who already have significant power and experience on Wikipedia.

Instead of more ethnographic work that considers only those who are highly active and visible on Wikipedia, there is a need to study the lacunae, the people who remain on the edges of Wikipedia because of disappointment, rejection or invisibility. What are missing from Wikipedia research are ethnographies of the dispossessed, the invisible and the subalterns. Ethnography is a useful tool in starting to shed light on the edges of Wikipedia's network for three core reasons. These include (1) ethnography's focus on multiplicity that suits the study of diverse and multifarious communities of practice within and outside of Wikipedia's domain, (2) the flexibility in ethnographic methods that enables the straddling of both the quantitative and qualitative traditions, as well as (3) the ethnographic tradition of highlighting those in the shadows of dominant systems of power.

1 Multiplicity

Wikipedia started as a small, well-defined community of individuals working towards a relatively simple set of goals, but as it has grown in number and in authority, Wikipedia's networks of individuals, technologies and policies have grown in numerous diverse directions.

Wikipedia is now constituted by multiple, striated communities and identities. In addition to discussions about Wikipedia articles taking place on talk pages, Wikimedia mailing lists and community pages, Wikipedia articles are the subject of discussion on social media sites, in the mainstream press and in sites such as Wikipediocracy that criticize Wikipedia's hidden power dynamics.

According to anthropologist, George Marcus:

> [A]ny cultural identity or activity is constructed by multiple agents in varying contexts, or places, and that ethnography must be strategically conceived to represent this sort of multiplicity, and to specify both intended and unintended consequences in the network of complex connections within a system of places.
>
> (1995, 25)

Wikipedia's complexity, the fact that it means many different things to many different people in multiple assemblages of humans and technological artifacts, makes it a particularly ripe field of study for ethnography.

2   Flexibility

Ethnographic research, with its focus on principles rather than specific methods, enables the researcher to employ a flexible suite of methods in order to study people and the meanings they ascribe to phenomena. Using the technique of "following the thing" suggested by Marcus (1995), Jenna Burrell (2009 and in this volume) suggests that we construct a network of human actors, non-human actants or objects, as well as the processes and practices that become enrolled as we follow the thing across numerous places, platforms or phenomena.

Applied to Wikipedia, such flexible approaches enable ethnographers to collect diverse sources of data, including trace data about who (or what, in the case of automated bot editors) has edited articles over which time periods, the rhetoric employed by editors in arguing for particular editorial or policy decisions, as well as to follow representations of phenomena to the subjects of such representation through interviews and participant observation. Mixed methods that employ the benefits of openly available trace data, but do not stop at such data, are useful to the ethnographer in order to fill in the gaps that remain invisible to the system. Such methods enable researchers to overcome challenges in being held to the study of a single platform when users and representations move dynamically between those platforms and, indeed, outside of those platforms in ways that the digital does not reach.

3   Shadows

There is a rich tradition in ethnographic research of engaging fully with the morality and ethics of particular systems. According to Nancy Scheper-Hughes (1992), ethnography calls on us to reveal our sympathies rather than trying to disguise them. By offering a lens for filtering the experiences of the dispossessed, ethnographers are in an important position to call for change to make systems more equitable in the light of their growing authority and power to represent.

In addition, participant observation enables the ethnographer to experience the position of the uninitiated, the newcomer and the powerless within the network. When one begins editing on Wikipedia, for example, one's edit count is low and so is one's authority within the network. I used such moments as opportunities to reflect on the challenges and problems faced by new editors in my own ethnographic study of Wikipedia (Ford 2015). There are individuals and communities who will always remain on the outside of the Wikipedia network. The ethnographic experience of the new editor puts researchers into a good position for documenting these narratives if ethnographers are sufficiently reflexive.

Conclusion

Although the Internet's liberatory potential is no longer a feature of commentary and scholarship in the same way that it was a decade ago, the excitement that has accompanied the vast availability of digital trace data has meant that those who have fallen on the dark side of the digital remain largely unheard. George Marcus writes that "the heart of contemporary ethnographic analysis is not in the reclamation of some previous cultural state or its subtle preservation despite changes, but rather in the new cultural forms to which changes in colonial subaltern situations have given rise" (1998, 79). Wikipedia is an example of a new cultural form that has arisen out of the global spread of the Internet and the dominance of Western epistemology and the logic of verifiable facticity. Understanding the political dynamics of those who remain outside of this logic is a critical job for ethnographers.

Rather than producing the final word on Wikipedia, ethnographic studies should seek to explore the edges of the Wikipedia network, to provide myriad alternative perspectives that shed light on the multiplicity of Wikipedia and its position as critical global representative infrastructure. Ethnographic studies should aim at achieving yet another alternative perspective, another frame with which to view what is produced out of Wikipedia's sociotechnical structures and what its place in our world is. In order to construct this frame, researchers must seek out the actors and phenomena that are in the shadow of the encyclopedia: the banned, the deleted and the disillusioned. In doing so, Wikipedia research will begin to take on the shape and voices of those who have a critical stake in its representations.

Note

1 *Encyclopaedia Britannica* criticized the report's methodology and refuted its conclusions but *Nature* refused to retract it (*Nature* 2006).

References

Benkler, Yochai. 2006. *The Wealth of Networks: How Social Production Transforms Markets and Freedom.* New Haven, CT: Yale University Press.

Bragues, George. 2007. "Wiki-Philosophizing in a Marketplace of Ideas: Evaluating Wikipedia's Entries on Seven Great Minds." SSRN Scholarly Paper ID 978177. Rochester, NY: Social Science Research Network. http://papers.ssrn.com/abstract=978177 (accessed August 18, 2016).

Burrell, Jenna. 2009. "The Field Site as a Network: A Strategy for Locating Ethnographic Research." *Field Methods* 21(2): 181–99. doi: 10.1177/1525822X08329699.

Ford, Heather. 2013. "How Wikipedia's Dr Jekyll Became Mr Hyde: Vandalism, Sock Puppetry and the Curious Case of Wikipedia's Decline." Paper presented at Internet Research 14: *Resistance and Appropriation.* Denver, Colorado, October 23–26, 2013.

———. 2015. "Fact Factories: Wikipedia and the Power to Represent." PhD dissertation. University of Oxford, 2015.

Ford, Heather, and R. Stuart Geiger. 2012. "Writing Up Rather Than Writing Down." In *Wikisym, 2012.* ACM Press. doi: 10.1145/2462932.2462954.

Ford, Heather, and Mark Graham. 2016. "Semantic Cities: Coded Geopolitics and the Rise of the Semantic Web." In *Code and the City*, edited by Rob Kitchin and Sung-Yueh Perng, 200–14. London: Routledge.

Forte, Andrea, and Amy Bruckman. 2005. "Why Do People Write for Wikipedia? Incentives to Contribute to Open-Content Publishing. GROUP 05 Workshop Position Paper." In *GROUP 05. Sanibel Island, FL.*

Fuchs, Christian. 2013. *Social Media: A Critical Introduction.* London: Sage.

Gallert, Peter, and Maja Van der Velden. 2013. "Reliable Sources for Indigenous Knowledge: Dissecting Wikipedia's Catch-22." In *At the Intersection of Indigenous and Traditional Knowledge and Technology Design,* edited by Nicola Bidwell and Heike Winschiers-Theophilus, 117–32. Santa Rosa, CA: Informing Science Press.

Geiger, R. Stuart, and Heather Ford. 2011. "Participation in Wikipedia's Article Deletion Processes." In *Proceedings of the 7th International Symposium on Wikis and Open Collaboration.* ACM Press. doi: 10.1145/2038558.2038593.

Geiger, R. Stuart, and David Ribes. 2010. "The Work of Sustaining Order in Wikipedia: The Banning of a Vandal." In *Proceedings of the 2010 ACM Conference on Computer Supported Cooperative Work,* 117–26. CSCW '10. New York: ACM. doi: 10.1145/1718918.1718941.

Giles, Jim. 2005. "Internet Encyclopaedias Go Head to Head." *Nature* 438(7070): 900–1. doi: 10.1038/438900a.

Gillmor, Dan. 2004. *We the Media: Grassroots Journalism By the People, For the People.* Sebastopol: O'Reilly Media.

Glott, Ruediger, and Rishab Ghosh. 2010. "Analysis of Wikipedia Survey Data." United Nations University MERIT. https://meta.wikimedia.org/wiki/Research:UNU-MERIT_Wikipedia_survey (accessed August 18, 2016).

Graham, Mark. 2011. "Wiki Space: Palimpsests and the Politics of Exclusion." In *Wiki Space: Palimpsests and the Politics of Exclusion,* edited by Geert Lovink and Nathaniel Tkacz, 269–82. Amsterdam: Institute of Network Cultures.

Graham, Mark, Bernie Hogan, Ralph K. Straumann, and Ahmed Medhat. 2014. "Uneven Geographies of User-Generated Information: Patterns of Increasing Informational Poverty." SSRN Scholarly Paper ID 2382617. Rochester, NY: Social Science Research Network. http://papers.ssrn.com/abstract=2382617 (accessed August 18, 2016).

Grossman, Lev. 2006. "You—Yes, You—Are TIME's Person of the Year." *Time,* December 25. http://content.time.com/time/magazine/article/0,9171,1570810,00.html (accessed August 18, 2016).

Halfaker, Aaron, R. Stuart Geiger, Jonathan T. Morgan, and John Riedl. 2013. "The Rise and Decline of an Open Collaboration System: How Wikipedia's Reaction to Popularity Is Causing its Decline." *American Behavioral Scientist* 57(5): 664–88. doi: 10.1177/0002764212469365.

Hargittai, Eszter, and Aaron Shaw. 2015. "Mind the Skills Gap: The Role of Internet Know-How and Gender in Differentiated Contributions to Wikipedia." *Information, Communication & Society* 18(4): 424–42. doi: 10.1080/1369118X.2014.957711.

Hill, Benjamin Mako, and Aaron Shaw. 2013. "The Wikipedia Gender Gap Revisited: Characterizing Survey Response Bias with Propensity Score Estimation." *PLoS ONE* 8 (6): e65782. doi: 10.1371/journal.pone.0065782.

Jemielniak, Dariusz. 2014. *Common Knowledge? An Ethnography of Wikipedia.* Stanford, CA: Stanford University Press.

Jenkins, Henry. 2006. *Convergence Culture: Where Old and New Media Collide.* New York: New York University Press.

Kriplean, Travis, Ivan Beschastnikh, David W. McDonald, and Scott A. Golder. 2007. "Community, Consensus, Coercion, Control: Cs*W or How Policy Mediates Mass Participation." In *Proceedings of the 2007 International ACM Conference on Supporting Group Work,* 167–76. GROUP '07. New York: ACM. doi: 10.1145/1316624.1316648.

Lam, Shyong (Tony) K., Anuradha Uduwage, Zhenhua Dong, Shilad Sen, David R. Musicant, Loren Terveen, and John Riedl. 2011. "WP: clubhouse? An Exploration of Wikipedia's Gender Imbalance." In *Proceedings of the 2011 International Symposium on Wikis and Open Collaboration,* 1–10. doi: 10.1145/2038558.2038560.

Leadbeater, Charles and Paul Miller. 2004. *The Proam Revolution: How Enthusiasts Are Changing Our Economy and Society.* London: Demos.

Lessig, Lawrence. 2011. *Code: And Other Rules of Cyberspace*. New York: Basic Books.

Lovink, Geert. 2012. *Networks without a Cause: A Critique of Social Media*. First edition. Cambridge, UK; Malden, MA: Polity Press.

Luyt, Brendan. 2011. "The Nature of Historical Representation on Wikipedia: Dominant or Alternative Historiography?" *Journal of the American Society for Information Science and Technology* 62(6): 1058–65. doi: 10.1002/asi.21531.

Marcus, George E. 1995. "Ethnography in/of the World System: The Emergence of Multi-Sited Ethnography." *Annual Review of Anthropology* 24(1): 95–117. doi: 10.1146/annurev.an.24.100195.000523.

———. 1998. *Ethnography through Thick and Thin*. Princeton, NJ: Princeton University Press.

Morozov, Evgeny. 2011. *The Net Delusion: How Not to Liberate the World*. London: Penguin.

Nature. Press release. 2006. "Encyclopaedia Britannica and Nature: A Response," March 23. www.nature.com/press_releases/Britannica_response.pdf (accessed August 18, 2016).

Niederer, Sabine, and José van Dijck. 2010. "Wisdom of the Crowd or Technicity of Content? Wikipedia as a Sociotechnical System." *New Media & Society* 12(8): 1368–87. doi: 10.1177/1461444810365297.

Okoli, Chitu, Mohamad Mehdi, Mostafa Mesgari, Finn Årup Nielsen, and Arto Lanamäki. 2012. "The People's Encyclopedia under the Gaze of the Sages: A Systematic Review of Scholarly Research on Wikipedia." SSRN Scholarly Paper ID 2021326. Rochester, NY: Social Science Research Network. http://papers.ssrn.com/abstract=2021326 (accessed August 18, 2016).

Pentzold, C., and S. Seidenglanz. 2006. "Foucault@ Wiki: First Steps towards a Conceptual Framework for the Analysis of Wiki Discourses." In *Proceedings of the 2006 International Symposium on Wikis*, 59–68. New York: ACM.

Reagle, Joseph. 2010. *Good Faith Collaboration: The Culture of Wikipedia*. Cambridge, MA: MIT Press.

———. 2013. "'Free as in Sexist?' Free Culture and the Gender Gap." *First Monday* 18(1). doi: 10.5210/fm.v18i1.4291.

Reagle, Joseph, and Lauren Rhue. 2011. "Gender Bias in Wikipedia and Britannica." *International Journal of Communication* 5: 21.

Rosenzweig, Roy. 2006. "Can History Be Open Source? Wikipedia and the Future of the Past." *The Journal of American History* 93(1): 117–46. doi: 10.2307/4486062.

Scheper-Hughes, Nancy. 1992. *Death without Weeping: The Violence of Everyday Life in Brazil*. Berkeley, CA: University of California Press.

Shirky, Clay. 2009. *Here Comes Everybody: How Change Happens when People Come Together*. London: Penguin.

Suh, Bongwon, Gregorio Convertino, Ed H. Chi, and Peter Pirolli. 2009. "The Singularity Is Not Near: Slowing Growth of Wikipedia." In *Proceedings of the 5th International Symposium on Wikis and Open Collaboration*, 8:1–8:10. WikiSym '09. New York: ACM. doi: 10.1145/1641309.1641322.

Sundin, Olof. 2011. "Janitors of Knowledge: Constructing Knowledge in the Everyday Life of Wikipedia Editors." *Journal of Documentation* 67(5): 840–62. doi: 10.1108/00220411111164709.

Viegas, F. B., M. Wattenberg, J. Kriss, and F. van Ham. 2007. "Talk Before You Type: Coordination in Wikipedia." In *40th Annual Hawaii International Conference on System Sciences, 2007. HICSS 2007*, 78. doi: 10.1109/HICSS.2007.511.

Weinberger, David. 2011. *Too Big to Know*. New York: Basic Books.

Wikimedia Foundation. 2011. "Editor Survey." https://commons.wikimedia.org/wiki/File:Editor_Survey_Report_-_April_2011.pdf (accessed August 23, 2016).

———. 2016. "Wikimedia Foundation Vision Statement." *Wikimedia Foundation Official Website*. https://wikimediafoundation.org/wiki/Vision (accessed January 26, 2016).

39

ENVIRONMENTAL SENSING AND CONTROL

Richard Beckwith and ken anderson

In the US, a community deployed air quality monitors in multiple locations across their neighborhood to collect data on industrial air pollution. These data could be used, for example, by asthma sufferers to avoid the areas with the worst pollution. Meanwhile, on the other side of the planet in Australia, farmers and fishers were gathering data to support their crops, cows, and oyster beds. All of these people, like many others, are working toward improving their lives or livelihoods with data. Yet, the impact of data goes well beyond improving health or supporting commerce. Considering this data collection to be environmental monitoring and nothing more would be easy but it would also be incomplete. To understand the role of these data and monitors in society, we must focus more keenly on the uses to which monitoring data are put. In doing so, we must also consider the impacts of these data on others. What we have seen in our fieldwork is that data were collected to influence policy, establish accountability, and exercise power.

Why Sensing?

We will start with a problem encountered in our fieldwork.

Robin connected her home computer to the free community network as soon as she heard about it. She used the network for what she described as the "usual things" (e.g., surfing and communications) but also to host an online streaming service and more. She was a power user, if ever there was one. Still, when she talked about the most important thing she did with the service, it was not a standard power user activity. She said that she really loved the community network because she could get online every morning and go to the state Environmental Protection Agency (EPA) website to check the Air Quality Index (AQI). She used the AQI so that she could make decisions about her son. Her son had deadly asthma and she used the data to decide on a path they would use to walk to his school. She would walk with him the long way on side roads if the AQI was bad. They would walk the short way, which was on a busier road, if the AQI was good that day.

This use of the AQI resulted in a significant problem for Robin and her son. The AQI reports on a system of sensors meant to characterize an area the size of a metropolitan region. The AQI cannot support the kinds of hyper-local decisions that Robin wanted to make regarding her son's health. The AQI for her region, covering over 145 square miles, used a network of US EPA-certified sensing stations the number of which you could count on two hands. The closest station to her home was five miles away while, at the same time, multiple factories and other pollution emitters were closer than that. What Robin really needed was better data, local data.

Robin needed data from a different kind of sensing system, one that provided data about differences between local streets, if not differences between sections of streets. She needed the kind of air quality data that you can only get from a dense deployment of networked, real-time sensors. The sensors from which the AQI is derived are quite expensive and, therefore, cannot be densely deployed. In the past few years, though, relevant sensors have become less expensive. There are now inexpensive network-connected air quality sensors that support remote measurements and the comparison of differences. Data can come from various sources, both personal and public, that are deployed within communities and be delivered to interested parties with ease. With current technologies, Robin's neighborhood can get the sensing technology she needs, finally providing her with the right information to make those choices she wants to make. But there is more to measuring community air quality data than is obvious.

Emerging Forms of Data/Emerging Shifts in Power

One of our fieldsites had an air quality sensor network that was designed to solve Robin's problem: How can a pedestrian avoid areas of high pollution? The deployment was in a neighborhood with an air quality problem. An analysis by the US EPA had shown that the neighborhood had a significant problem with air pollution, putting it in the second percentile nationally for air quality (that is, 98 percent of US communities had better air quality). One problem for those trying to avoid this pollution is that you cannot see it. Here is how a neighborhood activist (and mother of an asthmatic child) described the problem:

> The problem with air pollution today in America is that most of it is no longer visible. In the 1970s we were dealing with smog and envisioning L.A. and these basins of yellow smog. Today, the insidious air pollution problem is largely invisible to the naked eye, so having the technology that can make the invisible visible through data and numbers is important to realizing change because we need awareness before we have change.

Speaking of the network being deployed, she said:

> This technology gives the community a chance to have power and resources to get at issues that may seem intractable. If I can assess the risk, I can adapt, and having good data allows people to do that. This technology is a personal empowerment tool that puts information in the hands of individuals, and that knowledge can help motivate or otherwise give people tools to advocate for change.

Hearing her describe the technology does not actually reveal how the technology was to be used. When she says that the technology will allow her community "to advocate for change" or "to get at issues that may seem intractable," she means that the data will be used to bring attention to emitters and those emitters will be more easily forced to change their current practices. More simply, the data will be used to exercise power over emitters, a power that was not available to people/community/citizens/neighborhood without those data.

Data Ownership and the Commons

Speaking truth to power with data is not new. What is new is the idea that citizens can easily control data, both their collection and their flow. Citizen control over the collection and flow of data depends upon, loosely speaking, the individuals' ownership of these data.[1] Power, like control, is intertwined with ownership and the concept of ownership is in flux (Bezaitis and anderson 2011). This is especially true in the contentious area of data. Different people, institutions, and governments can have quite different opinions about who owns and has power over a particular piece of data. Using categories from the work of Helen Nissenbaum (2004), we might ask if the "owner" is an entity (e.g., a person) that is the *source* of the data in transaction and sends the data into circulation, or one that *receives* the data that have been sent, or one to *whom the data refer*. Recent legislation in the EU (i.e., "The Right to Be Forgotten") suggests we might start with the assumption that it is the person to whom the data refer—the person or entity that the piece of data is about—that is the rightful owner and has control.[2] In the example of air quality data, we must ask whether data about a public resource should also be considered public.

The air and water in a community's environment are paradigm examples of the commons and the need for stewardship. That is, these are public resources and are properly considered "the commons," which are resources shared by all within a community. The responsibility of stewardship of the commons is also shared by all members of the community. In fact, a paradigm example of the commons and the need for stewardship is the air and water in a community's environment. Polluting the air or drawing too much water is seen to be a violation of the rights of others within the community. Simply put, while society members are free to use the resources, they must leave them in such a state that others can use them as well.

Sensors are increasingly being used to collect data and track environmental quality and are likewise increasingly being used in the activity of stewardship. As a consequence, data about air and water could be seen to be part of the commons as well. The question of whether this "stewardship data" should be freely shared is crucial. We need to consider the impact of data sharing on community and the commons itself. Gudeman (2001, 27) says: "taking away the commons destroys community, and destroying a complex of relationships demolishes a commons." It is this complex of relationships, especially as reflected in stewardship practices with respect to data, to which we now turn.

Stewardship and the Commons: Inclosure, Regulation, and Oversight

In the past, when the resources of the commons were said to be under threat (particularly by public overuse), those properties were often privatized. That is, the commons were simply made into private property to be managed privately. These properties were, then, unavailable for locals to use. Such privatization of land is exemplified by the often-reviled Inclosure Acts in England, which granted ranking individuals ownership rights over what had been considered land to be used by any in the community. In lieu of "inclosure" to "protect" land, regulation is the more contemporary solution. Regulatory rules are enacted that restrict the use of a resource and, thereby, protect it. However, local users often believe that they can be more reasonable stewards of the local resources and should be trusted to do this on their own. Regulation, to some of the locals with whom we have worked, feels like a lack of freedom with respect to a resource over which they have been able to exercise control.

Inclusion and regulation are different solutions for stewardship problems but both share the restrictions on the practices of community members. Oversight is an interesting alternative. People are often willing to submit to oversight as a means to avoid regulatory constraint (Acheson 2003). As used here, "oversight" is voluntary monitoring or supervision over a situation. Basically, oversight can be used to prove that community members are doing nothing wrong. In the case of potential regulatory constraints vs. data collection, we see that people are often willing to collect and share information that will expose their practices to public scrutiny. This should not be surprising. In previous work (Beckwith and Mainwaring 2005), it was often found that people disclosed that they did not mind being "observed" through their data because they were "doing nothing wrong."[3]

Technological oversight, in particular, is seen as less onerous than regulatory constraint. If sensed data can be used to exact relief from government regulation, it can be quite attractive even if it seems as if it could not be. Troshynski et al. (2008) looked at data of a different sort. They looked at location tracking data collected by the ankle bracelets worn by convicted sex offenders in the US. Sex offenders are often released from prison with conditions on their behavior (such as not coming within a certain distance of schools). The tracking of these ex-offenders is meant to monitor all of their movement. Perhaps surprisingly, the researchers found that many ex-offenders liked the oversight that came from being technologically surveilled. Here's what one of their interviewees had to say about that:

> I travel a lot through southern California and this keeps me safe. It tracks me wherever I go. I like it. It's helped me and it's protected me. [The ankle monitor itself is] not going to stop me from re-offending. Like, it's not going to stop me from drinking, but it does protect me.
> (Troshynski et al. 2008, 489)

Surveillance or oversight, then, is not necessarily seen as a negative thing. In the case of these ex-offenders, who are frequently accused of violating the conditions of their release, they seek to show that they have not done so. Here, monitoring was put in place to support legal constraint but that same impulse to submit to oversight exists in other domains as well. The desire to avoid regulation drives at least some of this (Acheson 2003). It seems to be generally true that people prefer not to have their activities regulated by an external force such as a government. We had exactly this situation arise at one of our fieldsites.

A farming community we are researching wanted to avoid having the central government, which has little knowledge of local conditions, regulate their access to and use of water. Water is seen as part of the commons and, therefore, governments often assume the responsibility of stewardship when they deem it necessary. In the context of this community, the central government had responded to long-term drought conditions by establishing rules for water use across the nation. To support the development of rules, the government created hydrological models of every watershed. The models were created of the various watersheds from a distance, with relatively scarce data and without the deep knowledge of an area that comes from living somewhere. Most relevantly, the government did not have an intimate knowledge of our farmers' watershed, so the potential regulators did not know when their models made bad predictions, but the farmers *were* there and therefore knew when the models were wrong. For example, the government suggested that one farmer draw his water from a particular creek. The farmer had to tell the government that it would not be possible. That creek had long been dry.

Despite their distance, the government does know a lot about potential problems. Some watersheds are naturally problematic. The watershed in which our community is situated has one of those problems: there is sensitive estuary where the river comes down into the ocean. Other similar watersheds have oyster beds in the brackish water of their estuaries. Downstream "users" or protected lands often have problems that need to be addressed upstream. A downstream oyster farm has to worry about runoff from upstream farms because nutrient pollution is a common cause of algae blooms. Algae blooms can be harmful for oysters and can also mean that a harvest must be delayed until the bloom has cleared. An insufficiency of fresh water can lead to a salinification of the estuary and can threaten marine life. Regulations on water use and runoff are simple solutions to runoff or insufficient water flow and these regulations can be enacted from a distance. However, without an intimate knowledge of local conditions, the regulations typically need to be overly restrictive to make up for the lack of information and to ensure the commons are protected. Needless to say, our farmers did not want to be regulated under such conditions nor did they want to have their practices externally controlled.

The farmers came to an agreement with the government. They asked for permission to deploy their own sensors to augment the sensors deployed by the government and to have the data from those sensors included in the government database. Further, the farmers provided input into the existing government watershed models, too. Improving the models' accuracy and providing defensible data became tools for the farmers to use to fend off government regulation. One issue that needed to be resolved was that the government had to trust the data from the locals and the locals had to trust that the government would make the right decisions. There could easily be economic motivations for the farmers to alter their data, with government verification being difficult and costly. On the government side, incorporating farmer data was inconvenient and more costly than simply relying on existing models. We heard this from several farmers in the watershed:

> When we talk about this project statewide, nationally, or internationally, the thing that people always come back to, every single time, and the reason why this is generating so much interest is they all come back and they say, "Oh, there must be a huge trust issue there. This is all about trust." And it is all about trust. So, it's trust between all of you to manage your resource and that is unique. And I think that it's going to be very difficult for any government agency to argue against that kind of approach. Particularly when there's evidence behind it . . . so, at the moment, that's what we're doing. We're collecting that evidence . . . to make [our] group resilient when [we] have to deal with or negotiate with government.

In order to avoid regulation, this community has chosen to submit itself to oversight. They are using non-governmental, privately funded technologies to collect data about the watershed and their cultural practices. They are making that privately collected data public. In some ways, we might also imagine that these farmers are treating data about the watershed simply as part of the commons. The idea of data as part of the commons is a point we will next consider more closely.

The Commons and Governmental Policy: Accountability and Data

In one suburban community, we have worked with the residents, government agencies, and a non-profit advocacy group. These groups came together to address a problem with a public waterway, an issue of the commons. In particular, this community has a problem with flooding. While flooding occurs in many communities—and this one does have a long history of "excess water"—things have gotten much worse recently. Costly and dangerous floods have occurred multiple times a year. The water that flows down local streets is deep enough that children need to be picked up in boats at their school bus stop. People told us about yelling to children to get out of the rushing water but they could not be heard over the roar of the temporary river running down the street. Businesses in the flood plain had a hard time keeping their doors open and their stock safe. Storekeepers who rented were choosing to move away from their locations in this community. People who owned their own stores could not afford to simply move and had to move everything up off the floor if it seemed a flood might come. People left their homes due to flooding. Houses of new home owners re-flooded, causing significant loss of capital and even to the extent of forcing some of the homes into foreclosure, all of which reduced the value of neighborhood housing stock.

At first, residents' complaints were dismissed. Officials denied that anything was different and claimed that a few local rabble-rousers were simply trying to game the system for personal benefit. Because of governmental inaction, community members began to collect data and they collected a lot of it. When the community flooded, the "rabble-rousers" went out and walked around to find the boundaries of these floods, which allowed them to draw maps showing the extent of the flooding. One of the group members made maps that showed not only where the US Federal Emergency Management Agency (FEMA) had drawn 100- and 500-year flood boundaries (meaning how far the water would rise once every 100 or 500 years) but also showed the boundaries of actual recent floods. The community-developed maps were considerably different from the official maps and showed significantly more extensive flooding than had been predicted. In fact, the 500-year boundary had been under water many times in the previous few years. These citizen-generated maps, along with photographs of the floodwaters, were taken to public meetings and shown to anyone who would listen. The flooding finally got attention.

The initial response of local governments was defensive. Local government agencies were quick to point to global climate change and the more frequent threats from heavy and extreme precipitation events. The government explanation was that the infrastructure simply had not been modified to better handle the influx of rain. Climate change meant that the infrastructure had to change.

The community members did not believe the explanation. It did not account for all that they included in their data. The community told us that it was not that their infrastructure did not keep up. When they looked at upstream phenomena during the flooding events, they found less water input to the watershed than would have been the case if this were simply more rain. They told us that change in the infrastructure upstream from them was the primary culprit.

One of the public meetings that followed this increase in awareness included an employee of an upstream community. This is one of the ways in which the commons influences group membership. The communities interested in the stewardship of the commons' resource often must work together. Upstream and downstream communities each have an interest in the activities of the other. The upstream community that this person represented had not had much to do with the activities in this town until this meeting. Interestingly, the community that he represented is also the one that the residents held accountable for their recent flooding. He told the group that part of his job was to control the retention pond (which the residents said was not used to its capacity during floods) and he said that it, too, was overflowing. The residents produced photographs, the veracity of which he questioned, that showed the pond was not filled as it should have been during what they claimed were flooding events. This photographic evidence was open to being questioned—when were the photos actually taken?—but the accusation was now out there.

One of the responses to the massive amount of data collected by residents was actually the collection of even more data. Money started to come into the community both to facilitate monitoring conditions, as well as to change the infrastructure to help prevent future flooding. More gauge sites to monitor water depth were deployed in the watershed. More rain gauges were also deployed. Everyone watched with interest as the next flood season arrived. Interestingly, residents explained that the rain gauges showed the same amount of rain coming into the watershed as in the years with flooding. However, the flow gauges in the problematic creek were reporting less water during rain events. Most importantly, following the increase in monitoring there was less frequent flooding. Perhaps significantly, residents reported that the retention pond in the upstream community was clearly being used.

The residents declared—with good reason—that data collection had forced the use of existing infrastructure to mitigate the effects of flooding in their community. This past flood season saw fewer flooding events and money continued to come into the community to improve the infrastructure. More data are being collected—such as more flow gauges and rainfall monitors—and the watershed map is being updated with more accurate elevation information. Everything was great . . . up to a point.

Privacy and Datasheds: Sequestration

We have been addressing stewardship practices as they are supported by data. However, we must also address the stewardship of the data itself. Much of our research has looked at the ways in which data circulate (Beckwith et al. 2015). However, our research does not just look at data circulation, like we saw between the government and farmers (oversight) and between and among suburban neighborhoods and the government (commons accountability). We also look at times that data does not flow because individuals do not want it to. Borrowing from the notion of "watershed," we talk about a "datashed." A datashed is defined by the locations to which data flow or perhaps, more significantly, the locations to which some data do not flow. Often, when data do not flow it is because people want to avoid some of the effects of its "openness." People within a community might want to restrict the flow of data even with data about the commons. However, such data might not actually be under the control of the community associated with the commons and issues of control arise. That was the case in our field site in the flooding suburbs.

Something else interesting happened with the flood data we have discussed. Despite all of the attention and all of the data (or perhaps because of it), the community did not account for the ways that government agencies started to react. One of these reactions comes from the fact that FEMA flood maps do more than simply predict the extent of potential future events. These maps are also used to define the boundaries of where residents are required to have specific flood insurance, which can add thousands of dollars to the cost of owning a home. In fact, home equity loans and re-financing often depend on a person acquiring this insurance. In effect, the data about the watershed, the data about the commons, potentially have a negative economic impact on the people of the commons who actually collected some of the data themselves.

During our time in the community, we asked people if there was anyone with whom they did not want to share data about their community and flooding. The answer of one resident is a good representation of the community at large:

Well, one is the insurance company. They'll just use that against us. We pay enough on homeowners [insurance] to begin with and if they tie it up with flood insurance, I think it'd be really ridiculous. [We would need to pay] $2,300 in addition . . . for flood insurance over what we're paying for homeowners.

In meeting with community members, we heard many times that they felt it was unfair for their own data to be used against them. They wanted to withhold the data from the agencies that would use it to require additional insurance, while still using it to get benefits from the local government. They threatened to withdraw their data from public discussions and for improving the official maps. They can withhold their own maps, of course, but better maps are likely coming anyway. It is well known that FEMA maps are inadequate to the task of assigning risk to different residences; FEMA has been asked by the legislative branch of the US federal government to improve their maps. Community generated input is not necessary, though, in the creation of FEMA maps. Obviously, having good maps of recent events drawn by locals could help enormously in redrawing these official maps. However, the new water sensors in the community, which were deployed by the government, and new topological maps can be used to redraw the boundaries. The real question here is whether the community members have the right to withhold information about the commons from governmental bodies or, more accurately, can local community members insist that a governmental body not consider some information about their community if it is to be used against it.

The community members who had worked so hard to collect data about actual flooding were unhappy that their data might be used to redraw the official maps and place these same residents in the predicament of having to pay more money. Despite the fact that these data were fairly indisputably about the commons (water and flooding), these residents felt that these data should not flow to just anyone. They felt it was their data and they should be able to withhold access when they wanted.

It is important to remember that commons resources are often part of the lives of only a restricted community. The goal here seemed to be similarly restricting data. Recalling Gudeman's warning we cited earlier that "taking away the commons destroys community, and destroying a complex of relationships demolishes a commons" (2001, 27), we need to ask ourselves about the extent to which opening data about the commons to outsiders could disrupt community and whether the data itself is properly considered a part of the commons. Finally, we need to also ask the extent to which "the commons" may extend beyond the people, the commoners, for whom that commons is a shared resource.

Conclusion

Knowledge is power and it can command obedience. A man of knowledge during his lifetime can make people obey and follow him and he is praised and venerated after his death. Remember that knowledge is a ruler and wealth is its subject.

(Saying 146 from *Nahjul Balagha* by Imam Ali (1984))

It is commonplace to note that "knowledge is power." What we have seen in our field-work is that data collected from new affordable and consumer accessible sensors and stored data can also be used to influence power in relationships and even changes the composition of those relationships. While people do not often talk about how data will be used to achieve their ends, it has become apparent that data can be used to bring otherwise unwilling parties into an interaction. Data can even force others to enter into relationships. For example, people can collect all the air quality data they want, for whatever reason they want (health, environmental, personal reasons), however, having the data does not, in and of itself, result in an improved environment or health. One of the most powerful ways that air quality data improves health is a consequence of the fact that putting data into public circulation can force others to be accountable. Emitters and regulators can be brought to account for their behavior. Without the data, however, it is as if the emissions do not exist, and, while the air quality might impact the lives of residents, there is limited possibility of even having air quality as a topic of negotiation. With air quality data, residents can force the emitters to the table. Simply put, communities can monitor the commons to demand accountability.

We saw that those who wanted to demonstrate a willingness to be held accountable for their actions also used data. The farmers collected watershed data not simply to have the data, but rather so that they could demonstrate that they were good stewards and, thereby, avoid regulation. It is worth considering that regulation, which is a public affair, would itself require information from those regulated to demonstrate compliance to the regulatory body. Therefore, it is not clear that the farmers in this case were actually collecting less data than would have been required with regulation. However, it did allow the farmers with more intimate knowledge of the region to make decisions for use without the shackles of regulations. It enabled them to have a greater sense of agency in controlling the fate of their farms and their lives. Providing acceptable data to those who would otherwise argue for regulation allowed the farmers to avoid controls by self-surveillance.

Ownership and use of data (and, therefore, power) remains an issue, particularly when those data are about the commons. Does the community own those data in the sense that they can determine where and under what conditions that data flows? Does a community have "The Right to Be Forgotten" with respect to data where the community (through its commons) is the data subject? What does free access mean in a data commons?

Sensor data collected by community about a community's commons creates new social territory—what is the nature of those data? Do data collected by individuals about a commons resource (like air or water) become a new kind of commons—a data commons? Inclosure— removing control of a resource from a community—has a clear and devastating effect on community and the commons. Misunderstanding and mishandling the commons, whether environmental or digital, could be likewise troubling. The questions of who constitutes the community of the commons and who is granted privileges of access to and control over data are in flux as society comes to terms with what it means for an environment to be surveilled digitally by the community itself or an overarching authority. From our three field sites, it is clear that even these communities have not worked out all the ramifications of having sensor networks deployed in their communities. A data commons would be a new resource, a resource which society is still coming to terms with in understanding.

Some things are clear. The emerging technologies enabling environmental monitoring by citizens (communities) improve the quality and reduce the cost of data acquisition. The data have become a new resource for communities. But data are not collected for data's sake. These technologies are changing power relations within and for communities. People collect information in order to get things done and the control/ownership of data is power. Data achieves its value and power through circulation. Introducing information into the public discourse (or not), that is, controlling data flow, remains one of the more important capacities of digital technologies. We see time and again in our fieldwork that people understand not only the power of data to influence lives but also that people work to control information in contexts in which it can influence their lives. Even if we like to think that information wants to be free, it does not seem to want to be powerless.

Notes

1 We are talking about the conceptions of ownership as they are held by the people with whom we worked. Often these ideas are in conflict with legal issues of ownership and these conflicts are only being worked out with continued exposure. We do not have the space here to address the legal issues surrounding ownership and hope to address these in a later paper.

2 It is important to keep in mind that ownership and control of data are concepts that need to be worked out as people are more exposed to data collection and use. We assume here the perspective of most of those in our fieldwork: owners are the final arbiters and control data use and distribution.

3 Nevertheless, we also find that those who say they do not care often do have significant privacy concerns (Beckwith and Mainwaring 2005).

References

Acheson, James M. 2003. *Capturing the Commons: Devising Institutions to Manage the Maine Lobster Industry.* Hanover, NH: University Press of New England.

Imam Ali. 1984. *Peak of Eloquence (Nahjul Balagha) Sermons and Letters of Imam Ali Ibn Abi Talib,* Translated by Askari Jafri. Eleventh edition. New York: Islamic Seminary Publications.

Beckwith, Richard and Scott Mainwaring. 2005. "Privacy: Personal Information, Threats, and Technologies." Proceedings of ISTAS 2005: 9–16.

Beckwith, Richard, John Sherry, and David Prendergast. 2015. "Data Flow in the Smart City." Communities and Technology, Smart Cities Workshop. Limerick Ireland.

Bezaitis, Maria and ken anderson. 2011. "Flux: Changing Social Values and their Value for Business." *Proceedings of EPIC:* 12–17.

Gudeman, Stephen. 2001. *The Anthropology of Economy: Community, Market, and Culture.* London: Blackwell.

Nissenbaum, Helen. 2004. "Privacy as Contextual Integrity." *Washington Law Review,* 79(1): 119–57.

Troshynski, Emily, Charlotte Lee, and Paul Dourish. 2008. "Accountabilities of Presence: Reframing Location-Based Systems." *Proceedings of CHI:* 487–96.

Part IX

DESIGN

40

THE POLITICS OF DESIGN, DESIGN AS POLITICS

Christo Sims

Design is on the march. Terms and practices that once circulated primarily within the fairly circumscribed worlds of professional designers—"charrettes," "prototyping," "brainstorming," and so forth—have permeated worlds as diverse as business management, statecraft, and education reform. Ethnography has not been immune from this extension and, if anything, some of our most esteemed practitioners have helped to promote it. For Bruno Latour (2008), the spread of the word design attests to the collapse of faith in modernist narratives while also signaling more humble, democratic, and open-ended ways to make collective futures. For Paul Rabinow, George Marcus, James Faubion, and Tobias Rees (2008), the practices of professional designers offer promising ways for rethinking contemporary modes of anthropological inquiry and knowledge production, and the design studio represents an exciting model for teaching and learning ethnographic craft. For Alberto Corsín Jiménez (2013), "prototyping" is not only a term of art among select communities of practice; it is also a more general model for how a polity might mutually prefigure configurations of objects and sociality.

While ethnographers have recently advocated for design in different ways, they appear to share a desire to not just interpret the world but also to try to change it. Put differently, many ethnographers' recent interest in design can be seen in part as an attempt to explore new modes of doing a material politics.[1] Given this renewed interest in the political possibilities of design, this short chapter explores some of the ways that design does and can do political work. After offering a brief rationale for why ethnographers should examine design as a mode of doing politics, I primarily focus on three, often intra-related, political processes in which design might play a part: prescribing, publicizing, and proposing.[2] The chapter ends with a brief exercise in, and argument for, attending to the often undemocratic character of design-ethnography as a mode of doing politics.

Romancing Design

While couplings of professional designers and ethnographers have a long and complex history (cf. Dourish 2006; Suchman 2011), recent proponents of an ethnography-design courtship tend to be forward-looking, playful, and generally optimistic. It would not be an overstatement to suggest that romance is in the air. By saying as much I am not trying to dismiss the exciting possibilities that might be accomplished by ethnographers and designers working and learning with and from each other, nor do I want to cast a wet blanket on the excitement of making new friends. Ethnographers need enchantment as much as anyone else, and at one point in my career I certainly had a crush on design that I will return to at the end of this chapter. For me, the potential problem with ethnographers romancing design is not the vitality that such romances engender, but rather the tendency to idealize the object of affection. In particular, in romancing design I worry that we might be obscuring some of its politics.

As my colleague Lilly Irani (2013, 2015) has helped elaborate, the rising status and power of design and design practices is intimately entwined with the rising power of terms such as "innovation," "entrepreneurialism," and "disruption," as well as with the related feelings of awe that can accompany the ongoing proliferation of new media technologies into more and more facets of social life. Given these associations, it would be politically naive to embrace design without giving careful consideration to the political ideologies and programs of which design and designers are often integrally a part. And yet it would also be a mistake, it seems to me, to dismiss recent interest in design as just another instance of neoliberalism taking over the academy and the world. What is needed is not just recognition that design is political, but also a nuanced discussion about how design does and can do political work, in different situations, for and with differently located participants, including sometimes ethnographers.

Before jumping in, I want to be clear that the chapter does not offer a comprehensive or definitive account of design and politics. Given the brevity of the chapter, I do not address important questions about the power relations among and between designers and ethnographers—I do not address what some ethnographers might be getting from a partnership with design, nor what some designers might be getting by coupling with ethnography. Nor do I extensively address how design-ethnography can turn heads, win resources, and inspire respect in ways that neither could do as effectively on its own.

Rather, and in keeping with the analysis, the chapter takes a propositional stance that also attempts to remain committed to the situated character of all political practices, including practices of proposing. In that vein, I want to emphasize that the ideas put forth in this chapter are reworkings of ideas that have been relayed to me, first as someone who worked in the worlds of professional designers, then as someone who learned to become an academic ethnographer who, in part, studied professional designers trying to improve the world, and most recently as an assistant professor who sometimes teaches classes that experiment with doing design as politics and who has been in close correspondence with a couple of ethnographers who also care deeply about design and politics. On this last point I should note that almost everything that follows has emerged from ongoing conversations with two of my colleagues in the Department of Communication at UC San Diego: Lilly Irani and Fernando Domínguez Rubio. Both have addressed similar issues at greater length and with more eloquence than I do here. If these themes are of interest to you, then I heartily recommend consulting some of the ideas that have shaped my own.[3]

Prescribing

Perhaps the most thoroughly analyzed political faculty of design can be characterized as its potential for *prescribing*. The field of science and technology studies, in particular, has investigated how even the most mundane seeming artifacts and environments—from bridges (Winner 1980), to door-closers (Latour 1988), to phone books (Bowker and Star 1999)—can act in ways that enable, route, and generally micromanage the perceptions, actions, and interpretations of the other actors entangled in a given setting. As Madeleine Akrich and Bruno Latour (1992, 261) succinctly put it, prescription has to do with "what a device allows or forbids from the actors—humans and non-human—that it anticipates." Designed objects and environments, from this perspective, do not just limit and enhance actors; rather, they help constitute them as the sorts of actors that they are in particular situated activities. It is from this proposition that Akrich and Latour, as well as many others, have famously argued that designed objects and environments have a moral, and hence political, character.

At one level, the observation that designed objects exert a prescriptive force is hardly surprising. People know, for example, that a barbed-wire fence discourages certain activities for both humans and non-humans just as they know that an all-you-can-eat buffet encourages others. For many designers, prescribing—or more positively inflected synonyms such as "affording"—are the *raisons d'être* of design, and, indeed, designers and engineers tend to emphasize the prescriptive capacities of their designs as they attempt to promote and publicize them. What is more, perennially polarized public debates about the social implications of new technologies are in large part arguments over the presumed prescriptive forces that a new design exerts. And, if anything, both designers and those who engage in public debates about new technologies tend to overstate the presumed prescriptive capacities of design.

But the prescriptive capacities of design can also act in less noticed, and hence potentially more insidious, ways, and it is this insidiousness that critical analysts are keen to ferret out. Here, analysts tend to be concerned with how design, and the work of technoscience more generally, does political work that is not recognized as such. The concern in these cases is with the ways that designed objects and environments can be a mode of doing "politics by other means," to borrow a phrase from Donna Haraway (1984). Of particular concern is the way that design and technoscience can be a way of doing anti-politics, that is, with the ways in which political problems and concerns are translated into seemingly apolitical technoscientific problems that designers and other experts can manage and solve, a process that the anthropologist Tania Murray Li (2007) has characterized as "rendering technical."

Examples from the worlds of international development are especially helpful for illustrating how processes of rendering technical produce depoliticizing effects even when the prescriptions that designers inscribe in their interventions fail to work as planned. I did my PhD at an Information School, which, among other things, has become a fertile ground for the emergence of various fields that take researching and designing for "the other" as one of their professed areas of expertise. By attending such a program I became familiar with the emerging field of Information and Communication Technologies for Development (ICT4D), an effort to bring together technology designers, government officials, NGOs, and social scientists, including ethnographers, in an attempt to address perceived deficiencies and injustices in the global South. Through critical dialogs with graduate students who were trying to conduct ethnographic studies of and for ICT4D projects, as well as through my own involvement in projects that aimed to reinvent education for the digital age, I came to see how design could have deeply problematic depoliticizing effects even as a given intervention "failed" on its own terms. A political-economic problem, such as extreme poverty, was translated into a technical-informational problem—such as a lack of computers or Internet connectivity—that a designed intervention, like One Laptop Per Child or Facebook's Internet.org initiative, could supposedly remediate. Not only did these processes of rendering technical tend to depoliticize the sources of poverty, they often also reductively distorted the worlds that designers targeted for improvement. As such, when designers engaged in processes of rendering technical they tended to inscribe into artifacts and built environments prescriptions that did not fulfill designers' aspirations, but these "failed" interventions nevertheless produced effects that were very much political (cf. Ferguson 1994; Scott 1998; Li 2007; Sims 2017).

Design can also act in insidiously political ways in cases where an artifact or environment's prescriptive character is overlooked, forgotten, or treated as natural or normal. Once a designed artifact becomes integrated into webs of material practices—once it has been "black boxed," to use a term from science studies—its prescriptive character tends to disappear into the background of taken-for-granted experience, except in cases of crisis and breakdown. For Susan Leigh Star (1999), such "boringness" was precisely what made the study of designed infrastructures—from sewers to geographically distributed electronic laboratories—both interesting and politically important. It is in part because so many designed artifacts and infrastructures tend to fall into the background of everyday experience that design's prescriptive capacities can be an insidious way of doing "politics by other means."

Publicizing

Just as design can be a way of inscribing and concealing political prescriptions, so too can it help publicize issues, concerns, and actors that are typically excluded from the terrain of political debates and struggles. By using the term "publicizing" I mean to reference both recent invocations to use design as a means of "making things public" (Latour 2005), as well as the long history of design in the professions of public relations, advertising, and propaganda, the latter of which are the professional worlds through which I learned to practice design. While these two senses of publicizing sit uneasily with one other, they also resonate in ways that suggest some caution be taken before celebrating design for its capacities to make things public. For the sake of this chapter, however, I will focus on the more optimistic version of design as a means of publicizing.

Latour's vision of design as "the cautious Prometheus" puts forth a mode of doing politics that does not just criticize modernizing philosophies and schemes but also aims to supplant them. Latour's invocation can be read as an extension of his influential salvo *Why Has Critique Run Out of Steam?* (2004), which called into question the iconoclastic tendencies and political efficacy of social and cultural critique. For Latour, the urgency of the contemporary political and ecological situation requires critically inclined academics to not just diagnose what is wrong with other people's ideas and programs but also to go about attempting to change material conditions. Design, according to Latour, offers a humble and practical model for how to go about making social-material change in a way that is neither revolutionary nor modernizing; it suggests a way, Latour maintains, to "draw together" the conflictual and contradictory matters of concern that characterize any attempt to change material circumstances. Design can thus be a way of "making public" the complex human and non-human entanglements that modernist ideologies and political projects attempt to simplify and purify, in part through the processes of rendering technical discussed in the last section.

A concrete example will help clarify how some ethnographers and designers have responded to Latour's invocation. In an article titled, *Technifying Public Space and Publicizing Infrastructures* (2013), my colleague Fernando Domínguez Rubio, an ethnographer, and Uriel Fogué, an architect, describe a design proposal that Fogué's architecture firm produced for the city council of Madrid. The firm proposed redesigning Plaza del General Vara del Rey, a public square in Madrid, so that the energy and water infrastructures upon which city inhabitants depended would be transformed from taken-for-granted "matters of fact" into matters of public concern. Among other things, the proposal envisioned installing a collection of "hybrid urban trees" that would combine shade-giving solar panels with recreational artifacts such as swings. The energy captured and transformed by these solar panels would, in turn, help power the treatment and circulation of rainwater collected to irrigate the plaza's vegetation, and excess power would be sold back to the city's power grid in order to pay for the cost of redeveloping and maintaining the square. For Domínguez Rubio and Fogué, such an intervention would not only transform "a hitherto passive public space" into "an active urban power plant fully integrated into the infrastructural network of the city" (Domínguez Rubio and Fogué 2013, 1044). It would also transform the city's infrastructure, which is typically concealed from the public except in cases of breakdown, from a matter of fact into a matter of concern.

The architectural firm's plans for the plaza represent just one attempt to use design to make things, in this case infrastructures and ecological processes, public, and, in so doing, to transform seemingly settled matters of fact into matters of concern, the latter of which could be subject to public debates and more democratic political struggles. Like Latour, Domínguez Rubio and Fogué's example also focuses on politicizing the entanglement of sociotechnical systems and ecological processes. For readers who are sympathetic to these issues, including myself, these examples illustrate an optimistic case of how design can be used as a mode of doing politics by way of publicizing.

Proposing

A third, and related, political process in which design can play a role is that of *proposing*. Here, the challenge for the designer is not the modernist imperative to prescribe solutions, but rather a more modest attempt to put forth possible, but not necessarily probable, futures. Politically, the designer is trying to use design as a means for sparking reflection and debate about the sorts of futures people do and do not want. Using design as a way to help people imagine possible collective futures can in part be seen as an attempt to break out of the fatalisms, realisms, and cynicisms that often characterize contemporary politics, and especially the difficulty of imagining an alternative to neoliberalism (cf. Fisher 2009; Wright 2010). Proposing is similar to prescribing in that the designer is positioned as an expert who articulates a changed material reality, but proposals stop short of attempting to answer the modernist question "what is to be done?" and instead respond to the more modest question "what might be?" Proposing is also related to publicizing in that the designer aims to share resources for imagining futures, but proposing does not aim to simply transform matters of fact into matters of concern; rather, the designer attempts to catalyze imaginings of where those entanglements might lead, as well as how they might be changed.

While the design-as-proposing stance has a long history among designers, and particularly architects, it has recently gained momentum as a way of doing politics in part thanks to the "speculative design" movement, as exemplified by the works of designer-scholars such as Anthony Dunne and Fiona Raby (2013). An example speculative design project that Dunne and Raby produced with their students, titled "United Micro Kingdoms," can help illustrate the political possibilities of design as proposing.[4] The United Micro Kingdoms project imagines a not-too-distant future in which the United Kingdom has fractured into four "micro kingdoms," each of which pursues a different idealized version of political-economic and sociotechnical organization. To catalyze reflection, imagination, and discussion about the sorts of futures people do and do not want, the designers imagined, designed, and built models of the dominant modes of transport that would be used in each of these fictional worlds. Because designed artifacts inscribe the moral characteristics of the worlds of which they are a part, the designers hoped that speculative models of future modes of transport could catalyze reflection and discussion about the political, economic, social, natural, and technological entanglements that help constitute the worlds we inhabit and are helping to make. For example, for a speculative micro kingdom organized predominantly by market forces, digital surveillance, and technocratic efficiency, the designers built models of self-driving electric cars that rely on tracking technologies to optimize use of "public" roadways. In this imagined world, the state would lease public roads to private companies that, in turn, would rent consumer-citizens temporary access to public road-space through their fleets of self-driving vehicles. If a consumer wanted to take up more road-space-time, they could pay more to rent a self-driving vehicle with a larger spatial footprint, much like today's price gradations for seat-space on budget airlines. In such a world, transport technologies would be instrumental appliances governed by the technification of an economic rationality, all of which would be legitimated under the guise of consumer choice.

By designing a fictional vehicle tailored for this dystopian future world, Dunne and Raby aimed to *publicize* how moral *prescriptions* and modes of social organization are materially inscribed into our technologies and infrastructures; they did so in an attempt to catalyze debate about how many people live now as well as how people want to live in the future. In doing so, they attempted to use design as a way of doing politics that tries to evade the trappings of, on the one hand, the utopianism that characterizes so many tech-solutionist projects, as well as, and on the other hand, the fatalism of so many "realist" accounts.

Design Within (Whose) Reach?

Design's capacities for doing politics are no doubt part of what makes design alluring to many contemporary ethnographers. In my own case, I have studied the problematic political consequences of well-intended design initiatives while also remaining involved with designers so as to experiment with different ways of doing politically engaged work. I hope to keep up this exploration and I am glad to see that many other ethnographers are also experimenting along similar lines.

Yet I also worry that there is something politically important but often missing in many of the more enthusiastic calls for design-ethnography pairings. In particular, in romancing design I worry that some ethnographers risk overlooking the fact that design-ethnography courtships are often pairings of professional elites with overlapping but also different bases of spatialized privilege. Another way of putting this last point is that both design and ethnographic modes of scholarly production are always located somewhere, and these somewheres are both structured by and structuring of a spatialized, hierarchical, and often quasi-Tayloristic division of paid and unpaid labor.[5] While ethnographers and designers might criticize these arrangements, and particularly forces of bureaucratization, many have also done comparatively well living off these material and cultural divisions, and, as such, their politics of change might do more to remake and extend, rather than dismantle and transgress, the status quo.

My own trajectory through these intersecting worlds can help illustrate this last point. My romance with design began not long after I graduated college when I, like many other graduates of selective colleges on the east coast of the United States, moved to New York City to begin my career. When I arrived in New York I did not know much about the worlds of professional designers, nor did I have much interest in, nor an opinion about, what constituted good and bad design. And yet within two years of relocating to New York I had moved to design-conscious Brooklyn and I was spending much of my free time reading design books, learning design software, taking design classes, and visiting exhibitions at places like MoMA to learn about canonically revered designers such as Mies van der Rohe. Within a few years I had learned to identify and covet "well designed" items, including furniture that I could not afford from ironically named stores like "Design Within Reach."

What changed?

For one, my first job after college was in the rapidly growing professional field known nowadays as interaction or experience design. In this job I worked with numerous young professionals who had been trained at the Rhode Island School of Design, a prestigious design school in the United States. It was largely through my relationship with these budding professional designers that I came to learn about and appreciate the practices and products of their professional world. Like many others who have developed a crush on design, I found these designers' professional practices and lifestyles seductive. They seemed creative, culturally and technically sophisticated, and generally hip. It was pleasurable to playfully experiment, to think and act in imaginative ways, to make stuff with others, and to think that we were inventing the future. What we were actually doing was making marketing devices for organizations that could afford to pay us, but I was young and naive and for many years I was hooked on design.

Quite a few years, and a PhD, later, it is now somewhat embarrassingly obvious to me that my romance with design—and later, but hopefully to a lesser extent, with ethnography—was tied to my not-so-reflexive aspiration to belong to an elite and seemingly cosmopolitan professional class faction. I learned how to be more like a designer as I was trying to figure out what sort of professional adult person I could become, first in New York City and later in the San Francisco Bay Area where I moved for graduate school. Knowledge about, appreciation for, and being skillful at design were, and remain, markers of a cosmopolitan sophistication in many of the New York City and Bay Area circuits through which I traveled, and they remain esteemed knowledges and practices along many of the academic pathways that I now traverse.

For me, the important political question raised by these experiences is not whether ethnographers should try to build alliances with other professional elites—in many ways they must—but rather on how they do so, with whom else, and with what consequences for what and whom? If thinking and making practices are like a game of cat's cradle, as Donna Haraway (2013) suggests, then it is worth remembering that when we do design and ethnography, and hence politics, we are often doing so with partners that were already within our reach.

Notes

1 While echoing the sentiment of Marx's final thesis on Feuerbach, most contemporary ethnographers who advocate for design as a mode of doing material politics imagine a distinctively non-revolutionary mode of political change. Latour (2008, 2) is explicit on this point.

2 I thank my colleague Fernando Domínguez Rubio for first bringing to my attention the prescribing versus proposing distinction. For Domínguez Rubio, the political capacities of design can be characterized as "enfolding" and "unfolding" what counts as political. The former loosely corresponds to my discussion of prescribing whereas his notion of "unfolding" includes what I am characterizing separately as publicizing and proposing. I am using the terms prescribing, publicizing, and proposing—rather than enfolding and unfolding—in an attempt to emphasize that these are often rather ordinary and pedestrian processes in social life. By using more colloquial terms I also wish to draw attention to how recent design enthusiasts tend to overlook the long history of design in the not-so-inspiring professions of marketing, advertising, and public relations. For Domínguez Rubio's discussion of "enfolding" and "unfolding" see Domínguez Rubio and Fogué (2015).

3 See in particular Domínguez Rubio and Fogué (2013, 2015) and Irani (2013, 2015).

4 For an online version of this exhibition, see Dunne and Raby (2015).

5 Lucy Suchman, an anthropologist who has spent much of her career working inside the worlds of professional technology designers, has articulated a similar position with her call for a politics of design and scholarship as one of "located accountability" (Suchman 2002).

References

Akrich, Madeleine, and Bruno Latour. 1992. "A Summary of a Convenient Vocabulary for the Semiotics of Human and Nonhuman Assemblies." In *Shaping Technology/Building Society: Studies in Sociotechnical Change*, edited by Wiebe E. Bijker and John Law, 259–64. Cambridge, MA: The MIT Press.

Bowker, Geoffrey, and Susan Leigh Star. 1999. *Sorting Things Out: Classification and Its Consequences*. Cambridge, MA: The MIT Press.

Corsín Jiménez, Alberto. 2013. "Introduction: The Prototype—More than Many and Less than One." *Journal of Cultural Economy* 7(4): 381–98.

Domínguez Rubio, Fernando, and Uriel Fogué. 2013. "Technifying Public Space and Publicizing Infrastructures: Exploring New Urban Political Ecologies through the Square of General Vara Del Rey." *International Journal of Urban and Regional Research* 37(3): 1035–52.

———. 2015. "Unfolding the Political Capacities of Design." In *What Is Cosmopolitical Design?*, edited by Albena Yaneva and Polo Alejandro Zaera, 143–60. London: Ashgate.

Dourish, Paul. 2006. "Implications for Design." In *Proceedings of the ACM Conference Human Factors in Computing Systems*, 541–50. Montreal, Canada: ACM.

Dunne, Anthony, and Fiona Raby. 2013. *Speculative Everything: Design, Fiction, and Social Dreaming*. Cambridge, MA: The MIT Press.

———. 2015. "United Micro Kingdoms." www.unitedmicrokingdoms.org (accessed February 7, 2016).

Ferguson, James. 1994. *The Anti-Politics Machine: "Development," Depoliticization, and Bureaucratic Power in Lesotho*. Minneapolis, MN: The University of Minnesota Press.

Fisher, Mark. 2009. *Capitalist Realism: Is There No Alternative?* London: Zero Books.

Haraway, Donna. 1984. "Primatology Is Politics by Other Means." In *PSA: Proceedings of the Biennial Meeting of the Philosophy of Science Association, Volume 2*, 489–524. Chicago, IL: University of Chicago Press.

———. 2013. "SF: Science Fiction, Speculative Fabulation, String Figures, So Far." *Ada: A Journal of Gender, New Media, and Technology* (3).

Irani, Lilly. 2013. *Designing Citizens in Transnational India*. PhD dissertation, University of California, Irvine.

———. 2015. "Hackathons and the Making of Entrepreneurial Citizenship." *Science, Technology & Human Values* 40(5): 799–824.

Latour, Bruno. 1988. "Mixing Humans and Nonhumans Together: The Sociology of a Door-Closer." *Social Problems* 35(3): 298–310.

———. 2004. "Why Has Critique Run Out of Steam? From Matters of Fact to Matters of Concern." *Critical Inquiry* 30(2): 225–48.

———. 2005. "From Realpolitik to Dingpolitik, or How to Make Things Public." In *Making Things Public: Atmospheres of Democracy*, edited by Bruno Latour and Peter Weibel, 4–31. Cambridge, MA: The MIT Press.

———. 2008. "A Cautious Prometheus? A Few Steps Toward a Philosophy of Design (with Special Attention to Peter Sloterdijk)." In *Proceedings of the 2008 Annual International Conference of the Design History Society*, edited by Fiona Hackne, Jonathan Glynne, and Viv Minto, 2–10. Falmouth: Universal Publishers.

Li, Tania Murray. 2007. *The Will to Improve: Governmentality, Development, and the Practice of Politics*. Durham, NC: Duke University Press.

Rabinow, Paul, George E. Marcus, James D. Faubion, and Tobias Rees. 2008. *Designs for an Anthropology of the Contemporary*. Durham, NC: Duke University Press.

Scott, James C. 1998. *Seeing Like a State: How Certain Schemes to Improve the Human Condition Have Failed*. New Haven, CT: Yale University Press.

Sims, Christo. 2017. *Disruptive Fixation: School Reform and the Pitfalls of Techno-idealism*. Princeton, NJ: Princeton University Press.

Star, Susan Leigh. 1999. "The Ethnography of Infrastructure." *American Behavioral Scientist* 43(3): 377–91.

Suchman, Lucy. 2002. "Located Accountabilities in Technology Production." *Scandinavian Journal of Information Systems* 14: 91–106.

———. 2011. "Anthropological Relocations and the Limits of Design." *Annual Review of Anthropology* 40(1): 1–18.

Winner, Langdon. 1980. "Do Artifacts Have Politics?" *Daedalus* 109(1): 121–36.

Wright, Erik Olin. 2010. *Envisioning Real Utopias*. New York: Verso.

41

ETHNOGRAPHY AND THE ONGOING IN DIGITAL DESIGN

Elisenda Ardèvol and Débora Lanzeni

Introduction

This chapter rethinks the connections between ethnography, design and the digital in light of our position that ethnography is a process of knowledge, not about the world as it is, but processes of knowledge production that we learn with others (Ingold 2013). Drawing on our ethnographic work among Free Culture (FC) producers and technology designers in Barcelona, we question the idea that the digital is something "out there" in order to understand it as something that is becoming and which cannot be reduced to a thing, object, device, relationship or even a technology. In this way, we place the ethnographic exploration of "the digital" as part of the contemporary and of the ethnographies of the contemporary (Crapanzano 2004; Budka 2011; Pink et al. 2015). With this in mind, we seek to challenge how we develop an ethnographic approach to embrace the digital as unfinished and in movement. Thus, we argue that digital ethnography should not be defined by the digital as its object of study, nor should it be limited to its specific techniques, such as participant observation in virtual environments or online interviews.

Although the ethnographic methods have been fruitfully used to describe online social interactions (Baym 2000), video gamer cultures (Nardi 2010) and digital developers or software cultures (Kelty 2008; Coleman 2010), we propose that what defines digital ethnography is its flexible and transformative nature based on the relationship that ethnographers and their research partners engage in during the formation of the digital-material world. We therefore argue that the field of design and creative industries is a fruitful location to explore how ethnography and the digital actually bring each other to life.

The Digital Under Construction

In recent years, the digital has provided a broad agenda of topics and objects of study in the social sciences, from phenomena, expressions and performances that will be characteristic of "digital cultures," to methodological approaches to perform research in new media, Internet, social media, mobile phones and the social and cultural practices related to these technologies (Horst and Miller 2013).

Virtual worlds, online dating, video gamers, hackers, software developers, anonymous social media, social media, webpages, bitcoins, selfies, crowdfunding, electronic banking, teleworking, online shopping, and so on, are only a few of the objects of study categorized under the umbrella of "the digital." However, the digital in these disparate objects of study cannot be reduced to the set of technologies and infrastructures that they seem to share. Moreover, to characterize the digital by its elementary common composition of bits would be a "thin" description in Geertzian terms (Geertz 1973), or a definition that does very little to help us understand society's current transformations or the different ways that people make, feel, think, desire and fear, by this exchanging of bits.

Indeed, to define something as part of the "digital culture" (because it is made by bits) and then observe it in the real world to study its common traits, its new characteristics and its features is to draw an arbitrary division between "the digital" and everything else. Moreover, to delimitate the digital as a closed entity that interacts with culture or society in causal terms reifies technology (the bits, the digital devices) as the cause of the subsequent cultural or social transformations. The solution of defining our object of study as a new entity composed by the sum or combination of elements (hybridization) does not solve the analytical problem, because it does not dissolve the categorical concepts that we depart from. Thus, the first problem that we face with digital ethnography is what "the digital" means in the equation. We argue that digital ethnography should not be defined by the digital as its object of study nor as a specific methodology, just because things done by bits are different from those done by atoms. The problem that digital ethnographers must first address is how the digital is involved in the research questions we want to address.

The digital has become a well-established field of inquiry through its thoroughly conceptual constructive operations, vivid debates and accumulative work within the social sciences. In the first social studies of the Internet at the end of the century, researchers studied technological cultures, virtual worlds, online identities and social life in cyberspace (Ardèvol and Gómez-Cruz 2014). It was later that all of these particular objects of study were unified under the common umbrellas named digital anthropology, digital media, digital ethnography, etc. The digital emerges as an affiliated object (Suchman 2005) in the social sciences as it is recognized by practitioners as a field of inquiry, but it would be a methodological mistake to consider this pragmatic construct as an empirical reference. In other words, to understand the digital as a descriptive category of our inquiry pre-defines our object of study instead of opening it to interrogation. The challenge of digital ethnographers, then, is to develop useful questions for an ethnographic approach to embrace the concrete transformations, movements and uncertainties that entail what we call "the digital."

By formulating the digital as an open question of inquiry, we situate ethnographic exploration of the digital as part of the contemporary and of the ethnographies of the contemporary: contemporary in the sense that it is happening here and now, existing or occurring at the same period of time in its formation as the ethnographer (Crapanzano 2004; Budka 2011). The contemporary is a challenging conceptual category, as the present is a moment in which what is, what will be or what has been is at least potentially open (Rabinow et al. 2008, 7). For Rabinow and Marcus, "contemporary" usually refers to a mode of historicity whose scale and scope are relatively short in range, but it also can be crafted as an analytical concept that allows the ethnographer to conceptualize the emergent as a dynamic knot of co-temporalities. If ethnography is concerned with the emergent, what is current or emergent has nothing to do with just any totality, but with the combination of different traits that create new conjunctures that lead to evolving dynamics. Whatever the digital is (and we do not need to define it *a priori*), the digital is in flux, and visualizing what the digital entails depends on all concrete fieldwork.

This brings us back to methodology. In many handbooks and methodology companions, ethnography is depicted as a qualitative method for data gathering. This idea is reaffirmed in interdisciplinary realms, where ethnography is presented as a descriptive method that can be paired with the theory the researcher chooses (Dicks et al. 2006; Murthy 2011). We agree that the ethnographic method evolves within different theoretical frameworks, but we must insist that there are some epistemological grounds that cannot be driven out without discarding its pillars: displacement, denaturalization and open theory.

Ethnography is crucially driven by a kind of openness to the perspective of others, a perspective that entails other sorts of being in the world, ontological positions (Viveiros de Castro 2012), or epistemological constructions (Bohannan 1966). From the beginning, ethnography has involved a specific epistemological movement (among others) that is set to adopt a position of distance and closeness to what is studied. It is depicted as distant because of its scientific nature and close for two reasons: first, because of the inclusion of the researcher in the field, and, second, because of the inclusion of others (their thoughts, values, possessions and means of engaging with knowledge) both in the object of study and in the research questions.

Thus, what we study is not unrelated to our work, but rather is defined by what we do with others. Our research questions are not separate from how we produce them or from the questions and answers that others whom we engage in research produce. This foundational movement "is a shift from viewing scientific objects and cultural forms as things to be discovered, to recognizing that the process of 'discovery' is increasingly one of active production, of reconfiguring our worlds into new formations" (Fischer 2007, 556) with our informants, correspondents or travel companions. Ethnography, as born from anthropological tradition, has historically been a method of understanding "other peoples," and to grasp the diversity of life forms, even in colonialist conditions and, further on, embracing postcolonialism studies and developing research "at home," ruling out the misconception that cultures are homogeneous wholes (Comaroff and Comaroff 2001). This exercise of displacement and denaturalization mainly consists in experiencing the world with others as they do, and that means examining the sustainability of our own conceptualizations when entering into a dialog with the native or vernacular concepts of the people we encounter. There are certainly different theories and frameworks that inform our approach to others' knowledge and ways of life, but the researcher's ideas are always contrasted with the native concepts (denaturalization), and the comprehension that comes out of that comparison brings out ethnographic knowledge, as in Ginsburg (1999), a feminist anthropologist studying the Right to Life movement in the USA, or Rapp (1999), questioning her position regarding knowledge, power and practice in the US medical care system focusing on female decisions around amniocentesis. The outcome of these operations usually results in the adjustment and reformulation of the researcher's theories and conceptual frameworks. Thus, pre-concepts and theories must remain open to change during fieldwork. This open relationship between theory and fieldwork is therefore one of the keystones to understanding how research works in ethnography (Pink et al. 2015).

Digital ethnographers work with technicians, designers, Internet users and video gamers, but the fieldwork is not, or at least not exclusively, about technicians, designers, Internet users or video gamers. Like any "other cultures" that ethnographers study, from the Amazon forest to the Chicago streets, virtual world games, online chatting, FC creations, open source projects and technology design labs are engaging fields of inquiry that bring to existence emergent forms of life around us that challenge our epistemological common sense about the composition and attachments of the world. As Fischer posits (2007, 567), some of these emergent forms of life entail fundamental changes in the legal system that operates in virtual as well as real-life worlds, from IP rights and Creative Commons licenses to the market—the introduction of venture capital and new relations between government, university and industry—and the sense of physical body and social self. How the legal system, the market or social life changes depends on the people that are actively engaged in such transformations (designers, lawyers, economists, social and natural scientists, citizens, politicians), their things (laws, codes, artifacts, objects) and their aims, their skills and their expert and common-sense understandings. How we make sense of this emerging world also depends on the ethnographer's ability to learn what is going on from others.

We argue that what defines digital ethnography is its capacity to learn the nuances of the digital as it is expressed—or not expressed—in people's everyday lives. This is due to the flexible and transformative nature based on the relationship in which ethnographers and their research partners and their things engage. To illustrate this, in the following section we focus upon our digital ethnography with FC creators and activists.

On Digital Creation

Our work in FC focuses precisely on the aspects of digital that stretch, meld with and conform to the current processes of cultural creation and cross the categorical line between "digital" and "non-digital." Our research—specifically two ethnographic projects completed around groups of FC producers and open source developers in Barcelona—proposes a focus on the daily life of people related to FC privileging notions and practices that shape a way of life and a particular design approach to the world and technology. We approach digital creation in a broad sense to include both the design of artifacts, objects or media and the production of narratives, images and discourses that occur at different places and at different levels when researchers, politicians, citizens, artists, media producers, designers and technology developers meet and evolve to defend Internet neutrality. Specifically, we engage with software and hardware developers creating tools and methodologies that enable collective cooperation (Lanzeni 2012) and, in addition, audiovisual producers engaged in Creative Commons using tools such as crowdfunding, free software and social networking to produce, perform and publicize audiovisual collective work (Ardèvol 2013).

FC is a globally based Internet movement inspired by Lawrence Lessig (2004) that advocates for the neutrality of the Net and its basic structure (continuity and openness) as key principles for cultural creativity and innovation. In addition, people in FC drive the transformation of cultural production through the collaborative logic that the Internet opens, by the development of a new regulatory framework for the creation, circulation and consumption of cultural products based on P2P network models, open source and free software practices.

In the USA, the FC movement evolved mainly through legal policies, statements and controversies related with the Internet and authorship rights. In Europe, it was reduced to local and minor struggles, but progressively linked to broad social movements. Spain's FC movement reached a tipping point during 2011 and 2012, as several FC activists were aligned with broad social movements and citizens' demonstrations in the Spanish Occupy 15M movement (Postill 2013a, 2013b). Nevertheless, FC activists do not make up a homogeneous group. For example, the Free Culture Forum held in Barcelona in 2012 brought together people from different backgrounds (artists, engineers, lawyers, designers, academics, etc.) and commercial companies, pro-common P2P organizations, digital start-ups and new business models. If 15M cannot be understood without the collaboration of FC activists, FC vitality in Spain—and in Europe at large—cannot be understood without taking into account its multiple connections to grassroots social movements. Moreover, the relevance of FC in Spain during those years was due to the fact that it joined a wider citizen response to political and economic crisis, linking Internet issues and struggles to citizens' broader mobilizations and worries.

For FC activists, effective political action must be embedded in daily practices and doing things in specific ways. For them, creativity is not defined by an individual's mind, nor by a product or symbolic good, but as a collective work that entails collaboration, remixing and sharing, improvising and recycling the main sources of cultural innovation. Corporate enclosure and intellectual property legislations restrict the emergence of creative ideas and innovation from the grassroots and put the design for Internet neutrality and fair access to anyone in danger. What the Internet is and could be is not fixed, but is constantly being reworked. FC activists believe that the emergence of a world made of bits actually opens a universe of unlimited possibilities to create and share, but for this new world to exist, the active participation of citizens is necessary. As they say, "Don't ask what the Internet can do for you, but what you can do for the Internet." Thus, the digital is not only the technology or the bits that circulate, but includes what its methods of production and circulation are, how they can be shaped and how a culture of plenty and commonality can be realized. What surrounds FC and the development of open technologies is more than what they and we mean by "digital." As our interlocutors were intervening in some constitutive parts of a broader process, the digital exceeded technology and the Internet in becoming a strategy for a better future.

The digital—for them and for us—includes more than digital technology, practices and environments; it also includes changes and transformations in our relations with the world. The digital—for them and for us—is in motion; it is constantly becoming, and it is in its continuum that they and we are actively involved. Ultimately, it is this "in motion" that the digital ethnographer engages in and tries to understand.

Design and Digital Ethnography

Design and anthropological studies of science and technology bring to digital ethnography the understanding of the object of study as open and "in motion." Design ethnography attempts to develop a methodology to grasp the things and the processes that are not closed and are in an active course of formation, while digital ethnography has been largely centered in the media object and its uses (Pink et al. 2015). While the anthropology of science and technology opens up ways to study the contemporary and the emergent by redefining the site or the locus of ethnographic fieldwork, design anthropology teaches us that ethnographic observations can be involved in design practices to foster mutually interacting relations and recast assumptions insofar as ethnographic fieldwork can be a form of engagement and part of transitional practices (Gunn et al. 2013, 7). Again, it is easy to reduce "design" to another new field in which, ethnographically, anthropologists have a lot to say. Nevertheless, design anthropologists usually stress that design could offer much more to the ways that anthropologists do research than anthropology may offer to design, which is not trivial at all (Dourish 2006; Gunn et al. 2013; Akama and Pink 2014). Research on design offers anthropologists a particular manner of composing fieldwork that we also want to explore in this chapter. In other words, studying digital design ethnographically might involve a collection of techniques but also certainly entails a reconceptualization of how ethnographic research is involved in others' practices—that is to say, a practice that we might not completely participate in or could not even fathom by "being there"—in bringing something to the world together.

Design ethnography illuminates digital ethnography because this shift not only signifies an enhancement in the aim of ethnography from description to intervention, but also a reformulation of how participant observation is conceived and what kind of knowledge ethnography seeks. As Pink argues (2014, 9):

> Digital ethnography is a way of doing ethnography that is part of and participates in a digital-material-sensory environment rather than simply ethnography about the digital. When applying this point to design anthropology, this likewise refers to the environments we research in, seek to understand and whose future evolutions we seek to both intervene in and shape through design interventions.

In recent years, ethnography has been experimenting with adaptive changes in the tools (from text and drawings to audiovisual aids and digital forms of recording), the field (from single-site to multi-site) and the object (from studying cultures to the cultural flows of activity and to the emergent) but has maintained its scope (displacement, denaturalization and open theory) and, to some extent, its aims (to give a meaningful description of a human realities). However, the commitment to carry out anthropology with design has shifted the ways that we ultimately understand the ethnographic aim, which is not only to describe a world, but also to directly intervene in its formation through the very process of doing fieldwork.

The documentary aim of the ethnographic method has hidden the importance of the encounter with others for ethnographic description and to understand what happens in these encounters. Even so, it was in the early 1980s, and in the context of a turn in postcolonial studies and feminism, that Trinh T. Minh-ha (1989)—a documentary filmmaker—pointed out that her ethnographic production was an attempt to speak nearby instead of speaking about the others, and David MacDougall (1991) also called the ethnographic documentary the description of an encounter. Tim Ingold has been very critical of the ways that ethnography has become interdisciplinary, precisely because of the conflation of ethnography with method, and fieldwork with gathering data to obtain knowledge about others' lives (Ingold 2013, 386). Indeed, Ingold insists that while ethnography is associated with description, participant observation is a mode of knowledge created with others:

> To observe means to watch what is going on around and about, and of course to listen and feel as well. To participate means to do so from within the current of activity in which you carry on a life alongside and together with the persons and things that capture your attention. As with the encounter, anthropological participant observation differs only in degree from what all people do all of the time. . . . Knowledge grows from the crucible of lives lived with others. This knowledge, as we are well aware, consists not in propositions about the world but in the skills of perception and capacities of judgment that develop in the course of direct, practical, and sensuous engagements with our surroundings.
>
> (Ingold 2014, 387)

The site of knowledge production is not only found in the cabinet after fieldwork, but is forged in correspondence in the field. Moreover, the ethnographer is part of the world as it is being performed, and that has crucial implications in doing ethnography with digital technology designers as we explain in the following section.

On Smart City Technologies

In Débora Lanzeni's (2016) fieldwork with smart technology developers, she realized that the concept of "smart" could not be ethnographically defined at the outset. Smart is part of the ways in which cities are envisioned in market fairs, governmental policies and news reports, and stories about how future technologically enhanced and potentially automated cities, homes and lives are imagined. However, to gain an understanding of this concept and how it is mobilized in relation to constituting digital-material worlds, and how it is intermingled with the design of smart technologies, we need to unpack what "smart" means for people who are involved in the development of smart technologies. Learning how they do the things they do, how they think what they think, and learning from the products themselves in their ethnographic context allows us to situate concepts and categories to trace continuities and discontinuities in everyday life where the digital is produced and evolves, rather than trying to seek what smart technology gives to the world (Holbraad 2011).

The Smart City as a vision and as a program relies mainly upon two interrelated aspects that are categorized under the rubric of designable: technologies that enable things, buildings, routes, garbage containers, and so on, to produce valuable information for the organization of the city, and software applications that enable citizens, government, institutions and companies to sort out this information in productive ways (Lanzeni 2016). Both aspects involve a larger group of technologies that have been part of the many other systems, such as smoke detectors, door locks or industrial security detention, both known and new. The engagement of technology designers with these technologies emerged prior to the mass advent of the digital and most of the new technologies that are at the core of the Smart City project were already created before the contemporary digital moment (Lanzeni 2016). Nevertheless, for the Smart City program, all technologies that enable the city to be more organized and allow things to connect to each other are part of a kind of new digital momentum in the world. Design technology, by contrast, is more about continuities, re-connections and experimentation with existing technologies in order to make room for other possibilities than about seeking novelty. Therefore, through the relation with a continuum of ideas, things and programs, distinguishing between something digital and something not digital is both difficult and useless. Designers, through practice, make technologies that become part of our digital worlds.

Partners in the Intervention

Ethnographic research on smart technologies reveals that even if the researcher is not fully aware of everything that is happening, because she or he does not possess certain skills or lacks experience, she equally intervenes in the practice of making possible technologies, the design and the further intellection of the digital. In this sense, the digital is in motion and the ethnographic research that encompasses digital design takes part in creating it and in defining what the specificity of it in every case is. Because ethnography and design clearly collaborate with the formation of people's future (Gunn et al. 2013), they also collaborate with the elaboration of the digital in its artifacts, its technologies, and its conceptualizations and beliefs.

In design and in digital ethnography *contemporaneity* operates as encounter with others, as constellation for inquiring. Sometimes, the problem with the concept of contemporaneity is that it easily becomes "the condition of existence," as Englund and Leach suggest with reference to the word "modernity" (2000, 226). In consequence, most conceptualizations of "contemporary" imply a description of how things are now and here. It acts with a kind of *ceteris paribus* law that freezes in time and space one moment of existence; this contemporaneity opens up only what we are looking at, where the "openness" seems to positively occur and the "possible" emerges. In this sense, it might lead us to conceive the contemporary as an actual moment rather than a descriptor of existence or as a claim for openness. On the contrary, we understand the contemporary—like the digital—as what emerges from how our research partners and we, ethnographers, problematize the questions that we want to grasp. Consequently, the contemporary—as well as the digital—is what is ongoing in how we walk over the world together along with our partners and the other parts of what we pointed out as digitalities: a sensor, an interactive device, a repository of software or a vision of Smart City.

Sharing our understandings of doing ethnography among open source and FC creators and activists, designers and smart technology developers is a way to reflect on the ethnography of the contemporary, the interdisciplinary and forms of collaboration (Marcus 1995; Maurer 2002; Rabinow et al. 2008). Doing design ethnography means to be in the field by "doing things together" with our partners. That frames the fieldwork as a heterogenic process where partners are involved in different ways dissolving the homogeneity of the "other" and the presence of the ethnographer as the "stranger" in the field. Partnership helps us to avoid an understanding that the ethnographer is "collaborating" in the things that "others" are doing. Collaboration in this sense is potentially "ethnographer-centered" as it frames what others do in relation to the point of view of the ethnographer. The intersection between Design and Digital in Anthropology brings to the fore that ethnography is not any more a privileged stance from where to look at what the others do. Rather it is part of what is going on (Pink 2014; Gunn et al. 2013).

Co-presence in ethnographic fieldwork, then, is the way to explore knowledge co-creation in conversation with our research partners. In the case of digital ethnography, it is usually understood as an adaptation of the method to online environments. For example, in virtual ethnography (Hine 2000), the emphasis is put on adapting the ethnographer's reflexivity in relation to the experience of participating in online interactions and how to produce different means of co-presence based on non-physicality (Beaulieu 2010; Horst 2015). Forming a design perspective to engage in virtual worlds is to understand co-presence as a way to learn from another's practices and discover means of imagining oneself in another person's world. FC activists frame co-presence as a commitment based on horizontal relationships. Digital designers, on the contrary, frame the ethnographer's co-presence in relation to the task at hand; commitment is to be in the action.

Design ethnography merges with digital ethnography highlighting the openness and transformative nature of the ethnographic process. The digital does not mediate human relations but is part of the human imagination and the material and sensory world in daily activity. How the digital is defined takes shape in the ongoing; some understanding is perhaps contextual to fieldwork, while some will be elaborated as part of our monograph for further revisions.

Ethnography is part of an open process that does not end with ethnographic outputs and that transforms the ethnographer as well as the people and things engaged in the research process in many—and not always expected—directions. Ethnography works on an epistemological, methodological and intervention level simultaneously, and these three aspects cannot be sliced into unrelated units. And we have seen that this has special relevance when dealing with research in designing digital technologies.

In conclusion, merging digital and design ethnography sheds light on the ways we are doing ethnography *in the contemporary*. This merging speaks not only about the digital or about design, but it discloses an epistemological shift in ethnography at large that entails embracing the ongoing and the things in the course of formation. This epistemological shift in the configuration of the object of study—in the course of formation—renders a movement of de-centering ethnography itself as a privileged site of knowledge production, compromising the ethnographer and the ethnographic practice in the ongoing action.

References

Akama, Yoko and Pink, Sarah. 2014. "Design + Ethnography + Futures: Disrupting." PDC2014 Workshop: *Design Anthropology in Participatory Design: From Ethnography to Anthropological Critique.* 13th Participatory Design Conference. Namibia.

Ardèvol, Elisenda. 2013. *Cultura digital y prácticas creativas: Tientos etnográficos en torno a la Cultura Libre.* Barcelona: IN3-Working Paper Series.

Ardèvol, Elisenda and Gómez-Cruz, Edgar. 2014. "Digital ethnography and media practices." In *The International Encyclopedia of Media Studies.* Vol. 7, edited by Angharad N. Valdivia, John Nerone, Kelly Gates, Sharon Mazzarella, Vicki Mayer, Erica Scharrer, et al., 498–518. London: Wiley and Sons.

Baym, Nancy K. 2000. *Tune in, log on: Soaps, fandom, and online community.* Vol. 3. Thousand Oaks, CA: Sage.

Beaulieu, Anne. 2010. "Research note: From co-location to co-presence: Shifts in the use of ethnography for the study of knowledge." *Social Studies of Science* 40(3): 453–70.

Bohannan, Laura. 1966. "Shakespeare in the bush." *Natural History* 75(7): 28–33.

Budka, Philipp. 2011. "From cyber to digital anthropology to an anthropology of the contemporary." www.media-anthropology.net/file/budka_contemporary.pdf (accessed February 29, 2016).

Coleman, Gabriella, E. 2010. "Ethnographic approaches to digital media." *Annual Review of Anthropology* 39: 487–505.

Comaroff, Jean and John L. Comaroff. 2001. "Naturing the nation: Aliens, apocalypse, and the post-colonial state." *Social Identities* 7(2): 233–65.

Crapanzano, Vincent. 1977. "On the writing of ethnography." *Dialectical Anthropology* 2(1): 69–73.

———. 2004. *Imaginative horizons: An essay in literary-philosophical anthropology.* Chicago, IL: University of Chicago Press.

Dicks, Bella, Soyinka, Bambo, and Coffey, Amanda. 2006. "Multimodal ethnography." *Qualitative Research* 6(1): 77–96.

Dourish, Paul. 2006. "Implications for design." *Proceedings of the SIGCHI Conference on Human Factors in Computing Systems,* 541–50. ACM.

Englund, Harri and James Leach. 2000. "Ethnography and the meta-narratives of modernity." *Current Anthropology* 41(2): 225–48.

Fischer, Michael M. J. 2007. "Four genealogies for a recombinant anthropology of science and technology." *Cultural Anthropology* 22(4): 539–615.

Geertz, Clifford. 1973. *The interpretation of cultures: Selected essays.* New York: Basic Books.

Ginsburg, F. 1999. "Cuando los nativos son nuestros vecinos." In *Constructores de otredad,* edited by Mauricio Boivin, Ana Rosato and Victoria Arribas, 186–93. Buenos Aires: Antropofagia.

Gunn, Wendy, Ton Otto, and Rachel Charlotte Smith, eds. 2013. *Design anthropology: Theory and practice.* London: Bloomsbury.

Hine, Christine. 2000. *Virtual ethnography.* London: Sage.

Holbraad, Martin. 2011. "Can the thing speak?" Open Anthropology Cooperative Press, Working Papers Series, 7: 1–26. http://openanthcoop.net/press/http://openanthcoop.net/press/wp-content/uploads/2011/01/Holbraad-Can-the-Thing-Speak.pdf (accessed February 29, 2016).

Horst, Heather. 2015. "Being in fieldwork: Collaboration, digital media, and ethnographic practice." In *Fieldnotes: The makings of anthropology in the digital world,* edited by Roger Sanjek and Susan W. Tratner, 153–70. Philadelphia: University of Pennsylvania Press.

Horst, Heather A. and Daniel Miller eds. 2013. *Digital anthropology.* London: Bloomsbury.

Ingold, Tim. 2013. *Making: Anthropology, archaeology, art and architecture.* London: Routledge.

———. 2014. "That's enough about ethnography!" *HAU: Journal of Ethnographic Theory* 4(1): 383–95.

Kelty, Christopher M. 2008. *Two bits: The cultural significance of free software*. Durham, NC: Duke University Press.

Lanzeni, Débora. 2012. "Desde el diseño de Software a la acción política: un acercamiento etnográfico al movimiento de la Cultura Libre." M. Thesis, Barcelona: IN3 Md.

———. 2016. "Smart global futures: Designing affordable materialities for a better life." In *Digital Materialities, Design and Anthropology*, edited by Sarah Pink, Elisenda Ardèvol, and Débora Lanzeni, 45–60. London: Bloomsbury.

Lessig, Lawrence. 2004. *Free culture: The nature and future of creativity*. New York: Penguin.

MacDougall, David. 1991. "Whose story is it?" *Visual Anthropology Review* 7(2): 2–10.

Marcus, George E. 1995. "Ethnography in/of the world system: The emergence of multi-sited ethnography." *Annual Review of Anthropology* 24: 95–117.

Maurer, Bill. 2002. "Anthropological and accounting knowledge in Islamic banking and finance: Rethinking critical accounts." *Journal of the Royal Anthropological Institute* 8(4): 645–67.

Minh-Ha, Trinh, T. 1989. *Woman, native, other*. Bloomington, IN: Indiana University Press.

Murthy, Dhiraj. 2011. "Emergent digital ethnographic methods for social research." In *Handbook of Emergent Technologies in Social Research*, edited by Sharlene Hesse-Biber, 158–79. New York: Oxford University Press.

Nardi, Bonnie A. 2010. *My life as a night elf priest: An anthropological account of World of Warcraft*. Ann Arbor, MI: University of Michigan Press.

Pink, Sarah. 2014. "Digital–visual–sensory-design anthropology: Ethnography, imagination and intervention." *Arts and Humanities in Higher Education* 13(4): 412–27.

Pink, Sarah, Heather Horst, John Postill, Larissa Hjorth, Tania Lewis, and Jo Tacchi. 2015. *Digital ethnography: Principles and practice*. London: Sage.

Postill, John. 2013a. "Participatory media research and Spain's 15M movement." Hotspots, Cultural Anthropology website, February 14. http://culanth.org/fieldsights/86-participatory-media-research-and-spain-s-15m-movement (accessed February 29, 2016).

———. 2013b. "The uneven convergence of digital freedom activism and popular protest: A global theory of the new protest movements." Melbourne: RMIT University. http://rmit.academia.edu/JohnPostill (accessed February 29, 2016).

Rabinow, Paul, George E. Marcus, James D. Faubion, and Tobias Rees. 2008. *Designs for an anthropology of the contemporary*. Durham, NC: Duke University Press.

Rapp, Rayna. 1999. *Testing women, testing the fetus: The social impact of amniocentesis in America*. New York: Routledge.

Suchman, Lucy. 2005. "Affiliative objects." *Organization* 12(3): 379–99.

Viveiros de Castro, Eduardo. 2012. "Cosmological perspectivism in Amazonia and elsewhere." *HAU: Masterclass Series* 1: 45–168.

42

DISRUPTIVE INTERVENTIONS WITH MOBILE MEDIA THROUGH *DESIGN+ ETHNOGRAPHY+ FUTURES*

Yoko Akama, Katherine Moline, and Sarah Pink

Introduction

This chapter brings together digital ethnography with experimental art, speculative and participatory design research to consider what might be possible when they are blended together, and how this could provide insights into change-making initiatives. In entwining various disciplinary practices, we are interested in creating forms of research that surpass definitions. This exploration is undertaken through a research initiative, *Design+Ethnography+Futures*, where the not-yet-made is at the center of inquiry (Akama et al. 2015). For us, uncertainty is a welcome ingredient. By putting this at the forefront of our research process, we explore two issues to consider how contemporary societies approach the ubiquity and possibilities of digital technologies for change-making. These are (1) the growth of digital maker cultures and the human capacity for digital improvisation that is evident through their activity, and (2) the need to recognize uncertainties that pervade our knowledge about how digital futures will emerge. In doing so, we attempt to confront and undermine a techno-deterministic worldview where design is often synonymous with technological innovation, framed as a panacea for solving problems. Our approach is not just to critique these assumptions but also to carve out ways to investigate how we can remake new understandings together.

We first outline how we envisage the relationship between design and ethnography emerging through our work, as a critical response to debates about the use of ethnography in the Human Computer Interaction (HCI) field, and how we are inspired by design anthropology, speculative design, and participatory design that points a way forward. Next, we detail how *Design+Ethnography+Futures* develops approaches that are sensitive to how incremental changes to our self-awareness and socio-material relationship can be initiated, catalyzed, scaffolded, and imagined together. We share critical reflections of these early initiatives and describe the implications these have for digital ethnography. Rather than offering a "how to" guide, we propose considerations, questions, and disruptive strategies to navigate emergent and contested futures.

Inspirations and Departures

Design+Ethnography+Futures was conceived through a desire to advance new forms of experimental practice, rather than as a critical response to existing combinations of design, ethnography, and digital media. From December 2013 to 2014, Yoko Akama and Sarah Pink at RMIT University have been co-facilitating a series of workshops, which were the sites of our shared research explorations with participants. These workshops ranged in format and duration, from two full days to three hours long, between 12–30 researchers and postgraduate students from various universities. Each workshop invited a guest facilitator to frame a theme that was of interest to explore with others. In June 2014, Katherine Moline led a workshop called *Myths of the Near Future*, informed by an accumulation of 20 years of workshops, artworks, and exhibitions that explore social experiences mediated by technology (Moline 2011, 2012, 2014, 2015a, 2015b).

Like all *Design+Ethnography+Futures* workshop series, it pivoted around five key concepts— disrupting, unknowing, sharing, making, and moving—improvised with the participants who are often researchers from different disciplines beyond design or anthropology. *Myths of the Near Future* also employed improvisation as its key modality to co-explore socio-technical interaction to *disrupt* participants' relationships with their mobile phones—a familiar, practical, precious, and innocuous technology—by turning it into a research tool. *Unknowing* was explored by swapping phones with a workshop participant they knew little of to see what the interaction revealed about each other and about themselves. Participants were invited to *make*, using the props provided, which led to *sharing* of ideas, insights, feelings, photos, videos, and conversation. *Moving* explored emerging shifts in participants' understandings and practices of their smartphone interactions. Uncertainty is at the core of the workshop-based inquiry, requiring all to interrogate what we think we know and question the assumptions and paradigms that are taken for granted in our respective disciplines as we co-explore what their intertwined futures might be.

Design+Ethnography+Futures seeks to depart from traditional approaches in design ethnography and HCI, which have tended to design resolutions by incorporating ethnography-derived user insights during the tight locus of the formal design phase to create digital technologies. This transactional relationship whereby ethnography is seen to generate implications for design has been problematized by Paul Dourish (2006, 5) who argues that it "postulates design as the natural end-point of research inquiry, and therefore designers as the gatekeepers for that research" and thus removes ethnography, and those whom ethnographers study, outside of the design process itself. Instead, we advance discussions of how to surpass this relationship that separates ethnography and design as distinct stages and inquiry, to instead generate a design+ethnography+futures entanglement. Focusing on methodological issues is a necessary

Figure 42.1   The image *What the Phone Sees When No-One is Looking* by David Carlin demonstrates the disruptive potential of the invitation to leave behind the certainties associated with mobile phones

first step; while "results" are important, they have little meaning if the ways of knowing behind them are not critiqued or acknowledged.

Contemporary framings of design and ethnography (sometimes called design anthropology) have begun to create a form of practice that departs from the temporality of the ethnographic past, and that engages *with* design and people as they move into the future (Gunn and Donovan 2012; Gunn et al. 2013). They demonstrate that a future-focused and exploratory research could not be developed through a single disciplinary endeavor. This is resonant with many forms of interdisciplinary research, as explained by Rendell (2013, 119):

> In demanding that we exchange what we know for what we do not know, and that we give up the safety of competence and specialism, and instead enter a terrain beset with fears of inability, lack of expertise and the dangers of failure, the transformational experience of interdisciplinary work produces a potentially destabilizing engagement with existing power structures, allowing the emergence of fragile forms of new and untested experience, knowledge and understanding.

Similarly, *Design+Ethnography+Futures* is an attitude as well as a deliberative research strategy to step into such uncertain terrains. We situate our exploration here as substantively engaged in processual worlds where boundaries between ethnography and design are already dissolving. Design anthropology takes a step further to explore how this can be undertaken together with research participants. As researchers interested in creating and understanding change, we are always working *with* emergent qualities and *with* people with whom we share journeys into the immediate future. Thus, our agenda is not to do "better" design ethnography in order to improve digital technology. Nor are we attempting to experiment with design techniques or practice in order to produce novel ethnographic insights and do "better" ethnography, although we acknowledge that both of these can be side products of our endeavor.

Rather, *Design+Ethnography+Futures* is a step sideways which, prior to resolving its methodological or theoretical application, carves out a space akin to a "sand pit" or "research incubator" where a hybrid interweaving of disciplines is underpinned by a commitment to creating a common theoretical and conceptual foundation. Like our substantive engagements with future uncertainties, our exploration challenges what we habitually thought we already knew and did. Instead of defending boundaries and enshrining disciplinary approaches, our curiosity stems from rubbing up against and alongside other disciplines to create a productive dialog.

Arguably, designers have always been oriented toward future making and willingly embrace the unexpected. Discourses in speculative design and critical design (Dunne and Raby 2013; Michael 2012), and methods such as cultural probes (Gaver et al. 1999) emerged out of an inquiry to make ordinary and everyday things (products and services) extraordinary or strange, through the Surrealist technique of defamiliarization. For example, speculative design is a reflexive approach that critiques industry norms and engages people in contemplating the futures made possible with technological innovation. Dunne and Raby (2013) characterize it as a range of approaches in provoking "fictional worlds," "what-if scenarios," and "cautionary tales." In a similar vein, sociologist Mike Michael (2012, 173) describes the processual aspect of speculative design that aims to "throw up the peculiar, the unexpected, the troublesome, the incommensurable" that manifests otherwise unthought design routes or invites "inventive problem making." Moline's workshop draws upon these discourses.

Encouragingly, many others share these future-oriented concerns. Recent movements in participatory design echo its political heritage that sought to question, reveal, and deliberatively intervene in systems (e.g. workplace democracy) through the very people and technology that were part of such systems. The emergence of *Living Labs* (Björgvinsson et al. 2012) is one such speculative space. Instead of prototyping designs in artificial environments isolated from real-world people and contexts, the *Living Lab* places design directly into people's lives in order to provoke different ways of understanding and imagining.

Ethnographers have taken inspiration from such discourses in design. Joachim Halse's (2013, 194) "ethnographies of the possible" is a process of involving participants in materializing ideas, concerns, and speculations to "revitalize their pasts, reflect upon the present, and extrapolate into possible futures" through participatory design (PD). Halse is motivated by involving people in an open-ended dialog about future waste-handling practices, constituted through interactions in the present. In doing so, he raises concerns of his own disciplinary origins of anthropology and the absence of tools for exploring "an ethnography of the possible" with "articulate yet tentative forms" (ibid., 184) with which the possible is conceptualized and made material. When PD engages the imagination as "a fictive reality," it is moderated by "present resources and constraints" (ibid., 184). Halse recommends exploratory prototypes that focus on the user's lived experience as conducive to exploring issues with a product or service before the design is definitively resolved.

Similarly, *Myths of the Near Future* workshop and inquiry was motivated by a concern that design is implicated in a distributed social problem generated through changing patterns of phone usage, such as not answering a particular person's phone calls (blanking), dropping friends by text, and the ubiquitous ways in which a smartphone can monitor bodily functions and movements. These topics are also concerns for digital ethnographers, who are interested in, for instance: the use and experience of mobile and locative media intimacy and privacy (Hjorth et al. 2016 and Locating the Mobile[1]); the design, use, and future imaginaries related to body monitoring technologies (Fors et al. 2016; Pink et al. forthcoming); or social media (Miller 2010).

While ethnographies of mobile media open up new understandings of the ways in which relationships, experience, and everyday life are constituted and how they are changing, they confront different methodological, ethical, and procedural issues to design research in the same field. For ethnographers, ethics in this field is mainly concerned with issues around privacy, anonymity, informed consent, and ensuring minimal risk, harm, and discomfort for the research participants. In contrast, design research and practice confronts how it can be inadvertently implicated in mediating social interactions that might have been unintentional. How can design confront and disrupt what it takes for granted as a custodian of innovation and "future making?" While it is true that ethnographers never know what the actual impact of their research will be, for the designer whose role is to make interventions in the world, this position is exacerbated since they cannot know in advance the future implications of design's outcome. Indeed, we share Gatt and Ingold's (2013, 145) concern about predictive and prescriptive orientations to future making that seek "to conjecture a novel state of affairs as yet unrealized and to specify in advance the steps that need to be taken to get there." Similarly, these were some of the motivating factors for the *Myths of the Near Future* workshop.

Our approach resonates with Gaver's (2014) in embracing ambiguity, idiosyncrasy, and a disposition for risk, confusing, puzzling, or annoying participants, and through this process, precipitating new questions and thinking which contrast with over-determined practices of design. A similar intention is seen in *Myths of the Near Future*, and the broader *Design+Ethnography+Futures* inquiry where, with invited participants, we co-explored ways to question our own disciplinary methods, paradigms, and assumptions, instead of researching the "users" of different technologies. Led by Moline, the workshop sought to undermine participants' assumptions about mobile phones. The disruptive approach sought to produce new ways of knowing about phone use—a familiar, practical, precious, and innocuous technology—by turning it into a research tool. We were interested less in the social science concern with what people (think they) usually do, to instead explore what was made possible when they let go of the fundamental assumptions that frame what they do. This refers not only to assumptions that are articulated verbally, but also to tacit ways of knowing and doing that might not often be spoken about. The following section describes aspects of the workshop that addressed this.

Myths of the Near Future Workshop

The *Myths of the Near Future* workshop took place on June 11, 2014 at the Design Hub, RMIT University. It attracted 15 researchers and postgraduate students largely from RMIT University and several from other universities. The workshop began by acknowledging some of the concerns and assumptions that were part of the ways that people used and thought about their mobile phones. These conversations revolved around two key issues. The first proposed that we increasingly allow our phones to mediate and take charge of our lives, and there was a shared concern among the group about the expansion of images circulating via social media (Facebook, Instagram, and Pinterest), reflecting questions around privacy and control. The second was developed through a discussion about how algorithms mitigate the poor quality of cameraphone lenses and distinguish image from noise by aggregating previous photos taken and stored on the phone (Jordan and Hito 2014).

The first theme was explored through a collective story-telling approach called *spoken portraits* that related primarily to concerns around privacy and control. Moline invited participants to swap their phones with someone in the workshop to review the texts, images, and histories stored on their smartphones. If we understand mobile phones and much of the material that is stored on or shared through them to be subject to different levels of privacy, either in close social media groups or through password protection, this activity challenged assumptions about how mobile media materials are usually shared. Instead of the conventional ways in which mobile media privacy has come to be constituted, in this activity, the participants' privacy was protected through verbal agreements on the limits of access for each phone. This was a deliberate attempt to disrupt existing ways of negotiating privacy, and a few participants opted out of this exercise. The ways people experienced this activity and reported feelings such as discomfort, confusion, and self-consciousness, offers valuable insights into how mobile media privacy is constituted. It also implies interesting future routes of investigation into the creative ways in which privacy is reconstituted when familiar ways of constructing it are disrupted. This is discussed further below.

The second activity, called *visual narrative*, addressed the earlier discussion of how image algorithms are aggregated to create smartphone photographs, which had questioned the idea that such images represent a documentary *veritas*. The participants were invited to disrupt this image-making algorithm by taking photographs that were different to those they would usually make with smartphones, thereby attempting to interrupt the cameraphone's inbuilt system. Moline provided props for this task—rubber tubing, plumbing parts, and electrical wires—to co-construct visual narratives. Participants were invited to make images using their smartphone capabilities, which gave rise to spontaneous, improvised video, photography, and audio recordings of conversations. These were made as the visual narratives were constructed, which offered useful insights into how smartphones were used as part of these collaborations (see Figures 42.1–42.3). The open, playful, and informal approach also helped strangers break the ice, inviting participants to foster trust and spontaneous collaboration.

Participants' photographs of embodied ways of engaging with the props and technologies in the workshop triggered discussions of new ways in which smartphones and apps are becoming part of everyday life. For example, in Figure 42.2, *Image as Self as Code 4*, both through its title and the linear bodily arrangement alongside a composition of stacked boards reflects the earlier group discussion and was explained by a participant as a way of making sense by "visualizing loose concept[s] of how we deal with data, digital documents, and code."

The workshop opened up the possibility for participants to play out some of the core concerns that were revealed earlier in creative and imaginative ways. Props were pulled apart and made into new objects, while some were worn or wrapped around the body. Given license to abandon the conventions of what to do with mobile phones invited new forms of performativity. These emerged through participants' engagements as the workshop itself incorporated the contingencies of the environment in which it was situated. Images were created like digital memorabilia of the workshop experience and titled with evocative names, such as *Broadcasting Out*, *The Tensions of Desire and Repulsion*, *What the Phone Sees When No-One is Looking* (Figure 42.1), *Hidden Private Spaces on the Phone*, *Image of the Image of the Image*, and *Hungry Digital Ghost*. Once created, these were e-mailed to *Design+Ethnography+Futures* and posted on its website.[2] While digital ethnography practice offers us routes toward knowing people's experiences and aspirations relating to mobile media by exploring what they have actually done or think they usually do, a design+ethnography+futures approach engages with participants' experiences, imaginaries, and perceptions of the possible in alternative ways.

Figure 42.2   Image as Self as Code 4 by Laurene Vaughan where participants and boards are stacked together

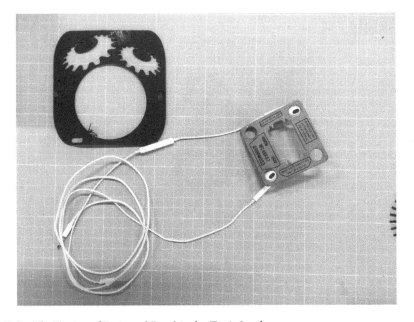

Figure 42.3   The Tensions of Desire and Repulsion by Tania Ivanka

A Process of Mutual Changing through Disruption

Moline's approach described here sought to make the familiar strange. However we were not seeking to simply enable a new way of analytically engaging with those everyday practices, things, and environments that are normally too close for us to see. Rather the approach developed in the workshop was intended to be more provocative, and to invite people to reflect on the uncertainties associated with the feeling that something that you thought you knew has become unfamiliar. The participants' reflective accounts suggest that swapping phones and creating *spoken portraits* with each other were both disruptive and productive strategies for enabling ways to provoke questions. The workshop opened up understandings of changes to social interactions created by technologically mediated communication.

Most participants valued the opportunity to disrupt and reflect on their phone usage. Their casual attitude toward storing personal information on their smartphones was only registered when someone else accessed it. This disruption prompted one participant's realization of how little she remembered about what was stored on her phone:

> As the mobile phone is a "thing" that assembles a lot of activities in my life, that both serves as a tool for organizing—and for disorganizing—I became a bit uncertain of my use of it. And to be quite frank—I had no idea of how little I know of what kind of traces I have left on the phone.

Such defamiliarization activities are summarized by another participant in that: "From that uncertain process the unexpected outcomes became new knowing"; and for her, "[t]he known was transformed from an individual experience of mobile use, to the collective memories created by sharing and making." One other participant described sharing as "naming; speaking out; knowing through naming," saying this was valuable for reflecting on phone usage. Thus such defamiliarization prompted participants to articulate new feelings about aspects of smartphones that they might previously have taken for granted.

The workshop brought forth participants' expertise and knowledge of smartphone use and drew out important implications for research on social communication through ubiquitous computing. As Mike Michael suggests, the socio-technical is more than distinct elements that retain separate identities, but is characterized by a "mutual changing" that "become together" (2012, 170). This relationality emerged in participants' accounts where they and their phones were no longer viewed as separate. They reflected on their relationship to their phones, and how the phone is changing their relationship and understanding. For example, one participant stated, "I know my phone collects and aggregates data of all kinds about me, but rarely see it revealed even in this basic way." He continued, "hearing myself represented through my photos [in the *spoken portrait* activity], . . . made me think about [the photos], and my phone in new ways." For this participant, this activity simultaneously revealed thoughts about other people interpreting his personal phone data:

> I learned a lot about what not only my phone "looks like" (and what I look like) through the specific lens of photos and my sporting apps, but [also] about how we understand phones to show things about people, all of this was also specific to the person doing the looking.

Another participant noted a revival of her awareness of how she communicated with herself, which opened up a new way to think about the phone: "not just as a communication device with other people and 'the world' but with us [ourselves], in the case of alarms, reminders, tracking apps, photos, and notes." The reflective accounts glimpses at the "mutual changing" described by Michael, a process of realization and understanding that they are changed by their phones as much as the phone is servicing their changing needs.

Design+Ethnography+Futures: Embracing Discomfort and Uncertainty

Conventional digital ethnography research into mobile phone use has prioritized interviews and observational research with users. Ethnographers at RMIT University's *Digital Ethnography Research Centre* such as Hjorth, Horst, Pink, and Tacchi have used methods such as re-enactment, video touring, and participant mapping to engage participants and their mobile devices more directly with researchers (Pink et al. 2016a). These have created ways to learn about the emotional, sensory, and often unspoken ways people experience and appropriate mobile technologies. The disruptive, improvisory, and co-exploratory methods in the *Myths of the Near Future* workshop rather differently posed new questions about the possible and the imagined relationships that could emerge between participants and their smartphones.

However, a disruptive research exploration to interrogate everyday habitual activities (like smartphone use) and fields (such as HCI, design, ethnography, research) does not necessarily feel comfortable, and can generate resistance. This was sensed most acutely in the phone swapping activity, something that disrupted social conventions, even when presented as a collaborative interrogation of these very norms and habits. Participants' observations about their "confusion" with the "open[ness] of the brief[s]" were explained in feedback as "discomfort." One participant noted that others needed "additional guidance about the purposes of that experimental making as a way of knowing more how to act, how to begin, what to do." This account of disorientation matched our own observation of a pronounced frustration in one participant who opted out from the phone swapping exercise, subsequently leading to three others on her table doing the same. Another commented that: "We were certain that our 'true self' would be revealed—but we were uncertain about what that would be in tangible, named terms," and, "it felt as a much more risky act—not because of risk of harassment, but because of the feeling of sharing a chaotic unknown—without the effort of shaping or curating it for communication." When we compare these comments and experiences that emerged from a design workshop-based research context with how participants have shared their private social media groups and cameraphone images with researchers in an ethnographic research context, there are interesting insights and comparisons to be drawn. As Pink and colleagues have shown through their research into privacy and locative media in families, when participants showed and shared their mobile media images and activities, they spontaneously demonstrated close emotional connections to these materials, which were not expressed in the spoken interviews. It invoked a sense of authenticity of feeling that was associated with the use of mobile media.

Such affective dimensions of smartphone usage also emerged in the feedback. One participant described a renewed attachment to the phone, claiming that he "left the workshop feeling a bit more affectionate towards my phone [because] it's not only the big data, what's collected about me through my use, but that as an object it can be revealing to another person." We see this as resonating with our own interpretations of the workshop outcomes and a characteristic that is important for collective experiences that build and institute conventions that comprise the social-technical world.

Indeed the workshop manifested the participants' self-consciousness about revealing themselves through their smartphone apps and content, despite being encouraged to "negotiate different boundaries (go and no go zones)" as one participant put it, to the point that it inhibited some from participating in certain activities. These accounts of discomfort and resisting the brief are interesting for us, not because we are concerned that they might reveal flaws in our approach, but because we rarely hear about them. Gaver (2014) is an exception here, willingly sharing projects that "aren't working," and labeling some as "failures." Halse (2013, 188) similarly alludes to the importance of research to reveal "conflicts of interest," refusals and disappointments and the danger of glossing over these for "idealized future stories." This indicates the risky, contested, and contingent nature of participatory and speculative design research.

Building on this, *Design+Ethnography+Futures* creates workshop-based research spaces through which it endeavors to explore disruptive emotions because they provoke questions of ourselves that we might not like to examine. They also reveal how neither the present nor change processes are simple to understand or to design for—thus showing how such work complicates any ambitions to use such research processes to inform "better" design, something that we had already rejected as a possibility from the outset. Instead the implication is that since the present is messy, and complex to research for ethnographers (see Law 2004), we need to regard processes of change, and possible futures as equally messy. They cannot be reduced to simple predictable contexts in which we might design neat future-oriented solutions.

Where To From Here?

Within the framework of ethnographies of the possible (Halse 2013) we consider improvisation, disruption, and uncertainty to be extremely valuable for understanding the affective dimensions of adjusting to the changing technological and emotional landscapes of digital media ecologies. As we have shown, the act of making the everyday strange, and inviting participants to innovate in an environment where their existing assumptions and certainties were challenged, enabled them to reimagine their relationships to their technologies. It also corresponded with our aim to disrupt overdetermined notions of design, technology, and how these shape our futures. This approach explored in *Design+Ethnography+Futures* opens up a productive extension to the mash up of research approaches in PD, speculative design, design anthropology, and Halse's ethnographies of the possible in ways that overlap with the interests of digital ethnography. The disruptive strategies we developed also therefore show the benefits of surrendering the expectations (Akama et al. 2015) of the disciplinary and social norms of design and ubiquitous technology.

For digital ethnography practice, *Design+Ethnography+Futures* is not intended to be an add-on or a way to make ethnographic practice or techniques better than they already are. Instead it creates a specific agenda that has different aims that orientate it toward exploring and performing the possible and the imagined, but yet is never completely disentangled from the practice of either discipline. In this chapter we have sought to examine this by putting smartphones—which are both a focus of digital ethnography research and featured in the *Myths of the Near Future* workshop—at the center of the discussion. Both research agendas have brought to the fore similar interests and concerns. This indicates that it would indeed be fruitful to bring together such methods and research questions in stronger relief to each other in future work. As such, our aim here has primarily been to present a proposal, some theoretical framing, and examples of disruptive techniques that sit at the interface between existing knowledge, practice, and interests of digital ethnography and design, and to demonstrate the possibilities for creative and future-focused thought and practice that emerge from this.

Acknowledgments

Thanks to the workshop participants, Shana Agid, Natalie Araujo, Craig Batty, Marsha Berry, David Carlin, Melisa Duque, Annie Fergusson, Nicholas Hansen, Christoph Hewett, Tania Ivanka, Alexia Maddox, Sean Redmond, Janine Sisson, Dagny Stuedahl, and Laurene Vaughan.

Design+Ethnography+Futures is a research program that spans the Digital Ethnography Research Centre, Design Futures Lab and the Design Research Institute at RMIT University. We thank these research clusters for providing funding and support to enable this work.

Notes

1 See http://locatingthemobile.net/
2 See http://d-e-futures.com/events/workshop-3-myths-of-the-near-future-2/

References

Akama, Yoko, Sarah Pink, and Annie Fergusson. 2015. "Design+Ethnography+Futures: Surrendering in Uncertainty." *Proceedings of the 33rd Annual ACM Conference Extended Abstracts on Human Factors in Computing Systems.* Seoul, Republic of Korea, April 18–23: 531–42.

Björgvinsson, Erling, Pelle Ehn, and Per-Anders Hillgren. 2012. "Design Things and Design Thinking: Contemporary Participatory Design Challenges." *Design Issues* 28(3): 101–16.

Dourish, Paul. 2006. "Implications for Design." *Proceedings of the SIGCHI Conference on Human Factors in Computing Systems*, Montréal, Québec, Canada, April 22–28: 541–50.

Dunne, Anthony and Fiona Raby. 2013. *Speculative Everything: Design, Fiction, and Social Dreaming.* Cambridge, MA: The MIT Press.

Fors, Vaike, Martin Berg, and Sarah Pink. 2016. "Capturing the Ordinary: Imagining the User in Designing and Using Automatic Photographic Lifelogging Technologies." In *Lifelogging: Digital Self-tracking and Lifelogging—Between Disruptive Technology and Cultural Transformation*, edited by Stefan Selke, 111–28. Springer VS.

Gatt, Caroline and Tim Ingold. 2013. "From Description to Correspondence: Anthropology in Real Time." In *Design Anthropology*, edited by Wendy Gunn, Tom Otto, and Rachel Charlotte-Smith, 139–58. London: Bloomsbury.

Gaver, Bill. 2014. "Recent Studio Research." Talk at UNSW. www.niea.unsw.edu.au/events/symposiumworkshops-feral-experimental (accessed September 1, 2014).

Gaver, Bill, Anthony Dunne, and Elena Pacenti. 1999. "Cultural Probes." *Interactions* 6, 1 January/February: 21–9.

Gunn, Wendy and Jared Donovan, eds. 2012. *Design and Anthropology.* Surrey, UK: Ashgate.

Gunn, Wendy, Tom Otto, and Rachel Charlotte-Smith, eds. 2013. *Design Anthropology: Theory and Practice.* London, New York: Bloomsbury.

Halse, Joachim. 2013. "Ethnographies of the Possible." In *Design Anthropology: Theory and Practice*, edited by Wendy Gunn, Tom Otto, and Rachel Charlotte-Smith, 180–96. London, New York: Bloomsbury.

Hjorth, Larissa, Heather Horst, Sarah Pink, Baohua Zhou, Fumitoshi Kato, Genevieve Bell et al. 2016. "Locating the Mobile: Genealogies of Locative Media in Tokyo, Shanghai and Melbourne." In *Lifestyle Media in Asia*, edited by Fran Martin and Tania Lewis. London: Routledge.

Jordan, Marvin and Steyerl Hito. 2014. "Politics of Post-Representation." *DisMagazine.* http://dismagazine.com/disillusioned-2/62143/hitosteyerl-politics-of-post-representation/ (accessed June 30, 2014).

Law, John. 2004. *After Method: Mess in Social Science Research.* London: Routledge.

Michael, Mike. 2012. "De-Signing the Object of Sociology: Toward an 'Idiotic' Methodology." *The Sociological Review* 60 (S1): 166–83.

Miller, Danny. 2010. *Tales from Facebook.* Oxford: Polity.

Moline, Katherine. 2011. "Equipment for the Actual Complexities and Intricacies of String: Super-Tube, Super-Suction, Super-String." Presented at *RED Objects—Research in Experimental Design*: Objects, COFASpace; College of Fine Arts, Paddington. http://redobjects.unsw.edu.au/people/dr-katherine-moline/.

———. 2012. "The Legacy of Historical Design Collectives in Contemporary Experimental Design: A Case Study of Global Tools and Digestion." In *The Design Collective: An Approach to Practice*, edited by Harriet Edquist and Laurene Vaughan, 121–40. Newcastle upon Tyne: Cambridge Scholars Publishing.

———. 2014. "Dingo Logic." In *Feral Experimental: New Design Thinking, National Institute for Experimental Arts and UNSW Galleries*, edited by Katherine Moline. Sydney: University of New South Wales.

———. 2015a. "Experimental Practice: Provocations." In *Experimental Practice: Provocations In and Out of Design*, edited by Katherine Moline, Brad Haylock, and Laurene Vaughan, 2–3. Melbourne: RMIT Design Hub.

———. 2015b. "Myths of the Near Future 2: Equipment." In *Experimental Thinking/Design Practices*, edited by Katherine Moline and Peter Hall. Brisbane: Griffith University Art Gallery.

Pink, Sarah, Heather Horst, John Postill, Larissa Hjorth, Tania Lewis, and Jo Tacchi. 2016a. *Digital Ethnography: Principles and Practice*. London: Sage.

Pink, Sarah, Kerstin Leder Mackley, Val Mitchell, Garreth Wilson, and Tracy Bhamra. 2016b. "Refiguring Digital Interventions for Energy Demand Reduction: Designing for Life in the Digital Material Home." In *Digital Materialities: Anthropology and Design*, edited by Sarah Pink, Elisenda Ardèvol, and Dèbora Lanzeni, 79–97. Oxford: Bloomsbury.

Pink, Sarah, Vaike Fors, and Martin Berg. Forthcoming. "Visual and Sensory Methodologies for Researching the Experience of Physical Activity." In *Routledge Handbook of Physical Cultural Studies*, edited by Michael Silk, David L. Andrews, and Holly Thorpe. London: Routledge.

Rendell, Jane. 2013. "A Way with Words: Feminists Writing Architectural Design Research." In *Architectural Design Research*, edited by Murray Fraser, 117–36. London: Ashgate.

43

MORE-THAN-HUMAN LAB

Creative Ethnography after Human Exceptionalism

Anne Galloway

Haere mai. Welcome.

This story starts with an introduction so that the reader can know who I am, and how I have come to know what I know. My name is Anne Galloway. My mother's family is Canadian and my father's family is British. Born and raised outside both places, for the past seven years I have been tauiwi, or non-Maori, a settler in Aotearoa-New Zealand. I have always lived between cultures and have had to forge my own sense of belonging. Today I am in my home, on a small rural block in the Akatarawa Valley of the Tararua ranges, at the headwaters of the Waikanae River, on the ancestral lands of Muaūpoko and Te Āti Awa, with my partner, a cat, seven ducks, five sheep—four of whom I hope are pregnant—and a multitude of extraordinary wildlife.

The only way I know how to understand myself is in relation to others, and my academic career has been dedicated to understanding vital relationships between things in the world. Most recently, I founded and lead the More-Than-Human Lab (http://morethanhumanlab. org/), an experimental research initiative at Victoria University of Wellington. Everything I have done has led me to this point, but for the purposes of this chapter I want to pull on a single thread. This is a love story for an injured world, and it begins with broken bones . . .

Thinking with the *BoneKnitter*

In the final year of a three-year research project I slipped, fell, snapped two bones, and looked down to see my foot facing the wrong direction. Although I did not know it at the time, in that moment my research bearing changed. There was surgery, and complications, and a long convalescence. As expected by others, and myself, I rallied and finished the project. But in the end, only one element of the research embodied the vulnerability I had felt, and captured the experience of care that had allowed me to get it done.

Counting Sheep: NZ Merino in an Internet of Things was a Royal Society of New Zealand Marsden-funded research project that explored how the production and consumption of New Zealand merino wool and meat might be (re)shaped by emerging technologies like the Internet of Things. The first part of the project comprised a multi-site ethnography of NZ merino breeding, and case study of industry production and marketing strategies. The second part of the project translated this ethnographic work into a set of four speculative design propositions for public engagement. They are archived online at: http://countingsheep.info/.

With one exception, our fictional design scenarios demonstrated a tacit acceptance of technological progress. Although sometimes quite fantastical they were also notably conservative, either maintaining the cultural status quo or, in the more dystopian versions, amplifying current inequalities. Put a bit differently, although couched in the language and imagery of individual empowerment, the primary beneficiaries of these technocultural futures would be corporations and governments. Perhaps predictably, these designs most often elicited polarized responses: people were either very much for or against them.

The *BoneKnitter* was different. Industrial design student Dani Clode and I designed it to radically reimagine relations among people, animals, and technology—and to use care as its driving ethic. We designed a set of physical models and imagined a fictional service, and the online scenario (http://countingsheep.info/boneknitter.html/) comprised a set of photographs with the following text:

> The *BoneKnitter* is a dream for slow technology that honors New Zealand's natural environment and pays tribute to generations of Māori and Pākehā merino growers, shearers and wool handlers.
>
> We envision a future where orthopedic casts are crafted from all natural materials and slowly knitted over broken bones. Where a medical caregiver offers us a comfy chair and brings us a hot cuppa with some gingernut biscuits, before running wool into the machine and hand-cranking it to life.
>
> Inspired by early twentieth-century home knitting machines, we imagine a *BoneKnitter* crafted from sustainable native rimu wood and naturally stained. Three rows of different sized needles knit three different weights of merino wool and native plant materials into three separate layers—one on top of the other (Figure 43.1).

Figure 43.1 More-Than-Human Lab, *BoneKnitter* detail. Copyright Anne Galloway

Each cast is made from single origin NZ merino wool, and as we comfortably wait for each layer of the cast to be knitted, we are invited to learn about the people, places, and animals that produced it.

Figure 43.2 More-Than-Human Lab, *BoneKnitter* detail. Copyright Anne Galloway

We see individual casts crafted from the range of natural merino wool colors, both plainly styled and patterned after the topographic contours of the land where the sheep were raised, or the genetic sequence of the sheep that produced the wool.

Each cast comes with data histories for each animal, and we are given personal collections of photos and stories to take home.

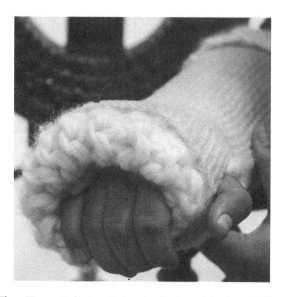

Figure 43.3 More-Than-Human Lab, *BoneKnitter* detail. Copyright Anne Galloway

The base layer of the cast uses ultra-fine 15-micron merino wool; the middle layer uses medium 21-micron merino wool; and the top layer of the cast uses fine 19-micron merino wool.

The gauze-like first layer is knitted from merino wool infused with medicinal manuka honey and kawakawa extract. The wool's natural lanolin helps keep the skin from becoming dry and itchy, and manuka and kawakawa plants have long been used in rongoā Māori to heal wounds and ease aches.

The second, middle layer of the cast takes full advantage of merino wool's natural ability to stay warm when it is cold, and cool when it is hot. The thick and chunky spin of the yarn also provides padding to protect the bones while they heal, along with a soft and attractive cuff over the edges of the hard cast.

The third, and top, layer uses merino wool spun with NZ flax or harakeke fibers, infused with native bio-resins that set as hard as fiberglass. In Māori songs, harakeke often evokes human relationships and bonds, and its presence in the cast symbolically ties producers to the people who live with—and heal through—their products.

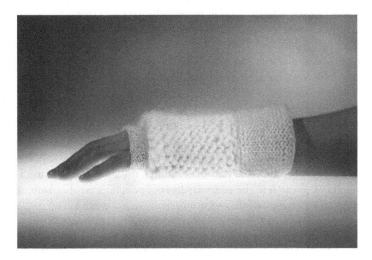

Figure 43.4   More-Than-Human Lab, *BoneKnitter* detail. Copyright Anne Galloway

Wool enters the *BoneKnitter* through holes in the top of the barrel, where it catches the first needle. The machine's knitting speed is controlled by the hand-crank, and a carved wooden platform is provided to rest the broken limb during the knitting process.

Looking to the future of medical products, we see timeless traditions of people caring for animals, the land, and each other.

The *BoneKnitter* is a highly technologized object set within a broader ecology of networked data technologies, but we strove to keep the technology in the background. As a product, the *BoneKnitter* is a beautiful wooden barrel mounted on a stand, but its story is found in the processes of being cared for by other people, animals, and technologies—and in its implicit invitation to care for other people, animals, and technologies.

The public survey responses to the *BoneKnitter* were also different. Some respondents focused on the object itself:

"Mixing modern and old fashioned technologies because there is value in both [is a good idea]."—Industry Respondent, NZ

"I think the idea is fabulous. I like the idea of using natural products, especially in a way that I would never have thought of, but make logical sense."—Farm Respondent, NZ

But, for me, the most interesting—and inspiring—responses went beyond the object:

"The BoneKnitter is beautifully crafted and I like that it is a low tech device. [It's a good] idea that it takes time, allowing the wearer and operator time to talk and share stories, something so often missing in the medical world where patients are seen as units of time and where medical professionals do not have the time to listen."—University Respondent, UK

"I am reminded of how, during treatment for cancer, I was advised against what turned out to be many smart choices—like eating from my own garden—and simply due to germophobia. It's sickening to think that necessary precautions against needless exposure to harmful pathogens can slide so easily into the kind of hysteria that reigns in current medical practice, and, I fear, is the main barrier to R&D of this kind of product."—University Respondent, US

"I remember having a plaster cast when I broke my arm when I was a kid and this seems like it would have been far more comfortable . . . I like the natural materials and the slow process of making the cast."—University Respondent, AU

In our other fictional scenarios, viewers responded to the technologies within the prescribed boundaries. The *BoneKnitter* instead conjured memories and evoked imagined futures beyond our vision. In other words, it moved people.

Looking back now, I see the *BoneKnitter* as the first instance of a promise I still strive to uphold: to ground my research in the everyday lives of people, animals, plants, and lands, and to imagine radical and caring possibilities for who and what we can become.

Interlude: Toward a Fantastic (Digital) Ethnography

For the past 30 or 40 years, ethnographers have explicitly acknowledged our role in writing culture, and many women anthropologists have explored different kinds of stories and different forms of storytelling (Abu-Lughod 1991; Behar and Gordon 1996). More recently, Underberg and Zorn (2013) argue that anthropologists bring "much-needed attention to considerations of power, embodiment, and identity markers in digital culture" (p. 8), and digital ethnography is a particularly fertile sub-field for the discipline as it "involves adapting and transforming . . . ethnographic storytelling techniques across multiple forms of new media" (p. 10). The work of the More-Than-Human Lab is situated within this broader sub-field, but through its connections with design research also seeks to push its boundaries.

To a certain degree ethnographers make up people every time we present a viewpoint or activity through a composite character, and fictional personas and locations have long provided anonymity for research participants as well as distance from difficult topics or contentious actions. But I am particularly interested in ethnographic fiction, which is often described as a story that could have been "discovered" and told by an anthropologist. Accordingly, even though made up, these narratives focus on cultural life as if it were actually experienced by real people. Within such a messy, border-crossing genre (Narayan, 1999) I would include novels written by anthropologists such as Camilla Gibb (see for example, 2005) and non-anthropologists such as Andrea Levy (see for example, 2004). Regardless of background, what these novels have in common is an emphasis on thickly descriptive realism.

But what if ethnography took inspiration from more speculative fiction and design? Novelists such as Ursula K. Le Guin (see for example, 1969) and Octavia Butler (see for example, 1993) are well known for stories with strong anthropological concerns, as well as their feminist critiques of techno-science. Similarly, Anab Jain, co-founder of Superflux studio, has said their speculative design "aims to cut through established narratives about the present and the future, often using stories, cautionary tales, super fictions, scenarios and arti-facts to engage with the breadth of often exciting, yet unsettling possibilities that lie ahead of us" (2013, n.p.). While works like these can be seen to bring together the interests of digital ethnography and ethnographic fiction described above, I wonder if we might also explore the potential of less realist narratives.

In her essay "The Critics, the Monsters, and the Fantasists," Ursula Le Guin (2009) argues for the value of fantasy narratives, a point to which I will return later. For now, I would like to high-light the essay's critique of fictional realism, as Le Guin reminds us that not only is our distinction between factual and fictional narrative historically quite recent, but that we have forgotten how to even read fantasy. Imagine, she suggests, if we were to "judge modern realist fiction by the standards of fantasy." We would find ourselves, she continues, faced with "a narrow focus on daily details of contemporary human affairs; trapped in representationalism, suffocatingly unimaginative, frequently trivial, and ominously anthropocentric" (p. 28). In other words, Le Guin's essay challenges us to probe what exists beyond realism, beyond anthropocentrism, and to carefully question what this space can and cannot bring forth. If "good" science fiction is often predicated on its ability to be scientifically plausible—just as "good" ethnographic fiction is meant to be culturally plausible—then to escape, or exceed, these ways of thinking and doing may require the incredible, unruly, premodern sensibility that infuses the fantastic. As Le Guin explains, the fantastic reminds us of "what we have denied, what we have exiled ourselves from" and that "humanity is not lord and master, is not central, is not even important" (pp. 38–9).

This concern with relationality is also integral to digital ethnography, as Pink et al. (2015) remind us that social relations are more and more often embodied in, and mediated through, digital technologies. The relationship between humans and nonhumans has become a funda-mental focus of ethnography and we continue to develop new methods for investigating the dynamic relations among people, places, and technologies. Nonetheless, I believe that most digital ethnography is still very human-centered and that we need to push ourselves to actively engage with more nonhuman animals, and with other forms of both organic and inorganic life.

Care After Human Exceptionalism

What if we refuse to uncouple nature and culture? What if we deny that human beings are exceptional? What if we stop speaking and listening only to ourselves?

The More-Than-Human Lab combines ethnography and creative research methods to explore more-than-human (Whatmore 2006) worlds through what Haraway (2015, 160) refers to as "webs of speculative fabulation, speculative feminism, science fiction, and scientific fact." We work to go beyond definition or judgment, in order to think *with* the world and not *for* the world.

I want to recognize "the vulnerability faced by certain human populations and ecologies" (Vaughn 2016, n.p.) and attend to the historical trajectories and impermanent assemblages (Tsing 2015; Yusoff 2016) that characterize life on earth. Following Braidotti, I see the posthuman Anthropocene "as an amazing opportunity to decide together what and who we are capable of becoming . . . [and] a chance to identify opportunities for resistance and empowerment on a planetary scale" (2013, 195). I also want to take seriously Todd's (2016) reminder that these dreams are not new, that Indigenous (and other oppressed) people have been "dreaming of an otherwise" for hundreds of years, and that our "ability to face the past, present, and future with care—tending to relationships between people, place, and stories— will be crucial as we face the challenges of the Anthropocene" (n.p.).

This focus on a feminist and decolonized ethics of care is, I believe, the direction that ethnographic critique needs to take if we want to thrive—or even just survive—in a wounded world. As Haraway put it, "caring means becoming subject to the unsettling obligation of curiosity, which requires knowing more at the end of the day than at the beginning" (2008, 36). And since caring is always also relational practice, or something we do with human/ nonhuman others, Mol et al. (2010) argue that a focus on actual, everyday practices allows us to ask questions about what constitutes "good" and "bad" care, or "too much" and "not enough" care.

Puig de la Bellacasa (2012, 209) also reminds us that *how* we care is very important, as:

[C]are can also extinguish the subtleties of attending to the needs of an "other" required for careful relationality. All too easily it can lead to appropriating the recipients of "our" care, instead of relating ourselves to them [. . .] Appropriating the experience of another precludes us from creating significant otherness, that is, from *affirming* those with whom we build a relation. How to care for the "oppressed" is far from being self-evident.

And, again, Mol et al. (2010, 13) distinguish care from justice, as care constitutes situated knowledges and practices rather than ethical principles:

In the ethics of care it was stressed that in practice, principles are rarely productive. Instead, local solutions to specific problems need to be worked out. They may involve "justice" but other norms (fairness, kindness, compassion, generosity) may be equally or more, important—and not in a foundational way, but as orientations among others.

It is this being and doing (differently) with others that underpins everything the More-Than-Human Lab seeks to explore.

Finale: Imagining Otherwise

As a way of wrapping up this story, I would like to briefly return to Le Guin's (2009, 40–1) argument for why we should take fantasy fiction seriously:

In reinventing the world of intense, unreproducible, local knowledge, seemingly by a denial or evasion of current reality, fantasists are perhaps trying to assert and explore a larger reality than we now allow ourselves. They are trying to restore the sense—to regain the knowledge—that there is somewhere else, anywhere else, where other people may live another kind of life. The literature of imagination, even when tragic, is reassuring, not necessarily in the sense of offering nostalgic comfort, but because it offers a world large enough to contain alternatives and therefore offers hope.

I believe this perspective is consistent with, and complementary to, the more-than-human ethics of care outlined above. I also see this kind of critique as a valuable addition to, or extension of, digital ethnography in the Anthropocene. As more technological devices connect people to things in the world, and as more data are collected about people and things, digital ethnography stands to make an important contribution to our understanding of constantly shifting relations. When combined with speculative design that translates realist narratives into fantastic stories, I also believe we can inject hope into spaces, times, and relations where it seems most unlikely.

Although the experiments being done through the More-Than-Human Lab are still in their early stages, I see incredible potential in developing more critical and creative ways of doing ethnography. Postgraduate students are pursuing a variety of multispecies ethnographies and technological interventions, and my own research is currently focused on how farmers and veterinarians care for livestock and ensure the animals have "good" deaths as well as "good" lives. It is my hope that telling fantastical stories about these practices will provide new and more sustainable possibilities for people to live with animals, plants, and the land. Our shared futures might depend on it.

References

Abu-Lughod, Lila. 1991. "Writing Against Culture." In *Recapturing Anthropology: Working in the Present*, edited by R. G. Fox, 137–62. Santa Fe: School of American Research Press.

Behar, Ruth and Deborah A. Gordon. 1996. *Women Writing Culture*. Berkeley, CA: University of California Press.

Braidotti, Rosi. 2013. *The Posthuman*. Cambridge: Polity Press.

Butler, Octavia. 1993. *The Parable of the Sower*. New York: Aspect Press.

Gibb, Camilla. 2005. *Sweetness in the Belly*. Toronto: Anchor Canada.

Haraway, Donna. 2008. *When Species Meet*. Minneapolis, MN: University of Minnesota Press.

——. 2015. "Anthropocene, Capitalocene, Plantationocene, Chthulucene: Making Kin." *Environmental Humanities* 6: 159–65.

Jain, Anab. 2013. "Staying with the Trouble." Conference presentation at Poptech 2013, 24–26 October, Camden, Maine, USA. Transcript available at: http://superflux.in/work/staying-with-the-trouble

Le Guin, Ursula K. 1969. *The Left Hand of Darkness*. New York: Ace Books.

——. 2009. "The Critics, the Monsters, and the Fantasists." In *Cheek by Jowl: Talks & Essays on How & Why Fantasy Matters*, 25–42, Seattle: Aqueduct Press.

Levy, Andrea. 2004. *Small Island*. London: Headline.

Mol, Annemarie, Ingunn Moser and Jeannette Pols. 2010. "Care: Putting Practice into Theory." In *Care in Practice: On Tinkering in Clinics, Homes and Farms*, edited by Annemarie Mol, Ingunn Moser and Jeannette Pols, 7–25. Bielefeld: Transcript-Verlag.

Narayan, Kirin. 1999. "Ethnography and Fiction: Where Is the Border?" *Anthropology and Humanism* 24: 134–47.

Pink, Sarah, Heather Horst, John Postill, Larissa Hjorth, Tania Lewis and Jo Tacchi. 2015. *Digital Ethnography: Principles and Practice*. London: Sage.

Puig de la Bellacasa, Maria. 2012. "'Nothing Comes Without its World': Thinking With Care." *The Sociological Review* 60: 197–216.

Todd, Zoe. 2016. "Relationships." *Theorizing the Contemporary*, Cultural Anthropology website. www.culanth.org/fieldsights/799-relationships (accessed January 21, 2016).

Tsing, Anna Lowenhaupt. 2015. *The Mushroom at the End of the World: On the Possibility of Life in Capitalist Ruins*. Princeton, NJ: Princeton University Press.

Underberg, Natalie M. and Elayne Zorn. 2013. *Digital Ethnography: Anthropology, Narrative and New Media*. Austin, TX: University of Texas Press.

Vaughn, Sarah. 2016. "Vulnerability." *Theorizing the Contemporary*, Cultural Anthropology website. www.culanth.org/fieldsights/791-vulnerability (accessed January 21, 2016).

Whatmore, Sarah. 2006. "Materialist Returns: Practising Cultural Geography in and for a More-Than-Human World." *Cultural Geographies* 13(4): 600–9.

Yusoff, Kathryn. 2016. "Anthropogenesis: Origins and Endings in the Anthropocene." *Theory, Culture & Society* 33(2): 3–28.

44

USING FICTION TO EXPLORE SOCIAL FACTS

The Laboratory of Speculative Ethnology

Elizabeth Chin

Here in the savage slot we are not occupants of your designated past we are steeping in our imagined futures, quilted together of pain and purpose, nipped and stitched, enwrapping our bruised, burnished limbs in swathes of Dutch wax fabric.

The Laboratory for Speculative Ethnology is a direct response to race and racism in the worlds of art, design, and anthropology. Built upon a commitment to explore realness guided by principles of antiracism and afrofuturism, the voice of the Lab is one that says those unsayable things, those things that tend to remain dirty secrets held inside ivory towers and white-walled studios. The notion of "the savage slot" was elegantly and thoughtfully delineated by Haitian anthropologist Michel-Rolph Trouillot (2003). His move was to identify the problematic ideological space occupied by anthropology as a discipline. (With this move a host of "native" anthropologists who may or may not slide into that savage slot so easily were also identified.) Trouillot situates the establishment of anthropology as a discipline and as an essential part of an emergent Western discourse he describes as "order-utopia-savagery" (28).

In historicizing the emergence of anthropology within a larger field of meaning-making, Trouillot identifies the *raison d'être* of anthropology as enmeshed within a Western ideological world ordering that relegated its "others" to the margins: the savage slot. In challenging both the realness and the necessity for such ordering, Trouillot calls anthropology to reexamine its own emergence and existence. "There is no savage slot," he argues, going on to assert, "the Other cannot be contained within a residual category" (27). The Laboratory explores, in part, the act of embodying this refusal to be contained.

We live now a centered time and place without margin. We lived then before you discovered us. You in your white worlds, white walls, white studios, white coats, white houses, white pages, freshly white, purely lightened to a clarity that obscures its own interiority you don't exist and you don't even know it.

There are few social spaces more unrelentingly white than the art or design studio. White walls, white people, white culture, white ideology. White, white, white. It is the profoundly unreflective whiteness typical of white normativity, typical of what DiAngelo (2011) identifies in her essay "White Fragility," a whiteness full of unique individuals, who also assign to themselves the ability to stand for the universal. This unreflective whiteness, in design territories, is unable to excavate (or is perhaps uninterested in excavating) the racist and sexist ideologies embedded in Bauhaus-derived aesthetics that for so many constitute "good design." These aesthetics are a materialization of chronopolitics, an ideological stance that positions whiteness toward the future and relegates blackness toward the past. In this space, white excellence is self-evident and self-perpetuating: as I write there are 100 full-time faculty staff at my institution. There are two women of color (I am one of them) and only one black man among that 100. Nearly 80 percent of the full-time faculty is white. We only hire the best, of course! Every department chair is white. Does this mean there are no good enough people beyond whiteness to fill their seats? I witnessed one department chair claim proudly that "everyone I have hired in my department is a personal friend of mine." The college does not, of course, have an affirmative action procedure.

Along with this unreflective whiteness is a practice and orientation based almost entirely on neoliberal values, which might help to explain why it is remarkably devoid of an articulated politics. The Lab materially and performatively asserts that the digital, design, and particularly what is called "design for good" require being situated contextually with relation to inequality, racism, colonialism, and sexism. This is a topic that rarely emerges in designerly spheres, except in realms that are highly academic and, thus, peripheral to mainstream design (here I am thinking of people such as Josh Berson, Benjamin Bratton, or Grant Kester, for instance, whose work addresses these politics in powerful ways (Bratton 2013; Berson 2015; Kester 2011)).

Technology is us it is how we see you. Sensor here sensor there, gps tracking activated, cameras capture your image and when we ride the trains we dance, fringe and leds light the way.

Historian Rayvon Fouché forces us to bear witness to the political heaviness of technology when he proposes four eras defining technology and race in the United States. Each of these eras is predicated on the centrality of blackness to his formulations. The first era is characterized by conditions where enslaved people themselves constitute technology. His fourth, and current, era is characterized by "devices that nostalgically reference the analog realm" accompanied by "a nostalgia of in-need ethnic others to be saved" (2008, 62). Fouché expressly identifies this saving impulse with missionary energies directed to those in-need ethnic others, occupants of Trouillot's savage slot.

I want to make a direct connection between this missionary impulse and Technology for development (T4D) and Information Computer Technology for Development (ICT4D) efforts. The digital is central to each of these, whether as a medium for production, or as an element of completed projects or products. In the current epoch, technology boosters are the new missionaries to the developing world, working on an assumption that Africans are empty vessels to be filled (Fouché 2008). Yet these empty Africans are as fictitious as white people themselves. James Baldwin (1984) claims that there are no white people, that whiteness is a moral choice and not a manifest reality. He might be right; he might be crazy, but looking at LifeStraw and other design objects proclaiming their ability to save lives in the third world, the self-serving moral implications of whiteness are hard to miss.

Your vision is the only one; your hunger to know others feeds your emptiness, your help is a generous, racist love that birthed the natural history museum packing the "past" behind glass frozen forms forever doing their pastness, the timeless then that never is now no matter how far we go.

Think Donna Haraway and "Teddy Bear Patriarchy" (1984)—the museum houses as much ideology as it does anything else. With their natural historical invention, *The Couple in the Cage* (1993), Coco Fusco and Gabriel Gómez Pena reanimated the human zoo experience that had been built into world's fairs and other expositions since the discovery of "natives." Dioramas as ideology under glass. We can see the ideology should we make the attempt. Anthropologists have discussed the problematics of museums in the ways they materialize race and racism (Weismantel 2001; Candelario 2007; Conklin 2013) yet we lack the tools to remake it effectively. For their part, designers too often mistake beautiful things for universal "meaning," and end up imposing colonial ideas and worse, without adequate recognition of the politics of their work (Tunstall 2013). The Laboratory of Speculative Ethnology is one attempt to take the best from each field and offer up something of theoretical sophistication that makes its argument from what it is, materially and digitally.

In other words, take your LifeStraw and shove it—into your composting toilet.

In the territory that might be shared by ethnography, design, and the digital, designers often take risks that anthropologists simply cannot imagine, and that is very often a good thing. From an ethnographic point of view, however, these risks are too often under-informed, drawing from first world sensibilities to solve problems in the developing world. Usually the focus is upon *problems that make first world people uncomfortable*. It is amazing, for instance, how many young designers have gone to Africa, discovered the problem of access to pure water, and created a solution to that problem. So many solutions! This origin story is shared both by LifeStraw and the Pure Water Bottle. Both won numerous design prizes and accolades: "Taking on the noble challenge of finding a cure for water sterilization, Timothy Whitehead's bottle cleans water in just 2mins flat," gushed Gizmodo (Hannaford 2015). *Forbes* magazine included LifeStraw among the "ten things that will change the way we live" (Ely 2015). The Pure Water Bottle, it turns out, was never a solution to anything, since it never went into production. Like so many water filtration projects, it was a wonderful design exercise. The self-confident enthusiasm for these solutions is invigorating, but has little foundation. There are hundreds of solutions to the water problem, each with a well-paid team of researchers, and often its own test site in Kenya or India or some other savage slot spot. In just a couple of minutes on Google I found LifeStraw, Life Sack, PureMadi, SteriPen, Solarball, a water purifying bike setup, ceramic filters, some coated with silver nanoparticles, particle embedded paper filters, cotton fabrics treated with nano inks, slow sand filters, carbon filters.

With so many problem-solving solutions around, why is it that the statistics about access to water have not changed appreciably? A key reason is that these are product-oriented solutions, and these kinds of solutions very neatly sidestep the infrastructure question. Moreover, nearly all these products have short lifetimes, need regular replacement, and in local terms are exorbitantly costly. LifeStraw attempts to do its part, distributing free family-sized devices in schools. Their website announces that in 2014 volunteers distributed 1,646 units that allow

157,975 students access to safe water. In April 2016 all of these will be due for replacement. There is no indication as to whether LifeStraw has a strategy in place to accomplish this.

Peter Redfield classifies LifeStraw among an emergent array of humanitarian life technologies that are premised on the failure of the state to safeguard populations (2012). He argues that these objects and the companies that produce them are embedded in an expressly moral assertion that human life matters. This moral assertion is, not surprisingly, quite similar to Fouché's missionary impulse. The goodness of both the enterprise and the (white) people who undertake it is presented as self-evident, with article titles like this one: "These Social Entrepreneurs Risked Their Lives to Produce Charcoal in Haiti" (Thorpe 2015). These projects look like nothing so much as a huge success on their promotional webpages, which do not show the storage rooms full of unused whatsits, or the piles of broken thingamajigs. It is not that they are ungrateful, those empty vessels. When it breaks and there are not parts to fix it because local materials were not used, or because nobody local was trained with the expertise necessary to make repairs (much less design something on their own), is that when you will rethink your design choices? When there are few adopters because the "low cost" facility equals half a person's yearly income, what will your response be? When the tribe over there rejects in-the-ground toileting completely because that is where you put your ancestors and shitting on your ancestors is more than undignified, it is utterly disrespectful, will you advocate behavior change or cultural adjustment? Whose behavior change? Whose cultural adjustment? Meaning well is not a great excuse for not having great ways to test and iterate on the ground from the get go. Wanting to help is not necessarily the best way to be helpful. Just take a peek at the website Humanitarians of Tinder.

> *See here, this sensor here, this one I'm wearing, yes place it to your tender curling organ and listen. Volume? Let me turn it up my fingertips touch face, my hand does not hold the microphone, my hand IS the microphone, speak into my palm. The future is us, and this future, this future of us, is about us, for us, and we make it through us. Those other futures you create about "people"? We do not exist in them. Utopia? Tapioca! Manioc. Tomato, potato, squash, peanut. We changed the world, you may think you conquered, you pacified, you laid out reservation lands, but we invaded you, your flesh is of our invention, we are what you have been eating, we are what you are made of, you have made yourself of us. 1492 was the beginning of your end, too. Maize, mayi, mais. High fructose obesity and ethanol your innovation-based gifts to the buffet of our shared future.*

If design tends to veer toward empty self-congratulation, anthropology has often indulged in the sport of self-critical reflection to the point of paralysis. The ethnographer's cautiousness and penchant for the cautionary tale primes anthropologists to shrink away from design's energetic zest for intervention and solution seeking. Immersed in a commitment to understanding problems, anthropologists may take up activism, but are loath to initiate cultural change, or at least loath to initiate cultural change *on purpose*. We talk a great game about how terrible this or that is, why it is wrong, why it is bad, but when asked "what can be done," retreat into the security of unpicking the knot as being in and of itself, enough. Anthropology has its own troubled history with racism and sexism, as well, a history that is as yet unfinished. At big anthropological conferences, I inevitably find myself huddled in a room with other anthropologists of color, where we swap stories generally running along the lines of I-can't-believe-this-racist-thing-just-happened-in-my-session, or inappropriate-comments-from-colleagues-who-ought-to-know-better, and generally despair the state of disciplinary cluelessness about the continuing racism within our ranks. "What has this got to do with digital ethnography?" you might ask. My answer would be: "Exactly."

That vision you value so much. When you observe, your objectivity that excuse for self-satisfaction for center-of-the-universe-you and you and you and you substitute your self for me. You do that you-niverse that you do so well. And here's the ~~voodoo~~ Vodou that I do: re-verse not reverse go far enough back and you end up in front again in the Mobius tide of time and space. I don't see you, I sense you.

What are the possibilities in the space between missionary-type doing good and knowing so much it is impossible to figure out how to be helpful? Speculation might be part of the answer. Being at the intersection of design and anthropology has allowed me to see and experiment with doing ethnography through the digital. Ethnography *of* the digital has grown tremendously in recent years, within anthropology and in such fields as Human Computer Interaction (HCI) and Science and Technology Studies (STS). The reliance on language for doing anthropology (talking as a primary fieldwork mode; writing fieldnotes as the signature field documentation activity; writing as the way to produce anthropological knowledge) belies the problematic politics of bodies, embodiment, the power of materiality itself and leads us right back to questions of race and sex.

Visual anthropology has a long and important history of expanding ways of anthropological knowing and communicating, but the reliance on vision as virtually the only sensory complement to writing needs to be questioned more robustly. This is being done, for instance, in the growing field of sensory ethnography. Sarah Pink points out that sensory ethnographic approaches "are not short-cuts to the same materials that would be produced in the classic approach" (2009, 10); in other words, moving beyond the visual offers new ways for ethnography to produce knowledge. Pink argues that contemporary conditions may not allow ethnographers to embed themselves as thoroughly as they did in Malinowski's day and sensory methods might have been developed in part as a response to these changing circumstances. Even so, she emphasizes, they have value independent from the more traditional ethnographic tools and approaches. In this age of sensors that can detect everything from CO_2 to heartbeats, light frequencies, pressure, and movement—among a host of other things—anthropologists could extend their methodological tool kit exponentially should they wish. Yet, by and large, anthropologists tend to use technology pretty much off the shelf.

What designers do, in contrast, is to re-imagine, re-make, or outright invent technologies that do what they want them to do. In the Laboratory of Speculative Ethnology, when we have our suits on, part of what we explore is the integration of body and technology: what if cloud-gathered data were manifested in the sensors we wear? It is not a cyborg thing, it is an exploration of what it means to move away from interposing the technology between the anthropologist and the subject, to make it skin, integral to the moment of touching, the point of contact, the medium of mediation.

Ethnography *through* the digital, from the Lab's perspective, means experimenting with the embodied relationship between ethnographer and technology in hacker-ish, playful, and speculative ways. This form of speculation critically reflects upon the practice of ethnography, the role of technology in making ethnographers and their others, and the cultural embeddedness of technology and its uses. Furthermore, speculation allows for serious exploration of "what if" scenarios that are rarely the stuff of the ICT4D approach, and pretty much never show up in anthropology.

Your way of knowing what do you know? Without touch you cannot feel. Without taste you cannot swallow, without smell you cannot follow your nose's knowing who is it who is behind the glass encased caught in time you in the forever nowness of your self satisfaction oh you. Yes you. But who are "we"?

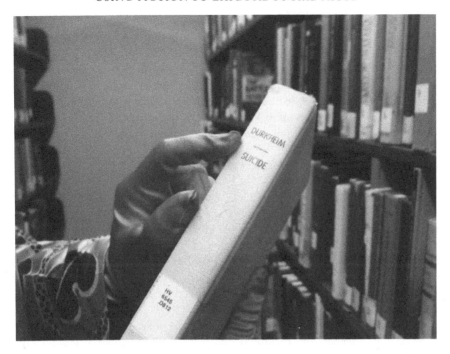

Figure 44.1   Laboratory of Speculative Ethnology *Suicide*

Sylvia Wynter (1995) saltily posed this question at the Smithsonian museum during a symposium examining the implications of 1492.

> *Just the facts ma'am, just the social facts. Suicide. Genocide. Suicide by cop. Fiction is not for the faint of heart, the faintly beating heart beneath the flesh made of new world wonders holy guacamole La Malinche, Anacaona, Pocahontas and the tragic octoroon Sally Hemings. They labored to push forth new nations. Race, the social fact extraordinaire, birther of social fact-lets aplenty: lynching, Jim Crow, Lost Bird, America itself all those "Americans" and those America-S and in the face of all that, ALL THAT, I say up with social fiction because #blacklives matter #Icantbreathe and you gotta admit social facts are a death trap. Fiction is that seed of truth rooting itself in fact and future daring us to sense the coming of an us you have failed to forecast. No, you are not white by nature. You have made the amoral choice to be white. James Baldwin said so.*

Speaking of Malinowski and the ins and outs of embedded long-term ethnography, let us address some of the problematic assumptions about classic participant observation, assumptions that become profoundly visible in a quick Google image search using the term "anthropology fieldwork." I am tempted to collectively title these images "Anthropologist as tool user," since in a plurality of images, the anthropologist is a starkly white person at the center of the frame, dutifully observing the natives from behind some form of technology whether the tried-and-true notebook and pencil, camera, or in Napoleon Chagnon's case, some complex and moderately incomprehensible doohickey. David Syring (2015) uses the evocative term "technopelli" for this same issue. Through the instrument of the Google image search, anthropology resolves into its own worst stereotype, the intrepid adventurer discovering primitive peoples in the jungles of time. From calipers and cameras to iPhones and big data, technology has been a means of fixing some people in the past, over there, in the savage slot. For anthropologists, the digital is nearly without exception interposed between us and them. The Lab works to trouble that boundary, digitally. Yes, technology has ideology built into it, just like the museum (Philip et al. 2012). Yet there is no reason that a given set of uses is hard-wired into the technology, predetermining the ways people make use of them: hacking, DIY, off-label use, and basic cussedness result in all kinds of surprising use-scenarios. The so-called digital divide is of our own making too much of the time. It is our burden and our responsibility to get subversive, decolonizing the digital and the forms of knowing it creates.

Now there's a fact for you to face. You, and you. But who are "we"?

In the afterword to the classic ethnography *Tally's Corner*, Elliot Liebow (1967) reveals a devastatingly simple realization: when seated at a restaurant table with three of his African American informants, he sees uniformity, a table full of black men. They, on the other hand, see black men and one white man. The visibility of his own whiteness is something he is unable to witness and experience, yet it is there for all to see. Anthropology is like that. We so often write as if we are invisible in the worlds we describe with such knowing and clarity and yet our own hypervisibility unacknowledged. It is there in that array of Google images, anthropologists at the center of every frame.

Rather than imagining observation as creating a cloak of invisibility, in the Lab we own our hypervisibility, celebrating it, tricking it out. It is not as if anybody is fooling anybody, after all. Which is more disruptive? Pretend invisibility or active visibilization? The anthropologist who interposes technology between their body and that of the observed, or the Lab of Speculative Ethnology member whose suit of hypervisibility houses inbuilt technologies through which the world can be alternately sensed, documented, and translated?

Document this. Racial violence. Detect its stains, the strains it places upon the beating heart, the breath you take.

Skinning speculation with Afro-ness, the Lab makes *everything* about race, instead of nothing. Our current speculative device under construction is the Racial Violence Documentator, or RVD. Using readily available biometric sensors, the device is as yet unbuilt. It works like this: a person would register their account, inputting information such as age, gender, etc. When the device is worn, it creates a running record of heart rate, blood pressure, skin conductance, respiration, and a handy camera shoots video from the wearer's point of view. Scanning incoming data, the proprietary software tags moments of stress. These moments are cross-referenced with video to geotag and assess what is happening in the moment, creating a living map as it goes. When a moment is detected, the system pings users to fill in additional information about the moment in question. What was happening? Who was there? What was said? Data from all users is anonymized, compiled, and aggregated. All sorts of things are possible: perhaps the device is worn visibly and proudly, so that the RVD operates as something of a visible deterrent to racist or discriminatory behavior. Perhaps it is worn invisibly, to clandestinely document everyday events. How do they make the user feel? We will create nonworking and various levels of working prototypes and have people use them. How sensitive are they? What kind of communication emerges when someone wears an RVD visibly? How are social dynamics influenced with a visibly announced RVD versus an invisible one? These are opportunities for us to learn as much about present-day experiences of race and racism as they are also moments to jump into imaginary trajectories for those social facts. Exploring the future, after all, is always also an exercise in examining the present. The modes of playfulness, creation, and imagination thus become rich grounds for anthropology and design to work conjointly. The basic technology, by the way, is not much different from what is used in a lie detector. That is on purpose, and serves to demonstrate that the ideology need not dictate the use of technology. Wear the RVD and answer this question: Are you white? This stance also emphasizes the importance of actively injecting race into the ways we think about and use technology, whether in the realm of anthropology or in design and digital realms.

> *Prebirth effects, weights and measures. Blood pressure spike: data sent. Skin conductance, heart rate, respiration, the algorithm plotting the daily toll that living takes when you are black or brown or yellow or Native or any other kind of ~~thing~~ being that exceeds whiteness. Because it is real. But what is "real"?*

Scientific data on the realness of race is contested and problematic (see McGlotten on "black data" (McGlotten et al., n.d.)). The spirometer is a case in point. Originally used during the antebellum period to demonstrate the lack of vitality in enslaved people, Braun demonstrates that across time and geography, the spirometer's most consistent use has been to shore up racial divides, achieving that consistent end only through inconsistent (and hence, unscientific) ways of deploying the instrument itself (Braun 2014). Measurement of biometrics has long had racial and racializing implications, the bulk of which have been quietly integrated into the digital mechanisms for measuring bodily functions and evaluating health (Montoya 2012). As Braun notes in her discussion of the uses of the spirometer, the issue is not so much whether or not the differences can be considered real. The issue is why are certain questions being asked and not others? The ongoing debate about the causes of hypertension in African Americans is an example. The medical approach is one that takes race as a given and tends to attribute hypertension to innate biological factors (Kaufman and Hall 2003).

In posing questions differently, Leith Mullings (2005) offers the Sojourner Syndrome to account for stress levels among African American women. The Sojourner Syndrome is "an interpretive framework that speaks to the historical dialectic of oppression, resilience and resistance" as a socially and historically contextualized way to understand differential infant mortality rates and other health issues more often attributed to genetic and biological difference among black women. Mullings' alternative framework challenges the notion that biological racial difference is at work in differential life outcomes for black women; one of the key implications of this argument is that if the problem is not founded in biology, neither then is the solution. This is one example of productive challenge to apparently neutral data, more and more of which is digitally created and documented. Without such challenges and alternative renderings, the racist underpinnings of biometrics in particular will continue to contribute to knowledge that is both partial and problematic at best.

> *What do you know of my needs? My desires? Your empathy, it is not you feeling what I feel, it is you inventing what I feel so you can feel good. We smile and dance in the face of death. You label it PTSD and teach us how to let the tears flow.*

Working in the space of the speculative, designers are free from the everyday rules and regulations of physics, of time/space, of here and now. It has so much possibility! And yet of course designers, like everybody else, work from within the confines of their particular cultures. Graphic design in the United States is estimated to be 86 percent white (Carroll 2015), and other design fields are just as un-diverse; recent figures released by leading tech firms document predominantly white workforces (Alba 2015). It should be no surprise, then, that design speculation overwhelmingly reflects whiteness. Racial inequality is virtually absent as a topic in speculative enquiry. Furthermore, speculation often fails to imagine an outside-of-capitalism scenario that is unmoored from the ideology of capitalism itself. Common speculative futures: So many three-tiered societies where the top exploits the bottom and the middle struggles to stay in place or rise, so many worlds where the machines take over.

Bianca Dahl (2009) shows how when in Botswana, Western aid workers' norms about expression of trauma could not accommodate the local constructions of grief. Interpreting children's smiles and laughter as psychopathology, they carefully and caringly coached the children in the proper behaviors, which included shedding of tears and public performances of sorrow. Haitians do not cry either, and death, in the form of the Gede spirits, is both uninvited and always present, ever bawdy, raucous, and ready to play. The gede, with their love of children and their jauntiness perform what most Haitians know: when death is so devastatingly familiar, it is hard to fear. When I arrived in Haiti in 2015, a friend told me that an American visitor to the village had created an ongoing ruckus because she was crying so much. (She was shocked by the poverty.) "She's making everyone upset," my friend said. "When she's crying it makes them feel like they've done something wrong." Thus this woman's tears might have provided her some emotional relief, but she was entirely unaware of the effect it was having on everyone around her.

> *Is that a tear in your eye? Don't look to me to justify your goodness as you reach toward me across the digital divide. Has your empathy filled my belly?*

The purported freedom of the Internet emerged right along with what Alondra Nelson (2002, 6) calls the "reified binary between blackness and technology." This is to say that the same racial politics, social inequalities, political failures, structures of power are at work in the digital realm as they are anywhere else, a point also made by van Dijk (2005). As Kali Tal pointed out early on (1996), the technology sphere has always been racialized, and in particular, the possibilities offered online for new lives was not much of a new idea to those who had long struggled with double consciousness. This question takes on particular features in the developing world, where the digital divide is being continually back-filled by aid efforts, technology for development, and other innovations tasked with providing solutions. Part of the problem here is that so many of these international aid efforts take for granted far too many of the problematic utopian claims made about technology and the future. Technology does not, and never has, all on its own, solved social problems. The history of technology is strewn with claims about how we are just this close to achieving freedom from work, from drudgery, from technology itself. None of that freedom ever seems to emerge. We are stuck with the same old problems with fancier technology to address them.

> *You make, you dispense, you distribute.*

ICT4D solutions nearly always push information, services, or capacities to people whose only job is to absorb, not create or contribute. Those wielding digital expertise remain the experts; the means through which people might build their own solutions are not required or, even, perhaps, desired in the way technology is constructed and deployed. Part of the problem with this dynamic is that it is firmly rooted in the designerly tradition of productification and marketing. Productification and marketing, in turn, are expressly dedicated toward the creation and expansion of markets. Digital interventions in the space of global development are not, then, ultimately about the eradication of need, but rather the creation of new needs, as any form of product development inevitably must be. The humanitarian element in ICT4D is, to a great degree, utterly irrelevant from the point of view of capital: a market is a market and a buyer is a buyer and a user is a user. The neoliberalization of the aid industry only intensifies the degree to which capital calls the shots (Daley 2013; Bornstein and Redfield 2011). It matters little that the market is in malaria prevention, the buyer is an international NGO, and the user is a rural peasant. As huge NGOs from UNICEF to USAID take on design methods and approaches in the interest of innovation, they do so within frameworks that are increasingly neoliberal.

Moving away from open granting mechanisms, funding for projects is shaped in entre-preneurial terms where the fast pitch, incubator and accelerator models dominate. These orientations offer speed and flexibility but they also mitigate against careful and time-intensive processes where collaboration on the ground might be encouraged. In defining so-called "grand challenges" or targeting specific areas, these agencies gain the advantage of seeking wide-ranging contributions to identified pressing issues. On the down side, the reduction of opportunities for pure research on seemingly marginal topics seriously reduces opportunities where serendipity produces unexpected applications or outcomes. Success is measured in terms of achieving preselected goals and measures; a mode of procedure that any ethnographer can attest is doomed to produce lackluster and uninteresting results.

As if we have no hands, no voices. But I have speakers here and here and here and when you approach, song bursts forth from me but not from my mouth this song is not an invitation but a protective shield.

Of course it is hard to label any solution as being bad. But are they any good, really? What alternatives might there be to what has been imagined? Digital solutions in the devel-oping world much too rarely engage people actively as people capable of contributing to the making and meaning of what is being produced. Even more rarely do these efforts venture into the realms of, much less indulging in joy, creativity, surprise, pleasure. The poverty of this bare life approach to people's needs is fueled primarily by a lack of imagi-nation on the part of the designers. I am dying to find out the unsolicited uses of a current object, the Talking Book. It is actually a pretty neat thing, a small, programmable device for playing audio files, aimed at rural African populations who are "the poorest of the poor" and where literacy is low (Kelion 2014). It comes loaded with lots of useful information and currently targets rural farmers and new mothers. Where I get interested, though, is in the part where it can record. How many young kids, do you think, get their hands on those talking books and sing their hearts out, tell silly stories, record all sorts of stuff that has nothing to do with agriculture or new mothers but is profoundly interesting, creative, and if all that energy were harnessed, where might it go?

Keep your distance. Enter my world on my terms or not at all. In the land of America, streets paved in gold mobile money is years behind, years behind where we are now in the country of Africa and the nation of Haiti where every mile is the last mile. You preach democracy, we prac-tice necromancy. Survival of the most fit, the well-fitted, the exquisitely tailored custom cut and hand-sewn organic and fair trade stuff of dreams. You built it and you came. Whose dreams are dreaming? We were here then we will be there then we will have been there and here. There you are. Here we are. But who are we?

References

Alba, Davey. 2015. "Microsoft Releases More Diversity Stats, and They Aren't Pretty." *WIRED*. January 5. www.wired.com/2015/01/microsoft-diversity/ (accessed November 11, 2015).

Baldwin, James. 1984. "On Being White . . . and Other Lies." *Essence* 14 (April): 90–2.

Berson, Josh. 2015. *Computable Bodies: Instrumented Life and the Human Somatic Niche*. London: Bloomsbury Academic.

Bornstein, Erica, and Peter Redfield. 2011. *Forces of Compassion: Humanitarianism between Ethics and Politics*. Santa Fe, NM: SAR Press.

Bratton, Benjamin. 2013. "Some Trace Effects of the Post-Anthropocene: On Accelerationist Geopolitical Aesthetics." *E-Flux*, 46. www.e-flux.com/journal/some-trace-effects-of-the-post-anthropocene-on-accelerationist-geopolitical-aesthetics/ (accessed November 11, 2015).

Braun, Lundy. 2014. *Breathing Race into the Machine: The Surprising Career of the Spirometer from Plantation to Genetics*. Minneapolis, MN: University of Minnesota Press.

Candelario, Ginetta E. B. 2007. *Black behind the Ears: Dominican Racial Identity from Museums to Beauty Shops*. Durham, NC: Duke University Press Books.

Carroll, Antoinette. 2015. "Diversity & Inclusion in Design: Why Do They Matter?" *AIGA | the Professional Association for Design*. www.aiga.org//diversity-and-inclusion-in-design-why-do-they-matter/ (accessed November 11, 2015).

Conklin, Alice L. 2013. *In the Museum of Man: Race, Anthropology, and Empire in France, 1850–1950*. Ithaca, NY: Cornell University Press.

Dahl, Bianca. 2009. "The 'Failures of Culture': Christianity, Kinship, and Moral Discourses about Orphans during Botswana's AIDS Crisis." *Africa Today* 56(1): 23–43.

Daley, Patricia. 2013. "Rescuing African Bodies: Celebrities, Consumerism and Neoliberal Humanitarianism." *Review of African Political Economy* 40(137): 375–93.

DiAngelo, Robin. 2011. "White Fragility." *The International Journal of Critical Pedagogy* 3(3): 54–70.

Ely, Breckinridge. 2015. "Ten Things That Will Change the Way We Live." *Forbes*. www.forbes.com/2006/02/16/sony-sun-cisco-cx_cd_0217feat_ls.html (accessed December 16, 2015).

Fouché, Rayvon. 2008. "From Black Inventors to One Laptop Per Child: Exporting a Racial Politics of Technology." In *Digitizing Race: Visual Cultures of the Internet*, edited by Lisa Nakamura and Peter Chow-White, 61–84. Minneapolis, MN: University of Minnesota Press.

Hannaford, Kat. 2015. "High-Tech Water Bottle Uses UV Light to Sterilize Water." *Gizmodo*. http://gizmodo.com/5604142/high-tech-water-bottle-uses-uv-light-to-sterilize-water (accessed November 25, 2015).

Haraway, Donna. 1984. "Teddy Bear Patriarchy: Taxidermy in the Garden of Eden, New York City, 1908–1936." *Social Text*, no. 11 (Winter, 1985): 20–64.

Heredia, Paula, and Coco Fusco. 1993. *The Couple in the Cage*.

Kaufman, Jay S., and Susan A. Hall. 2003. "The Slavery Hypertension Hypothesis: Dissemination and Appeal of a Modern Race Theory." *Epidemiology* 14(1): 111–18.

Kelion, Leo. 2014. "Talking Book Trial to Help 'Poorest of Poor' in Ghana." *BBC News*. Online (accessed November 20, 2015).

Kester, Grant H. 2011. *The One and the Many: Contemporary Collaborative Art in a Global Context*. Durham, NC: Duke University Press.

Liebow, Elliott. 1967. *Tally's Corner: A Study of Negro Streetcorner Men*. Boston, MA: Little, Brown.

McGlotten, Shaka, and E. Patrick Johnson. n.d. "Black Data." In *No Tea, No Shade: New Queer of Color Critique*. Durham, NC: Duke University Press.

Montoya, Michael. 2012. "Bioethnic Conscription: Genes, Race, and Mexicana/o Ethnicity in Diabetes Research." *Cultural Anthropology* 22(1): 94–128.

Mullings, Leith. 2005. "Resistance and Resilience: The Sojourner Syndrome and the Social Context of Reproduction in Central Harlem." *Transforming Anthropology* 13(2): 79–91.

Nelson, Alondra. 2002. "Future Texts." *Social Text* 71: 1–15.

Philip, Kavita, Lilly Irani, and Paul Dourish. 2012. "Postcolonial Computing: A Tactical Survey." *Science, Technology & Human Values* 37(1): 3–29.

Pink, Sarah. 2009. *Doing Sensory Ethnography*. London: Sage.

Redfield, Peter. 2012. "Bioexpectations: Life Technologies as Humanitarian Goods." *Public Culture* 24(1): 157–84.

Syring, David. 2015. *With the Saraguros: The Blended Life in a Transnational World*. Austin, TX: University of Texas Press.

Tal, Kali. 1996. "Life behind the Screen." *WIRED*. October 1. www.wired.com/1996/10/screen/ (accessed February 17, 2016).

Thorpe, Devin. 2015. "These Social Entrepreneurs Risked Their Lives to Produce Charcoal in Haiti." *Forbes*. November 10. www.forbes.com/sites/devinthorpe/2015/11/10/social-entrepreneurs-risk-lives-for-charcoal-in-haiti/ (accessed February 17, 2016).

Trouillot, Michel-Rolph. 2003. "Anthropology and the Savage Slot: The Poetics and Politics of Otherness." In *Global Transformations: Anthropology and the Modern World*, 7–28. New York: Palgrave Macmillan.

Tunstall, Elizabeth (Dori). 2013. "Decolonizing Design Innovation: Design Anthropology, Critical Anthropology, and Indigenous Knowledge." In *Design Anthropology: Theory and Practice*, edited by Wendy Gunn, Ton Otto, and Rachel Charlotte Smith, 2114–230. London: Bloomsbury Academic.

van Dijk, Jan A. G. M. 2005. *The Deepening Divide: Inequality in the Information Society*. Thousand Oaks, CA: Sage.

Weismantel, Mary. 2001. *Cholas and Pishtacos: Stories of Race and Sex in the Andes*. Chicago, IL: University of Chicago Press.

Wynter, Sylvia. 1995. "1492: A New World View." In *Race, Discourse, and the Origin of the Americas: A New World View*, edited by Vera Lawrence Hyatt and Rex Nettleford, 5–57. Washington, DC: Smithsonian.

INDEX